The Operational Auditing Handbook

The Operational Auditing Handbook

Auditing Business and IT Processes

Second Edition

Andrew Chambers
Graham Rand

A John Wiley and Sons, Ltd., Publication

This edition first published 2010
© 2010 John Wiley & Sons, Ltd

Registered office
John Wiley & Sons Ltd, The Atrium, Southern Gate, Chichester, West Sussex, PO19 8SQ,
United Kingdom

For details of our global editorial offices, for customer services and for information about how to apply for permission to reuse the copyright material in this book please see our website at www.wiley.com.

The right of the author to be identified as the author of this work has been asserted in accordance with the Copyright, Designs and Patents Act 1988.

All rights reserved. No part of this publication may be reproduced, stored in a retrieval system, or transmitted, in any form or by any means, electronic, mechanical, photocopying, recording or otherwise, except as permitted by the UK Copyright, Designs and Patents Act 1988, without the prior permission of the publisher.

Wiley also publishes its books in a variety of electronic formats. Some content that appears in print may not be available in electronic books.

Designations used by companies to distinguish their products are often claimed as trademarks. All brand names and product names used in this book are trade names, service marks, trademarks or registered trademarks of their respective owners. The publisher is not associated with any product or vendor mentioned in this book. This publication is designed to provide accurate and authoritative information in regard to the subject matter covered. It is sold on the understanding that the publisher is not engaged in rendering professional services. If professional advice or other expert assistance is required, the services of a competent professional should be sought.

Library of Congress Cataloging-in-Publication Data
Chambers, Andrew D.
  The operational auditing handbook : auditing business and IT processes / Andrew Chambers, Graham Rand.—2nd ed.
      p. cm.
  Includes bibliographical references and index.
  ISBN 978-0-470-74476-5 (H/B)
 1. Management audit. I. Rand, G. V. (Graham V.) II. Title.
  HD58.95.C48 2010
  658.4′013—dc22
                                                                                    2009054377

A catalogue record for this book is available from the British Library.

Typeset in 10/12 Times by Laserwords Private Limited, Chennai, India
Printed in Great Britain by CPI Antony Rowe, Chippenham, Wiltshire

Library
University of Texas
at San Antonio

Contents

Preface	xv
Acknowledgements	xvii

Part I Understanding Operational Auditing 1

1 APPROACHES TO OPERATIONAL AUDITING 3

Definitions of "Operational Auditing"	3
Scope	4
Audit Approach to Operational Audits	12
Resourcing the Internal Audit of Technical Activities	16
Productivity and Performance Measurement Systems	19
Value for Money (VFM) Auditing	22
Benchmarking	23

2 BUSINESS PROCESSES 27

Introduction	27
An Audit Universe of Business Processes	28
Self Assessment of Business Processes	30
A Hybrid Audit Universe	30
Reasons For Process Weaknesses	30
Identifying the Processes of an Organisation	32
Why Adopt a "Cycle" or "Process" Approach to Internal Control Design and Review?	35
Business Processes in the Standard Audit Programme Guides	35
The Hallmarks of a Good Business Process	36
Academic Cycles in a University	37

3 DEVELOPING OPERATIONAL REVIEW PROGRAMMES FOR MANAGERIAL AND AUDIT USE — 40

Scope — 40
Practical Use of SAPGs — 41
Format of SAPGs — 45
Risk in Operational Auditing — 50

4 GOVERNANCE PROCESSES — 75

Introduction — 75
Internal Control Processes being Part of Risk Management Processes — 75
Risk Management Processes being Part of Governance Processes — 76
Objectives of Governance, Risk Management and Control Processes — 77
The COSO View of Objectives — 78
Should there be a Single Set of Objectives? — 80
The Internal Governance Processes — 81
The Board and External Aspects of Corporate Governance — 81
The Board's Assurance Vacuum — 82
Risk and Control Issues for Internal Governance Processes — 84
Risk and Control Issues for the Board — 87
Risk and Control Issues for External Governance Processes — 90

5 RISK MANAGEMENT PROCESSES — 95

Introduction — 95
Objectives of Risk Management — 95
Essential Components of Effective Risk Management — 98
The Scope of Internal Audit's Role in Risk Management — 99
Tools for Risk Management — 101
The Risk Matrix — 101
Risk Registers — 106
Risk Management Challenges — 107
Control Issues for Risk Management Processes — 112

6 INTERNAL CONTROL PROCESSES — 116

Introduction — 116
Paradigm 1: COSO on Internal Control — 118
Paradigm 2: Turnbull on Internal Control — 128
Paradigm 3: COCO on Internal Control — 129
Paradigm 4: A Systems/Cybernetics Model of Internal Control — 130
Paradigm 5: Control by Division with Supervision — 135
Paradigm 6: Control by Category — 137

	The Objectives of Internal Control	139
	Determining Whether Internal Control is Effective	141
	Control Cost-Effectiveness Considerations	142
	Issues for Internal Control Processes	143
7	**REVIEW OF THE CONTROL ENVIRONMENT**	**147**
	Introduction	147
	Control Objectives for a Review of the Control Environment	147
	Risk and Control Issues for a Review of the Control Environment	148
	Fraud	149
8	**REVIEWING INTERNAL CONTROL OVER FINANCIAL REPORTING—THE SARBANES-OXLEY APPROACH**	**151**
	Introduction	151
	Costs and Benefits	154
	2007 SOX-LITE	155
	Revised Definitions of "Significant Deficiency" and "Material Weakness"	156
	Using a Recognised Internal Control Framework for the Assessment	157
	Risk and Control Issues for the Sarbanes-Oxley s. 302 and s. 404 Compliance Process	171
9	**BUSINESS/MANAGEMENT TECHNIQUES AND THEIR IMPACT ON CONTROL AND AUDIT**	**178**
	Introduction	178
	Business Process Re-Engineering	178
	Total Quality Management	181
	Delayering	187
	Empowerment	189
	Outsourcing	191
	Just-In-Time Management (JIT)	195
10	**CONTROL SELF ASSESSMENT**	**199**
	Introduction	199
	Survey and Workshop Approaches to CSA	200
	Selecting Workshop Participants	200
	Where to Apply CSA	200
	CSA Roles for Management and for Internal Audit	201
	Avoiding Line Management Disillusionment	202
	Encouragement from the Top	203

Facilitating CSA Workshops, and Training for CSA	204
Anonymous Voting Systems	205
Comparing CSA with Internal Audit	205
Control Self Assessment as Reassurance for Internal Audit	206
A Hybrid Approach—Integrating Internal Auditing Engagements with CSA Workshops	206
Workshop Formats	207
Utilising CoCo in CSA	208
Readings	210
Control Self Assessment	210

11 EVALUATING THE INTERNAL AUDIT ACTIVITY 214

Introduction	214
Ongoing Monitoring	214
Periodic Internal Reviews	215
External Reviews	216
Common Weaknesses Noted by Quality Assurance Reviews	217
Internal Audit Maturity Models	218
Effective Measuring of Internal Auditing's Contribution to the Enterprise's Profitability	219
Control Objectives for the Internal Audit Activity	232

Part II Auditing Key Functions 237

12 AUDITING THE FINANCE AND ACCOUNTING FUNCTIONS 239

Introduction	239
System/Function Components of the Financial and Accounting Environment	239
Control Objectives and Risk and Control Issues	240
Treasury	241
Payroll	243
Accounts Payable	246
Accounts Receivable	248
General Ledger/Management Accounts	251
Fixed Assets (and Capital Charges)	253
Budgeting and Monitoring	256
Bank Accounts and Banking Arrangements	258
Sales Tax (VAT) Accounting	261
Taxation	263
Inventories	266
Product/Project Accounting	268

Petty Cash and Expenses 270
Financial Information and Reporting 272
Investments 274

13 AUDITING SUBSIDIARIES, REMOTE OPERATING UNITS AND JOINT VENTURES 276

Introduction 276
Fact Finding 277
High Level Review Programme 278
Joint Ventures 279

14 AUDITING CONTRACTS AND THE PURCHASING FUNCTION 285

Introduction 285
Control Objectives and Risk and Control Issues 285
Contracting 289
Contract Management Environment 290
Assessing the Viability and Competence of Contractors 295
Maintaining an Approved List of Contractors 297
Tendering Procedures 299
Contracting and Tendering Documentation 302
Selection and Letting of Contracts 304
Performance Monitoring 306
Valuing Work for Interim Payments 308
Contractor's Final Account 310
Review of Project Outturn and Performance 313

15 AUDITING OPERATIONS AND RESOURCE MANAGEMENT 317

Introduction 317
System/Function Components of a Production/Manufacturing
 Environment 318
Control Objectives and Risk and Control Issues 318
Planning and Production Control 318
Facilities, Plant and Equipment 321
Personnel 324
Materials and Energy 327
Quality Control 330
Safety 332
Environmental Issues 335
Law and Regulatory Compliance 338
Maintenance 339

16 AUDITING MARKETING AND SALES — 343

- Introduction — 343
- System/Function Components of the Marketing and Sales Functions — 343
- General Comments — 344
- Control Objectives and Risk and Control Issues — 344
- Product Development — 345
- Market Research — 348
- Promotion and Advertising — 350
- Pricing and Discount Policies — 353
- Sales Management — 355
- Sales Performance and Monitoring — 359
- Distributors — 362
- Relationship with the Parent Company — 366
- Agents — 368
- Order Processing — 371
- Warranty Arrangements — 375
- Maintenance and Servicing — 377
- Spare Parts and Supply — 380

17 AUDITING DISTRIBUTION — 383

- Introduction — 383
- System/Function Components of Distribution — 383
- Control Objectives and Risk and Control Issues — 384
- Distribution, Transport and Logistics — 384
- Distributors — 388
- Stock Control — 392
- Warehousing and Storage — 395

18 AUDITING HUMAN RESOURCES — 399

- Introduction — 399
- System/Function Components of the Personnel Function — 399
- Control Objectives and Risk and Control Issues — 399
- Human Resources Department — 400
- Recruitment — 404
- Manpower and Succession Planning — 408
- Staff Training and Development — 410
- Welfare — 413
- Performance-Related Compensation, Pension Schemes (and other Benefits) — 415
- Health Insurance — 422
- Staff Appraisal and Disciplinary Matters — 424
- Health and Safety — 427

Labour Relations	430
Company Vehicles	432

19 AUDITING RESEARCH AND DEVELOPMENT — 437

Introduction	437
System/Function Components of Research and Development	437
Control Objectives and Risk and Control Issues	437
Product Development	438
Project Appraisal and Monitoring	442
Plant and Equipment	445
Development Project Management	447
Legal and Regulatory Issues	450

20 AUDITING SECURITY — 453

Introduction	453
Control Objectives and Risk and Control Issues	454
Security	454
Health and Safety	457
Insurance	460

21 AUDITING ENVIRONMENTAL RESPONSIBILITY — 463

Introduction	463
Environmental Auditing	465
The Emergence of Environmental Concerns	465
EMAS—The European Eco-Management and Audit Scheme	466
Linking Environmental Issues to Corporate Strategy and Securing Benefits	467
Environmental Assessment and Auditing System Considerations	468
The Role of Internal Audit	470
Example Programme	470

Part III Auditing Information Technology — 477

22 AUDITING INFORMATION TECHNOLOGY — 479

Introduction	479
Introduction to Recognised Standards Related to Information Technology and Related Topics	480

System/Function Components of Information Technology and
Management 486
Control Objectives and Risk and Control Issues 488

23 IT STRATEGIC PLANNING — 489

24 IT ORGANISATION — 493

25 IT POLICY FRAMEWORK — 496

26 INFORMATION ASSET REGISTER — 502

27 CAPACITY MANAGEMENT — 511

28 INFORMATION MANAGEMENT (IM) — 514

29 RECORDS MANAGEMENT (RM) — 524

30 KNOWLEDGE MANAGEMENT (KM) — 542

31 IT SITES AND INFRASTRUCTURE (INCLUDING PHYSICAL SECURITY) — 554

32 PROCESSING OPERATIONS — 559

33 BACK-UP AND MEDIA MANAGEMENT — 562

34 REMOVABLE MEDIA — 566

35 SYSTEM AND OPERATING SOFTWARE (INCLUDING PATCH MANAGEMENT) — 570

36 SYSTEM ACCESS CONTROL (LOGICAL SECURITY) — 576

37 PERSONAL COMPUTERS (INCLUDING LAPTOPS AND PDAs) — 580

38	REMOTE WORKING	585
39	EMAIL	590
40	INTERNET USAGE	598
41	SOFTWARE MAINTENANCE (INCLUDING CHANGE MANAGEMENT)	605
42	NETWORKS	609
43	DATABASES	613
44	DATA PROTECTION	616
45	FREEDOM OF INFORMATION	627
46	DATA TRANSFER AND SHARING (STANDARDS AND PROTOCOL)	636
47	LEGAL RESPONSIBILITIES	645
48	FACILITIES MANAGEMENT	648
49	SYSTEM DEVELOPMENT	651
50	SOFTWARE SELECTION	655
51	CONTINGENCY PLANNING	658
52	HUMAN RESOURCES INFORMATION SECURITY	661
53	MONITORING AND LOGGING	667
54	INFORMATION SECURITY INCIDENTS	671
55	DATA RETENTION AND DISPOSAL	680

56	ELECTRONIC DATA INTERCHANGE (EDI)	688
57	VIRUSES	691
58	USER SUPPORT	694
59	BACS	696
60	SPREADSHEET DESIGN AND GOOD PRACTICE	699
61	IT HEALTH CHECKS	707
62	IT ACCOUNTING	710

Appendix 1	Index to SAPGs on the Companion Website	712
Appendix 2	Standard Audit Programme Guides	719
Appendix 3	International Data Protection Legislation	729
Appendix 4	International Freedom of Information Legislation	763
Appendix 5	Information Management Definitions	835
Appendix 6	IT and Information Management Policies	839

Bibliography	852
Index	859

Preface

The durability of this Handbook is indicated by the fact that the previous edition, first published in 1997, was in print until this second edition appeared. The Handbook was designed to fill a gap by providing an up-to-date guide to operational auditing, taking a business process approach. The format makes the book friendly as a practical Handbook.

New content for this edition includes in-depth consideration of governance processes, risk management processes and internal control processes. We have radically updated and much extended the content on auditing information technology, and our treatment of international data protection legislation and international freedom of information legislation does, we believe, give thorough and innovative coverage of these important contemporary topics. Indeed, users of this Handbook will find it gives them most of the up-to-date toolkit they need to provide an effective audit service in the field of information technology. Because compliance with s. 404 of the Sarbanes-Oxley Act has resulted in a widely applied approach to assessing the effectiveness of internal control over financial reporting, we have given that attention too. Readers will find more detailed coverage of control self assessment, and we have also included a chapter on assessing the internal audit activity. Where appropriate we have aligned this edition to the latest *Standards* of The Institute of Internal Auditors and to the pronouncements of other bodies.

The Handbook is intended as a companion for those who design self assessment programmes of business processes to be undertaken by management and staff. Likewise it is a mentor for internal auditors and consultants who conduct audits on behalf of others. We have developed the book to cater for private, public and not-for-profit sectors and to be a basis for designing value-for-money audit approaches. We also believe that external auditors dealing with financial and accounting systems and often engaged in management audits will find the book of value and should have it in their libraries.

At the same time we have had in mind the professional qualification requirements in this subject area of The Institute of Internal Auditors, with the intention that this book will be a suitable standard text. Particularly with the student in mind we have where appropriate supported specific points with cross-referenced notes which appear at the end of each chapter, and there is a comprehensive bibliography.

The book's timeliness comes partly from the mix of business processes included, and the contemporary treatment given to each. In part it comes from the ways we have attempted to weave in the contemporary approaches and issues of, for instance, business process re-engineering, just-in-time management, downsizing, delayering, empowerment, environment, ethics, control self assessment and IT. In part it is a matter of the risk evaluation techniques which we describe as often being appropriate aids for those who must review and evaluate business processes.

The Handbook aims to raise the consciousness of the underlying issues, risks and objectives for a wide range of operations and activities. In other words, it aims to stimulate creative thought about the business context of operational audit reviews. In practice, it would be an extremely difficult task to define a set of universal panacea approaches to the audit of the various operational areas of any organisation, as the driving motivations and the contexts into which they are set would vary between entities. In adopting a business oriented stance supported by practical examples of the key questions to resolve, we hope that audit creativity will be encouraged rather than stifled by over-prescriptive programmes and routines. Readers will need to take account of their own experiences and the relevant aspects of the cultures prevailing within their organisations, and bring these to bear on the contents of this book, so that a suitably tailored approach to auditing operations emerges.

We have attempted to distinguish between on the one hand approaching audit work according to the way a business is structured, and on the other hand seeking to identify and then assess the natural business processes that step across organisational parts. It is often the latter approach to audit work that has the greatest potential to add value.

We are confident that the "real world" pedigree of this book will make it eminently useful for practising auditors, line managers, consultants, and those who intend to become qualified as operational auditors.

We would appreciate readers' comments and advice for future editions.

Andrew Chambers
Management Audit LLP
The Water Mill
Moat Lane
Old Bolingbroke
Spilsby
Lincolnshire
PE23 4ES
England

Tel. & fax: +44 (0)1790 763350
Internet tel.: +44 (0)207 099 9355
Internet fax.: +44 (0)207 099 3954
Email: ProfADC@aol.com
Web: www.management-audit.com

Graham Rand

grahamrand@btinternet.com
Mobile: +44 (0)7729 374074

Acknowledgements

We thank our many clients and friends who have been the stimulus for much of the content and approach of this book. We are grateful to those who have kindly read through the full manuscript with care, making many useful suggestions which we believe have led to a better book. We have quoted from many sources: in every case we have endeavoured to provide full attribution for the material we have used and to obtain the appropriate permissions. If there has been any oversight on our part we apologise and would like to correct it at our first opportunity.

Andrew Chambers
Graham Rand

Part I:
Understanding Operational Auditing

1

Approaches to Operational Auditing

DEFINITIONS OF "OPERATIONAL AUDITING"

Business processes often step across the frontiers between sections within a business, requiring high standards of coordination between different organisational parts. Control is often weaker where coordination is required between sections that are organisationally separate. Internal auditors are likely to be more productive if they focus considerable attention to the points of interface between organisational parts where coordination is required but is more difficult to achieve than within a single section of the business. Furthermore, internal auditors are likely to be more productive if a significant proportion of the audit engagements they perform are of natural business processes that step across the business's organisational frontiers. We state this up front as it is so important, and we shall explore this innovative audit approach in detail in Chapter 2 when we have established some fundamentals in this chapter.

The term "operational auditing" conjures up different images for internal auditors. It may be used to mean any of the following:

The audit of *operating units* such as manufacturing plants, depots, subsidiaries, overseas operating units, and so on. While the audit scope may cover only accounting, financial and administrative controls it may be broadened in scope to cover the administrative and operational controls, risk management and governance processes of the operating unit under review. To impose general scope limitations for internal audit activities is inconsistent with the global *Standards* of The Institute of Internal Auditors (www.theiia.org).

The audit is how the *functional areas of a business* (such as sales, marketing, production, distribution, HR, etc.) account for their activities and exercise financial control over them. This meaning of operational auditing acknowledges that the internal auditing activity should review all the operational areas of the business, but too narrowly specialises in the audit of accounting and financial controls. It is likely to imply that the internal auditing activity is representing only the finance director or the chief accountant in providing assurance about accounting and financial control across the business.

The audit of *any part of the business* (operating unit, functional area, section, department or even business process, etc.) where the audit objective is to review the effectiveness, efficiency and economy with which management is achieving its own objectives. Depending upon how broadly one defines internal control, the approach to operational auditing goes further than a review of detailed internal control procedures since management's objectives are not achieved merely by adhering to satisfactory systems of internal control.

The classic management writers, Koontz, O'Donnell and Weihrich, endorsed this approach to operational auditing:

An effective tool of managerial control is the internal audit, or, as it is now coming to be called, the operational audit... Although often limited to the auditing of accounts, in its most useful aspect operational auditing involves appraisal of operations generally... Thus operational auditors, in addition to assuring themselves that accounts properly reflect the facts, also appraise policies, procedures, use of authority, quality of management, effectiveness of methods, special problems, and other phases of operations.

There is no persuasive reason why the concept of internal auditing should not be broadened in practice. Perhaps the only limiting factors are the ability of an enterprise to afford so broad an audit, the difficulty of obtaining people who can do a broad type of audit, and the very practical consideration that individuals may not like to be reported upon. While persons responsible for accounts and for the safeguarding of company assets have learned to accept audit, those who are responsible for far more valuable things—the execution of the plans, policies and procedures of a company—have not so readily learned to accept the idea.[1]

SCOPE

A key issue for a business and its internal audit function to decide upon is whether the scope of internal audit work in an operational area of the business should be restricted to a review of the appropriateness of, and extent of compliance with, key internal controls or should be a more comprehensive review of the operation generally.

The Committee of Sponsoring Organizations (COSO) view of internal control rightly sees one of the three objectives of internal control as being to give "reasonable assurance" of "effectiveness and efficiency of operations":

Internal control is broadly defined as a process, effected by the entity's board of directors, management and other personnel, designed to provide reasonable assurance regarding the achievement of objectives in the following categories:

- Effectiveness and efficiency of operations.
- Reliability of financial reporting.
- Compliance with applicable laws and regulations.[2]

So COSO's broad view of internal control is that internal control (i.e. management control) is everything that management does in order that there is reasonable assurance the business will achieve all of its objectives. A narrower view of internal control is that it is only one of a number of facets of management—among others being planning, organising, staffing and leading. It is true that these facets overlap and an internal audit which intends to focus more narrowly on key internal controls is likely to need to address planning, organising, staffing and/or leadership issues to some extent, since deficiencies in these may weaken control. But there will be many aspects of planning, organising, staffing and leading which are neutral in their effect on the functioning of key controls but which contribute to providing reasonable assurance of the achievement of efficient and effective operations.

The important issue is whether internal audit may legitimately draw management's attention to deficiencies in planning, organising, staffing and leading which, while not weakening the design and operation of key controls, nevertheless impede the achievement of objectives more generally. In the past internal audit was often defined as *the independent appraisal of the effectiveness of internal control*. The Institute of Internal Auditors' current (2009) definition of internal auditing, subscribed to globally, is that:

Internal auditing is an independent, objective assurance and consulting activity designed to add value and improve an organization's operations. It helps an organization accomplish its objectives by bringing a systematic, disciplined approach to evaluate and improve the effectiveness of risk management, control, and governance processes.[3]

So, should an enlightened enterprise restrict internal audit to narrow internal control matters, or should internal audit be encouraged to review and report on *any matters* which may be unsound? Differing positions are adopted in different enterprises. The middle-of-the-road approach is to encourage internal audit to interpret its mission as being the *appraisal of internal control* (in all its component parts,[4] in all operational areas of the business and at all levels of management). If during the course of audit work, other matters are noted which should be of management concern but do not directly have a control dimension, internal audit should be encouraged to report on them.

Beyond the consideration of the point of focus for audit reviews of operational areas, the audit function will have to define those aspects of the organisation which are to be subject to review. In practice, of course, this will vary considerably between organisations, and will be related directly to the nature of the business and the way the organisation is structured. For example, a multinational pharmaceutical company may have its principal manufacturing bases and research and development activities in only those few countries where the economic and commercial environments are most suitable, whereas sales and marketing operations (of varying scale) may exist in every country where there is a proven market for the products.

Although the focus of operational auditing is likely to be on those activities which are most strongly associated with the main commercial markets of the organisation (for example, production, sales, after sales support, service provision, etc.), it is likely that the supporting or infrastructure operations will also need to be reviewed on the basis that they too contribute to the well-being of the organisation as a whole. At the top level, one possible categorisation of all these areas could be as follows (although this classification will not fit every business or service-provision scenario):

- management and administration
- financial and accounting
- personnel and human relations
- procurement
- stock and materials handling
- production/manufacturing
- marketing and sales
- after sales support
- research and development
- information technology
- contracting.

This particular top level classification would be appropriate for a large organisation involved in product development, manufacturing and sales activities. A modified model would emerge for an organisation (public or private) associated with providing a service (for example, a public health authority or a roadside vehicle repair service).

Below this level of categorisation, there would be specific or discrete activities or systems, each of which may be the subject of a separate operational audit review. The subsequent chapters of this book will predominantly examine operational areas from this systems/activities orientation. For each of the above classifications there will be a number of discrete functions, systems or activities which may be defined within a particular organisation and be subject to examination by the internal auditors. This breakdown of the organisation into a set of separate audit reviews could be said to form the *audit universe* of potential audit projects. For example, the top level classifications noted above could be broken into the constituent systems or activities listed below, each of which could be the subject of an audit review. In some cases the noted subjects may readily align with a department within the organisation (i.e. payroll, human resources, purchasing, etc.). Alternatively, the activities may require coordination between a number of departments or functions (for example, the development of a new product may involve, *inter alia*, the marketing, accounting and research functions). Each organisation will be different and the internal audit function will need to adopt the most suitable definition of their *universe* of potential review assignments in order to match the prevailing structure and style.

A breakdown of the above top level classification into constituent systems or activities is given below:

Management and administration:

- the control environment
- organisation (i.e. structure)
- management information
- planning
- risk management
- legal department

- quality management
- estates management and facilities
- environmental issues
- insurance
- security
- capital projects
- industry regulations and compliance
- media, public and external relations
- company secretarial department.

Financial and accounting:

- treasury
- payroll
- accounts payable
- accounts receivable
- general ledger/management accounts
- fixed assets (and capital charges)
- budgeting and monitoring
- bank accounts and banking arrangements
- sales tax (i.e. VAT) accounting
- taxation
- inventories
- product/project accounting
- petty cash and expenses
- financial information and reporting
- investments.

Personnel/Human relations:

- human resources department (including policies)
- recruitment
- manpower and succession planning
- staff training and development
- welfare
- pension scheme (and other benefits)
- health insurance
- staff appraisal and disciplinary matters
- health and safety
- labour relations
- company vehicles.

Procurement (see also Contracting (below)):

- purchasing
- contracting (NB: this subject may be further broken down into a number of discrete subsystems, such as tendering, controlling interim and final payments, etc. see below).

Stock and materials handling:

- stock control

- warehousing and storage
- distribution, transport and logistics.

Production/manufacturing:

- planning and production control
- facilities, plant and equipment
- personnel
- materials and energy
- quality control
- safety
- environmental issues
- law and regulatory compliance
- maintenance.

Marketing and sales:

- product development
- market research
- promotion and advertising
- pricing and discount policies
- sales management
- sales performance and monitoring
- distribution
- relationship with parent company (for overseas or subsidiary operations)
- agents
- order processing.

After sales support:

- warranty arrangements
- maintenance and servicing
- spare parts and supply.

Research and development:

- product development
- project appraisal and monitoring
- plant and equipment
- development project management
- legal and regulatory issues.

Information Technology (IT):

- Auditing Information Technology
- IT Strategic Planning
- IT Organisation
- IT Policy Framework
- Information Asset Register
- Capacity Management
- Information Management (IM)
- Records Management (RM)

- Knowledge Management (KM)
- IT Sites and Infrastructure (Including Physical Security)
- Processing Operations
- Back-up and Media Management
- Removable Media
- System and Operating Software (Including Patch Management)
- System Access Control (Logical Security)
- Personal Computers (Including Laptops and PDAs)
- Remote Working
- Email
- Internet Usage
- Software Maintenance (Including Change Management)
- Networks
- Databases
- Data Protection
- Freedom of Information
- Data Transfer and Sharing (Standards and Protocol)
- Legal Responsibilities
- Facilities Management
- System Development
- Software Selection
- Contingency Planning
- Human Resources Information Security
- Monitoring and Logging
- Information Security Incidents
- Data Retention and Disposal
- Electronic Data Interchange (EDI)
- Viruses
- User Support

- performance monitoring
- arrangements for subcontractors and suppliers
- materials, plant and project assets
- valuing work for interim payments
- controlling price fluctuations
- monitoring and controlling variations
- extensions of time
- controlling contractual claims
- liquidations and bankruptcies
- contractor's final account
- recovery of damages
- review of project outturn and performance
- maintenance obligations.

Governance, risk management, internal control:

- internal governance processes
- the board
- external governance processes
- risk management processes
- issues for internal control.

For each of the above constituent activities there is available on the companion website a detailed standard audit programme guide (SAPG) in Word format, which readers can adapt to be more closely applicable to their business activities.[5] This is available on a password protected accompanying website. See Appendix 1 for details. The above list of constituent activities is by no means exhaustive, so we also provide a blank SAPG in Word format for readers to use to develop further business activities.

We also provide in Word format a set of 24 SAPGs relating to some of the activities within financial institutions and a set of 27 applicable to the health sector. The activities covered in these sector-specific sets are:

Sector: Financial institutions

- branch security
- branch operations
- management
- treasury dealing
- investments—new accounts
- investments—account maintenance
- investments—account statements
- secured personal loans
- unsecured loans
- commercial lending—new business
- commercial lending—account maintenance
- cheque accounts
- ATM services
- credit and debit cards

- new mortgage business
- mortgage account maintenance
- mortgage arrears
- mortgage possessions and sales
- mortgage mandates
- mortgage annual statements
- treasury environment
- staff accounts
- securities.

Sector: Health

- purchaser contracting
- provider contracting
- general practitioner fund holding
- charitable funds
- use of health centres
- private patients
- welfare foods
- residential accommodation
- joint finance
- residents' monies
- cashiers
- family health service authority
- road traffic accidents
- nursing homes
- trading agencies
- insurance products
- pharmacy stores
- risk management
- cash collection—car parks
- cash collection—telephones
- cash collection—prescriptions
- cash collection—shops/restaurants
- cash collection—staff meals
- cash collection—vending machines
- income generation
- staff expenses
- losses and compensations.

It is unwise to restrict one's thinking of these systems or activities as either existing or operating in isolation. This is rarely true. Any organisation will be formed from a number of interacting activities with points of interface. For example, in the case of ordering and receiving goods from external suppliers, there needs to be a coordinated flow of accurate information between the purchasing department, the stock warehouse and the accounts payable section. Whereas the control processes operating within a function or department may be well defined and applied, there is the potential for control weaknesses at the point of interface with other related functions. There are alternative ways of dividing up the *audit universe* of activities within an organisation and Chapter 2 examines such approaches in some detail.

It is important to stress that the listing of possible systems and activities given above is but one example of the way in which an organisation can be defined for audit or review purposes. Not all the items will be appropriate in every organisation. Additionally, although a listed activity may be relevant to a particular scenario, the scale and significance of it will vary between organisations. This matter of degree should be taken into account when the audit function is determining its priorities for planning purposes.

When approaching the review of operational areas of the organisation, it is important that the auditor has an accurate appreciation of the related key issues. If necessary, prior research should be conducted in order to provide the auditor with an acceptable level of understanding. Beyond the auditor's self-interest in being able to tackle confidently the review project, there is also the matter of the auditor's credibility in the eyes of operational management. It is interesting to note that The Institute of Internal Auditors' *Standards* place even more stress on planning an audit engagement than on performing it, expending twice as many words on the former. Unless the auditor can readily demonstrate a pragmatic awareness of the critical issues and set these against the objectives of senior management for the area under review, any subsequent work and findings may be in danger of not being treated seriously by management due to inaccuracies, misinterpretations and an inappropriate focus. The auditing approach to be adopted during operational reviews needs to be both professional and practical, and these elements will need to be set into the context of the formal auditing procedures. The practical and behavioural aspects of auditing are beyond the scope of this book. However, unless management can be suitably assured that the reviews conducted by internal audit are objective, professional and based upon an accurate understanding of the issues, they may question the worth of such activities to the organisation.

AUDIT APPROACH TO OPERATIONAL AUDITS

Auditors of operations should keep firmly in their mind the objectives of management for the operations being audited. At an early stage in planning the audit engagement, the audit team need to establish what are management's objectives. If management are unclear as to their objectives, then these objectives must be worked out with management before the audit engagement can process. During the planning phase of the audit engagement the audit objectives need to be established. "Audit objectives" are not synonymous with "management's objectives" as the audit objectives specify the particular focus that the auditors will have during the audit engagement. Even so, each audit objective must be determined because it will potentially add value in assisting management to achieve one or more of their objectives. No time should be expended during the audit engagement on issues which are immaterial to the achievement of management's objectives. Nothing should appear in the audit report of the engagement which is immaterial to the achievement of business objectives by management.

An audit approach which places management's objectives at its centre[6]

The group internal audit department of a domestic products multinational company headquartered in London is undertaking an audit engagement of the multinational's operating unit in Tokyo. At an early point in the planning process of this engagement, the audit team establishes who has oversight responsibility for the Tokyo operating unit. Let us say that this is the production director located in London, to whom the head of the Tokyo operating unit reports.

In a real sense the audit engagement is being conducted for the production director. The production director has a number of direct reports spread across the world, with oversight responsibility for each. The production director needs to know that all is in order within each of these operating units. He or she can go and find out for himself or herself. But the production director will rarely find the time to do so, and would hardly know how to set about doing so effectively. Internal auditing has been defined as doing what management would do if management had the time and knew how to do it. Internal auditors are experts at auditing—which management usually is not. An internal audit function does, of course, have the time to audit. Internal audit looks round corners that management are unable easily to look round for themselves.

At a later stage, the emerging audit findings will be discussed with the head of the Tokyo operating unit, whose responses will be built into the final audit report; the audit report will be *addressed* to the production director in London who may be regarded as the main client of this particular audit engagement. The report will be *copied* to the head of the Tokyo operating unit. In this way, the audit findings will be addressed to the level of management that needs to know and that is capable of ensuring appropriate action on audit findings is taken. Should the production director fail to ensure this, the chief audit executive will then need to consider whether the audit results, together with reference to the CAE's view that insufficient action has been taken upon them, should be communicated to an even higher level.[7] However, the CAE may consider that the degree of importance of the audit findings, when matched to the seniority of the production director, means that escalation above the level of the production director is not warranted as it may be legitimate for the production director to decide whether to live with a level of risk identified during the audit engagement.

Meanwhile, early during the planning of the audit engagement, having established that the production director has oversight responsibility for the Tokyo operating unit, the audit team arrange to meet with the production director. Initially the auditors ask the production director to explain:

"What are your objectives for the Tokyo operation?"

As with all information offered to the audit team during the course of the audit engagement, the auditors will consider how they can independently verify the validity of the statement of management's objectives that the team has been given. If the production director points out to the audit team that he or she has not thought much about the Tokyo operation for a while and cannot immediately recall whether there are any established objectives for Tokyo, then audit findings are already starting to emerge as clearly this is unsatisfactory. Nevertheless, the audit engagement cannot proceed further until the audit team has hammered out with the production director an agreed upon set of objectives for the Tokyo operation.

Next, in effect the audit team asks the production director the following question:

"OK, we are agreed on your objectives for the Tokyo operating unit. What information do you need to be receiving so that you know whether these objectives are being achieved?"

Again, if the production director is uncertain, then further provisional audit findings are starting to emerge—even though this discussion is taking place only during the planning phase of the audit engagement, before the audit team have left London for Tokyo. But planning the engagement cannot proceed further until the audit team has hammered out with the production director an agreement on the nature of the information he or she needs to be in receipt of in order to monitor whether management's objectives for the Tokyo operation are being achieved.

The next step is for the audit team to ask to see the information the production director is receiving:

"OK, we are agreed on the information you need to get from Tokyo to monitor that management's objectives for Tokyo are being achieved. Can you show us the information you are receiving about the Tokyo operation, please?"

When the audit team reviews this information they may discover that it is incomplete, unclear, inconsistent or untimely. So, further important provisional audit findings are starting to emerge. Nevertheless, the audit team endeavours to interpret the information so as to determine the most valuable focus for the audit fieldwork in Tokyo—that is, their audit objectives. They will discuss their proposed audit objectives with the production director with the intention of getting his "buy-in" to them. But being an assurance engagement, not the provision of a consulting service, it should be the decision of the chief audit executive what the audit objectives are to be: internal auditors do not subordinate their judgement on professional matters to that of others.[8]

Having determined the audit objectives for the engagement, the audit team are then able to draw up their audit programme which sets out how they plan to spend their fieldwork time in Tokyo. The approach they will take in Tokyo will include:

- confirming the reliability of the management information of importance submitted to the oversight function in London;

> - undertaking audit fieldwork so as to develop audit recommendations on issues they are already aware of with respect to incompleteness, lack of clarity, inconsistency and untimeliness;
> - determining whether other significant events are occurring in Tokyo which should be reported to the oversight function.
>
> While this case study describes a slightly novel approach to operational auditing, it does illustrate the importance of being clear about management's objectives for the operation being audited, and how management's objectives are woven through the engagement from beginning to end. The case study interprets a classic article which defined internal auditing as:
>
> "Internal auditing is the process of appraising the information flow to the monitoring function of a system for its quality and completeness. It is carried out by checking that the information is both self consistent and mutually consistent and by the irregular generation of test information flows."

Auditing for the Three and Six Es

Operational auditors are auditing for the "three Es"—effectiveness, efficiency and economy. They are looking for opportunities for business processes to be done differently so as to improve their effectiveness, efficiency and economy. At the very least they are intending to provide assurance to management and to the board that business processes *are* effective, efficient and economic. Too often auditors fail to appreciate the distinctiveness between each of these "three Es" with the risk that auditors fail to address all three separately. The COSO definition of internal control, given earlier in this Chapter, fails to highlight 'Economy' separately, choosing instead to subsume it within 'Efficiency'.

Figure 1.1 helpfully shows the distinctions, as well as the relationships, between the three. How *economic* we are is best considered in terms of the ratio between what we planned to spend on each unit of resource of given quality, and what we actually spent. Every organisation (whether a manufacturing or service entity), and every function or process within an organisation, has conversion processes that turn the actual inputs available into actual outputs. If staff are poorly trained, incompetent, poorly motivated or poorly supervised it will be likely that the ratio of usable outputs to the actual resources input into the conversion process will be unsatisfactory: in other words we do not have an adequately *efficient* (or smooth) conversion process. It is not just the quality of staff that contributes to efficiency: the design of processes, the quality of technology and so on are other factors. We are *effective* if our actual outputs correspond to the outputs we planned.

Figure 1.1 presumes that our economy, efficiency and effectiveness are each measured against economy, efficiency and effectiveness targets we set ourselves. If we are insufficiently demanding we may achieve 100% outcomes against the modest targets we set ourselves. Clearly we need ways of avoiding falling into this trap by:

- benchmarking against other organisations for indications as to whether we are "economic enough", "efficient enough" and "effective enough";
- comparing with other parts of our organisation;
- measuring and interpreting trends over time;
- aiming for continuous improvement.

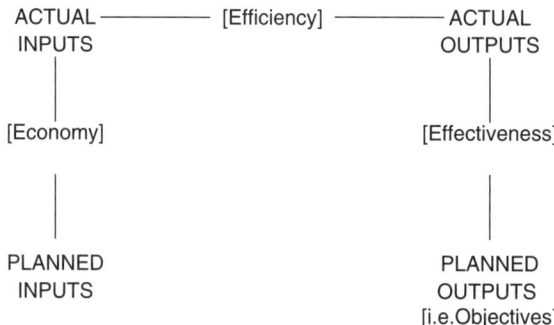

- *Economy* – means "doing them cheap" – with, for instance, unit costs for labour, materials, etc. being under control. *Economy* is the ratio between planned inputs and actual inputs in terms of unit costs of given quality.
- *Efficiency* – means "doing things well" – smoothly, for instance with good systems which avoid waste and rework. *Efficiency* is the ratio of actual inputs to actual outputs. Every organisation, whether a service organisation or a manufacturing business, has such a conversion process.
- *Effectiveness* – means "doing the right things" – i.e. achieving objectives. *Effectiveness* is the ratio of actual outputs to planned outputs (i.e. planned objectives).

Figure 1.1 The three Es

These three Es can be related to each other as shown in the model in Figure 1.1.

Internal auditors have now added a further "three Es" to their portfolio of matters of audit interest, particularly as a consequence of their role in the audit of governance processes as set out in Standards 2110 to 2110.C1 of The Institute of Internal Auditors:[9]

- *Equity*—avoidance of discrimination and unfairness; acceptance and promotion of diversity.
- *Environment*—acting in an environmentally responsible way.
- *Ethics*—legal and moral conduct by management and staff.

RESOURCING THE INTERNAL AUDIT OF TECHNICAL ACTIVITIES

Standard 1210 of The Institute of Internal Auditors on "Proficiency" reads:

"Internal auditors must possess the knowledge, skills, and other competencies needed to perform their individual responsibilities. The internal audit activity collectively must possess or obtain the knowledge, skills, and other competencies needed to perform its responsibilities."

and Standards 1210.A1 and 1210.C1[10] respectively read:

"**1210.A1**—The chief audit executive must obtain competent advice and assistance if the internal auditors lack the knowledge, skills, or other competencies needed to perform all or part of the engagement. . . .

"**1210.C1**—The chief audit executive must decline the consulting engagement or obtain competent advice and assistance if the internal auditors lack the knowledge, skills, or other competencies needed to perform all or part of the engagement."

Business objectives are achieved through successful processes within the operational areas of the business. The internal audit scope should not be merely to explore how operations are accounted for and administered. Business operations often include elements which are highly technical and which are essential if operational objectives are to be achieved. To audit such operations successfully, the audit team must collectively possess an understanding of those technical activities. While this understanding generally need not be to the level of an expert, it must be sufficient for the audit team to be able to determine whether the governance processes, risk management and internal control give reasonable assurance of the achievement of objectives and, if not, what measures might be introduced to rectify the situation. Beyond that, it is not necessary for the internal auditor to be expert in the technicalities of the operation being audited. Indeed it can be counterproductive and unconvincing for the auditor to try to project an expert image in the technicalities of the operation under review. Operational management are the operational experts. Internal auditors are expert at conducting audits and have general expertise in the principles of governance processes, risk management and internal control.

Where there is an inadequate balance between the technical complexity of the operation to be audited and the available, relevant technical competence of the in-house internal auditors, a number of options are available to the chief audit executive.

One option is to decline to include the operation within the future audit plan, or to approach the engagement with a limited scope so as to skirt round the challenging technical aspects of the operation . . . Standards 1130 on "Impairment to Independence or Objectivity" requires that . . .

"If independence or objectivity is impaired in fact or appearance, the details of the impairment must be disclosed to appropriate parties . . ."

and the Interpretation to this Standard makes "scope limitations" one of these impairments. Standard 2020 on "Communication and Approval" requires that the chief audit executive communicate to senior management and to the board the impact of resource limitations.

Another option is to adjust the competencies of the internal audit function so that all the principal technical disciplines which are core to the operations of the business are represented within the audit team. This often requires foresight—long-range planning to adjust the complement of internal auditors to the future needs of the business. Modern internal auditing activities should be multidisciplinary. The bias towards accountancy expertise is largely a consequence of the accountancy profession being one of the few sources of recruits of staff who have been trained in auditing. It is likely that the chief audit executive will favour recruiting internal auditors who are familiar with more than one of the requisite technical areas.

A further option is to buy-in temporarily the technical expertise to work alongside in-house internal auditors so as to build their competence to perform audits in particular technical areas. Such bought-in expertise may be sourced from outside the organisation or from technical areas within the entity but divorced from the particular operation to be audited. A similar but not identical approach was followed within British Petroleum for the internal audit of plant safety—of refineries, depots, terminals, pipelines and so on.

> ### BP's approach after the Texas refinery explosion
>
> Non audit staff, selected by BP's process safety advisor for the refining business from technical staff who were external to the subject site but were almost always BP employees, were used to undertake these so-called gHSEr audits.[11] The role of BP's Group Internal Audit was to conduct internal reviews of this gHSEr process but generally not to undertake the audit engagements themselves. Following the explosion at BP's Texas refinery early in 2005, and pipeline spillage at Prudhoe Bay, Alaska at about the same time, BP's board asked James Baker, previously Secretary of State in George Bush Snr's Administration and previously an oil industry specialist, to enquire and report to the board. The Baker Panel's report[12] suggested that BP's approach to resourcing their gHSEr audits had led to an internalised view of how things were done in BP and that third-party reviews by a qualified outside party would offer a different level of assurance. BP's board accepted the Baker Panel's suggestion that the Panel be mandated by the board to appoint an external expert to undertake this audit work for at least a five-year period, reporting directly to the board of BP.[13,14]

Indeed, sometimes the approach is followed to outsource completely the audit of highly technical areas. IT auditing is often so outsourced. While it is a moot point whether the work done by an outside expert and his or her team (as with the BP example) is to be regarded as internal audit work, The Institute of Internal Auditors' *Standards* make it clear that overall responsibility remains with the chief audit executive even when entire parts of internal audit work have been outsourced:

The chief audit executive is responsible for all internal audit engagements, whether performed by or for the internal audit activity, and all significant professional judgements made throughout the engagement. The CAE also adopts suitable means to ensure this responsibility is met. Suitable means include policies and procedures designed to:

- minimize the risk that internal auditors or others performing work for the internal audit activity make professional judgements or take other actions that are inconsistent with the CAE's professional judgement such that the engagement is impacted adversely.
- Resolve differences in professional judgement between the CAE and internal audit staff over significant issues relating to the engagement. Such means may include

discussion of pertinent facts, further inquiry or research, and documentation and disposition of the differing viewpoints in engagement working papers. In instances of a difference in professional judgement over an ethical issue, suitable means may include referral of the issue to those individuals in the organization having responsibility over ethical matters.

Another approach to obtaining assurance about highly technical activities is to rely, to a greater or lesser extent, on a programme of control self assessment (CSA) by technical management and staff, most probably in the form of CSA workshops facilitated by internal audit. This is different from traditional internal auditing—in particular as it is a less independent, less objective self assessment by management and staff. It has the advantage that it taps into the technical expertise of management and staff active in running the technical operation. Furthermore, these staff are probably already aware of the deficiencies of the operation and will have their own ideas as to how to make rectification going forward. We address control self assessment in Chapter 10.

PRODUCTIVITY AND PERFORMANCE MEASUREMENT SYSTEMS

Overview

Organisations are likely to have in place a number of key performance measures, so as to, among other things, assess the achievement of their objectives and goals, assess their progress, and compare relative performance (for example, over time). The nature and form of such measures will, of course, vary between types of organisation and indeed specific specialised forms of measurement may apply in certain industries or sectors. However, there are a number of general measures of effectiveness, efficiency and economy which usually apply universally and we shall look at some examples later in this chapter.

Measurement methods can be applied in order to identify whether there is any initial potential for improvement, and then subsequently used to monitor that the required levels of performance are maintained. The need to apply effective and realistic performance measurement methods is often generated as a by-product of fundamental change processes where, for example, an organisation is refocusing its strategy and position.

The Audit Implications for Measurement

During the course of a review of an operational area, the auditor is often faced with the need either to set the review findings into an appropriate context, or to indicate the performance of the area under review against the criteria previously established by management.

In most cases, it is preferable to utilise the measurement standards and criteria put in place by management as this results in the auditor using a common and compatible language when communicating results and points of concern. Conversely, if the auditor chooses to use a new, alternative or perhaps radical form of performance measure, this may influence or jeopardise management's view of the auditor's findings. This is not to say that auditors should only adopt the prevailing measurement criteria established by management, as there may be a compelling reason for introducing another objective form of performance assessment in some cases. Whatever the form of measurement applied, its use must be founded on both accurate and reliable data and a proven method, otherwise the credibility of internal audit will suffer.

Although it is important to establish a reliable and meaningful vocabulary for the measurement of performance in key operations, auditors must not lose sight of the fact that such measures can only point to potential areas of improvement and do not of themselves offer solutions. Assuming that the conclusions drawn from the review of such criteria are accurate and relative, they can then be used to frame and support audit recommendations and the appropriate corrective action(s).

In their use of performance measurement, auditors should be careful not to supplant management's use and interpretation of the same criteria. On the one hand, it may be legitimate for an auditor to investigate further the lack of management response to an adverse measurement indicator, but this does not necessarily mean that management has abdicated their basic responsibility for monitoring and control. This underlines a basic truism, in that measurement data is provided for interpretation and unless there is a formal measurement protocol in place, there may be the potential for differing conclusions to be drawn from the same data. This stresses the importance of formally establishing, for the organisation, a performance measurement policy and framework so that all concerned are clear about the nature of the data and how to use it in practice. Additionally, the creation and communication of corporate targets and goals can remove (or at least contain) some of the ambiguity associated with the required level of performance and expected level of associated achievement.

Each operational audit review project will present the auditor with a challenge to identify the most appropriate and meaningful performance measures to utilise, whether or not such criteria are already applied within the organisation.

Example Performance Measures

When establishing performance measures, it is logical to structure them on a hierarchal basis with the macro level indicators being broken into more detailed (micro level) measures relative to specific areas or subdivisions of either the operations or organisation. This should be borne in mind when considering the following example performance measures.[15]

Workload/Demand Performance Measures

Indicate the volume of output, whether services, products or other, and when linked to measures of input of resources, give useful information on quality or quantity matters.

Examples:

- Number of users

- Number of units produced
- Number of books in a library
- Percentage of first class degrees in a university.

Economy Performance Measures

These may highlight waste in the provision of resources indicating that the same resources may be provided more cheaply or that more enterprise may be conducted at the same cost.
   Examples:

- Cost of actual input in comparison with planned input
- Cleaning costs per hour worked
- Maintenance costs per unit area
- Cost of the finance function per 100 staff
- Cost of the chief executive's department per 1000 clients.

Efficiency Performance Measures

These may highlight potential opportunities to convert given resources to end product with less waste. Many performance measures will point to either uneconomic or inefficient practices, or both. It is often not possible to distinguish between one and the other.
   Examples:

- Ratio of actual input to actual output
- Breakdown per production day
- Accidents at work per 1000 personnel
- Degree success in comparison to school examination grades.

Effectiveness Performance Measures

These performance measures focus on how objectives are being achieved—regardless of economy, efficiency or equity (except where the objectives relate specifically to economy, efficiency and equity).
   Examples:

- Actual output in comparison to planned output
- Degree success (in a college or university)
- Research output per 100 research staff
- Ratio of customer complaints to sales.

Equity Performance Measures

These performance measures draw attention to unfairness or potential social irresponsibility in terms of corporate policy and practice.

Examples:

- Departmental grant per member of staff
- Number of library books per category of user
- Proportion of female employees
- Proportion of disabled employees.

VALUE FOR MONEY (VFM) AUDITING

Earlier in this chapter we gave the generally accepted definition of internal auditing to which internal auditing *Standards* require internal auditors to conform. The definition states that internal auditing is designed "to add value and improve an organization's operations". So, internal auditors should add value in all of their work. The Institute of Internal Auditors defines "add value" as:

Value is provided by improving opportunities to achieve organizational objectives, identifying operational improvement, and/or reducing risk exposure through both assurance and consulting services.[16]

A better definition of 'add value' would be:

The internal audit activity adds value when the organisation and its stakeholders benefit from the results of internal audit work. Benefit arises when the internal audit activity provides objective and relevant assurance, and contributes to the effectiveness and efficiency of governance, risk management and control processes.

Value for money auditing is sometimes used in a different context to refer to a style of operational auditing which makes extensive use of key performance indicators to explore the cost of achieving standards of efficiency and effectiveness and whether these costs represent good value.

Value for money auditing takes account of the three Es. It frequently makes extensive use of performance indicators in the form of ratios and other statistics to give an indication of value for money—especially when trends are explored in these performance indicators over time, or variations in performance are identified and explained between different operating units.

The term value for money is often applied to public sector spending in the UK, where there is an implied obligation placed on public bodies to ensure that they obtain and provide services on the most economic grounds. This process invariably involves elements of competition where cost comparisons are made between parties being invited to supply goods and services. For example, many services within UK local government have been put out to tender in order to obtain the "best deal", and very often this tendering process has also included the internal department or function that had previously been supplying the service.

This striving for procurement on a *least cost* basis appears to be very logical and represent common sense, especially where the expenditure of public funds is involved. However, it is equally important to consider whether the potential service provider (or supplier or contractor) can meet the required quality and performance standards as well. Therefore, any consideration of value for money must take in quality and performance achievement factors as well, as there may be serious commercial or operational implications if the relevant services/goods are not up to a given standard.

Value for money auditing will involve the assessment of an appropriate range of performance measurement criteria. It could be asked that unless management have clearly established their own basis for measuring and assessing the supply of goods and the provision of services, why did they embark on the process in first place? In other words, what was their driving motivation in either fulfilling the requirements or seeking alternatives?

In both the management and audit assessment of matters of value for money, the usual approach is to make comparisons with a range of options or possible solutions to the principal problem. These comparisons should be conducted as scientifically and objectively as possible and utilise appropriate measurement means. This part of the process begins with realistically identifying all the practical options and alternatives (perhaps including doing nothing at all).

In a more formal environment (for example, where acquiring new computing facilities) it may be necessary and desirable to go through a detailed feasibility study as part of an overall project appraisal process. This can then incorporate the appropriate cost and performance comparisons which underline the determination of value for money. In such scenarios, it is important that the auditor is content with the chosen assessment mechanism and measurement criteria so that, taken together, the appropriate reassurance can be derived that the process is sound and accurate. In some instances it may be necessary for the auditors to recommend improvements in these areas to add value to the process, whilst avoiding usurping management's ultimate responsibility for their system.

Whether or not a formal procedure is in place to determine generally the achievement of value for money, the internal audit function may be required (or indeed obliged) independently to assess such matters on behalf of management. Auditors should always avoid taking on activities which should, in the first place, be the responsibility of management. However, where internal audit has a legitimate role to play, auditors should endeavour to identify all the probable options and the most suitable basis on which they should be measured and assessed in value terms.

In order to avoid any potential problems at the conclusion of their assessment, auditors should consider discussing their proposed assessment and measurement criteria with management at the outset, and furthermore to obtain the agreement of management on the applied methodology. In certain sectors and industries, recognised criteria may already exist and so it may not be necessary for auditors to develop their own process.

BENCHMARKING

Benchmarking can be defined simply as a comparison of one's own performance in a specific area with that applied by others in compatible circumstances. As a technique it is founded on the premise that there may be viable alternative ways of performing a process and fulfilling a requirement.

For a benchmarking exercise to be meaningful, it is necessary to understand fully the existing processes, systems and activities as a firm basis for subsequent comparison with external points of reference (such as industry or professional standards). This process of realisation often incorporates the establishment of critical success factors for an operation (or part thereof). The principal objectives of benchmarking are likely to include:

- maintaining a competitive advantage in the appropriate market;
- establishing current methods, best practice and related trends;
- ensuring the future survival of the organisation;
- maintaining an awareness of customer expectations (and being able to address them);
- ensuring that the organisation has the appropriate approach to quality issues.

The focus of a benchmarking exercise can be varied in relation to the fundamental justification and objectives of the process. For example, if the objective was primarily to examine the existing processes within the organisation as a means of identifying common factors and best practices to apply throughout the company, the focus could be said to be downward and inward. Alternatively, if the organisation was seeking views on the strengths and weaknesses of competitors this is outward looking in nature, and could involve one-to-one competitor benchmarking, industry benchmarking or best-in-class benchmarking methods.

Internal audit departments can often benefit from participating in benchmark comparisons with other audit functions; such involvement can contribute to their understanding of:

- the internal auditing trends and practices as applied by the companies surveyed;
- the implications and potential of the findings for the participant's own organisation;
- the validity of the participant's own stance on internal auditing in relation to that apparent from the survey data.

Involvement in such exercises will enable participants to take a view of the need for change or review of their own organisation's approach to internal auditing in light of the survey data.

Of course, benchmarking is not an end in itself, but rather one platform used to identify and subsequently launch the required or necessary processes of change within a department, function, activity, process or organisation.

NOTES

1. Koontz H., O'Donnell, C. and Weihrich, H. (1976) *Management*. 8th edition. McGraw-Hill, Singapore, pp. 670–671.
2. Committee of Sponsoring Organizations (COSO) (September 1992) *Internal Control–Integrated Framework*.
3. This generally accepted definition of internal auditing is to be found in the preamble to The Institute of Internal Auditors' (The IIA) Code of Ethics which is part of their International Professional Practices Framework (IPPF). Members and candidates for the professional certifications of The IIA commit to observing the Code of Ethics which, *inter alia*, requires conformance with their *Standards*.

The *Standards*, also part of the IPPF, make it clear in several places that conformance with the *Standards* requires that internal auditing corresponds to this Definition of Internal Auditing.

4. COSO *Internal Control–Integrated Framework* study (1992) identified the five components of internal control as being (1) control environment, (2) risk assessment, (3) control activities, (4) information and communication, and (5) monitoring.
5. Word is a trademark of the Microsoft Corporation.
6. The example we give of the audit engagement of the Tokyo operating unit by a London-based group internal audit department team is based on a rather novel approach to internal auditing, as set out in a classic article by Dr Graham Hibbert and Margaret Graham, titled "The Boundaries of Internal Auditing" which appeared in *Accountancy* (the monthly journal of the Institute of Chartered Accountants in England & Wales) as long ago as September 1979, pp. 95–100. In that article they defined their style of internal auditing as follows:

   > Internal auditing is the process of appraising the information flow to the monitoring function of a system for its quality and completeness. It is carried out by checking that the information is both self consistent and mutually consistent and by the irregular generation of test information flows.

   While this definition on its own is rather hard to understand, the example we give should make it clear.
7. Standard 2600 of The Institute of Internal Auditors reads:

   2600—Resolution of Senior Management's Acceptance of Risks

   When the chief audit executive believes that senior management has accepted a level of residual risk that may be unacceptable to the organization, the chief audit executive must discuss the matter with senior management. If the decision regarding residual risk is not resolved, the chief audit executive must report the matter to the board for resolution.
8. The mandatory interpretation to The Institute of Internal Auditors' Standard 1100 on "Independence and Objectivity" includes the words: "Objectivity requires that internal auditors do not subordinate their judgement on audit matters to others. Threats to objectivity must be managed at the individual auditor, engagement, functional, and organizational levels" and the *Standards*' Glossary definition of "Objectivity" reads:

   Objectivity

   An unbiased mental attitude that allows internal auditors to perform engagements in such a manner that they have an honest belief in their work product and that no significant quality compromises are made. Objectivity requires internal auditors not to subordinate their judgement on audit matters to others.
9. **2110—Governance**

   The internal audit activity must assess and make appropriate recommendations for improving the governance process in its accomplishment of the following objectives:

   - Promoting appropriate ethics and values within the organization;
   - Ensuring effective organizational performance management and accountability;
   - Communicating risk and control information to appropriate areas of the organization; and
   - Coordinating the activities of and communicating information among the board, external and internal auditors, and management.

      2110.A1—The internal audit activity must evaluate the design, implementation, and effectiveness of the organization's ethics-related objectives, programs, and activities.

      2110.A2—The internal audit activity must assess whether the information technology governance of the organization sustains and supports the organization's strategies and objectives.

      2110.C1—Consulting engagement objectives must be consistent with the overall values and goals of the organization.

10. Standards with the alpha character "A" within the Standard number indicate a Standard relating to the internal audit *assurance* role. Those with "C" relate to the internal audit *consulting* role.
11. gHSEr—"getting Health, Safety and the Environment right".
12. The Report of the BP U.S. Refineries Independent Safety Review Panel ("The Baker Report"), 2007, *vide*, in particular, pp. 14 and 211.
13. *Vide* Chambers, A. D. (2008) "The board's black hole—filling their assurance vacuum: can internal audit rise to the challenge", *Measuring Business Excellence*, Vol. 12, No. 1, pp. 47–63.
14. *Vide* Chambers, A. D. (April 2009) "The black hole of assurance", *Internal Auditor*, Vol. 66, No. 2, pp. 28–29.
15. The examples in this section were drawn from Chambers, A. D., Selim, G. M. and Vinten, G. (1987, 1988 and 1990) *Internal Auditing*. Pitman Publishing, pp. 361–362.
16. Entry in the Glossary to the *Standards* of The Institute of Internal Auditors (2009).

2
Business Processes

INTRODUCTION

In Chapter 1 we adopted primarily a functionally oriented approach to defining the activities for operational audit review. In other words, we looked at the whole organisation as a set of discrete and definable activity areas, such as treasury, production, payroll, etc. This is one traditional and convenient way of approaching audit assignments, but there are some associated drawbacks, which we are discussing here.

One of the shortcomings of the functional approach to defining the audit universe is that it often fails to identify very significant activities that naturally span departments. For example, the process of launching a new product or service may be extremely significant for a company. This will normally involve the appropriately coordinated contributions of a number of functions, including finance, research and development, marketing, sales, production, accounting, legal department, and so on. As a consequence, launching new products and services is often done in a very poorly controlled way. The auditor is unlikely to find an entry on the internal telephone directory called "product launch", and so it is possible that this critical area would be missed if a purely functional approach to assignment definition were adopted.

Whenever an auditor draws a boundary (or scope) around an audit review project, there will inevitably be loose ends or points of onward interconnection to consider. One way of avoiding this eventuality is to consider the business operations as a series of "cradle to grave" processes or cycles, where a chain of interrelated events or activities is plotted from the origin to the conclusion.

Where an internal audit engagement corresponds to an organisational part of the business, the internal auditor should expect that many of the opportunities for improvement will lie at the points of interface between that part of the business and other parts of the business with which there needs to be effective coordination. The audit programme for the audit engagement should reflect this probability. Thus, by way of example, when the audit subject is "payroll" the auditor might expect to find the principal control weaknesses at the periphery of payroll, for instance where payroll staff rely on the timely, accurate and complete notification by operations management of overtime hours worked, and where they rely on the HR department to notify payroll about joiners and leavers as well as about changes in rates of pay.

AN AUDIT UNIVERSE OF BUSINESS PROCESSES

How do auditors decide upon the most appropriate way to define their universe of audit review projects? There are obviously a number of ways that an organisation can be divided up. One way would be to separate the "productive" or commercial aspects of the business (such as manufacturing or sales) from the support or infrastructure activities (such as accounting, photocopying or security). This type of subdivision is generally geared to the fundamental nature of the business or operations of the organisation and tends to lend a natural priority to those more significant areas of activity.

The simplest (although not necessarily the best) way to define the audit universe is to look at the internal telephone directory. This will identify the discrete departments and may, if viewed alongside any organisation charts, lend a definable form to the company. However, this approach perpetuates the misguided view that such departments operate in isolation of each other within their own orbit.

Two apparent advantages of using this "departmental" or "functional" basis for defining audit reviews are: (1) the area under review is clearly bounded, and (2) reporting lines to responsible management are clear-cut. However, although this may suggest that the audit administration may theoretically be straightforward, this is not necessarily true in practice. It is unlikely that any one department, system or activity will operate in complete isolation, but each will need to interact with other data and systems in order to be fully effective.

At a simple level, such interaction could relate to the input of data from a source system (outside of the department) which is then processed in some way so that some form of enhanced or amended data is generated for output to the next process or department. For example, taking coded transactions from an accounts payable system into the general ledger as the basis for producing management accounts information—all the stages being handled by discrete domains. There is something inherently unnatural and disturbing about self-perpetuating departments/functions that lack points of interconnection with others!

It is often at the point of interaction between systems or departments where controls are critical. This is where the custody of data, etc. changes hands. Auditors should be aware of these points of interaction and satisfy themselves that the data moving between systems is consistent, complete and accurate, so that the subsequent processes are undertaken on a reliable basis.

The way in which defined functions are mapped and interconnected across an organisation will obviously differ considerably between organisations, and may be influenced by best practice, sector-specific practice and the requirements of legislation and regulation. In any event, the auditor will need to establish and communicate the boundary or scope of each review project, partly as a means of ensuring that all concerned are aware of what is being examined (and equally important, what is not being included) within the review.

Dividing up the audit universe for review purposes into a number of business processes, rather than according to how the organisation is structured into departments, divisions, operating units, HQ functions and so on, has great potential to reveal opportunities to improve economy, efficiency and effectiveness. Governance processes, risk management and internal control are usually much weaker over business processes which cut across departmental frontiers. Quite commonly the process has not been considered in an integrated way, and controls may have been formalised only for operating each part of the process which occurs within a single section of the organisation. User manuals of required procedures have often not been developed so thoroughly as to describe processes that step across departmental frontiers.

A business process way of defining the internal audit universe of auditable units is also likely to result in an audit universe of fewer auditable units although each, corresponding to a process which requires coordination between a number of parts of the organisation, is likely to be a more complex audit engagement. For instance, the internal audit department of a large clearing bank redefined its audit universe away from comprising, *inter alia*, each of the many hundreds of bank branches to become each of the bank's processes—such as opening current accounts, managing overdrafts, and so on. Once redefined in this way, branches were visited not because they represented audit engagements to be performed but on a sample basis to test that controls over the bank's processes were operating satisfactorily across the bank.

We concede that an advantage of defining the audit universe according to the way the organisation is structured (into departments, divisions, operating units, HQ functions and so on) is that it is usually more straightforward to determine where to go to perform the audit engagement and also more straightforward to determine to whom to address the audit report. An audit of, for instance, launching a new product or an audit of handling customer complaints will involve the auditor in undertaking audit fieldwork in a number of different parts of the organisation and is likely to generate audit results which must be communicated to a number of senior managers, none of whom may be able to take ownership of dealing with all of the audit results. Where it is ambiguous who has the ownership responsibility to take action on an audit finding, *prima facie* a problem of authority and responsibility has been identified which indicates that the overall process lacks sufficient control.

The auditor who chooses the business process method of defining the scope of audit reviews is faced with the need to identify all the relevant managers responsible for the activities within the scope of the engagement. This will be necessary in order to ensure that they are duly consulted about the review and so the auditor is clear about the reporting lines for the report and auditor's recommendations.

The main benefit of this approach is that it should encompass all the relevant issues and aim to provide reassurance to management on the effectiveness of the internal control measures in place across the whole process. On the down side, this method requires auditors to plan very carefully how they approach the engagement and to ensure that the fieldwork is adequately coordinated in order to initially identify and consider all the risks and control issues, which will potentially span a number of organisationally separate areas. These considerations will have implications for the general manageability of the audit review project.

In the course of examining the various approaches to defining the audit universe and performing audit engagements, you should be aware of the practical advantages and disadvantages from the auditor's point of view. We do not necessarily promote or suggest any specific method as the ideal, as the environment and culture of organisations will vary considerably in practice and no one approach can ever be universally appropriate. Auditors will need to assess the risks inherent within their organisations as the primary basis for allocating audit review resources, and accordingly adopt the most suitable review methods for their specific circumstances.

The role played by internal audit within organisations will also vary in practice, and their chosen review basis will need to meet the specific needs of the relevant organisation and adapt to the prevailing management culture while addressing the requirements of professional internal audit practice. The nature of the organisation's operations is likely to have the greatest influence here, and unless the internal audit function can ensure that their review activities are suitably aligned with the corporate approach and objectives, the credibility of the auditing service may be adversely affected.

SELF ASSESSMENT OF BUSINESS PROCESSES

Reviewing business processes using the control self assessment (CSA) approach can sometimes be a workable alternative to the traditional internal audit approach though CSA provides a lesser level of objective assurance. CSA is discussed in Chapter 10. A representative can be invited to attend the CSA workshop from each of the parts of the organisation that need to coordinate in the business process. It may be the first time they have got together to discuss the process in an integrated way. They will each be well aware of the coordination problems they have been experiencing and will have their own ideas as to how to address them. The workshop generates its own report and it then naturally falls to those who attended the workshop to implement most of the agreed actions arising from the workshop.

A HYBRID AUDIT UNIVERSE

In reality, an internal audit activity is likely to have an audit universe where some of the potential audit engagements are of subjects which correspond to the organisational parts of the business (departments, divisions, operating units, HQ functions and so on) while others are of business processes which cross over the structural frontiers. This poses a challenge to avoid "double auditing" where the internal audit activity addresses the same issues as part of a process audit and also as part of a functional audit.

REASONS FOR PROCESS WEAKNESSES

It is not just that formal, laid-down procedures tend not to be so thoroughly defined to address requirements for coordination between sections of the business. Control is likely to be weaker *between* sections than *within* sections for behavioural reasons as well. Staff are sociable people. Everyone values his or her membership of groups. The workgroup that someone belongs to is usually important to that individual. Staff tend to identify with their immediate workgroup more strongly than they identify with the organisation as a whole. Indeed, this *intra-group loyalty* is likely to contrast strongly with *inter-group rivalry*. It is a responsibility of management to use their best endeavours to mitigate this likely default mentality. If a member of a workgroup sees a workgroup colleague making a mistake, he or she will tactfully endeavour to rectify it in a timely way—through a sense of loyalty to a colleague and because the reputation and good fortune of the entire workgroup depends on the team's productivity. If one group sees another group making a mistake, it is quite likely that the first group will relish the misfortune of the other group and merely observe as they dig a deeper and deeper hole for themselves. However, it is more likely that the workgroup will not notice the errors being made by a linked workgroup until the associated group's output becomes this workgroup's input—at which point its defects will be labelled as "nothing to do with us—not our fault". On the other hand, an internal auditing function should have unrestricted rights of access and can follow an operation wherever it goes. Since control is likely to be weakest where there is a requirement for coordination between sections, it follows that many internal audits should be of auditable units that correspond to natural business processes rather than to the formal, structural organisational subdivisions of the business.

We have already pointed out that formal, laid-down procedures are likely to be more fully developed to describe the work undertaken within a section of the business than between sections. The manager of a section is likely to make sure that this is so but may have no authority to ensure that procedures spanning sections of the business are similarly robust. Furthermore if the formal procedures within a section turn out to be inadequate, there is a better prospect for them to be compensated for by the development of informal procedures by the members of that workgroup. It is true that one observes informal coalitions developing within a business when, for instance, staff in different sections which need to coordinate with each other take the trouble to have lunch together—and so on. But it is easier for relationships to work constructively *within* a section than *between* sections.

In whatever way the organisation is structured (into divisions, departments, sections and so on) it is always a subjective and often an evolutionary compromise and could have been done differently. It is to be hoped that the structure has been designed so as to put together in a single section the staff that are engaged in a common task or a series of closely related tasks requiring a maximum of interaction between the members of the workgroup. But by putting staff together in a single section, management has divided them organisationally from a number of other staff in other sections with whom interaction, to some extent, is still required. The implications of these group dynamics led Likert[1] to develop the idea of the *linking pin*. He postulated, no doubt correctly, that for an organisation to function properly there is a need not only to have cohesive workgroups. In addition there is a need for groups to be linked together by competent, trained group coordinators, called *linking pins* with membership of two or more groups. The linking pin, who may not be the most senior person in any of the groups, does the following:

- helps a group achieve consensus;
- communicates the consensus to the other group(s);
- facilitates resolution of conflict between groups.

Lawrence and Lorsch showed that linking pins who share the norms of the interfacing groups are likely to be more effective than those who are more closely aligned to just one of the groups being linked.[2] Use of familiar jargon is often important in this. It is the problem of divergent norms between linked workgroups that often accounts for the lack of effective coordination and control between the workgroups. What is valued as important by one group may be disregarded by the other workgroup. For instance, sales and marketing people place a premium on creativity and discount the value of economy and control which tend to be prized by accountants and production staff.

IDENTIFYING THE PROCESSES OF AN ORGANISATION

We now turn our attention to defining the organisation as a number of processes or cycles each of which potentially may be the subject of an audit engagement.

This approach focuses on a number of related economic events that occur within an organisation that in turn may generate transactions and interactions with systems. It is often referred to as the "business cycle" approach. Its prime aim is to take account of the lifecycle of a series of events within the business operations and review them in their entirety across all functional and organisational boundaries.

Before going on to look at this approach in some detail, we should pause for a moment to deal with a matter of basic terminology. The term "cycle" in this context may be potentially confusing as not all the economic activities that form the backbone of this method are truly cyclical in nature. It may be preferable to use the term "business processes" as many are linear and do not significantly loop back in a cyclical way.

It is impractical to suggest a standard division into processes that will hold true for organisations generally. Each organisation is significantly unique. It will be necessary for chief audit executives to brainstorm with their colleague auditors, with management and even with the audit committee of the board in order to identify the principal business processes of their organisation and to determine which should be the subject of an audit engagement.

Here we suggest first a basic and then a more detailed list of business processes commonly found in organisations, offered as a starting point for chief audit executives to develop their own tailored list applicable to their organisations.

Beyond this, in Chapter 14 we show how contracting can be interpreted as a process with a number of sub-processes linking together.

Six Ubiquitous Processes

The following simple definitions can be applied to six principal processes commonly found within organisations.

1. The Revenue Process

Related to those activities that exchange the organisation's products and services for cash, and therefore include (*inter alia*) the following elements:

- credit granting;

- processing orders;
- delivery and shipping;
- billing to customers;
- maintaining accurate and reliable inventory records;
- the activities associated with accounts receivable;
- bad debt (including pursuing debtors and writing off balances);
- reflecting the related transactions correctly in the accounting systems.

2. The Expenditure Process

Those activities/systems that acquire goods, services, labour and property; pay for them; and classify, summarise and report what was acquired and what was paid. For example:

- ensuring that suppliers are stable, reliable and able to provide the appropriate goods/services on time, at the right price and to the required quality;
- the requisitioning of goods, services, corporate assets and labour;
- receiving, securely storing and correctly accounting for goods;
- all the activities associated with accounts payable (e.g. matching orders to suppliers' invoices and confirming the accuracy of pricing, etc.);
- recruiting and correctly paying staff;
- ensuring that all taxes due are correctly calculated and disbursed;
- ensuring that all the related accounting records are accurate, up to date and complete.

3. The Production/Conversion Process

In this context, the term "conversion" relates to the utilisation and management of various resources (inventory stock, labour, etc.) in the process of creating the goods and services to be marketed by the organisation.

The key issues in this process include accountability for the movement and usage of resources up to the point of supply which is then dealt with in the revenue cycle. Conversion cycle activities include product accounting/costing, manufacturing control, and stock management.

4. The Treasury Process

This process is fundamentally concerned with those activities relating to the organisation's capital funds, such as:

- the definition of the cash requirements and cash flow management;
- allocation of available cash to the various operations;
- investment planning;
- the outflow of cash to investors and creditors (i.e. dividends).

5. The Financial Reporting Process

This process is *not* based on the basic processing of transactions reflecting economic events, but concentrates upon the crucial consolidation and reporting of results to various interested parties (i.e. management, investors, regulatory and statutory authorities).

6. The Corporate Framework Process

This process incorporates those activities concerned with ensuring effective and appropriate governance processes and external accountability. It is to do with the development and maintenance of values, culture and ethics, and effective management, strategic, infrastructure and control frameworks that should aim to give form to the underlying direction, structure and effectiveness of an organisation. This category can also include issues such as specific industry regulations and compliance.

An Alternative, More Detailed Classification of Business Processes

This more detailed classification into processes draws upon Johnson and Jaenicke.[3] It covers in more detail the six overall "ubiquitous" processes set out above. Johnson and Jaenicke say that the four cycles (marked with an asterisk below) form the internal accounting control system for most enterprises.

1. Cash process: The flow of cash into the business principally through payments from customers, the custodial function with regard to that cash and the conversion of the cash in settlement of debts due principally to suppliers.

2. Information process: The gathering of data and its conversion into information; the analysis of that information leading to decisions which in turn result in data on performance.

3. Integrity process: "[the] controls over the creation, implementation, security and use of computer programs, and controls over the security of data files. These controls, technically referred to as integrity controls, constitute a cycle because they operate continuously from the time programs are instituted and data are introduced into the computer records."[3]

4. Launching a new product process: The cycle that includes market research, R & D, provision of necessary finance, tooling up (or the equivalent), commencement of production and the sales launch.

5. Payments process:* "Transaction flows relating to expenditures and payments and related controls over (among other activities) ordering and receipt of purchases, accounts payable, and cash disbursements."[3]

6. Planning and control process: Planning a course of action, executing that action, measuring the results, comparing actual performance with planned performance and deciding upon corrective action.

7. Production process:* "Transaction flows relating to production of goods or services and related controls over such activities as inventory transfers and charges to production for labour and overhead."[3]

8. Product life process: Commencing with the processes of launching a new product, through the routine production phase, product revision and relaunch, product price adjustments, and termination or decline of the product line.

9. Revenue process:* "Transaction flows relating to revenue generating and collection functions and related controls over such activities as sales orders, shipping, and cash collection."[3]

10. Time process:* "Not strictly related to transaction flows, this cycle includes events caused by the passage of time, controls that are applied only periodically, certain custodial activities, and the financial reporting process."[3]

A useful text which explores the cycle approach to understanding business systems is *Accounting Information Systems—A Cycle Approach* by James R. Davis, C. Wayne Alderman and Leonard A. Robinson; the third edition was published in 1990 by John Wiley & Sons Inc., New York. While this book has a student orientation, professional people will find it valuable too.

WHY ADOPT A "CYCLE" OR "PROCESS" APPROACH TO INTERNAL CONTROL DESIGN AND REVIEW?

An further advantage of viewing business activity as a number of processes is that it affords a more natural, systems oriented view by following a business process through its entire "life span" from inception to ultimate disposition. This avoids the more limited perspective which results if business activities are viewed (or audited) only to the extent that they occur *within* a section of the business such as within a department.

To some extent, auditors have always appreciated the idea of natural processes or flows, as one definition of "audit trail" indicates, *viz*:

Audit trail implies the preparation and retention within an organisation (a) for an adequate period, (b) in a reasonably accessible form, and (c) in enough detail to satisfy the auditors, of records which allow each detailed element of any transaction to be tracked from its source through each intermediate stage to its final disposition (or dispositions); and vice versa—that is, the facility to use records to trace back in detail from the final outcome (or outcomes) through the intermediate stages back to the initial source (or sources) of the transaction.[4]

BUSINESS PROCESSES IN THE STANDARD AUDIT PROGRAMME GUIDES

The **Standard Audit Programme Guides** [SAPGs] which accompany this Handbook in Word format on a password protected accompanying website (see Appendix 1 for details), accommodate to the concept of the business as a number of processes, in two ways.

First, each SAPG indicates other SAPGs with which the subject of the SAPG interacts—either because what happens in that other area of the business impacts on the subject of the SAPG, or what happens within the subject covered by the SAPG impacts upon other areas of the business. This is indicated in a table at the end of each SAPG.

Secondly, Appendix 2 classifies each SAPG as belonging in a major or secondary way to one or more of the six "ubiquitous" processes explained above. We recognise that the first four SAPG process categories are built around a range of related economic events which may in turn generate transactions and interactions with systems. It should be noted that there is likely to be selective interaction between the defined processes, for example the general management of cash is one of the key issues of the Treasury Process, but the Revenue Process is associated with cash receipts and the Expenditure Process will involve cash disbursements. In instances where a particular system or activity has a relevance to more than one of the named processes, the SAPG methodology differentiates between the Main (or primary) and Secondary relationships. This discrimination is intended to further assist users in selecting the appropriate combinations of SAPGs which can readily support the structural objectives of their adopted audit universe approach.

THE HALLMARKS OF A GOOD BUSINESS PROCESS

In this chapter we have discussed understanding the organisation as a number of fundamental business processes, each of which is likely to require involvement of several parts of the organisation. So far we have not addressed the characteristics of a robust business process. The following are some of the hallmarks of a sound business process:

1. designed to meet objectives which are clear;
2. has regard to competitive issues;
3. performance can be (and is) measured;
4. unsatisfactory performance is rectified;
5. activities are completed in a timely way;
6. processes are cost effective;
7. controls are "preventative" rather than merely "permissive";
8. as few "movements"/"stages" as possible;
9. unnecessary steps have been eliminated;

    - nothing is done which is unimportant to the achievement of objectives;

10. proper authorisations;
11. controls positioned as early as possible in the process;
12. documented;
13. has an audit trail;
14. right people doing the right job;
15. room for adaptation;
16. defines risks within the process itself.

ACADEMIC CYCLES IN A UNIVERSITY

By way of an illustrative case study, we show here some of the cycles which would apply in a university.

ACADEMIC CYCLES IN A UNIVERSITY

1. The Course Cycle

The course goes through a design process which is subject to quality control mechanisms. When approved it is run for the first time. Participants in the course, especially the students, evaluate their experience of the course and make suggestions for improvement. In the light of their assessments the programme is reviewed, invariably leading to adjustments in course design to address opportunities for improvement.

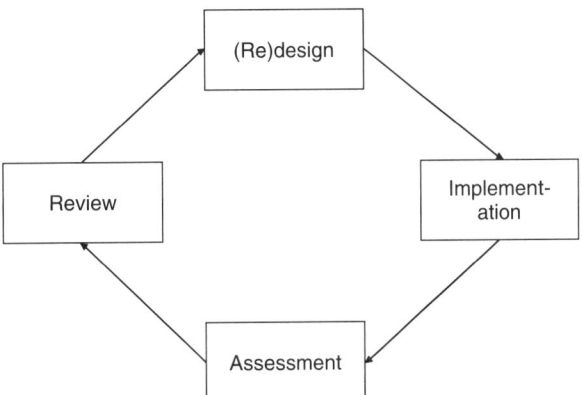

2. The Student Cycle

The University markets the course to market sectors likely to be interested, leading to applications to join the course from prospective students. From these applicants a number are selected and enrol. As students of the University, and of this course in particular, they are tutored and cared for so that they can progress their studies satisfactorily. At points during the programme of study, the level of attainment of each student is assessed so that eventually the student has achieved the completion standard required and becomes a graduate of the University. The University's graduates are important ambassadors for the University, not least for marketing purposes, and so the University endeavours to ensure the goodwill of their alumni by providing them with alumni services, including the opportunity to network with other graduates.

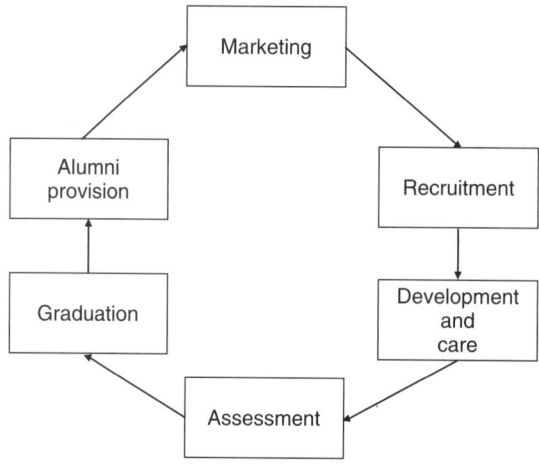

3. Teacher Cycle

Academic staff share teaching, research and administrative duties on an equitable basis, and each is given an indication of his or her future teaching. This enables the academic staff member to plan and execute the preparation of his or her future teaching, leading to the development of teaching materials in good time for the actual delivery of the teaching. A process of student assessment of teaching quality is applied to enable the academic staff member, in liaison with his or her academic manager, to review his or her performance and take steps to make necessary improvements. This may lead to adjustment of the quantity and content of the staff member's future load.

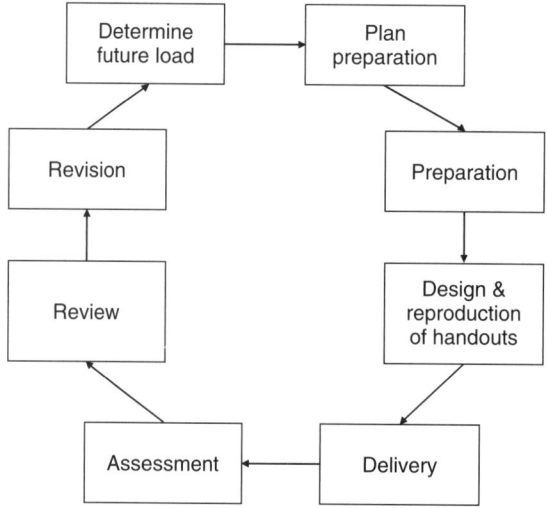

4. Teaching Space Cycle

For traditionally delivered taught programmes, classroom and other space is required. This has to be estimated, planned for and then provided sufficiently to cater for all of the University's traditional taught programmes, having regard to the number of registered students on each taught programme. Importantly, the space must be equipped with appropriate teaching resources which also need to be determined and planned for. Timetabling available space to particular courses needs to be done efficiently to avoid under-utilisation and must be communicated to parties clearly and in a timely way. Care must be taken to ensure that timetabled slots are properly utilised. This cycle is revisited annually, or before the start of each semester, in order to maintain efficient allocations.

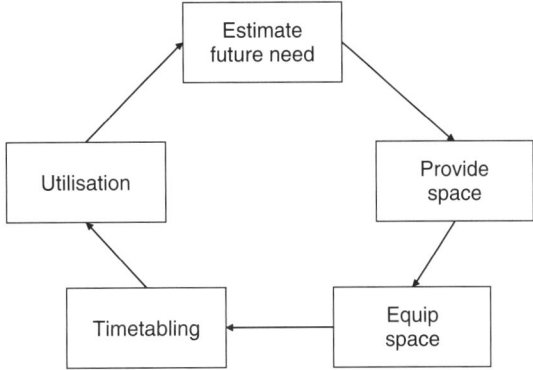

NOTES

1. Likert, Rensis (1956) *New Patterns of Management*. McGraw-Hill, New York.
2. Lawrence, Paul and Lorsch, Jay (1967) *Organization and its Environment*. Harvard University Press, Cambridge, MA.
3. Johnson, K. P. and Jaenicke, H. R. (1980) *Evaluating Internal Control—Concepts, Guidelines, Procedures, Documentation*. John Wiley & Sons Inc., New York, p. 29.
4. Chambers, Andrew and Court, John M. (1991) *Computer Auditing*. 3rd edition. Pitman, London, p. 38 (*vide* also 1st edition, 1981, p. 13).

3
Developing Operational Review Programmes for Managerial and Audit Use

SCOPE

In this chapter we start by introducing a practical method of documenting all the elements of an operational audit review in a form which resembles the traditional internal control questionnaire (ICQ). We have called this method **Standard Audit Programme Guides (SAPGs)**. The chapter concludes with a discussion on the subject of risk in operational auditing and features a control matrix approach to assessing risk and control effectiveness.

The original concept of SAPGs was built around their use within word processing software, where each discrete program was a separate document file that could easily be updated and maintained using the facilities of the word processing environment. This form of usage had the principal advantage of being a familiar software environment supported by extensive functionality. However, printed blank proformas can be used as an alternative.

In this chapter we shall discuss the format of the SAPG and how to use it. The landscape format of the SAPG illustrated in this chapter is, of course, but one possible layout, and users of this technique can create their own design within the word processing system of their choice.

To save space, we will in subsequent chapters give listings of relevant control objective and risk/control issues taken from some of the SAPG documents, but not in the full SAPG landscape format. Our general aim is to highlight the salient points of audit concern for the functions and activities rather than to emphasise any particular SAPG document layout.

The full set of almost 200 SAPGs, in landscape Word format, is available on a password protected website accompanying this Handbook. Those available in this way when this Handbook went to print are listed in Appendix 1.

PRACTICAL USE OF SAPGs

SAPGs are intended for use during management and audit reviews of activities within an organisation.

Today an increasing amount of auditing is done in a self-audit context where management, together with their staff, consider in quite a formalised though participative way (a) the risks of not achieving their objectives now and into the future, and (b) whether internal control is equal to the task of giving reasonable assurance of achievement of objectives. We discuss control self assessment (or control risk self-assessment as it is often called) fully in Chapter 10. SAPG documents offer an ideal basis for control self assessment. They raise the right questions and encourage management and staff to consider whether controls are satisfactory to address the issues raised. They provide a self-documenting record of the progress of the control self-assessment which is available for subsequent audit or senior management review. The classification of SAPGs into a wide variety of business activities means that a suitable SAPG is likely to be available for most functional areas. Where the scope of the self assessment is a complete operating unit, a high level review programme, which we discuss later in this chapter, is likely to be appropriate.[1] In other chapters of this Handbook we provide checklists of control issues which are as relevant to managers for self-audits as for auditors to use during their audits.

In the auditing context, there are obviously a number of ways that the organisation can be divided for the purposes of reviewing the effectiveness of internal controls. For example, *functionally* based on the organisational structure, or *operationally* based on the prime activities of organisation. SAPGs can be used in a variety of ways, and each SAPG can be suitably scoped to meet the method of defining the discrete audit review projects. For example, an audit department could choose to view the organisation as noted in the following listing, and accordingly create a separate SAPG for each activity or system. This example structure is based on the division of the audit universe of potential review projects into 12 main areas.

1. **Management and Administration**

    - The control environment
    - Organisation (i.e. structure)
    - Management information
    - Planning
    - Risk management
    - Legal department
    - Quality management
    - Estates management and facilities
    - Environmental issues
    - Insurance
    - Security
    - Capital projects
    - Industry regulation and compliance
    - Media, public and external relations
    - Company secretarial department.

2. **Financial and Accounting**

   - Treasury
   - Payroll
   - Accounts payable
   - Accounts receivable
   - General ledger/management accounts
   - Fixed assets (and capital charges)
   - Budgeting and monitoring
   - Bank accounts and banking arrangements
   - Sales tax (i.e. VAT) accounting
   - Taxation
   - Inventories
   - Product/project accounting
   - Petty cash and expenses
   - Financial information and reporting
   - Investments.

3. **Personnel**

   - Human resources department (including policies)
   - Recruitment
   - Manpower and succession planning
   - Staff training and development
   - Welfare
   - Pension scheme (and other benefits)
   - Health insurance
   - Staff appraisal and disciplinary matters
   - Health and safety
   - Labour relations
   - Company vehicles.

4. **Procurement**

   - Purchasing.

5. **Stock and Materials Handling**

   - Stock control
   - Warehousing and storage
   - Distribution, transport and logistics.

6. **Production/Manufacturing**

   - Planning and production control
   - Facilities, plant and equipment
   - Personnel
   - Materials and energy
   - Quality control
   - Safety
   - Environmental issues

- Law and regulatory compliance
- Maintenance.

7. **Marketing and Sales**

   - Product development
   - Market research
   - Promotion and advertising
   - Pricing and discount policies
   - Sales management
   - Sales performance and monitoring
   - Distribution
   - Relationship with parent company (for overseas or subsidiary operations)
   - Agents
   - Order processing.

8. **After Sales Support**

   - Warranty arrangements
   - Maintenance and servicing
   - Spare parts and supply.

9. **Research and Development**

   - Product development
   - Project appraisal and monitoring
   - Plant and equipment
   - Development project management
   - Legal and regulatory issues.

10. **Information Technology**

    - IT strategic planning
    - IT organisation
    - IT sites
    - Processing operations
    - Back-up and media
    - Systems/operating software
    - System access control
    - Personal computers
    - Software maintenance
    - Local area networks (LANs)
    - Databases
    - Data Protection
    - Facilities management
    - System development
    - Software selection
    - Contingency planning
    - Electronic data interchange (EDI)
    - Viruses
    - Electronic office

- User support
- Spreadsheet design
- Expert systems
- IT accounting.

11. **Contracting**

- Contract management environment
- Project management framework
- Project assessment and approval
- Engaging, monitoring and paying consultants
- Design
- Assessing viability/competence of contractors
- Maintaining an approved list of contractors
- Tendering procedures
- Contract and tender documentation
- Insurance and bonding
- Selection and letting of contracts
- Management information and reporting
- Performance monitoring
- Sub-contractors and suppliers
- Materials, plant and project assets
- Valuing work for interim payments
- Controlling price fluctuations
- Monitoring and controlling variations
- Extensions of time
- Controlling contractual claims
- Liquidations and bankruptcies
- Contractor's final account
- Recovery of damages
- Review of project outturn and performance
- Maintenance obligations.

12. **Governance, Risk Management, Internal Control**

   (Note that this group is numbered as Set 14 in Appendix 1 and in the web-based SAPG resource.)

- Internal governance processes
- The board
- External governance processes
- Risk management processes
- Issues for internal control.

During the course of an audit review there will be a number of common factors to record and evaluate. For example, the control objectives for the activity being reviewed, the risks or operational issues, the controls and measures in place to address the risks and issues, the results of audit testing and the conclusions drawn. The SAPG format illustrated later in this chapter will cater for all these factors and we will subsequently describe how the SAPG can be completed and used to document these key review elements.

Once they have been developed for use, the SAPGs can be used either singly or in various combinations to provide detailed guidance and direction during audit projects and field visits. They should aim to define the key and essential knowledge about a given subject, and thus form a key part of the audit documentation.

The scope and nature of each audit project may be different. This variability is driven by such practical aspects as availability of audit resources, the relative scale of the target business operations, logistical considerations, areas of specific management concern, etc. SAPGs can be used in combinations to match the audit coverage to the specified business systems and activities. Although each SAPG can be used in a "free-standing" context, they can also be linked in a number of ways to support the objectives established by audit management:

- Most SAPGs will be designed to cover systems which have interfaces with other systems (for example, there are logical linkages between purchasing, accounts payable and stock control). It follows, therefore, that perceived weaknesses in one system/activity may have implications for issues in another related system or activity. Each SAPG can be provided with a table of such interrelationships so that the user can promptly determine the knock-on effects of any noted concerns.
- The principal activities of an operating unit or overseas subsidiary can also be flexibly related to a number of individual activity or system-based SAPGs.
- Away from the use of individual SAPGs to support the examination of discrete activities, there is the alternative view of a business expressed in terms of business processes (or alternatively cycles, although not every process is actually cyclic in form). These business processes can be described as being a series of related or interlinked economic events. The structure of individual SAPGs can also be used as the basis of using them in combinations supporting auditing on a business process basis. Appendix 2 shows how SAPGs can be combined to cover fundamental business processes.

In any event, it is likely that most audit visits will be the subject of some prior research and preparation so that the audit time spent on site is optimised for efficiency and direction, and that the auditors are focused on the most worthwhile investigations. In order to assist with such deliberations, special forms of SAPG can be developed which support the gathering of such research information. For example, users of the SAPG approach may choose to develop a "fact finding programme"[1] or a "high level review programme"[2] to meet such requirements. (Refer to Chapter 13, which discusses the use of such programmes in the context of auditing subsidiaries and remote operating units.)

FORMAT OF SAPGs

In our proposed SAPG format, the critical contents of each SAPG are a number of **risk or control issues** relevant to the specific system. These are expressed in the form of questions which raise the issues in the context of what is being done either to achieve a desired outcome or to avoid an unwanted one. Examples of such questions would be:

- How does management ensure that the business activities of the organisation are conducted in accordance with all the prevailing and relevant legislation and regulations?
- What processes would ensure that any failures to fully comply with current legal requirements were promptly identified and resolved?

This form of question structure supports the use of the format in either the traditional audit situation where the direction is set by "What can go wrong?", or where a management orientation is adopted where the emphasis is placed on "What do we need to achieve?"

The risk and control issues are further divided into two groups, namely **key issues** and **detailed issues**. The former are the more significant and crucial points about the system under review and the aim should be always to take them into account during the audit. The latter category of issues takes the user into more of the underlying system considerations, and would be utilised only if there was a potential weakness revealed as a consequence of considering the key issues. We will return to the context of this division of issues later in this chapter.

The purpose of the SAPG is to guide the auditor through an examination of the issues specific to the system or activity with the intention of recording the nature of measures and controls in place to ensure either that business objectives are achieved, or that risks and exposures are successfully avoided. The auditor will need not only to record the nature of measures and controls in place, but also to consider their effectiveness, and dependent upon that interpretation record the nature and results of any audit testing applied to determine whether the situation needs to be reported to management.

The suggested form of the SAPG is divided into three distinct sections:

- title page
- the risk/control issues
- system interfaces.

The format and use of each of these are described in following sections.

Note that in all the examples that follow, the text in *italics* relates to that entered by the user during the course of the audit review, whereas the normal text relates to the information entered at the initial design stage.

SAPG Title Page

The title page has three separate areas:

- an area which records the details of the subject matter covered by the SAPG and a reference number (see Figure 3.1).
- an area used to record details about the specific audit project (see Figure 3.2).
- a section which describes the control objectives for the relevant system (see Figure 3.3). In practical usage, the text in this last section of the page can be edited and updated whenever necessary by the user.

DEVELOPING OPERATIONAL REVIEW PROGRAMMES FOR MANAGERIAL AND AUDIT USE 47

SAPG Ref.: *0102*	**Function:** *Management & Administration*	**Activity/System:** *Organisation*

Figure 3.1 SAPG title page—subject matter covered

Company: *Acme Corporation*	**Division:** *Orthopaedics*	**Country:** *USA*	**Site:** *New York*
Audit Ref.: *USA01-2007*	**Date:** *3 January 2007*	**Completed by:** *John Brown*	**Reviewed by:** *G. V. Rand*

Figure 3.2 SAPG title page—details about audit project

CONTROL OBJECTIVES

(a) To ensure that the organisational structure is appropriate to the business and the achievement of strategic objectives; (b) To ensure that the organisational structure is determined by the business and operational needs and avoids needless sub-divisions and excessive levels; (c) To ensure that the structure enables the flow of key information upwards and outwards within the organisation and across all the business activities; (d) To ensure that relevant responsibilities, authorities and functional terms of reference are defined and in place; (e) To ensure that responsibilities and authorities are adequately segregated in order to avoid conflicts of interest and the potential for fraudulent practices; (f) to ensure that the structure is periodically reviewed and any changes are agreed and authorised at a senior level; (g) To ensure that each manager's span of control is optimised and avoids either over- or under-utilisation; (h) To ensure that adequate staff resources are determined, authorised and provided in order to achieve the functional and business objectives; (i) To ensure that the prevailing organisational structure is suitably documented and communicated to all relevant staff; and (j) To ensure that the organisational structure and the related functional divisions of responsibility are accurately and adequately reflected in the accounting and management information systems.

Figure 3.3 SAPG title page—control objectives

The Risk/Control Issues

This is the main part of the SAPG and consists of a table based on the headings noted in Figure 3.4. If the table facilities within a word processor have been used to develop this format, it should be possible for all the cells to expand down the page as text is entered. On this and subsequent pages, the use of each column is discussed.

Seq.	Risk/Control Issue	Current Control/ Measure	WP Ref.	Effective Yes/No	Compliance Testing	Substantive Testing	Weakness to Report
1	Key Issues						
1.1	What measures are in place to ensure that management are kept informed of production activities as the basis for their decision making?						
2	Detailed Issues						
2.1	How can management be assured that production downtime caused by plant breakdown is minimised?						

Figure 3.4 SAPG—outline of risk/control issues

The **Seq.** column contains a sequential number used to identify each risk/control issue. These issues are divided into two groups, **Key Issues** which are identified by being both in the sequence starting **1.1** and printed in **bold** text, and **Detailed Issues** which are in the sequence starting at 2.1. (Refer to Figure 3.4). The Key Issues reflect the top level and critical aspects of the system/activity under review and should always be considered by the auditor. There are normally between six and ten key issues noted on each system/activity SAPG. The detailed issues examine the relevant subject in greater elemental detail and should be addressed by the auditor only if the responses obtained in relation to the key issues suggest that there could be further inherent weaknesses in control. There can be any number of detailed issues recorded within an SAPG dependent on the complexity and relevance of the system/activity.

The **Current Control/Measure** column is used by the auditor to record a brief description of any controls or measures that are in place to address the issues raised in the Risk/Control Issue column. (Refer to Figure 3.5.) Try to avoid going into too much detail in this column. This type of information can be obtained in a number of ways, for example, as a result of discussion with departmental staff, from a review of documented procedures, or from previous audit working papers. In practice there may be more than one control or measure in place which has an effect on the issue raised; any number of these can be noted in the Current Control/Measure cell.

The **WP Ref.** column can be used to note any working paper cross-reference, such as a system flowchart or procedure manual.

Seq.	Risk/Control Issue	Current Control/ Measure	WP Ref.	Effective Yes/No	Compliance Testing	Substantive Testing	Weakness to Report
1	**Key Issues**						
1.1	What measures are in place to ensure that management are kept informed of production activities as the basis for their decision making?	Regular management report (type PRO78X) produced and circulated to unit managers. Contents are reviewed, discussed, and signed off at weekly team meetings.	Flow chart PRD04 page 8	YES			

Figure 3.5 SAPG—example of a partly completed risk/control issues

The **Effective Yes/No** column is used to note whether the recorded current control or measure is likely to be effective in either supporting the required objective or counteracting any underlying risk posed by the issue. This judgement, which may need to be applied by the audit manager or supervisor, is an opinion on likely effectiveness. The responses recorded in this column can be used to determine those areas which should be subject to audit testing. The decision whether or not to apply audit testing will, of course, be relative to the user's own auditing standards, but a number of logical tactics could apply. For example, the consideration that a particular control or measure would be effective (i.e. a YES response), may obviate the need for any testing; however, at this stage, the auditor does not know whether the control is actually being applied correctly and/or consistently. This suggests that some limited compliance testing is desirable to ascertain if the control is actually being applied appropriately in every instance. In order to contain the amount of audit time spent on compliance testing, it is often desirable to identify the key controls and measures which represent the greatest potential and target these for compliance tests. The **Compliance Testing** column can be used to record the test applied and a summary outcome. (Refer to Figure 3.6.) Because space is limited, the user can elect just to record a working paper cross-reference to the detailed testing schedules rather than a full explanation.

In instances where either the compliance testing revealed an inadequate application of the measure or the control/measure was judged unlikely to be effective, further substantive testing may be justified to evaluate if a potential weakness has been exploited. Summary details of such substantive testing can be noted in the **Substantive Testing** column. By way of illustration, Figure 3.6 incorporates example entries in the **Compliance** and **Substantive Testing** columns.

The last column (**Weakness to Report**) can be used to note any points of audit concern arising from the audit review and testing which should either be discussed

Seq.	Risk/Control Issue	Current Control/ Measure	WP Ref.	Effective Yes/No	Compliance Testing	Substantive Testing	Weakness to Report
1	Key Issues						
1.1	What measures are in place to ensure that management are kept informed of production activities as the basis for their decision making?	Regular management report (type PRO78X) produced and circulated to unit managers. Contents are reviewed, discussed, and signed off at weekly team meetings.	Flow chart PRD04 page 8	YES	WP: Test 23 Reports for November 2010 examined—no evidence of examination or review	WP: Test 54 November and December 2010 reports examined in detail—13 instances of production shortfall reported with no apparent follow-up action.	Recommend to management that they ensure that this control is applied as defined in the procedures manual and that all reports are monitored for evidence of action taken to address reported problems. Discussed with Production Manager 01.01.2010

Figure 3.6 SAPG—example of a completed risk/control issues

further with management or formally reported to them as a recommendation for action. The contents of this column can be interfaced with the reporting processes used by the audit function.

The completed SAPG file can be saved as a word processing document file and printed out to form part of the audit working papers and permanent file.

System Interfaces

This page of the SAPG (as illustrated in Figure 3.7) is intended to alert auditors to the likely interfaces between the system or activity being addressed in the SAPG and any others. Where weakness and control problems have been revealed during the system review, there may be consequences or implications for other systems either "downstream" or "upstream" of the system under review. The System Interfaces Table is intended to draw auditors' attention to systems with input or output connections. These connections may be based solely on data flow or have additional operational implications. The example Systems Interface Table featured in Figure 3.7 is provided for illustrative purposes and is related to an accounts receivable system.

RISK IN OPERATIONAL AUDITING

Matters of risk have traditionally been of concern to auditors and although the profession has also embraced other business oriented approaches, risk is likely to remain a potent determinant in directing audit work.

DEVELOPING OPERATIONAL REVIEW PROGRAMMES FOR MANAGERIAL AND AUDIT USE

SYSTEM INTERFACES FOR ACCOUNTS RECEIVABLE

It is unlikely that any activity or system will operate in complete isolation, but will need to interact with other data and systems in order to be fully effective. At a simple level, such interaction could relate to the input of data from a source system and the generation of amended or enhanced data which can be output to the next process. For example, taking coded transactions from an accounts payable system into the general ledger as the basis for subsequently producing management accounts information.

It is often at the point of interaction between systems where controls are critical. Auditors should be satisfied that the data moving between systems is consistent, complete and accurate, in order that the subsequent processes are undertaken upon a reliable basis.

The following table aims to plot, for the subject system of this Standard Audit Programme Guide, the potential interfaces with other systems which may require audit attention. Indicators are provided to differentiate between those interfaces which act as input sources to the subject system and those which are potential output targets. The "SAPG Ref." column records the reference number of the Programme Guide which addresses the issues for the related system

System	SAPG Ref.	Input Source	Output Target	System	SAPG Ref.	Input Source	Output Target
Management Information	0103		✓	Stock Control	0501	✓	
Treasury	0201		✓	Warehousing/Storage	0502	✓	
General Ledger & Management A/Cs	0205		✓	Sales Performance/ Monitoring	0706	✓	✓
Budgeting & Monitoring	0207		✓	Warranty Arrangements	0801	✓	
Bank Accounts/ Arrangements	0208	✓	✓	Maintenance and Servicing	0802	✓	
VAT Accounting (where applicable)	0209		✓	Spare Parts and Supply	0803	✓	
Inventories	0211	✓	✓				
Product/Project Accounts	0212		✓				
Financial Information & Reports	0214		✓				

Figure 3.7 SAPG—System Interfaces page and Systems Interfaces table

The internal auditor's use of risk assessment can operate at different levels of audit planning and activity:

At a **tactical** level the auditor may choose to apply risk assessment techniques to the potential universe of possible audit projects as a means of setting relative priorities, and thus determine those higher risk audit projects for inclusion into the annual audit plan. This approach normally involves the development of an audit risk formula.

At the **operational** level (i.e. during the course of a specific audit project), risk assessment linked to an evaluation of control effectiveness can focus the auditor's attention on aspects of the subject under review which are more deserving of his or her attention. With audit resources under pressure, it is important that auditing efforts are concentrated on the highly risky, poorly controlled aspects where management action may be required.

Two proven risk assessment methods for audit planning, which can be computerised using spreadsheet software, were explored in *Effective Internal Audits*,[3] in *Auditing the IT Environment*[4] and in *Auditing Contracts*.[5] We shall, later in this section, briefly explore an operational level risk and control assessment technique using a control matrix methodology. However, before doing so, we shall consider (in the next section) general matters of risk and control in operational auditing.

The Nature of Risk

In simplistic terms, risk can be defined as a function of *what is at risk* and *how likely is it to be at risk*. In other words, the extent (or size) of the risk and the probability of that risk actually occurring. An alternative term for the size dimension would be *inherent risk*. An alternative term for the probability dimension would be the *control risk* or the *system risk*.

Whereas the size of a given risk may be relatively easy to determine objectively, for example the known value of stock held or the actual level of cash turnover at a retail outlet, the probability element is generally a more subjective dimension. In the auditing context, the probability of a given risk occurring is fundamentally seen as a by-product of the effectiveness of the controls put in place by management. Put simply, the poorer the level of control exercised over a process or function, the greater the probability of risk *exposure* occurring. However, the interpretation of the effectiveness of controls can be subjective and the subject of some debate between auditors and their client managers. In all honesty it is very difficult, if not impossible, to remove totally the subjectivity in risk assessment, especially where matters of effectiveness, quality and opinion are involved. All parties to a risk assessment process should recognise any such limitations and take practical steps towards reducing and/or understanding the potentially subjective aspects of the process.

The term "exposure" in relation to risk could be defined as "an unwanted event or outcome that management would wish to avoid". Although it is perhaps usual for auditors to relate risks primarily to financial values (i.e. value of cash lost, extent of additional costs, etc.), initial exposures can also be nonfinancial in nature, although most exposures may have a related or ultimate financial impact. An example of a primarily nonfinancial exposure, would be the loss of reputation and the impact on the corporate image following a well-publicised breach of regulations (such as unauthorised discharge of a harmful substance into the environment). It could be said that any resultant loss of business will have a financial dimension, as will any operational restrictions imposed by the regulatory authorities over and above any fines or penalties. Auditors, when considering risk exposures during a project, should take a broad view of the potential impacts on the organisation and not concentrate solely on financial aspects.

Each organisation may have specific sector or operational aspects which need to be considered in risk terms; for example, the ability of a hospital trust to maintain the required levels of contracted services could be affected by the public reputation of the medical facilities offered, or the continuing operation of a chemical plant will be governed by the continued adherence to the laid-down health, safety and environmental regulations.

Measuring Risk

For any given system, process, activity or function there are likely to be a number of possible risk exposures. However, when these exposure elements are compared with each other, they may exhibit variable degrees of inherent (or size) risk for the organisation, and we should aim to take account of this risk variability in our determination of risk. So we need to identify ways of measuring the various aspects of risk. For instance, in a review of the payroll function, the following two possible risk exposures could, *inter alia*, apply:

1. Errors in the calculation and payment of net salaries due to the incorrect application of annual pay review data to the payroll records.
2. Payments made to unauthorised or invalid people set up on the payroll.

It may be considered that the impact of risk (1) might be potentially much greater than that of risk (2). For instance, it is likely to affect a greater number of employees (indeed, possibly all employees' payroll records), whereas risk (2) is more likely to be restricted to a relatively few fraudulent or erroneous payroll records. Clearly risk (1) also has the potential for a wider range of exposure types when compared to risk (2); for instance, beyond the financial impact of such a risk, the following aspects may also apply, each with its own degree of relativity for the organisation beyond the size extent:

- the reaction of the taxation authorities to such a large-scale error (i.e. casting doubts over the accuracy and reliability of the other payroll processes);
- the cost and disruption involved in recovering from the error;
- the processing of overstated transactions through the company bank account and the attendant effects on cash flow;
- the effects on staff morale given the scale of error in salary payments;
- the effect of adverse publicity on the organisation's reputation and image.

In the control matrix we discuss later in this chapter, two elements of inherent (or size) risk are accounted for. First, an expression of the type of exposure, on a category scale of likely relative importance to the business; and secondly, the likely extent (or the measure of the size) of the exposure. For example, the first element could be related to a scale of type of effect for the company as follows, using a category scale of 1 to 6, where a score of 6 represents the greater degree of relative risk:

6 (most serious)   Financial impact with implications for the achievement of corporate objectives and financial targets.
5   Loss of cash or other asset, or increase in liability.
4   Political sensitivity or loss of reputation.
3   Loss or exaggeration of profit.
2   Distortion of the balance sheet.
1 (least serious) Accounting error with no effects on profit and loss or balance sheet.

We could term this measure as a *type* (of risk) score.

If, for instance, we had an exposure which reached point 5 on the above *type* scale because there was a potential loss involved, we then have to give substance to the likely extent of that loss should it occur, and we do this by allocating an additional measure of the likely *size* of that loss. We could relate this size element either to a scale of actual loss values or to a summary form of scale such as small, medium and large degrees of actual impact represented on a three-point scale, where 3 is the largest potential loss. So, for our example, we could conclude that the likely extent of our loss (*Type* score 5) would be high (*Size* score 3), and these may be combined mathematically to produce a composite measure of the relative inherent risk. One such method would be to multiply the two scores; i.e. $5 \times 3 = 15$ (as a measure of inherent risk).

We shall return to this approach in our subsequent examination of the control matrix method. However, we have dealt with only one part of the risk equation, i.e. that part relating to inherent risk (or *what is at risk*). We will now turn our attention to the measurement of control effectiveness, which is a moderator of the real risk position.

Measuring Control Effectiveness

In the same way that varying degrees of inherent risk will apply to the constituent exposures for a given system, activity, process or function, control effectiveness also has a variability. Overall control effectiveness can be said to be the product of two dimensions, namely:

1. the potential effectiveness of a control activity[6] assuming that it is applied correctly all the time by staff and management

    combined with

2. the actual extent it is complied with.

This viewpoint supports the premise that however *potentially* effective a control may be, it becomes effective only when it is complied with; and even if a control is complied with all the time it may not be 100% effective in eliminating an exposure. Just as there are varying degrees of inherent risk, there will, in the real world, be differing extents of potential control effectiveness and variations in the way that controls are complied with. Additionally, the effectiveness of a control will vary between the exposures it impacts upon.

It is possible to apply a simple mathematical approach to these related measures of control effectiveness, by expressing each of the two aspects as percentages, i.e.:

- The potential effectiveness of the control (i.e. if applied correctly all the time) can be expressed on a scale of 1 to 5, where a score of 5 equates to 100% effective (4 = 80%, 3 = 60%, 2 = 40%, 1 = 20%, and a score of zero means no effect at all in addressing the related risks).
- The extent to which the control is actually complied with can be determined by the auditor during initial compliance testing and scored using the same five-point scale. For example, if the compliance test examination of a sample of transactions suggested that the control was complied with for only 60% of the time, the score of 3 for compliance would be given.

The two scores can then be combined as a measure of the contribution made by this control for reduction or eradication of the related risk exposures. For example, if a control has an 80% level of potential effectiveness but is only complied with for 60% of the time, this could be expressed as a resultant control contribution of 48% (i.e. 60% of 80).

Using such an approach it is a simple matter for the auditor (and management) to conclude on the type of action required. If the potential effectiveness of a control is high, but compliance is poor, the obvious solution is to improve the level of compliance. Alternatively, if the potential effectiveness level is low, then irrespective of the level of actual compliance, the related risk will remain unaddressed, thus suggesting that alternative control action is required.

It is necessary to be aware of the subjectivity associated with these forms of measurement, especially in respect of potential control effectiveness. It could be said that this method facilitates the painting of a more precise picture of the control situation when compared to the internal control questionnaire (ICQ) approach—in shades of grey (or indeed in colour) as opposed to black and white. But, the down side is that care is required in the determination of the relative scoring, otherwise the conclusions can easily be challenged by auditee management. Although there is no escaping fundamental subjectivity, a great deal can be achieved by prior discussion of the technique with management and getting them to "buy into" the method. In any event, the use of any method of risk assessment by the internal audit function should ideally have the sanction of the audit committee.

Earlier in this chapter we considered the traditional use of ICQs by auditors as means of evaluating control effectiveness against predefined control objectives for a given system or function. When using an ICQ, the auditor is expected to evaluate control effectiveness in a fairly restrictive way—i.e. normally by responding *Yes* or *No* to the question "*Is this control effective?*" Presumably behind the answer to this question, are a number of facts and findings which aid the auditor in responding to the rather blunt answering parameters.

ICQs don't cater especially well for the varying extents of inherent risk, potential control effectiveness and control compliance. Additionally, in reality a particular control process may address a number of different risk exposures—to different degrees of effectiveness; and a particular risk exposure may be addressed by a number of controls, all operating at different levels of potential effectiveness and compliance. However, the traditional ICQ format does not readily facilitate the mapping of such interactions.

In the following section we shall introduce a control matrix method which incorporates some of the principles of risk and control measurement we have examined so far.

A Control Matrix Approach to Risk and Control Evaluation

In this section we will outline the mechanics of the control matrix method using a simple example and building up the required data in stages. The processes used are based on the concepts of risk and control measurement noted in the earlier sections. For a more comprehensive exploration of this and other risk-based audit planning methods, see *Effective Internal Audits*.[3] At the end of this section we provide two examples of more realistic and comprehensive matrices.

The control matrix technique is ideally suited to the spreadsheet environment. The control matrix can be used by auditors during any audit project or review. The aim of the control matrix method is to bring together, in a mathematically sound way, the dimensions of risk and control as a means of calculating a *risk score* for each of the component risk exposures. This *risk score* can then be used to direct the auditor's attention to those aspects of the system under review which may, among other things, require substantive testing, discussion with management, the agreement of the required corrective action, etc.

Although our simple example matrix will focus on the previously discussed risk and control approach to audit review, it should be noted that this method can also equally be applied to reviews using an alternative, positive, approach (i.e. "What do we need to achieve in respect of this system, function or process?", and "What measures have we put in place in order to ensure that achievement?"). This form of the method aligns more readily with the view of the business adopted by management, who see their role as primarily relating to the achievement of objectives and not solely geared to countering risks. The comprehensive example matrix shown in Figure 3.17 uses Objectives (as opposed to exposures) and measures (as opposed to Controls) in order to illustrate this positive orientation of the control matrix method.

The Development of an Example Control Matrix

For the purposes of our simplified example, we will consider a limited number of risks and controls applicable to a management information system (MIS). The items we have selected for our illustration of the method are not intended to be comprehensive, and you will easily be able to define additional and alternative examples that more realistically fit the prevailing scenario in your own organisation.

First, it is necessary to identify the likely risk exposures associated with an MIS. Figure 3.8 lists five possible top level exposures. In practice there will be others, but this reduced list serves to illustrate the technique.

The process of identifying the possible exposures for the system under review will normally be undertaken early in the audit project as a basis for the work

> **EXPOSURES**
>
> A Unable to maintain/amend the MIS
>
> B Inaccurate, incomplete, or out-of-date information
>
> C Data corruption
>
> D Inaccurate system parameters, variables and assumptions
>
> E Leak of sensitive company data—competitive disadvantage, malpractice

Figure 3.8 Selected *exposures* for a management information system

that follows. In doing so, it is important to ensure that the identified items are comprehensive, realistic and pitched at the appropriate level.

It is important when noting exposures that cause and effect are differentiated. For example, a failure to ensure adequate segregation of duties is not essentially an exposure, but the possibility of introducing false accounting transactions by taking advantage of poor segregation is an exposure. Remember the earlier definition of an exposure: an unwanted event or outcome that management would wish to avoid.

Although we have given only one-line descriptions of the exposures, further implications can be assumed; for example, in respect of exposure B (which relates to inaccurate information) we could also assume that the quality of management decisions will be affected by the poor data quality.

The accurate identification of the risk exposures associated with the system under review is a crucial stage as all that follows will be dependent on the foundation of possible risk components. In practical situations, the process of recording the exposures may be undertaken under the auspices of audit management or in a brainstorming session. Furthermore, the auditor may wish to involve management from the area under review, so that the perceptions of inherent risk are accurate, realistic and mutually agreed at the outset of the audit project. The prevailing management culture and the way in which internal audit is perceived will obviously affect the decision to involve auditee managers in the risk assessment process.

The next stage would be to identify the controls in place for the system under review. Details of these controls may be obtained from a number of possible sources, for example:

- previous audit working papers (where they exist), updated with any amended or additional practices;
- interviews with staff and management;
- review of official policies, procedures and/or operations manuals (subject to confirmation that they are correctly applied in practice).

Figure 3.9 lists five possible control activities relevant to an MIS. This is an abbreviated listing and many other controls are likely to apply in practice.

> **CONTROLS**
>
> 1. System specification is documented and any amendments are updated and verified.
>
> 2. 90% of data input is via feeder systems direct interfaces—thus minimising keying errors.
>
> 3. System access is controlled by user-ID and password. Access system is maintained by the systems administrator.
>
> 4. Standing data and parameters are entered and verified by the financial accountant prior to the use of the MIS.
>
> 5. Access to standing data and parameters is further protected by the use of an additional (higher level) password control system.

Figure 3.9 Limited selection of example controls for a management information system

We have now gathered the basic elements for the construction of our control matrix for the subject of the MIS. Figure 3.10 depicts the basic form of the matrix incorporating the example exposures and controls taken from Figures 3.8 and 3.9.

Before moving on, we'll look generally at the structure and purpose of the matrix format of Figure 3.10.

The vertical columns of the matrix relate to the exposures. In our example, the five exposures (as noted in Figure 3.8) are represented in the columns labelled **A** to **E**. In the adjacent box at the top of the matrix, the exposure descriptions are repeated.

The horizontal rows of the matrix represent the example controls which should be in place (as noted in Figure 3.9).

There are a number of points of intersection between the vertical (exposures) and horizontal (controls) elements. We will step through the completion of these cells and provide, where necessary, a description of the underlying theory and simple mathematics.

We need to apply the previously discussed measures of inherent risk to each of the five noted exposures as a means of reflecting their relative significance. We do this in the two rows near the top of the matrix columns labelled *Type* and *Size*. First, the *Type* score, which accounts for the degree of significance of the risk to the organisation, needs to be determined. In order to ensure consistency in the application of such scores, an agreed scale is required, such as the six-point scale shown in Figure 3.11.

Each of the noted exposures needs to be considered against this scale, which in nature resembles a ladder to be climbed until the highest relevant point is reached for the exposure under consideration—i.e. the most serious type or category of unwanted outcome which this exposure represents. For example, when considering exposure A (MIS not adequately documented—unable to maintain/amend) it might

DEVELOPING OPERATIONAL REVIEW PROGRAMMES FOR MANAGERIAL AND AUDIT USE

Management Information System—Abbreviated Example Matrix		EXPOSURES				
		A	B	C	D	E

Exposures:

A Unable to maintain/amend the MIS
B Inaccurate, incomplete, or out of date information
C Data corruption
D Inaccurate system parameters, variables and assumptions
E Leak of sensitive company data—competitive disadvantage, malpractice

			A	B	C	D	E
	Calculated Risk Score	Risk					
	Scale 3 (6 is the most serious)	Type					
	Size (3 is the maximum)	Size					
	CONTROLS						
1	**System specification is documented and any amendments are updated and verified**	Best					
		Test					
		Both					
2	**90 % of data input is via feeder systems direct interfaces—thus minimising keying errors**	Best					
		Test					
		Both					
3	**System access is controlled by user-ID and password. Access system is maintained by the systems administrator**	Best					
		Test					
		Both					
4	**Standing data and parameters are entered and verified by the financial accountant prior to the use of the MIS**	Best					
		Test					
		Both					
5	**Access to standing data and parameters is further protected by the use of an additional (higher level) password control system**	Best					
		Test					
		Both					

Figure 3.10 Blank control matrix for a management information system

> Start climbing this ladder scale from the bottom until you reach the highest relevant point for the exposure.
>
> Point of scale:
>
> 6   Failure to achieve business objectives, and/or loss of credibility.
>
> 5   Systems failure.
>
> 4   Loss of control of the corporate database.
>
> 3   Damaging delay.
>
> 2   Unnecessary financial costs.
>
> 1   Delay of no commercial significance.

Figure 3.11   Example exposures oriented category scale for determining the *Type* score

be relevant to climb the ladder scale (depicted in Figure 3.11) up to position 4; this can then be entered into the *Type* score cell on the matrix corresponding to exposure A. Refer to Figure 3.12, which depicts possible scores for the example exposures A to E.

The second dimension of inherent risk is its *Size* ranking based (in our example) on a simple three-point scale where the value chosen reflects the size extent of the unwanted outcome (i.e. 1 = small, 2 = medium, 3 = large) which we selected from the ladder scale. We have inserted in Figure 3.12 the possible *Size* scores for our chosen exposures. You will note that values have now appeared in the *Calculated Risk Score* row of the matrix in Figure 3.12. The formula used to generate these scores is discussed later, but this *Risk* score is one of the key outputs of the matrix process as it aims to reflect the residue risk of each exposure taking into account the inherent risk dimensions (i.e. a combination of the *Type* and *Size* scores) and the effects of the controls in place. Of course, at this stage of data entry into our matrix, only the inherent risk values have been entered and the Risk score calculation is incomplete. The *Risk* score is generated in the range 1 to 4, where a score of 1 means an insignificantly low degree of residue risk, whereas a score of 4 equates to a high risk exposure which is poorly controlled and which therefore may require additional audit investigation, etc. We shall subsequently return to consider the *Risk* score after we have entered the score data for the controls in place.

We have concluded that control effectiveness consisted of two elements, namely: (1) the potential effectiveness of a control assuming it was being followed by staff and management as intended, and (2) the extent to which the control is actually being complied with. Taken together, these two factors will give an indication of the actual contribution made by the control in addressing the inherent risk. The matrix technique facilitates the recording of these factors.

Management Information System—Abbreviated Example Matrix			EXPOSURES				
			A	B	C	D	E
Exposures:							
A Unable to maintain/amend the MIS							
B Inaccurate, incomplete, or out of date information							
C Data corruption							
D Inaccurate system parameters, variables and assumptions							
E Leak of sensitive company data—competitive disadvantage, malpractice							
	Calculated Risk Score	Risk	3	4	3	3	3
	Scale 3 (6 is the most serious)	Type	4	6	5	4	6
	Size (3 is the maximum)	Size	3	3	2	2	2

Figure 3.12 Entry of *Type* and *Size* scores to determine the inherent risks for the noted exposures

Figure 3.13 shows some example *Best* scores inserted into the matrix. These relate to a measure of potential control effectiveness based on a scale of 0 to 5, as follows:

5	Would eliminate the risk if followed (i.e. 100% effective)
4	80% effective
3	60% effective
2	40% effective
1	20% effective
0	No effect (or not applicable to this exposure)

Figure 3.13 reveals that a *Best* score of 5 for control 1 in addressing exposure A suggests a very optimistic expectation for its effects, whereas a less optimistic stance is taken with the application of a *Best* score of 2 for control 3 in relation to exposure B. Also by looking at the mapping of the interactions of controls and exposures as represented in Figure 3.13, we can see that:

- one control (i.e. number 3) is capable of addressing (to differing extents) a number of exposures (i.e. references B, C and E);
- one exposure can be addressed by a number of controls to varying degrees of potential effectiveness (i.e. exposure B is targeted by controls 2, 3, 4 and 5).

This mapping also aids the identification of the more significant (or key) controls and their interaction with the underlying (or inherent) risks. If audit time is limited, it may be more practical to concentrate on such key controls. This method also graphically indicates where there may be redundant controls.

Management Information System— Abbreviated Example Matrix			EXPOSURES				
			A	B	C	D	E
Exposures:							
A Unable to maintain/amend the MIS							
B Inaccurate, incomplete, or out of date information							
C Data corruption							
D Inaccurate system parameters, variables and assumptions							
E Leak of sensitive company data—competitive disadvantage, malpractice							
	Calculated Risk Score	Risk		3	4	3	3	3
	Scale 3 (6 is the most serious)	Type		4	6	5	4	6
	Size (3 is the maximum)	Size		3	3	2	2	2
	CONTROLS							
1	**System specification is documented and any amendments are updated and verified**	Best		5				
		Test	?	?				
		Both						
2	**90 % of data input is via feeder systems direct interfaces—thus minimising keying errors**	Best			4			
		Test	?		?			
		Both						
3	**System access is controlled by user-ID and password. Access system is maintained by the systems administrator**	Best			2	5		3
		Test	?		?	?		?
		Both						
4	**Standing data and parameters are entered and verified by the financial accountant prior to the use of the MIS**	Best				3	4	
		Test	?			?	?	
		Both						
5	**Access to standing data and parameters is further protected by the use of an additional (higher level) password control system**	Best				2	3	
		Test	?			?	?	
		Both						

Figure 3.13   Example control potential (*Best*) scores

Wherever there is an interaction of an exposure with a control a question mark is inserted in the *Test* score cells as a reminder that data concerning control compliance is required. The *Test* score aims to reflect the other dimension of control, namely the degree to which each control is actually complied with, as determined by normal compliance testing methods. The degree of compliance is measured using the following 0 to 5 scale:

5	100% compliance
4	80% compliance
3	60% compliance
2	40% compliance
1	20% compliance
0	No compliance

The degree of compliance for each of the featured controls is determined and then entered into the matrix along the *Test* score row where a Best *score* has been previously entered. Figure 3.14 shows the matrix after the entry of the required *Test* scores.

The following important points should be noted from Figure 3.14:

1. The insertion of the *Test* scores has resulted in the calculation of the *Both* scores for each control in the cells below. The *Both* score is a mathematical combination of the *Best* and *Test* scores with the intention of representing the contribution made by the relevant control in addressing the inherent risk to exposure. The *Both* score is calculated using the following formula where B represents the *Best* score and T relates to the *Test* score:

$$B - (5 - T) = Both$$

2. The *Calculated Risk Scores* at the top of each **Exposure** column have also changed and now take into account all the data in the column. The following formula is used to compute the *Risk* scores and it takes account of the *Type*, *Size* and all of the *Both* scores in the relevant columns, where B is the sum of the cubes of the *Both* scores in the column:

$$Type \times Size \times [125 - B]$$

The output of this calculation is related to a Risk *score* scale of 1 to 4 as follows:

Result	Score
if greater than 1500	4
between 751 and 1500	3
between 1 and 750	2
if less than or equal to 0	1

The *Risk* score is the key output of the matrix technique, in that it indicates those exposure elements (and their related controls) which are more deserving of further audit attention. A *Risk* score of 4 suggests an important exposure (due to its high inherent risk value) and the relative absence of effective control exercised over it. Having completed the control matrix to the point depicted in Figure 3.14, the auditor can allocate the remaining audit time in proportion to the *Risk* scores for the component aspects of the system under review (i.e. more time to those exposures with *Risk* scores of 4 and 3, and less (or none at all) on those with *Risk* scores of 2 and 1).

Figure 3.15 again shows the completed matrix with the addition of some data at the bottom in the form of overall inherent risk (size) and overall control scores. The inherent risk score has been calculated from all the *Type* and *Size* scores in the matrix as an indication of the overall level of risk for the system under review. The overall control score is generated from all the *Both* score data as an indication of the general level of control effectiveness. Both these scores can be useful as overall ratings for the subject under review, especially where there is a requirement to measure the output of the current audit examination against previous reviews.

So far we have deliberately used a limited range of exposures and controls in our examples in order to illustrate the control matrix technique. However, in practical use, the matrices created are likely to be much more comprehensive than the one in Figure 3.15. Figures 3.16 and 3.17 are more typical examples of matrices.

Figure 3.16 is an exposures oriented matrix which, like our simplified examples above, addresses the subject of a management information system. However, it contains suggested exposures and controls.

Figure 3.17 addresses the subject of planning, and uses the alternative orientation of the matrix method which replaces exposures and controls with objectives and measures. The objectives in the vertical columns relate to *what needs to be achieved* in relation to planning; the measures represent the steps taken to aid the achievement of the given objectives. In this context, the term "measures" is broader in scope than the "controls" used in the former example, in that management will implement a wide range of measures in order to achieve their objectives, which although they may include control activities, are not restricted to only controls. For example, staff will need to be trained in preparation for a new business venture or computer software will be acquired/developed to address an operational requirement.

The objectives are assessed using a type scale which aims to reflect their relative significance to the organisation and the size score reflects the level (or scale) of that contribution (i.e. small, medium or large). Measures are given *Best* scores which reflect the extent of the potential contribution to the achievement of the related objective and the *Test* scores represent the extent to which they are followed and applied. The *Risk* score indicates the extent to which the measures in place address the driving objectives. The higher the generated *Risk* score, the more significant the objective and the less likely it is that it will be achieved. The auditor's attention is therefore focused on those aspects of the subject under review that are worthy of additional audit attention. Management can also use this technique to assess and monitor their progress and the likelihood of achieving their objectives.

Management Information System—Abbreviated Example Matrix			EXPOSURES				
			A	B	C	D	E
Exposures:							
A Unable to maintain/amend the MIS							
B Inaccurate, incomplete, or out of date information							
C Data corruption							
D Inaccurate system parameters, variables and assumptions							
E Leak of sensitive company data—competitive disadvantage, malpractice							
	Calculated Risk Score	Risk	1	4	2	3	3
	Scale 3 (6 is the most serious)	Type	4	6	5	4	6
	Size (3 is the maximum)	Size	3	3	2	2	2
	CONTROLS						
1	**System specification is documented and any amendments are updated and verified**	Best		5			
		Test	5	5			
		Both		5			
2	**90 % of data input is via feeder systems direct interfaces—thus minimising keying errors**	Best		4			
		Test	3	3			
		Both		2			
3	**System access is controlled by user-ID and password. Access system is maintained by the systems administrator**	Best		2	5		3
		Test	4	4	4		4
		Both		1	4		2
4	**Standing data and parameters are entered and verified by the financial accountant prior to the use of the MIS**	Best		3		4	
		Test	2	2		2	
		Both		0		1	
5	**Access to standing data and parameters is further protected by the use of an additional (higher level) password control system**	Best		2		3	
		Test	4	4		4	
		Both		1		2	

Figure 3.14 Control matrix after inserting the compliance (*Test*) scores

Management Information System— Abbreviated Example Matrix			EXPOSURES				
			A	B	C	D	E

Exposures:

A Unable to maintain/amend the MIS
B Inaccurate, incomplete, or out of date information
C Data corruption
D Inaccurate system parameters, variables and assumptions
E Leak of sensitive company data—competitive disadvantage, malpractice

				A	B	C	D	E
	Calculated Risk Score		Risk		1	4	2	3	3
	Scale 3 (6 is the most serious)		Type		4	6	5	4	6
	Size (3 is the maximum)		Size		3	3	2	2	2
	CONTROLS								
1	System specification is documented and any amendments are updated and verified	Best		5				
		Test	5	5				
		Both		5				
2	90 % of data input is via feeder systems direct interfaces—thus minimising keying errors	Best			4			
		Test	3		3			
		Both			2			
3	System access is controlled by user-ID and password. Access system is maintained by the systems administrator	Best			2	5		3
		Test	4		4	4		4
		Both			1	4		2
4	Standing data and parameters are entered and verified by the financial accountant prior to the use of the MIS	Best			3		4	
		Test	2		2		2	
		Both			0		1	
5	Access to standing data and parameters is further protected by the use of an additional (higher level) password control system	Best			2		3	
		Test	4		4		4	
		Both			1		2	

Inherent Risk (Size) Score [5 is worst risk; 1 best] — 3
Overall Control Score [5 is worst risk; 1 best] — 3

Figure 3.15 Completed Control Matrix with Overall *Risk and Control* scores

DEVELOPING OPERATIONAL REVIEW PROGRAMMES FOR MANAGERIAL AND AUDIT USE

Management Information System—EXPOSURES

Exposures:

A   MIS not adequately documented—unable to maintain/amend
B   Inadequate operating instructions—error, system failure
C   Use of inaccurate, incomplete or out of date information
D   Re-keyed data contains errors—affect on decision making
E   Unable to trail/prove data to source(s)—affects decisions
F   Unauthorised access to/use of MIS—error, leakage, etc.
G   Inadequate specification & testing of MIS—credibility, etc.
H   Unable to recover use of MIS in event of system failure
I   Inadequate management reporting facilities—additional effort
J   Inaccurate system parameters, variables and assumptions
K   Failure to back-up MIS data—delay, cost, unable to recover
L   Leak of sensitive company data—competitive disadvantage
M   Insecure or poorly designed spreadsheets—logic errors, etc.
N   Absence of spreadsheet model documentation and/or testing

SCALE 3 (ABRIDGED)
6   Loss of information
5   Loss of cash or other asset, or increase in liability
4   Political sensitivity or loss of reputation
3   Loss or exaggeration of profit
2   Distortion of the balance sheet
1   Accounting error without P & L or balance sheet effect
(Exposures oriented scale)

Management Information System—		EXPOSURES													
		A	B	C	D	E	F	G	H	I	J	K	L	M	N
Calculated Risk Score	Risk	3	2	4	3	2	3	2	4	3	3	4	3	2	2
Scale 3 (6 is the most serious)	Type	6	6	6	6	6	6	6	6	6	6	6	6	6	6
Size (3 is the maximum)	Size	2	1	3	2	1	2	1	3	2	2	3	2	1	1
CONTROLS																
1 System specification is documented and any amendments are updated	Best	4														
	Test	?	?													
	Both															
2 User & operating manuals have been developed—contents agreed with users & IAD	Best	4	4													
	Test	?	?	?												
	Both															
3 Analysis & reporting module handbooks are available	Best	4	4													
	Test	?	?	?												
	Both															
4 90 % of data input is via feed system direct interfaces—therefore no keying errors	Best			4												
	Test	?		?												
5 Input data is reconciled back to source system(s)	Best			4												
	Test	?		?												
	Both															

(continued)

Management Information System—			EXPOSURES													
			A	B	C	D	E	F	G	H	I	J	K	L	M	N
	Calculated Risk Score	Risk	3	2	4	3	2	3	2	4	3	3	4	3	2	2
6	Update file headers validated to prevent incorrect or duplicate loading of data	Best			4											
		Test	?		?											
		Both														
7	Limited re-keying is necessary—all such input is reconciled to source control values	Best				5										
		Test	?			?										
		Both														
8	Operations log maintained for all MIS processing & activity—source file input is recorded	Best					4									
		Test	?				?									
		Both														
9	System reports on "missing" data input files to ensure MIS update is complete	Best			3		3									
		Test	?		?		?									
		Both														
10	System operates on restricted access Novell network located in Executive suite	Best							4					4		
		Test	?						?					?		
		Both														
11	System access is controlled by user-ID and password	Best						5						4		
		Test	?					?						?		
		Both														
12	Network PC based MIS was developed per user management requirements specification	Best							4							
		Test	?						?							
		Both														
13	MIS was tested by users and IT Dept. before live use—all modifications also tested	Best						5								
		Test	?					?								
		Both														

DEVELOPING OPERATIONAL REVIEW PROGRAMMES FOR MANAGERIAL AND AUDIT USE

Management Information System—EXPOSURES (continued)

Exposures:

A	MIS not adequately documented—unable to maintain/amend	H	Unable to recover use of MIS in event of system failure
B	Inadequate operating instructions—error, system failure	I	Inadequate management reporting facilities—additional effort
C	Use of inaccurate, incomplete or out of date information	J	Inaccurate system parameters, variables and assumptions
D	Re-keyed data contains errors—affect on decision making	K	Failure to back-up MIS data—delay, cost, unable to recover
E	Unable to trail/prove data to source(s)—affects decisions	L	Leak of sensitive company data—competitive disadvantage
F	Unauthorised access to/use of MIS—error, leakage, etc.	M	Insecure or poorly designed spreadsheets—logic errors, etc.
G	Inadequate specification & testing of MIS—credibility, etc.	N	Absence of spreadsheet model documentation and/or testing

SCALE 3 (ABRIDGED)
6 Loss of information
5 Loss of cash or other asset, or increase in liability
4 Political sensitivity or loss of reputation
3 Loss or exaggeration of profit
2 Distortion of the balance sheet
1 Accounting error without P & L or balance sheet effect
(Exposures oriented scale)

Management Information System—			EXPOSURES													
			A	B	C	D	E	F	G	H	I	J	K	L	M	N
	Calculated Risk Score	Risk	3	2	4	3	2	3	2	4	3	3	4	3	2	2
	Scale 3 (6 is the most serious)	Type	6	6	6	6	6	6	6	6	6	6	6	6	6	6
	Size (3 is the maximum)	Size	2	1	3	2	1	2	1	3	2	2	3	2	1	1
	CONTROLS															
14	Contingency plan allows for emergency use of alternative network	Best								4						
		Test	?							?						
		Both														
15	Source files are backed-up to tape in relevant department	Best								4			4			
		Test	?							?			?			
		Both														
16	MIS data backed up to tape streamer on a daily basis	Best								4			4			
		Test	?							?			?			
		Both														
17	Flexible reporting, analysis & query software interfaces have been incorporated into design	Best									5					
		Test	?								?					
		Both														
18	Standing data & parameters are verified by Financial Accountant before system use	Best											4			
		Test	?										?			
		Both														

(continued)

Management Information System—			EXPOSURES													
			A	B	C	D	E	F	G	H	I	J	K	L	M	N
	Calculated Risk Score	Risk	3	2	4	3	2	3	2	4	3	3	4	3	2	2
19	Access to standing data and parameters is protected by additional password control	Best											4		2	
		Test	?										?		?	
		Both														
20	Use of MIS facilities is restricted on a "need to know" basis	Best						4						4		
		Test	?					?						?		
		Both														
21	Back-up media stored in Financial Accounts Dept. safe	Best												4		
		Test	?											?		
		Both														
22	MIS hard copy circulated is restricted and in sealed confidential packets	Best												3		
		Test	?											?		
		Both														
23	IT Dept. develop all critical company spreadsheets—ICAEW best practical standards	Best													4	
		Test													?	
		Both														
24	User specifications produced for all spreadsheets—delivered systems are signed-off by users	Best													3	4
		Test	?												?	?
		Both														
25	IT Dept. and users conduct testing of all spreadsheets—results & amendments documment	Best												4		
		Test	?											?		
		Both														
26	Documentation is incorporated into spreadsheets for ease of use—updated as required	Best														4
		Test	?													?
		Both														

Figure 3.16 Management Information System

Planning—OBJECTIVES

A	Establish a suitable & robust Strategic Planning framework	H	Ensure action plans & adequate resources are provided
B	Ensure planning processes & models are rigorously tested	I	Ensure actual progress is monitored against the plan(s)
C	Ensure company mission/objectives are clearly communicated	J	Maintain awareness of organisations' strengths & weaknesses
D	Ensure all plans (i.e. IT, Manpower, etc.) are co-ordinated	K	Ensure all planning activity remains realistic/objective
E	Ensure mechanism addresses sustained competitive advantage	L	Ensure adequate staff involvement in planning process
F	Ensure that corporate goals are realistic & measurable	M	Ensure senior management are committed to planning process
G	Provide accurate/reliable information for planning purposes	N	Ensure commercially sensitive data remains confidential

SCALE 3 (ABRIDGED)
6   Management must be able to understand what is happening at a strategic level
5   Medium to long term corporate objectives must be achieved
4   Budgets and profit targets must be achieved
3   Management must be taking appropriate action to correct performance
2   Management must understand what is happening at operational level
1   Motivation must be high
(Exposures oriented scale)

Planning			\multicolumn{14}{c}{Objectives}													
			A	B	C	D	E	F	G	H	I	J	K	L	M	N
	Calculated Risk Score	Risk	4	2	4	4	4	4	3	3	2	2	3	3	3	3
	Scale 1 (6 is the most serious)	Type	6	6	5	6	6	5	6	5	2	2	5	3	3	5
	Size (3 is the maximum)	Size	3	1	3	3	3	3	2	2	3	3	2	3	3	2
	Measures															
1	**Planning Dept. established with the brief to develop & implement a suitable planning method**	Best		3												
		Test	?	?												
		Both														
2	**External consultants to assist in initial process & provide objectivity during reviews**	Best		4										4			
		Test	?	?										?			
		Both															
3	**Planning method/procedures are documented in manual—copies are supplied to affected staff**	Best		4	3				2								
		Test	?	?	?				?								
		Both															
4	**Initial pilot exercise conducted for subsidiary X—procedure amendments incorporated**	Best			5												
		Test	?		?												
		Both															
5	**Overview mission statement & key objectives circulated to all staff**	Best			5										2		
		Test	?		?										?		
		Both															

(continued)

THE OPERATIONAL AUDITING HANDBOOK

Planning			OBJECTIVES													
			A	B	C	D	E	F	G	H	I	J	K	L	M	N
	Calculated Risk Score	Risk	4	2	4	4	4	4	3	3	2	2	3	3	3	3
6	Key senior managers involved in the planning process	Best			4			3		4			3	4	4	
		Test	?		?			?		?			?	?	?	
		Both														
7	Methodology links all aspects of planning & ensures compatibility of goals, etc.	Best				4										
		Test	?			?										
		Both														
8	Divisional plans are subject to review to ensure compliance with Group plan objectives, etc.	Best				4										
		Test	?			?										
		Both														
9	All plans are ratified by the board	Best				4		3								
		Test	?			?		?								
		Both														
10	Each business activity is analysed in respect of internal & external influences	Best					3									
		Test	?				?									
		Both														
11	All potential projects are subject to feasibility study & assessment	Best						4	3							
		Test	?					?	?							
		Both														
12	Measurable targets are allocated to each goal—monitored for progress, achievement, etc.	Best							4		3					
		Test	?						?		?					
		Both														
13	MIS established as source for company planning data—contents reconciled to source(s)	Best								4						
		Test	?							?						
		Both														

DEVELOPING OPERATIONAL REVIEW PROGRAMMES FOR MANAGERIAL AND AUDIT USE

Planning—OBJECTIVES (continued)

A Establish a suitable & robust Strategic Planning framework
B Ensure planning processes & models are rigorously tested
C Ensure company mission/objectives are clearly communicated
D Ensure all plans (i.e. IT, Manpower, etc.) are co-ordinated
E Ensure mechanism addresses sustained competitive advantage
F Ensure that corporate goals are realistic & measurable
G Provide accurate/reliable information for planning purposes
H Ensure action plans & adequate resources are provided
I Ensure actual progress is monitored against the plan(s)
J Maintain awareness of organisations' strengths & weaknesses
K Ensure all planning activity remains realistic/objective
L Ensure adequate staff involvement in planning process
M Ensure senior management are committed to planning process
N Ensure commercially sensitive data remains confidential

SCALE 3 (ABRIDGED)
6 Management must be able to understand what is happening at a strategic level
5 Medium to long term corporate objectives must be achieved
4 Budgets and profit targets must be achieved
3 Management must be taking appropriate action to correct performance
2 Management must understand what is happening at operational level
1 Motivation must be high
(Exposures oriented scale)

Planning			Objectives													
			A	B	C	D	E	F	G	H	I	J	K	L	M	N
	Calculated Risk Score	Risk	4	2	4	4	4	4	3	3	2	2	3	3	3	3
	Scale 1 (6 is the most serious)	Type	6	6	5	6	6	5	6	5	2	2	5	3	3	5
	Size (3 is the maximum)	Size	3	1	3	3	3	3	2	2	3	2	3	3	3	2
	MEASURES															
14	External information gathered from documented and reliable official sources	Best							4							
		Test	?						?							
		Both														
15	Specific expertise/research data acquired as necessary	Best							4							
		Test	?						?							
		Both														
16	Method requires production of action plans & resource requirements for Board approval	Best								4						
		Test	?							?						
		Both														
17	Divisional Managers agree action plans & are held responsible for implementation within deadlines	Best								4				4	4	
		Test	?							?				?	?	
		Both														
18	Monthly progress reports are presented to the board	Best									5					
		Test	?								?					
		Both														

(continued)

Planning			OBJECTIVES													
			A	B	C	D	E	F	G	H	I	J	K	L	M	N
	Calculated Risk Score	Risk	4	2	4	4	4	4	3	3	2	2	3	3	3	3
19	Market Analyst canvasses customers, etc. for external opinion of company/performance	Best										4				
		Test	?									?				
		Both														
20	Key performance factors are monitored & fed into the planning process	Best										4				
		Test	?									?				
		Both														
21	Cross-functional involvement in the planning process provides broad basis for contents review	Best											3	4	3	
		Test	?										?	?	?	
		Both														
22	Complete copies of interim & final planning reports only circulated to Board members	Best														4
		Test	?													?
		Both														
23	All research data/reports held on secure PC protected by access control system	Best														4
		Test	?													?
		Both														

Figure 3.17 Management Information System

NOTES

1. A suggested fact finding programme can be found in Chambers, A. D. (2009) *Tolley's Internal Auditor's Handbook*. LexisNexis, pp. 480–483.
2. A suggested high level review programme can be found in Chambers, A. D. (2009) *Tolley's Internal Auditor's Handbook*. LexisNexis, pp. 484–491.
3. Chambers, A. D. (1997) *Effective Internal Audits—How to Plan and Implement*. Management Audit, www.management-audit.com.
4. Chambers, A. D. and Rand, G. (1997) *Auditing the IT Environment—Assessing and Measuring Risk and Control*. Management Audit, www.management-audit.com.
5. Chambers, A. D. and Rand, G. (1997) *Auditing Contracts*. Management Audit, www.management-audit.com.
6. We use the expression *control activity* loosely here in the sense that it might refer to any element of internal control. The COSO *Internal Control—Integrated Framework* identified five components of internal control of which they called one "control activities"—see Chapter 6. Our use of the term here could refer to a control element in any one of COSO's five components of internal control.

4
Governance Processes

INTRODUCTION

This is the first of three consecutive chapters that tackle, respectively, governance processes, risk management and internal control. Each contains, towards the end, a practical guide on the objectives and the audit issues. In this chapter we set out to explain the role of internal audit in corporate governance. The position we take is that internal audit is primarily involved with (a) internal governance processes but is increasingly active in (b) reviewing the board and (c) providing a service with respect to the accountability of the organisation to its stakeholders. The practical guides towards the end of this chapter cover each of these three dimensions.

INTERNAL CONTROL PROCESSES BEING PART OF RISK MANAGEMENT PROCESSES

COSO's 1992 *Internal control—Integrated Framework* allowed some to regard risk management as being part of internal control since "risk assessment" was shown in the 1992 framework as being one of the five essential components of internal control (see Figure 6.1 in Chapter 6). Since the advent of COSO's 2004 *Enterprise Risk Management* framework, the generally accepted view is the reverse of that—internal control is now perceived as part of risk management, albeit a large part of how risks are managed. This is illustrated by Figure 5.2 of Chapter 5 and is referred to in the 2004 Framework publication, as follows:[1]

Encompasses Internal Control

Internal control is an integral part of enterprise risk management. This enterprise risk management framework encompasses internal control, forming a more robust conceptualization and tool for management. Internal control is defined and described in Internal Control—Integrated Framework. Because that framework is the basis for existing rules, regulations and laws, that document remains in place as the definition of and framework for internal control. While only portions of the text of Internal Control–Integrated Framework are reproduced in this framework, the entirety of that framework is incorporated by reference into this one.

The Institute of Internal Auditors' Definition of Internal Auditing, developed through due process as a prelude to modelling their new 2001 *Standards*, so far remains unchanged in the 2009 International Professional Practices Framework (IPPF) and reads (bolding added):

Internal auditing is an independent, objective assurance and consulting activity designed to add value and improve an organization's operations. It helps an organization accomplish its objectives by bringing a systematic, disciplined approach to evaluate and improve the effectiveness of **risk management, control, and governance processes**.

RISK MANAGEMENT PROCESSES BEING PART OF GOVERNANCE PROCESSES

Since risk is seen as including internal control, the definition refers to these two in a logical order. It is "governance processes" that is out of sequence in the definition, meaning that the definition is due for revision. Indeed the 2009 release of the *Standards* for the first time uses the sequence "governance, risk management, and control processes" in both the Standard on the nature of internal audit work and also in the order in which these three issues are addressed throughout the *Standards*.[2] Arguably, the *Standards* are now accepting not only that internal control processes are amongst the risk management processes of an organisation but that the risk management processes are amongst the governance processes of an organisation, as shown in Figure 4.1.

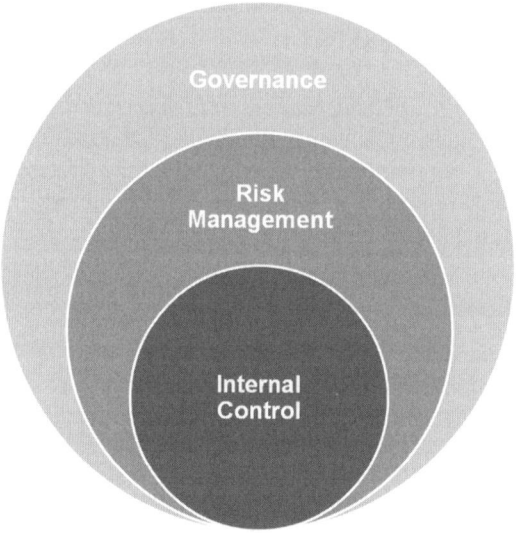

Figure 4.1 The relationship between governance processes, risk management and control

The conciseness of the wording of the Definition and also of Standard 2100—Nature of [Internal Audit] Work[2] make it unclear whether the scope of internal audit work is limited to the review of the *processes* of risk management and internal control, although it is clear that it is the internal processes of governance which are within the scope of internal audit. If the scope went further than "processes", internal audit might, for instance, advise the board and senior management on the specific internal and external risks that the organisation is facing rather than restrict their advice to whether the process of risk management is sound. However, other *Standards* make it clear that for both "governance" and "risk management" it is the *process* that is within the scope of internal audit:

Standard 2110—Governance

The internal audit activity must assess and make appropriate recommendations for improving the governance process . . .

Standard 2120—Risk Management

The internal audit activity must evaluate the effectiveness and contribute to the improvement of risk management processes.

Standard 2130—Control

The internal audit activity must assist the organization in maintaining effective controls by evaluating their effectiveness and efficiency and by promoting continuous improvement.

OBJECTIVES OF GOVERNANCE, RISK MANAGEMENT AND CONTROL PROCESSES

Since internal control is deemed to be an important part of risk management, it is not surprising that the Institute's *Standards* are quite repetitive in the parts that address risk management and internal control. In particular, the *Standards* have adopted COSO's objectives of internal control as being the objectives of risk management and internal control—though showing separately the "safeguarding of assets" rather than blending this into the "effectiveness and efficiency of operations" objective as COSO has done.

Standard 2120.A1 on Risk Management *and* Standard 2130.A1 on Control

The internal audit activity must evaluate . . . regarding the:

- Reliability and integrity of financial and operational information;
- Effectiveness and efficiency of operations;
- Safeguarding of assets; and
- Compliance with laws, regulations, and contracts.

The Institute's *Standards* give different objectives for governance processes. The equivalent Standard to 2120.A1 (above) and 2130.A1 (on internal control) reads:

2110—Governance

The internal audit activity must assess and make appropriate recommendations for improving the governance process in its accomplishment of the following objectives:

- Promoting appropriate ethics and values within the organization;
- Ensuring effective organizational performance management and accountability;
- Communicating risk and control information to appropriate areas of the organization; and
- Coordinating the activities of and communicating information among the board, external and internal auditors, and management.

We summarise the Institute's position in Figure 4.2.

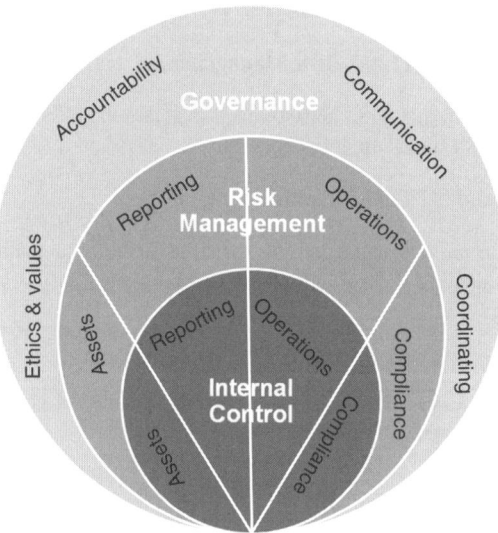

Figure 4.2 The Institute of Internal Auditors' objectives of governance processes, risk management and control

THE COSO VIEW OF OBJECTIVES

There is no COSO framework on corporate governance or on internal governance processes, but there is a considerable need for one. The COSO position is summed up in Figure 4.3, with governance still to be developed by COSO.

We cannot be sure whether COSO would adopt the distinctive objectives of governance processes that The Institute of Internal Auditors has identified (Standard 2110 and Figure 4.2) or would settle for objectives which align with risk management and internal control. COSO added a fourth, "strategic" objective to risk management forming what they termed "a more robust conceptualisation" than their internal control framework, implying that the "strategic" objective should have been included in their internal control framework, with a result which would have

Figure 4.3 COSO's objectives of risk management and control

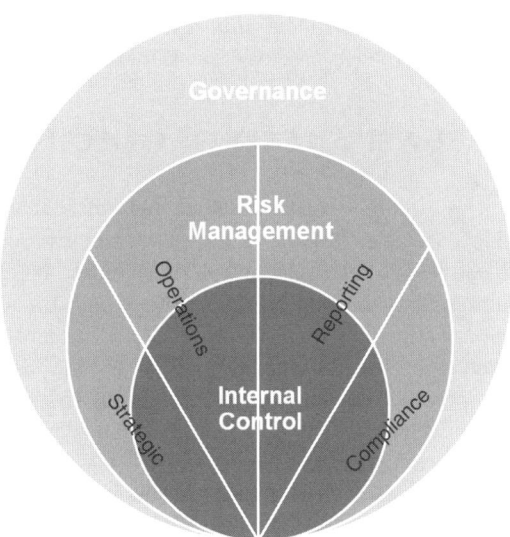

Figure 4.4 The Institute of internal Auditors' objectives of risk management and control

been as illustrated in Figure 4.4. Had that been the case, then possibly the same four objectives would apply to governance processes as well, as illustrated in Figure 4.5.

If the objectives of internal governance processes were to be the same as the objectives of risk management and internal control, and bearing in mind that internal governance processes include risk management and internal control, it could be

80 THE OPERATIONAL AUDITING HANDBOOK

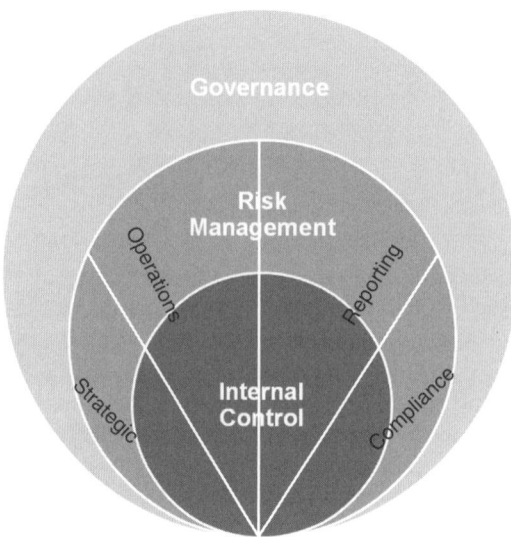

Figure 4.5 A scheme for one set of objectives, modelled on COSO's risk management framework

argued that it would be unnecessary for the Institute's *Standards* to address these three (governance processes, risk management and internal control) separately.

SHOULD THERE BE A SINGLE SET OF OBJECTIVES?

If it is sound to conceptualise that internal control is part of risk management which, in turn, is part of the governance processes of the organisation, then the objectives of internal control must either be the same as the objectives of risk management or must be incorporated into broader objectives for risk management that are consistent with those of internal control though broader. In the case of The Institute of Internal Auditors, they are the same. In the case of COSO they are incorporated into broader objectives for risk management. Similarly, if it is sound to conceptualise that risk management is part of the governance processes of the organisation, then the objectives of risk management must either be the same as the objectives of governance processes or must be incorporated into objectives for governance processes that are consistent with those of risk management, though broader. As we have said, COSO is silent on this.

The Institute of Internal Auditors' objectives for risk management (see above) are much narrower than those for governance processes, but we are satisfied that the former all fit into the latter. In view of this, should a common set of objectives be desirable for each of governance processes, risk management and internal control, consideration should be given to utilising the governance processes objectives for this purpose, as set out in Figure 4.6.

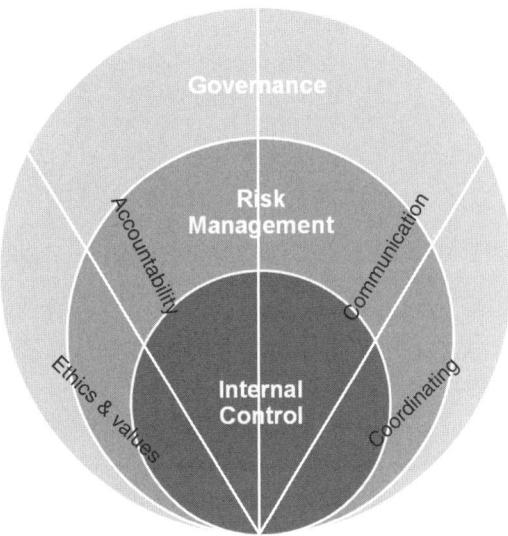

Figure 4.6 A scheme for one set of objectives modelled on The Institute of Internal Auditors' governance processes objectives

THE INTERNAL GOVERNANCE PROCESSES

It will be apparent from the Institute's list of four objectives of governance processes in Standard 2110 that the intention is that the scope of internal audit with respect to governance is limited to the *internal* governance processes of the organisation. Figure 4.7 points out that governance processes (i.e. corporate governance) additionally include *external* governance processes and also those charged with governance (*the board*) who hold the ring between the internal and external governance processes.

THE BOARD AND EXTERNAL ASPECTS OF CORPORATE GOVERNANCE

The board is clearly an important governance process. The board sets the direction of the organisation and oversees that management implements the direction set. The board has an accountability obligation to the shareholders and other stakeholders of the organisation. Shareholders and other stakeholders exercise control from outside (external control).

We need to take a view on the extent, if at all, that internal audit scope runs beyond the internal governance processes as set out in Standard 2110 to embrace review of the board and also review of external aspects of corporate governance—per Figure 4.5.

There are indications that internal audit is becoming more involved in the external aspects of corporate governance. Any assistance that internal audit provides to

82 THE OPERATIONAL AUDITING HANDBOOK

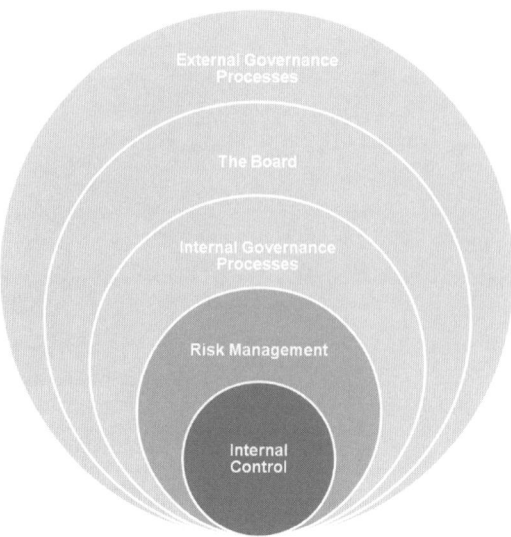

Figure 4.7 Corporate governance is internal and external processes, with the board between

the external auditors belongs to the external aspects of corporate governance since external auditors report to the external shareholders. There are many cases when internal auditors are required to report to regulators who are one category of stakeholder. Overall opinions, expressed by internal audit to their audit committees, assist boards in formulating their own statements on internal control for publication. Specific internal audit engagements conducted directly for, and at the request of, the board's audit committee are often another example of internal audit serving the needs of external stakeholders, at least indirectly. The important interface between the chief audit executive and the audit committee of independent directors is evidence that internal audit is contributing to the accountability of the board to its shareholders since a primary role of independent directors is to safeguard the interests of shareholders. There have been occasions when chief audit executives have included their own report within the published annual report of the organisation. Management often asks the internal audit activity to provide them with assurance on the reliability of assertions within the annual report that are not subject to other independent verification. Analysts and shareholder pressure groups often express surprise that internal audit had not been more effective at uncovering unreliable reporting to shareholders.

THE BOARD'S ASSURANCE VACUUM

The global financial crisis and deep recession that commenced in 2007 brought into sharp relief that many boards had been unaware of the nature and scale of many of the internal and external risks that their organisations were running. This failing was not limited to financial institutions. It was widely commented upon that too many directors lacked the ability to readily understand what was happening within their businesses. But apart from that, there were indications that management teams were being selective about the information they fed through to their boards, the timing of that information flow and whether potentially bad news had been given the right emphasis. The question arises, "How can boards get the assurance they need that the policies of the board are being implemented by management and that there are no banana skins round the corner, known or not to management, over which the organisation may slip in the future?" Arising from that question are the lead-on questions, "Do boards need independent assurance on these matters?", and "To what extent can internal audit fill the board's assurance vacuum?"

The extent to which internal audit can fill this assurance vacuum depends on the degree of confidence that the board, and its audit committee, can have about the independence, objectivity and competence of internal audit. It is already the case that the chief audit executive generally has a direct reporting relationship to the audit committee, but reporting administratively ("for pay and rations") is almost invariably to management. "He who pays the piper calls the tune!" Unfortunately there have been too many examples of chief audit executives allowing their reports to the audit committee to be, in effect, edited by management before they reach the audit committee, so that their contents are what management wishes them to be rather than what they would have been had the chief audit executive followed his professional judgement. Audit committees may be unaware that reports to them in the name of the chief audit executive are not as independent as they appear to be. Internal auditing *Standards* require that internal auditors do not subordinate their judgement to that of others,[3] but this is hard to sustain if internal audit is too closely aligned with management.

We suggest that the time has come for chief audit executives to report "for pay and rations" (*"administrative reporting"*) to the chairman of the board or, if the chairman was not independent when appointed to the chair, to the board itself. A satisfactory alternative would be for the chief audit executive to report to the company secretary or legal counsel if, as is sometimes the case, that person is independent of management, drawing their budget from the chairman or from the board. The costs of the internal audit activity would be regarded as one of the costs of running the board. Of course internal audit would continue to report on the results of their work (*"activity reporting"*) to the board or to its audit committee, and would continue to account for its professionalism (*"functional reporting"*) to the board on to its audit committee. In this way, management will be unable to control the reporting of internal audit to the board, and boards will have more confidence in what internal audit reports to them. Reporting to the board in this way would not diminish the value of internal audit to management. Over the years internal audit has graduated to providing assurance to higher and higher levels of management, but that has not diminished the value of internal audit work to junior levels of management. Indeed, the assurance that internal audit is able to provide can be enhanced if internal audit is independent of those to whom the assurance is provided. Clearly, from what we are suggesting, internal audit would not be independent of the board since internal audit would report to the board administratively. But, in assessing the degree of assurance the board can receive from the results of internal audit work, it is much to be preferred that internal audit no longer reports administratively to management below the level of the board.

RISK AND CONTROL ISSUES FOR INTERNAL GOVERNANCE PROCESSES

Control Objectives for Internal Governance Processes

> (a) To promote appropriate ethics and values within the organisation.
>
> (b) To ensure effective organisational performance management and accountability.
>
> (c) To communicate risk and control information to appropriate areas of the organisation.
>
> (d) To coordinate the activities of and communicating information among the board, external and internal auditors, and management.

(a) Promoting Appropriate Ethics and Values within the Organisation

1 Key Issues

1.1 Does the evidence indicate that the organisation has high ethical standards?

1.2 Are ethical standards and values consistent across the organisation?

1.3 Are ethical policies and codes of conduct complete, appropriate and applied?

- Code of Business Conduct
- Code of Scientific Conduct
- Fraud Policy Statement
- Etc.

1.4 Does the organisation have a clear policy that outlaws bribery?

1.5 Are ethical policies and values communicated effectively and accepted across the organisation and at all levels?

1.6 Do the board and top management set the right tone in their personal conduct and by reacting appropriately and consistently to wrongdoing within the organisation?

1.7 Does the organisation have a suitable whistleblowing policy which is known to staff and contractors, and reviewed regularly by the audit committee of the board?

2 Detailed Issues

2.1 Does the organisation have the skills and competencies to assess and develop appropriate organisational ethics and values?

2.2 How does the organisation set about obtaining assurance on ethics and values?

2.3 Are best practices elsewhere evaluated with a view to adapting for the organisation if appropriate?

2.4 Does internal audit inform the board on matters such as culture, tone, ethics and transparency?

2.5 Is the process for ethical investigations and employee disciplinary matters well defined, appropriate and followed?

2.6 Does the organisation report publicly on its values and ethical policies?

(b) Ensuring Effective Organisational Performance Management and Accountability

1 Key Issues

1.1 Is a common understanding of the purpose of the organisation shared by the board and the owners?

1.2 How does the board ensure that the organisation is keeping to its defined purpose?

1.3 Does the board appropriately empower executive management?

1.4 Does the board receive regular, reliable and clear reports to measure attainment of performance targets and to monitor management's progress?

1.5 Does the organisation's structure promote effective performance management and accountability?

1.6 Is there proper assignment of accountabilities and performance management responsibilities?

1.7 Do remuneration arrangements align individual performance with organisational performance and avoid perverse incentives that encourage excessive risk taking?

2 Detailed Issues

2.1 Does the organisation have the skills and competencies needed to assess and develop appropriate performance management and accountability systems?

2.2 How does the organisation set about obtaining assurance on the appropriateness and effectiveness of performance management and accountability?

2.3 Are best practices elsewhere evaluated with a view to adapting for the organisation if appropriate?

2.4 Are job descriptions, performance appraisals and rewards fully aligned?

(c) Communicating Risk and Control Information to Appropriate Areas of the Organisation

1 Key Issues

1.1 Does the evidence indicate that risk and control information is communicated appropriately?

1.2 Are the board's and top management's concerns about major enterprise risks communicated downwards so as to inform risk management at lower levels?

1.3 Are operating personnel's perceptions about risk communicated upwards, and ultimately to top management and to the board where appropriate?

1.4 Is an enterprise-wide view of risk taken?

1.5 Has the organisation defined its risk appetite—overall and for its component parts?

1.6 Is risk management embedded into the culture and approach of the organisation?

1.7 Does the audit committee of the board concern itself both with the risk management process of the organisation, and also with the specific high-level risks that the process has (or has not) identified?

2 Detailed Issues

2.1 How does the organisation set about obtaining assurance that risk and control information is communicated effectively to appropriate areas of the organisation?

2.2 Are best practices elsewhere evaluated with a view to adapting for the organisation if appropriate?

2.3 Is there a shared risk management methodology across the business, including use of common risk terminology?

2.4 Does the scope of internal audit work allow some time to review parts of the business that are perceived as being low risk, in case there may be significant concealed risks in those areas of the business?

2.5 Is the future plan of internal audit engagements based on a risk assessment?

(d) Coordinating the Activities of and Communicating Information among the Board, External and Internal Auditors, and Management

1 Key Issues

1.1 Does the evidence indicate that coordination between these parties is to a high standard?

1.2 How does the organisation ensure that external and internal auditors do not subordinate their judgement on professional matters to that of anyone else?

1.3 How does the audit committee effectively oversee the external audit so as to ensure its quality and independence?

2 Detailed Issues

2.1 Does the organisation have the skills and competencies to coordinate and communicate information on internal governance processes among the board, external and internal auditors, and management?

2.2 Who is responsible for this coordination and is it recognised in their job description(s) and terms of reference/charter?

2.3 Are best practices elsewhere evaluated with a view to adapting for the organisation if appropriate?

2.4 Is there an avoidance of unnecessary duplication of work between the different review agencies, including external and internal audit?

2.5 Has the external auditor expressed concern about the timing of information flow from management to the external auditor?

RISK AND CONTROL ISSUES FOR THE BOARD

Control Objectives for the Board

> (a) To ensure the board sets the direction of the organisation.
>
> (b) To ensure the board effectively oversees management.
>
> (c) To ensure that appropriate policies are in place to fully support the achievement of the objectives of the organisation.
>
> (d) To ensure that the composition and functioning of the board fully support the achievement of the objectives of the organisation.

(a) To Ensure the Board Sets the Direction of the Organisation

1 Key Issues

1.1 Does the board have effective oversight of the development and adoption of strategy?

1.2 Is the quality of information that comes to the board appropriate, timely, clear and reliable?

1.3 Does the board collectively possess the competencies it needs to direct and oversee the business?

1.4 Do board committees possess the appropriate skills?

1.5 Do individual directors exercise skill, care and diligence?

1.6 Do nonexecutive directors act in the best interests of the organisation, or wrongly promote their own interests or the interests of those who nominated them?

1.7 Do executive directors align themselves with the best interests of the organisation, or seek to promote their executive interests above all else?

2 Detailed Issues

2.1 Is there a well maintained board policy manual/directors' handbook, readily accessible to all directors, that includes:
- the constitutional documents of the organisation
- terms of reference of board committees
- summary of current policies of the board
- delegation of authority guidelines
- statement of matters reserved to the board
- copy of policy statement on directors taking independent advice at organisation's expense
- summary of key covenants entered into with third parties
- statement of high-level external and internal risks and their mitigation (risk register)
- copy of directors' contracts with the company

2.2 Is the balance of boardroom time, as between direction and oversight, about right?

2.3 Does internal audit undertake audit engagements on specific aspects of governance?

(b) To Ensure the Board Effectively Oversees Management

1 Key Issues

1.1 Is the independent element on the board sufficient to be an effective challenge to management?

1.2 Are the nonexecutive members of the board well informed about the business?

1.3 Does the board work as a team, with outside members contributing to strategy as well as overseeing executive performance?

1.4 How does the board obtain assurance that the policies of the board are being implemented by management, and that there are no banana skins round the corner, known or unknown to management, over which the organisation may slip in the future? Is this assurance in part independent of management?

1.5 Does the audit committee collectively possess the appropriate recent and relevant financial experience?

1.6 Do board committees report fully to the board, so that the board is not insulated from the important deliberations that take place at board committee level?

1.7 Does the audit committee express a periodic opinion (at least once a year) to the board on:
- the effectiveness of organisational risk management and internal control?
- the reliability of financial and other information used internally and published?
- the professionalism of the organisation's external auditors?

- the professionalism, independence and scope of internal audit and of other internal review agencies?

2 Detailed Issues

2.1 Does the board give due consideration to the results of internal audit work?

2.2 Do nonexecutive directors get significantly involved with the organisation between board and board committee meetings?

(c) To Ensure that Appropriate Policies are in Place to Fully Support the Achievement of the Objectives of the Organisation

1 Key Issues

1.1 Has the board provided sufficient resources to enable executive management to achieve the goals of the organisation?

1.2 Does the board review the policies framework of the organisation periodically?

1.3 Are any policies ignored in practice?

1.4 Are different polices on the same issues being followed in different parts of the organisation?

1.5 Are some policies incompatible with other policies?

1.6 Are there any examples of policy statements that are intended only for "public consumption", but not for practical use.

2 Detailed Issues

2.1 How are board policies communicated throughout the organisation, and is this done effectively.

2.2 Do "grass roots" levels of the organisation contribute appropriately to the formulation of organisational policies?

(d) To Ensure that the Composition and Functioning of the Board Fully Support the Achievement of the Objectives of the Organisation

1 Key Issues

1.1 Is the board the right size to be most effective?

1.2 Is there an avoidance of excessive concentration of power at the top of the business?

1.3 Does the board collectively possess the appropriate experience, expertise and personal qualities?

1.4 Does the board meet with the frequency needed to discharge its responsibilities effectively?

1.5 Is there openness and candour at board meetings and an absence of excessive formality?

1.6 Is the board supported by the right board committees with appropriate terms of reference and competent membership?

1.7 Is the performance of the following assessed sufficiently regularly and robustly—
The board?
The chairman of the board
Each board committee?
The chairman of each board committee?
Each executive and nonexecutive director?

2 Detailed Issues

2.1 Are total board costs known and monitored?

2.2 Is attendance of board and board committee meetings good?

2.3 Is there an adequate budget for, and programme of, ongoing training for directors?

2.4 Are board and board committee agenda papers and minutes of a high standard with appropriate retention?

2.5 Are board and board committee agenda papers circulated sufficiently in advance of meetings?

2.6 Are members well prepared for board and board committee meetings.

2.7 How effective is the induction programme for new nonexecutive directors, with the bias likely to be on learning about the organisation?

2.8 How effective is the induction programme for new executive directors, with the bias likely to be on the responsibilities of directors and boards?

2.9 Does the membership of the board and of board committees correspond to best practice corporate governance guidance?

RISK AND CONTROL ISSUES FOR EXTERNAL GOVERNANCE PROCESSES

Control Objectives for External Governance Processes

(a) To ensure that the organisation is mindful of the interests of its owners and other stakeholders.

> (b) To ensure that the organisation's accountability to its stakeholders is transparent.
>
> (c) To ensure, so far as is possible, that stakeholders exercise well informed control over their stakes in the organisation.

(a) To Ensure that the Organisation is Mindful of the Interests of its Owners and other Stakeholders

1 Key Issues

1.1 Has the organisation formally identified its stakeholder groups (e.g. owners, creditors, customers, suppliers, staff, local community, tax authorities, trades unions, pressure groups, politicians, the media, trade associations, etc.)?

1.2 Has the organisation established the state of health of its relationship with each significant stakeholder group, including by enquiry to these groups?

1.3 Does the organisation have a strategy to improve stakeholder relationships which are unhealthy, and to preserve and leverage off the healthy stakeholder relationships?

1.4 Has the organisation set out to understand and mitigate its reputational risks?

1.5 Does the organisation have a policy with respect to selecting, preparing, conducting and reviewing meetings with investors, analysts and the media?

1.6 Does the organisation have a policy to determine when it should publish a trading update or a profits warning?

1.7 How does the organisation focus on its corporate social responsibilities?
- Board CSR committee?
- Sustainability audit?
- Internal CSR policies and procedures?
- Commitment to continuous improvement?

2 Detailed Issues

2.1 Does the organisation analyse the composition of its ownership body and track changes?

2.2 Who fronts the relationship of the organisation with different stakeholder groups, and are they competent and trained to do this well?

2.3 Does the organisation have a crisis response plan, including within it a communications strategy—with responsibilities clearly assigned to key players who will be instantly accessible?

(b) To Ensure that the Organisation's Accountability to its Stakeholders is Transparent

1 Key Issues

1.1 Does the organisation engage in regular dialogue with significant stakeholder groups?

1.2 Does the organisation have a satisfactory policy with respect to selecting, preparing, conducting and reviewing meetings with investors, analysts and the media?

1.3 Does the organisation have a satisfactory policy to determine when it should publish a trading update or a profits warning?

1.4 Are the directors' corporate governance assertions verging on "box ticking" of corporate governance requirements, or are they fully informative?

1.5 Does the organisation publish an annual sustainability report?

1.6 What is the perception of stakeholders as to the organisation's transparency of accountability?

2 Detailed Issues

2.1 Does the incidence of prior year adjustments to financial statements (etc.) indicate a lack of transparent accountability?

2.2 How does the organisation's annual report compare with that of other organisations—in terms of clarity, attractiveness, conciseness, informativeness and timeliness?

2.3 How does the organisation's website compare with that of other organisations—in terms of clarity, attractiveness, content, ease of use, informativeness and being up to date?

(c) To Ensure, so Far as is Possible, that Stakeholders Exercise Well Informed Control over their Stakes in the Organisation

1 Key Issues

1.1 Does the board encourage and welcome that owners, and in some cases other significant stakeholders, hold the board to account for its performance, behaviour and financial results?

1.2 Does the board encourage the organisation's principal owners to explain to the board their views when they do not accept the position of the organisation on an issue?

1.3 Does the organisation facilitate that shareholders can exercise their rights significantly?

2 Detailed Issues

2.1 Is the AGM staged to maximise attendance by shareholders?

2.2 Is the website used well to communicate with shareholders?

(d) To Ensure the Organisation has a Sound Reputation for Responsible Governance

1 Key Issues

1.1 Does the organisation's share price command a premium on account of its reputation for good corporate governance?

1.2 Does the organisation enter its annual report and accounts and its annual sustainability report for "best in class" awards?

1.3 Is it the organisation's policy to apply best practice corporate governance principles and to comply with best practice corporate governance provisions/guidelines?

1.4 Has the organisation identified areas for improvement in its corporate governance, with a view to implementing the requisite changes?

1.5 Does the organisation invest in public relations to explain its corporate governance policies?

1.6 Are directors chosen in part for their corporate governance track record?

1.7 Is the board enriched through its diversity—with respect to gender, ethnicity, etc.

2 Detailed Issues

2.1 Does the board have a corporate governance committee?

2.2 What is the view of investor groups about the organisation's corporate governance?

NOTES

1. Committee of Sponsoring Organizations of the Treadway Commission (COSO) (2004) *Enterprise Risk Management—Integrated Framework*, Executive Summary, p. 5.
2. 2009 "**Standard 2100—Nature of Work**

The internal audit activity must evaluate and contribute to the improvement of **governance, risk management, and control processes** using a systematic and disciplined approach.

Prior to 2009 this Standard read:

The internal audit activity should evaluate and contribute to the improvement of **risk management, control, and governance processes** using a systematic and disciplined approach.

(Our bolding).

3. The mandatory Interpretation to Standard 1100 on Independence and Objectivity includes the words: "Objectivity requires that internal auditors do not subordinate their judgement on audit matters to others" and the Glossary definition of Objectivity states: "... Objectivity requires internal auditors not to subordinate their judgement on audit matters to others."

5

Risk Management Processes

INTRODUCTION

In Chapters 4, 5 and 6 we address respectively governance processes, risk management and internal control, the three overlapping areas that correspond to the scope of internal audit's review as set out in The Institute of Internal Auditors' *Standards* and Definition of Internal Auditing, the latter reading (bolding added):

Internal auditing is an independent, objective assurance and consulting activity designed to add value and improve an organization's operations. It helps an organization accomplish its objectives by bringing a systematic, disciplined approach to evaluate and improve the effectiveness of **risk management, control, and governance processes**.

Each of these three chapters contains, towards the end, a practical guide on the objectives and the audit issues.

OBJECTIVES OF RISK MANAGEMENT

We have modelled the practical guide on risk management around the Institute's *Standards* specification of what constitutes risk management effectiveness. Effectiveness means the achievement of objectives, and so this specification is a useful guide to the objectives of risk management:

2120—Risk Management

The internal audit activity must evaluate the effectiveness and contribute to the improvement of risk management processes.

Interpretation:

Determining whether risk management processes are effective is a judgment resulting from the internal auditor's' assessment that:

- Organizational objectives support and align with the organization's mission;

- Significant risks are identified and assessed;
- Appropriate risk responses are selected that align risks with the organization's risk appetite; and
- Relevant risk information, enabling staff, management, and the board to carry out their responsibilities, is captured and communicated in a timely manner across the organization, enabling staff, management, and the board to carry out their responsibilities ...

The Interpretations within the *Standards* have the same mandatory force as the other parts of the *Standards*.

In this chapter we could have adopted the Institute's use in their *Standards* of COSO's objectives of internal control[1] as also being the objectives of risk management, since the *Standards* reproduce these in both the internal control and the risk management sections of the *Standards*:

2120.A1—The internal audit activity must evaluate risk exposures relating to the organization's governance, operations, and information systems regarding the:

- Reliability and integrity of financial and operational information.
- Effectiveness and efficiency of operations.
- Safeguarding of assets; and
- Compliance with laws, regulations, and contracts.

Using the Interpretation of Standard 2120 (see above) to give us the objectives of risk management for use in this chapter allows us to differentiate from Chapter 6, especially in the practical guide at the end of this chapter compared with the guide at the end of Chapter 6. Note that our use of the Institute's stated objectives of risk management means we are diverging from COSO's 2004 objectives of enterprise risk management.[2] Unlike COSO's definition of internal control (Chapter 6), COSO's definition of enterprise risk management does not itself contain a statement of the objectives of risk management:

Enterprise risk management is a process, effected by an entity's board of directors, management and other personnel, applied in strategy setting and across the enterprise, designed to identify potential events that may affect the entity, and manage risk to be within its risk appetite, to provide reasonable assurance regarding the achievement of entity objectives.

COSO states their objectives of risk management separately:

This enterprise risk management framework is geared to achieving an entity's objectives, set forth in four categories:

- Strategic—high-level goals, aligned with and supporting its mission
- Operations—effective and efficient use of its resources
- Reporting—reliability of reporting
- Compliance—compliance with applicable laws and regulations.

...

Another category, safeguarding of resources, used by some entities, also is described.

THE MARCONI CASE

Lord Weinstock dominated GEC (not to be confused with the US GE) for thirty years as its chief executive. By the time he retired from GEC in 1996 he was out of favour with institutional investors who had been chiding him to do something constructive with GEC's legendary cash mountain, or to return it to the shareholders. In truth Lord Weinstock had presided over a rather sleepy giant conglomerate, underperforming other major companies. Its strengths were its balance sheet and its strong but not leading position in, amongst other things, the manufacture of defense equipment, locomotives, heavy industrial products and electrical equipment. Marconi was just one of their companies.

Perhaps it was predictable that Lord Weinstock's successor as chief executive, and the latter's appointee as finance director, shortly to become deputy chief executive, would listen to the institutional shareholders. They took to the board a proposed strategy to transform GEC into a telecoms hardware and software company, renaming the group Marconi. The allure of the dotcom sector was irresistible. The board, comprising famous names with excellent business backgrounds, agreed—and the institutional shareholders approved.

The group divested itself of the operating companies it no longer wished to retain, moving out of defense and heavy industrial manufacture. They used the proceeds from these divestments, together with their cash mountain and significant loans from financial institutions, to finance near the top of the market an aggressive, expensive acquisition spree of telecoms businesses. Marconi's shareholders benefitted in the process to some extent, both in terms of Marconi's rising share price for a while and their holdings of shares and loan notes in BAE who had acquired GEC's defense companies.

When Marconi had succeeded in repositioning itself as a telecoms company, it became apparent that it was vulnerable. Its balance sheet was now much more heavily geared. It was not large enough in telecoms to dominate the market. It had repositioned itself just when mobile phone companies were cutting back their investment budgets, having overextended themselves paying governments for 3G mobile telephony licenses.

Marconi's executive team proposed to their board that a merger should be sought with another leading telecoms company as a matter of urgency before Marconi's share price collapsed. The board refused. The board had not agreed previously to that as a fallback position should the transformation strategy fail.

The rest is history. The banks moved in. The shareholders lost almost everything. The CEO and Deputy CEO were ousted in 2001.

Figure 5.1 (continued)

> The banks did not emerge unscathed. A proud, independent, financially strong but unspectacular (in terms of shareholder return) company bit the dust.
>
> There are a number of lessons from this tale. An important one is that strategies that take a big punt on the very future of the company are too risky to prudently adopt. Strategic options should be stress tested for risk before they are adopted. Risk management approaches must be applied carefully at the strategy formulation stage, as well as to managing risks during strategy implementation. At the strategy formulation stage possible risky events should be identified and approaches devised to reduce the risk of those events occurring. Should any of those events occur, there should be effective contingency plans developed *and agreed in advance by the board at the strategy formulation stage* which can be expected to effectively mitigate the consequences.

Figure 5.1 Adopting an excessively risky strategy

So the COSO objectives of risk management are the same as the COSO objectives of internal control with the exception of the addition of the strategic objective which, arguably, should have been one of COSO's internal control objectives since strategies should be developed in a well controlled way. We discuss this in Chapter 6. COSO is right to add the strategic objective to their enteprise risk management framework: strategic options need to be weighed up having regard to risk. An adopted strategy should have been stress tested for risks which should have been assessed as being within the organisation's risk appetite. It is likely to be unacceptable to adopt a new high risk strategy that would lead to the collapse of the organisation should the strategy fail and if there is more than an outside possibility that it might fail. We illustrate this with a brief case study at Figure 5.1.

ESSENTIAL COMPONENTS OF EFFECTIVE RISK MANAGEMENT

Having defined the objectives of risk management, COSO then goes on to identify eight essential components which must be in place and working effectively if risk management is to be effective. They are summarised on the front face of COSO's enterprise risk management "rubik cube" (Figure 5.2). In reality they are little different from the five CSO internal control components (Figure 6.1). The three differences are:

1. The "Control Environment" component under the 2002 internal control framework is now termed the "Internal Environment", though its meaning is unchanged. Not being a framework on internal control, the title "Control Environment" was not thought to be ideal, but choosing to label it "Internal Environment" has resulted in an ugly oxymoron.

2. COSO's 1992 internal control framework explained that the single internal control component on "Risk Assessment" entails (a) identifying events which represent risk, (b) measuring/understanding/assessing the risk associated with those

RISK MANAGEMENT PROCESSES

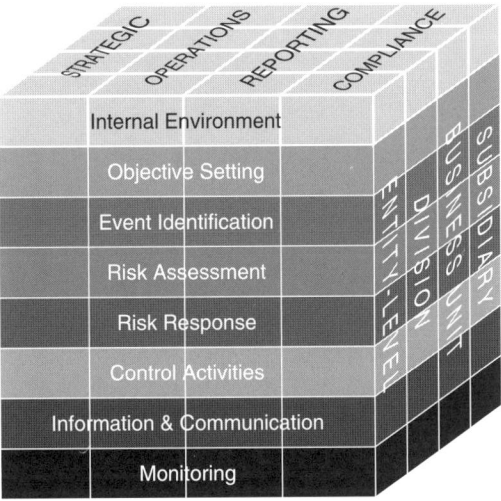

Figure 5.2 COSO's enterprise risk management "Rubik cube". Copyright 1992–2004 by The Committee of Sponsoring organizations of the Treadway commission. All rights reserved. Reprinted with permission

events, and (c) deciding how to respond to them. (Figure 6.1). Now, under the 2004 COSO enterprise risk management framework, this has been split into three separate essential components—justified as the ERM framework is placing more emphasis on risk.

3. The addition of the "Strategic" objective of enterprise risk management, results in a need for an additional, essential component of enterprise risk management—"Objective setting". "Objective setting" on the front face of the COSO cube (Figure 5.2) is the equivalent of "Strategic" on the top face. This represents the only real change from COSO's internal control components. It makes the enterprise risk management framework, in COSO's words, "a more robust conceptualisation"[3] than the internal control framework since it includes the setting of objectives.

Chapter 6 examines these components in detail.

THE SCOPE OF INTERNAL AUDIT'S ROLE IN RISK MANAGEMENT

Note that Standard 2120.A1 (above) extends the internal audit remit beyond providing assurance on risk management *processes* (Interpretation of Standard 2120, above) to an internal audit responsibility to evaluate all sorts of risk exposures facing the organisation. The implication is that internal audit must advise the board and management on the adequacy of risk management processes, *and also draw their attention to significant risks that they may be overlooking or focusing upon inadequately in the estimation of internal audit.*

There is a range of enterprise risk management activities some of which fit into the internal auditor's assurance role and others into their consulting role, while of course others are the responsibility of management and should not be undertaken by internal audit. Figure 5.3 provides a useful summary of the position.[4]

100 THE OPERATIONAL AUDITING HANDBOOK

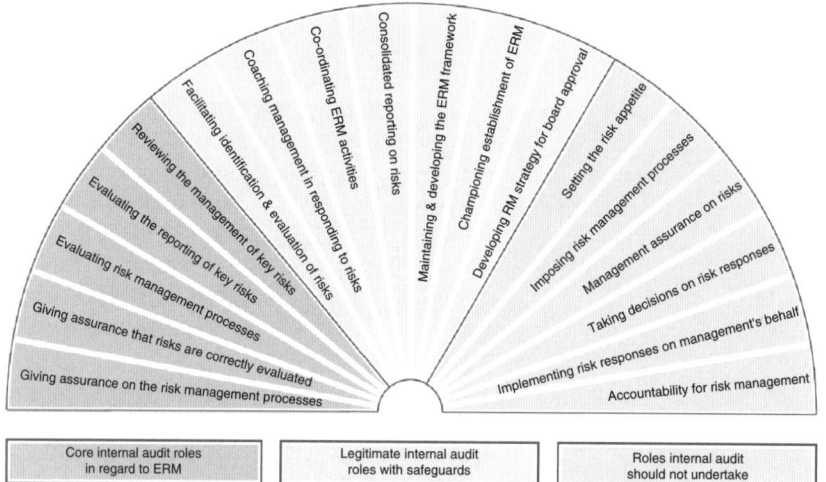

This diagram is taken from "Position Statement: The Role of Internal Audit in Enterprise-wide Risk Management", reproduced with the permission of the Institute of Internal Auditors – UK and Ireland. For the full Statement visit www.iia.org.uk.

Correspond to internal audit's assurance role[5]	Correspond to internal audit's consulting role[6]	Represents management responsibilities[7]
Giving assurance on the risk management process.	Facilitating identification and evaluation of key risks.	Setting the risk appetite.
Giving assurance that risks are correctly evaluated.	Coaching management in responding to risks.	Imposing risk management processes.
Evaluating the risk management processes.	Coordinating ERM activities.	Management assurance on risks.
Evaluating the reporting of key risks.	Consolidating the reporting on risks.	Taking decisions on risk responses.
Reviewing the management of key risks.	Maintaining and developing the ERM framework.	Implementing risk responses on management's behalf.
	Championing the establishment of ERM.	Accountability for risk management.
	Developing risk management strategy for board approval.	
Core internal auditing roles in regard to ERM	**Legitimate internal auditing roles - *with safeguards***	**Roles internal auditing should not undertake**

Figure 5.3 The audit risk management activities fan. © The Institute of Internal Auditors–UK and Ireland Ltd, July 2008

TOOLS FOR RISK MANAGEMENT

In this chapter we suggest two useful tools to apply in risk management—first, the risk matrix and secondly, the risk register. Using tools such as this enables all participants to focus more closely on the same issues, enables subjectivity to be exercised methodically, simplifies and makes attractive what would otherwise be a difficult task and ensures there is a record being kept of the judgements made which can be refined over time.

THE RISK MATRIX

Risk is usually defined as the possibility that an event will occur (that is, a threat will materialise) and adversely affect the achievement of objectives. It is measured in terms of the degree of likelihood that the event might occur, coupled with the probable impact should the event occur. So an individual risk may be plotted graphically using a graph, sometimes known as a risk map or matrix, such as is shown at Figure 5.4.

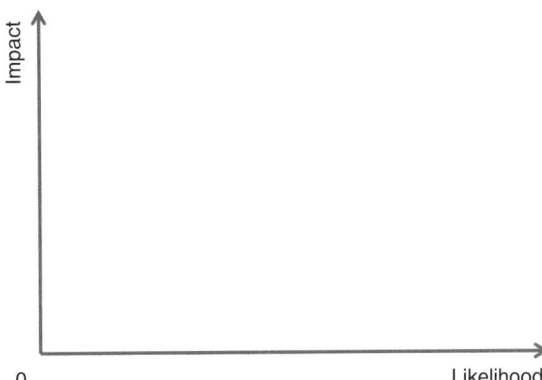

Figure 5.4 A risk matrix graph

Several risks may be plotted on a single graph; in Figure 5.5 we have plotted just one threat. The circle represents *either* the inherent risk (which is the level of risk that the organisation would be exposed to if there were no mitigating measures in place) *or* the gross risk (which is the level that the organisation is exposed to if it takes no further mitigating actions). The triangle is the level of risk remaining after the chosen mitigating actions have been introduced and applied. The issue then is whether this level of residual risk is acceptable. In Figure 5.5 the residual risk of this threat is shown to be within the organisation's risk appetite—the broad-based amount of risk the organisation is willing to accept in pursuit of its mission or vision. Sometimes an organisation will have to accept, at least for a while, a level of risk which is beyond its risk appetite—when there is no action that can be taken. Other times an organisation may not accept a level of risk which is within its risk

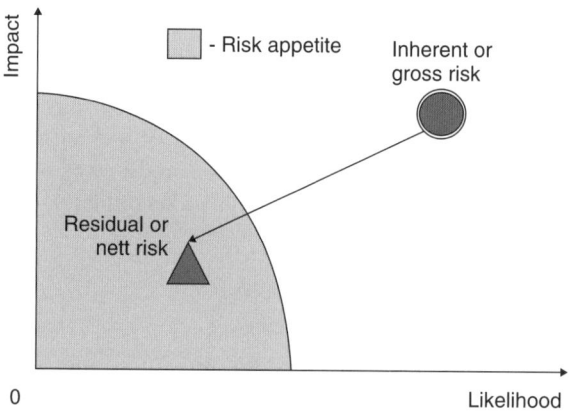

Figure 5.5 A risk plotted on a risk matrix graph

appetite—when doing things differently will readily reduce the risk still further at no significant extra cost.

Appropriate Ways of Mitigating Risk

We have made the distinction between "inherent risk" and "gross risk". Imagine a simple case. An organisation has a large amount of loose cash. The inherent risk is how much damage would probably be done to the organisation if the cash were carelessly left lying around in full view and completely accessible to strangers. The gross risk is the risk that the organisation is exposed to after taking account of the active and passive controls that, fortuitously or by design, are in place. In practice, when management and staff brainstorm about risk, they usually find it easier to conceptualise about gross risk than about inherent risk as they naturally factor into their consideration what they know about active and passive controls that are in place. For instance "This is not much of a risk as nobody knows we are holding this cash", or "This is not much of a risk because we keep it in the safe." An assessment of gross risk is therefore usually the starting point of any exercise to consider whether threats are being managed effectively. This is something to bear in mind when a control self assessment (sometimes termed "control risk self assessment") approach is being followed (see Chapter 10).

Nevertheless, on occasion it can be useful to start with an assessment of inherent risk as this can indicate whether a threat is being mitigated excessively, extravagantly or in inappropriate ways. To start at the inherent risk position requires answering the question: "Imagine we had no active or passive controls at all: what would we judge the scale of the threat to be, in terms of likelihood and impact?" If we were then to plot the inherent risk on our graph, Figure 5.6 suggests the appropriate control approach to concentrate upon in order to mitigate inherent risks most effectively.

A. An inherent risk judged to be within quadrant A of the graph is very likely to occur and to have a large impact on the organisation. Overlaid upon a judicious

RISK MANAGEMENT PROCESSES

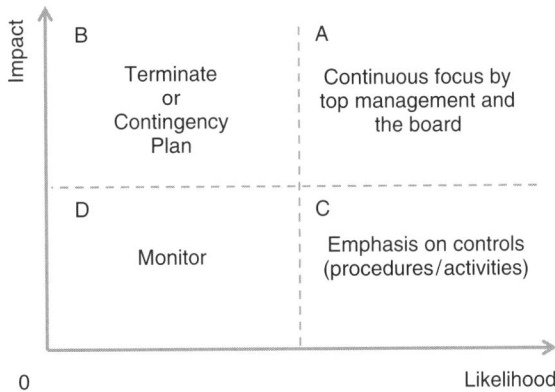

Figure 5.6 Possible appropriate responses to inherent risks

application of control approaches appropriate to the mitigation of inherent risks plotted as being within the other quadrants of the graph, there must be constant attention to the mitigation of this threat by top management, with review by the board.

B. An inherent risk within quadrant B is not very likely to occur but will have a large impact on the organisation were it to occur. There are alternative control approaches here. The organisation may seek to *terminate* this risk, for instance by having duplicate data centres in different geographic regions, so that a physical disaster or a withdrawal of staff at one location will enable essential data processing to continue at the other location. Alternatively, or additionally, the organisation may develop and test a contingency plan, thereby putting in place the exceptional measures that will be followed contingent upon the threat materialising.

C. An inherent risk plotted as being within quadrant C is one that is very likely to occur, perhaps repeatedly, in the absence of measures to mitigate the risk, but is unlikely to have a large impact on the business. An example might be invoicing with incorrect unit prices. Clearly it is necessary to get these things right first time, and so organisations largely depend on control procedures (what COSO calls "control activities") to achieve this.

D. A risk in quadrant D has been judged not very likely to occur and of no great likely significance if it does. It is likely to be enough to develop and apply monitoring measures which are largely intended to check that the threat remains within this quadrant and so does not require other mitigation approaches to contain the threat. Monitoring may be a matter of management reviewing exception reports, of software monitoring exceptions and trends over time, of the compliance function reviewing processes and outturns, and so on.

Categorising Risks

If different categories of risky event are plotted on the same risk matrix it can become confusing; for instance IT risks may be very different in character from funding risks or from HR risks, so that it will usually be more appropriate to categorise risks and use one or more graph for each category of risk. One categorisation of risks might be as per Figure 5.7.

> Strategic
> Structural
> People related
> General systems
> Regulary and legal
> New business and markets
> The market and competition
> Funding
> etc.

Figure 5.7 Risk categories

Subjective Judgement in Managing Risk

There is much judgement in most risk management, including in risk assessment. Some organisations with respect to some of their risk assessment can reduce the amount of judgement involved. For instance, a financial institution may be able to use its database of historical information to assess quite accurately the likely impact of relaxing credit terms, but even this relies on the future corresponding to the past upon which the historical data is based. It will usually be largely a matter of judgement to identify the risky events to which the organisation is exposed, and then to judge the degree of likelihood and impact that applies to them. There could be differences of perception as to the units (whether monetary or other) which calibrate the vertical *impact* axis, and the units (whether time or other) that calibrate the horizontal axis. It will be a matter of judgement to assess the extent to which mitigating actions reduce the level of risk. Deciding the organisation's risk appetite also entails the exercise of judgement, and it may be decided that the risk appetite should vary between different parts of the same organisation. A further limitation of the approach shown in Figure 5.5 is that risk is being plotted on the graph as a single point estimate whereas in reality the risk will be on a range with respect to both the horizontal and vertical axis. We discuss later how this limitation can be circumvented. The subjectivity and over-simplification of this technique should be recognised but it does not invalidate using this tool.

A More Sophisticated Example of a Risk Matrix

A more sophisticated application of the graphical approach is illustrated in Figures 5.8 and 5.9. Threats plotted on the graph are given a score by multiplying their horizontal and vertical positions together. The score determines the seriousness of the risk, as indicated in Figure 5.9, and colour coding is applied to give a visual representation of the degree of criticality. When colour coding is used it is conventional to apply a traffic light approach of "red", "amber" and "green"; but this organisation has chosen to use four categories.

RISK MANAGEMENT PROCESSES 105

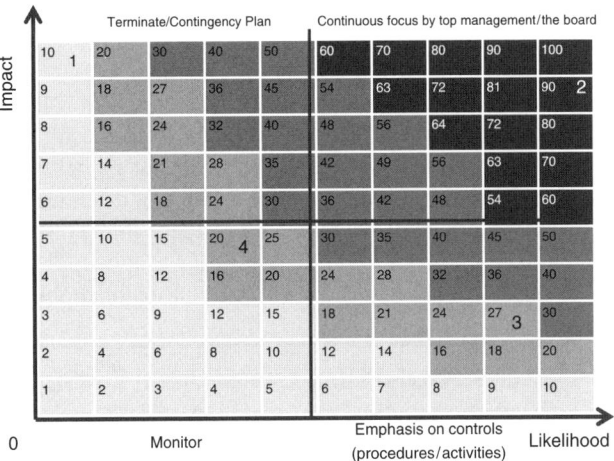

Sample threats:
1. Plane hitting the computer centre
2. Failure of a high profile venture
3. Keying errors
4. Bad weather keeping staff from working

Figure 5.8 Numeric scores and colour coding. Reproduced by permission of Kelsey Walker

SCORE	RISK CATEGORY	COLOUR
60 +	CRITICAL	RED
30–59	HIGH	ORANGE
16–29	MEDIUM	YELLOW
1–15	LOW	WHITE

Figure 5.9 Risk scale for Figure 5.8. Reproduced by permission of Kelsey Walker

We should note an important point with respect to the four illustrative risks, numbered 1 to 4, and plotted as "gross risks" in particular cells of the matrix at Figure 5.8. The threat of a plane hitting the computer centre has been given a risk score of just ten, which places it as a much lower threat to the organisation than either the risk of a high profile venture failing (90) or even the threat resulting from keying errors (27). In practice it is difficult to assess the degree of gravity of a threat and it requires a careful exercise of judgement to do so. It is worthwhile debating the issue as a team and, where there is significant disagreement, considering the threat as being within a range rather than as a single point. We discuss this in our consideration of Figure 5.11 (below). It is both "Likelihood" and "Impact" which may be assessed inaccurately. For instance, few predicted the collapse in late 2007 of the wholesale bond and securitisation markets which resulted in the credit crunch—a failure accurately to assess the likelihood of that global crisis occurring. The likelihood of external risks such as this materialising is often harder to predict accurately than the likelihood of internal risks; indeed these threats may be more difficult to identify in the first place. Potential "Impact" may also be underestimated: there have been many examples of keying errors resulting in major problems, as illustrated at Figure 5.10.

THE SECURITIES COMPANY CASE

In December 2005 a Japanese securities trader transposed two numbers he encoded into his online PC. The effect was that instead of instructing the sale for 600 000 yen of a single share in a new telecoms company, the instruction was to sell 600 000 shares at one yen each. That was more shares than the company had issued. The trader immediately realised his error but the Tokyo Stock Exchange's computers repeatedly prevented him from correcting his mistake. It resulted in the Stock Exchange, the world's second largest, closing for four hours—which in turn led to the resignation of the Exchange's chief executive and two other senior staff. Variously estimated as costing the securities company between £190m and £285m, it meant that their staff had to forego their Christmas bonuses—not something that staff in that sector appreciate!

Figure 5.10 The risk of underestimating a threat

Plotting Ranges of Risk

Plotting threats as single points on the graph is, of course, an oversimplification but to do otherwise often introduces a degree of complexity that vexes management and staff using this technique to consider risks. Figure 5.11 illustrates that the impact dimension can be shown as a range of potential impacts—in the case of threat "1" the intention has been to indicate it has no upper limit. If it was also considered necessary to show "likelihood" (the horizontal axis) as a range of possible likelihoods, then the result would be neither a single point estimate, nor a line, but a curve. Note that the horizontal axis in Figure 5.11 is also being used in a more sophisticated way.

RISK REGISTERS

The graphical approach discussed above in this chapter is an excellent tool to use when brainstorming in workshops about the threats to the organisation or to parts of it. The risk register approach is less visual in its representation, but is

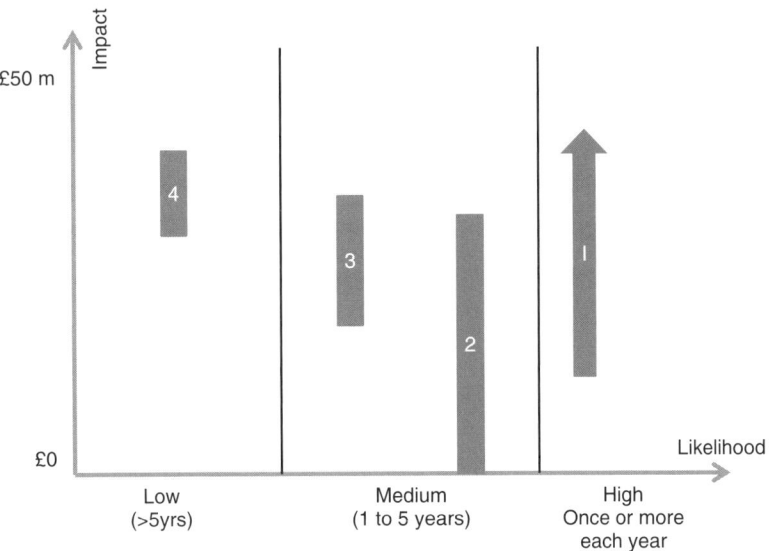

Figure 5.11 Showing "Impact" as a range of financial values

widely used to create and maintain a record of threats and their management at all levels and in all parts of the organisation. The risk register allows a more detailed description of the approaches being taken to manage risks. Figure 5.12 provides one layout for a risk register which captures information broadly similar to that shown on the graphs we have discussed.

Figure 5.12 uses the phrase "board accountability". Some organisations usefully distinguish between the "risk sponsor" and the "risk owner" roles. The risk sponsor is the most senior person (or committee) with overall responsibility for overseeing the mitigation of the threat. The risk owner is the member of staff to whom day to day management of the risk has been assigned.

RISK MANAGEMENT CHALLENGES

We end this chapter by pointing out some of the limitations of risk management as practised by most organisations today.

Major Risks that are Concealed

Major risks that organisations are exposed to may not be on top management's radar screen. Top management may tend to be focused on achieving their goals to the extent of being blind to the unanticipated consequences of their policies. Major risks in effect may be buried in the woodwork of the organisation, like a woodworm invisibly weakening the organisation. Figure 5.13 illustrates this. It is possible that some staff, even some with management responsibilities, may be aware of the problems but do not consider that they are responsible for doing anything about them.

108 THE OPERATIONAL AUDITING HANDBOOK

Risk	Gross Risk		Board Accountability	Control description	Control effectiveness	Net/residual risk		Action	Responsibility	Review Date
	Im-pact	Likeli-hood				Im-pact	Likeli-hood			
1										
2										
3										
4										
	Numeric scale 1 to 5				Strong, Good, Weak or Poor	Numeric scale 1–5				

Figure 5.12 Sample layout of a risk register

FALSIFICATION OF QUALITY DATA

The regulator of a nationalised UK nuclear company announced that four production workers had been dismissed for falsifying quality data. One of their duties had been to measure samples of reprocessed nuclear rods and to enter the measurement data on a schedule. The schedule was then reviewed by a quality inspector to ascertain that the measurements had been taken and that the rods were within acceptable quality tolerances. After a while the quality inspector realised that the production workers had been fabricating the measurement data.

A consequence was that customers cancelled their contracts out of concern for the quality of the rods they had been receiving from this nuclear company. This led to jeopardising the commercial future for reprocessing spent nuclear fuel. The government insisted that a new MOX plant for reprocessing spent nuclear fuel was mothballed. One Japanese power generator was paid many £ millions in compensation; the rods of suspect quality already supplied to that company had to be shipped back to the UK. One calculation put the total cost to the UK nuclear company at some £ 300m.

Another consequence was that the privatisation of the nuclear company was put "on hold" by the government. Arguably it had been top management's determination to make the company attractive for privatisation that had been the cause of this problem. Some claimed that corners had been cut in order to improve the bottom line, and that production workers had as a consequence become overworked and demoralised. Others claimed that there was a penal "command culture" within the business which discouraged staff from discussing their problems and was antipathetic to what was required in an industry where safety should have been paramount.

A further consequence was the impact upon the board. The government fired the executive directors and declined to renew the appointments of the nonexecutive directors. Only the newly appointed chairman of the board survived but he had to wait until he retired before he was awarded his knighthood.

A moral to this tale is that perhaps the largest risks the business is running may be buried in the woodwork. A second moral to this tale is that significant risks can be a direct consequence of the priorities that top management is imposing upon the business. A third moral is that boards, especially their nonexecutive directors, are severely challenged to know whether the policies of the board are being implemented by management and whether there may be banana skins round the corner over which the organisation may slip in the future. A further moral to this tale is that controls may have been designed into business processes and may appear to be working, but in fact are failing completely to be effective.

Figure 5.13   The risk of concealed risk

A risk-based approach to audit planning should not mean that the internal audit activity only undertakes audits of business processes that are considered (by the board, top management and the chief audit executive) to be of high risk. A proportion of internal audit time should be allocated to undertake audits of areas of the business not perceived to represent significant risk—in case there are concealed risks in those parts of the organisation.

The Extra Risks of Less Democratic Organisations

Hierarchically organised businesses, and those with more of a command culture than a participative culture, are less likely to ventilate their problems. If staff find they are penalised for being frank about weaknesses, then they will not be frank. Clearly the culture of the organisation can, of itself, pose a threat to the organisation.

Multiple Simultaneous Risks Materialising

When organisations fail or almost fail it is often because several threats come to fruition at the same time. These threats may or may not be independent of each other. Figure 5.14 illustrates this. In most organisations, risk management is inadequate to identify and assess the risk of multiple simultaneous failures. The techniques of risk management, including those discussed in this chapter, would become too complex to use, understand and rely upon if they were adapted to accommodate the risk of multiple simultaneous failures. But the human mind can almost intuitively process the complexity of such scenarios quite well. Every organisation should consider what risks they face that more than one untoward event might happen at the same time, what those events might be and whether the organisation has in place what will be needed to manage a way through the multiple crises, should this occur.

A CRISIS FOR A HOME LOANS COMPANY

The government announced the end of tax relief on mortgage repayments. At the same time interest on domestic mortgages reached 15%. The national economy was in crisis, with a consequence that unemployment reached 10%. Arguably these threatening events were connected but a fourth was not: a significant secondary bank collapse and there was a "flight to quality" by depositors who deserted the home loans company in favour of safer havens for their deposits.

The home loans company declared to their own banks that a material adverse change in circumstances had occurred. The share price of the home loans company collapsed by about 99%.

Figure 5.14 Simultaneous threatening events

Opportunities as well as Threats

We should note that this chapter's discussion of risk management has been in the context of *threats* to the business which must be identified, assessed and responded to. We should not overlook that the tools of risk management can and should be applied to *opportunities* as well as to threats. Organisations should seek to identify what might happen in the future which could offer an opportunity to an organisation if that organisation was positioned to exploit that opportunity at the time, notwithstanding that it might not be within the organisation's business plan. Consideration should be given to advance development of the capability to exploit such an opportunity should it occur. Any opportunity missed can be interpreted as a threat that has not been avoided, as Figure 5.15 illustrates.

> **A PORTABLE BUILDING MANUFACTURER LOSES OPPORTUNITIES**
>
> A manufacturer of high quality portable accommodation was unable to take advantage of the opportunity that the tsunami in the Far East presented for the immediate supply of large quantities of temporary housing. Six months later they missed out on a similar opportunity following the earthquake in Northern Pakistan. A consequence was that the competition moved in and the company lost market share and failed to acquire commercial experience.

Figure 5.15 Opportunities missed

Too Risk Averse?

Finally, we should not be too risk averse. Profit is the reward for taking risk. Drucker (1977)[8] said:

The main goal of management science must be to enable business to take the right risk. Indeed, it must be to enable business to take greater risks—by providing knowledge and understanding of alternative risks and alternative expectations; by identifying the resources and efforts needed for desired results; by mobilizing energies for contribution; and by measuring results against expectations; thereby providing means for early correction of wrong or inadequate decisions. All this may sound like mere quibbling over terms. Yet the terminology of risk minimization does induce a hostility to risk-taking and risk-making—that is, to business enterprise.

COSO (2004)[9] takes a more cautious view:

No entity operates in a risk-free environment, and enterprise risk management does not seek to move towards such an environment. Rather, enterprise risk management enables management to operate more effectively in environments filled with risk.

CONTROL ISSUES FOR RISK MANAGEMENT PROCESSES

Control Objectives for Risk Management Processes

> (a) Organisational objectives support and align with the organisation's mission
>
> (b) Significant risks are identified and assessed
>
> (c) Appropriate risk responses are selected that align risks with the organisation's risk appetite
>
> (d) Relevant risk information, enabling staff, management, and the board to carry out their responsibilities, is captured and communicated in a timely manner across the organisation, enabling staff, management, and the board to carry out their responsibilities.

(a) Organisational Objectives Support and Align with the Organisation's Mission

1 Key Issues

1.1 Have the organisation's objectives been defined?

1.2 Have the organisation's objectives been mapped to the organisation's mission statement, and is there a close fit?

1.3 Are the mission and objectives of the organisation consistent with the organisation's purpose as set out in the constitutional documents of the organisation?

1.4 Do the owners and other stakeholders of the business share with the board and senior management a common view about the mission and objectives of the organisation?

1.5 Is the mission, and are the objectives, of the organisation clearly communicated from the top downwards, and is there commitment at all levels to deliver on both?

2 Detailed Issues

2.1 Do the defined organisational objectives correspond to what the organisation is focusing upon?

2.2 If the organisation achieves its objectives, will it fulfil its mission?

2.3 How does the organisation revisit and redefine its mission and objectives?

(b) Significant Risks are Identified and Assessed

1 Key Issues

    1.1 Is there a formal process of risk management (identification, assessment and response)?

    1.2 Is risk management applied at the strategy formulation stage (to avoid adopting high risk strategies) as well as to the implementation of adopted strategy?

    1.3 Is risk management embedded into the culture of the business, so that it is an attitude of mind of management and staff?

    1.4 Does the organisation endeavour to identify and assess *external* as well as *internal* risks?

    1.5 Does the organisation's risk management appropriately classify risks into appropriate categories (e.g. funding, marketing, HR, IT, reputational, etc.)?

    1.6 Does the organisation employ effective risk management methodologies/tools?

    1.7 Is the plan of future internal audit engagement based on a risk assessment?

2 Detailed Issues

    2.1 Does the organisation's risk management process embrace extend to considering the risk to the organisation of failing to exploit opportunities which may arise in the future?

    2.2 Have there been any events occurring to the organisation which indicate that not all significant risks were anticipated, and what lessons should be learnt from this?

    2.3 Does the organisation consider the likelihood, consequences and effective mitigation of a number of threats materialising simultaneously?

    2.4 Does internal audit invest some audit time reviewing areas of the business which are perceived to be of low risk, in case significant risks are concealed in those areas of the business?

(c) Appropriate Risk Responses are Selected that Align Risks with the Organisation's Risk Appetite

1 Key Issues

    1.1 Is responsibility for the ownership and control of risks clearly assigned to appropriate staff?

1.2 Has the organisation defined its overall risk appetite and its varying risk appetites for the parts (e.g. divisions, processes, operating units, product ranges) of the business?

1.3 Is the organisation running a level of risk which is unacceptable, being beyond the organisation's risk appetite?

1.4 In assessing risk, is allowance made for the degree of subjectivity involved in identifying, assessing and deciding how to respond to risks?

1.5 Is there a risk that the organisation may be too risk averse?

2 Detailed Issues

2.1 Are the optimal means used to mitigate risks depending upon the character of the risk?

2.2 Are there cost-effective opportunities to mitigate risks still further, even though they are assessed as being within the organisation's risk appetite?

(d) Relevant Risk Information, Enabling Staff, Management, and the Board to Carry out their Responsibilities, is Captured and Communicated in a Timely Manner across the Organisation

1 Key Issues

1.1 How are insights about risks communicated effectively upwards so as to inform top level assessments of risk?

1.2 How are the concerns about risk at senior levels communicated downwards so as to be factored into risk assessments at operational levels?

1.3 Does the organisation capture and monitor effectively appropriate risk information to determine whether the key risks to the business are under control?

1.4 Does the audit committee of the board review (a) the risk management process of the organisation, and (b) the high level risks to the organisation that the process has identified and assessed?

1.5 Does the audit committee report on risk to the board, so that the board itself addresses risk management?

1.6 Is available risk information sufficient to enable the business to manage risk effectively?

1.7 Is the risk management role of internal audit confined to providing assurance and consulting advice on risk management, rather than having the responsibility (a) to be the specialist risk management function of the business, or (b) to take management decisions and action with respect to risk management?

1.8 Does the organisation maintain adequate risk registers at all levels and across all of the business?

1.9 Does the culture of the organisation encourage a frankness about risks being run?

2 Detailed Issues

2.1 Has the organisation endeavoured to develop and use "leading indicators" to give timely warnings of the likely development of unacceptable levels of risk?

NOTES

1. The Institute of Internal Auditors has adapted the COSO internal control objectives slightly by separating out the "safeguarding of assets" from the "effectiveness and efficiency of operations" and by stating that the compliance objective includes compliance with contracts. In regard to the latter, it would have been preferable if the Institute had also highlighted the importance of complying with the policies of the board and with the overall purpose of the organisation.
2. Committee of Sponsoring Organizations of the Treadway Commission (COSO) (2004) *Enterprise Risk Management—Integrated Framework*, "Executive Summary", p. 3, reproduced by permission.
3. Committee of Sponsoring Organizations of the Treadway Commission (COSO) (2004) *Enterprise Risk Management—Integrated Framework*, Executive Summary, chapter 1 on "Definition", p. 33 and also "Executive Summary", p. 25.
4. This diagram is taken from "Position Statement: The Role of Internal Audit in Enterprise-wide Risk Management", reproduced with the permission of The Institute of Internal Auditors—UK and Ireland. For the full Statement visit www.iia.org.uk. See also The Institute of Internal Auditors (January 2009): The Role of Internal Auditing in Enterprise-wide Risk Management, Position Paper, revised, p. 4 at www.theiia.org.
5. The Glossary to The Institute of Internal Auditors' *Standards* defines 'Assurance Services' [by internal auditors] as:
   > An objective examination of evidence for the purpose of providing an independent assessment on governance, risk management, and control processes for the organization. Examples may include financial, performance, compliance, system security, and due diligence engagements.
6. The Glossary to The Institute of Internal Auditors' *Standards* defines "Consulting Services" [by internal auditors] as:
   > Advisory and related client service activities, the nature and scope of which are agreed with the client, are intended to add value and improve an organization's governance, risk management, and control processes without the internal auditor assuming management responsibility. Examples include counsel, advice, facilitation, and training.
7. The definition of "Consulting Services"—see Note 6 (above) makes it clear that internal audit does not assume any management responsibilities.
8. Drucker, P. F. (1977) *Management: Tasks, Responsibilities, Practices*. 1979 Pan UK edition, p. 433.
9. Committee of Sponsoring Organizations of the Treadway Commission (COSO) (2004) *Enterprise Risk Management—Integrated Framework*, "Executive Summary", p. 2.

6
Internal Control Processes

> "If you look at all the failures of quoted companies in the past, they have all been failures of internal control."
>
> Sir Adrian Cadbury

INTRODUCTION

Business processes need to be well controlled. The purpose of this chapter is to explain how this control may be achieved, and how to assess whether this is so. We will do this by introducing a number of internal control paradigms, or frameworks. In covering these matters we will, of course, need to explain what is understood by the phrase "internal control".

"Internal control" as an expression is distinctive from "external control", the latter being control exercised over the business from outside by owners and other stakeholders. "Internal control" is the control exercised *within* the business by management and overseen by the board. It also includes the control of activities that have been outsourced.

The Developing Concept of Internal Control

Fayol, the "father of management theory" was the first to describe "control" as a function of management along with other functions which he set out as being planning, organising, commanding, coordinating, controlling.[1] Fayol's concept of control was different from, and narrower than, the contemporary, general understanding of the meaning of internal control as set out in 1992, for instance, by COSO,[2] as we shall see.

The narrow concept of "check", "internal check" or "internal cross check" had predated[3] the introduction by AICPA in the 1940s of the phrase "internal control".[4] Indeed "internal check" remains an important means of control, although it is a phrase rarely used today. In 1948 AICPA recognised that their definition of internal control was "broader than the meaning sometimes attributed to the term". At that time AICPA defined internal control as:

Internal control comprises the plan of organisation and the co-ordinate methods and measures adopted within a business to safeguard its assets, check the accuracy and reliability of its accounting data, promote operational efficiency, and encourage adherence to prescribed managerial policies.

Later (1958), AICPA distinguished between accounting and administrative control, largely for pragmatic reasons as they needed to provide a focus on the controls most relevant to their members engaged as external auditors:[5]

Accounting control comprises the plan of the organisation and the procedures and records that are concerned with the safeguards of assets and the reliability of financial records.

Administrative control includes, but is not limited to, the plan of organization and the procedures and records that are concerned with the decision processes leading to management's authorization of transactions. Such authorization is a management function directly associated with the responsibility for achieving the objectives of the organization and is the starting point for establishing accounting controls of transactions.

Contemporary Understanding of Internal Control

By then the concept of internal control was shaping up in a way which paralleled to some extent the 1992 COSO definition of internal control which is the generally accepted current definition of today:

Internal control is broadly defined as a process, effected by the entity's board of directors, management and other personnel, designed to provide reasonable assurance regarding the achievement of objectives in the following categories:

- Effectiveness and efficiency of operations.
- Reliability of financial reporting.
- Compliance with applicable laws and regulations.

The Securities & Exchange Commission's Rule for the implementation of s. 404 ("Management's Assessment of Internal Controls") of the 2002 Sarbanes-Oxley Act requires that the CEO and CFO use a recognised internal control (see Chapter 8) for the purpose. The framework to be used for s. 404 purposes must have been developed by due process, externally to the organisation using it. The SEC mentions three frameworks which would be acceptable—COSO (US), CoCo (Canada) and Turnbull (UK). The CoCo and Turnbull definitions of internal control, while not identical to COSO, have much common ground;[6,7] we discuss this further in the section of Chapter 8 on "Using a recognised internal control framework for the assessment". In this chapter we introduce each of these three frameworks and also a further three internal control paradigms. Which paradigm to select to use will depend upon a number of circumstances and auditors and systems designers may "mix and match" between the paradigms. One of the first three paradigms is likely to have to be applied when there is a mandatory or other requirement to use an externally developed paradigm, developed as a result of an acceptable due process. The second three paradigms are compatible with the COSO, Turnbull and CoCo frameworks as they largely elaborate in particular ways upon the "control activities" component of internal control which is to be found in the COSO, Turnbull and CoCo frameworks.

PARADIGM 1: COSO ON INTERNAL CONTROL

During the 1980s five US bodies,[8] known as COSO (Committee of Sponsoring Organizations) invited Treadway to head a commission of enquiry in the wake of concern about fraudulent financial reporting. The so-called Treadway Report[9] was published in 1987. Treadway recommended that management should include a report on internal control with their published financial statements. Adoption of this proposal was deferred pending clarification of the meaning of internal control and the form and process of any such report by management, and it now looks as if it will continue to be a voluntary, though frequently followed, practice in the USA. To provide this clarification, COSO funded a further project, the fieldwork of which was conducted by Coopers & Lybrand, which led to the publication in 1992 of *Internal Control—Integrated Framework*. This gives us a new definition of internal control which is supplanting the 1948 AICPA definition and its derivatives. COSO also gives guidance on how internal control is achieved—by means of five interrelated control components. Finally, COSO gives guidance on the process and form of public reports by management on internal control.

The COSO internal control concept, as with CoCo and Turnbull, regards internal as being very broad, as the COSO definition indicates. It is all of the management process except for the setting of objectives. It is as if one replaces one's ordinary spectacles by internal control ones which permit viewing the management process through the lens of internal control. This provides a modified perspective and a modified focus. In essence the focus is on all that management does but from the perspective of the control impact.

It is justifiable for COSO to define internal control broadly. Control depends on each of the other functions of management. There is no control without:

- Planning—for instance, design of the right procedures (which is part of planning) is essential for effective control. There has to be a plan against which to exercise control. Without a plan there can be no control.
- Organising—for instance, structuring the business into subdivisions and determining reporting arrangements. To illustrate the proximity between *organising and controlling* it is illuminating to remember that Fayol used the label "span of control" to describe the issue of how many subordinates one boss might supervise—yet this is clearly a matter of organisation as well as of control.
- Directing and leading—few would question that the quality of leadership impacts upon control.
- Staffing—too few or too many staff can lead to things getting out of control—as can incompetent, disloyal, dishonest or lazy staff.
- Co-ordinating—is the art of ensuring that happenings occur in harmony with each other—without which things will be out of control.

That COSO excluded the setting of objectives from internal control was problematic. It indicates that the concept of internal control is artificially articulated and could have been described differently. The problem is that the achievement of overall objectives requires the setting of lesser objectives—and so on downwards to more and more detailed levels. So, while COSO sets out the objective of internal control as the achievement of management's objectives, to do so entails the setting of lesser objectives. It is because of this deficiency in the COSO concept of internal control that COSO is able to describe their 2004 enterprise risk management framework as "a more robust conceptualisation" as it does not have this deficiency. Thirdly, "other personnel" are crucial for effective internal control for a number of reasons: they are the ones who operate control procedures and, from their vantage point, they have valuable insights into where internal control is ineffective and how it might be improved. Every organisation should endeavour to tap into the resource of "other personnel" perhaps through a programme of control self assessment (Chapter 10).

Note that COSO defines internal control as being *all* aspects of *all* processes that give reasonable assurance of the achievement of *all*, not just some, of the organisational objectives. Note that internal control is regarded by COSO as a process, not a state of affairs; and note that the definition acknowledges that effective internal control requires a conscious process of design (and redesign) as it cannot be expected to happen by chance. "Reasonable assurance" is a code phrase; it means much more than a sporting chance. It means we should design our processes so that we are confident that they are robust enough to ensure that the organisation will achieve its objectives—although we can never be 100 % confident that unanticipated events, particularly unexpected external risks, may thwart the achievement of organisational objectives. Nevertheless it is prudent to design our controls with a margin to cope with the unexpected—even if this means we settle for bottom-line performance that is less spectacular than it might otherwise be.

The analogy of a ship, sailing across an ocean to a distant port, is useful. On board should be everything needed to give reasonable assurance that the ship will reach its destination. If internal control had been defined more narrowly (as, for instance, is implied by paradigms 4, 5 and 6 below) we would be referring just to the navigation and direction control systems on board. Instead, the COSO concept and also paradigms 2 and 3 include within internal control everything that contributes to getting the ship to where it is heading—the navigation and direction control systems and also the design of the hull, the strength of the motors, the maintenance of the craft, the training and motivation of the crew, the quality of leadership and so on. When internal auditors report opportunities to improve internal control over business processes, they may be drawing attention to any elements of the management process.

Note that the COSO definition assigns responsibility for internal control to three parties. It is impressive that a definition dating back to 1992 put the board in pole position. The board is responsible for the policies of the organisation that impact upon internal control; the board is also responsible to oversee that management has effective internal control. Management is responsible to design, implement, monitor and maintain effective systems of internal control across the business and over activities which have been outsourced.

COSO's internal control definition sets out that there are three objectives of internal control. In reality there is one overall objective—to provide reasonable assurance that the organisation will achieve all of its objectives. COSO has chosen to classify this objective into three parts. But the "objectives cake" could have been cut into any number of slices, with the cuts in different places—and it would be the same objectives cake. Later in this chapter (at **Objectives of internal control**) we explore how other proponents have categorised the objectives of internal control.

COSO on Achieving Effective Internal Control

We have discussed how COSO defines internal control. COSO then goes on to explain that, according to the COSO internal control framework, internal control is achieved by means of five essential components of internal control that must be in place and must be functioning well.

1. Control environment
2. Risk assessment
3. Control activities
4. Information and communication
5. Monitoring

COSO's five internal control components have also been adopted over time by Rutteman, Turnbull, the SEC, PCAOB[10] and so on as the criteria to be used to assess internal control effectiveness. We explain the meaning of these components later. It is COSO's conceptual representation of these five components, along with the definition and further COSO guidance, which qualifies the COSO publication to be termed an internal control *framework*.

COSO has represented their internal control framework in the form of the cube at Figure 6.1. The three COSO objectives of internal control, per their internal control definition, are shown on the top face, with the five essential components on the front face. The other face is intended to indicate that this internal control framework can be applied in the design or review of the organisation as a whole or of any function or process of the organisation.

Although COSO acknowledges that a "directed focus" will be possible if internal control effectiveness is being considered with respect to only one or two of the COSO internal control objectives, it is gratifying for auditors and audit committees that any obligation to consider internal control effectiveness "in the round" (i.e. whether internal control is effective to provide reasonable assurance of the efficiency and effectiveness of operations, of reliable financial reporting *and* compliance with laws and regulations) does not multiply their work pro rata. For instance, a good code of business conduct is likely to impact positively on each of the objectives of internal control.

COSO's "Control Environment" Component

In their 2004 *Enterprise Risk Management* study (see Chapter 5) COSO labelled "the control environment" as "the internal environment". Some use the term differently to refer to all the components of internal control. As used by COSO and others, it is to

INTERNAL CONTROL PROCESSES 121

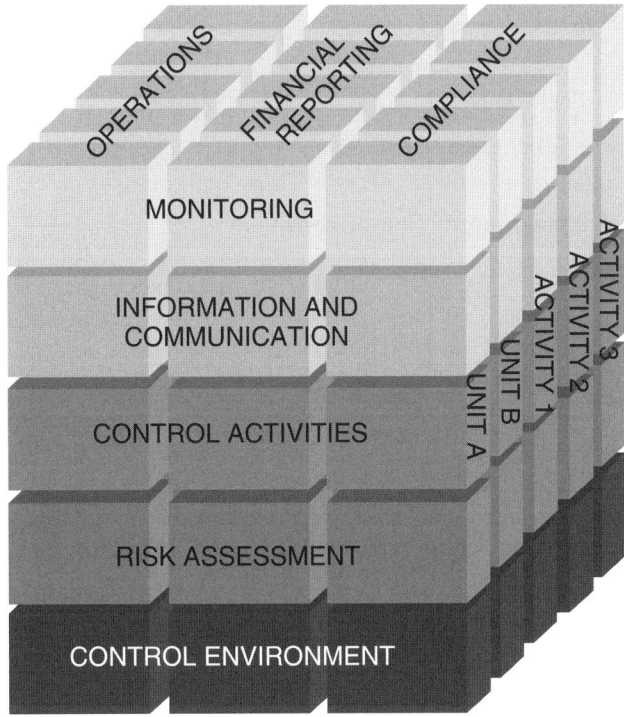

Figure 6.1 COSO's internal control "rubik cube". Copyright 1992–2004 by the Committee of Sponsoring Organizations of the Treadway Commission. All rights reserved. Reprinted with permission

do with the "tone at the top" in terms of the example set by top management and the board, whether they tend to override controls in their own interests and whether they act consistently and appropriately to wrongdoing. The control environment includes the values, ethics, culture and commitment of the organisation and its members. IT embraces the policies of the board which relate to internal control—such as the organisation's code of business conduct, its whistleblowing policy, its internet security policy and so on. It includes the way the organisation has been structured.

Of the five essential internal control components, the control environment can be regarded as the foundation component: if the control environment is unsound it is most likely that the other four components will also be inadequate. A good control environment provides the setting necessary for effective internal control arrangements to be established and applied.

The Institute of Internal Auditors, in their *Standards* Glossary defines "control environment" in a closely similar way to PCAOB,[10] as:

Control Environment—The attitude and actions of the board and management regarding the significance of control within the organization. The control environment provides the discipline and structure for the achievement of the primary objectives of the system of internal control. The control environment includes the following elements:

- Integrity and ethical values.
- Management's philosophy and operating style.
- Organizational structure.
- Assignment of authority and responsibility.
- Human resource policies and practices.
- Competence of personnel.

COSO's "Risk Assessment" Component

COSO included within risk assessment the identification of threats to the organisation, their assessment or measurement and deciding how they should be responded to. In COSO's 2004 *Enterprise Risk Management* framework, "event identification" "risk assessment" and "risk response" are shown as three separate components (see Chapter 5, Figure 5.2). Risk assessment is an essential component of internal control as we need to assess where the risks are greatest in order to focus our scarce resources in those areas.

Risk is present in every activity and we all, to varying degrees, continually evaluate the relative significance of risk in our lives and take appropriate steps to counteract the potential implications.

In a business context, risk can be an inherent feature of the operations of an organisation, especially where there is notable change taking place. The nature of risk may be, on the one hand, critical to the continued survival of the organisation, or a matter of a positive commercial image on the other hand. There are, of course, numerous shades of grey in respect of the relative impact of risks, and each entity will be likely to have a unique mapping of implications and consequences.

In order to plan effectively and economically for the reduction or containment of business-related risks, an organisation will need to identify all the risks that may apply in the course of their operations. In the case of launching new business ventures, an assessment of risk will normally feature as part of the strategic level of planning. Although the risks associated with established business activities may be (or thought to be) well known, there is always the necessity to ensure that changes in business objectives, legislation, etc. are catered for in the organisation's view of relative risks.

The identification of risk within a business should be an ongoing process sensitive to the implications of changed market conditions, operational workloads, macroeconomic parameters, and so on. Effective management should be able to anticipate the need for change and accordingly evaluate the amendments to the corporate risk profile.

Given that the control awareness and philosophy of an organisation should ideally be driven from the top and have the express commitment of senior management, then it logically follows that the associated assessment of risk should also emanate from a high level within an organisation. This is especially relevant when an organisation is undergoing radical or far-reaching change, perhaps as a matter of continued survival.

Data on risks should be accurate and viewed in the context of likelihood of occurrence. For existing activities there may be historic risk data available based on past achievements to draw upon. Risks can be represented by either quantitative or qualitative factors and will certainly have differing degrees of potential impact.

Identified risks should be prioritised and control objectives established in every case. The objectives can reflect the required performance indicators applicable to each risk as a means of establishing the thresholds of tolerance. Taken collectively the ranking and objectives data will drive the definition and design of the required control systems.

Objectives may be classified in a number of ways, for example:

Operations Objectives	(e.g. performance/profitability goals)
Financial Reporting Objectives	(e.g. accurate statements prepared in accordance with prevailing requirements)
Compliance Objectives	(e.g. adherence to relevant sector regulations, legislation, board policies, covenants entered into with third parties, etc.)

In basic terms, one measure of success for any system of internal control is that there is reasonable assurance that the established control objectives have been achieved, and will be in the future.

Business and society are not static entities, they are subject to all manner of changes initiated from both within and outside an entity. The assessment of risks should be an ongoing process with reappraisal of the implications for the business. Changes in either the nature or priority of risk should then be carried through to the setting of control objectives and the modification/creation of the system of internal control.

COSO's "Control Activities" Component

This control component refers to all the procedures the organisation operates which have a control purpose—such as locking doors, undertaking reconciliations and so on. If organisations did none of these things, there could not be effective internal control.

The establishment of a system of control benefits from being approached afresh, but it is more likely that, in practice, the mechanisms will have evolved progressively over a considerable time.

The creation of a high-profile control environment, the undertaking of a risk assessment of an entity's operations, and the setting of a range of control objectives will naturally lead to, or flush out, the required control mechanisms. It is too simplistic to say that every exposure and control objective will need to be matched with a control activity, as there may be inevitable overlap with both objectives and control activities, with the potential for varying degrees of significance when viewed in combination.

There are two dimensions to control activities. First, there is the establishment of a policy which defines what has to be done to achieve the related business objective. Secondly, a procedure is required which defines the processes necessary to meet the policy requirements. Generally speaking, policies are normally defined at a fairly high level, while procedures have a tendency for a markedly lower or detailed level of definition. The policies may specify the best form of control type to achieve the desired effect, whereas the procedures will be concerned with the elemental mechanism of the preferred approach. Ensuring that the spirit of both these elements remains compatible is therefore essential if the underlying objectives are to be achieved.

Control activities/procedures will need to be accurately defined and effectively communicated to those involved. It is always preferable to establish written procedures which remove the possibility of misinterpretation so often associated with verbal instructions. Control activities may be defined in the form of procedures, user manuals, job descriptions, etc. Any timing requirements, reporting criteria or authority thresholds should be clearly incorporated into such documents. Operational changes should be subject to prompt review so that any required procedural changes can be accommodated and communicated.

The nature and extent of control activities will need to be considered against the balance between the costs of implementing them and the benefits derived. Where there are compensating controls, any redundant processes should be pruned out, but only after achievement of control objectives is assured.

The form of control activities employed will obviously be dependent upon the nature of the associated risks and control objectives and there are few hard and fast rules that can be brought to bear. The generic form of controls (i.e. preventative or detective) and their eventual form (i.e. authorisation, reconciliation, segregation of duties, etc.) will need to be matched to both the risks and objectives.

In key areas, it may be essential that some form of trail of control activities is maintained as evidence of appropriate application of the procedure. Such trails can be monitored by management to provide some assurance that the control is being complied with.

Where the control activity requires a specific or specialised skill, there should be a mechanism in place to ensure that the requisite knowledge levels are maintained, perhaps through ongoing training and staff development programmes.

With the increasing influence of information technology upon all manner of everyday business activities, it is crucial for the integrity of corporate data and continuation of service provision that specific control objectives and activities are targeted at computer systems. Data is often the lifeblood of an organisation and steps should be taken to ensure that it remains accurate, complete, secure and authorised.

COSO's "Information and Communication" Component

In order to function efficiently and successfully, an organisation requires that relevant information is provided to the right people at the right time. It is inconceivable that a modern business could run and achieve its objectives without a flow of relevant information. Additionally, it is essential that such information is reliable in terms of accuracy and completeness. Inaccurate or outdated data will affect management's ability to make the appropriate decisions and control the business. Where necessary, data should be authorised and secure, especially where it is commercially sensitive.

In a contemporary business, all manner of data will be gathered, analysed and distributed; it may for example, relate to operational matters, performance statistics, financial status or matters of control compliance.

Selected staff will require the receipt of information in order to perform their specific tasks. Working with outdated or incomplete data may jeopardise both their performance and the achievement of corporate objectives.

Corporate information should not be considered purely from the internal viewpoint, as relevant data received from, and sent out to, external bodies can also be crucial; for example, ordering call-off details from a major customer will impact upon both production and stock functions, whereas the timely release of invoices will potentially benefit cash flow, etc. Matters such as data accuracy can take on a different significance when there are external dimensions, in that the image and reputation of an organisation can be severely damaged if incomplete or invalid information is distributed to customers or suppliers.

Inevitably in the present business environment, information directly relates to some form of computerised process. Of course, information technology brings great benefits to the business world, but unless carefully controlled and monitored there is the potential for severe adverse impacts. A cynic may be inclined to say that computers have an unnerving knack of generating rubbish a lot faster than human beings. As a general rule there should be independent proof that a system has generated accurate and complete data, and the fact that "the computer produced this report" should not be taken as positive evidence that the data is reliable.

There is normally a key set of data elements which form the heart of a business, and whereas the systems (or applications) which process and manipulate such data may change over time, the nature of this crucial data is likely to remain fairly consistent. As part of a corporate level information technology strategic plan, a form of data modelling can be undertaken which seeks to identify the required data structure and assign factors such as ownership, access rights and security levels for each element.

In the appropriate circumstances they may be benefits associated with the development of a formal information policy defining the key components of the business information system. Having established a management information system (MIS) or equivalent, it is relatively easy to build in required controls aimed at ensuring the accuracy, integrity and timeliness of data.

In the context of a control environment, information sources may have a discrete control implication in that, for example, they provide the means to either operate a control or highlight the failure of a control condition. When defining and building a control environment and associated control activities, the use of key information elements is inevitable. Reconciliation and testing routines can provide management with assurances that systems are operating correctly.

The term "communication" has a broader significance than pure information. For example, communication systems can relate key messages about the culture and control awareness of an enterprise, and engender a collective responsibility for control matters if handled appropriately.

Internal communications can cater for flows in various directions, i.e. up the hierarchy, across functions or down through all layers of management and responsibility. Although any organisation should have a healthy regard for the sensitivity and confidentiality of information flowing through lines of communication, it is as important to ensure that staff do receive the information they require to fulfil their responsibility as it is to prevent unauthorised access to data.

The communication routes to utilise in the event of either a problem or failure occurring should be clearly defined so that the prompt reporting of anomalies is facilitated.

External communication requirements will cater for both inward and outward flows. For example, in a service industry context, it may be crucial to ensure that customer complaints or operational failures are swiftly and accurately routed to the appropriate personnel. Alternatively, periodic performance or compliance reports may have to be sent out to a regulatory body.

We are presented with a variety of means of communication, where speed, accessibility and security will all vary with the method. Defining standards for the use of an appropriate method in specific circumstances can provide greater assurance that communications will be effectively achieved.

It will often be worthwhile to undertake a review project to explore the "information balance" of the organisation as a whole or of any of its parts, as illustrated in Figure 6.2. The balance is most likely to be inefficient with respect to business processes that cut across structural boundaries of the organisation. Many organisations and parts of organisations expensively gather and retain a surfeit of data far beyond the extent to which this data is used to extract potentially useful information. On the other hand, an organisation may have inadequate records to derive the information that management needs. Then again, an organisation or any part of it, may have implemented processes that generate plentiful information but the quality and quantity of the use of that information for analysis purposes means that much of the available information is not being utilised. Alternatively, the analysis of the available information may be stretched beyond that which the inadequate information can support rigorously. We all recognise the organisation, or part thereof, that analyses available information from all angles but appears incapable of taking the decisions

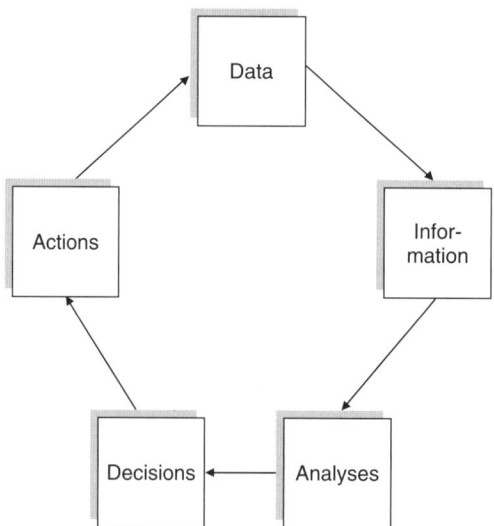

Figure 6.2 Harnessing information efficiently

suggested by the analysis. Others take decisions "on the seat of their pants" with insufficient recourse to rigorous analysis, notwithstanding that it has often been said that "wrong decisions may be better than no decisions"! But a decision is pointless unless it is auctioned: many managers seem to lack the follow-through to ensure their decisions are implemented, and in a timely and effective way. Other organisations or their component parts may tend to rush around like scalded hens taking random and inconsistent actions that were never decided upon.

The message from this is that, in the interests of economy, efficiency and effectiveness there needs to be a controlled balance between data, information, analysis, decision and action.

COSO's "Monitoring" Component

We have discussed the development of the control environment, the establishment of control activities geared to the risks present in the organisation and the required flow of business-related information. Each organisation will further need to consider how these components contribute to top management's and the board's need for assurance.

Information systems should provide the principal means of monitoring the effectiveness of internal control systems. Equally important is the establishment of mechanisms which, having identified either a problem or control failure, ensure that management is made aware so that the necessary corrective action can be promptly taken.

As to who should undertake the responsibility for monitoring the internal control system, this should fall ultimately to the board, who in any event have the final responsibility for the operations of the organisation. In practical terms, directors cannot operate all aspects of monitoring on their own. Line management should have defined responsibilities for ongoing or day-to-day monitoring of operations, financial performance, etc. Ideally a degree of independence should be brought to bear on the monitoring process. Nonexecutive directors can play a vital role in monitoring, for example through an audit committee of the board with specific responsibilities for reviewing financial statements and assessing the effectiveness of the internal control system and the activities of the internal audit function.

The board should further monitor the identification of business risks and the development of control objectives and priorities, although the initial detailed work may be undertaken by more junior management.

The internal audit function has the potential to play a vital role in independently assessing the effectiveness of controls and reporting upon same to the board perhaps through the auspices of the audit committee. Compliance functions, especially within financial institutions, also play a key role.

The processes of ongoing and/or periodic review, whoever conducts them, should not only consider the effectiveness of the existing control system, but should also question whether the system itself is still relevant and suitable. Businesses and operations will invariably change and have to adapt to external forces, so that it is probable that practices and therefore control will have to be modified to meet the new demands. Whether the reviewer has detected a failure of the existing control system or the requirement for that system to be updated, there needs to be a defined mechanism and a route that enables prompt and effective reporting of the shortcomings. Management should have in place a system for receiving feedback from a number of sources about control-related problems, etc. These may be formal in nature such as would apply to internal and external auditors' reporting channels, but should also cater for more junior members of staff who may suspect that an improper act has been perpetrated.

A procedure for dealing with reported shortcomings and ensuring that appropriate corrective action is applied by management will also be necessary to avoid either a recurrence or more significant breach of policy.

Evidence of review of the system of internal control should be available; this may be in the form of internal audit reports, summaries of significant control issues coordinated by the audit committee, or minutes of board meetings, etc.

The consolidation and reporting of the conclusions of control self assessment programmes, especially in the absence of an internal audit function, are likely to have a significant role to play in assessing internal control effectiveness within an enterprise.

PARADIGM 2: TURNBULL ON INTERNAL CONTROL

The UK's Turnbull guidance[7] is closely similar to the COSO internal control framework, though developed in much less detail. We really need to cross refer to COSO in order to understand the Turnbull framework. It does however have a greater emphasis on risk. It defines internal control broadly, as does COSO, to cover everything that management does other than the setting of objectives. The guidance was developed to interpret the internal control part of the UK Corporate Governance Code which makes it best practice for boards to assess the effectiveness of all of internal control and also risk management systems—in contrast to the US requirement for the CEO and CFO to assess the effectiveness of internal control just over financial reporting and other disclosures, per s. 302 and s. 404 of the 2002 Sarbanes-Oxley Act. The UK Corporate Governance Code[11] has this to say about internal control:

C.2 Internal Control

Main Principle

The board should maintain a sound system of internal control to safeguard shareholders' investment and the company's assets.

Code Provision

C.2.1 The board should, at least annually, conduct a review of the effectiveness of the group's system of internal controls and should report to shareholders that they have done so. The review should cover all material controls, including financial, operational and compliance controls and risk management systems.

The Turnbull guidance[7] suggests means of applying this part of the Code. Turnbull defines internal control as:

An internal control system encompasses the policies, processes, tasks, behaviours and other aspects of a company that, taken together:

- facilitate its effective and efficient operation by enabling it to respond appropriately to significant business, operational, financial, compliance and other risks to achieving the company's objectives. This includes the safeguarding of assets from inappropriate use or from loss and fraud, and ensuring that liabilities are identified and managed;
- help ensure the quality of internal and external reporting. This requires the maintenance of proper records and processes that generate a flow of timely, relevant and reliable information within and outside the organisation;
- help ensure compliance with applicable laws and regulations, and also with internal policies with respect to the conduct of business.

The appendix to the Turnbull guidance repeats the COSO essential components of internal control, except that it confusingly combines "control environment and control activities".

PARADIGM 3: COCO ON INTERNAL CONTROL

The internal control framework of the Canadian Institute of Chartered Accountants' Criteria of Control Board ("CoCo") is less "mechanical" and more "behavioural" than the COSO internal control framework and, arguably, has advantages in application within organisations that are more participative and less hierarchical, as well as being a valuable control framework to use in control self assessment situations.[6] CoCo also defines internal control broadly, as does COSO, to cover everything that management does other than the setting of objectives. CoCo defines internal control as follows:

Control comprises those elements of an organization (including its resources, systems, processes, culture, structure and tasks) that, taken together, support people in the achievement of the organization's objectives. These objectives fall into one or more of the following categories:

- **Effectiveness and efficiency of operations** includes objectives related to an organization's goals, such as customer service, the safeguarding and efficient use of resources, profitability and meeting social obligations. This includes the safeguarding of the organization's resources from inappropriate use or loss and ensuring that liabilities are identified and managed.
- **Reliability of internal and external reporting** includes objectives related to matters such as the maintenance of proper accounting records, the reliability of information used within the organization and of information published for third parties. This includes the protection of records against two main types of fraud: the concealment of theft and the distortion of results.
- **Compliance with applicable laws and regulations and internal policies** includes objectives related to ensuring that the organization's affairs are conducted in accordance with legal and regulatory obligations and internal policies.

Reflecting the more behavioural orientation of the CoCo control framework, their internal control components are as the four indicted in Figure 6.3:

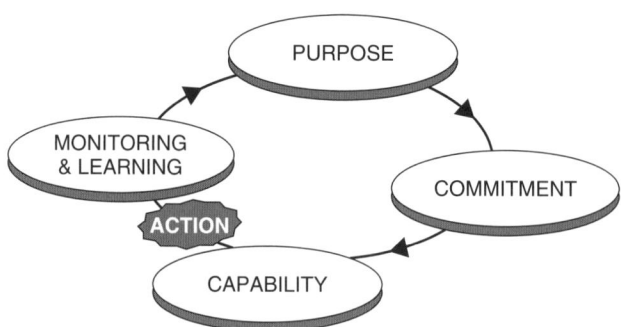

Figure 6.3 The CoCo internal control framework. Reprinted with permission from *Guidance on Control* (The Canadian Institute of Chartered Accountants, 1995, Toronto, Canada)

CoCo explains:

A person performs a task, guided by an understanding of its **purpose** (the objectives to be achieved) and supported by **capability** (information, resources, supplies and skills). The person will need a sense of **commitment** to perform the task well over time. The person will **monitor** his or her performance and the external environment to **learn** about how to do the task better and about changes to be made. The same is true of any team or work group. In any organization of people, the essence of control is purpose, commitment, capability, and monitoring and learning.

CoCo has identified 20 criteria of control grouped into the four sets referred to in Figure 6.3. "Purpose" groups the criteria that provide a sense of the organisation's direction—that is, "what to do". "Commitment" groups the criteria that provide a sense of the organisation's identity and values—that is, "wanting to do it". "Capability" groups the criteria that provide a sense of the organisation's competence—that is, "Tools to do it". "Monitoring and learning" groups the criteria that provide a sense of the organisation's evolution—that is, "Are we doing it?" The identification and assessment of internal and external risks is one of the criteria belonging to the "Purpose" grouping. Matters relating to ethical values belong to a criterion within the "Commitment" grouping. Information and communication are two of the criteria within the "Capability" grouping. Readers should refer to the CoCo publications[6] for further detail, and we discuss the CoCo internal control framework further in Chapter 18 where we address the control self assessment approach.

PARADIGM 4: A SYSTEMS/CYBERNETICS MODEL OF INTERNAL CONTROL

Conceptually this paradigm views the organisational process as analogous to, for instance, an air conditioning system. The plan is the room temperature setting of the thermostat. Actual performance is monitored and compared to the plan. If a significant variance between "plan" and "actual" occurs, then the control system makes a decision to switch the fan on or off in order that, and until, room temperature is within an acceptable tolerance of the planned temperature. So the control system is continuously interpreting information available to it. In this system the monitoring and decision taking is automated or programmed into the programmer or controller. In business automated, electronic monitoring and decision taking is excellent if it is feasible to do it in this way while taking appropriate account of all of the variables, and so long as customers and others are prepared to tolerate, even welcome, interfacing with impersonal systems. Electronic controls tend to be more reliable than mechanical controls and mechanical controls tend to be more reliable than controls that require manual oversight. In practice, effective internal control is likely to rely on a combination of manual and automated activities.

Ashby's cybernetics law of requisite variety has relevance here. It states that the control mechanism must be designed to accommodate the variety of what is to be controlled. So, if a light is only to be "on" or "off" the switch must be able to handle these two states. The programmer of an air conditioning system is likely to be required to accommodate humidity as well as temperature, a time clock function and also manual override—so the control process quickly becomes quite complex. Ashby's law also suggests that the control mechanism of a system will tend to utilise technology as complex as the technology of what it is controlling. Ashby's law has implication for business control: organisations should expect to need to invest in control technology which corresponds to the technology they are utilising to run their business processes; and organisations should be open to investing in audit technology similar to the technology they are using to run their business processes.

Systems/cybernetics theory has developed its own terminology—see Figures 6.4, 6.5, 6.6 and 6.7.

```
Input
Process
Output
Boundary
Closed systems
Open systems
Variable
Internal
External
Environment
```

Figure 6.4 General systems terms

Basic System Concepts[12]

A system is a set of related elements with a purpose. A system has three main elements (Figure 6.5):

The "process" changes the "input" into "output". The parts of the elements which may change are termed "variables". A system conceptually has a "boundary" within which the functioning of the system [Input > Process > Output] takes place. A subsystem is a smaller system within a larger system.

The term "internal" is used to refer to what happens *within* a system, and "external" if the variable enters from outside the system boundary, or exits to beyond

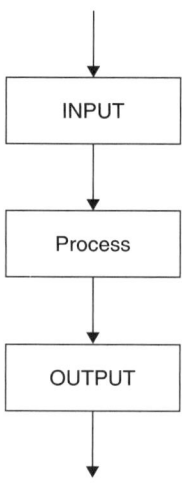

Figure 6.5 Main elements of a system

Control object
Detector
Reference point
Comparator (analyser)
Activator
Feedback
Feedforward

Figure 6.6 Systems control concepts

the system boundary. The environment of a system is what takes place beyond its boundary. A turbulent environment often requires a system to be more "open" to the environment in order to cope with rapid change.

A system is like an onion, or perhaps like a garlic. There are systems (subsystems) within systems. Particularly with open systems we use our discretion to draw the boundaries depending upon the focus of our interest. We can invariably "peel off the skin" and see other, smaller systems within an outer boundary.

Basic Elements of a Control System

With reference to Figure 6.6, the "control object" is the variable of the system's behaviour which is to be monitored and controlled. The "detector" is the part of the system which measures (or monitors) the control object. The "reference point" is the standard against which the actual performance of the control object is compared.

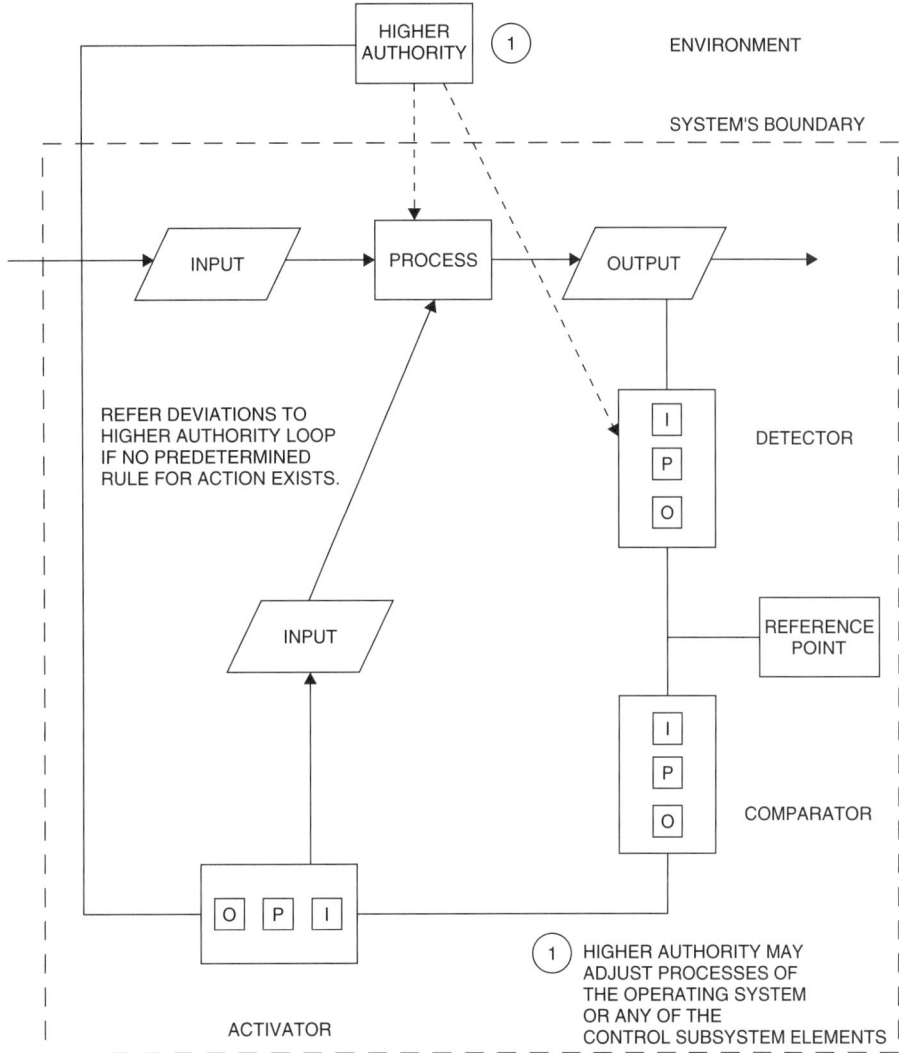

Figure 6.7 An illustration of an open, adaptive control system (from Gleim's CIA Review Book Part III on Management Control and Information Technology (10th edition, December 2001, ISSN: 1099-8837, ISBN 1-58194-182-X, p. 35, www.gleim.com).

The "comparator (analyser)" makes the comparison and assesses whether or not it is significant. The "activator" takes the decision which is intended to restore actual performance to what is desired.

An Example

Imagine a central heating system, or an air conditioning system. These are the basic control elements in our example:

Control Object	–	temperature
Detector	–	temperature gauge on the thermostat
Reference Point	–	22°C
Comparator (Analyser)	–	relative temperature sensor in thermostat
Activator	–	control switch in thermostat

The temperature setting (= the "control object") is put at the desired output (say 22°C = the "reference point") by adjusting the temperature gauge (= the "detector") on the thermostat. The thermostat continuously measures actual performance (that is, room temperature) and compares it with the 22°C planned performance (= the "comparator"). If a significant variance has developed between actual and planned performance, the micro switch in the thermostat (= the "activator") takes a programmed decision to switch the main mechanism on or off in order to bring actual performance back in line with planned performance.

The "control" part of the system is to ensure that desired states are achieved. The control part of the system invariably relies upon "feedback". "Feedforward" passes information forward to an activator which is then able to adjust processes which have not yet taken place in the light of the actual outputs which have been achieved from earlier processes.

"Input", "Process" and "Output" each need to be controlled. A more elaborate schematic of this is shown as Figure 6.7.

Business systems, indeed all social systems, are open systems in that their performance is sensitive to external variables. Simple chemical reactions within a controlled environment (mixing hydrogen with oxygen, for instance) would be an example of a closed system. A rigorous definition of a closed system would be a system that does not have any inputs or outputs from and to the system, but this is theoretical and does not exist in the real business world. A perpetual motion machine would be an example. It is better for us to use the definition that "a closed system is one that does not accept uncontrolled inputs, whereas an open system is subject to uncontrolled inputs". Even this is rather theoretical in a business context as, according to this definition, most systems are "open" systems. Nevertheless we can frequently obtain a better initial understanding of a business activity by "oversimplifying" our analysis of the way it behaves, describing it, at least initially, in closed system terms.

The expression "internal control" is therefore understood by systems theory to refer to the regulation of variables which occur *within* a system; consequently "external control" would be the regulation of variables which originate from outside the system or have destinations outside the system.

Open systems are harder to control than closed systems.

Controls may sometimes be automated ("programmed controls"), but the complexity of the control process may preclude this (i.e. "discretionary controls" are applied). Discretionary controls are more likely to be essential when it is necessary to control inputs and outputs to and from the system, as in the case of an open system.

A "corrective" system is one that can adapt in order to achieve desired states. In other words it can follow different processing paths according to prescribed rules. This may be applicable for either an "open" or a "closed" system. An "adaptive" system has the flexibility to modify its processes in response to changes in the environment;

so an adaptive system is always an open system. This is like learning—it goes beyond simply following a particular path according to prescribed rules.

Corrective control systems are sometimes called first-order control systems. In these the control responses are entirely predictable being based on predetermined system rules and functioning with no regard to environmental changes. On the other hand, adaptive control systems (sometimes called second-order control systems) can take control steps in response to changes in the environment, and can learn from their experience.

PARADIGM 5: CONTROL BY DIVISION WITH SUPERVISION

This model of internal control is based on the premise that effective control may be achieved by means of an appropriate combination of various opportunities to "divide" ("separate off" or "segregate"), together with supervision. Designing our control processes to take advantage of sensible opportunities to divide may be a costless way of achieving effective internal control as it may be just a matter of allocating work in ways that reduce the likelihood that errors and losses, deliberate or accidental, will occur. However, there may be possible intangible costs: for instance, if in order to improve control we design our process so that whomsoever physically handles cash does not also account for it, then we may be reducing the potential for job satisfaction and for those involved to take an intelligent 360° interest in the business process. Specialisation, which some of these divisions entail, can however result in greater productivity.[13] On the other hand, if we rely on supervision to achieve effective control, additional costs will be involved and the supervision may also not be very reliable.

So this view of internal control counsels that we should endeavour to achieve effective control by means of judicious divisions of various sorts; but if we judge that inadequate control has been achieved by divisions, then we should rely to a greater extent on supervision. It follows that the need for effective supervision will be greatest over processes that are control sensitive and in particular when we have been unable to establish satisfactory internal control through a mix of "divisions".

We set out here the different division opportunities that can be utilised, solely or in combination and in conjunction with supervision where necessary, to achieve effective internal control.

Division of Duties

Ensure that two or more people work together on tasks where there is a risk of a lack of control, so that they act as a cross-check on each other. This also has the advantage of avoiding excessive dependence upon one member of staff. Examples might include issuing passwords, granting and adjusting credit limits, the database administrator role, requiring two staff to open a vault, and so on.

Division of Fundamentally Incompatible Responsibilities

Control will be strengthened if authorisation is required from someone who does not execute the task, and if both the authorisation and the execution are separated from the accounting for this activity. This can often be applied to custodial activities such as the cashier function or the warehousing function. The cashier should not be the person who authorises the release of cash or the replenishment of the cash float; neither the cashier nor the authorising person should maintain the control account for cash. Another, noncustodial example would be that the purchasing manager places orders against someone else's authorisation and neither have a hand in accounting for purchases.

Division of Operations

Some activities conflict with each other if undertaken by the same person or group. For example, selling should be divided from making decisions about levels of credit extended to customers; if this is not done, then the control weakness needs to be compensated for by supervision—perhaps by review of sales staff's credit limit adjustment decision by a credit control committee.

Division of Staff

Be aware of the control weaknesses that may arise when the effect of other divisions is negated because of personal relationships. For instance when two members of staff undertaking segregated tasks share the same office and informally substitute for each other, or when they strike up a personal relationship outside work.

Division of Data

Modern IT databases mean that data is held once only on IT databases, to be accessible to all users from different parts of the organisation who need to access that data. Artificial walls need to be built into IT systems. At the design stage, for each category of data it should be determined who has the authority to add, change, delete and merely to look at that category of data. Controls should then be built into the software to limit activity in that desired way—e.g. by means of password control. Internal auditors should have unrestricted authority to look at data but no opportunity to add, change or delete any data.

Division of Data Entry and Accounts Postings

Consider whether control may be improved if certain "bookkeeping" activities are divided. For instance the posting of debits from the post of credits to personal accounts; the posting of adjusting entries from the posting of original entries; the submission of corrections to rejected input data from the original submission of the input errors, etc.

Division of Authority

There are different ways in which authority to commit the organisation can be allocated with varying degrees of control effectiveness. It could be allocated to one person; or to one person with review by another; or by two people jointly, or to a committee, or to nobody. Who these individuals are, and their degree of independence from each other, also impacts upon the effectiveness of the authorisation control.

Division of Time

Often "time is of the essence" in modern businesses. To complete a transaction promptly tends to speed up business cycle times and increase the volume of business while lowering costs. But sometimes it can be sensible to build deliberate time delays into transactions and to make other uses of time in order to improve control. Examples include delaying shipment until the payment has cleared, time locks on vaults, "log off after time out", etc.

Control may be improved if the system provides after the event evidence of control sensitive activity, and also if after the event authorisation is required before a change can be implemented. For example if a customer's credit limit is changed, the system may be programmed to require after the event authorisation by a supervisor before the changed credit limit can be used.

PARADIGM 6: CONTROL BY CATEGORY

A particular type of control may be appropriate in a certain circumstance, and indeed more than one type of control may be needed to bear down effectively on a particular risk. Some categories of control are as shown in the table. As with most categorisations, there is overlap between some of them.

	Category of control	Risk target	Nature	Examples	Reference
1.	Preventive	Cause	Designed to limit the possibility of an undesirable outcome being realised. "Preventive" (Steering) controls anticipate unwanted consequences and take corrective action *before the system's processes are completed* in order to prevent the unwanted consequences occurring. The more important it is that	Separation of duty, whereby no one person has authority to act without the consent of another (such as the person who authorises payment of an invoice being separate from the person who ordered goods prevents one person securing goods at public expense for their own benefit); or limitation of action to authorised persons (such as only those	UK HM Treasury,[14] Gleim[15]

	Category of control	Risk target	Nature	Examples	Reference
			an undesirable outcome should not arise, the more important it becomes to implement appropriate preventive controls. The majority of controls implemented in organisations tend to belong to this category.	suitably trained and authorised being permitted to handle media enquiries prevents inappropriate comment being made to the press).	
2.	Pre-emptive	Cause	Yes/No controls that require approval before processing can proceed	Authorisation to raise a credit limit, to accept an order, to make a payment—and so on.	Gleim[15]
3.	Directive	Cause	Designed to ensure that a particular outcome is achieved. They are particularly important when it is critical that an undesirable event is avoided—typically associated with Health and Safety or with security.	A requirement that protective clothing be worn during the performance of dangerous duties, or that staff be trained with required skills before being allowed to work unsupervised.	UK HM Treasury,[14] Gleim[15]
4.	Performance	Cause	Designed to orientate and motivate the organisation's people to focus on the achievement of targets that are appropriate for the achievement of the entity's objectives.	A target to despatching all orders on day of receipt of order, or within 24 hrs. A target to respond to all e-mail or postal mail on day of receipt. A target that less than 2 % of production should fail quality control checks.	This Handbook
5.	Detective	Effect	"Post-action" or "post-event" controls, taking place after the other system's processes have been completed and detecting unwanted consequences which have already occurred.	Stock or asset checks (which detect whether stocks or assets have been removed without authorisation), reconciliation (which can detect unauthorised transactions), "Post Implementation	UK HM Treasury,[14] Gleim[15]

Category of control	Risk target	Nature	Examples	Reference
			Reviews" which detect lessons to be learned from projects for application in future work, and monitoring activities which detect changes that should be responded to.	
6. Corrective	Effect	Designed to correct undesirable outcomes which have occurred and have been detected.	Design of contract terms to allow recovery of overpayment. Insurance can also be regarded as a form of corrective control as it facilitates financial recovery against the realisation of a risk. Contingency planning is an important element of corrective control as it is the means by which organisations plan for business continuity/ recovery after events which they could not control.	UK HM Treasury;[14,15]
7. Investigative	Cause and effect	To try to understand how the undesirable outcome occurred, to ensure that it does not happen next time, and to provide a route of recourse to achieve some recovery against loss or damage.		IIA[16]

THE OBJECTIVES OF INTERNAL CONTROL

Earlier in this chapter we pointed out that the objective of internal control can be broken down into any number of sub-objectives. It is just a matter of how one categorises the objectives of management. This ranges from a single objective (The Institute of Internal Auditors' *Standards* Glossary definition of control), two objectives (the UK Corporate Governance Code), three objectives (COSO, 1992 and 2004), four objectives (The Institute of Internal Auditors' *Standards*), five objectives (the old Institute of Internal Auditors' Standards, 1978–2001) and six objectives (The King Report on Corporate Governance for South Africa, 2002).

The Institute of Internal Auditors' Standards Glossary Definition of Control

Any action taken by management, the board, and other parties to manage risk and increase the likelihood that established objectives and goals will be achieved. Management plans, organizes, and directs the performance of sufficient actions to provide reasonable assurance that objectives and goals will be achieved.

The UK's Combined Code on Corporate Governance (2008), C.2 on Internal Control

Main Principle:

The board should maintain a sound system of internal control to:

- safeguard shareholders' investment, and
- safeguard the company's assets.

Code Provision

C.2.1 The board should, at least annually, conduct a review of the effectiveness of the group's system of internal controls and should report to shareholders that they have done so. The review should cover all material controls, including financial, operational and compliance controls and risk management systems.

COSO (Internal Control—Integrated Framework, (1992), and Enterprise Risk Management, (2004)

Internal control is broadly defined as a process, effected by the entity's board of directors, management and other personnel, designed to provide reasonable assurance regarding the achievement of objectives in the following categories:

- Effectiveness and efficiency of operations.
- Reliability of financial reporting.
- Compliance with applicable laws and regulations.

The Institute of Internal Auditors' Standards (post 2001)

2130—Control The internal audit activity must assist the organization in maintaining effective controls by evaluating their effectiveness and efficiency and by promoting continuous improvement.

2130.A1—The internal audit activity must evaluate the adequacy and effectiveness of controls in responding to risks within the organization's governance, operations, and information systems regarding the:

- Reliability and integrity of financial and operational information.
- Effectiveness and efficiency of operations.
- Safeguarding of assets.
- Compliance with laws, regulations, and contracts.

The Old Standards of The Institute of Internal Auditors (1978–2001), in the Superseded Statement on Internal Auditing Standards

The primary objectives of internal control are to ensure:

- The reliability and integrity of information.
- Compliance with policies, plans, procedures, laws, regulations, and contracts.
- The safeguarding of assets.
- The economical and efficient use of resources.
- The accomplishment of established objectives and goals for operations and programs.

The King Report on Corporate Governance for South Africa, 2002

The board should make use of generally recognised risk management and internal control models and frameworks in order to maintain a sound system of risk management and internal control to provide a reasonable assurance regarding the achievement of organizational objectives with respect to:

- Effectiveness and efficiency of operations;
- Safeguarding of the company's assets (including information);
- Compliance with applicable laws, regulations and supervisory requirements;
- Supporting business sustainability under normal as well as adverse operating conditions;
- Reliability of reporting; and
- Behaving responsibly towards all stakeholders.

DETERMINING WHETHER INTERNAL CONTROL IS EFFECTIVE

The CoCo programme of the Canadian Institute of Chartered Accountants has stated that control is effective to the extent that it provides reasonable assurance that an organisation will achieve its objectives reliably; or, control is effective to the extent that the remaining (uncontrolled) risks of the organisation failing to meet its objectives are acceptable.

Authoritative guidance, for instance the Turnbull Report or the SEC rule on implementing s. 404 of the Sarbanes-Oxley Act, make it clear that two questions must be answered before a conclusion can be made about the effectiveness of internal control.

1. Have any outcomes occurred which indicate that internal control has been ineffective?
2. Is the internal control process robust enough to give reasonable assurance of the achievement of management's objectives?

We are not entitled to conclude that there is effective internal control (over the whole business or over a process which is the subject of our review) just because after careful investigation we have uncovered nothing that has gone wrong. Organisations may be unaware of significant failures that have occurred. But if we have discovered something of significance that has gone wrong, it is likely to mean that we have to conclude that internal control has not been effective.

A sound approach to addressing the second question is to review the robustness of COSO's five essential components of internal control (control environment, information and communication, risk assessment, control activities, monitoring) so as to be able to conclude that internal control can be expected to be effective. This will include confirming that these control components are being applied in the manner that they have been designed to be. A frequent mistake is to focus just on an assessment of control activities, but to overlook the criticality of the other four essential components of internal control.

It is to be preferred that the second question (above) is addressed by reference to COSO's eight enterprise risk management components (see Chapter 5) as this broadens the assurance that the auditor can give to embrace both risk management and internal control.

CONTROL COST-EFFECTIVENESS CONSIDERATIONS

Regardless of whether costly failures are prevented, a process with good control, for instance through segregation of duties, may not cost more to run than one with weak control. There may be opportunities to achieve effective control in more economical ways. Duplicate controls may mean that some controls are redundant and can be eliminated.

Management make many judgement calls as to the extent to which it is worthwhile investing in enhanced control to provide greater assurance of the achievement of objectives. Certainly control should be sufficient to mitigate risks so that the residual risks remaining are within the organisation's risk appetite. Again, that involves judgement as to the potential effectiveness of control(s) and also as to what the risk appetite should be.

It is desirable to make control as watertight as is practical. Events judged to be unlikely to occur or of little consequence if they do occur, may turn out to have major repercussions upon the organisation. It is prudent to reconsider the efficacy of the business approach which accepts that control is imperfect, say to prevent fraud, but rather cynically endeavours to build the ongoing, routine cost of the fraud into the price of the organisation's products or services. It is not always possible to assess the potential top-side cost of breakdowns in control. Fraud can be regarded as a particular type of breakdown in the system of internal control. Then there is the ethical and practical business challenge of the moral hazard that the organisation is allowing by permitting its business processes to be insufficiently controlled.

ISSUES FOR INTERNAL CONTROL PROCESSES

Objectives of Internal Control Processes

> To provide reasonable assurance of:
> (a) The reliability and integrity of financial and operational information.
> (b) The effectiveness and efficiency of operations.
> (c) The safeguarding of assets.
> (d) Compliance with laws, regulations, policies and contracts.

1 Key Issues

1.1 Is a control framework applied to the design and assessment of internal control within the organisation?

1.2 Have there been significant errors and/or losses due to control weaknesses that have not been corrected?

1.3 Over time, are all significant business processes reviewed for their control effectiveness?

1.4 Does management understand that they are responsible for the effectiveness of internal control?

1.5 Does the audit committee of the board report to the board the committee's overall opinion of the effectiveness of internal control?

1.6 Is the chief audit executive required to report to the audit committee, or to the board, internal audit's overall opinion of the effectiveness of internal control?

1.7 Are key processes documented, highlighting their key controls; and is the design adequacy of these key controls evaluated?

1.8 Is there a satisfactory programme for testing the operation of key controls, executed by management and by internal audit?

1.9 What is the level of risk that management may override controls, and if this were to occur would it be reported to an independent level?

2 Detailed Issues

2.1 Does the control framework used measure up to COSO, CoCo or Turnbull?

2.2 When necessary, is the internal control of outsourced processes within the scope of the organisation's design and assessment of internal control?

2.3 Are management and staff trained to understand the meaning of internal control and how it is achieved?

2.4 Is there evidence that controls are dysfunctional in that they are hampering the achievement of objectives?

2.5 Is internal control achieved in a cost-effective way?

2.6 Is there over-control through unnecessarily costly control processes, or through duplicate controls?

2.7 Is line management required to regularly assess, and certify to, the control effectiveness of their areas of responsibility?

2.8 When the chief audit executive believes that senior management has accepted a level of residual risk that may be unacceptable to the organisation, and has not resolved the matter through discussion, does the chief audit executive report the matter to the board, or to the audit committee, for resolution?

2.9 Does a lack of effective internal control create a moral hazard for management, staff, contractors, customers, suppliers or other parties?

2.10 Would errors, fraud or other avoidable losses be detected?

2.11 Is responsibility for the prevention, detection and investigation of fraud clearly assigned within the job descriptions of appropriate staff?

NOTES

1. Fayol, Henri (1916) *Administration Industrielle et Générale* (Principles of Industrial Administration).
2. COSO (September 1992) *Internal Control—Integrated Framework*, www.coso.org.
3. See, for instance, Collins, Arthur (1904) *The Municipal Internal Audit*. Gee & Co., London.
4. American Institute of Certified Public Accountants (AICPA) (1948, published in 1949) *Internal Control—Elements of a Co-ordinated System and its Importance to Management and the Independent Public Accountant*. AICPA, New York.
5. AICPA (October 1958) *Statement on Auditing Procedure No. 29*. AICPA, New York. See, for example, AICPA (November 1972) SAP 54 (*Statement on Auditing Procedure, No. 54*); also AICPA: SAS No. 1 and No. 55 (*Statement on Auditing Standards, No. 1 and No. 55*); and more recently the distinction is continued in the US COSO (1992) report (ibid.), and the UK exposure draft *Internal Control and Financial Reporting* 1993.
6. *Guidance on Control* (November 1995), ("The CoCo programme"), The Criteria of Control Board (CoCo) of The Canadian Institute of Chartered Accountants,

still in print. See also CoCo's *Preface to Guidance issued by the Criteria of Control Board* (November 1995) and *Guidance for Directors—Governance Processes for Control* (December 1995).

7. The Financial Reporting Council (1999 and 2005, revised): *Internal Control—Guidance for Directors on the Combined Code* ("The Turnbull Report"). Copies are available at www.frc.org.uk/corporate/internalcontrol.cfm.

8. American Institute of Certified Public Accountants; American Accounting Association; The Institute of Internal Auditors; The Institute of Management Accountants; The Financial Executives Institute.

9. "The Treadway Commission Report" (1987) *Report of the National Commission on Fraudulent Financial Reporting*. National Commission on Fraudulent Financial Reporting, New York, available on COSO's website: www.coso.org.

10. PCAOB's Auditing Standard No. 2 *"An audit of internal control over financial reporting performed in conjunction with an audit of financial statements"* (March 9, 2004), superseded by Auditing Standard No. 5, www.praobus.org.

11. The Financial Reporting Council, (2008 and 2010): The Combined Code on Corporate Governance; commencing 2010 titled The UK Corporate Governance Code, http://www.frc.org.uk.

12. We are grateful to Irvin Gleim. Professor Emeritus in the Fisher School of Accounting at the University of Florida, for permission to reference into Gleim's CIA Review Book Part III on Management Control and Information Technology (10th edition, December 2001). The diagram at the end of this article comes from p. 35 of that publication. Gleim Publications provides a study guide for each of the four parts of The Institute of Internal Auditors' international Certified Internal Auditor examinations which, in the editor's opinion, are undoubtedly the best available and the best way to prepare for these examinations. Gleim Publications offer similar guides for several other professional examinations which are popular in the US—such as Certified Public Accountant and Certified Management Accountant. The Gleim guides are also excellent for continuing professional development. Further particulars from Gleim Publications Inc., P.O. Box 12848, University Station, Gainesville, Florida 32604 [tel.: (352) 375-6940, email: admin@gleim.com, Internet: www.gleim.com].

13. *Vide*, e.g. Adam Smith (1776) *The Wealth of Nations*:
    > In the progress of the division of labour, the employment of the far greater part of those who live by labour, that is, of the great body of the people, comes to be confined to a few very simple operations, frequently only one or two. ... The man whose whole life is spent in performing a few simple operations, of which the effects too are, perhaps, always the same, or very nearly the same, has no occasion to exert his understanding, or to exercise his invention in finding out expedients for removing difficulties which never occur. He naturally loses, therefore, the habit of such exertion, and generally becomes as stupid and ignorant as it is possible for a human creature to become. ... His dexterity at his own particular trade seems, in this manner, to be acquired at the expense of his intellectual, social, and martial virtues. ... this is the state into which the labouring poor, that is, the great body of the people, must necessarily fall, unless government takes some pains to prevent it.

14. HM Treasury (October 2004) *The Orange Book—Management of Risk, Principles and Concepts*, http://www.hm-treasury.gov.uk/d/orange_book.pdf, §6.4, pp. 29 and 30.

15. Gleim's CIA *Review Book Part III on Management Control and Information Technology*. 10th edition, December 2001, www.gleim.com. Gleim also refers to further control types: first order (corrective) controls, second order (adaptive) controls, programmed controls and discretionary controls.

16. The Institute of Internal Auditors Inc. (May 2009) Practice Advisory 2010–12: *Using the Risk Management Process in Internal Audit Planning*, para. 4. The meaning PA 2010-2 gives to "investigative controls" is not identical to the meaning we have given in this chapter.

7
Review of the Control Environment

INTRODUCTION

In this chapter we set the scene for conducting a review of the control environment. We shall be using the following definition of the term "control environment" provided by the Committee of the Sponsoring Organizations (COSO) in their publication *Internal Control—Integrated Framework*:

The control environment sets the tone of an organisation influencing the control consciousness of its people. It is the foundation for all other components of internal control, providing discipline and structure. Control environment factors include the integrity, ethical values and competence of the entity's people; management's philosophy and operating style; the way management assigns authority and responsibility, and organises and develops its people; and the attention and direction provided by the board of directors.)[1]

First we shall establish the top level control objectives for this subject and then examine the relative risk and control issues posed in the form of questions. During the course of their review, auditors will be seeking to answer these questions by, first, determining the controls and measures that are in place in each instance, and secondly to evaluate the effectiveness of these controls/measures by performing compliance and substantive testing as appropriate.

CONTROL OBJECTIVES FOR A REVIEW OF THE CONTROL ENVIRONMENT

The following two objectives are deliberately pitched at a top level view of the control environment. However, it would be straightforward to break these down to a more detailed set.

1. To ensure that management conveys the message that integrity, ethical values and commitment to competence cannot be compromised, and that employees receive and understand that message.
2. To ensure that management continually demonstrates, by word and action, commitment to high ethical and competence standards.

RISK AND CONTROL ISSUES FOR A REVIEW OF THE CONTROL ENVIRONMENT

In order to evaluate whether the two control objectives listed above are being met, the auditor will need to consider the underlying risks and control issues. Noted below are a set of questions related to the risk and control issues that are inherent to the subject of the control environment.

The issue questions have been divided into two sets, namely the key issues (numbered 1.1 to 1.7) and the detailed issues (numbered 2.1 to 2.15). The auditor should always seek to answer the key issue questions, turning to the detailed set either when there is a noted weakness in the controls in place for the key set or whenever time permits.

1 Key Issues

1.1 Are there in place satisfactory Codes of Conduct and other policies which define acceptable business practice, conflicts of interest and expected standards of integrity and ethical behaviour?

1.2 Do management (from the top of the business downwards to all levels) clearly conduct business on a high ethical plane, and are departures appropriately remedied?

1.3 Is the philosophy and operating style of management consistent with the highest ethical standards?

1.4 Do the human resource policies of the business adequately reinforce its commitment to high standards of business integrity, ethics and competence?

1.5 Has the level of competence needed been specified for particular jobs, and does evidence exist to indicate that employees have the requisite knowledge and skills?

1.6 Are the board and its committees sufficiently informed and independent of management such that necessary, even if difficult and probing, questions can be explored effectively?

1.7 Is the organisation structure such that (a) all fully understand their responsibilities and authorities, and (b) the enterprise's activities can be adequately monitored?

2 Detailed Issues

2.1 Are Codes of Conduct comprehensive, addressing conflicts of interest, illegal or other improper payments, anti-competitive guidelines and insider trading?

2.2 Are Codes of Conduct understood by and periodically subscribed to by all employees?

2.3 Do senior managers frequently visit outlying locations for which they are responsible?

2.4 Is it the impression that employees feel peer pressure "to do the right thing"?

2.5 Is there sufficient evidence that management moves carefully in assessing potential benefits of ventures?

2.6 Does management adequately deal with signs that problems exist (e.g. hazardous by-products) even when the cost of identification and remedy could be high?

2.7 Are sufficient efforts made to deal honestly and fairly with business partners (e.g. employees, suppliers, etc.)?

2.8 Is disciplinary action sufficiently taken and communicated in the case of violations?

2.9 Is management override of controls appropriate when it occurs, and sufficiently authorised, documented and explained?

2.10 Are there job descriptions (which adequately define key managers' responsibilities) and performance appraisals with follow-up action to remedy deficiencies?

2.11 Is management and staff turnover reasonable, i.e. not excessive?

2.12 Are staffing levels adequate but not excessive?

2.13 Do staff recruitment procedures sufficiently enhance the enterprise's commitment to high standards of integrity, ethics and competence?

2.14 Do training programmes sufficiently enhance the enterprise's commitment to high standards of integrity, ethics and competence?

2.15 Do sufficient lines of communication exist to obviate the temptation of "whistleblowing"?

When examining questions from both the key issues and the detailed issues you should consider how, as an auditor, you would go about answering them. Additionally, you should also apply some thought as to what sort of controls and measures need to be in place to adequately address the inherent risks.

FRAUD

Fraud is an intentional, deceitful act for gain with concealment. As such, it is more than theft. Defalcation is theft by a person in a position of trust. Fraud may be perpetrated by one person working on his or her own, but many frauds are able to occur only as a result of collusion—between collateral associates working in different positions within the business, between a manager and someone reporting to that manager, or between an insider and an outsider. There may be mass collusion, for instance, between many salespeople and many customers, even to the extent that the fraud tacitly may have become regarded as a regular perk.

It is frequently because of the collusion characteristic that fraud is so difficult to prevent and detect since effective systems of internal control often become ineffective when collusion circumvents the segregation features of a control system. This illustrates that an effective system of internal control requires much more than a good set of control activities such as segregation of duties—it also always requires the other components of internal control as the COSO report called them: control environment, risk assessment, information and communication, and monitoring.

We may classify fraud as:

- management fraud, for instance fraudulent financial reporting
- employee fraud
- outsider fraud
- collusive fraud.

Some fraud, especially computer program frauds, may be continuous, working for the defrauder indefinitely into the future. Some continuous frauds require no further direct action by the defrauder once they have been set up, as they continue working automatically. Some continuous frauds require constant maintenance by the defrauder, such as teeming and lading frauds. Other frauds are not continuous but have a "smash and grab" character with the defrauder absconding with the gains in a carefully timed way just before the perhaps inevitable detection.

One important deterrent for fraud is for the business to have a good record of detecting fraud. If a prospective defrauder knows there is a high risk of detection and that the consequences upon detection will not be pleasant, then that person will be less likely to engage in the fraud. Given a personal need, an opportunity to perpetrate a fraud and a conviction that detection is most unlikely or that the consequences upon detection would not be too disgraceful, then many ordinary people will be sorely tempted to engage in fraud. It is up to management to make sure that these ingredients are not present in their business.

Difficult though it is to achieve, the most effective antidote to fraud is a strong system of internal control in all its component parts. Of course, good internal control also reduces the risk of accidental error or loss. Both fraud and accidental errors and losses share the characteristic of occurring in part due to a breakdown in the system of internal control.

8

Reviewing Internal Control over Financial Reporting—The Sarbanes-Oxley Approach

"There is a delicious irony in this which illustrates the unintended consequences of regulation. Sarbanes-Oxley has provided a bonanza for accountants and auditors, the very professions thought to be at fault in the original scandals."

Tony Blair, UK Prime Minister, 26 May 2005, speech on the compensation culture delivered at the Institute of Public Policy Research, University College, London.[1]

INTRODUCTION

Of the 67 sections within the US Sarbanes-Oxley Act of 2002, it is the approach to implementing s. 404 (Management assessment of internal controls) that is the main focus of this chapter (Figure 8.1). Section 404 requires management of US quoted companies to establish, maintain, assess and certify to an adequate internal control structure for financial reporting. It also requires the company's external auditors to attest to, and report on, management's assessment. Since 2002 the approach to assessing the business process of internal control over financial reporting has been articulated in particular by the SEC and those with oversight of auditing, and this Handbook would be deficient without a detailed consideration of the resultant methodology. By extension, the methodology also can be applied to the audit of other business processes.

We shall also be referring to s. 302 (Corporate responsibility for financial statements) which requires the signing officers of a published report to certify, *inter alia*, that they have designed and evaluated internal controls over reporting and that the report is reliable in all respects (Figure 8.2), not just with respect to internal controls over financial reporting but other disclosure controls as well. Section 302, at (6), also requires signing officers to certify in their companies' published reports

> **SECTION 404. MANAGEMENT ASSESSMENT OF INTERNAL CONTROLS**
>
> (a) RULES REQUIRED.—The Commission shall prescribe rules requiring each annual report required by section 13(a) or 15(d) of the Securities Exchange Act of 1934 (15 U.S.C. 78m, 78o(d)) to contain an internal control report, which shall—
>
> (1) state the responsibility of management for establishing and maintaining an adequate internal control structure and procedures for financial reporting; and
>
> (2) contain an assessment as of the end of the most recent fiscal year of the issuer, of the effectiveness of the internal control structure and procedures of the issuer for financial reporting.
>
> (b) INTERNAL CONTROL EVALUATION AND REPORTING.—With respect to the internal control assessment required by subsection (a), each registered public accounting firm that prepares or issues the audit report for the issuer shall attest to, and report on, the assessment made by the management of the issuer. An attestation made under this subsection shall be made in accordance with standards for attestation engagements issued or adopted by the Board. Any such attestation shall not be the subject of a separate engagement.

Figure 8.1 s. 404 of the Sarbanes-Oxley Act: management's assessment of internal control

that they have indicated whether or not there have been any significant changes in internal controls or in other factors that could significantly affect internal controls subsequent to the date of their evaluation, including any corrective actions with regard to significant deficiencies and material weaknesses.

Section 906 (Corporate responsibility for financial statements) is also relevant in that it introduces severe criminal sanctions for breaches of s. 302 and s. 404 up to a maximum of a $1 000 000 fine and imprisonment for not more than 10 years for *knowingly* breaching s. 302 or s. 404 or $5 000 000 and as much as 20 years' imprisonment for *wilful* breach (Figure 8.3).

Thus, the criminalisation of lapses in these aspects of corporate governance is now a significant risk. Companies incorporated and listed outside of the US are caught by the Sarbanes-Oxley Act if they have any secondary listing in the US. Executives based outside of the US could therefore find themselves subject to the criminal legal processes of the US. Overseas operating units of US listed companies must also observe the requirements arising from s. 302 and s. 404 unless they are so immaterial to the group results as to be outside the scope of the assessment to be done by the group.

Other sections of the Sarbanes-Oxley Act (ss 201, 206, 301, 303, 406 and 407) will also be explained in this chapter since they touch on certain attributes of a company's control environment and risk management that the Act requires to be in

SECTION 302. CORPORATE RESPONSIBILITY FOR FINANCIAL REPORTS

(a) REGULATIONS REQUIRED.—The Commission shall, by rule, require for each company filing periodic reports under section 13(a) or 15(d) of the Securities Exchange Act of 1934 (15 U.S.C. 78m, 78o(d)), that the principal executive officer or officers and the principal financial officer or officers, or persons performing similar functions, certify in each annual or quarterly report filed or submitted under either such section of such Act that—

(1) the signing officer has reviewed the report;

(2) based on the officer's knowledge, the report does not contain any untrue statement of a material fact or omit to state a material fact necessary in order to make the statements made, in light of the circumstances under which such statements were made, not misleading;

(3) based on such officer's knowledge, the financial statements, and other financial information included in the report, fairly present in all material respects the financial condition and results of operations of the issuer as of, and for, the period presented in the report;

(4) The signing officers—

(A) are responsible for establishing and maintaining internal controls;

(B) have designed such internal controls to ensure that material information relating to the issuer and its consolidated subsidiaries is made known to such officers by others within those entities, particularly during the period in which the periodic reports are being prepared;

(C) have evaluated the effectiveness of the issuer's internal controls as of a date within 90 days prior to the report; and

(D) have presented in the report their conclusions about the effectiveness of their internal controls based on their evaluation as of that date;

(5) the signing officers have disclosed to the issuer's auditors and the audit committee of the board of directors (or persons fulfilling the equivalent function)—

(A) all significant deficiencies in the design or operation of internal controls which could adversely affect the issuer's ability to record, process, summarize, and report financial data and have identified for the issuer's auditors any material weaknesses in internal controls; and

(B) any fraud, whether or not material, that involves management or other employees who have a significant role in the issuer's internal controls; and

(6) the signing officers have indicated in the report whether or not there are any significant changes in internal controls or in other factors that could significantly affect internal controls subsequent to the date of their evaluation, including any corrective actions with regard to significant deficiencies and material weaknesses.

Figure 8.2 s. 302 of the Sarbanes-Oxley Act: corporate responsibility for financial reports

> **SECTION 906. CORPORATE RESPONSIBILITY FOR FINANCIAL REPORTS.**
>
> (a) IN GENERAL.—Chapter 63 of title 18, United States Code, is amended by inserting after section 1349, as created by this Act, the following:
>
> "§ 1350. Failure of corporate officers to certify financial reports
>
> (a) CERTIFICATION OF PERIODIC FINANCIAL REPORTS.—Each periodic report containing financial statements filed by an issuer with the Securities Exchange Commission pursuant to section 13(a) or 15(d) of the Securities Exchange Act of 1934 (15 U.S.C. 78m(a) or 78o(d)) shall be accompanied by a written statement by the chief executive officer and chief financial officer (or equivalent thereof) of the issuer.
>
> "(b) CONTENT.—The statement required under subsection (a) shall certify that the periodic report containing the financial statements fully complies with the requirements of section 13(a) or 15(d) of the Securities Exchange Act of 1934 (15 U.S.C. 78m or 78o(d)) and that information contained in the periodic report fairly presents, in all material respects, the financial condition and results of operations of the issuer.
>
> "(c) CRIMINAL PENALTIES.—Whoever—
>
> > "(1) certifies any statement as set forth in subsections (a) and (b) of this section knowing that the periodic report accompanying the statement does not comport with all the requirements set forth in this section shall be fined not more than $1,000,000 or imprisoned not more than 10 years, or both; or
> >
> > "(2) Willfully certifies any statement as set forth in subsections (a) and (b) of this section knowing that the periodic report accompanying the statement does not comport with all the requirements set forth in this section shall be fined not more than $5,000,000, or imprisoned not more than 20 years, or both.
> >
> > ..."

Figure 8.3 s. 906 of the Sarbanes-Oxley Act: Criminal sanctions

place, and which thus have to be assessed in coming to a conclusion on the adequacy of internal control over financial reporting and over other published disclosures.

Other countries, including Canada,[2] Japan[3] and France[4] have moved towards their own SOX approach, with varying degrees of resolution, in some cases targeted more towards regulated financial institutions.

COSTS AND BENEFITS

There has been considerable concern about the added costs to companies of complying with s. 404. These costs have been relatively evenly spread between internal costs to position management to be able to attest to the effectiveness of internal control over financial reporting, external costs to supplement these internal resources, and additional audit fees. Since the introduction of s. 404 the external audit has been described as "the triple audit"—(a) the traditional audit of the financial statements, (b) the audit by the external auditor of internal control over financial reporting, and (c) the auditor's attestation of management's assessment of and certification to the effectiveness of internal control over financial reporting. The Sarbanes-Oxley Act requires that it is the external auditor of the company, rather than another firm of public accountants, who must undertake the s. 404 audit work.

To some extent the costs have been reducing as "first time through" costs have washed through, and now as a result of SOX-Lite (see below). FEI[5] has undertaken annual surveys of this. Their fourth survey of 2007/8 year ends polled 185 companies with average annual revenues of $4.7 billion. They found that companies that were accelerated filers required an average of 11 100 people hours internally to comply with s. 404 in 2007, a decrease of 8.6% from the previous year. In addition they retained an average of 1244 outside people hours to support management's obligations under s. 404, a decrease of 13.7%. 23.7% ($846 000) of external auditor fees were down to s. 404 audit work—a decrease of 5.4% from the previous year.

It is imperative that companies seek to obtain as much benefit as possible from complying with this statutory requirement. The FEI 2007 survey found that only approximately half of companies considered the s. 404 process had made financial reports more accurate and reliable and that compliance with s. 404 has helped to prevent or detect fraud, although more (69%) acknowledged that investors had more confidence in their financial reports. However, an institute of Internal Auditors survey of 171 chief audit executives found that 72% considered the costs of s. 404 compliance exceeded or greatly exceeded the benefits.[6]

The original SEC rule setting out how companies should approach compliance and PCAOB[7] Auditing Standard No. 2 arguably went further than the legislators had intended. This led to many companies listing in, for instance, London or Hong Kong rather than in the US. Other companies, especially overseas registrants, withdrew from the US market. Following their withdrawal British Airways' 2007 annual report showed that their external auditing costs reduced from £4.3m to £3m and costs for "other services pursuant to legislation" primarily being Sarbanes-Oxley s. 404 work reduced from £1.27m to £57 000.

2007 SOX-LITE

In response, in 2007 the SEC[8] and PCAOB[9] introduced amended guidance[10] respectively to management and to external auditors in the form of what has become known as SOX-Lite. The Sarbanes-Oxley Act itself remains unchanged from its introduction in 2002. PCAOB missed an opportunity to abandon their requirement that external auditors undertake their own audit of internal control over financial reporting which is not specifically demanded by s. 404 and which represents the most significant proportion of the external audit costs resulting from s. 404 implementation.[11]

REVISED DEFINITIONS OF "SIGNIFICANT DEFICIENCY" AND "MATERIAL WEAKNESS"

Section 302 (above) requires the company's signing officers to state in their public reports that they have disclosed to the external auditors and to the audit committee "significant deficiencies" and that they have identified for the issuer's auditors any "material weaknesses in internal controls"; and they must indicate in their public reports "any corrective actions with regard to significant deficiencies and material weaknesses". How these terms are defined therefore impacts upon the burden of complying with s. 404. From 2007 the definitions have been relaxed, as indicated in Figure 8.4:

Significant deficiency—PCAOB Auditing Standard No. 2 (2004)
A control deficiency (or a combination of internal control deficiencies) should be classified as a significant deficiency if, by itself or in combination with other control deficiencies, it results in more than a remote likelihood of a misstatement of the company's annual or interim financial statements that is more than inconsequential will not be prevented or detected.

Significant deficiency—PCAOB Auditing Standard No. 5 (2007)
A significant deficiency is a deficiency, or a combination of deficiencies, in internal control over financial reporting that is less severe than a material weakness, yet important enough to merit attention by those responsible for oversight of the company's financial reporting.

Material weakness—PCAOB Auditing Standard No. 5 (2007)
A significant deficiency should be classified as a material weakness if, by itself or in combination with other control deficiencies, it results in more than a remote likelihood that a material misstatement in the company's annual or interim financial statements will not be prevented or detected.

Material weakness—PCAOB Auditing Standard No. 5 (2007)
A material weakness is a deficiency, or a combination of deficiencies, in internal control over financial reporting, such that there is a reasonable possibility that a material misstatement of the company's annual or interim financial statements will not be prevented or detected on a timely basis... A material weakness in internal control over financial reporting may exist even when financial statements are not materially misstated.

PCAOB Auditing Standard No. 5 (2007) also defines "significant misstatement" as "a misstatement that is less than material yet important enough to merit attention by those responsible for oversight of the company's financial reporting."

Figure 8.4 Definitions of "significant deficiency", "material weakness" and "significant misstatement"

Relaxing these definitions is helpful in moderating the level of detail to which s. 404 work has to be done. It is also helpful that it makes it less likely that companies will have to report that they "failed" the s. 404 scrutiny. It has been shown that reporting failure depresses share price by some 4% within 60 days.[12] Intriguingly, it has also been observed that while the mean failure rate has been 6% for companies audited by a "Big-4" firm, the failure rates of clients of one of these firms is only 3% while the failure rate of clients of another is 9%.[13]

USING A RECOGNISED INTERNAL CONTROL FRAMEWORK FOR THE ASSESSMENT

Resulting from the SEC's final rule, the US Securities Exchange Act of 1934 has been amended to require management to base their evaluation of the issuer's internal control over financial reporting upon a suitable, recognised control framework that has been established by a body or group that has followed due-process procedures, including the broad distribution of the framework for public comment.[14] This is different from conventional internal auditing for which there is no obligation to use an external framework.[15]

The SEC gives *Internal Control—Integrated Framework* (1992) created by the Committee of Sponsoring Organizations of the Treadway Commission ("COSO") as an example of a suitable framework for s. 404 purposes (see Chapter 6). They also cited the *Guidance on Control* published by the Canadian Institute of Chartered Accountants ("CoCo"—see Chapters 6 and 10) and the report published by the Institute of Chartered Accountants in England & Wales *Internal Control: Guidance for Directors on the Combined Code* (known as the Turnbull Report—see Chapter 6) as examples of other suitable frameworks that issuers could choose in evaluating the effectiveness of their internal control over financial reporting.

The SEC draws attention to the fact that both the COSO framework and the Turnbull Report state that determining whether a system of internal control is effective is a subjective judgement resulting from an assessment of whether the five components (that is, control environment, risk assessment, control activities, monitoring, and information and communication) are present and functioning effectively. The SEC points out that although CoCo states that an assessment of effectiveness should be made against 20 specific criteria, CoCo acknowledges that the criteria can be regrouped into different structures, and that CoCo's *Guidance on Control* includes a table showing how the criteria can be regrouped into the five-component structure of COSO.[16]

The SEC encouraged companies to examine and select a framework that may be useful in their own circumstances. The SEC also encouraged the further development of existing and alternative frameworks.[16] Certainly, COSO's *Enterprise Risk Management—Integrated Framework* (2004) would be an acceptable framework to use since it incorporates all of COSO's internal control framework while going further (see Chapter 5).

Most companies complying with s. 302 and s. 404 of the Act use the COSO (1992) framework, since this is a US statutory obligation and the COSO (1992) framework, while globally authoritative, is the accepted US framework. The UK Turnbull framework is very close to the COSO (1992) framework.

An important point to note is that the whole framework must be applied to the assessment that management and the external auditors make under s. 404. In Chapter 6 we considered COSO's the five essential components of internal control. One of those components is "Control activities" (or control procedures). This component will feature most prominently in the s. 404 assessments that management and external auditors perform. Often overlooked is that the other internal control components must also be within the assessment—the control environment, information and communication, risk assessment and monitoring. We consider each of these five components of internal control in turn in the context of s. 302 and s. 404 compliance. We do not repeat what we covered in Chapters 5 (Risk Management) and 6 (Internal Control) which provide detailed, relevant guidance applicable to s. 302 and s. 404 compliance. Here we restrict ourselves to (a) focusing what the Sarbanes-Oxley Act itself stresses with respect to the components of internal control, and explaining the methodology that has developed for complying with s. 302 and s. 404 consequent upon the SEC rule and PCAOB Auditing Standard No. 5.

The "Control Environment" Component of Control in SOX Compliance

Chapters 6 and 7 cover general control environment issues. Elements of the control environment stressed in the Sarbanes-Oxley Act relate to the duties, independence and competence of companies' audit committees and the ethics of companies' senior financial officers. These matters should certainly be formally considered by management and external auditors as part of their s. 302 and s. 404 work. The consideration by management should be documented and reported to the board and to the audit committee. External auditors should draw any concerns to the attention of the board and its audit committee.

Section 301 of the Act (Figure 8.5) makes an audit committee a statutory listing requirement and sets out other statutory requirements for audit committees. These include, but are not limited to, giving the audit committee direct responsibility for the appointment, compensation and oversight of the external auditor, unlike the UK position.[17] Section 301 also establishes a statutory independence definition for audit committee members, including that they must receive no fees from the company other than for their board service[18] and must not be an "affiliated person"[19] of the issuer or any subsidiary.

Section 407 (Figure 8.6) requires disclosure, with reasons, if the company does not have a financial expert as a member of the audit committee. The SEC's Final Rule[20] has defined an audit committee financial expert as a person with all of the five following attributes:

1. An understanding of generally accepted accounting principles and financial statements;
2. The ability to assess the general application of such principles in connection with the accounting for estimates, accruals and reserves;

TITLE III—CORPORATE RESPONSIBILITY

SECTION 301. PUBLIC COMPANY AUDIT COMMITTEES.

Section 10A of the Securities Exchange Act of 1934 (15 U.S.C. 78f) is amended by adding at the end the following:

"(m) STANDARDS RELATING TO AUDIT COMMITTEES.— "(1) COMMISSION RULES. — H. R. 3763—32

"(A) IN GENERAL.—Effective not later than 270 days after the date of enactment of this subsection, the Commission shall, by rule, direct the national securities exchanges and national securities associations to prohibit the listing of any security of an issuer that is not in compliance with the requirements of any portion of paragraphs (2) through (6).

"(B) OPPORTUNITY TO CURE DEFECTS.—The rules of the Commission under subparagraph (A) shall provide for appropriate procedures for an issuer to have an opportunity to cure any defects that would be the basis for a prohibition under subparagraph (A), before the imposition of such prohibition.

"(2) RESPONSIBILITIES RELATING TO REGISTERED PUBLIC ACCOUNTING FIRMS.—The audit committee of each issuer, in its capacity as a committee of the board of directors, shall be directly responsible for the appointment, compensation, and oversight of the work of any registered public accounting firm employed by that issuer (including resolution of disagreements between management and the auditor regarding financial reporting) for the purpose of preparing or issuing an audit report or related work, and each such registered public accounting firm shall report directly to the audit committee.

"(3) INDEPENDENCE.—

"(A) IN GENERAL.—Each member of the audit committee of the issuer shall be a member of the board of directors of the issuer, and shall otherwise be independent.

"(B) CRITERIA.—In order to be considered to be independent for purposes of this paragraph, a member of an audit committee of an issuer may not, other than in his or her capacity as a member of the audit committee, the board of directors, or any other board committee—

"(i) accept any consulting, advisory, or other compensatory fee from the issuer; or

"(ii) be an affiliated person of the issuer or any subsidiary thereof.

"(C) EXEMPTION AUTHORITY.—The Commission may exempt from the requirements of subparagraph (B) a particular relationship with respect to audit committee members, as the Commission determines appropriate in light of the circumstances.

Figure 8.5 (*continued*)

> **"(4) COMPLAINTS.**—Each audit committee shall establish procedures for—
>
> **"(A)** the receipt, retention, and treatment of complaints received by the issuer regarding accounting, internal accounting controls, or auditing matters; and
>
> **"(B)** the confidential, anonymous submission by employees of the issuer of concerns regarding questionable accounting or auditing matters.
>
> **"(5) AUTHORITY TO ENGAGE ADVISERS.**—Each audit committee shall have the authority to engage independent counsel and other advisers, as it determines necessary to carry out its duties.
>
> **"(6) FUNDING.**—Each issuer shall provide for appropriate funding, as determined by the audit committee, in its capacity as a committee of the board of directors, for payment of compensation—
>
> **"(A)** to the registered public accounting firm employed by the issuer for the purpose of rendering or issuing an audit report; and
>
> **"(B)** to any advisers employed by the audit committee under paragraph (5)."

Figure 8.5 s. 301 of the Sarbanes-Oxley Act: audit committees

3. Experience preparing, auditing, analyzing or evaluating financial statements that present a breadth and level of complexity of accounting issues that are generally comparable to the breadth and complexity of issues that can reasonably be expected to be raised by the registrant's financial statements, or experience actively supervising one or more persons engaged in such activities;
4. An understanding of internal controls and procedures for financial reporting; and
5. An understanding of audit committee functions.

Under the Final Rules, in order to qualify as an audit committee financial expert a person must have acquired the above listed attributes through any one or more of the following:

- Education and experience as a principal financial officer, principal accounting officer, controller, public accountant or auditor or experience in one or more positions that involve the performance of similar functions;
- Experience actively supervising a principal financial officer, principal accounting officer, controller, public accountant, auditor or person performing similar functions;
- Experience overseeing or assessing the performance of companies or public accountants with respect to the preparation, auditing or evaluation of financial statements; or
- Other relevant experience; and, if other relevant experience is what qualifies the director, that experience must be described.

> **SECTION 407. DISCLOSURE OF AUDIT COMMITTEE FINANCIAL EXPERT.**
>
> **(a) RULES DEFINING "FINANCIAL EXPERT".** — The Commission shall issue rules, as necessary or appropriate in the public interest and consistent with the protection of investors, to require each issuer, together with periodic reports required pursuant to sections 13(a) and 15(d) of the Securities Exchange Act of 1934, to disclose whether or not, and if not, the reasons therefor, the audit committee of that issuer is comprised of at least 1 member who is a financial expert, as such term is defined by the Commission.
>
> **(b) CONSIDERATIONS.** — In defining the term "financial expert" for purposes of subsection (a), the Commission shall consider whether a person has, through education and experience as a public accountant or auditor or a principal financial officer, comptroller, or principal accounting officer of an issuer, or from a position involving the performance of similar functions —
>
> (1) an understanding of generally accepted accounting principles and financial statements;
>
> (2) experience in —
>
> (A) the preparation or auditing of financial statements of generally comparable issuers; and
>
> (B) the application of such principles in connection with the accounting for estimates, accruals, and reserves;
>
> (3) experience with internal accounting controls; and
>
> (4) an understanding of audit committee functions.
>
> **(c) DEADLINE FOR RULEMAKING.** — The Commission shall —
>
> (1) propose rules to implement this section, not later than 90 days after the date of enactment of this Act; and
>
> (2) issue final rules to implement this section, not later than 180 days after that date of enactment

Figure 8.6 s. 407 of the Sarbanes-Oxley Act: audit committee's financial expert

Section 406 (Figure 8.7) requires a US issuer to disclose whether it has a Code of Ethics for its senior financial officers and, if not, why not. Any changes to the Code of Ethics must be disclosed. The Act requires that the Code cover honest and ethical conduct, including the ethical handling of actual or apparent conflicts of interest between personal and professional relationships; full, fair, accurate, timely, and understandable disclosure in the periodic reports required to be filed by the

> **SECTION 406. CODE OF ETHICS FOR SENIOR FINANCIAL OFFICERS**
>
> (a) CODE OF ETHICS DISCLOSURE. — The Commission shall issue rules to require each issuer, together with periodic reports required pursuant to section 13(a) or 15(d) of the Securities Exchange Act of 1934, to disclose whether or not, and if not, the reason therefor, such issuer has adopted a code of ethics for senior financial officers, applicable to its principal financial officer and comptroller or principal financial officer, or persons performing similar functions.
>
> (b) CHANGES IN CODES OF ETHICS. — The Commission shall revise its regulations concerning matters requiring prompt disclosure on Form 8-K (or any successor thereto) to require the immediate disclosure, by means of the filing of such form, dissemination by the Internet or by other electronic means, by any issuer of any change in or waiver of the code of ethics for senior financial officers.
>
> (c) DEFINITION. — In this section, the term "code of ethics" means such standards as are reasonably necessary to promote —
>
> (1) honest and ethical conduct, including the ethical handling of actual or apparent conflicts of interest between personal and professional relationships;
>
> (2) full, fair, accurate, timely, and understandable disclosure in the periodic reports required to be filed by the issuer;
>
> and
>
> (3) compliance with applicable governmental rules and regulations.
>
> (d) DEADLINE FOR RULEMAKING. — The Commission shall —
>
> (1) propose rules to implement this section, not later than 90 days after the date of enactment of this Act; and
>
> (2) issue final rules to implement this section, not later than 180 days after that date of enactment.

Figure 8.7 s. 406 of the Sarbanes-Oxley Act: code of ethics

issuer; and compliance with applicable governmental rules and regulations. The SEC in their Rule[20] has expanded the requirement to cover:

1. Honest and ethical conduct, including the ethical handling of actual or apparent conflicts of interest between personal and professional relationships;
2. Avoidance of conflicts of interest, including disclosure to an appropriate person or persons identified in the code of any material transaction or relationship that reasonably could be expected to give rise to such a conflict;

3. Full, fair, accurate, timely, and understandable disclosure in reports and documents that a company files with, or submits to, the Commission and in other public communications made by the company;
4. Compliance with applicable governmental laws, rules and regulations;
5. The prompt internal reporting to an appropriate person or persons identified in the code of violations of the code; and
6. Accountability for adherence to the code.

The SEC's rule further extends the intent of s. 406 to cover the principal executive officer of the company as well as the principal financial officer (etc.) and to require the company to make the Code available, which s. 406 did not specifically address:

We therefore are adopting rules that will allow companies to choose between three alternative methods of making their ethics codes publicly available. First, a company may file a copy of its code of ethics that applies to the registrant's principal executive officer, principal financial officer, principal accounting officer or controller, or persons performing similar functions and addresses the specified elements as an exhibit to its annual report. Alternatively, a company may post the text of its code of ethics, or relevant portion thereof, on its Internet website, provided however, that a company choosing this option also must disclose its Internet address and intention to provide disclosure in this manner in its annual report on Form 10-K, 10-KSB, 20-F or 40-F. As another alternative, a company may provide an undertaking in its annual report on one of these forms to provide a copy of its code of ethics to any person without charge upon request. [20]

The "Risk Assessment" Component of Control in SOX Compliance

Chapters 5 and 6 of this Handbook cover general risk assessment issues that should be applied as appropriate to s. 302 and s. 404 compliance. Elements of risk assessment stressed in the Sarbanes-Oxley Act relate to conflicts of interest, improper influence on the conduct of audits and avoidance of the provision of most non audit services by a company's external auditors. Section 301 of the Act (above) makes the audit committee of the board responsible for overseeing these risks. Applying the COSO internal control framework to a company's obligations under s. 302 and s. 404 means that management certifying under s. 302 and s. 404 must satisfy themselves that the audit committee has considered these and other risks and concluded that they are being addressed satisfactorily. The audit committee will expect to receive from management representations on these matters, but it will be inadequate for the audit committee to accept these representations on face value without probing more deeply. It is "the principal executive officer or officers and the principal financial officer or officers" who certify under s. 302, and so they must also satisfy themselves directly that these risks have been mitigated effectively, rather than merely relying on the audit committee to have done so.

To safeguard the independence of the external auditor, s. 206 (Figure 8.8) outlaws a firm continuing as the external auditor of a company that has recruited into one of a number of senior company positions a member of the audit firm who

> **SECTION 206. CONFLICTS OF INTEREST**
>
> Section 10A of the Securities Exchange Act of 1934 (15 U.S.C. 78j–1), as amended by this Act, is amended by adding at the end the following:
>
> "(l) CONFLICTS OF INTEREST.—It shall be unlawful for a registered public accounting firm to perform for an issuer any audit service required by this title, if a chief executive officer, controller, chief financial officer, chief accounting officer, or any person serving in an equivalent position for the issuer, was employed by that registered independent public accounting firm and participated in any capacity in the audit of that issuer during the 1-year period preceding the date of the initiation of the audit."

Figure 8.8 s. 206 of the Sarbanes-Oxley Act: recruiting from the audit firm

had been involved in the audit over the previous 12 months. Since companies are unlikely to be able to wait at least 12 months before filling such a vacancy, this effectively blocks recruitment into the company from the external audit team.

Section 303 (Figure 8.9) makes it an offence to put pressure on the external auditor which may result in materially misleading financial statements.

Section 201 (Figure 8.10) excludes the external auditor from undertaking most non audit services for their listed company audit clients, obligating the companies to ensure that this is observed. An exception is the provision of tax advice. Those non audit services not excluded by s. 201 must be approved by the audit committee on an item by item basis at any time in advance of the activity. The writing of comfort letters is regarded as an audit service not requiring audit committee approval. Non audit services must be specifically identified: a blanket general approval by the audit committee is prohibited. This pre-approval may be delegated to individual audit committee members subject to disclosure to the next audit committee meeting. There is no requirement to pre-approve fees, but a prudent audit committee would wish to know about these as they could impact the effective independence of the external auditor with respect to the audit. There is a *de minimus* exception in that if a service was not recognised as a non audit service at the time it was provided, then it may be approved by the audit committee retrospectively but only if (a) the aggregate amount of all such non audit services is less than 5% of the total paid to the firm in the financial year, (b) the company did not recognise the services as 'non audit services' at the time they were provided and (c) the services are brought to the attention of the audit committee promptly and before the completion of the audit. All approved non audit services performed by the external auditor must be disclosed to investors.

The "Control Activities" Component of Control in SOX Compliance

Most of the effort involved in meeting the requirements of s. 404, by both management and the external auditors, is focused on the controls built into processes

> **SECTION 303. IMPROPER INFLUENCE ON CONDUCT OF AUDITS**
>
> **(a) RULES TO PROHIBIT.**—It shall be unlawful, in contravention of such rules or regulations as the Commission shall prescribe as necessary and appropriate in the public interest or for the protection of investors, for any officer or director of an issuer, or any other person acting under the direction thereof, to take any action to fraudulently influence, coerce, manipulate, or mislead any independent public or certified accountant engaged in the performance of an audit of the financial statements of that issuer for the purpose of rendering such financial statements materially misleading.
>
> **(b) ENFORCEMENT.**—In any civil proceeding, the Commission shall have exclusive authority to enforce this section and any rule or regulation issued under this section.
>
> **(c) NO PREEMPTION OF OTHER LAW.**—The provisions of subsection (a) shall be in addition to, and shall not supersede or preempt, any other provision of law or any rule or regulation issued thereunder.
>
> **(d) DEADLINE FOR RULEMAKING.**—The Commission shall—
>
> (1) propose the rules or regulations required by this section, not later than 90 days after the date of enactment of this Act; and
>
> (2) issue final rules or regulations required by this section, not later than 270 days after that date of enactment.

Figure 8.9 s. 206 of the Sarbanes-Oxley Act: improperly influencing the external auditor

that contribute to the reliability of financial statements. A SOX methodology has developed which is a sound approach to be followed more generally in audit work.

In general terms the approach that may be followed is set out in Figure 8.11.

The scope of s. 404 is the assessment of internal control for financial reporting, leading to the CEO and CFO to be able to certify under s. 302 as to its effectiveness (etc.). The scope of s. 302 is broader in that it covers all forms of disclosures made in the annual report as the certification covers, *inter alia*, 'any untrue statement of material fact [in the published report]'.

It is usual to start from two points—"top-down" and "bottom-up". First, identify (a) the lines in the financial statements of the listed company that have the potential to be significantly misstated and also which could conceal significant fraud, and (b) any other "material facts" in the published report ("top-down"). Secondly, identify the critical business processes which may potentially impact the financial statements and "the material facts" significantly ("bottom-up"). With one qualification, all the accounting systems which could significantly impact these lines in the financial statements and "the material facts", or which account for these critical business

TITLE II—AUDITOR INDEPENDENCE SECTION 201. SERVICES OUTSIDE THE SCOPE OF PRACTICE OF AUDITORS.

(a) PROHIBITED ACTIVITIES.—Section 10A of the Securities Exchange Act of 1934 (15 U.S.C. 78j—1) is amended by adding at the end the following:

"(g) PROHIBITED ACTIVITIES.—Except as provided in subsection (h), it shall be unlawful for a registered public accounting firm (and any associated person of that firm, to the extent determined appropriate by the Commission) that performs for any issuer any audit required by this title or the rules of the Commission under this title or, beginning 180 days after the date of commencement of the operations of the Public Company Accounting Oversight Board established under section 101 of the Sarbanes-Oxley Act of 2002 (in this section referred to as the 'Board'), the rules of the Board, to provide to that issuer, contemporaneously with the audit, any non-audit service, including—

"(1) bookkeeping or other services related to the accounting records or financial statements of the audit client;

"(2) financial information systems design and implementation;

"(3) appraisal or valuation services, fairness opinions, or contribution-in-kind reports;

"(4) actuarial services;

"(5) internal audit outsourcing services;

"(6) management functions or human resources;

"(7) broker or dealer, investment adviser, or investment banking services;

"(8) legal services and expert services unrelated to the audit; and

"(9) any other service that the Board determines, by regulation, is impermissible.

"(h) PREAPPROVAL REQUIRED FOR NON-AUDIT SERVICES.—A registered public accounting firm may engage in any non-audit service, including tax services, that is not described in any of paragraphs (1) through (9) of subsection (g) for an audit client, only if the activity is approved in advance by the audit committee of the issuer, in accordance with subsection (i)."

(b) EXEMPTION AUTHORITY.—The Board may, on a case by case basis, exempt any person, issuer, public accounting firm, or transaction from the prohibition on the provision of services under section 10A(g) of the Securities Exchange Act of 1934 (as added by this section), to the extent that such exemption is necessary or appropriate in the public interest and is consistent with the protection of investors, and subject to review by the Commission in the same manner as for rules of the Board under section 107.

Figure 8.10 s. 201 of the Sarbanes-Oxley Act: prohibition of non audit services

1. Engage the board, management and other personnel in the ownership of internal control
2. Adopt and understand a recognised internal control framework.
3. Identify the objectives to be achieved.
4. Identify the "mission critical" business processes (the processes that are key to the achievement of objectives).
5. Consider standardising processes across all business units.
6. Learn about each key process, documenting it in narrative, spreadsheet and/or flowchart form.
7. Within a key process, identify and document the key controls.
8. Judge the potential of each key control to be effective, if followed as intended. Modify the control approach if necessary.
9. Design and document tests to be conducted to assess compliance with each control.
10. Conduct these tests.
11. Interpret the results of these tests; where necessary ensure better compliance or modify the control approach if satisfactory compliance is judged impractical.
12. Interpret the control significance of unwanted outcomes that have occurred.
13. Conclude on the effectiveness of internal control at the process level
14. Draw overall conclusions

Figure 8.11 Assessing the effectiveness of internal control

processes, are "in-scope" for s. 404 assessment. The exception would be any part of the business which could be judged immaterial to the group results and therefore out-of-scope for s. 302 and s. 404 assessment. Care needs to be taken not to be beguiled into inappropriate complacency, as Figure 8.12 challenges. There is therefore a risk of defining the scope of s. 302 and s. 404 assessments too narrowly. If we add to this the desirability to ensure the company benefits to the maximum from their SOX work, it is unlikely to be in the best interests of the company to define the work as narrowly as possible while still operating within the law.

Having identified the processes, operational as well as accounting, that are in-scope, the next step is to learn about those processes and document them. Styles of documentation used vary between narrative write-ups, process maps (flowcharts) and control registers (usually spreadsheet-based). The flowcharting conventions used would have special symbols to denote controls which are critical for s. 302 and s. 404

1. Might it be possible for a major error or malpractice to impact significantly on a line in the financial statements which has been assessed as being immaterial?	If so, the processes that contribute to the make-up of this line in the financial statements must be in-scope for s. 404 purposes.
2. Could a very small operating unit's conduct, unknown at group level, significantly impact group results?	If so, those processes within this small operating unit that could impact significantly on the group results must be in-scope for s. 404 purposes.
3. Does the operation of certain physical controls impact on the reliability of accounting data, or on the disclosure of material facts in the published report?	If so, these physical controls must be 'in-scope' for s. 404 purposes. An example of such a physical control might be a gauge that monitors leakage from an oil pipeline, or a mole that inspects for internal corrosion of an oil pipeline.

Figure 8.12 The risk of defining the scope of s. 302 and s. 404 assessment too narrowly

purposes. A control register for a business process might have columns to specify the following, with a row for each key SOX control:

- Control numeric code
- SOX control number (if different)
- Sub-process
- The objective of the control
- How it may impact the financial statement (line and whether completeness, valuation, existence or occurrence, etc.)
- Financial statement risk
- Description of the control
- Control type (preventative, detective, corrective etc—see Chapter 6)
- Control category (system access, procedural, authorisation, etc.)
- Transaction type (e.g. routine, period end, etc.)
- Frequency of operation of the control
- Control operator
- Control owner.

It is conventional to conduct a walkthrough test to confirm one's understanding of the process flow and the design of the controls, to verify the completeness of the control documentation, and to facilitate the identification of the controls which are key to the s. 302 and s. 404 assessment. A walkthrough test is likely to be from cradle to grave, with just one transaction. It is not an alternative to the more detailed testing we describe later.

Having learnt about, and having documented, the SOX processes judgement must now be applied to conclude whether these processes are under effective control—on the assumption that the key controls are operating as intended. The process may need to be amended in order to improve the effectiveness of internal control over reporting. In practice, one of the challenges is likely to be that the control documentation is insufficiently precise or detailed to indicate whether a control has the potential to be effective if it is operating as intended, and it may be ambiguous as to whether this is because the control has been described carelessly and incompletely, or whether the control really is a weak control. Staff recording systems of control will need training to do so effectively.

At this point, tests of controls to be conducted should be designed and the nature of these tests documented. The documentation of the tests to be performed is sometimes termed "test scripts". A test script would include:

- Sub-process
- Control objectives
- Financial statement risk
- Actual control number and description
- Test designer and date
- Sample size and selection test description
- Documentation required by the test.

The extent of testing needed is a matter of judgement, though guidance to management along these lines has emerged from audit firms. If the control operates with the frequency shown in Figure 8.13, take the number of periods indicated in the sample size column; then take a sample from each period of the size indicated in Figure 8.14 depending on the total size of the population to be tested in that period.

Questions the auditor should ask management and staff are:

- What do management and staff do if they find an error?
- How do they determine if there is one?
- Have they found any, and what happened?
- Have they been asked to override processes, and why? What happened?

Frequency of control	Sample size
Annually	1
Quarterly	2
Monthly	2
Weekly	5
Daily	20
Multiple times a day	25

Figure 8.13 Frequency of the control

Population size	Sample size
1—3	1
4—11	2
12—50	3
51—100	5
101—200	15
201—300	20
Above 300	25 max

Figure 8.14 Sample size to be tested

It will be apparent that the Sarbanes-Oxley Act incentivises companies with international operations to standardise their systems across the world. Otherwise the burden becomes much more complex of identifying in-scope key processes, documenting them, considering the adequacy of key controls and strengthening them if necessary, designing test scripts, conducting tests, documenting the results of tests and concluding on control effectiveness and reporting the results. US and German parents, for example, may find this easier than UK parent companies as the former have tended to impose standard systems of control across their operations worldwide. The UK approach has often been to hold dispersed operating units to account for bottom-line performance, but to give them more latitude as to how they produce acceptable results. Arguably it is unfortunate that a US statute skews the management approach of multinationals.

Companies caught by the Sarbanes-Oxley Act have complained that it tends to lead to less flexibility in modifying business processes as the potential impact upon internal control over financial reporting and other disclosures of any proposed changes has to be carefully assessed before the changes are made. Clearly this has advantages but can lead to excessive bureaucracy and a propensity not to change processes even when they need to be amended. It is important to consider changes in a timely way, when possible not leaving things to the last minute, and to build into the change process a Sarbanes-Oxley impact assessment as a matter of routine at an early stage.

The "Information and Communication" Component of Control in SOX Compliance

The purpose of s. 302 and s. 404 compliance work is to assess the reliability of financial and other information that is published. So far in this chapter we have placed most emphasis on control activities (key control procedures) as means of ensuring this. It is possible that not everything of relevance will be identified and assessed by reference to the control environment, risk assessment and control activities components of internal control. Some time should be spent considering the quality of information used by management and the board and which is the basis of published information. It should not only be accurate and complete, it should be timely, clear, mutually consistent and useful as well.

The "Monitoring" Component of Control in SOX

The theme of this chapter has been the assessment of internal control over financial and other public reporting. This fits into the "monitoring" component of COSO's and Turnbull's internal control frameworks. This monitoring can be done by a number of parties. Internal audit is often tasked with setting up the s. 302 and s. 404 assessment processes which fall within the remit of management. In one multinational oil company, of 250 internal auditors in total, 70 were given this task. Resources were also bought in from outside to supplement this internal resource. The medium to long-term intention should be to transfer most of the s. 302 and s. 404 work "into the line", making it an ongoing responsibility of line management and staff. The internal audit role can then be to assure senior management and the audit committee of the board that s. 302 and s. 404 compliance work is being done satisfactorily, rather than for internal audit to perform that work themselves. On an ongoing basis it would be an unacceptable overhead to do otherwise, even allowing for the amelioration of resources required after the set-up stage of s. 302 and s. 404 compliance. There is also the issue of internal audit independence in that providing assurance about the adequacy and effectiveness of the SOX process is important but cannot be done well by internal audit if internal audit is charged with the responsibility of undertaking the SOX process. The Institute of Internal Auditors' Standard 1130.A2 states:

Assurance engagements for functions over which the chief audit executive has responsibility must be overseen by a party outside the internal audit activity.

PCAOB Standard No. 5 requires the external auditor to evaluate the extent to which he or she will use the work of others, such as internal auditors, to reduce the work the auditor might otherwise perform himself or herself to meet the audit requirements of s. 404. The Standard explains that the degree of competence and objectivity of the other party has to be assessed to determine the extent the auditor may use their work. In practice, the company should set out to achieve a maximum amount of coordination between internal and external auditors with respect to s. 404. The external auditor is likely to be able to place more reliance on internal audit if internal audit is auditing the SOX process rather than performing the process of designing, documenting and testing the control processes. On the other hand there is a greater risk that the SOX process will not be done so diligently if it is a line responsibility of management and staff.

The Institute of Internal Auditors has published useful guidance to management on complying with their requirements under s. 404.[21]

RISK AND CONTROL ISSUES FOR THE SARBANES-OXLEY S. 302 AND S. 404 COMPLIANCE PROCESS

Control Objectives for the Sarbanes-Oxley s. 302 and s. 404 Compliance Process

(a) To achieve ongoing compliance with s. 302 and s. 404 and associated sections of the Act.

(b) To secure and maintain a reputation with investors and others for exemplary Sarbanes-Oxley performance.

(c) To ensure that the company maximises the benefit arising from s. 302 and s. 404 work.

(d) To control the costs of s. 302 and s. 404 compliance.

1 Key Issues

1.1 Has the company defined and implemented a programme for SOX compliance?

1.2 Is the SOX programme embedded into the business as a managerial responsibility, or is it reliant on internal audit and/or bought-in resources to achieve?

1.3 How has it been ensured that management and staff understand the meaning of internal control?

1.4 Have the processes relevant to the SOX programme been documented, with the key SOX controls highlighted and described?

1.5 Has the company scripted the tests to be conducted of key SOX controls?

1.6 Is the level and nature of testing sufficient to allow reliable conclusions to be drawn about the effectiveness of internal control over financial and other reporting?

1.7 Do identified "material weaknesses" and "significant deficiencies" indicate an unacceptable lack of priority being placed upon effective internal control?

1.8 Are identified "material weaknesses" and "significant deficiencies" remedied in a timely way, and usually before the publication of the annual report?

1.9 How does the company ensure that management does not override controls?

1.10 Does the company have a code of ethics for the chief executive officer and senior financial and accounting officers, and how does the company ensure it is appropriate and applied?

1.11 Does the chief audit executive provide assurance to senior management and to the audit committee of the board as to the effectiveness of the SOX process?

1.12 Does the audit committee of the board diligently oversee the external audit process, including the independence of the external audit firm and their provision of any nonaudit services?

1.13 Does the audit committee possess appropriate financial expertise?

1.14 Does the company coordinate well with the external auditor in the SOX process?

2 Detailed Issues

2.1 Are the company costs of the SOX programme (a) monitored, (b) justified and (c) trending downwards?

2.2 Are the external audit costs of the SOX programme (a) monitored, (b) justified and (c) trending downwards?

2.3 Does the company benchmark their SOX programme against other companies?

2.4 Has the SOX programme resulted in improved internal control processes?

2.5 Is the scope of the SOX programme appropriate in that all the financial statement lines, business units and business processes are in-scope that could result in "material weaknesses" and "significant deficiencies" in public reporting?

2.6 Is a recognised internal control framework applied and does it include an assessment of all of the components of internal control, not just "control activities"?

2.7 Why did the company choose the internal control framework it uses for the SOX process?

2.8 Is there a control register which sufficiently describes the key SOX controls, and is it kept up to date?

2.9 Is the certification by the CEO and CFO supported by timely certifications from all the relevant lower levels of the company?

2.10 Is the consolidation of SOX work across the company done effectively to support the CEO's and CFO's overall certifications?

2.11 Is the company standardising its SOX processes across the business in all locations, to the extent appropriate?

2.12 Is there a SOX review of intended changes to business processes before their introduction?

2.13 Are key SOX controls documented clearly so that the nature and quality of these controls can be discerned from the documentation?

2.14 Are the results of testing clearly recorded and retained?

2.15 Have any restatements of prior year results meant that the CEO's and CFO's certification for the year in question was erroneous and, if so, were appropriate lessons learnt and approaches modified?

NOTES

1. http://www.number10.gov.uk/output/Page7562.asp.
2. Bill 198 (2003), Ontario, known as "CSOX".
3. The Financial Instruments and Exchange Law (*Kin'yūshōhin torihiki-hō*), 14 June 2006, known as J-SOX.
4. Loi de sécurité financière, 2003.
5. Financial Executives International, www.financialexecutives.org.
6. The Institute of Internal Auditors Inc. (2005) *Sarbanes-Oxley Section 404 Work: Looking at the Benefits*. The IIA's Research Foundation.

7. Public Companies Accounting Oversight Board (PCAOB), set up as a consequence of s. 101 of the Sarbanes-Oxley Act to oversee the audit of US public companies.
8. Securities and Exchange Commission: 17 CFR Parts 210, 228, 229 and 240, Release Nos 33-8809; 34-55928; FR-76; File No. S7-24-06, RIN 3235-AJ58: *Amendments to Rules Regarding Management's Report on Internal Control Over Financial Reporting*: Final rule; and 17 CFR Part 241, Release Nos 33-8810; 34-55929; FR-77; File No. S7-24-06: *Commission Guidance Regarding Management's Report on Internal Control Over Financial Reporting Under Section 13(a) or 15(d) of the Securities Exchange Act of 1934*: Interpretation.
9. Public Companies Accounting Oversight Board (PCAOB), (2007), Auditing Standard No. 5: An Audit of internal control over financial reporting that is integrated with an audit of financial statements, www.pcaobus.org/.
10. The SEC acknowledges that there are many different ways to conduct an evaluation of the effectiveness of internal control over financial reporting to meet the requirements. They say that an evaluation conducted in accordance with the interpretive guidance issued by the Commission in Release No. 34-55929 will satisfy the requirements.
11. The wording of s. 404 is that a company's external auditors should attest and report on management's assessment of internal control over financial reporting, not that the external auditors should undertake their own assessment of the effectiveness of internal control over financial reporting. However, it is the former that has been formally abandoned, namely their attest and report on management's assessment of internal control over financial reporting. It is impossible to escape the conclusion that PCAOB has tinkered with the auditor's obligations under s. 404(b), making only a cosmetic change here whereas they might have interpreted the Act as enabling the abandonment of their own separate audit of internal control. We cannot therefore expect external audit costs to reduce significantly since what has been abandoned was not an onerous task for the external auditors in view of the fact that they had been undertaking their own assessment of the effectiveness of internal control over financial reporting.

The Institute of Chartered Accountants in England & Wales (ICAEW) concurs that PCAOB has misinterpreted s. 404. In their response to the SEC on proposed PCAOB Auditing Standard No. 5, ICAEW wrote:

> Section 404(a) of the Sarbanes-Oxley Act places a clear responsibility on management to assess and report on internal control over financial reporting. Section 404(b) states, in respect of the internal control assessment required of management under section 404(a), that the auditor '.... shall attest to, and report on, the assessment made by the management of the issuer.' The wording of the Act does not require an audit of internal control over financial reporting.
>
> Whilst we respect the SEC's and the PCAOB's intended clarification of section 404(b)—in conjunction with section 103(a)(2)(A)(iii)—so that the wording in the Act is now interpreted to mean 'the audit of internal control', we remain of the view that: there has never been any public justification offered by the SEC or the PCAOB of why the attestation required by the Sarbanes-Oxley Act should take the form of an audit; and of the two opinions required by AS 2, the wrong opinion has been eliminated.
>
> The choice of the auditors' opinion required by AS 5 will result in more testing and higher costs than would have been the case if the opinion on management's assessment had been retained and the current opinion had been removed. Such outcomes must be of concern to US authorities as they seek to enhance the effectiveness and reduce the costs of section 404 and to maintain the competitiveness of US capital markets"

[ICAEW's response to File No. PCAOB-2—7-02: Proposed Auditing Standard on an Audit of Internal Control over Financial Reporting that is integrated with an Audit of Financial Statements (12 July 2007), letter addressed to Nancy M. Morris, Secretary, SEC].

PCAOB explains their Auditing Standard No. 5's rationale for retaining the audit of internal control, and abandoning their attest and report on management's assessment of internal control over financial reporting in the following terms [SECURITIES AND EXCHANGE COMMISSION, (Release No. 34-55876; File No. PCAOB-2007-02) (June 7, 2007): Public Company Accounting Oversight Board; Notice of Filing of Proposed Rule on Auditing Standard No. 5, An Audit of Internal Control Over Financial Reporting That is Integrated with an Audit of Financial Statements, and Related Independence Rule and Conforming Amendments]:

> Although Auditing Standard No. 2 [required] the auditor to evaluate management's process, the auditor's opinion on management's assessment is not an opinion on management's internal control evaluation process. Rather, it is the auditor's opinion on whether management's statements about the effectiveness of the company's internal controls are fairly stated.
>
> ...
>
> In [PCAOB Auditing Standard No. 5, PCAOB] attempted to address concerns that the separate opinion on management's assessment required by Auditing Standard No. 2 contributed to the complexity of the standard and caused confusion regarding the scope of the auditor's work. Accordingly, to emphasize the proper scope of the audit and to simplify the reporting, [Auditing Standard No. 5 requires] that the auditor express only one opinion on internal control—a statement of the auditor's opinion on the effectiveness of the company's internal control over financial reporting. The proposal eliminate[s] the separate opinion on management's assessment because it was redundant of the opinion on internal control itself and because the opinion on the effectiveness of controls more clearly conveys the same information—specifically, whether the company's internal control is effective.
>
> Many commenters agreed with the Board that eliminating the separate opinion on management's assessment would reduce confusion and clarify the reporting. Some commenters, however, suggested that the Board should instead require only an opinion on management's assessment. These commenters expressed their belief that the Act requires only that the auditor review management's assessment process and not the company's internal control. ...
>
> The Board has determined, after considering these comments, to adopt the provision requiring only an opinion on internal control. The Board continues to believe that the overall scope of the audit that was described by Auditing Standard No. 2 and [Standard No. 5] is correct; that is, to attest to and report on management's assessment, as required by Section 404(b) of the Act, the auditor must test controls directly to determine whether they are effective."

PCAOB also points out [Footnote 29, Release No. 34-55876; File No. PCAOB-2007-02, (June 7, 2007)]. that, in addition, s. 103 of the Sarbanes-Oxley Act requires PCAOB's standard on auditing internal control to include "testing of the internal control structure and procedures of the issuer ..." PCAOB also asserts that under s. 103, PCAOB's Standard must require the auditor to present in the audit report, among other things, "an evaluation of whether such internal control structure and procedures ... provide reasonable assurance that transactions are recorded as necessary to permit preparation of financial statements in accordance with generally accepted accounting principles".

The SEC has also adopted corresponding changes to its own rules that require the auditor to express an opinion directly on internal control.

12. Source: Glass Lewis, FactSet.

13. Source: Compliance Week/Raisch Financial Internal Control Scorecard.
14. Securities and Exchange Commission: 17 CFR PART 241, Release nos 33-8810; 34-55929; FR-77; File No. S7-24-06]: *Commission Guidance Regarding Management's Report on Internal Control Over Financial Reporting Under Section 13(a) or 15(d) of the Securities Exchange Act of 1934*: Interpretation, p. 11.
15. Nowhere in The Institute of Internal Auditors' *Standards* is there any suggestion that an externally developed framework should be used to evaluate internal control. Interpretation of Standard 2010 requires the chief audit executive to take account of the organisation's own risk management framework or, in the absence of one, to use his or her own judgement when planning what to audit. Standard 2210.A3 states that internal auditors should use management's own criteria to evaluate controls, if they are adequate. If they are inadequate the Standard requires that internal audit should work with management to develop adequate criteria. Standard 1100 and the Glossary definition of 'Objectivity' require the chief audit executive not to subordinate professional judgement to that of anyone else. New Interpretation to Std 2120.
16. Securities and Exchange Commission: 17 CFR PART 241, Release nos 33-8810; 34-55929; FR-77; File No. S7-24-06]: *Commission Guidance Regarding Management's Report on Internal Control Over Financial Reporting Under Section 13(a) or 15(d) of the Securities Exchange Act of 1934*: Interpretation, p. 11, footnote 24.
17. The UK's 2008 Combined Code on Corporate Governance (www.frc.org.uk) contains a provision (C.3.6) that sets out the audit committee's role with respect to the appointment (etc.) of the external auditors: "The audit committee should have primary responsibility for making a recommendation on the appointment, reappointment and removal of the external auditors. If the board does not accept the audit committee's recommendation, it should include in the annual report, and in any papers recommending appointment or re-appointment, a statement from the audit committee explaining the recommendation and should set out reasons why the board has taken a different position."
    UK listed companies are not required to comply with Combined Code provisions but are required under the Listing Rules to explain their reasons if they do not. The UK, as this provision indicates, has always been careful not to elevate the audit committee above the board, unlike s. 301 of the Sarbanes-Oxley Act. Indeed, for UK listed companies it is ultimately the shareholders who vote the external auditors into office and approve their remuneration, unless this power has been devolved by the shareholders to the board.
    Where there is a corporate governance conflict for an overseas registrant between their country of incorporation requirements and those of the US, as in this example, their US filings should address the conflict and explain the practice being followed by the company, which is permitted to follow the requirements of its country of incorporation. Pragmatically, the best way round this particular conflict is likely to be for the board and the shareholders to accept the advice of its audit committee on the appointment and remuneration of the company's external auditors.
18. Director fee supplements may be paid for belonging to the audit committee and for chairing it, but no consulting fees or performance-related remuneration is permitted.
19. The SEC defines an affiliate as: "a person that directly, or indirectly through one or more intermediaries, controls, or is controlled by, or is under common control with, the person specified".

20. Securities and Exchange Commission, 17 CFR PARTS 228, 229 and 249, Release nos 33-8177; 34-47235; File No. S7-40-02], RIN 3235-AI66, Disclosure Required by Sections 406 and 407 of the Sarbanes-Oxley Act of 2002, Final rule.
21. The Institute of Internal Auditors Inc. (January 2008): Sarbanes-Oxley Section 404: A Guide for Management by Internal Controls Practitioners. 2nd edition, www.theiia.org.

9

Business/Management Techniques and their Impact on Control and Audit

INTRODUCTION

In this chapter we will examine selected business management approaches in respect of their nature allied to an awareness of their potential impact on the control of operations and internal audit.

The following approaches will be discussed:

- business process re-engineering (BPR)
- total quality management
- delayering
- empowerment
- outsourcing
- JIT (just-in-time management).

BUSINESS PROCESS RE-ENGINEERING

Definition

BPR is normally a strategically driven programme of change which concurrently affects the organisation's structure, human resources, systems and processes. The process is usually both far-reaching in its effects and normally represents a quantum leap in change terms.

It is often a realignment of the business processes to the core organisational strategy of the business because they are regarded as unsound. Frequently it is the strategy itself which is being changed significantly so that the business processes need to be brought in line with the modified strategy.

BPR is not essentially an IT project. It is driven by the business and IT takes its place in the process as an enabling factor along with employees, key business processes, etc. Indeed, one cornerstone of the BPR approach is that it is holistic in nature, in that change and development are viewed across a spectrum of people, processes and technology, with the implications for all being assessed and addressed. Of course, the rapid pace of information technology change has, of itself, offered greater and more flexible opportunities to the business community.

Continuous Improvement

An alternative approach, which is less cataclysmic, is to apply a gradual programme of continuous improvement to operations over a longer time period. In this situation, the affected operations may basically be sound and only require small degrees of change to be applied, and then only to selected elements of the overall process, for example the modification of information technology systems. Continuous improvement is normally a fundamental component of total quality management (which we discuss next). However, there really is no reason why an organisation should not implement a suitable cocktail of different techniques in order to achieve its objectives.

The Radicalism of BPR

Business process re-engineering is the re-engineering of business systems. It has been called a radical change programme which is designed to:

- reduce costs significantly
- make operations significantly more efficient
- find a competitive advantage.

The need for BPR is often driven by acutely unfavourable business circumstances, but even without these a prudent management will consider the competitive advantages which may follow from BPR. It is better to be proactive rather than be forced to respond when a crisis is upon the company.

BPR can be said to be a high risk technique as the aim is to achieve high levels of improvement in a short timescale.

The Driving Force for BPR

The motivations for applying this technique will be varied, but the continuing survival and development of the organisation are normally at the heart of such radical change methods. There may be, on the one hand, the fundamental need to refocus the strategy of the organisation or alternatively external forces (such as a new competitor in the market or changed economic conditions) may be brought to bear. The following general examples may apply:

- increasing cost burdens squeezing profit margins;

- declining income levels from a given product or service, suggesting that additional or improved service is necessary;
- inefficient usage of resources possibly linked to funding limitations;
- poor productivity and efficiency levels when compared to industry norms;
- the need to maintain or improve customer loyalty.

As with the application of any form of strategically driven technique, top management should be seen as the driving force and be responsible for the re-engineering initiative. In order to enhance the possibility of success, the BPR project team should include suitably senior and experienced managers.

Benefits from BPR

Very frequently, post BPR, the business is likely to be more closely aligned with customer needs ("customer focused") than before BPR. All processes become geared to the customer. Staff and management are likely to benefit from increased empowerment. (We examine empowerment later in this chapter.) The IT systems will more closely correspond to need. Business costs will have been reduced through downsizing, better asset management, better supplier relationships and productivity benefits.

How BPR May Affect the Business

Although the results of BPR are intended to be beneficial, the process has risks associated with it. Staff are likely to be resistant to major change and morale may suffer. The efficiency of running existing systems may be impaired as staff resources are diverted to the BPR project. The transition from the old systems to the post-BPR approach can be unsettling and, unless planned with very great care, lead to major breakdowns in business performance. This is especially so as BPR usually involves the redesign of IT systems. Customers may suffer in the short term even though they should notice perceptible improvements after implementation of BPR. In the short term BPR will be expensive as it is likely to entail major investment of time by management and staff, and of capital by the business itself. If consultants are used, the business must be careful to ensure that it does not lose ownership of the programme.

The following 11 general principles for a BPR project are taken from *Business Process Re-Engineering—A Practical Handbook for Executives*, by Stephen Towers:[1]

1. A BPR programme will take strong leadership, substantial time and real commitment.
2. Begin with a baseline assessment of your processes today.
3. Consultants are extremely useful in moving a BPR programme forward.
4. Define BPR in quantitative terms, and set up a BPR directorate.
5. BPR should be institutionalised through structural changes including "working groups".

6. BPR means revised and revamped technology.
7. Successful BPR begins internally, within an organisation, before it moves out to your business partners and customers.
8. Your organisation's training budget will increase considerably, but it's worth it because BPR rests on the shoulders of your staff.
9. Staff motivation remains the most difficult aspect of BPR to get right.
10. Expect that a percentage of your staff will not be able to measure up.
11. Evaluate your risks, but don't let them deter you.

The Implications for Internal Audit

The more major the change within a business, the greater the risk to effective internal control. BPR is intrinsically linked to major change. It is major change which results in staff being more process or project oriented and less functionally oriented: this very often reduces the extent to which internal control is achieved through segregation of functions and duties—and so alternative ways of achieving satisfactory control must be implemented.

Internal auditors are often rightly asked to participate in the BPR process. When BPR is being designed and implemented, invariably the resources of the internal audit function will be targeted in large measure to the new systems being developed. Internal auditors must understand the BPR process in order to advise on the control quality of the new systems. Internal auditors should also be in a position to review the BPR change process itself and advise whether that process has effective controls built into it. One particular risk is that of escalating costs associated with the BPR project. Internal auditors should be alert to the risk that established controls may not be operated effectively during the BPR project as management and staff resources are diverted to the BPR project itself.

The internal audit function itself may be the object of a BPR project, perhaps as a part of a larger BPR exercise.

TOTAL QUALITY MANAGEMENT

Total quality management (TQM) is a way of managing to improve the effectiveness, flexibility and competitiveness of a business as a whole. More specifically, TQM is a management philosophy embracing all the activities through which the needs and expectations of the customer, the community, and the objectives of the organisation are satisfied in the most efficient and cost effective way by maximising the potential of all employees in a continuing drive for improvement. A strategy can involve significant changes to an organisation's attitudes, priorities and controls. It is therefore a decision for management. It is not the responsibility of internal audit. However, internal audit departments will often take charge of the appraisal of the organisation's systems of control to monitor and assess the implementation and operation of the new quality operations.

Quality Systems

Quality assurance systems are systems which set out to demonstrate to customers that a business is committed to quality and able to supply its customers' quality needs. Standards[2] for quality systems have been established which place an emphasis on formalising individual systems, procedures and associated quality controls. Considerable emphasis is placed on documenting systems and establishing what the standards of performance are to be.

One criticism of the quality assurance systems movement is that the business seeking registration determines what its own systems will be and what standards of performance will be achieved—these are not externally imposed—they may not be very impressive in terms of quality. But they will be documented and registration is only achieved after they have been appraised by accredited external independent reviewers. Periodic external reviews will be conducted to ascertain whether the established quality systems are being complied with—as a requirement for continued registration. Many companies insist on using suppliers who are registered for quality systems.

Since registration is dependent upon *external* assessment, internal audit is not in a position to provide this service within their company. They can, however, advise the company on how to set about the process of obtaining registration, and assist the company to meet the requirements for registration. An internal auditing unit may make arrangements for one or more of its staff to be trained and approved as ISO/BS assessors: they will not be able to act as assessors within their business but the experience of what is involved will be helpful to the business, assisting in avoiding the cost of employing fee charging assessors over a period of many weeks to analyse the improvements necessary to reach the standards required for ISO/BS certification.

Either the whole business can seek registration covering the organisation as a whole, or sections of the business may do so. Many internal auditing units have gone for registration for a variety of reasons:

- The high level of existing standardisation of internal audit methods often means that an internal auditing unit is well placed to prepare for and seek registration.
- Registration by internal audit sets a good example to the business as a whole.
- Registration by internal audit gives internal audit practical experience of what is involved—which it can then make use of in the advice it gives to the rest of the company.
- Being a service department, registration by internal audit may give its clients, as well as the company's external auditors and regulators, more confidence in the quality of the internal audit unit.
- registered internal audit unit gains a competitive advantage in several ways, for example, in bidding for outsourced internal audit work, or in recruitment and retention of audit staff.

One familiar element of a TQM programme is promotion of a culture of continuous improvement which is based on the premise that those involved in applying the various processes have the detailed knowledge and are therefore best placed to improve them. Although the initiative for TQM and related continuous improvement programmes will invariably stem from senior management (and be actively endorsed by them), the basic responsibility for improvements lies with employees at the sharp end of the business.

In order to ensure that continuous improvement programmes are successful, staff will need to be supported by suitable training in such relevant techniques as effective team working, brainstorming, problem identification, problem solving, and so on.

As with any rudimentary cultural re-orientation, it will take time to achieve the necessary changes in roles and to generate the anticipated benefits.

The Cost of Quality

Unavoidably there are costs associated with maintaining a quality environment, just as there are financial implications in instances of poor quality. Here we are concerned with categories of quality cost beyond those associated with setting up the TQM environment and accreditation processes. Managers will need to identify quality costs in a number of categories if they are to be in position to quantify the effects of possible improvement and prioritise their improvement efforts in areas which are likely to achieve significant savings.

Quality costs may apply in the following example areas:

- the prevention of defects (i.e. improved design and production techniques/practices);
- the monitoring of ongoing quality through inspection and appraisal activities;
- the cost of correcting defective products or services *prior* to delivery to the customer (i.e. internal failures);
- the costs associated with correcting defective products/services detected *after* delivery to the customer (i.e. external failures). This may include the cost of refunds, discounts, repairs or replacements.

The last category should be of special concern as the reputation and image of the organisation can be adversely affected and future trading relationships put in jeopardy.

Quality Audits

Quality auditing is established in many businesses that have adopted TQM and/or sought and obtained ISO/BS registration for quality systems. The quality audit process seeks to establish and maintain high standards of TQM and/or quality systems.

Some of the options for approaching quality auditing are:

- address these matters as part of the programme of work of the internal auditing unit;
- run a separate quality audit function discrete from the internal audit unit but with a full level of coordination between the two so as to avoid duplication of work;
- have one audit department divided into two principal sections—one for conventional internal auditing, the other for quality auditing.

ISO/BS standards stipulate the incorporation of self-audit procedures into quality systems. This represents an element of auditing with cost implications.

Quality auditing is not the same as internal auditing. It is an essential part of TQM management philosophy and of a dedication to quality systems. The internal audit approach ideally should be:

- to reassure management and the board that quality auditing is being done effectively, and therefore to conduct internal audits of the quality auditing processes. If internal audit are conducting the quality audits itself, this will have to be done by others.
- to assess the extent to which internal audit can rely on work done by quality audit where it overlaps with the scope of internal audit, thereby avoiding unnecessary duplication.

In concluding this discussion of TQM, we note below a set of control objectives and risk and control issues for the subject, which could be used as the basis for developing an internal audit review programme.

Control Objectives for Quality Management

(a) To ensure that quality management techniques are appropriately considered and utilised in order to improve competitive advantage and the quality of service to customers.

(b) To ensure that the quality management approach is suitably justified, authorised and documented.

(c) To ensure that senior management are committed to the relevant quality strategy.

(d) To ensure that the costs of achieving and maintaining the quality regime are accurately assessed and subject to monitoring.

(e) To ensure that suitable quality and performance criteria are established, which are capable of measurement.

(f) To accurately determine customer requirements for products and services.

(g) To ensure that, whenever justified, nationally or internationally recognised quality standard accreditations are obtained and retained.

(h) To ensure that actual performance against the required quality standards is monitored and managed.

(i) To ensure that staff are suitably motivated to contribute to the quality programme and provided with the appropriate skills.

> (j) To ensure that defined objectives and tangible benefits are actually achieved.
>
> (k) To ensure that the quality management programme is subject to regular monitoring and review, and remains up to date and relevant.

Risk and Control Issues for Quality Management

1 Key Issues

1.1 Has the use of quality management techniques been the subject of adequate research, justification and authorisation (and how is this evidenced)?

1.2 Has the quality management policy/programme been documented?

1.3 Have the objectives of the quality programme been clearly defined (i.e. in terms of potential competitive advantage, improved customer satisfaction, etc.)?

1.4 How has senior management demonstrated its commitment to the quality programme?

1.5 Have all the costs associated with the quality programme been accurately and realistically identified, agreed and authorised?

1.6 Have realistic and measurable quality and performance criteria been defined for all the affected activities, and are the relevant staff aware of the requirements?

1.7 How has the involvement and motivation of staff been signified in the development of the quality programme?

1.8 What steps have management taken to ensure that the appropriate national or international quality standard accreditation will be achieved and maintained?

1.9 How does management ensure that all the relevant staff training requirements have been identified and suitably addressed?

1.10 Are all the quality initiatives subject to ongoing monitoring in order to ensure that targets and objectives are realised?

1.11 How is management to be made aware of performance and quality shortfalls against the defined expectations, and what measures ensure that such problems are adequately followed up?

2 Detailed Issues

2.1 Have all the relevant operational procedures and policies been updated in light of the documentary requirements of the quality management scheme?

2.2 What processes has management applied in order to select the most suitable areas for the quality initiatives?

2.3 What mechanisms prevent unsuitable business operations being targeted with quality initiatives?

2.4 What prevents the implementation and operation of unauthorised or unjustified quality schemes?

2.5 Have customer requirements been accurately identified and taken into consideration?

2.6 How has the quality scheme been justified?

2.7 How does management verify that it has identified all the costs and operational requirements of applying the quality management programme?

2.8 Are the costs associated with the quality programme subject to suitable authorisation (and how is this evidenced)?

2.9 What processes prevent unauthorised expenditure for quality-related activities?

2.10 Are all the costs associated with the quality programme adequately reported and subject to suitable monitoring and reaction?

2.11 Have suitable and justifiable quality control and testing facilities been provided?

2.12 Are quality control defect and rejection rates identified and monitored?

2.13 What action is taken if quality control defect and rejection rates fail to improve as a result of the quality programme?

2.14 How does management ensure that staff are adequately trained to fulfil their quality obligations?

2.15 What mechanisms are in place to identify and promptly resolve quality problems?

2.16 Where applicable, how did management justify the adoption of national or international quality standards?

2.17 Have the costs of obtaining and maintaining recognised quality standards been accurately identified and authorised?

2.18 Have suitably experienced external examiners been appointed to conduct the required reviews of the quality programme?

2.19 How can management be sure that the examiners' fees represent good value for money and are competitive?

2.20 How are shortcomings noted by the external examiners brought to the attention of management, and what measures are in place to ensure adequate follow-up and that action is taken?

2.21 How would the failure to achieve the potential benefits of the quality programme be detected and reported?

2.22 How does management ensure that the quality programme remains relevant, effective and justifiable?

2.23 How does management ensure that serious failures in the quality programme are dealt with?

2.24 Have nonproductive or wasteful processes been identified through the quality scheme and what has been done in such instances?

2.25 How does management ensure that external suppliers and agencies are able to contribute effectively to the achievement of the required quality standards adopted by the organisation?

2.26 Are customer satisfaction levels subject to ongoing monitoring so that the success (or otherwise) of the quality initiative can be accurately assessed?

2.27 How are existing customer service concerns identified and effectively addressed?

2.28 How is the accuracy of data input from other systems (e.g. quality control) confirmed?

2.29 How is the data output to other systems (e.g. planning) confirmed?

DELAYERING

Definition

Delayering simply means removing one or more levels of management from the enterprise, or from a part or parts of it.

Potential Implications of Delayering for the Enterprise

Even within very modern organisations where organisation structure is fluid and the structural emphasis is on project organisation or on matrix organisation, you will find a hierarchical organisation structure.

The number of levels of management and staff will vary according to the historical evolution of the business and also according to the type of business it is. Some enterprises, or parts of enterprises, are appropriately very flat. An implication of being flat is that each manager supervises a larger number of subordinates. This is called "the span of control" of the manager—an expression first coined by Henri Fayol [1916].[3] How wide the span of control of a manager can be depends largely on these features:

- the extent to which subordinates are doing similar jobs;
- the extent to which subordinates need to be monitored and helped;

- the degree to which the supervisory task is streamlined by techniques such as IT-based reporting by exception;
- the extent to which the manager has fundamental work to complete which does not involve supervising others;
- the extent to which the manager invests time reporting upwards;
- the extent to which the manager expends time liaising with collateral associates within the business;
- the extent to which the manager has a communication role *external to the business* such as with the media and customers;
- the degrees of personal assistance the manager has in performing his or her duties.

The principal underlying theme behind these features is that of *limited cognitive ability*. In business almost everyone suffers from information overload. Managers resort to various devices to handle information overload, which occurs because our minds are unable to process rationally all the information that needs to be processed in order to make optimal decisions. Clearly, the more staff a manager has to supervise, the more information the manager is required to process. The risk is that supervision becomes nominal—that delegation becomes abdication.

Many businesses have little idea how many levels of management and staff they have. They have an even vaguer idea as to how they stack up in this regard compared to their competitors. It is an even more difficult decision to determine how many levels of management and staff the business *should* have.

Removing a layer of management and staff broadens the span of control of the managers involved. It generally therefore leads to greater *empowerment* of those being supervised (see the following section for a discussion of empowerment). Generally it should be associated with the development of modern IT-based systems which make it easier for managers to supervise more subordinates, perhaps through IT-generated *reporting by exception*.

Delayering usually has a dramatic impact on lowering staffing costs. So it is often part of a business process re-engineering project (discussed earlier). It can be one way of achieving productivity gains. It is often made feasible when a factor of production other than staff (such as automation or outsourcing) becomes more economic than investment in staff, which perhaps becomes too costly or unreliable.

Yet its other advantages may be even greater. We have mentioned the greater empowerment inherited by the level of management or staff beneath the level which has been removed. This should ideally lead to greater job satisfaction and to greater work motivation.

Equally dramatic can be the speeded up responsiveness which occurs within the business as a consequence of delayering. Instructions communicated downwards to operating levels have one less layer to filter through. Each layer usually represents a time delay and a potential for distortion of the message which was originally intended to be communicated downwards. Likewise, information communicated upwards about the results of operations, reaches decision-making levels more quickly and with less corruption en route. So a faster moving, more responsive enterprise is created.

Each unnecessary level of management or staff is a superfluous, unproductive and costly overhead. Delayering simplifies the business. For instance, to mention just one example, a smaller personnel function will be required if there are fewer staff employed.

The Informal Organisation

It is probable that every enterprise has an informal organisation as well as a formal one. Where staff find they need to interact with certain other staff in order to do their job, they will tend to find a way of doing so—even if the formal structure does not provide this opportunity. They may get into the habit of having lunch together, for instance, or a junior executive may bypass a boss to report a matter of concern to a higher level. In turn, the higher level may interact directly with staff several levels more junior, bypassing intermediate levels of management. Some businesses are very formal in defining and applying reporting relationships; others are much more informal. Some businesses have formal codes of business practice and some of these will specify that junior staff may address matters of concern directly to much more senior levels of management (and to internal audit as well) if they perceive a need to do so.

The informal organisation structure is as real as the formal one. Any analysis of structure and of levels of management and staff may need to take both the informal and the formal aspects of organisation structure into account.

In addition to having an informal organisation structure, staff tend to develop informal procedures when the formal laid-down procedures prove to be inadequate.

Internal Audit Implications

Questions for internal audit include:

- How many levels of management and staff does the enterprise have, and how many should it have? This is a question that should be asked during any operational audit.
- Does management have the information it needs to supervise effectively, and is management supervising effectively?
- Will a proposed delayering project lead to a loss of control, (a) temporarily while the project is in progress, and (b) after it has been implemented—and what can the auditor recommend to avoid this?
- Are there too many levels of management and staff in the internal auditing department?

EMPOWERMENT

Definition

The delegation of responsibility to and trust of staff for making business decisions, without the need for close, detailed review and approval of those decisions. This approach is based on the premise that employees, at all levels, are responsible for their own actions and should be given the authority to make decisions about their work.

Rationale for Empowerment

Determined cost-cutting (perhaps as one of the objectives of a business process re-engineering project and prompted often by acute competitive pressures) frequently has the effect of giving more responsibility to most staff. Since there are likely to be fewer staff, it follows that the responsibilities of most are likely to be greater. This will also generally be the effect of greater automation, although we should not overlook that many decisions are now "programmable"—meaning they can be automated so that no member of staff may have the responsibility to make these decisions. Of course, the development of systems for programmed decision making is itself a responsibility that has to be taken very seriously by any business. The operation of programmed decision making should also be monitored by management who have the responsibility to note unsatisfactory programmed outcomes and intervene so as to override them on a timely basis.

So, to some extent "empowerment" is a likely by-product of several of the new approaches to management which we are discussing in this chapter.

But "empowerment" is also an objective in its own right as it is perceived to have many positive outcomes. Herzberg's[4] bipolar analysis of job satisfaction factors divided them into two groups. The *hygiene factors* are to do with the surroundings of the job (such as good working conditions, pleasant colleagues to work with, easy travel to work, etc.) whereas the *motivators* are more closely to do with the job itself (such as job interest, opportunity for achievement, recognition of achievement, advancement). Herzberg maintained that if management attended well to the hygiene factors which related to their staff, then this would only remove negative feelings of dissatisfaction: in themselves the hygiene factors would not positively motivate staff. For positive motivation, the motivators had to be in place. And if staff were motivated to perform well, then outputs would improve—in effect the business would be buying-in to the potential of its people.

Maslow's[5] view of satisfaction was not bipolar: it was uni-polar. He perceived of a hierarchy of needs. At the lowest level people have (a) physiological needs (for food, water, warmth, etc.). At progressively higher levels are (b) security needs, (c) social needs, (d) esteem needs, (e) autonomy needs and (f) self-actualisation (or self-fulfilment) needs. Maslow found that most people display some degree of dissatisfaction with the extent to which their needs are satisfied. He found that an acute level of dissatisfaction with the extent to which a lower level need was satisfied would often lead to a major preoccupation by the individual designed to alter things and meanwhile the higher level needs would signify little in that person's consciousness. For instance, a starving person will be preoccupied with the need to find food and will not indulge in concern about their level of self-actualisation. Maslow found that most occupational groups in the developed world have achieved levels of satisfaction which mean that most or all of Maslow's needs are a matter of concern to them.

Autonomy is the need that most closely corresponds to the concept of "empowerment". Autonomy means taking decisions and being able to see the results which follow from those decisions.

If managers and staff are able to obtain more of their lives' needs through their work experiences, they are likely to be motivated to focus on their job so as to fulfil themselves. If their jobs provide inadequate opportunities to fulfil their needs, they will not identify with their work so much and will seek to obtain fulfilment in their leisure activities. The half-hearted focus of such employees on their work will result in much less effective levels of performance. "Empowerment" is seen as an important way of providing staff with the opportunity to fulfil themselves more at work. From the organisation's viewpoint there is likely to be the additional objective of increasing motivation to do the job well (for example, to satisfy customers and participate more fully in the "life" of the organisation).

If empowerment confers the authority to make decisions, it is possible that varying levels of service (i.e. to customers) will result through the differing interpretations applied by individual members of staff. In addition, there may be an attendant lack of clarity, in that it is more difficult to discern who is responsible for what.

We should not overlook the other perspective which suggests that many people do not want responsibility; many people may be happier not to have to make decisions; many people may be happier in a job that enables them to focus on non work activities, such as hobbies, family, voluntary work, church etc. And a happy employee is better than an unhappy one.

Internal Audit Implications

- Has "empowerment" weakened control by weakening supervision—and, if so, are there effective compensating controls?
- Has "empowerment" removed or weakened *segregation of duties* controls—and, if so, are there effective compensating controls?
- Has "empowerment" increased the potential for employee or management fraud—and, if so, what are the safeguards?
- Has "empowerment" led to excessive dependence on one or a few key members of staff?
- Has "empowerment" led to the motivational and productivity gains expected of it—or are management and staff disillusioned by excessive responsibilities and excessive work loads?

OUTSOURCING

Meaning

Sometimes termed "contracting out", outsourcing occurs when services previously provided by in-house personnel are supplied by an outside contractor. This often takes place after a due process of market testing, which requires that a fully specified tender document is prepared and potential outside contractors are invited to tender for the work against the specification. The in-house personnel who previously provided the services (sometimes known as the direct labour) may be invited to tender for the work in competition with the outside tenderers.

Impact on In-house Personnel

Very often, a condition of tendering imposed on the outside tenderers is that they must agree to take on the direct labour personnel. The drawback for those whose contract of employment transfers in this way from the business to the outside contractor is that their terms and conditions of service and their job security are often not so good with the outside contractor as they were previously, when perhaps they had been insulated from the effect of market forces. Large organisations often end up paying premium employment costs (such as profit-sharing and pension schemes) to peripheral employees for whom they were not originally intended; outsourcing their work can eliminate that premium.

Broadening Scope of Outsourcing

In recent years there has been a general trend to outsourcing noncore activities such as catering, security, office cleaning and, in the case of local authorities, refuse collection. More recently, more fundamental activities such as accounting, computer operations and site maintenance have been seen as candidates for outsourcing. Outsourcing computer operations is normally termed *facilities management* (see Chapter 17).

Cost–Benefit Issues

In the public sector, the push towards outsourcing is often initiated to inject a competitive element into the tendering for services. It is believed that this can lead to lower costs of public services as well as higher quality. Management must, however, take great care to ensure that it is not *just* costs that determine the choice of outsourcer—essential standards of service provision must be maintained. An outside contractor is unlikely to provide any service unless it is part of the contract, and the contract must specify the standard of service expected, with penalty clauses for shortfall. Outsourcing also has the effect of reducing the size of (or at least reducing the rate of growth of) the public sector in a national economy, which is perceived as having certain macroeconomic advantages.

Cost Escalation

At first, outsourced services may be provided on favourable terms, but once well established, and as soon as the contractual terms permit, the contractor may raise the price of providing the service. Then, with the in-house provision no longer being available, the organisation may be in a weak position to resist escalating costs of ensuring that the service continues to be provided. Of course, if there is an open market in the provision of these services, the services can be market tested again so that a competitive provider is found.

Contractors may be able to justify low-price tenders as they can often be costed on a marginal cost basis for a while. For instance, firms of public accountants may tender for outsourced internal audit work in anticipation that they will be able to resource that work using staff at a time of the year when they are not heavily engaged with year-end external audit work.

A common practice is to bid for a market-tested service at cost price and, once the contract has been won, to charge at expensive rates for services that the client needs but did not include in the tender document and which are therefore not covered by the contract. Careful specification of the job and careful wording of the contract can reduce this risk.

Re-invigorating a Business through Outsourcing

The cultural implications of outsourcing are considerable. The net effect of a significant amount of outsourcing is to make the organisation smaller and simpler to run. There is a reduced requirement for staff functions such as a large personnel department, so there are these indirect cost savings as well. Many of the popular approaches to contemporary management are designed to achieve this.

Outsourcing can help a business keep or regain its dynamism—its ability to adapt more rapidly. Management have more freedom to make changes without the problem of having to overcome staff who may be resistant to change, or at least have to be managed effectively during times of change. Management are able to focus more single-mindedly on the main issues.

Impact on Human Resource Inventory

By using outside contractors, the reservoir of in-house trained and experienced staff will be reduced and consequently the organisation may become less competent, more vulnerable and perhaps less able to competently handle a future need to change. On the other hand, outsourced activities provide outside contractors with learning experience *on the job*. This may be a potential competitive threat, as in effect the business is developing outsiders who may set up in competition or take their resultant know-how to a rival business for which they also provide outsourced services.

Outsiders working for the business may also represent a security risk. For example, most businesses take incredible risks with their contract cleaners who may have virtually unrestricted access to premises out of hours.

The Decision to Outsource

How does management decide what and whether to outsource? First, they apply cost–benefit principles to the decision. Secondly, they consider which of their noncore activities might be done better by outsiders who specialise in those activities—in other words, by outsiders for whom those activities *are* core. For example, an automobile manufacturer might not regard its core business as involving machining—it may buy in all its components and merely assemble and market its products. Much of the marketing is also likely to be contracted out.

It is not always immediately apparent what are the core activities of a business—and they may change over time. One way of identifying what is the business's core activity is to determine what it is that it is consistently able to do at greatest profit in terms of return on capital employed. For instance, a domestic home loan company may develop special expertise in collecting overdue debts—to the extent that it becomes the market leader in collections. In such a case its core business might be regarded as changing from having been a home loans company to having become a collections company, which may tender for the collections work of other home loans and consumer credit companies.

Strategic Implications

The decision to outsource may have strategic implications. Businesses must consider the security of their supplier and distribution lines. Outsourcing may make the organisation more dependent on outside suppliers and distributors and so it might opt for vertical integration instead. Vertical integration is the process whereby a business expands so that it absorbs other businesses in the supply and distribution chain. Since each of these businesses intends to make a profit, gathering them together so that they are all "in-house" ensures that all the profit margins are retained. However, the business may not be so successful at making a profit on noncore activities in which it has relatively low expertise. In any case, if outside contractors are in plentiful supply the strategic risks are fewer, and vertical integration may be neither attractive nor appropriate.

There may be broader issues at stake which militate against outsourcing. For instance, customers and clients of the business might *expect* that certain elements of the service they receive are provided internally and not outsourced.

Implications for Internal Audit

You can see from the above discussion that outsourcing poses control risks of particular interest to the internal auditor. We summarise some of them here:

- Do the tender document and the subsequent contract specify an adequate minimum standard of service, and ensure that unanticipated contingencies will be serviced effectively?
- Are the contracting procedures for outsourcing adequate to ensure the contractor is selected objectively, and are these procedures followed?
- Is it evident that contracted-out services are value for money?
- Has management considered and is management managing the security risk associated with utilisation of outsiders for contracted out work?
- Is contracted-out work periodically market tested to ensure the service is provided competitively?
- Are all services currently performed by in-house personnel considered on an impartial basis for market testing?

- Has the business a clear strategic grasp of what is its core activity and so should not be regarded as a candidate for outsourcing?
- Is partial outsourcing (whereby contract staff work alongside in-house staff) rationally considered as an option wherever it may be applicable?
- Is contracting out leading to excessive dependence on one supplier, and does management regularly consider this risk?
- Does management review the discharge of contracts for outsourced services with a view to learning lessons from cost overruns, etc.?

JUST-IN-TIME MANAGEMENT (JIT)

The driving objectives of JIT are to eliminate wasteful or non value-added activities, and by doing so achieve improvements (such as increased quality, reduced work-in-progress stock levels, improved productivity and reduced costs). The radicalism of the technique will invariably mean the reassessment and/or the casting aside of existing practices, and it is, therefore, important that those involved approach the exercise with open minds.

The conceptual origins of JIT have a connection with the work of Frederick Taylor[6] early in this century and were really brought into wider prominence by Japanese industry as an extension of their struggles to survive after the Second World War. One of the first practical working examples was implemented by Toyota in the early 1960s. What emerged was an integrated approach to managing production which brought together a number of techniques, including JIT.

In 1982, Schonberger[7] listed the 14 concepts associated with a streamlined and focused approach to production, including such elements as quality at the source, automation and robotics, minimised set-up time, quality circles and just-in-time production. Information technology systems, particularly those which are capable of interfacing with suppliers' IT systems, have made the contemporary development and use of JIT feasible.

It is important to understand that JIT manufacturing systems are driven by the principle of being "demand-pulled" through the production process, i.e. production activities are governed (or "pulled") by downstream processes requiring subassemblies from upstream processes. This is the reverse of more traditional production systems where the flow is "pushed" through the production chain. Smaller production batches will usually apply in JIT systems and this more readily facilitates other related aspects of the method to be accommodated. For example, the concurrent employee responsibility for ensuring that the required quality criteria are met at the conclusion of each discrete production stage, rather than relying on the more traditional quality control inspection after the final production stage has been completed and when it is more difficult to pinpoint the source of any quality problem. In tandem with the allocation of responsibility for quality matters, employees can also halt the production process if a defect or problem is discovered, thus permitting the (hopefully) prompt resolution of the problem. This approach is referred to as "quality at the source" and is based on the Japanese concept of *Jikoda* which translates to "stop everything when something goes wrong". The aims here are to minimise defects as an important contribution to quality and to coincidently empower employees to identify and solve them.

Coordination of the JIT process is clearly critical and this is influenced, in turn, by effective communication along the production chain. A simple system of cards called *Kanbans* is normally used to send signals between production workers. The *Kanban* cards are used to instruct workers either to obtain the parts required for their stage of the process (i.e. using the so-called "move" cards) or to actually produce a number of parts (i.e. utilising the so-called "production" cards). Both types of card are attached to (and associated with) standardised containers which physically flow through the production processes, "pulled" by the downstream demands.

So far, we have primarily looked at JIT from a theoretical or concept viewpoint. We should hasten to point out that information technology usually has a vital role to play in the technique, especially in respect of the provision of up-to-date and accurate information about the current state of the production process. Data about the units of production and their progress is not only held on the physical *Kanban* cards but tracked using IT systems which can provide timely interactions with inventory records, accounting systems, planning processes, and so on.

The JIT concept can apply beyond the in-house world of production and have links to suppliers, in which case it is normally referred to as just-in-time purchasing (JITP). The principal aims of JITP are to reduce and contain stockholding levels, improve the quality of parts and minimise all the associated costs (i.e. of storage facilities). JITP has implications for the selection of suitable suppliers who can meet all the demands of the system of supply. Suppliers participating in JITP schemes will have to become more flexible to enable the call-off of smaller delivery quantities on a swift turnround basis.

Figure 9.1 features a simple example to illustrate the primary advantages and disadvantages of a JIT relationship with a supplier.

Applying new techniques, such as JIT, will require that staff and managers adopt a more flexible attitude to their thinking about the processes under review. They may have to reposition their existing concept of the situation and embrace alternative viewpoints so that the revision will be successful. The successful adoption of such philosophies presupposes that the in-house culture is tuned to the same harmonious frequency, where the employees' contributions are also seen as coincidently contributing to their motivation, fulfilment and self-esteem. If so, the organisation can potentially benefit from a more committed and creative workforce. One manifestation of this enlightened attitude is the concept of *bottom-round management*, which is typified by a consensus management stance supported by the participation of workers in the discussion and resolution of problems, which may have been historically viewed as the sole concern of management.

Implications for Internal Auditors

The following are implications of JIT management for internal auditors:

- Auditors must have a suitable understanding of the associated techniques in order that their reviews are both effective and credible. The inclusion of internal auditors in the development of manufacturing systems will go towards helping address this potential shortcoming, but only if the organisation is at the stage of

> **An example of JITP**
>
> An automobile manufacturer will design deliveries from suppliers so that the correct number and type of components needed for perhaps only today's production arrive just-in-time and in the right sequence from the component suppliers.
> By doing this, the automobile manufacturer achieves the following:
>
> - inventory space and carrying costs are minimised
> - in-house inventory management is simplified (for instance, a search for a missing component is a search through a smaller inventory of parts)
> - some risks are transferred to suppliers (such as risk of damage to components while in storage, etc.)
> - suppliers become more "locked in" to the automobile manufacturer's business
> - changes in production schedules and product mix may become easier to make
> - there is less risk of redundant, surplus or obsolete stock of components
> - less working capital is needed as less is invested in inventory
> - JIT contributes to making the business less complex and easier to change (in a similar way to outsourcing).
>
>   But the automobile manufacturer risks:
>
> - assembly line stoppages through late arrival of components
> - production losses due to industrial disputes at component suppliers or their distributors
> - higher component costs to compensate suppliers for their carrying costs.

Figure 9.1 Examples of the advantages and disadvantages associated with a JIT approach to procuring supplies

introducing new or revised methods, thus offering the audit function the opportunity of early involvement.
- Auditors should be aware of the cultural implications for the organisation of introducing and using production management methods such as JIT. Unless both management and workforce are adequately prepared to adopt a more contributive and collaborative approach, the successful implementation of such methods can be jeopardised.
- There may be broader control implications associated with the devolution of responsibilities to employees. Unless the wider (environmental) levels of controls are effective, they may easily be overridden (or ignored) by employees empowered to act within the confines of collective initiative (as typified by the concept of bottom-rounded management).
- Consider the cost-accounting implications of a JIT or JITP system. For example, with the emphasis placed on minimising waste and avoiding activities that do

not add value, how does management accurately identify the associated costs as the basis for taking appropriate corrective action?
- Auditors will need to coordinate their approach to operational reviews of JIT systems so as to take into account such diverse aspects as product planning, cost accounting, process design, related information flows, quality issues and relationships with suppliers.
- The use of JIT manufacturing systems leads to a reduction in paperwork and this can present problems for auditors when tracking processes along a production chain unless there are compensating points of reference (for example, the use of barcodes to facilitate the recording of the flow of products, subassemblies, etc.). The contrary situation can apply in JITP systems, in that more frequent and smaller order quantities are common and can generate more transaction paperwork to flow between the organisation and the supplier. Electronic data interchange (EDI) between business partners may be used to reduce physical paperwork and speed up the flow of relevant data (see Chapter 17).
- Increased use of automation throughout the production chain theoretically supplants the need for more traditional forms of control. Auditors will, however, need to ensure that automated processes take due account of any control implications.

NOTES

1. Towers, S. (1994) *Business Process Re-engineering—A Practical Handbook for Executives*. Stanley Thornes, Cheltenham.
2. Now known in the UK as the ISO/BS EN 9000: 2000 family of quality management systems standards.
3. Fayol, H. ([1916] 1949) *General and Industrial Management*. Trs. Constance Storrs. Pitman, London. First published in France as *Administration Industrielle et Générale*.
   Henri Fayol was born in France in 1841 and graduated, aged 19, as a mining engineer to be appointed engineer of the Commentry pits of the Commentry-Fourchambault, from which he retired as managing director in 1918. In his retirement he propounded his Theory of Administration.
4. Herzberg, F. *et al*. (1959) *The Motivation to Work*. 2nd edition. Harper & Row, London.
5. Maslow, A. (1954) *Motivation and Personality*. Harper & Row, London.
6. Frederick Taylor (1856–1915) was an American engineer who worked for the Midvale Steelworks in Philadelphia. He introduced time-and-motion study to improve output and management. In 1893 he became an independent consultant in what he termed "scientific management". His publications include *Shop Management* (1903) and The Principles of Scientific Management (1911).
7. Schonberger, R. J. (1982). *Japanese Manufacturing Techniques—Nine Hidden Lessons in Simplicity*. Free Press, New York.

10
Control Self Assessment

INTRODUCTION

Control Self Assessment (CSA) developed during the 1990s as an alternative to, or more generally an adjunct to, conventional internal auditing. It is generally considered to have been born in a multinational Canadian oil company. Their business processes were being re-engineered. Implications of this business process re-engineering were that internal audit was being downsized and greater empowerment was being given to line management and staff. It followed that some of the responsibility for the review of business processes would be transferred to management and staff with less reliance on the internal audit activity. The internal audit activity devised a process of control self assessment by management and staff, facilitated by internal audit. The CSA movement gathered momentum when the senior members of that company's internal audit activity became consultants specialising in CSA.[1]

The carefully defined approach to CSA owes much to that genesis—especially with regard to the methodologies that emerged at that time. Some would say that the CSA approach became over-defined and too rigid. Of course, something as generic as management and staff undertaking their own assessments of internal control cannot realistically be attributed to a particular origin, nor confined to a particular approach. Indeed IBM with their self assessment programme (SAP) and British Petroleum with their internal control review programme (ICRP) both predated the development referred to above, and both were facilitated by internal audit.

During the 1990s extravagant claims were made for CSA by some of its proponents, notably that CSA added more value than conventional internal auditing and would supersede the latter. Now a more balanced perspective applies as the limitations of CSA are more readily appreciated alongside the benefits, based on experience. Nevertheless CSA, in tandem with conventional internal auditing, has much to commend it and it is our purpose in this chapter to set out an approach in straightforward, practical terms.

SURVEY AND WORKSHOP APPROACHES TO CSA

Broadly speaking, any self assessment of internal control by line management and staff can be termed "control self assessment". Key line managers across the business may be required to certify annually to the effectiveness of internal control by returning a completed certificate or questionnaire. Part of the management obligation might be to consult staff as part of this process and certify that all the concerns of staff have been addressed. In CSA parlance, this approach is usually termed "a survey approach to CSA".

A more demanding, ambitious style of CSA is workshop-based. A small number of managers and staff are selected to form the workshop. Each member of the workshop should play an approximately equal role in the process that is the subject of the workshop and all the most significant elements of the process should be represented between the differing expertise and experience of the workshop members. The relative seniority of those belonging to the workshop is unlikely to be uniform as very junior members of staff may play key roles in a process and should therefore be represented at the workshop alongside more senior people. The requirement to cover the elements of the process amongst the workshop members is likely to be the main driver to determine the size of the workshop. Workshops with more than about ten members become unwieldy, meaning that the process being covered by the workshop should probably be subdivided into a number of subprocesses addressed in more than one workshop.

SELECTING WORKSHOP PARTICIPANTS

One consideration in selecting those to attend the workshop is whether the presence of a senior manager is likely to inhibit the workshop in that more junior members may defer to the judgement of the more senior. Much depends on the personality of the particular senior people and also on the management style. Organisations, and parts thereof, that are managed hierarchically rather than participatively, and are managed as it were "more by the stick than the carrot" will always find it harder to benefit from CSA. Members of the workshop need to feel uninhibited at drawing attention to their own and others' failures. If acknowledgement of control weaknesses is unwelcome, then the workshop is unlikely to be successful.

WHERE TO APPLY CSA

It will be apparent that the CSA approach lends itself naturally to the review of business processes that step across structural boundaries of the business (see Chapter 2). Workshop members can be drawn from each of the parts of the businesses that need to coordinate effectively to achieve the purposes of the subject business process. Conventional internal auditing can be challenged to review these types of business process in that it may be difficult to conduct such an audit engagement and challenging to know to whom to address the resultant audit report. Of course, CSA can also be applied to the review of activities which correspond to the responsibilities of a single section of the business.

CSA may also be an effective approach to follow to review the quality of control in highly technical areas of the business that the internal audit activity lacks the competence to understand adequately. The technical personnel working in these areas of the business probably have valid insights about the inadequacies of control and how it might be improved, and the CSA approach can tap into this experience that they have.

In its fully fledged form, CSA is intended to cover the entire organisation and to work to an annual cycle of workshops across the organisation. That is often not practically achievable. Workshop members often find an annual interval between workshops is too short. If internal audit is to provide one or two facilitators for each CSA workshop, the internal audit overhead is likely to be unmanageable for such a comprehensive CSA programme. Just as conventional internal auditing rarely if ever covers the entire organisation annually, neither need a CSA programme. When both approaches are being applied, the future plan of each should be based on a risk assessment conducted at least annually.[2] The risk assessment of each should factor in an assessment of the degree of assurance that can be relied upon from the other programme.

It will usually be wise to commence CSA in "easy win" parts of the organisation, which are likely to have some of these characteristics:

- There is likely to be considerable opportunity to make improvements.
- The process steps across departmental frontiers and is difficult to review as a conventional internal audit assignment.
- Internal auditors have insufficient technical skills to master the activity to be reviewed.
- The activity is performed in a participative, nonthreatening part of the organisation so that workshop participants are unlikely to be reluctant to be frank.

CSA ROLES FOR MANAGEMENT AND FOR INTERNAL AUDIT

Ideally it should be management who have the responsibilities to decide:

- the subjects to be covered by CSA;
- the approach, whether survey of workshop, to be used;
- the frequency of the workshops;
- who should be invited to be members of the workshops;
- the action to be taken based on the workshop results;
- what to report, and to whom.

The role of internal audit is usually:

- to facilitate to CSA programme;
- to facilitate CSA workshops;
- to review the assurance that management and the board can place on the CSA programme;
- to report the results of their assurance review to senior management and to the board.

Facilitation is the art of enabling others to achieve better results for themselves. CSA is control *self* assessment, effective facilitation of CSA by internal audit should ensure that an optimal programme of CSA workshops is decided upon by management, and appropriate workshop members are chosen.

Many proponents of CSA have aimed to achieve a life for the CSA programme that is independent of the internal audit activity, so that management drive the programme forward and facilitate the workshops. Practical experience indicates that CSA momentum is unlikely to be maintained without significant facilitation by internal audit. It is analogous to achieving effective risk management by line management and staff in an organisation without a risk management function (Chapter 5). It is also analogous to endeavouring to transfer into the line the process of Sarbanes-Oxley s. 302 and s. 404 compliance (Chapter 8). Nevertheless, to the extent that internal audit can safely step into the CSA shadows and leave management to run the CSA programme, then internal audit should do so.

AVOIDING LINE MANAGEMENT DISILLUSIONMENT

Beyond the achievement of the first cycle of the CSA programme, it is possible that managers will assume that the exercise is now complete and that there is no further justification for their continued involvement. In any case, they may not see their main mission as being driven by control, but rather to ensure that their (and the organisation's) objectives are achieved.

Management and staff often misguidedly assume that control is the prime domain of the internal auditing function, and they fail to recognise that they have the prime responsibility for control activities and that control is an integral part of their management processes. Therefore, it follows that cost-effective internal control activities are often positive means of achieving the required targets and objectives.

A realistic (and healthy) view of the related risks will need to be developed against which control activities can be set. Line managers should be encouraged to acknowledge ownership of their systems and processes, and to aim to reduce, counter or eradicate the related risks as one mechanism for contributing to improved performance. All parties need to recognise that control activities should be cost-effective and therefore in proportion to the underlying risks.

Among the many stated benefits of CSA are that line managers accept their control responsibilities and are "empowered" to determine such controls and influence how they are applied in practice (rather than being imposed). However, the success (or otherwise) of CSA is heavily dependent on how the concept is "sold" to management, for example:

- what is the agenda? (Cost saving, quality and performance improvements, corporate survival through the achievement of objectives, linkages with other concurrent initiatives, such as quality, etc.);
- the prevailing attitude of senior management and whether they are seen to be committed to the process;
- the past and future role of internal auditing within the organisation;
- whether the CSA process is, in itself, unduly cumbersome and bureaucratic;

- the extent to which line management and their staff are able to influence the process and "have their say" (i.e. a partnership approach);
- the degree of preparation and support provided to managers and their staff (i.e. training workshops and the clear communication of the objectives of the CSA programme).

CSA is an opportunity for management and internal audit to establish a common perception of the organisation through its procedures and control activities. It is fundamentally important to have a clear idea of where the organisation is going (objectives) and the underlying key factors that will influence the way there (i.e. cost containment/reduction, quality achievements, maintaining customer/client relationships, etc.).

Line managers and their staff may view the need to identify and document the controls as an onerous task. However, this initial administrative overhead is reduced in subsequent years as only amendments and refinements need to be documented.

Managers may be concerned that any detected control weaknesses in their domain will be used against them in some way. Unless this perception is corrected, they may be reluctant to be open and honest about control shortcomings. Taking into account the prevailing management ethos, managers may not be inclined to reveal potential control problems within their area in case they are penalised. This negative perception will need to be corrected so that managers are positively encouraged (perhaps even rewarded) to draw attention to weaknesses in control and to openly contribute their ideas for future improvements.

The CSA process should be forward-looking; recognising and accepting the need to improve control processes as a success factor, rather than negative reactions to past oversights. Without an open and honest approach to the review and assessment of control, the results are likely to be half-hearted and the opportunity to reap real benefits will be missed.

The CSA process should be built on, promoting a collective responsibility for internal control as a partnership between line management, who are accountable for control as part of their responsibilities, and internal audit, who objectively appraise the effectiveness of controls in place on behalf of senior management.

Where possible, forms of measuring achievements can be devised that enable performance comparisons to be assessed over time, as a means of marking improvements and gains. Internal audit should consider formally reporting the positive aspects of their findings in the context of attaining the strategic and operational goals set for the organisation.

ENCOURAGEMENT FROM THE TOP

Senior management need to demonstrate commitment to the CSA process and encourage line management to buy-in to the fact that internal controls can support the achievement of corporate goals. Senior management should clearly communicate the motivation and purpose for the CSA process, as a way of focusing personnel towards good practice, etc.

In order to provide the direction and focus for CSA, it will be necessary to identify the strategic and operational objectives for the organisation. These may be linked to other related initiatives, such as TQM, safety or environmental assessments. Staff taking part in the CSA programme should be well informed about its purpose and provided with training (perhaps through workshops facilitated by internal audit).

Management should aim to engender a positive and contributive environment, where CSA participants can have their say and influence outcomes. This can be reinforced by adopting constructive attitudes, perhaps linked to team building concepts. Using a "team building" approach can emphasise that the CSA process is about assessing "real world issues", and empowering people to take effective action(s). Managers should be encouraged to reveal potential control weaknesses in their departments without the fear of recriminations. However, they also need to be aware of the related need to suggest effective and justifiable control solutions.

CSA offers unique opportunities for a new and more proactive relationship to be established between line managers and the internal audit function, with all parties focusing their attention on positive achievement through an effective internal control environment. If they haven't already done so, internal auditors should recognise that their service should be tuned to the needs of the business, and coordinate their work accordingly.

Internal audit management can, through the auspices of CSA, raise the profile of the internal audit service and help promote the significance of internal control as a device for ensuring corporate success.

Self assessment can be considered as a necessary activity aimed at self preservation. Finding and correcting weaknesses in a company's operations, before such weaknesses cause the business to fail. It is an indicator as to the health and fitness of an organisation and a gauge to its ability to survive and prosper.[3]

FACILITATING CSA WORKSHOPS, AND TRAINING FOR CSA

Facilitation of CSA workshops by internal audit may involve two internal auditors at a workshop—one as the facilitator and the other as the "scribe" drafting the report of the workshop "in real time" as the workshop progresses. A workshop may last half a day or a short working day with a break at lunchtime. The last 30 to 45 minutes of the workshop is usually taken up by going through the report that has been drafted, getting the agreement of those attending to its contents. Trying to get agreement subsequent to the workshop leads to excessive delays.

An issue of concern for chief audit executives collaborating in the introduction of CSA is whether their existing internal audit staff have appropriate facilitation skills, and also an understanding of control self assessment so that they can act as effective CSA facilitators. Many chief audit executives have been pleasantly surprised how well their staff have taken to CSA facilitation—even if it uses skills which may have been largely latent beforehand. The Institute of Internal Auditors offers a Certification in Control Self Assessment programme: holders of the CCSA designation have passed a single multi-choice exam and are also able to demonstrate facilitation experience or the attendance at a facilitation training course comprising at least 14 hours. CCSA holders gain exemption from one of the four examination papers (Paper 4) that lead to the main, global professional designation for internal auditors—Certified Internal Auditor (CIA).

It has also been suggested that it is necessary to provide training for those who will attend CSA workshops. The training would cover risk management and internal control principles and the CSA approach that the organisation has adopted. Clearly such training adds to the cost of running the CSA programme. It is certainly necessary for those amongst the management team who may be assuming responsibilities for the CSA progamme and for facilitating CSA workshops.

Facilitation of CSA by the internal audit activity fits into the "consulting services" rather than the "assurance" role of internal audit.[1]

ANONYMOUS VOTING SYSTEMS

In addition to drafting the report, the "scribe" is likely to be running any hardware and software used by the workshop. Anonymous voting hardware and software, often termed "audience response systems", are frequently used, with each workshop participant having a cordless keypad. During the workshop the facilitator suggests participants vote on particular issues. A vote taken generally allows the workshop to progress to the next issue. The vote may crystallise the level of concern held collectively by the participants. It may highlight differing perceptions that need to be explored further. The votes result in collected data, presented attractively perhaps in graphs or pie charts that can be incorporated where relevant into the report of the workshop. Importantly, anonymous voting results in candid expressions of opinion, unalloyed by a voters' concern about the reception their vote will be given by their peers or managers who are also participating in the workshop: nobody need know how anyone has voted. So, anonymous voting is more important in nonparticipative, threatening, hierarchically governed organisations. It is also enjoyable to use, making the workshop less of a chore.

There are a number of anonymous voting products on the market.[4] They usually have built within them functionality designed to aid identifying, prioritising and then plotting risks by likelihood and impact, using the graphical/matrix approach we described in Chapter 5 (Figure 5.4 *et seq.*) or other suitable approaches.

COMPARING CSA WITH INTERNAL AUDIT

We do not consider that CSA can be a satisfactory alternative to a conventional internal audit activity, although at its outset many wondered whether it would prove to be so. Our reasons are these:

- the relative lack of independence and consequential objectivity that characterises CSA;
- the importance of management receiving dependable assurance on governance processes, risk management and internal control—at the audit engagement level, as well as overall assurance on these to top management, the board and the audit committee;
- the need for internal audit to encourage the CSA programme and to facilitate the CSA workshops;
- the value to top management, the board and the audit committee of internal audit reporting to these parties on the quality and scope of the CSA programme;

- the need to provide management and staff with training in order that they approach CSA effectively, and the likely need for internal audit to do this.

It will be apparent that CSA differs from conventional internal auditing in a variety of ways. The participants in CSA are less independent than internal auditors and thus the results are likely to be less objective. CSA workshop participants bring to the workshop what they know and what they are willing to disclose, perhaps overlaid by a subjective and unreliable gloss. Good facilitation of CSA by internal audit can reduce the impact of this potential weakness which may also be counterbalanced by the in-depth knowledge of CSA workshop participants of the operation under review and their level of expertise and experience. Internal auditors conducting conventional audit engagements learn about the operation under review through extensive engagement planning and by working through a detailed audit programme during perhaps extensive audit fieldwork. Whereas the engagement records of a conventional internal audit contain the evidence to support the results of the engagement, there may be no evidence gathered prior to a CSA workshop. On the other hand, there is no reason why requisite evidence should not be identified in advance and brought to the workshop. Other work can be done prior to the workshop itself, as we discuss below under 'Workshop formats'.

The results of the CSA workshop are the results of the participants, not of the internal auditor facilitator. We mentioned earlier that the report of the workshop is usually drafted during the workshop and approved by the participants before the workshop closes. Experience shows that it is better to complete a Word table rather than generate lengthy narrative prose in order to record the workshop results. These results will include a proposed action plan. This report of the workshop will need to be approved by senior management outside of the workshop. Those who attended the workshop are likely to feature prominently in implementing the agreed action, though other managers and staff are also likely to be involved in this.

CONTROL SELF ASSESSMENT AS REASSURANCE FOR INTERNAL AUDIT

The results of the control self assessment process can be used by internal audit once the head of the internal auditing unit is satisfied that the quality of the control self assessment work means that it can be relied upon. Internal audit has always had a professional obligation to avoid duplication of audit work where the work of others can be relied upon to meet internal audit objectives at least in part. Involvement of internal audit as an adviser in the control self assessment process will provide internal audit with the confidence to draw conclusions as to the effectiveness of the control self assessment process and the extent to which it can be relied upon to meet internal audit objectives.

A HYBRID APPROACH—INTEGRATING INTERNAL AUDITING ENGAGEMENTS WITH CSA WORKSHOPS

Some internal auditors report successfully combining otherwise conventional internal audit engagements with control self assessment workshops. When this approach is followed, a CSA workshop may be convened either during the planning phase of the audit or at the commencement of the audit fieldwork, facilitated by the internal audit team. The issues highlighted by that workshop will be followed up by the internal audit team, to the extent that they are relevant to the objectives of the audit. At the end of the audit fieldwork, instead of or additional to the usual exit meeting, the CSA workshop reconvenes and considers the issues afresh, taking account of the findings of the audit team. This reconvened CSA workshop may generate a report of the workshop, with an agreed action plan. Alternatively the report may be made in the conventional way by the internal audit activity.

WORKSHOP FORMATS

There are various objectives for CSA workshops and each determines how workshop time will be expended. Hubbard calls this "workshop formats". Hubbard's book *Control Self-Assessment: A Practical Guide* explores these in detail.[5] The commonest intention of a CSA workshop is to determine whether and how internal control needs to be improved in the subject area of the workshop. This requires a clear understanding of the objectives of the activity under consideration and the risks (internal and external) to the achievement of those objectives (Figure 10.1).

Figure 10.1 The assurance flowline

It is only then that the adequacy of controls can be considered together with whether and how they may be improved. Control can be judged effective if:

- the controls that are in place have the potential to mitigate the risks if they are applied;
- the controls that are in place are being applied effectively; and
- the extent to which the controls do not mitigate risk is acceptable to the organisation.

Our experience is that it is usually too demanding to cram into a single workshop a comprehensive brainstorming of everything covered in Figure 10.1. It is usually possible to define prior to the workshop the objectives of the activity to be reviewed in the workshop. Then the objectives need only be recapped upon at the start of the workshop. Likewise, it is helpful if the principal risks that the activity faces can be identified and agreed upon prior to the commencement of the workshop. This permits the workshop to give early focus to assessing those risks, for impact and likelihood, perhaps using anonymous voting after discussion and recording the results in the style of Figure 5.4 (Chapter 5). Experience shows that it is hard to control a workshop that is spending time identifying risks as participants' imaginations are hard to hold in check, and consequently time runs out before much progress is made. Assuming it is possible to complete the assessment of risks at an early stage of the workshop time can be spent considering whether internal control is adequate to mitigate those risks effectively and, if not, the changes to internal control that should be made.

Generally it is better that participants are asked to assess risks based on the state of affairs that they believe applies, rather than based on inherent risk. "Inherent risk" is the risk that would apply if there were no controls. Residual risk is the risk that remains after the application of controls. The issue the participants need to consider is whether the level of residual risk is satisfactory, that is within the organisation's risk appetite, and whether controls need to be modified (in design and/or application) in order to reduce the level of residual risk. We discuss this in Chapter 5—see especially the section on "Appropriate ways of mitigating risk".

Again, it is preferable that in advance of the workshop there is an agreed upon definition of the organisation's risk appetite for the activity under review. This can then be briefly summarised early in the workshop, without having to be debated and developed from scratch.

We started this section by pointing out that there are different "formats" for CSA workshops. There may be occasions when the focus of the workshop should be on identifying risks, or even on determining the objectives of the activity under review. Sometimes there needs to be a sequence of three linked workshops for the same business activity, covering respectively each of the elements in Figure 10.1.

UTILISING CoCo IN CSA

We have found that the CoCo internal control framework is often very useful in CSA. Figure 10.2 sets out the essential CoCo elements (or components) of internal control which we considered in Chapter 6 at "Paradigm 3: CoCo on internal control".

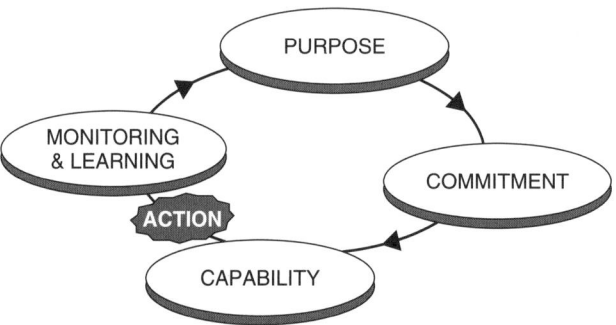

Figure 10.2 The CoCo internal control framework[6]. Reprinted with permission from *Guidance on Control* (The Canadian Institute of Chartered Accountants, 1995, Toronto, Canada)

The CoCo guidance includes a useful set of standard questions grouped according to "purpose", "commitment", "capability" and "monitoring and learning"—see Figure 10.3. We have found they can be used for any CSA workshop, regardless of the subject. If participants are asked to vote on each question, illuminating

PURPOSE

1. Do we clearly understand the mission and vision of the organization?
2. Do we understand our objectives, as a group, and how they fit with other objectives in the organization?
3. Does the information available to us enable us to identify risk and assess risk?
4. Do we understand the risk we need to control and the degree of residual risk acceptable to those to whom we are accountable for control?
5. Do we understand the policies that affect our actions?
6. Are our plans responsive and adequate to achieve control?
7. Do we have manageable performance targets?

COMMITMENT

1. Are our principles of integrity and ethical values shared and practised?
2. Are people rewarded fairly according to the organization's objectives and values?
3. Do we clearly understand what we are accountable for, and do we have a clear definition of our authority and responsibilities?
4. Are critical decisions made by people with the necessary expertise, knowledge and authority?
5. Are levels of trust sufficient to support the open flow of information and effective performance?

CAPABILITY

1. Do we have the right people, skills, tools and resources?
2. Is there prompt communication of mistakes, bad news and other information to people who need to know, without fear of reprisal?
3. Is there adequate information to allow us to perform our tasks?
4. Are our actions coordinated with the rest of the organization?
5. Do we have the procedures and the processes to help ensure achievement of our objectives?

Figure 10.3 *(continued)*

> **MONITORING AND LEARNING**
> 1. Do we review the internal and external environment to see whether changes are required to objectives or control?
> 2. Do we monitor performance against relevant targets and indicators?
> 3. Do we challenge the assumptions behind our objectives?
> 4. Do we receive and provide information that is necessary and relevant to decision-making?
> 5. Are our information systems up to date?
> 6. Do we learn from the results of monitoring and make continuous improvements to control?
> 7. Do we periodically assess the effectiveness of control?

Figure 10.3 CoCo's self assessment questions[6]

comparisons can be made with the votes of other CSA workshops on the same questions: it is often whether something is better or worse than the mean, rather than the absolute score, that is most informative. CoCo suggests that for each of these self assessment questions, a supplementary question "How do we know?" can be asked so as "to trigger identification and discussion of the control processes". We find that the answers to these self assessment questions usually suggest other relevant questions to be debated.

READINGS

Hubbard's book is concise and highly regarded.[5] Although published in 2000 it continues in print. It is an excellent guide for CSA practitioners and also strongly recommended for preparing to sit the examination for The Institute of Internal Auditor's Certification in Control Self Assessment. A collection of 24 essays by leading CSA practitioners, edited by Wade and Wynne, is also very worthwhile.[7]

CONTROL SELF ASSESSMENT

Control Objectives for Control Self Assessment

> (a) To contribute to ensuring that risks are managed to be within the organisation's risk appetite.

> (b) To tap into the knowledge and experience of management and staff who run business processes.
>
> (c) To empower management and staff to assess and improve the mitigation of risks.
>
> (d) To provide a practical means to assess business processes that cut across structural boundaries of the organisation.

(a) Template

1 Key Issues

1.1 Do management and staff participate in their own self assessments of risks and controls?

1.2 Does line management take ownership of the CSA programme?

1.3 Is there a formal programme of control self assessment?

1.4 Is there enthusiasm across the organisation for the CSA process?

1.5 Is the coverage of the CSA programme satisfactory?

1.6 Is the CSA programme applied to highly technical activities that are difficult for internal audit to audit in a conventional audit way?

1.7 Is the CSA programme applied to business processes that step across structural boundaries of the organisation?

1.8 Are CSA workshops facilitated effectively?

1.9 Does the board or its audit committee approve the CSA programme in advance?

1.10 Does the board or its audit committee learn about the results of the CSA programme, as appropriate?

1.11 Does internal audit advise the board or its audit committee on the level and scope of assurance that they might reasonably place on the results of the CSA programme?

1.12 Does the CSA programme add sufficient value?

2 Detailed Issues

2.1 Is there appropriate advance preparation and compilation of information before workshops take place?

2.2 Does the culture of the organisation contribute to unrestrained exchanges of views during CSA workshops?

2.3 Is there appropriate coordination between the internal audit activity and the CSA programme, to avoid unnecessary duplication?

2.4 Is the CSA programme based on (a) workshops and/or (b) surveys, as appropriate?

2.5 Have line management and staff received appropriate training in the CSA process, and in risk management and internal control?

2.6 Is the interval appropriate before a CSA workshop is repeated on the same business process?

2.7 Does it appear that CSA participants are inhibited from being frank about control weaknesses?

2.8 Is the CSA programme a true self assessment by management and staff, or is it in effect dominated by internal audit?

2.9 Has experience shown that appropriate people are invited to be members of CSA workshops.

2.10 Are CSA workshops facilitated well?

2.11 Are CSA workshop reports developed by the end of the workshop?

2.12 Do CSA workshop reports include action plans for change in order to improve the management of risks?

2.13 Are CSA workshop action plans promptly approved by management and effectively implemented?

NOTES

1. The Glossary to the *Standards* of The Institute of Internal Auditors defines "consulting services" as:
   Advisory and related client service activities, the nature and scope of which are agreed with the client, are intended to add value and improve an organization's governance, risk management, and control processes without the internal auditor assuming management responsibility. Examples include counsel, advice, facilitation, and training.
   "Assurance Services" are defined as:
   An objective examination of evidence for the purpose of providing an independent assessment on governance, risk management, and control processes for the organization. Examples may include financial, performance, compliance, system security, and due diligence engagements.
2. Standard 2010.A1 of The Institute of Internal Auditors reads:
   The internal audit activity's plan of engagements must be based on a documented risk assessment, undertaken at least annually. The input of senior management and the board must be considered in this process.
3. Beasley, K. (1994) *Self Assessment—A Tool for Integrated Management*. Stanley Thornes, Cheltenham.
4. For instance, "Communicator" by IML (http://www.iml.co.uk/), or "PPVote" by Option Technologies (www.ppvote.com).
5. Hubbard, Larry (2000) *Control Self-Assessment: A Practical Guide*. The Institute of Internal Auditors, www.theiia.org.

6. Reprinted by permission from *Guidance on Control* (1995) The Canadian Institute of Chartered Accountants, Toronto, Canada. Any changes to the original material are the sole responsibility of the author (and/or publisher) and have not been reviewed or endorsed by the CICA.
7. Wade, Keith and Wynne, Andy (1999) *Control Self Assessment—for Risk Management and Other Practical Applications*. John Wiley & Sons Inc., New York.

11

Evaluating the Internal Audit Activity

"Quis custodiet, ipsos Custodes?"
"Who audits the auditors?"[1]

INTRODUCTION

It is widely held that there is value in auditing business processes generally, and so it should follow that there is value in assessing the quality of that audit process. The internal audit activity should be reviewed. Indeed, the *Standards* of The Institute of Internal Auditors require that this should be done.

The requirement is addressed in the section of the *Standards* titled "Quality Assurance and Improvement Program". There are two main parts to this programme, the first part of which is divided into two:

- Internal Assessments, comprising (a) ongoing monitoring of the performance of the internal audit activity, and (b) periodic reviews performed by self assessment or by other persons within the organisation with sufficient knowledge of internal audit practices.
- External Assessments.

ONGOING MONITORING

"Ongoing monitoring" is done in a variety of ways and is a natural management responsibility. It is done by internal audit management and by senior general management as part of their oversight role of internal audit. It should also be a regular responsibility of the audit committee of the board. The later section of this chapter on measuring internal auditing's contribution to the business gives suggestions designed to be relevant both to ongoing monitoring and periodic internal reviews, as well as to external assessments. Nevertheless the quality assurance and improvement programme, in each of its three aspects, should be:

... designed to enable an evaluation of the internal audit activity's conformance with the Definition of Internal Auditing and the Standards and an evaluation of whether internal auditors apply the Code of Ethics. The program also assesses the efficiency and effectiveness of the internal audit activity and identified opportunities for improvement.[2]

PERIODIC INTERNAL REVIEWS

A periodic review, as one of the two mandatory approaches to internal assessments, can best be described as an internal audit engagement of the internal audit function itself, performed by one or more member(s) of the internal auditing function or by others from within the organisation who are capable of undertaking this engagement effectively. If the latter, then it is likely that one or more members of the organisation who had been internal auditors earlier in their career will be selected to undertake this audit engagement.

Auditor independence, and thus the objectivity of the audit results, is challenged when periodic internal reviews are conducted, especially when these are undertaken by members of the internal audit activity. This is one reason why internal auditing *Standards* require that there should also be periodic external reviews undertaken by independent and competent parties. A periodic internal review should however be conducted in the manner of any other internal audit engagement, and it should be impressed upon the internal auditors in the team that they are expected to come to an unbiased assessment. Choice of team member can be crucial. For instance, an experienced internal auditor recently hired from outside may be more likely to have an independent perspective. There may be other internal auditors of longer standing who are known to have a particularly independent style.

The Code of Ethics of The Institute of Internal Auditors includes this "Principle" on "Objectivity":

Internal auditors exhibit the highest level of professional objectivity in gathering, evaluating, and communicating information about the activity or process being examined. Internal auditors make a balanced assessment of all the relevant circumstances and are not unduly influenced by their own interests or by others in forming judgments.

There is no longer a stipulation within the International Professional Practices Framework of The Institute of Internal Auditors that a periodic internal review must be conducted at least annually. We suggest that an annual interval will usually be appropriate but the incidence, and the scope of this internal audit engagement will, along with other potential internal audit engagements, be subject to the *Standard* that states:

The internal audit activity's plan of engagements must be based on a documented risk assessment, undertaken at least annually. The input of senior management and the board must be considered in this process.[3]

There are likely to be grounds to dispense with a periodic internal review in the year that an external review is conducted.

EXTERNAL REVIEWS

External reviews are required to be conducted at least once every five years and possibly more frequently. They must be conducted by a competent individual or team from outside the organisation. An external reviewer should neither be an employee from elsewhere within the same group of companies, nor someone from the regulator of the organisation or from any other associated party such as the organisation's external auditor. The Institute of Internal Auditors is likely to be able to put together a suitable external assessment team, and many consultants specialise in this. Firms of public accountants are often positioned well to do this work, though the firm that undertakes the external audit of the financial statements of the organisation should not be used. The *Standard* reads:

External assessments must be conducted at least once every five years by a qualified, independent reviewer or review team from outside the organization. The chief audit executive must discuss with the board:

- The need for more frequent external assessments; and
- The qualifications and independence of the external reviewer or review team, including any potential conflict of interest.

Interpretation:

A qualified reviewer or review team consists of individuals who are competent in the professional practice of internal auditing and the external assessment process. The evaluation of the competency of the reviewer and review team is a judgment that considers the professional internal audit experience and professional credentials of the individuals selected to perform the review. The evaluation of qualifications also considers the size and complexity of the organizations that the reviewers have been associated with in relation to the organization for which the internal audit activity is being assessed, as well as the need for particular sector, industry, or technical knowledge.

An independent reviewer or review team means not having either a real or an apparent conflict of interest and not being a part of, or under the control of, the organization to which the internal audit activity belongs.[4]

An organisation may decide to "convert" a periodic internal assessment into a quasi external assessment by subjecting the periodic internal assessment to an external validation; but the guidance is that it should be the organisation's intention to undertake a full external assessment as soon as the opportunity occurs thereafter.

Usually it will be the audit committee of the board that hires the external assessor or team and the report on the assessment will be addressed to the audit committee. Where this is not the case, the chief audit executive has an obligation under internal auditing standards to ensure that the results are communicated both to senior management and to the board, or to the board's audit committee.[5]

Internal auditors will be familiar with the challenge that frequently confronts them of being under some pressure to provide an overall conclusion to an audit engagement which is satisfactory at least. The same applies to a periodic internal review and to an external assessment. The chief audit executive and his or her colleagues will be disappointed if the overall conclusion is that the internal audit activity is not conforming to the Code of Ethics, Definition of Internal Auditing and *Standards*. They will also be disappointed if, despite an overall conclusion of conformance, there are many significant expressions of concern contained within the report.

In our experience, detailed instances of non conformance with *Standards* are always encountered during these internal and external assessments. This need not lead to an overall conclusion of non conformance though it is likely that these detailed instances will be referred to in the report of the assessment. The crucial test that the assessor has to make is whether the non conformance has impacted, or is likely to impact, on the performance of internal audit activity to the extent that it has significantly compromised the achievement of the internal audit activity's objectives, or is likely to do so. The objectives of the internal audit activity should be set out in the Charter of the activity:

1000—Purpose, Authority, and Responsibility

The purpose, authority, and responsibility of the internal audit activity must be formally defined in an internal audit charter, consistent with the Definition of Internal Auditing, the Code of Ethics, and the Standards. The chief audit executive must periodically review the internal audit charter and present it to senior management and the board for approval.

Interpretation:

The internal audit charter is a formal document that defines the internal audit activity's purpose, authority, and responsibility. The internal audit charter establishes the internal audit activity's position within the organization; authorizes access to records, personnel, and physical properties relevant to the performance of engagements; and defines the scope of internal audit activities. Final approval of the internal audit charter resides with the board.

> **1000.A1**—The nature of assurance services provided to the organization must be defined in the internal audit charter. If assurances are to be provided to parties outside the organization, the nature of these assurances must also be defined in the internal audit charter.
>
> **1000.C1**—The nature of consulting services must be defined in the internal audit charter.

1010—Recognition of the Definition of Internal Auditing, the Code of Ethics, and the Standards in the Internal Audit Charter

The mandatory nature of the Definition of Internal Auditing, the Code of Ethics, and the Standards must be recognized in the internal audit charter. The chief audit executive should discuss the Definition of Internal Auditing, the Code of Ethics, and the Standards with senior management and the board.

COMMON WEAKNESSES NOTED BY QUALITY ASSURANCE REVIEWS

In our experience, very common failings of internal auditing activities which feature in reports of periodic internal reviews and external assessments, include:

- scope of work that does not embrace everything set out in the Definition of Internal Auditing.
- Charter that does not exist, or is out-of-date, or inadequate in its coverage.
- Insufficient internal audit resources to provide adequate assurance to management and to the board.
- Restricted scope of internal audit activity, with some "no go" areas.
- Inadequate independence from management.
- Only indirect or no reporting to the board or to its audit committee.
- Inadequate or no handbook setting out the internal audit activity's methods of work.
- Inadequate on-going training for internal auditors.
- Inadequate basis for determining the plan of future audit engagements.
- Routine failure to complete the planned programme of audit engagements.
- Insufficient planning (including documentation of the plan) for individual audit engagements.
- Common failure to complete the planned programme of work at the level of individual engagements.
- Insufficient or inconsistent evidence to support audit findings contained within engagement reports.
- Inadequate audit engagement records.
- Inadequate evidence of audit supervision contained within audit engagement records.
- Superficial audit work, usually with inadequate testing of controls.
- Lack of timeliness in audit reporting.
- Inadequate use of audit tools, such as audit software.
- Poor coordination with other review agencies (such as external audit, the compliance function, quality assurance, etc.).

INTERNAL AUDIT MATURITY MODELS

Recently much effort has been devoted to developing internal audit quality assessment frameworks to enable the maturity of internal audit activities to be assessed. An early attempt to do this is the UK HM Treasury's framework (2006)[6] designed for use with governmental internal audit activities. It is often used in external assessments of governmental internal audit activities. For some time The Institute of Internal Auditors' Research Foundation sponsored a study led by lead researcher Elizabeth McRae that appeared in 2010.[7] Useful guidance, regularly updated, can also be found on Protiviti's website.[8]

Just as with the assessment of internal control or the assessment of enterprise risk management, it can be appreciated that it is valuable if there is a framework to be used against which the assessment of an internal audit activity can be made. If the framework has been developed independently and externally, it has a special value. A relevant question is whether any framework is needed other than the Definition of Internal Auditing, Code of Ethics and *Standards* of The Institute of Internal Auditors.

A further question is to enquire as to the empirical rigour with which the framework has been developed and, in particular, the validity of (a) the specification of the characteristics of each of the levels of maturity (e.g. Initial, Infrastructure, Integrated, Managed, Optimising) and (b) the categories in which each of these levels should be assessed (e.g. Services & Role of Internal Audit, People Management, Professional Practices, Performance Management & Accountability, Organizational Relationships & Culture, and Governance Structures). It is possible that an internal audit activity should not aspire to be most mature (Level 5) across each of these categories.

EFFECTIVE MEASURING OF INTERNAL AUDITING'S CONTRIBUTION TO THE ENTERPRISE'S PROFITABILITY

At a time when internal auditing is being challenged by outsourcing alternatives and by other methods of reviewing managerial effectiveness, it is particularly important to be able to measure its contribution to the enterprise's profitability.

In this section we take a look at performance measures for internal auditing—measures of inputs (*economy*), process (*efficiency*) and especially outputs (*effectiveness*). Appropriate specific measures are recommended. In doing this we will be identifying the key aspects of internal auditing which need to be focused upon in order to improve internal auditing's contribution to the enterprise's profitability. We consider the difficulties of reaching reliable measures of internal audit performance, and distinguish between qualitative and quantitative measures. We suggest a value for money approach to assessing internal audit performance.

It will be necessary to identify the categories of performance measures which may be used to evaluate internal audit performance and the strengths and weaknesses of each. We give advice on their interpretation. We place the measurement of internal audit in context with: (a) the general business environment, (b) professional standards for internal auditing and (c) good management practice on planning and control. Lastly, we present a particular approach to the use of performance measures in value for money auditing which may be applied to assessing internal auditing performance.

The General Business Environment—The Recession

Historically the growth of internal auditing as a business service has been "counter cyclical", though there are indications that this may not be so during the present recession. By this we mean that in the past internal auditing has developed most strongly during times of economic constraint. It may be that directors and managements consider that investment in internal auditing is particularly important in constrained times as an antidote to the control risks sometimes associated with stringent cost cutting. Or it may be that managements have turned their attention away from financial, accounting and operational control (to which internal audit can contribute) when extra profits have been more easily secured by burgeoning sales.

Whether or not internal audit prospers in constrained times, it certainly behoves internal audit to be able to demonstrate that its function is cost-effective and is managed so as to maximise its cost-effectiveness. Where internal auditing is not a mandatory requirement by statute law or by regulation, there is added pressure for audit to be able to demonstrate its worth.

There are indications that managements are now placing internal auditing under a microscope with the intention of determining whether it pays its way. Internal auditing is a costly service to run. Each productive day of internal auditor time expends a sizeable amount of profits from sales needed to resource an internal audit function.

Competitive Tendering

Even where internal auditing is a mandatory requirement the vogue for competitive tendering makes internal auditing a prime candidate for market testing and contracting out.[9] Established in-house internal auditing functions find they are tendering competitively against firms of public accountants, consultants specialising in internal auditing and other in-house internal auditing functions who have been given the freedom to tender for external work. To win the contract, these outside parties may be willing to bid at marginal cost—especially if they have surplus capacity.

The many arguments for and against an enterprise contracting out its internal auditing are summarised below. An aspect that has been largely overlooked is that performance measures for internal audit are particularly important for providing the means of establishing performance-related contracts for internal audit provision, and for monitoring its ongoing provision after the contract has been let.

With the bias being towards accepting lowest cost bids, it is particularly important to devise and use internal audit performance measures which focus upon *outputs* first, *process* second and *inputs* last—this categorisation is followed in this discussion. Each of these three is, of course, important. Senior general management and the board responsible for contracting out decisions should ensure that this sort of internal audit performance monitoring is in place. In-house heads of internal audit can influence management and the board towards this and, in so doing, should be maximising their own opportunities for securing into the future the internal audit work for their in-house internal audit departments.

If management and the board allow decisions on letting contracts for internal audit work to be made on price alone, rather than value for money, they are acting irresponsibly. Decisions on price alone betray a lack of commitment to the value of internal auditing—perhaps merely a resignation to the provision of a skeletal internal audit service due to statutory or regulatory obligations. Even in enterprises with acute cash flow problems, decisions on price alone are unjustified as it is especially important that such businesses maximise value.

Since (a) mandatory obligation to have internal auditing and (b) cash flow difficulties often come together within the public sector, it is within that sector that we are currently experiencing most pressure to contract out internal auditing on price grounds alone.

Potential Advantages of Contracting out Internal Auditing

1. The business can more readily vary its spend on internal auditing, according to what it can afford, from time to time.
2. The contractor is motivated to perform well and can be held to account for that performance.
3. The provider can be changed more easily.
4. The service may be provided at a lower price.
5. An external provider may have a wider understanding as to how other enterprises tackle similar business issues.
6. An external provider may have more extensive audit support resources to draw upon.
7. An external provider may be able to develop the enterprise's own staff.
8. The actual and perceived independence of an external provider may be greater—leading to more confidence in the results of the audit work.

Potential Advantages of In-house Internal Audit Provision

1. A deeper grasp of the enterprise's affairs.
2. A finer adjustment of internal audit emphasis to the enterprise's needs.
3. "On the spot" responsiveness to management and the board; better able to take on unplanned work.
4. A training ground for the future senior executives.
5. Confidentiality.
6. More likely to have a genuine internal audit orientation as distinct from an external orientation.
7. Unable to "walk away".

Categories of Performance Measures

Measures of internal audit performance have tended to focus upon *input and process* rather than upon *output*. Auditors will understand the association between these three and *economy, efficiency and effectiveness*, respectively, as illustrated in Figure 1.1. The greatest challenge is now to develop a range of measures which throw light upon internal audit effectiveness (i.e. output measures).

Quantitative, Quasi-quantitative and Qualitative Measures

Another way to categorise performance measures is according to whether they are quantitative or qualitative. In reality each performance measure can be conceived as

CLIENT SATISFACTION SURVEY

Please answer each of the following questions with a score 1–5 on the following scale:

1 = not at all; 2 = barely; 3 = adequately; 4 = very; 5 = excellently.

1. How useful do you find internal audit?
2. How appropriate have been the objectives and scope of internal audit's work In your area?
3. How useful have been your discussions with audit *at the commencement* of the audit?
4. How useful have been your discussions with internal audit *during* the audit?
5. How open and communicative were the auditors with you and your staff?
6. How satisfactory was the timing of the audit fieldwork?
7. How satisfactory was the duration of the audit?
8. How satisfied were you with the time it took for internal audit to issue an agreed audit report?
9. How fair and balanced do you consider the audit report to have been?
10. How fully do you consider you were consulted on matters which were included within the audit report?
11. How useful did you find the audit report?

Figure 11.1 Client/management satisfaction survey

being somewhere on a gradation between the extremes of objective (quantitative) and subjective (qualitative). An important characteristic of quantitative performance measures is that their measurement is objectively determined. Yet even in a very clear-cut case of a quantitative performance measure[10] subjectivity is not avoided as the selection and design of that performance measure will have been based upon a judgement that it provided relevant guidance on relative internal audit performance, and the interpretation of the resulting data also will be very subjective. Soft, subjective measures are often given an aura of objectivity, so that they may be termed *quasi-quantitative*.

For instance, a satisfaction survey of internal audit clients, asking questions similar to those suggested in Figure 11.1, may be analysed numerically and trends compared over time or between different audit sections. The numeric presentation of the data tends to mask the high degree of subjectivity inherent within this performance measure. The client satisfaction survey is discussed further below.

Performance measures with a higher degree of objectivity than others are not necessarily the preferred ones to use: the criteria for selection of a performance measure should include a matching to the aspects of internal audit performance which are most important and which need to be monitored most.

Of crucial importance is to determine which aspects of internal audit performance are most important and which need to be monitored most. Strictly speaking, an aspect of internal audit performance could be of first importance while not needing to be monitored so closely as other aspects—*if* its achievement were assured *or*, occasionally, if it were outside the scope of management to regulate its achievement.

Using our model of *input*, *process* and *output*, we now consider for each of these categories the most important aspects of performance as they relate to internal audit. Some measures of performance inform about more than one of these categories. For instance, the success of the internal auditing function in completing its planned programme of audits relates closely to whether the function has achieved its objectives (planned outputs) but it also gives potential insights as to whether the function has approached its work efficiently (process).

Another example of this overlap between categories of performance measure is the client *satisfaction survey* (see Figure 11.1 for an example) which provides data on the reputation of audit. To some extent this will result from the judgement that management has made about the professionalism of internal auditors they have observed in action (audit process); to some extent the answers will depend on management's experience of the value of audit findings and recommendations (audit output). Some of the questions put to management in the survey will be targeted more to process than to output, and vice versa; but the impressions that management have about the professionalism of the audit process are likely to colour their answers to questions targeted at audit output; and their satisfaction with the audit output is likely to colour their impression of the audit process.

Input Measures

These performance measures throw light upon the economy with which the internal auditing activity is provided—whether by in-house provision or by external providers. Possible candidates for use as economy measures are:

- Numbers of auditors per 1000 staff compared to sector average.
- Levels of expenditure:
  - budget: actual
  - cost per auditor day
  - ratio of payroll to other costs
  - comparison between audit sections
  - comparison with previous periods.
- Allocation of productive time according to type of work (audit type; audit and non audit work [such as fire fighting] etc.)
- Extent to which audit staff are stretched.

Those measures selected may need to be adapted if internal auditing is contracted out. For instance the "number of auditors per 1000 staff compared to the sector average" would require a conversion to full-time staff equivalents based on the time that the outside consultants were spending in performing internal audit work. Data on the norms for each business sector are available from the impressive surveys of internal auditing conducted by The Institute of Internal Auditors. A ratio of one internal auditor to every 50 or 100 total staff employed by the enterprise might be typical of financial institutions where tight control is an absolute priority, whereas 1:1000 or 1:2000 is more typical of civil engineering constructing firms—probably on account of other personnel, such as quantity surveyors, being engaged in quasi-internal auditing tasks.

As a bald measure of economy, the number of auditors employed is useful, but there may still be diseconomies to be identified. Audit expenditure may be out of control—either audit payroll expenditure or nonpayroll costs. Some sections of the audit department may be more costly than others, perhaps without justification. Even where there is justification for differential costs between audit sections, this is useful information for management as it may point to possible opportunities to obtain better value for money in certain parts of the total audit programme than in other parts. Whether or not this is so will depend not just on cost considerations, but also on the potential for audit effectiveness in the various parts of the total audit programme. So measures of economy must be interpreted together with measures of effectiveness (outputs) and efficiency (process) before appropriate management action can be determined.

We suggest among our input measures a measure of the extent to which audit staff are stretched. It is arguable that this should be categorised as an efficiency (process) measure. If audit staff are not being extended it is likely that the staff input is unduly costly. Ensuring that audit staff are extended is a matter of managing the audit function efficiently. If staff are extended they are likely to perform better and the effectiveness (outputs) of the audit function may be improved.

Audit departments are now frequently calculating the cost of each audit. Audit reports often highlight this figure. An increasing number of audit functions are charging out the cost of the audit to the activity which has been audited. This practice encourages auditors to perform well in order to keep clients satisfied, and encourages clients to take the audit process more seriously as they are paying for it. It also more accurately reflects the total costs of running the different parts of the business. On the other hand, since line management should not determine whether or not an audit is conducted, nor what resources are allocated to it, it is arguable that those costs should not be charged against their budgets.

Process Measures

The emphasis with respect to *process* measures is the *efficiency* with which the internal audit activity functions. The *efficiency* analogy with an automobile is whether it runs as a well-oiled, well-maintained machine. This is distinct from the costs associated with running the automobile, which are matters of *economy*. It is also distinct from whether or not the automobile achieves the objectives set for it—such as luxury, prestige, timeliness, etc.—which is a matter of *effectiveness*. Of course, these three overlap, as we have said before: a poorly maintained automobile is less likely to be effective, for instance.

See Figure 11.2 for a breakdown of process performance measures.

PROCESS PERFORMANCE MEASURES

- Training
- Professional activities
- Rotation of audit staff
- Extent of real responsibility—or is audit work specified in detail?
- Compliance with *Standards*
- Proportion of time which is productive
- Categorisation of productive time according to the stages of audit
- Target dates for various stages of an audit
- Time delay between end of fieldwork and issuance of final audit report
- Time spent on individual audits in comparison with planned time
- Comparison of time with results
- Time spent on total audits—in comparison with planned time
- Rate of completion of audits on schedule
- Reputation of internal audit (client satisfaction survey results)

Figure 11.2 Process performance measures

Our model in Figure 1.1 shows that *efficiency* links *economy* with *effectiveness*. Perhaps a good overall measure of audit efficiency is therefore the average cost of each implemented audit recommendation.

Insight into the audit function's overall efficiency will come from exploring the achievement of target dates and the extent that audit management has been successful in maximising auditors' time actually spent conducting audits and, within that productive time, the way it has been allocated and supervised.

The audit client may also have some useful impressions about the professionalism of the audit approach which can be explored in a survey—see Figure 11.1. The main measure of professionalism of internal auditing is generally held to be *The International Professional Practices Framework* of The Institute of Internal Auditors, which includes their *Standards*: performance measures can be devised to assess the extent to which an internal auditing function conforms to these *Standards*. It should be pointed out that conformity requires commitment to them by the internal auditing function, but also needs support by senior general management and the board.

Output Measures

Here we are considering (a) whether or not internal audit achieves its objectives, and (b) indeed, even *whether it achieves the right objectives*.

The Charter of the internal auditing function, as a statement of the distinctive rights and obligations of the audit function, is an important yardstick against which audit effectiveness or output should be measured. Certain elements of the *Standards* also relate to audit effectiveness as distinct from audit process.

Audit output is hard to measure. Internal auditors are knowledge workers whose output is not always tangible. Knowledge workers conventionally issue reports, and internal auditors are no exception. Internal audit reports are a repository of information on audit output. Perhaps the principal objectives of internal auditors are to reassure management that their systems of internal control are sound and, where they are not, to persuade management to implement their recommendations. Figure 11.3 summarises the implicit or explicit objectives of internal auditing.

The implicit and explicit objectives of internal auditing:

1. To reassure management that internal control is sound.
2. To identify non compliance and urge future compliance.
3. To identify system weaknesses and make recommendations for improvement.
4. To persuade management to accept and implement successfully the audit recommendations for improvement.

Figure 11.3 The objectives of internal auditing

Figure 11.4 outlines output performance measures.

The existence of an audit function with broad coverage provides a measure of reassurance to management and the board with respect to point 1 in Figure 11.3 and discourages future abuse due to the deterrent effect of audit. Perhaps the nearest we can get to measuring this type of audit effectiveness is to measure the planned coverage of internal audit and the extent to which internal audit succeeds in completing its planned programme of work.

An analysis of the findings in audit reports can measure the success of the department in identifying non compliance with essential controls—perhaps comparing with the previous year, or comparing the success of different audit teams, or comparing the success of the audit function in certain areas of audit work compared to other areas.

With regard to points (3) and (4) in Figure 11.3, a similar analysis of (a) past audit reports and (b) audit records of audit follow-up should allow a measurement similar to the example in Figure 11.5. Admittedly this is an inexact set of

OUTPUT PERFORMANCE MEASURES

- **Reporting success**
- **Cost savings achieved**
- **Increased opportunities identified by audit**
- **Completion of audit plan**
- **Client satisfaction**
- **Compliance with internal audit charter**
- **Audit staff advancement**
- **Occasions on which internal audit is consulted on systems changes**
- **Level of requests for special audit assignments**

Figure 11.4 Output performance measures

	Recommendations	Acceptances	Implementations	Successes
Number	1000	800	700	650
Losses	200	100	50	
Loss rate (%)	20	12.5	7.1	

Figure 11.5 Example of internal audit reporting success

measures—it presumes, for instance, that success can be assessed. Even where it can be assessed, the time delay is likely to be too great to make it a useful measure of internal audit performance. So it might be more practical to measure in accordance with Figure 11.5 but stopping short of trying to evaluate whether or not an implemented audit recommendation was successful.

It may be possible to attach money values to cost savings which follow management's acceptance and subsequent correction/implementation of audit findings and recommendations in points (2), (3) and (4) of Figure 11.3. It will, however, never be possible to account for the total value of the audit function to the business as a whole in terms of cost savings. The impact on costs of many accepted and implemented audit recommendations is indeterminable, as usually we will never know what would have happened if management had not so acted. Nevertheless, a historical record of known cost savings which have followed from audit work can give *one* indication of audit value for money. It is, however, human nature to overlook the additional costs which are often associated with points (2), (3) and (4). Internal audit also tends to take credit for good suggestions from line staff. Certainly, management and staff should be given credit for successful implementation of audit recommendations.

In measuring cost savings it is difficult to determine the length of time into the future that the audit department should compute the saving: the decision is arbitrary. For instance, if the audit department takes credit for savings over a

12-month period, this overlooks that the business may continue to benefit from that audit finding indefinitely. Despite these objections, measuring cost savings does have a place in the assessment of audit effectiveness.

Interpretation of Performance Measures

Any performance measure may mislead if it is interpreted on its own. For instance, the number of internal auditors per 1000 staff employed may show a very economic approach to internal auditing, but other measures may indicate that internal auditing is not very effective. Completion of all audits and reports by their target dates may be at the expense of useful findings and recommendations being made. Measures of reporting success should be linked with measures of cost savings, time utilisation and the achievement of audit plan.

We also need to be cautious about placing too much confidence in our performance measures. It might be that they indicate a high degree of audit success and yet overlook important issues which bear upon internal audit effectiveness. Here we highlight just two possible issues of this sort.

First, *audit independence*. This is a prerequisite of successful internal auditing. Secondly, the *scope* of internal auditing work. Two quotations are helpful here:

Whether or not audit is able to perform the full range of audit functions effectively and efficiently largely depends upon management attitude and support which is itself largely influenced by status and independence. The real sign of independence is that auditors are not impeded in their efforts to examine any area within the organisation whereas status often determines the significance attached to audit findings by management.[11]

There is no persuasive reason why ... internal auditing should not [appraise operations generally, weighing actual results in the light of planned results]. Perhaps the only limiting factors are the ability to afford so broad an audit, the difficulty of obtaining people who can do a broad type of audit, and the very practical consideration that individuals may not like to be reported upon. While persons responsible for accounts and for the safeguarding of company assets have learnt to accept audit, those responsible for far more valuable things—the execution of plans, policies and procedures of a company—have not so readily learnt to accept the idea.[12]

Figure 11.6 highlights some of the issues which affect audit independence.

Integrating Performance Measures with Good Management Practice

The performance measures we use to evaluate internal audit should harmonise with those applicable to the enterprise as a whole. The importance of the objectives identified for audit is that these should underpin an organisation's overall aims and objectives, so that audit's achievements aid the development of the organisation as a whole.

Top management and the board should take the trouble to satisfy themselves that this is so. The Chartered Institute of Public Finance and Accountancy (CIPFA)

INTERNAL AUDIT INDEPENDENCE

1. Is internal audit organisationally distinct from any part of the enterprise In which it conducts audits?
2. Does internal audit derive its authority from the board?
3. Does Internal audit have a direct working relationship with the audit committee of the board, and does the head of internal audit have a right of access to the chair of that committee?
4. Does the head of audit have direct access to the chief executive, and does the chief executive receive reports on audit assignments from the head of audit?
5. Does the head of audit have unrestricted access to the organisation's external auditors and to relevant regulatory authorities?
6. Is the recognised scope of internal audit consistent with the resources allocated to it?
7. Are there no operational areas or levels which are precluded from internal audit review?
8. Does internal audit have unrestricted access to personnel and information?
9. Is internal audit free of any responsibilities for conducting any operations other than independent reviews of internal control, and does internal audit avoid detailed involvement in system design?
10. Is it clearly management's as distinct from Audit's responsibility to accept and implement audit recommendations?
11. Are the audit assignments conducted, and their timing, consistent with the assessment of the head of audit as to relative audit need?
12. Is the content of audit reports entirely at the discretion of the head of audit?
13. Is the organisational status of the audit department, and the executive seniority of the head of the audit and its staff, sufficient to underwrite the above requirements?
14. Is it policy to staff the audit function with professionally competent and qualified personnel, and to require observance of the Code of Ethics and compliance with the standards of The Institute of Internal Auditors?
15. Is the assignment of auditors to particular audit assignments done with due regard to the need to maintain effective independence?
16. Is there a charter which sets out the distinctive rights and obligations of the audit function which is consistent with the above needs and is generally understood throughout the enterprise?

Figure 11.6 Factors affecting internal audit independence

suggested there are four fundamental questions to be asked of internal auditing, without which performance measures for internal audit have little meaning:

1. Does internal audit have agreed and established goals?
2. Is the work planned and resourced in such a way as to make achievement a realistic possibility?
3. Does the achievement of these goals contribute to the attainment of the corporate objectives, i.e. establishing and maintaining internal control?
4. Does internal audit achieve its defined goals?[13]

These questions should be addressed by the audit committee, by management, by the head of internal audit and by external audit. The charter of the internal auditing department should ensure positive answers to these four questions.

A Value for Money Approach to Evaluating Internal Audit, Using Performance Measures

In essence, value for money auditing endeavours to assess economy, efficiency and effectiveness, making use of carefully chosen and carefully interpreted performance measures. So the approach we have taken is a value for money approach to evaluating the internal auditing function.

A refinement of the value for money audit approach is to organise the chosen performance measures into three hierarchies, where the more junior levels of performance measures are intended to interpret the measurement of the more senior ones. The most senior measure in each hierarchy is intended to most accurately reflect the most important measure of economy (or efficiency, or effectiveness). Examples of these structures are given in Figures 11.7, 11.8 and 11.9.

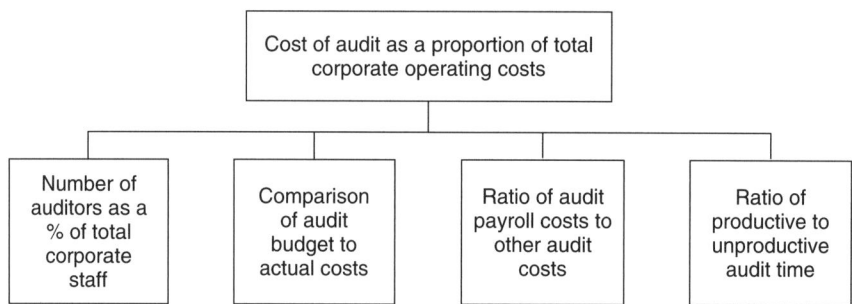

Figure 11.7 Economy (*inputs*) measures in the context of a value for money approach

It is no longer sufficient for audit to view the historic reasons for its establishment as justification for its continued existence. Audit must and should be prepared to provide proof of its worth and value for money to the organisation as part of the organisation's continual growth.[14]

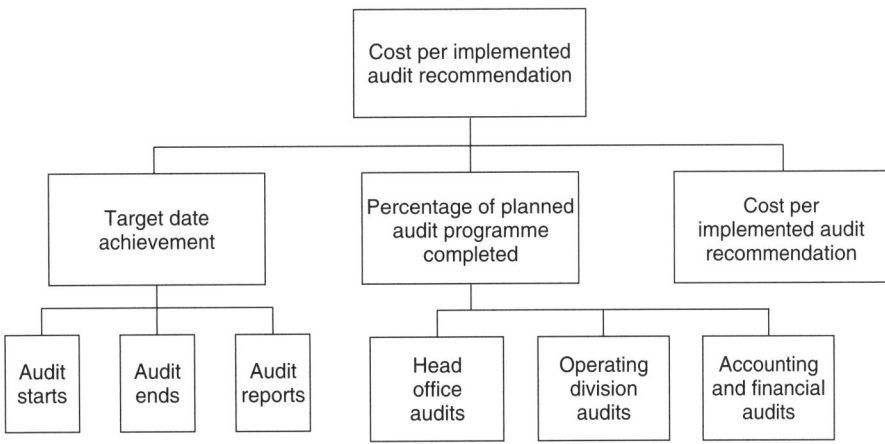

Figure 11.8 Efficiency (*process*) measures in the context of a value for money approach

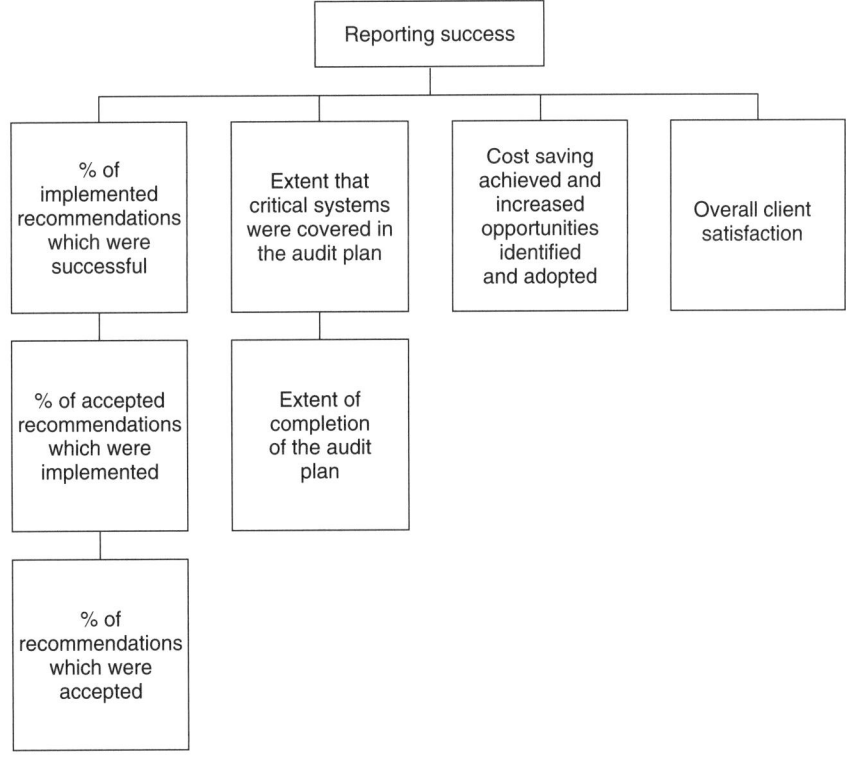

Figure 11.9 Effectiveness (*outputs*) measures in the context of a value for money approach

CONTROL OBJECTIVES FOR THE INTERNAL AUDIT ACTIVITY

> (a) To ensure that the internal audit activity provides sufficient and reliable assurance to the board and to management on governance processes, risk management and internal control.
>
> (b) To provide quality consultancy services to the organisation within the competence of the internal audit activity to do so, without assuming management responsibilities.
>
> (c) To achieve a scope for internal audit that is unrestricted across the organisation at all levels.
>
> (d) To be organisationally and operationally independent so that the judgement of internal audit on professional matters is never subordinated to that of others.
>
> (e) To conform to applicable ethical codes and professional standards.
>
> (f) Generally, to add value to the organisation.

1 Key Issues

1.1 Is there a Charter for the internal audit activity, consistent with the Definition of Internal Auditing, The Code of Ethics and *The Standards* of the Institute of Internal Auditors, and with the pronouncements of any other applicable body with whose requirements the internal audit activity should conform?

1.2 Does the chief audit executive determine the future plan of audit engagements following a risk assessment?

1.3 Does the scope of internal audit activity extend right across the organisation and at all levels?

1.4 Does the chief audit executive ever have to subordinate his or her judgement to that of management with respect to (a) the future plan or audit engagements, (b) access to records and personnel, (c) the content of audit engagement communications and (d) to whom audit results are communicated?

1.5 Does the chief audit executive (a) have unrestricted access to the chair of the board's audit committee at all times, (b) attend audit committee meetings and (c) meet privately from time to time with the audit committee in the absence of any executives?

1.6 Does the chief audit executive provide, at least annually, an overall assurance opinion to the board or its audit committee and to senior management?

1.7 Are the resources available to internal audit sufficient to support its responsibilities?

1.8 Are internal audit processes up to a high professional standard?

1.9 Does the audit committee of the board approve the future plan of audit engagements and then monitor progress against plan.

1.10 Is the reporting to the audit committee of audit results and audit follow-up sufficient for the audit committee to be appraised of the matters arising?

1.11 Is there general agreement that significant value is added as a result of internal audit work?

1.12 Is there an internal audit quality assurance and improvement programme in place comprising ongoing monitoring, periodic internal reviews and external assessments; and is this programme consistent with the requirements of professional internal auditing *Standards*.

2 Detailed Issues

2.1 Has the Charter of the internal audit activity been agreed with management and approved by the board or the board's audit committee?

2.2 Does the Charter set out that the internal audit activity adds value to the organisation by undertaking both assurance and consulting engagements?

2.3 Does the internal audit activity avoid assuming any managerial or operational responsibilities?

2.4 Does the audit committee concur in advance with decisions to do with the appointment, reappointment, termination and remuneration of the chief audit executive?

2.5 Does the internal auditing activity generally complete its future plan of work—to schedule and on budget?

2.6 Are engagements planned thoroughly so that management's objectives and the principal risks are identified during the planning stage and a programme of work to be followed during the audit fieldwork is designed?

2.7 Do engagement records clearly and fully support engagement findings?

2.8 Is supervision of audit work sufficient, and is adequate evidence of supervision documented?

2.9 Are internal audit activity reports (including communications of engagement results) of a high standard?

2.10 Does the internal audit function monitor the status of engagement results and follow up outstanding actions which are placing the organisation at risk?

2.11 Are audit methodologies leading edge?

2.12 Does the internal audit activity have sufficient skills and competences to discharge its responsibilities, either with in-house staff or through buying in the skills needed?

2.13 Is there a satisfactory ongoing development programme for all internal audit staff?

2.14 Is the performance of internal audit staff appraised?

2.15 Is feedback obtained from audited parties, and evaluated, on the acceptability and value of internal audit work?

2.16 Are the results of the quality assurance programme communicated appropriately and acted upon satisfactorily?

NOTES

1. Juvenal (c AD 55–127) (6th Satire): "Pone seram, prohibe. Sed quis custodiet ipsos Custodes? Cauta est et ab illis incipit uxor"—"Put on a lock! Keep her in confinement! But who is to guard the guards themselves? Your wife is as cunning as you, and begins with them." "Quis custodiet ipsos Custodes?" has also been loosely used to ask "Who judges the judges?" etc.
2. Quoted from the Interpretation to Standard 1300 (2009) of The Institute of Internal Auditors. The Definition referred to can be found in the Code of Ethics, and reads:
   > Internal auditing is an independent, objective assurance and consulting activity designed to add value and improve an organization's operations. It helps an organization accomplish its objectives by bringing a systematic, disciplined approach to evaluate and improve the effectiveness of risk management, control, and governance processes.
3. Standard 2010.A1 (2009).
4. Standard 1312 and its Interpretation (2009).
5. Standard 1320 (2009).
6. HM Treasury (December 2006): *Internal Audit Quality Assessment Framework—A Tool for Departments*, http://www.hm-treasury.gov.uk/psr_governance_risk_iaqaf.htm.
7. MacRae, Elizabeth (2010): *Internal Audit Capability Maturity Model (IA-CMM)*, The Institute of Internal Auditors Research Foundation.
8. Protiviti (2009) *2009 Internal Audit Capability and Needs Survey*, (www.protiviti.com), and *Capability Maturity Model Based on the IIA Standards*.
9. The UK expression *contracting out* is the equivalent to the US expression *outsourcing*.
10. Such as, for instance, *the elapsed time between ending audit fieldwork and issuing the audit report*. The decision to include this as one of the performance measures would be bound to be a matter of judgement; similarly there may be judgement involved in deciding the start and end points of the elapse time which is being measured. Judgement also has to be exercised in interpreting the resultant data—for instance, what elapse time is acceptable?

11. Chartered Institute of Public Finance and Accountancy (1981) *An Approach to the Measurement of the Performance of Internal Audit*, Audit Occasional Paper No. 3.
12. Koontz, Harold and O'Donnell, Cyril (1976) *Management—A Systems and Contingency Analysis of Managerial Functions*, 6th edition (International student edition). McGraw-Hill, Tokyo, pp. 670–671.
13. CIPFA (1981) *An Approach to the Measurement of the Performance of Internal Audit*, Audit Occasional Paper No. 3, p. 2.
14. CIPFA (1981) *An Approach to the Measurement of the Performance of Internal Audit*, Audit Occasional Paper No. 3, p. 1.

Part II:
Auditing Key Functions

12
Auditing the Finance and Accounting Functions

INTRODUCTION

In this chapter we consider the financial and accounting aspects of an organisation. First, we will consider the systems and functions that are likely to constitute this area of activity. Secondly, we shall examine each of these component functions and highlight the relative control objectives and the risk and control issues arising from the various activities.

The finance and accounting areas have long been the traditional domain of the internal auditor, perhaps to the extent that management only thought of internal auditing in terms of conducting reviews of accounting records. As this book seeks to demonstrate, the auditor has a legitimate role to play in all the operational areas of the organisation, but invariably even this broader view of the auditor's universe leads back to the accounting functions and the records they maintain. All operations have to be accounted for and so the operational areas of the organisation involve interfaces with the accounts, for example in terms of operating costs, income levels, budget and actual comparisons, and so on.

For discussion of related issues, refer to the Contents pages or to the Index to identify relevant topics. Although you may consider this to be familiar ground, this material should hopefully stimulate you into considering the implications from the organisation's standpoint that are inherent within the accounting and finance functions.

SYSTEM/FUNCTION COMPONENTS OF THE FINANCIAL AND ACCOUNTING ENVIRONMENT

Defining the Finance and Accounting Universe

There are a number of ways an auditor can define the constituent elements of finance and accounting within an organisation, for example:

- *functionally*, based upon the discrete accounting departments that are in place (and perhaps as recorded on the internal telephone list); or
- in terms of the *financial cycles*, such as the revenue cycle, the expenditure cycle or the treasury cycle.

In the latter approach, the term "cycle" can be misleading as the processes are not always cyclic in nature; perhaps the term "process" would be more apt. We discuss the process or cycle approach to auditing in Chapter 2. This approach does have one potential benefit when compared to the functional approach in that it takes account of the inevitable flow of data across functional boundaries where control is often at its weakest. This could be referred to as "a cradle to grave" review. Using the functional approach means that the internal auditor should always be alert to the input and output interfaces that usually exist between the function under review and those which interact with it.

We have chosen to use the *functional* approach to define the financial and accounting audit universe, which gives us the following possible breakdown of the key functions, systems or activities:

- treasury
- payroll
- accounts payable
- accounts receivable
- general ledger/management accounts
- fixed assets (and capital charges)
- budgeting and monitoring
- bank accounts and banking arrangements
- sales tax (VAT) accounting
- taxation
- inventories
- product/project accounting
- petty cash and expenses
- financial information and reporting
- investments.

CONTROL OBJECTIVES AND RISK AND CONTROL ISSUES

We shall now examine the control objectives and the related risk and control issues (divided into key issues and detailed issues) for each of the finance and accounting areas listed above. The data can be used within the format of the Standard Audit Programme Guides (SAPG) looked at in Chapter 3. To save space we have concentrated on the objectives to be set and the questions to be asked and have not presented them within the SAPG format.

The data supplied in the following sections are deliberately general and broad in nature, so that they can be related to a range of possible organisational scenarios. However, in practice, all manner of specific industry or sector factors may apply and these should be suitably incorporated into the data. Conversely, some of the issues raised may not apply (either in organisational or national terms) and these can accordingly be disregarded. The overall aim of the supplied data is to provide a general awareness of the likely elements for each activity.

TREASURY

Here we are primarily concerned with the adequacy of funding and the accountability for transactions, which are normally, by their nature, of high value. Given these two high-profile attributes, it is preferable that treasury operations are driven by authorised policies and procedures.

Control Objectives for Treasury

(a) To ensure that the organisation's funds are appropriately managed with the aim of providing adequate levels of working capital.

(b) To ensure that suitable and secure investments, financial instruments, etc. are utilised to the maximum benefit of the organisation and within the constraints of the prevailing laws and regulations.

(c) To ensure that treasury staff are suitably experienced and qualified, and operate within the limits of established policy and practices.

(d) To ensure that treasury activities are monitored as part of an overall view of risk management.

(e) To prevent the processing of unauthorised and fraudulent transactions.

Risk and Control Issues for Treasury

1 Key Issues

1.1 Has senior management (i.e. the board) established and issued a written policy governing treasury operations, authorised transaction types, financial limits, etc.?

1.2 Has management established and clearly communicated their objectives for the treasury function?

1.3 Have formal written treasury procedures been established which support the aims of the agreed treasury policy?

1.4 Have adequate independent and timely treasury monitoring facilities been established?

1.5 Has management provided suitably trained treasury personnel and the other necessary resources to ensure that their objectives are achieved?

1.6 Are working capital requirements defined, communicated, monitored and reacted to?

1.7 How does management ensure that all the relevant laws and regulations are being complied with?

1.8 Are treasury staff provided with adequate, accurate, relevant and timely data to support their decision-making and trading activities?

1.9 Are all treasury transactions supported with accurate documentation, authorisation (if required), and effective audit trails?

1.10 Are all treasury transactions and fund movements accurately accounted for, correctly recorded in the accounting system, and reported to management?

1.11 How does management verify that all treasury transactions are of the approved type and within the established limits for individual transactions?

1.12 Are all maturing funds/investments, income and interest receipts identified, recorded and correctly accounted for?

2 Detailed Issues

2.1 Are the Treasury Policy and operational procedures regularly reviewed, maintained and kept up to date?

2.2 What mechanisms prevent unauthorised treasury transaction types being processed?

2.3 Would unauthorised or fraudulent transactions be highlighted, reported and promptly reacted to?

2.4 How are unauthorised staff prevented from initiating and processing unauthorised treasury transactions?

2.5 What prevents the processing of unauthorised and invalid transaction types?

2.6 What prevents trading with unsuitable, financially unstable, or nonapproved counterparties?

2.7 Are all transactions subject to suitable authorisation before processing?

2.8 Are sensitive transactions assessed for inherent risk and subject to additional authorisation?

2.9 Are market trends and fiscal indicators monitored as part of management's ongoing assessment of the most appropriate treasury policy?

2.10 What prevents the payment of invalid or inaccurate fees and commissions?

2.11 How is unauthorised use of all electronic fund transfer facilities prevented?

2.12 Are security and financial instrument documents securely stored and adequately protected from loss, damage or misuse?

2.13 If market or financial conditions change, can the organisation promptly identify the potential exposures and take speedy remedial action?

2.14 How does management confirm that all income from treasury activities is accurately reported and accounted for?

2.15 Are treasury staff suitably aware of their obligations and responsibilities in respect of the prevailing policy, laws and regulations governing their activities?

2.16 How is management sure that non compliance with current regulations will be detected promptly?

2.17 How is the accuracy of data input from other systems confirmed?

2.18 How is the accuracy of data output to other systems confirmed?

2.19 How does management make sure that payments of interest and dividends are valid, accurate and complete?

2.20 Are all foreign currency transactions suitably authorised?

2.21 Are all "hedging" activities suitably authorised and reported to management?

2.22 Are all funding debts identified, accounted for, and correctly administered/ discharged?

2.23 Are changes in the relative values of investments and debts accurately ascertained and reflected in the accounts?

PAYROLL

In most cases it is likely that personnel costs will represent the greatest proportion of total overheads for an organisation. The scope of the following review points incorporates the initial authorised set-up of new employees, the processing of suitably authorised amendments (such as salary increases, holiday payments, bonuses), periodic payroll runs, payment arrangements, the correct accounting for taxation and national insurance deductions, reconciliation of the payroll, and the removal of employees from the payroll.

The payroll function has strong functional links with the human resources (or personnel) department. (Chapter 18 examines related personnel areas, such as recruitment.)

Control Objectives for Payroll

(a) To ensure that only valid employees are paid and at the correct and authorised rate.

> (b) To ensure that the calculations of all payments and deductions are correct and in accord with the relevant taxation and other regulations and requirements.
>
> (c) To ensure that all deductions are correctly disbursed.
>
> (d) To ensure that unauthorised access to the payroll system and data is prevented.
>
> (e) To ensure that all payroll transactions are accurately reflected in the accounting system.
>
> (f) To ensure that regular and accurate management and statutory information is produced.

Risk and Control Issues for Payroll

1 Key Issues

1.1 What mechanisms prevent payroll payments being made to invalid or unauthorised persons?

1.2 How does management ensure that amounts paid via the payroll are correctly calculated?

1.3 How does management confirm that income taxation and other deductions are accurately calculated and disbursed?

1.4 Is management provided with accurate payroll cost data on a regular basis to support their decision making, etc.?

1.5 How does management verify that all payroll transactions are correctly reflected in the accounting system in the proper accounting period?

2 Detailed Issues

2.1 Is the payroll system adequately protected from either misuse or unauthorised access?

2.2 What mechanisms prevent the set-up of fictitious employees on the payroll system?

2.3 How does management ensure that only valid employees are being paid via the payroll?

2.4 What prevents the set-up of incorrect or inaccurate payroll data (e.g. salary rates)?

2.5 Are payroll salary rates correct in relation to agreed pay scales/national rates, etc.?

2.6 How does management ensure that employees are not paid for work not done?

2.7 Are payroll payment transactions (overtime, bonus, salary increases, etc.) adequately authorised (prior to data entry) and correctly entered?

2.8 What prevents the entry and processing of duplicated payroll payment data?

2.9 How does management obtain assurance that the payroll system accurately calculates net salary and accounts for all disbursements?

2.10 What mechanisms prevent the incorrect calculation of income tax and any other statutory deductions?

2.11 How is management certain that all the necessary taxation and other deductions are correctly accounted for and paid over to the relevant authorities?

2.12 Are all holiday and sickness payments accurate, valid and within both the company policy and legislative requirements?

2.13 Are all exceptional payments adequately authorised?

2.14 Are pension and any other welfare deductions accurately calculated, deducted from salary and accounted for as inputs to their target systems?

2.15 What mechanisms prevent staff fraud or malpractice in relation to payroll activities?

2.16 Are payroll runs adequately reconciled to the accounting system and anomalies promptly identified and resolved?

2.17 What processes prevent the generation of inaccurate, incomplete or duplicated bank credit data (e.g. for automated fund transfer systems such as BACS in the UK)?

2.18 Are payroll payments, automated fund transfer data or salary cheques subject to adequate levels of authorisation?

2.19 What prevents payroll payments continuing to be made to former staff members who have left the organisation?

2.20 Is sensitive or confidential payroll data adequately protected from unauthorised access?

2.21 Are all the necessary/statutory payroll outputs and forms accurately produced and distributed in accordance with the required timetables?

2.22 Are comprehensive and up-to-date payroll procedures available?

2.23 Have specific responsibilities for the payroll function been suitably defined and allocated?

2.24 If wage/salary payments are made in cash, are the security precautions adequate to prevent theft and/or injury to staff distributing the pay?

ACCOUNTS PAYABLE

In this area, auditors should be taking an overview which incorporates related processes such as linking to the original purchase orders or instructions, confirmation of the receipt of goods/services, confirming the accuracy and validity of invoices, obtaining the authority to pay, maintenance of accurate creditor records, and account settlement. Accordingly there are natural functional linkages with the purchasing function, which is further discussed in Chapter 11.

Control Objectives for Accounts Payable

(a) To ensure that all payments are for valid and suitably approved creditor accounts for goods and services actually received.

(b) To ensure that all payments are correct and accurately reflected in the accounting system.

(c) To ensure that the prevailing sales tax or VAT regulations are correctly complied with.

(d) To ensure that good relationships are maintained with key suppliers.

(e) To prevent the possibility of supplier or staff malpractice.

Risk and Control Issues for Accounts Payable

1 Key Issues

1.1 How does management ensure that only valid invoices are paid where the goods and services have been correctly and fully received?

1.2 What mechanisms prevent the payment of inaccurately priced/calculated or duplicated invoices?

1.3 Are all invoices authorised prior to payment and confirmed as being within the agreed budget?

1.4 How does management ensure that the application and accounting treatment of VAT (or local sales tax) and duty is correct and in accord with the prevailing legislation or requirements?

1.5 What processes ensure that the values of paid accounts and outstanding invoice liabilities are accurately and completely reflected in the accounting system?

2 Detailed Issues

2.1 Is the organisation adequately protected from the payment of invalid or fraudulent invoices?

2.2 What would prevent staff from introducing false invoices into the system and these subsequently being paid?

2.3 Are all invoices identified, recorded, trailed and accounted for?

2.4 How does management ensure that the goods and services being charged for have actually been fully received?

2.5 What prevents payment of invoices where the goods were returned or proved to be unsatisfactory?

2.6 What prevents invoices from being paid more than once?

2.7 What prevents copy invoices from being paid?

2.8 Are invoice payments only made to valid and approved suppliers?

2.9 Would all invoice pricing and calculation errors be detected and resolved prior to payment?

2.10 Are all invoices subject to authorisation at the appropriate management level prior to payment and how is this process evidenced?

2.11 Is there adequate segregation applied between those originating purchase orders and those authorising the relevant invoice for payment?

2.12 Are VAT (or the equivalent sales taxes) and duty charges checked for validity and mathematical accuracy?

2.13 How does management verify that all VAT (or the equivalent sales tax) and duty is being correctly and accurately accounted for and recovered (if applicable)?

2.14 How does management confirm that all invoice transactions are correctly coded and accurately reflected in the financial records?

2.15 Are cheques or other methods of payment confirmed as correct and suitably authorised by an appropriate official before release?

2.16 Are all settlement cheques or payments accurately recorded, confirmed as being promptly despatched and subsequently accounted for through the relevant bank accounts?

2.17 Are individual supplier accounts accurately maintained so as to reflect the current situation?

2.18 Are foreign currency payments accurately calculated using the correct exchange rates?

2.19 Are invoices from overseas suppliers correctly treated in respect of sales tax or VAT recovery, etc.?

2.20 Are staff (and others) prevented from applying unauthorised amendments to the accounts payable system data?

2.21 How is the integrity of the accounts payable system assured?

2.22 Is management provided with accurate and relevant data from the accounts payable system on a timely basis?

2.23 Are credit notes and other adjustments (i.e. balance write-offs) confirmed as being correct and authorised for entry?

2.24 Are all transactions adequately trailed and supported by the relevant documentation?

2.25 Are discounts (including settlement discounts) correctly applied whenever relevant?

2.26 Are invoice payments made at the appropriate time (i.e. avoiding premature or overdue payment)?

2.27 Have comprehensive and up-to-date procedures been produced and circulated governing the accounts payable function?

2.28 Do the current procedures accurately define the requirements for ensuring compliance with any applicable regulatory requirements?

2.29 Are staff aware of their specific obligations and responsibilities?

2.30 How is the accuracy of data input from other systems confirmed?

2.31 How is the accuracy of data output to other systems confirmed?

ACCOUNTS RECEIVABLE

This area of activity has linkages to the vetting of customers for their stability and sales order processing, both of which are further addressed as part of Chapter 16.

The use of electronic data interchange (EDI) between large-scale trading partners is still growing. The objectives and issues for EDI are discussed in Chapter 56.

Control Objectives for Accounts Receivable

> (a) To ensure that all income generating activities are identified and accurately invoiced to customers.
>
> (b) To ensure that all invoices are paid and the income is correctly identified and accounted for and reflected in the accounts.
>
> (c) To minimise the extent of debt and provide for the prompt follow-up of overdue accounts.
>
> (d) To maintain the integrity of the accounts receivable system and data.

Risk and Control Issues for Accounts Receivable

1 Key Issues

1.1 How does management ensure that all goods delivered and services performed are identified and duly invoiced to customers?

1.2 What steps are taken to avoid trading involvement with financially unstable or unsuitable customers?

1.3 What procedures ensure all the required invoices are correctly raised using the appropriate prices and discounts, and that they are recorded, despatched and accounted for within the accounting system?

1.4 How is management certain that all customer remittances are correctly identified, recorded and accounted for?

1.5 Is management provided with adequate, timely and accurate information on potential and actual debt cases to enable prompt reaction?

1.6 Are overdue accounts promptly identified and effectively progressed?

1.7 Is output VAT (or equivalent sales taxes) correctly and consistently applied in accordance with the prevailing legislation?

2 Detailed Issues

2.1 Are all goods and services provided by the organisation accurately identified as the basis for subsequent customer billing?

2.2 How does management verify that all invoices are raised using the correct/appropriate prices and discounts?

2.3 What processes prevent the generation of duplicate invoices?

2.4 What would prevent the generation and despatch of an incorrectly completed invoice?

2.5 Are all invoices and credit notes identified and accounted for?

2.6 Are all invoices and credit notes correctly posted to an individual customer account?

2.7 What steps are taken to ensure that the correct rate of output VAT (or equivalent sales tax) is applied to all relevant invoices?

2.8 What mechanisms ensure that all the required invoices are printed and promptly despatched to customers?

2.9 Are potential customers appraised for creditworthiness and financial stability prior to trading relations being established?

2.10 What other measures are taken to prevent future bad debt situations?

2.11 Are there adequate procedures for the authorisation and setting of realistic customer credit limits?

2.12 What measures ensure that agreed credit limits are not exceeded?

2.13 What action is taken if an invoice is returned as undelivered by the postal service?

2.14 How does management ensure that all invoice values are posted to the accounts receivable system?

2.15 What prevents staff raising invalid or false credit notes in order to manipulate an account?

2.16 Are all credit notes checked for validity/accuracy and authorised by an appropriate member of staff?

2.17 Are all credit notes accounted for and confirmed as despatched?

2.18 Are all other account adjustments authorised as valid and confirmed as being processed?

2.19 Are all accounts receivable transactions accurately reflected in the general ledger for the appropriate accounting period?

2.20 How does management ensure that all customer remittances are identified, accounted for, correctly entered into the system against the relevant customer and promptly banked?

2.21 Is someone responsible for reconciling all transactions passing through the accounts receivable system to the relevant source and target systems?

2.22 How does management ensure that the individual customer account balances are correct?

2.23 Are customer remittances banked as soon as possible?

2.24 Are queries raised by customers logged and promptly resolved?

2.25 Are rejected or unidentified payments highlighted and promptly reacted to?

2.26 Are unauthorised members of staff prevented from accessing and amending the accounts receivable system and data?

2.27 Are statements accurately produced for all relevant customers and confirmed as despatched?

2.28 Have specific responsibilities been allocated for the speedy identification and follow-up of overdue accounts?

2.29 Are all overdue accounts (and those approaching being overdue) highlighted for action?

2.30 Is adequate, accurate and timely information produced and circulated for debt follow-up purposes?

2.31 Are all reasonable and permitted courses of action taken to pursue outstanding accounts and how is the action taken evidenced?

2.32 Are levels of bad debt accurately and regularly reported to management?

2.33 Are all bad debt write-offs authorised by an appropriate member of staff or management?

2.34 Can invalid or false write-off entries be processed?

2.35 Are the more serious and significant bad debt cases adequately and cost-effectively pursued?

2.36 Are all transactions adequately trailed and supported by appropriate documentation?

2.37 Have documented operational procedures been provided for the accounts receivable department?

2.38 Have specific responsibilities and authorities been clearly defined and allocated?

2.39 How is the accuracy of data input from other systems confirmed?

2.40 How is the accuracy of data output to other systems confirmed?

GENERAL LEDGER/MANAGEMENT ACCOUNTS

The accounting effects of all the economic events within the organisation are eventually reflected in the general ledger system and therefore both the overall structure and integrity of the system are critical issues. The general ledgering system will be used to generate financial information for both internal (i.e. management accounts) and external (i.e. the statutory accounts) consumption, and therefore it must operate in a stable and secure environment.

Control Objectives for General Ledger/Management Accounts

(a) To ensure that the general ledger and management accounts are accurate, reliable, and appropriately reflect the structure and operations of the organisation.

(b) To ensure that the accounting data is capable of meaningful and accurate analysis in order to support management decisions and actions.

(c) To ensure that the accounting records are maintained in accordance with the prevailing laws, regulations and professional good practice.

(d) To ensure that the accounting information can be used to generate all the required statutory published accounting statements.

Risk and Control Issues for General Ledger/Management Accounts

1 Key Issues

1.1 Has the chart of accounts been approved by senior management and does it suitably reflect the organisation and operations of the company?

1.2 How does management ascertain that the general ledger accounting data is accurate, complete and up to date?

1.3 How does management ensure that the accounting records and systems comply with the prevailing laws, regulations and accountancy good practice?

1.4 How does management verify that all summaries and analyses of accounting data are accurate and reliable?

1.5 How is the accuracy of published and statutory accounting statements confirmed?

1.6 What mechanisms protect the organisation's accounting data from loss, unauthorised amendment or leakage?

1.7 Is management provided with timely, accurate and relevant accounting information to support decisions and actions?

2 Detailed Issues

2.1 How does management make sure that all relevant economic events are identified and correctly reflected in the accounts?

2.2 How is the accuracy of data input from other systems confirmed?

2.3 How is the accuracy of accounting data output to other systems and external sources confirmed?

2.4 What prevents the processing of unauthorised or invalid accounting entries?

2.5 Is someone responsible for the accuracy and completeness of accounting data?

2.6 Are there mechanisms to prevent the unauthorised set up of accounts?

2.7 Has management approved the current chart of accounts and exercised adequate control over subsequent changes?

2.8 How does management ensure that transactions are being correctly posted to the appropriate nominal accounts?

2.9 How does management confirm that the correct and appropriate accounting treatment is being applied (e.g. for fixed assets)?

2.10 Would posting errors be identified and corrected?

2.11 Are key, control and suspense accounts regularly scrutinised and reconciled?

2.12 Are there mechanisms in place to ensure that transactions are correctly posted in the appropriate accounting period?

2.13 Are all source departments aware of the general ledger processing timetable and their specific data submission deadlines?

2.14 How is unauthorised access to the accounting system prevented?

2.15 What measures are taken to prevent the unauthorised production and circulation of accounting system reports and printouts?

2.16 Are journal adjustments subject to a suitable level of authorisation?

2.17 What prevents the processing of unauthorised or invalid journal adjustments?

2.18 What prevents the duplicate processing of accounting entries and journals?

2.19 How does management ensure that all required adjustments have been correctly processed?

2.20 Have written accounting procedures been provided for the guidance of the relevant staff?

2.21 Is management provided with adequate, timely and accurate accounting data to enable it to discharge its responsibilities?

2.22 What processes ensure that all the required published and statutory accounting statements are accurately produced on time?

2.23 Are the accounting records maintained in accordance with the prevailing laws and regulations?

2.24 Is management capable of detecting any material errors in the accounts and published statements?

2.25 Is someone given responsibility for keeping up to date with current accounting and related legislative requirements and ensuring ongoing compliance?

FIXED ASSETS (AND CAPITAL CHARGES)

In this section we are concerned with notable investments in such items as buildings, motor vehicles, plant and machinery, and office and computer equipment. Initially there should be appropriate authorisation for capital acquisitions, followed by accurate and complete accounting processes covering the purchase, depreciation, verification and eventual disposal of the assets.

Control Objectives for Fixed Assets (and Capital Charges)

> (a) To ensure that assets are correctly and accurately reflected in the accounts.
>
> (b) To ensure that all capital expenditure is justified and approved.

> (c) To ensure that all assets are identified, recorded and regularly verified.
>
> (d) To ensure that depreciation is appropriate and in accordance with both company policy and the prevailing regulations.
>
> (e) To ensure that all asset disposals and write-offs are valid, authorised and correctly reflected in the accounts.
>
> (f) To ensure that assets are appropriately protected and insured.

Risk and Control Issues for Fixed Assets (and Capital Charges)

1 Key Issues

1.1 Has management implemented an authorised policy governing capital acquisitions and expenditure and is it subject to review and update?

1.2 How is management assured that all capital expenditure and asset acquisitions are authorised?

1.3 How does management confirm that all assets are identified and correctly reflected in the accounts?

1.4 Are assets subject to regular verification, with the follow-up of anomalies?

1.5 Has management established and implemented a depreciation and accounting treatment policy for assets which reflects current and permitted accounting practices?

1.6 What mechanisms ensure that the correct depreciation is being calculated and reflected in the accounts?

1.7 Are fixed assets adequately protected against loss or damage?

1.8 Are asset disposals and write-offs suitably approved and conducted in the best interests of the organisation?

1.9 Where appropriate, are assets adequately insured?

1.10 Does management ensure that suitable reserves are calculated for the replacement of key assets?

2 Detailed Issues

2.1 Are documented procedures available governing all aspects of asset acquisition, accounting treatment, disposal, etc.?

2.2 Has the organisation developed an approved policy affecting assets and their management?

2.3 How are all asset purchases identified?

2.4 Are all asset purchases approved at the appropriate level and how is this evidenced and confirmed?

2.5 Is the correct reflection of assets in the accounts confirmed and how is this evidenced?

2.6 Are adequate and accurate asset registers maintained and subjected to regular reconciliation?

2.7 How does management ensure that the appropriate depreciation charges are being calculated in all cases?

2.8 How does management verify that all the relevant depreciation charges are being accurately reflected in the accounting system?

2.9 Are amendments to the asset or depreciation policies suitably approved and documented?

2.10 What processes are in place to protect the assets records and accounting information from loss or unauthorised access?

2.11 Would management be able to detect promptly the loss or misplacement of an asset item?

2.12 Are the assets values that are contained in published or statutory accounting data confirmed as being accurate and fair representations?

2.13 How is compliance with any prevailing regulations or accounting practice confirmed?

2.14 How is the accuracy of asset data output to other systems confirmed?

2.15 Are asset transfers (i.e. inter-company) suitably approved, documented and trailed?

2.16 Are assets adequately identified and protected from theft, loss, damage, etc.?

2.17 Are all relevant staff made aware of their responsibilities to safeguard and protect asset items?

2.18 Is the existence of assets regularly verified?

2.19 Are apparently missing or unaccounted for assets investigated and resolved?

2.20 Are key assets adequately insured and does management ensure that insurance cover is maintained and at the appropriate level?

2.21 Is sales tax, VAT and/or duty on fixed asset transactions determined and accounted for in accordance with the relevant regulations?

2.22 Are all asset disposals subject to adequate levels of authorisation, and how is this evidenced?

2.23 How is management assured that the best terms and conditions are obtained in respect of asset disposals?

2.24 Are all asset disposal proceeds accounted for and posted to the appropriate accounts?

2.25 Could an asset item be disposed of without the knowledge of management or without the relevant proceeds being accounted for?

2.26 Are the asset records/registers correctly updated on the disposal of an asset item?

2.27 Are all accounting adjustments applied to asset accounts approved at the appropriate level and how is this evidenced?

2.28 If permitted, are all pledges of assets as security suitably authorised, documented and confirmed as allowable under the prevailing regulations?

2.29 Are key assets suitably identified in order to plan for their replacement?

2.30 How does management ensure that future budgets incorporate accurate estimates for replacing key assets?

BUDGETING AND MONITORING

Here we are interested in both the general budgeting framework (i.e. how the budgets are initially generated, authorised and rolled out) and the allocated responsibilities for subsequently monitoring actual performance against budgets (i.e. identifying and reacting to significant variances, authorising budget amendments, etc.).

Control Objectives for Budgeting and Monitoring

(a) To provide an accurate and reliable budgeting system as a means to ensure that agreed financial and business objectives are achieved.

(b) To provide a realistic and accurate budgeting framework and plan which accurately reflects the structure and operations of the organisation.

(c) To provide management with a means to monitor progress against financial targets.

(d) To ensure that variations, deviations and failures to achieve targets are promptly identified for management action.

Risk and Control Issues for Budgeting and Monitoring

1 Key Issues

1.1 Has management developed and implemented a documented budgeting process for use throughout the organisation and does this clearly allocate responsibilities for action and follow-up of variances, etc.?

1.2 How is management certain that the budgeting model and processes adequately and accurately reflect the structure and operations of the organisation?

1.3 Are the budgeted figures agreed by the relevant members of management and how is this signified?

1.4 How is the accuracy and completeness of data input from other source systems confirmed?

1.5 How is the budget and actual data reflected by the budget system confirmed as accurate and complete?

1.6 Is the budget information produced and circulated on a timely basis?

1.7 How does management ascertain that all subsequent amendments to the budgeted data are justified, authorised and accurately applied?

1.8 Are significant budget versus actual variations identified and promptly acted upon?

1.9 How is the action taken in reaction to variations, shortfalls, etc. verified as complete and effective?

2 Detailed Issues

2.1 What mechanisms ensure that the budget model/system remains up to date with structural and operational changes?

2.2 How does management ensure that the assumptions and factors underlying the budgeting system are relevant and accurate?

2.3 How does management ensure that the data contained in the budgeting system accurately and completely reflects all the processes and events taking place in the business?

2.4 Does the budgeting system underpin the key objectives for the business?

2.5 Does line management have sufficient input into the process of determining accurate and realistic budgets?

2.6 How does management ensure that the system appropriately reflects the agreed financial scenario?

2.7 What prevents the application of unauthorised or invalid adjustments to the budget model data?

2.8 How does management ensure that the budget system data is an accurate reflection of the source systems?

2.9 How are subsequent amendments to the budget figures and targets confirmed as being suitably authorised and correctly applied?

2.10 Is the budget versus actual data circulated on a timely and prompt basis?

2.11 How is commercially sensitive or confidential accounting data protected from unauthorised exposure?

2.12 Has management clearly defined the level of variances that require follow-up action and the nature of the action required?

2.13 Have specific responsibilities been allocated for the monitoring and follow-up of budget versus actual data?

2.14 Are purchase commitments confirmed as being within budget prior to being processed?

2.15 Are all potential budget revisions identified and approved prior to update of the budgeting system?

BANK ACCOUNTS AND BANKING ARRANGEMENTS

This subject area affects all businesses. The variety of account types and the range of other services offered by the wider financial services community make the selection of the appropriate account arrangements critical. There is a fundamental requirement to consider the type of banking facilities best suited to both the operational and financial needs of the business (for example, in retailing situations where there are likely to be considerable levels of cash lodgements to be made on a daily basis).

Due attention should be paid to the control and monitoring of account usage, especially where there are in terms of devolved authorities for such activities as cheque signatories and fund transfers. Regular, independent and effective account reconciliations to internal records are essential, as they can limit the possibility of defalcation passing undetected.

Control Objectives for Bank Accounts and Banking Arrangements

(a) To ensure that banking arrangements and facilities are appropriate and adequate for the business.

(b) To ensure that all banking transactions are bona fide, accurate and authorised whenever necessary.

> (c) To ensure that overdraft facilities are authorised and correctly operated within the limits defined by management and the organisation's bankers.
>
> (d) To ensure that fund transfers and automated methods of effecting banking transactions are valid, in the best interests of the organisation, and authorised.
>
> (e) To ensure that the potential for staff malpractice and fraud are minimised.
>
> (f) To ensure that all income is banked without delay.
>
> (g) To ensure that banking charges are effectively monitored and minimised.

Risk and Control Issues for Bank Accounts and Banking Arrangements

1 Key Issues

1.1 Is management aware of all active corporate bank accounts, their purpose, and current status?

1.2 Are corporate bank accounts established only at the request of senior management for a defined and authorised purpose (and how is this process evidenced)?

1.3 What mechanisms prevent the unauthorised set-up and operation of a bank account?

1.4 Are the prevailing banking terms and conditions optimised in terms of account type, transaction levels, interest payable on balances, levels of charges, etc.?

1.5 How is management assured that all banking transactions are accurate, complete and authorised whenever necessary?

1.6 Have written procedures governing the set-up and use of banking facilities been established and implemented?

1.7 Do the prevailing banking arrangements maximise the return on surplus cash balances?

1.8 Would management be aware of impending overdraft situations and are all overdraft arrangements negotiated and suitably authorised in advance?

1.9 Have suitable and realistic cheque-signing mandates been established and what prevents an unauthorised member of staff from raising and issuing a cheque drawn against a corporate account?

1.10 How does management ensure that all bank account activities and balances are taken into account within the treasury function?

1.11 How does management ensure that only authorised bank loans and financing arrangements are established?

2 Detailed Issues

2.1 Have responsibilities for monitoring bank account balances been defined and allocated?

2.2 Has senior management clearly defined and communicated their objectives in respect of the operation of all bank accounts?

2.3 How does management ensure that the current banking arrangements adequately meet objectives?

2.4 Are bank accounts monitored in order that required changes in terms and conditions can be identified and implemented?

2.5 Are all bank account movements accurately reflected in the accounting system(s)?

2.6 Are bank accounts regularly reconciled and how is this evidenced?

2.7 Are reconciliation anomalies promptly identified, investigated and resolved?

2.8 Are excess balances promptly identified and authorised for transfer?

2.9 Are inter-account movements optimised to the benefit of the organisation or to avoid shortfalls?

2.10 How are unauthorised overdrafts avoided?

2.11 What prevents the processing of a transaction that would place an account in overdraft?

2.12 Are overdraft limits established, and if so what prevents the limit being exceeded?

2.13 How are banking entries input from other source systems confirmed for accuracy and validity?

2.14 How is the validity of direct debits, standing orders and other automated transactions verified (for both debits and credits to the corporate accounts)?

2.15 What controls are in place over the storage and usage of blank company cheques, and are all company cheques accounted for?

2.16 Have effective measures been put in place to ensure that all cheques are authorised (before release) by a mandated member of staff?

2.17 Are all defaced and void cheques accounted for?

2.18 Would instances of blank cheques being pre-signed be detected?

2.19 Are cheque-signing mandates in place and applied which define various levels of authority limit?

2.20 Are all cheques raised adequately trailed to the supporting accounting event/transaction (and do cheque signatories know what the cheque is for)?

2.21 Are all customer payments processed directly into a corporate bank promptly identified and allocated to the appropriate debtor account?

2.22 How is the accuracy and completeness of all transaction data relevant to the input to other systems confirmed?

2.23 Have adequate levels of transaction authorisation been defined and applied in practice?

2.24 How is management assured that all income is correctly identified and banked without delay?

2.25 Would management be aware of a missing or significantly delayed bank lodgement?

2.26 What measures are in place to prevent unauthorised use of electronic transaction facilities (such as CHAPS, BACS and telegraphic transfer)?

2.27 If cheques are signed using a signature printing system, what mechanisms prevent unauthorised use of the plates?

2.28 What action is taken to avoid the issue of incorrectly completed cheques?

2.29 Are cheques rejected as "refer to drawer", etc. promptly identified and effectively dealt with?

2.30 Are adequate precautions taken to protect members of staff involved in making bank lodgements?

2.31 Are banking charges reviewed, authorised and followed up if in error?

2.32 What processes prevent the establishment of unauthorised or unfavourable bank loan facilities?

2.33 Are all borrowing terms adequately documented?

2.34 How does management ensure that all borrowings are paid at the due time?

2.35 If relevant, how are exposures to interest rate and/or foreign currency exchange rate movements identified and minimised?

SALES TAX (VAT) ACCOUNTING

This section uses the value added tax environment as the standard model; however, the issues raised can easily be modified and applied to other sales taxation regimes. All aspects of mainstream VAT accounting are considered, including registration, the calculation of and accounting for input and output tax, compliance with the regulations, the production and submission of regular VAT returns, and the settlement of any taxes due. There are special VAT schemes (e.g. for retailers) and some activities have specific VAT implications (such as property development), but such considerations are not specifically considered here as we concentrate upon general issues.

The ability of VAT systems to cope with the current demands has also to be balanced against their flexibility to react effectively to, as yet unspecified, future changes (e.g. the introduction of a range of taxation rates for different goods and services). Most (if not all) recognised accounting systems do allow for multiple sales taxation rates, but there is still a necessity to ensure that all the other administrative activities can accordingly respond (perhaps very quickly) to changes.

Control Objectives for Sales Tax (VAT) Accounting

(a) To ensure that all valid input and output VAT is accurately identified at the appropriate rate, recorded and reported.

(b) To ensure that the correct net value of VAT is either reclaimed or paid over and supported by the relevant return.

(c) To ensure that the prevailing VAT regulations are correctly observed at all times.

(d) To ensure that the business remains correctly registered for VAT and correctly displays its registration number on all relevant documentation.

Risk and Control Issues for Sales Tax (VAT) Accounting

1 Key Issues

1.1 How does management ensure that all output VAT and duty on applicable sales is accurately identified, accounted for and duly reported?

1.2 How does management ensure that all input VAT and duty on applicable purchases is accurately identified, accounted for and duly reported?

1.3 What processes ensure that all the required VAT returns are accurately prepared in accordance with the current legislation?

1.4 How does management ensure that the correct net value is either reclaimed or paid over to Customs and Excise (C & E) (or equivalent regulatory body)?

1.5 Is the current company registration for VAT correct and up to date?

1.6 Have contingency plans and practical arrangements been made to cater for implementing variations in VAT rate?

1.7 What mechanisms ensure that all the required VAT returns are correctly completed and despatched on time?

1.8 Does the correct VAT registration number appear on all the relevant company stationery and documentation?

2 Detailed Issues

2.1 Have written procedures been established and implemented covering all VAT matters?

2.2 How does management ensure that exempt and invalid VAT entries are excluded from the accounting records and subsequent VAT returns?

2.3 Would errors in the calculation and accumulation of both input and output VAT be detected and corrected as necessary?

2.4 Is the content of the regular VAT return checked for completeness and accuracy before release (and how is this process evidenced)?

2.5 Would non completion or non submission of the VAT return be detected promptly?

2.6 How does management confirm that all company invoices consistently reflect the correct calculation of output VAT?

2.7 Are the company accounting systems capable of coping simultaneously with a number of different VAT rates?

2.8 Has management established contingency plans in the event of a VAT rate change at short notice (e.g. following a government budget)?

2.9 Does the accounting system adequately cater for zero-rated and exempt items?

2.10 Has management confirmed that the current accounting system complies with the requirements of Custom and Excise, and has the C & E formally acknowledged their acceptance of the system?

2.11 What would prevent the incorrect determination of the relevant tax point for a VAT-related transaction?

2.12 Are all imported purchases from other EU states correctly documented and accounted for?

2.13 Are all export sales to other EU states correctly documented and accounted for?

2.14 Are all VAT-related transactions adequately trailed (i.e. to facilitate an inspection by the C & E)?

2.15 Has management allocated a responsibility to maintain an accurate awareness of current VAT legislation as a means of ensuring ongoing regulatory compliance?

TAXATION

This area of accounting practice is potentially very complex and there are no general panacea solutions available. Therefore it is assumed that each organisation will have in place a taxation policy which takes into account all the factors relevant to its own trading and fiscal situation. Many larger organisations will either employ someone suitably experienced, or use the services of an external taxation specialist to ensure that they have an appropriate (and legal) taxation strategy.

The subject of taxation management can be viewed simply as a balance between minimising liabilities and ensuring compliance with often very complex regulations.

Control Objectives for Taxation

(a) To ensure that all tax affairs are appropriately planned and managed.

(b) To ensure that clear objectives are established in relation to taxation matters with a view to minimising tax liabilities within the confines of the prevailing legislation and regulations.

(c) To ensure that all tax liabilities are accurately determined and supported by accounting data.

(d) To ensure that all required taxation returns are correctly completed and filed on time.

(e) To ensure compliance with all relevant taxation legislation and regulations.

(f) To ensure that allowances and concessions are identified, accurately assessed and accordingly claimed.

(g) To ensure that all tax payments are suitably authorised.

(h) To provide management with adequate and accurate information on taxation matters and liabilities.

Risk and Control Issues for Taxation

1 Key Issues

1.1 Has management identified all the potential taxation liabilities for the organisation and defined a planned approach to ensuring that the relevant requirements are correctly met?

1.2 How does management ensure that all taxation liabilities are correctly calculated and discharged?

1.3 What measures ensure that taxation liabilities are minimised within the prevailing regulations?

1.4 How does management ensure that all the required regulations are satisfactorily complied with?

1.5 Is management supplied with regular and accurate data on corporate taxation liabilities as a means to support decision making?

1.6 Are all tax payments subject to suitable authorisation and how is this evidenced?

1.7 What processes prevent the unauthorised or incorrect settlement of taxes?

1.8 Are all taxation returns accurately supported by the underlying accounting system data?

2 Detailed Issues

2.1 Have suitably experienced staff been allocated the responsibilities of preparing and submitting all the necessary taxation returns?

2.2 How does management remain abreast of changing taxation requirements and ensure that the adopted approach is up to date and correct?

2.3 Has management taken adequate account of the taxation implications of the established relationships with either their parent or subsidiary companies?

2.4 Are complex taxation situations referred to independent taxation specialists for advice?

2.5 How is management sure that assessments of taxation liability are accurate and complete?

2.6 Has management issued and implemented a clear policy on taxation matters?

2.7 How is management certain that the correct/current rate of tax is being calculated?

2.8 Are affected staff aware of the required methods to reduce or contain the organisation's taxation liabilities?

2.9 What mechanisms ensure that all the relevant concessions and allowances are identified and taken into account?

2.10 How are breaches of current regulations prevented?

2.11 What prevents the submission of an incorrect taxation return?

2.12 What prevents the late submission of a taxation return?

2.13 How is the accuracy of the underlying accounting information confirmed?

2.14 How does management confirm that all relevant tax credits are correctly identified and reclaimed?

2.15 Would management be made aware of abnormal or significant variations in tax liability (and what action would they take in such instances)?

2.16 What prevents the premature or overdue settlement of taxes?

2.17 Are all new business operations reviewed in respect of their potential taxation implications?

2.18 How is accuracy of taxation payments data output to other systems confirmed?

2.19 How are taxation data, records and documentation protected from loss or damage?

2.20 Are taxation entries and data adequately documented and trailed to facilitate inspections undertaken by the relevant regulatory bodies?

INVENTORIES

In this section we primarily focus on the accounting dimensions of inventories. Chapter 17 includes a specific section on Stock Control in the operational context.

Control Objectives for Inventories

(a) To ensure that the accounting system and statutory accounts accurately reflect the value of current inventory stocks.

(b) To ensure that all stock purchases, issues and other movements are valid and correctly reflected in the inventory accounts.

(c) To ensure that stocks are correctly priced.

(d) To ensure that inventory values are periodically verified as correct.

(e) To ensure that all adjustments to stock valuations are suitably investigated and authorised.

(f) To ensure that inventory items utilised in production and customer sales activities are correctly charged out of the inventory accounts and accounted for in target systems.

(g) To ensure that write-offs of excess, scrap or obsolete stocks are valid and authorised.

(h) To provide adequate accurate and timely management information.

Risk and Control Issues for Inventories

1 Key Issues

1.1 How does management make sure that the accounting system accurately reflects the values of inventory stocks?

1.2 How does management confirm that the year end and statutory accounts contain accurate stock valuations?

1.3 What processes ensure that all processed stock movements are valid, correctly priced, and accurately posted to the relevant stock accounts?

1.4 Are stock values adequately and regularly verified, and how is this evidenced?

1.5 How does management ensure that all amendments to stock values are valid and correctly applied?

1.6 What measures ensure that all stocks used in production or sold to customers are correctly accounted for?

1.7 What prevents stocks being incorrectly priced?

1.8 Are all stock write-offs, disposals and adjustments suitably authorised and how is this evidenced?

1.9 Is management regularly provided with current and accurate information on stock holdings?

1.10 Does the accounting and management information provide the means to identify anomalies, and if so are such queries actively followed up?

2 Detailed Issues

2.1 What processes ensure that all stock movements are correctly reflected in the relevant stock accounts?

2.2 How is management assured that the stock accounts adequately identify and account for all stocks at all possible locations (e.g. in production, out with subcontractors)?

2.3 What prevents authorised stock entries and movements being processed?

2.4 How is unauthorised access to the stock accounting system prevented?

2.5 How is the accuracy of data input to the stock accounts system from other systems confirmed?

2.6 What prevents stock movements being incorrectly priced, and what prevents the set-up of an invalid or unauthorised stock price?

2.7 Are stock levels regularly and effectively verified by independent staff?

2.8 Is effective and adequate action taken in respect of stock variances revealed during stocktaking exercises?

2.9 Are all stock adjustments authorised and how is this evidenced?

2.10 What prevents the acceptance and processing of invalid, incorrect or unauthorised stock adjustments?

2.11 Is the quality of the underlying stock records assessed and verified?

2.12 Are adequate facilities provided to ensure that levels of stock losses, shrinkage, adjustments, etc. are regularly reported to management for action (and how is their reaction evidenced)?

2.13 Would excessive stock levels be promptly identified and corrective action taken?

2.14 What prevents the unauthorised write-off or disposal of stock items?

2.15 What mechanisms ensure that the income from stock disposals is maximised and fully accounted for?

2.16 What prevents stock items being despatched to customers without an invoice being raised?

2.17 Would processing errors, duplications, etc. be detected and corrected?

PRODUCT/PROJECT ACCOUNTING

The general issues raised in this section can be equally applied to accounting for products or specific projects. Chapter 19 (which addresses subjects relevant to research and development), includes a separate section on product development in the wider context, incorporating the marketing and technical issues.

Control Objectives for Product/Project Accounting

(a) To ensure that all projects and product developments/launches are suitably authorised as part of the strategic direction of the organisation.

(b) To ensure that the appropriate costing method is selected.

(c) To ensure that all the relevant costs are identified and accurately recorded.

(d) To ensure "local" factors are appropriately taken into consideration, such as market share, price sensitivity, price controls, etc.

(e) To establish budgets based on reliable data and assumptions.

(f) To ensure that actual costs and progress are adequately monitored and that variances are identified and acted upon.

(g) To ensure that actual sales or project outturn performance is monitored and managed.

(h) To ensure that the accounting system accurately reflects all the relevant economic events associated with each product/project.

Risk and Control Issues for Product/Project Accounting

1 Key Issues

1.1 Are all product developments or projects authorised and ratified by senior management as part of the long-term strategic direction of the organisation, and what prevents unauthorised product/project activity?

1.2 Have key objectives been set for the product/project (such as the required rate of return on the investment or target sales income) as the basis for performance and achievement monitoring?

1.3 Has management established the most appropriate costing method for the product/project and ensured that all the relevant cost elements and underlying assumptions have been identified and incorporated?

1.4 How is management certain that all the relevant cost data is accurate, complete and being correctly accumulated in the accounting system?

1.5 Has management taken adequate account of local factors, such as taxation, pricing controls, competitors' strategies, available subsidies and grants, etc.?

1.6 Have the key project stages, milestones and deliverables been identified and incorporated into a workable progress monitoring system for management review and action?

1.7 How is management certain that cost overruns, failures to achieve target objectives, etc. will be promptly detected and followed up?

1.8 How does management verify that it has accurately identified, and made available, all the required resources?

1.9 Has management defined the break even point for the product/project and established adequate monitoring of actual sales/performance to ensure achievement of their objectives?

2 Detailed Issues

2.1 Does management undertake a full appraisal of all potential products and projects and how is this evidenced?

2.2 Has management developed and agreed an authorised pricing policy based on market share, action by competitors, local pricing considerations, supply and demand, geographic differences, and so on?

2.3 Are all product developments/launches considered in relation to the established pricing policy?

2.4 Has management determined targets and objectives for each product/project, and established a mechanism to monitor actual performance against the targets?

2.5 How does management confirm that products/projects are achieving the required objectives?

2.6 How does management ensure that it has accurately identified all the direct and indirect costs associated with the product/project?

2.7 How does management confirm that all the resources (labour and material) actually expended are being identified and accurately costed?

2.8 Have all special costs (such as special tooling, capital equipment, employing external consultants, etc.) been taken into account?

2.9 If the product/project involves materials or services provided by external suppliers, has management taken due regard of the consequences of variations in the related costs?

2.10 Has the most relevant and appropriate costing method been applied?

2.11 How does management ensure it has accurately and realistically determined the profit level for the product (and is this linked to a critical and realistic level of sales activity)?

2.12 How is the accuracy of costing data input from other source systems confirmed for completeness and correct coding?

2.13 How is the accuracy of output costing data (budget and actual) confirmed?

2.14 Have all of the discrete production and other stages been identified, and how can management be certain that the associated costs are accurately reflected in the accounting/costing systems?

2.15 What processes prevent the inclusion of invalid or incorrect costs for a product or project?

2.16 Have cost targets been established for all the key stages of the project, and are actual costs monitored against the targets?

2.17 Are all cost overruns or performance shortfalls promptly brought to management's attention?

2.18 Is the impact of standard cost variances considered in relation to the inventory and cost of sales?

2.19 Are significant problems or cost variances recorded together with the proposed courses of management action?

2.20 How does management ensure that all identified problems, shortfalls, overspends, etc. are followed up and resolved?

PETTY CASH AND EXPENSES

Petty cash reviews are generally related to questions of scale. The levels of petty cash and general expense expenditure will vary considerably between organisations. Taking account of the possible low level scale of petty cash costs, management may feel content with the application of common sense controls and cost containment principles, as it will consider that there are more pressing business issues to address. However, given the relatively simple processes involved and the possible proliferation of an attitude that "everybody fiddles their expenses, don't they?" a lack of basic control can very easily lead to losses and staff behaving unethically.

Control Objectives for Petty Cash and Expenses

> (a) To ensure that all expenses are valid and authorised.
>
> (b) To ensure that all expenses are correctly identified, recorded and accurately reflected in the accounting system.
>
> (c) To ensure that all expense payments are in accord with company policy and any relevant external regulations (e.g. for sales tax or VAT).

Risk and Control Issues for Petty Cash and Expenses

1 Key Issues

1.1 How does management monitor that only valid, accurate and authorised expenses are processed?

1.2 What mechanisms prevent the acceptance and processing of invalid, unauthorised or incorrect expenses?

1.3 Are all petty cash floats identified and accounted for?

1.4 Has management established clear policies and procedures for recording, authorising and processing petty cash and expense claims?

1.5 How does management confirm that all petty cash and expenses are correctly reflected in the accounting system?

1.6 How is compliance with the prevailing VAT (or the equivalent sales tax) regulations for expenses confirmed?

2 Detailed Issues

2.1 Are expenses claims and petty cash returns supported by the relevant receipts?

2.2 Have expense authority levels and mandates been established, and how is their correct application evidenced?

2.3 Are petty cash and personal expense floats accounted for and regularly verified?

2.4 How does management ensure that petty cash/expense floats are appropriately recovered when an employee leaves the organisation?

2.5 Have staff been made aware of their responsibilities in respect of petty cash and expenses, especially their guardianship of floats?

2.6 What prevents the processing of personal cheques, loans and IOUs through the petty cash float?

2.7 Is the VAT or sales tax content being correctly identified and accounted for, and how are errors prevented?

2.8 Are all petty cash/expense claims adequately supported and trailed?

2.9 Are floats accurately determined, and how are excessively large floats avoided?

2.10 Have adequate and secure storage facilities been provided for petty cash and expense floats?

2.11 Has management determined and implemented standard rates for selected expense categories (e.g. meal allowances or mileage rates) and what prevents the processing of a claim for an invalid rate?

2.12 Have procedures been established governing the use of company fuel cards and credit cards?

2.13 What processes prevent the misuse of fuel cards (e.g. to cover private journeys)?

2.14 What processes prevent the misuse or inappropriate use of company credit cards?

FINANCIAL INFORMATION AND REPORTING

The issues raised in this section take account of both internal and external financial reporting requirements. The key concerns relate to accuracy, completeness, timeliness and security of the information.

Control Objectives for Financial Information and Reporting

> (a) To ensure that management (and others within the organisation) are provided with accurate and timely financial information to support their decision making and activities.
>
> (b) To ensure that all the relevant financial reports and returns are accurately prepared and distributed to external bodies in accordance with the prevailing legislation, regulation and contractual obligations.

> (c) To ensure that accounting records and statements are correctly maintained and prepared in accordance with the prevailing accounting standards and good practice.
>
> (d) To ensure that all financial information is adequately protected from loss, misuse or unauthorised leakage.
>
> (e) To ensure that sensitive or confidential corporate financial information is adequately protected.

Risk and Control Issues for Financial Information and Reporting

1 Key Issues

1.1 Has management identified and documented all its financial information requirements?

1.2 How is management certain that all the required financial information is accurate and provided on time?

1.3 What processes prevent the creation and circulation of inaccurate, invalid or out-of-date financial data?

1.4 How is management assured that all the required external and statutory financial reports/returns are accurately generated and released on time?

1.5 What mechanisms prevent the release of inaccurate financial data to external bodies?

1.6 How does management monitor that all accounting records are maintained in accordance with the current accounting regulations, standards and professional good practice?

1.7 What measures are in place to ensure that financial data is adequately protected from loss, distortion, misuse or unauthorised leakage?

2 Detailed Issues

2.1 Are internal financial information requirements regularly reviewed and updated so as to ensure that information flows are relevant, current and adequately address the needs of management and staff?

2.2 Are redundant and out-of-date information flows identified and terminated?

2.3 How does management ensure that information is being accessed only by authorised and relevant employees?

2.4 Are those managers responsible for maintaining the corporate financial records kept aware of all current and forthcoming requirements, accounting regulations, etc. in order to ensure ongoing compliance?

2.5 Would the failure to produce and distribute statutory financial information be detected and reacted to?

INVESTMENTS

Given the notable financial and timing implications associated with investment activities, it is crucial that authorised policies are in place and adhered to.

Control Objectives for Investments

> (a) To ensure that all investment decisions are adequately researched and authorised in accordance with the established objectives.
>
> (b) To ensure that investment commitments do not interfere with the required cash flow and that sufficient working funds are maintained.
>
> (c) To ensure that the timescale and liquidity implications of investments are adequately considered and catered for.
>
> (d) To ensure that invested funds and the income generated are correctly accounted for.
>
> (e) To ensure that all relevant regulations, exchange controls and accountancy standards are complied with.
>
> (f) To ensure that investment documentation is adequately and securely stored.

Risk and Control Issues for Investments

1 Key Issues

1.1 Has management established an approved investment policy which clearly defines their objectives (i.e. required levels of return, timescale, etc.)?

1.2 How does management ensure that investment income is maximised within the prevailing law and regulations?

1.3 How does management ensure that only suitable and authorised investments are made, which accord with the established objectives?

1.4 What processes prevent investment commitments from adversely interfering with the day-to-day cash requirements of the business?

1.5 Are all invested funds and the income generated from them accurately accounted for?

1.6 How does management confirm that all investments comply with the relevant laws, regulations and accounting standards?

1.7 Is investment documentation securely and adequately stored and protected from loss, misuse or damage?

2 Detailed Issues

2.1 What prevents the set-up of an unauthorised investment?

2.2 What prevents the set-up of an investment that is outwith the defined policy and management objectives?

2.3 How are the cash flow implications of proposed investments assessed so as to avoid shortages of day-to-day funding across the lifetime of the investment?

2.4 How is management authorisation for investments evidenced?

2.5 Are investment considerations adequately assessed for inherent risk?

2.6 Are investments aimed at achieving the highest yield and are they assessed in respect of achieving defined objectives?

2.7 Are all investments correctly recorded in the accounting system?

2.8 How does management ensure that all income due from investments is received in full and at the appropriate time?

2.9 Is investment income correctly identified and appropriately recorded in the accounting system?

2.10 Would investment activities which fail to comply with the prevailing regulations be prevented or promptly detected and reported?

13
Auditing Subsidiaries, Remote Operating Units and Joint Ventures

INTRODUCTION

In this chapter we will examine the specific practical considerations that apply in the auditing of subsidiaries or remote operating units (such as those located in other countries).

The modern corporation is increasingly organised into decentralised profit centres, some of which may be located overseas. It is normally the role of the centre to provide leadership, inspiration and direction in order to achieve the necessary performance potential. This presupposes that the required objectives and performance standards have been established, agreed and accurately communicated to those affected.

The degrees to which functions are devolved to the subsidiary and remote units will, of course, vary. Senior management will have to decide what business aspects remain the prerogative of the centre; for example, these could include:

- approving budgets
- setting production schedules
- reviewing divisional strategies
- allocating capital resources
- responsibility for research and development
- defining standards
- appointing divisional managers.

The roles and responsibilities of group and subsidiary management will need to be defined and clear policies generated; for example, on such matters as trading within the group, where the stances on sourcing from within the group and selling on to other subsidiaries will need to be defined.

For the most part, the fundamental audit approach to the bulk of the audit field work will be the same in this type of operational review as it would be for those conducted within the parent company or head office. In other words, the systematic review and assessment of the controls and measures in place both to counteract the inherent risks within the operation(s) being examined and to ensure that the established objectives are achieved. On the ground there may be some potential additional practical matters to address, such as the local language and legislative considerations. However, of prime concern to the audit manager will be how he/she can ensure that the time spent during the audit visit is productive and focused upon the appropriate things. This will be especially true if this is to be the first audit of the operation.

The audit manager may be under pressure to deploy precious resources in a cost-effective manner and in proportion to the perceived level of risks. This may be especially true when the additional costs of travel, accommodation and subsistence have to be added to the fixed payroll costs of the audit function. In the eyes of senior management there can be no justification for wasting audit time on low-risk operations with little overall significance to the organisation.

When contemplating the total audit universe of possible review projects, the audit manager may apply some form of relative risk assessment in order to identify auditing priorities as the basis for forming the audit plan for the coming year. We do not examine such formal risk assessment methods here,[1] but rather suggest two possible techniques for gathering key data about any subsidiary or remote operation as the basis for assessing the audit priorities within a review project.

FACT FINDING[2]

In the course of preparing for an audit visit, one method of gathering the key background and performance data and environmental facts about a potential audit review target would be to use a fact finding programme. The data collected during this process may be obtained from a number of sources including existing management information and accounting records, senior management representatives and local operating reports.

It may be possible to gather the required facts and data without visiting the target operation and thus avoid the costs associated with field visits. Where the required information is only available on-site, a form of brief reconnaissance trip may be justified. In either case, the intelligence obtained should aim to provide a reliable basis for subsequently scoping and focusing the planned audit visit activities on the key areas of the target operations.

The information gathered during this sort of fact finding exercise can be used to ensure that appropriate arrangements are put in place for the detailed audit review visit and that key circumstances are taken into account during the creation of the detailed audit review programmes. By following this sort of process, the possibility of wasting valuable time during the site visit is potentially reduced (although there is no guarantee that it can be completely eradicated).

Where the data is related to financial or performance matters, care should be taken to ensure that the sources are reliable and the data is both accurate and up to date. Where there is the likelihood of a prolonged delay between the date the data was gathered and the intended date of the audit field visit, the contents may have to be reviewed in the interim so that more current and credible information is made available to support the determination of audit coverage.

Particular attention should be paid to the appropriate interpretation of data trends or performance variances, as these may be influenced by legitimate events, such as seasonal sales patterns or the effects of local fiscal regulations. Where necessary, unusual data or underlying implications should be subject to further validation enquiries.

When the auditor is compiling the fact finding document, care should be taken to ensure that commercially sensitive and confidential data is adequately protected from unauthorised access and leakage.

One other practical consequence of using the fact finding approach is that it should ensure that the auditors engaged in the project and the subsequent review visit are suitably aware of the key environmental considerations. This will hopefully demonstrate to local management that the audit function has taken the time and effort to set the operation in context and obtained an accurate impression of the business under review. This sort of informed preparation can enhance the perceived credibility of the auditing function.

HIGH LEVEL REVIEW PROGRAMME[3]

Having concluded that a particular subsidiary or operation should be subject to operational audit review, it will be necessary to obtain an accurate impression of the relative risk priorities within the organisation, so that audit review resources can be suitably targeted. In the real world, this may present practical difficulties, especially where the chosen operation is located overseas. In such circumstances, the auditor may have to resort to a range of information sources so that a comprehensive picture of the operations can be formed. These sources may include:

- reviewing and analysing accounting, performance and other data sent to the parent company;
- conducting interviews with senior (parent company) executives with line responsibility for the relevant operation;
- getting local senior management to complete and return questionnaires covering the key areas of audit interest;
- where available, reviewing previous audit working papers and reports.

One possible solution to gathering the relevant data about the prevailing condition of internal controls and management attitudes is to conduct a high level review of the operation. This can be undertaken either by the audit department as a reconnaissance exercise prior to the main audit visit, or by soliciting the cooperation of local managers to provide the necessary data. This latter option may be more pragmatic in the case of an overseas operation where the associated travelling and accommodation costs may prevent two audit visits, especially where audit management are keen to ensure that any review time spent on site is productive and not used to gather background facts. If the responses were to be completed by local management, they would obviously require some guidance as to the purpose of the process and the type and level of information required.

Audit management also has the option to use the fact finding programme to bring together a wide range of relevant facts about the nature and type of business operation being considered for an audit review. The data contained in that programme could, in itself, indicate selected activities which could benefit from a full-scale audit review (for example, by virtue of the level and significance of a particular business activity or trading relationship). However, the additional use of the high level programme approach can provide yet further insight into the underlying quality and effectiveness of management within the business.

JOINT VENTURES

Any organisation must be alert to commercial opportunities that either support their objectives or have the potential to profitably exploit new areas. The maintenance of strategic and competitive advantage will drive organisations to seek new, improved, alternative and innovative ways of doing business. The search for such expansion opportunities may indeed be driven by the simple and basic expediency of ensuring the continued survival of the entity.

In some instances the cost of entering a new market area can be prohibitive and there may be other entry barriers to surmount (for example, technical and regulatory issues). Where another organisation has developed either a specific area of expertise or a market presence in a particular business operation, it may be more worthwhile considering a formal alliance with them, rather than struggle to enter the same marketplace singlehandedly. For example, a small software development company may enter into a joint marketing arrangement with a larger hardware company, and thereby take advantage of an established infrastructure. However, such concepts presuppose that there can be tangible benefits for both parties, otherwise why should the organisation with the established business or specific knowledge share their crock of gold with others? The business development strategy adopted by an organisation may have been historically cautious in nature, and any move into activities associated with higher risk and potentially high returns can be tempered if additional partners can be found to share the risk load, and of course share the profits if the exercise is successful.

The partners to a joint venture need not be solely restricted to commercial organisations. Financial institutions and government agencies can also be involved. Indeed, any other party with similar or shared objectives and goals could have a legitimate role to play. However, some partners may wish to impose specific conditions which may prove onerous (for instance, government agencies may be in the position to demand that prospective partners conform to their standards and practices). Alternatively, the parties may bring together their own specific, different and possibly specialised attributes, which amalgamate to form an innovative solution.

The nature of joint venture exercises can vary, for example:

- cooperation on a particular development project (e.g. a new computer software system, a new pharmaceutical product, or an oil pipeline);

- the co-ownership of a separate new company, operated and owned by all the parties;
- the operation of a business venture by one organisation on behalf of another.

The joint pooling of resources and efforts towards a mutually beneficial goal may have other potential benefits, such as economies of scale, improved efficiency levels, shared capital investment programmes and gaining access to areas of specialist knowledge. However, there are also attendant disadvantages, for instance only taking a share of the income and profits (if applicable), possible conflicts over the individual partner's strategic direction, onerous levels of communication, the absence of appropriate trust, the threats of competition in other areas of business, a disproportionate amount of time spent on resolving corporate cultural differences, and so on.

Wider economic factors will also have an effect on the market for joint venture exercises. Whenever the general or national economy is under pressure and trading conditions are affected, it may be more prudent for businesses to cooperate on joint ventures.

The nature and form of international trading relationships may become important (or indeed vital) to an organisation's survival strategy; for example, the opening up of the European market will give companies operating in different countries further opportunities for cooperative ventures while drawing on local market know-how and/or familiarity with diverse national business practices. However, involvement in international joint ventures does present additional potential problems, such as:

- localised business practices, laws, ethics, accounting standards, taxation and other regulations (e.g. conforming to local requirements, selecting the appropriate legal jurisdiction for contractual arrangements);
- the prevailing economic and political circumstances (e.g. possible effects on business operations and/or performance expectations);
- problems associated with time zone differences (e.g. disruption and elongation of lines of communications);
- difficulties concerning languages (e.g. clarity of communications, ensuring the uniformity and acceptability of documentation, regular reporting);
- currency and foreign exchange implications;
- internal auditors will be particularly interested in the role played by statutory auditors in overseas locations and the extent to which cooperation can be expected.

On the global business stage, there have been significant developments which could influence the general environment for joint venture relationships. The break-up of the former Soviet Union may offer western businesses trading and development opportunities with local partners, who have an appreciation of the emerging economic situation but perhaps lack the necessary skills and leading edge techniques to exploit their potential. The same situation applies to the former eastern bloc countries, who, having shed communism, are now seeking to take their place in a free global marketplace.

When considering joint ventures, managements are faced with fundamental questions about levels of investment, involvement, ownership, responsibility and control. Although all these elements can be defined in contractual terms and agreed procedures, there should always be a balance in allocation of risks, responsibilities, duties, liabilities and obligations.

It is crucial for any organisation to have a defined strategic plan which maps out the future development and growth of the business. All the day-to-day activities of the organisation should be linked to the agreed strategic plan, and this includes the role to be played by joint ventures. Joint ventures may be the only viable option for an organisation to achieve the required diversity and flexible growth within the required timescale; but such important steps should always be driven by sound and stable strategic thinking.

In the establishment of any relationship, it is easy to become distracted from the real issues and to lose a sense of informed realism. This may be because the parties view their contribution as but one part of the whole, and unless the roles and responsibilities of each participant are clearly defined, there is the danger that some issues will fall between the ensuing cracks.

Whenever two (or more) parties come together for a given purpose there is always the possibility that the specified venture may fail (or at least flounder). Very often an absence of clear communication leads to a breakdown fundamentally caused by a lack of accurate appreciation of the other parties' objectives. In the commercial world, joint business ventures are essentially partnerships of effort bound by contractual obligations and rights, but there can be a real chasm of difference between the high level business objectives and the detailed reality of the situation on the ground. One solution is to define (in the contractual and operating documentation) the requirements for regular meetings and the exchange of significant information about the venture and its progress.

Once the venture is up and running, its day-to-day operations are potentially influenced by all the different factors affecting all the partners. Some of these forces may either have implications for the joint venture (e.g. the need to concentrate resources on a crisis nearer to home) or potentially have simultaneous effects for all the parties to the joint venture. Lines of communication and planning should be flexible enough to enable a prompt response to such events, so as to ensure that the possible effects on the venture are communicated, understood and adequately reacted to.

In common with all business activities, management involved in joint ventures will need to ensure that controls form part of the target environment in order that investments in capital, resources and time are duly protected. The stance taken on internal control within joint ventures will depend, in part, on the attitudes to corporate governance and accountability that prevail in the partners' business environment, especially where they are overseas partners operating in different national arenas. If the basis of the joint venture is predominantly entrepreneurial in nature, there could be implied resistance to the application of too much control (e.g. control processes may be viewed as an unnecessary overhead or as an impediment to progress and growth). The need for incorporating internal control into the joint venture may be seen (especially by internal auditors) as self-evident; however, as in all operations there must be a realistic balance drawn between providing adequate, effective control and avoiding burdensome or suffocating control levels.

Many of the points raised so far in this section will need to be addressed during the period of negotiation prior to the formalisation of the joint venture relationship.

The Internal Audit Role in Joint Ventures

Where both (or all) parties to a joint venture arrangement have their own internal auditing functions, it will, at least, be necessary to ensure adequate cooperation and coordination of internal audit review activities. Given the loyalty expected of auditors to their employers, complete frankness and openness with their counterparts in other organisations is unlikely. However, internal auditors in one organisation should have a fundamental right of access to the records, premises and staff of the venture partners. Such access rights should clearly be defined in the contractual agreements and any definitions of auditing scope and timing should also be incorporated. Auditors may also be called upon to assess whether the business objectives established for the venture are likely to be achieved. If the audit review work is to be conducted in accordance with established auditing standards (such as those promoted by The Institute of Internal Auditors), this requirement should also be defined, together with any other qualitative factors, in the agreement documents.

The driving criteria for internal audit assessment of the joint venture operations will be to assure management that appropriate control activities are in place and that they are effective in protecting the organisation's investment and interests.

Internal audit management will need to maintain an up-to-date awareness of the general business plans for their organisation, so that they can anticipate the implications for audit planning and establish the foundation of audit assignments in the future. The chief internal auditor (or director of auditing) will need to consider the risks associated with the proposed joint venture(s) and agree with management the scope, extent and timing of any proposed audit involvement. When assessing the relative significance of the proposed venture, audit management should take into account the following prime factors:

- the financial impacts of the venture (i.e. levels of investment, projected income/ benefits, etc.);
- the inherent nature of the venture (i.e. familiar environment or new ground?)
- the extent of possible risks (i.e. external influences such as economic conditions, political stability);
- known control factors (i.e. the experience and ability of management, the stance taken on internal control responsibilities, previous track record, etc.).

It will be necessary to develop an audit strategy and plan for assessing the venture which is linked to the implementation timetable and designed to intermesh with the key stages of the project so that the auditor's contribution and impact are maximised.

It could strongly be argued that internal audit involvement at the inception of a joint venture relationship (i.e. prior to the live implementation of the exercise) should ensure that adequate attention is paid to matters of internal control and accountability. Whereas auditors should always avoid taking over the prime responsibility of management in matters of control, their involvement at this early stage can, at least, ensure that control is considered as an important issue.

As the negotiations progress and policies, responsibilities and procedures start to emerge, it is proper for auditors to review these outputs and comment on them from a control standpoint.

Early involvement in the venture development processes also enables the internal auditors to acquire an appreciation of the key business and operational issues of the proposed association. This is valuable intelligence for application in subsequent audit reviews, and additionally promotes the impression that the auditors are well informed and capable of conducting a targeted review.

Once the venture is implemented, the audit review programme is likely to be divided into two principal areas, namely:

- those aspects which relate generally to all business activities (i.e. the accuracy and timeliness of accounting information, the protection of assets, the banking arrangements, management information arrangements, compliance with regulations, laws, and so on);
- those aspects which are very specific to the nature of the joint venture operations.

In the case of the former category, the auditors can usually rely on the programmes that they apply elsewhere in the organisation, with suitable amendments to take account of any specific local or national conditions. The business issues arising from the latter category may be very specific (perhaps even unique in the organisation), and will therefore require the auditors to develop tailored programmes of work. In order to come up with realistic and high-quality programmes for the venture-specific activities, auditors will need to be fully acquainted with the driving objectives and goals established for the operation. Auditors may be called on to independently assess the progress being made with the venture and in doing so they will need to be familiar with the relevant performance criteria.

It is extremely likely that the audit reviews will involve visits either to the jointly owned site or to the premises of the venture partners. In either case, there is an obvious requirement for the audit staff to project a professional, purposeful and informed image.

If the venture was of a fixed term nature (such as a building development), the auditors may be required to undertake a post-completion and outturn review, where the actual performance achieved at the conclusion of the project is compared to the related objectives established at the outset. Such a review will be of use if the organisation is contemplating similar ventures or wishing generally to improve its procedures for forming and managing other joint schemes as there may be lessons to learn in the handling of particular aspects of the process which can then be incorporated into future procedures.

NOTES

1. Risk analysis techniques for audit planning are explored in Chambers, A. D. (1997) *Effective Internal Audits—How to Plan and Implement*. Management Audit, www.management-audit.com.

2. A suggested fact finding programme can be found in Chambers, A. D. (2009) *Tolley's Internal Auditor's Handbook*. LexisNexis, pp. 480–483.
3. A suggested high level review programme can be found in Chambers, A. D. (2009) *Tolley's Internal Auditor's Handbook*. LexisNexis, pp. 484–491.

14
Auditing Contracts and the Purchasing Function

INTRODUCTION

In this chapter we look at the purchasing function through an examination of the relative control objectives, and the related risks and control issues.

Purchasing activities can take many forms, ranging from the comparatively straightforward acquisition of the consumable items required for everyday business, through sourcing supplies required to keep a production process running smoothly, to sophisticated procurement contracting processes perhaps involving the selection of appropriate suppliers and tendering procedures.

The first section of this chapter concentrates on the issues related to the simpler forms of general purchasing. In the later sections we suggest a possible universe of contract auditing projects, and then examine in detail some of the more common activities associated with contracting.[1]

Consult other chapters for discussion of related issues (refer to the Contents and the Index). For instance, just-in-time (JIT) management, which may be applied by management to purchasing, is discussed in Chapter 9.

CONTROL OBJECTIVES AND RISK AND CONTROL ISSUES

For each area, we shall examine the component functions and highlight the relative control objectives and the risk and control issues (divided into key issues and detailed issues) arising from the various constituent activities. This data can be used within the Standard Audit Programme Guides (SAPGs) looked at in Chapter 3. To save space, we have concentrated on the objectives to be stated and the questions to be asked and have not presented them within the SAPG format.

Control Objectives for Purchasing

(a) To ensure that all purchasing activities are supported by authorised and documented policies and procedures.

(b) To ensure that purchasing appropriately supports the business objectives of the organisation.

(c) To ensure that the appropriate goods/services are obtained at the optimum price and at the relevant time.

(d) To ensure that all purchasing activity is valid, justified and authorised within the prescribed budgets.

(e) To ensure that suppliers are reliable, financially stable and able to satisfy the organisation's purchasing demands.

(f) To ensure that all goods and services are of an appropriate quality to satisfy the organisation's objectives.

(g) To ensure that supplier's trading terms and conditions are appropriate.

(h) To ensure that purchasing activities comply with all the prevailing legislation and regulations.

(i) To ensure that all purchasing activity is correctly reflected in the organisation's stock control records and accounts.

(j) To ensure that overdue and late deliveries are progressed.

(k) To ensure that supplier performance is adequately monitored and reacted to.

(l) To provide management with adequate, accurate and timely information on purchasing activities.

These control objectives are deliberately broad in nature. The purchasing motivation and approaches of various organisations will be subject to variation in respect of scale, nature, market pressures and potential operational impacts. For example, there will inevitably be different emphasis placed on the approach adopted for purchasing between the public and private sectors or between a service organisation and an engineering company.

Risk and Control Issues for Purchasing

1 Key Issues

1.1 Have authorised and documented purchasing policies and procedures been developed, implemented and adequately communicated to all affected parties?

1.2 How does management verify that all purchase orders are justified, authorised, within budget and accounted for within the correct accounting period?

1.3 What mechanisms prevent the invalid, unauthorised and fraudulent use of official orders?

1.4 How does management ensure that adequate and appropriate supplies are obtained to sustain the required business activities?

1.5 How does management ensure that goods and services are always obtained at the most economical and fair price?

1.6 How does management verify that all suppliers are stable, reliable and capable of meeting the organisation's needs at the optimum price?

1.7 What processes ensure supplies are to the required standard, specification and quality?

1.8 What mechanisms ensure that all goods are received on time and that overdue deliveries are identified and progressed?

1.9 How does management verify that all purchases are correctly reflected in stock control and accounting records?

1.10 What processes ensure that all purchasing activities fully comply with all the relevant legislation and regulations?

2 Detailed Issues

2.1 Have purchasing authority limits (financial and type) been established, and what mechanisms prevent such limits being exceeded?

2.2 Are adequate purchasing procedures in place and what processes ensure that they are kept up to date?

2.3 What measures ensure that purchase orders are issued only from authorised sources?

2.4 What mechanisms prevent the processing of purchase orders outwith the established policy conditions?

2.5 Are all purchase orders formally justified and suitably authorised, and how is this evidenced?

2.6 How is management assured that all purchasing activity across the organisation is suitably coordinated in order to avoid waste and maximise purchasing terms, etc.?

2.7 Are purchase orders confirmed to be within the agreed budgets at the point of commitment, and how is an unauthorised commitment prevented?

2.8 How does management verify that the format and content of all official orders conform to the required standards and legislation?

2.9 Are purchase orders adequately supported with sufficient details, descriptions, specifications, prices, delivery location, call-off and freight terms in order to ensure that the precise requirements of the business are met?

2.10 What processes prevent the despatch of inaccurate, incomplete or ambiguous purchase orders?

2.11 What processes prevent the raising and despatch of duplicate purchase orders?

2.12 What mechanisms ensure that the appropriate quantities of goods are ordered to support the operational requirements of the business?

2.13 What mechanisms ensure that all subsequent purchase order amendments are valid, authorised and correctly applied?

2.14 What mechanisms are in place to prevent over-ordering of items?

2.15 How are potential suppliers selected and what prevents the use of unstable or poor quality suppliers?

2.16 How is management certain that the purchasing function fully researches the optimum sources for their requirements?

2.17 Where approved suppliers have been identified, what mechanisms prevent the use of unauthorised sources of supply?

2.18 Are suppliers adequately and independently assessed for "approved" status, and what prevents staff/supplier misuse of the process?

2.19 Are accurate and up-to-date records of approved/suitable suppliers maintained, and what mechanisms prevent unauthorised and invalid access or amendment of such records?

2.20 Is the performance of suppliers monitored against all requirements and expectations so that unsuitable, unreliable or poor quality suppliers can be promptly identified and the appropriate action taken?

2.21 Would management be alerted if there was undue preference being given to a specific supplier, or there was an unreasonable demand being placed on any one supplier, or if there was potential for an unethical relationship being established between a supplier and purchasing management?

2.22 Is there adequate liaison between the purchasing function and all other affected activities (production, sales, stock control, etc.) and how are problems and conflicts avoided?

2.23 How does management verify that delivery requirements and call-offs are accurate, up to date and complied with?

2.24 Does the purchasing function maintain an adequate awareness of market conditions, prices, etc. in order to ensure the placement of orders at the optimum price?

2.25 How does management ensure that all available discounts are suitably exploited?

2.26 Are all relevant purchase versus leasing options adequately appraised to ensure that the most advantageous purchase terms are utilised?

2.27 How does management monitor that all the required quality and standards for supplied goods are achieved?

2.28 Would the supply of substandard, inadequate or poor quality goods be detected?

2.29 Are all rejected and returned goods correctly identified and a suitable credit claimed and accounted for?

2.30 How does management confirm that all the goods ordered and invoiced have in fact been received on time?

2.31 How is accuracy of data input from other systems (e.g. sales or production requirements) confirmed?

2.32 How is the accuracy of data output to other systems (e.g. stock control, warehousing) confirmed?

2.33 What steps are in place to ensure that the value of all order commitments and the associated cash flow impact is accurately calculated and accounted for?

2.34 Are the processes of ordering, accounting and receiving goods adequately segregated to prevent staff malpractice?

2.35 If staff purchase orders are processed, what mechanisms ensure that they are correctly and separately accounted for, and correctly and fully settled by the employee?

2.36 Where goods are obtained from overseas suppliers, how does management ascertain that all the relevant import and foreign exchange regulations have been identified and correctly addressed?

2.37 Is management provided with accurate, timely and relevant information on purchasing activities to support their decision making, etc.?

CONTRACTING

For many organisations in both the private and public sector, contracting activities can represent a significant degree of risk. In this section we will define a comprehensive universe of functions and activities associated with contracting, and from that broad universe make a selection of the more generally applicable processes for further, detailed examination of the related issues.

Contractual relationships can take many forms and indeed relate to a wide range of activities; for example, major civil engineering projects in the public sector or specialised goods and service procurement in the private sector. The contracting approaches applied in these differing scenarios will vary in form and scale, and may be affected by sector-specific regulations and practices. In order to take account of this potentially wide-ranging scope of contracting activities, we offer below a suggested audit universe structure divided into three distinct areas. Not all the activities listed will apply in every organisation.

Suggested Audit Universe

1. Contract management environment and pre-contract processes:

    - contract management environment (i.e. procedures and methods)*
    - project management framework
    - project assessment and approval
    - engaging, monitoring and paying consultants
    - design
    - assessing the viability and competence of contractors*
    - maintaining an approved list of contractors*
    - tendering procedures*
    - contract and tendering documentation*
    - insurance and bonding
    - selection and letting of contracts.*

2. During the currency of the contract:

    - management information and reporting
    - performance monitoring*
    - arrangements for sub-contractors and suppliers
    - materials, plant and project assets
    - valuing work for interim payments*
    - controlling price fluctuations
    - monitoring and controlling variations
    - extensions of time
    - controlling contractual claims
    - liquidations and bankruptcies.

3. Upon and after contract completion:

    - contractors final account*
    - recovery of damages
    - review of project outturn and performance*
    - maintenance obligations.

CONTRACT MANAGEMENT ENVIRONMENT

In situations where the level of contracting activity justifies the establishment of an overall contract management environment, there is a broad range of component issues to take account of. For example, matters of project viability, authority to

---

*These activities represent the more generally applied contracting processes and will be examined in more detail in the remainder of this chapter.

proceed, contractor competence and reliability, fair tendering processes, regulatory compliance, and so on. Certain sectors have long-established protocols for dealing with contracting, for instance the public sector and the civil engineering industry. However, not all contracting processes are correct for every situation, and some (such as tendering) may not be economically viable options.

Consider the level of contracting prevailing within your own organisation in the context of the potential risks (i.e. what is at stake).

Control Objectives for Contract Management Environment

(a) To ensure that contracting activities support the cost-effective achievement of agreed business objectives.

(b) To provide and maintain suitable documented procedures in order that contracting activities are effectively administered and so that staff malpractice and fraud are prevented.

(c) To ensure that contract requirements are correctly identified, appraised, justified and documented.

(d) To ensure that the optimum contracting solution is selected.

(e) To ensure that contracts awarded represent value for money and meet the required quality and performance standards.

(f) To ensure that only stable, financially secure and appropriately qualified contractors are engaged.

(g) To ensure that there is a fair and equitable basis for selecting contractors.

(h) To ensure that all requirements and objectives are identified, documented and met.

(i) To ensure that all payments against the contract are valid, authorised and correctly accounted for.

(j) To ensure that contracts are completed on time, within budget and to the required standard.

(k) To ensure that responsibilities are identified and allocated.

(l) To ensure that management information is accurate, appropriate, complete and timely.

(m) To ensure that progress is adequately monitored and that problems are promptly reacted to.

(n) To ensure that all statutory and regulatory issues are identified and correctly addressed.

(o) To ensure that the most appropriate form of contract is utilised and that the organisation is adequately protected in the event of contractor default.

(p) To ensure that any design requirements are fully explored and accurately communicated.

(q) To ensure that subsequent design changes are authorised and/or minimised.

(r) To ensure that delays and extensions of time are reported, minimised and authorised where necessary.

(s) To ensure that price fluctuations throughout the course of the contract are justified, authorised and correctly applied.

(t) To ensure that contractual claims are minimised, controlled and satisfactorily resolved.

(u) To ensure that all project assets, plant and materials are adequately protected and correctly accounted for.

(v) To ensure that valid claims for damages are correctly raised, pursued and settled.

Risk and Control Issues for Contract Management Environment

1 Key Issues

1.1 How does management ensure that significant contract activity is in accord with, and supports the achievement of, the business objectives of the organisation?

1.2 What steps ensure that all potential contracts or projects are fully appraised for viability, cost-effectiveness and justification (and how is this evidenced)?

1.3 How is management assured that realistic and accurate contract cost estimates are generated and subject to adequate ongoing monitoring throughout the contract?

1.4 What processes ensure that the most appropriate form of contract/project funding is selected and authorised (and how is this evidenced)?

1.5 How is management assured that the most suitable form of contract is used, and that the clauses represent a fair balance of the risks between the parties?

1.6 How does the organisation avoid the engagement of unstable, financially insecure or inadequately skilled contractors?

1.7 What measures ensure that contractors are selected on a fair and equitable basis (and how is staff malpractice and fraud prevented)?

1.8 How are all the relevant requirements, design, performance and quality criteria accurately identified and reflected in the contracting documentation?

1.9 What measures ensure that contracts are completed on time, within budget and to the required standards?

1.10 How is management assured that all contract and related management information is accurate, complete, up to date and appropriately routed to all affected parties?

1.11 What steps ensure that all contract payments are for work actually completed and are correctly calculated in accordance with the contract conditions?

1.12 When applicable, what measures are in place to deal effectively with price fluctuations during the course of a contract (and how is the organisation protected from unreasonable amendments to contract costings)?

1.13 Does management take steps to prevent or minimise the effects of potential contractor default?

1.14 Are all extensions of time subject to management authorisation, and what prevents unauthorised extensions?

1.15 What steps are taken to minimise contractual claims and potentially costly disputes?

1.16 What measures ensure that all contractual claims for damages against the contractor are fully assessed, accurately costed, and authorised to proceed (and how is this evidenced)?

1.17 What processes ensure that all valid/authorised damage claims are pursued, settled and correctly paid?

1.18 How does management ascertain that all contractor claims are identified, assessed and authorised (and what prevents the settlement of unauthorised or invalid claims)?

1.19 How does management ensure that all project/contract assets, plant and materials are accounted for and adequately protected from loss or damage?

1.20 How does management confirm that the anticipated benefits arising from contract activities are actually subsequently achieved, and what action is taken to address weaknesses in both the specific and general contract administration processes?

2 Detailed Issues

2.1 What specific measures would prevent any contractual activities which do not comply with the strategic direction of the organisation?

2.2 How are management and staff made aware of their responsibilities with regard to contracting activities, and has a suitable and workable procedural framework been provided for their guidance?

2.3 Are all the potential options and solutions explored as part of the appraisal process (and what prevents options being overlooked)?

2.4 What specific measures are in place to prevent and/or reveal staff malpractice, bias or fraud?

2.5 What measures ensure that only suitably justified and authorised contracts are progressed (and what specifically prevents the establishment of unauthorised contract relationships)?

2.6 What measures ensure that all the implications and costs are identified and reviewed (i.e. including ongoing running or maintenance costs)?

2.7 How does management ensure that all relevant insurance arrangements are optimised and current throughout the life of the contract?

2.8 How does management ensure that contractors under consideration have adequate and suitably skilled resources to meet the demands of the contract?

2.9 Whenever appropriate (or when required by legislation) are fair and properly controlled tendering procedures applied, and if so, what measures ensure that all the bids are impartially reviewed?

2.10 How does management ensure that the design and specification processes are adequate in order to avoid subsequent (and potentially costly) design changes?

2.11 Are measures in place to review and specify the required design and technical standards?

2.12 What steps are taken to ensure that realistic and workable targets and milestones are established and communicated as the basis for subsequent progress monitoring?

2.13 What measures ensure that contract/project progress and the achievement of contractual obligations are accurately and effectively monitored (and how can management be assured that problems, delays and shortcomings would be promptly identified and dealt with)?

2.14 How does management ensure that adequate and appropriate resources are provided (at the correct time) by the organisation in order to fulfil its obligations?

2.15 What steps are taken to ensure that the organisation's staff resources are adequately skilled and trained to discharge their contractual and administrative obligations?

2.16 What measures ensure that key contract/project activities are adequately documented and trailed?

2.17 What measures prevent the processing of unauthorised, invalid, duplicated or incorrect contract payments (i.e. for work not completed or for goods not supplied)?

2.18 What measures ensure that all contract payments are accurately reflected in the project and main accounting systems?

2.19 What action is taken to provide for adequate and accurate channels of communication and representation (both between the employer and contractor, and between affected areas within the employing organisation)?

2.20 Are actual costs adequately monitored against authorised budgets, and would variances promptly be identified for follow-up?

2.21 If subsequent design changes prove necessary, are they subject to accurate costing and authorisation (and how is this evidenced)?

2.22 What measures are in place to avoid the excessive cost and disruption of litigation for disputed contract claims?

2.23 Whenever necessary, what measures ensure that all statutory and regulatory issues are correctly addressed (and would non compliance promptly be identified)?

ASSESSING THE VIABILITY AND COMPETENCE OF CONTRACTORS

Irrespective of the scale of contracting activity, there is a generally universal justification for ensuring that the potential contractor is at the least capable, financially stable, and operates to recognised standards. Where the contracted activity or project is critical to the ongoing survival and operations of employing organisation, it becomes essential that a detailed assessment of contractors is conducted.

Control Objectives for Assessing the Viability and Competence of Contractors

(a) To ensure that only stable, financially secure and appropriately qualified contractors are engaged.

(b) To ensure that contractors have sufficient and appropriately skilled resources in order to meet the contract obligations.

(c) To ensure that contractors are selected fairly and without bias or favour.

(d) To ensure that adequate security is available in case of contract breach.

(e) To ensure that the contractor has appropriate and adequate insurance cover, and that this is maintained throughout the contract.

(f) To ensure that contractors with a propensity for contractual claims are identified and avoided.

Risk and Control Issues for Assessing the Viability and Competence of Contractors

1 Key Issues

1.1 What general measures are in place to evaluate the quality of contractors bidding for work?

1.2 What specific measures does management apply to confirm the financial stability of contractors (and what is the evidence for this)?

1.3 How does management ensure the reliability and reputation of potential contractors?

1.4 What measures are applied to ensure that contractors are appropriately qualified and hold membership of the relevant professional or trade organisations?

1.5 How is management assured that potential contractors have sufficient staff (and other) resources for the duration of the contract?

1.6 What measures ensure that contractors are selected on a fair and equitable basis (and how is staff malpractice prevented in the selection process)?

1.7 How does management confirm that adequate security or surety is available in the event of a contract breach?

1.8 How does management ensure that the contractor has in place sufficient and appropriate forms of insurance cover?

1.9 What specific measures would prevent the engagement of a contractor with a reputation or propensity for making contractual claims?

2 Detailed Issues

2.1 Are accurate and up-to-date records of contractors maintained as the basis for evaluating their suitability?

2.2 How does management specifically avoid the engagement of financially unstable contractors?

2.3 How does management ensure that engaged contractors remain financially stable for the duration of the contract?

2.4 Where applicable, does management obtain guarantees from parent companies or the contractor's bankers?

2.5 How is the technical suitability of contractors assessed (and against what benchmarks)?

2.6 How does management ensure that their records of contractors are accurate, up to date and relevant?

2.7 What measures ensure that the contractor's insurance cover remains valid and effective throughout the duration of the contract period?

2.8 Is the contractor's current and projected workload taken into account when assessing their ability to meet the contract demands?

2.9 If the contractor has been previously engaged by the organisation, how does management take account of the contractor's previous performance?

MAINTAINING AN APPROVED LIST OF CONTRACTORS

In the previous section we discussed the general issues which should be taken into account when an organisation is considering the engagement of an external contractor. However, where an organisation (such as a local authority) is regularly involved in seeking contractors for similar projects, it may prove necessary for them to maintain an approved list of reliable, trustworthy and stable contractors as the basis for selection, perhaps using tendering.

This section examines the objectives and issues surrounding the maintenance of approved lists and includes such related matters as selection criteria, maintaining the accuracy of the data, and compliance with regulations.

Control Objectives for Maintaining an Approved List of Contractors

(a) To facilitate the selection of financially stable, competent and reliable contractors.

(b) To ensure that contractors can achieve the required quality and technical standards.

(c) To ensure the selection of contractors with sufficient and appropriate resources.

(d) To ensure that the selection of contractors is based on fair and realistic criteria.

(e) To ensure that the relevant data is accurate, complete and maintained up to date.

(f) To ensure that the data is protected from unauthorised access, amendment and leakage.

(g) To ensure that all regulatory and statutory requirements are addressed.

Risk and Control Issues for Maintaining an Approved List of Contractors

1 Key Issues

1.1 How does management ensure that only financially stable, reliable and technically competent contractors are selected?

1.2 What specific measures ensure that the list of approved contractors is accurate and up to date?

1.3 How does management consistently assess contractors for the following attributes:

- financial status
- technical competence
- previous performance
- resources?

1.4 How does management ensure that the listing and selection criteria are fair and realistic?

1.5 Having established an approved contractor list, what specific measures prevent the engagement of an unlisted contractor?

1.6 What measures are in place to ensure that only valid contractors are entered on to the approved list?

1.7 What general measures are in place to ensure that only valid and authorised data amendments (including deletions) are applied to the approved list?

1.8 How does management ensure that all the prevailing regulatory and statutory requirements are correctly addressed?

2 Detailed Issues

2.1 Has management developed and documented formal procedures for maintaining an approved list (and have these been authorised for use)?

2.2 Who is responsible for assessing contractors and recommending their inclusion on to the list (and is adequate accountability and independence demonstrated)?

2.3 What specific measures prevent the inclusion of an unauthorised entry on to the list?

2.4 Are contractors subject to progressive evaluation in order to ensure that the listed data is relevant and accurate?

2.5 Would the engagement of an unlisted contractor be subject to specific authorisation (and how would this be evidenced)?

2.6 How is the listing data protected from unauthorised access or amendment (and how does management ensure that all amendments are authorised and accurately applied)?

2.7 What specific measures prevent staff malpractice (e.g. through collusion or bias) affecting the listing of a contractor?

2.8 What steps does management take to prove the accuracy and objectivity of the listing data?

2.9 How is confidential or commercially sensitive data protected from unauthorised leakage or access?

TENDERING PROCEDURES

Where an organisation (such as a local authority) has an obligation to demonstrate both fairness and value for money when selecting contractors, it may choose to put contract bids out to tender. The principal aim is to ensure that the optimum contractor is selected for the job, having regard for economic, quality, stability and technical issues along the way.

Tendering is not appropriate in every case, mainly because it can be costly for employer and contractor alike.

Control Objectives for Tendering Procedures

(a) To ensure that tendering is the most appropriate and cost-effective form of contractor selection in the circumstances.

(b) To ensure that the best value for money is obtained when selecting contractors.

(c) To ensure that the most suitable and appropriate form of tendering is applied and justified.

(d) To ensure that matters of contractor reliability, stability and technical competence are adequately addressed.

(e) To ensure that authorised and documented tendering procedures are in place.

(f) To ensure that the tendering process incorporates adequate competition.

(g) To ensure that the tendering process is fair and free from personal bias or undue influence.

(h) To ensure that the tendering instructions are accurate, complete and unambiguous.

(i) To ensure that the tendering documentation is accurate and complete.

(j) To ensure that an adequate and workable tendering timetable is applied and adhered to.

(k) To ensure that the tendering process is fairly conducted and that fraud and collusion are prevented.

(l) To ensure that the tendering process is relative to the type of contract and conforms to any legislative or regulatory requirements.

> (m) To ensure that appropriate internal procedures are in place to protect the recording, handling, storage and assessment of submitted tenders.
>
> (n) To ensure that submitted tenders are adequately protected from unauthorised access, opening, amendment or leakage.
>
> (o) To ensure that all contractors are treated equally and fairly.
>
> (p) To ensure that all tenders are impartially and appropriately reviewed as the basis for selection.
>
> (q) To ensure that errors, qualifications and omissions are detected and objectively dealt with.
>
> (r) To ensure that the optimum tender is authorised for selection.

Risk and Control Issues for Tendering Procedures

1 Key Issues

1.1 How does management ensure that tendering is justified as the most appropriate method of awarding contracts?

1.2 Has management established comprehensive, documented and authorised tendering procedures (and how is compliance with these assured)?

1.3 How does management target the tendering process and ensure that only suitable and reliable contractors are considered?

1.4 How does management ensure that the tendering procedure incorporates adequate and appropriate competition?

1.5 What selection criteria has management established as the basis for tender review and selection?

1.6 What measures are in place to ensure that the tendering procedure is fair, equitable and free from personal bias and influence?

1.7 How does management ensure that the tendering process complies with any prevailing legislation or regulations (e.g. as for EU contracts)?

1.8 How does management ensure that the tendering instructions are accurate and complete, and that a workable tendering timetable is in place?

1.9 How does management ensure that the tendering documentation accurately incorporates all the required information and correctly complies with the chosen form of contract?

1.10 How does management ensure that tenders received are impartially handled, recorded and securely stored awaiting assessment?

1.11 How are tenders protected from unauthorised opening, access, amendment or leakage?

1.12 How does management guarantee that all submitted tenders are impartially and equitably reviewed and assessed?

1.13 What measures ensure that the optimum tender solution is selected and authorised to proceed (and what is the evidence of the authorisation)?

2 Detailed Issues

2.1 Does management take appropriate account of the costs of tendering when choosing the optimum method of awarding contracts?

2.2 How does management ensure that the most suitable form of tendering (for the circumstances) is adopted?

2.3 How is the authorisation for applying a tendering approach evidenced?

2.4 How does management ensure that potential contractors are financially stable, reliable and technically competent?

2.5 What specific measures has management established to prevent staff malpractice or collusion with bidding contractors?

2.6 Has management established minimum competition criteria for the tendering process, and clearly identified the key objectives of the process beforehand?

2.7 How does management ensure that all contractors submitting bids will be treated equally and fairly (for example, in responding to specific enquiries)?

2.8 Are the costs associated with the tendering process accurately assessed, justified and monitored throughout?

2.9 How is management assured that the tendering timetable is adhered to?

2.10 How does management ensure that all submitted tenders are recorded/ acknowledged on receipt, and remain secure from tampering while awaiting review?

2.11 What specific measures are applied to the opening of tenders and the recording of key data, so that all are accurately logged and accounted for?

2.12 What action does management take with late and/or incomplete tenders?

2.13 How are tenders stored and what specifically prevents unauthorised access or amendment?

2.14 How does management ensure that any additional information (e.g. that resulting from a specific contractor enquiry) is fairly circulated to all bidding contractors?

2.15 In order that all tenders can be consistently reviewed, does management clearly establish the necessary review criteria (and if so, how can they be assured that these have been taken into account for all submitted tenders)?

2.16 How does management ensure that any errors, omissions or qualifications added by contractors will be detected and effectively dealt with?

2.17 What steps are taken to ensure that the tender review committee or team is balanced, unbiased and suitably qualified for the task?

2.18 Does the review committee document its recommendations and deliberations?

2.19 In what way is management assured that all submitted tenders are fully reviewed and assessed?

2.20 Where required, are unsuccessful contractors given access to anonymous details of the other tenderers?

CONTRACTING AND TENDERING DOCUMENTATION

Here we are concerned with the accuracy, completeness, legality and security of the documentation which supports the contracted activity.

Control Objectives for Contracting and Tendering Documentation

(a) To ensure that all stages of contract administration are supported by accurate, complete and legible documentation.

(b) To prevent and minimise the disruption, delay and additional costs caused by documentation errors and omissions.

(c) To ensure that all contract documentation is prepared in accordance with the relevant form of contract and regulations.

(d) To ensure that all documentation is securely stored and adequately protected from loss, damage, unauthorised amendment or leakage.

(e) To ensure that the location of all documents can be promptly traced.

(f) To ensure that only authorised and valid amendments are correctly applied to contract documents.

(g) To ensure that only current versions of documents are utilised.

(h) To ensure that all supporting information is correctly incorporated and to the required standard.

(i) To ensure that bonds, securities, completion certificates, correspondence, etc. are accounted for and securely filed.

(j) To prevent the premature or accidental disposal of contract documentation.

> (k) To ensure that the status of all contracts can be determined promptly and supported by the relevant documents.
>
> (l) To ensure that all relevant documents are retained and remain available for the required period.

Risk and Control Issues for Contracting and Tendering Documentation

1 Key Issues

1.1 How does management ensure that all the required contract documentation is generated at the appropriate time?

1.2 What measures are taken to ensure that documents are accurate, complete and legible?

1.3 What specific action does management take to avoid and detect errors and omissions?

1.4 What steps are in place to ensure that all relevant contract documentation is produced in the appropriate form and to the required standard?

1.5 What measures does management take to ensure that contract documents are securely stored and protected from loss, damage and unauthorised access?

1.6 How are contract documents filed, and are they able to be traced promptly?

1.7 Where it is necessary to apply amendments to contract documents, how can management be assured that only authorised and valid changes are applied?

1.8 Where several versions of a document may exist, what steps ensure that the correct and valid version is utilised and circulated?

1.9 How does management ensure that, where necessary, documents are produced to the required technical or professional standard (i.e. as for drawings or technical specifications)?

1.10 How does management ensure that documents with a financial or specific significance (such as bonds or securities) are adequately protected and kept secure until release?

1.11 What specific measures would prevent the premature or accidental destruction/disposal of contract documents?

1.12 What is the procedure for retaining contract documentation securely and for the appropriate period?

1.13 Does management maintain records which accurately indicate the current status of all contracting activities (and how is the accuracy and integrity of such records assured)?

2 Detailed Issues

2.1 How does management accurately identify all the documentation requirements?

2.2 Would errors and omissions be detected prior to the release of tendering and contract documents?

2.3 Where errors are noted, what steps are taken to ensure that all the affected documents are recalled and accurate replacements distributed to all affected parties?

2.4 What is the procedure for tracing and accounting for all copies of contract documentation?

2.5 What specifically prevents any unauthorised (or additional) copies being taken?

2.6 Would the loss or misplacement of contract documentation be capable of prompt detection?

2.7 How does management ensure that all copy sets are complete and legible throughout?

2.8 Are document storage conditions suitable for long-term retention?

2.9 How does management confirm that amendments are correctly applied?

2.10 What measures ensure that amended documents are correctly circulated and received?

2.11 What physically happens to outdated document copies (i.e. those that have been subject to subsequent amendment)?

2.12 How does management monitor that all bonds, securities, completion certificates, etc. are accounted for and traceable?

SELECTION AND LETTING OF CONTRACTS

Contracts represent the balancing of risks between the parties, and these are expressed in the form of documented rights and obligations. Selecting the most appropriate form of contract is often crucial in ensuring a fair balance of risks and rights, and this section examines the related issues. Additionally, it is necessary to ensure that the chosen contract is correctly enacted.

Control Objectives for Selection and Letting of Contracts

(a) To ensure that the most appropriate form of contract is utilised and that risks are fairly balanced between parties.

(b) To ensure that the optimum contract pricing method is selected for the circumstances.

(c) To ensure that the organisation is adequately protected in the event of contractor breach.

(d) To ensure that the contract conditions offer suitable remedies.

(e) To ensure the accurate and correct completion of all contract documentation.

(f) To aim to settle disputes within the contract conditions by mutual agreement.

(g) To ensure that stable and reliable contractors are selected to be parties to the contract.

(h) To ensure that all the key requirements, timings and obligations are defined in the contract.

(i) To ensure that all contractual relationships are authorised.

(j) To ensure that contracts are correctly and legally enacted.

(k) To ensure that all applicable European and international legal implications are correctly addressed.

(l) To ensure that all contract documentation is securely stored and adequately protected from loss, theft or damage.

Risk and Control Issues for Selection and Letting of Contracts

1 Key Issues

1.1 How does management ensure that the most suitable and appropriate form of contract is selected for the circumstances?

1.2 How is management assured that the relevant contract clauses represent a fair balance of the associated risks between the parties?

1.3 What specific measures ensure that the optimum contract pricing method is applied?

1.4 What steps does management take to ensure that contracts provide adequate protection for the organisation in the event of contractor breach?

1.5 What measures ensure that contract documentation is accurately, correctly and fully completed?

1.6 In order to avoid the potentially high costs of litigation, how does management ensure that contracts facilitate alternative dispute remedies (e.g. arbitration)?

1.7 What general measures are applied to ensure that only reliable, stable and suitably qualified contractors are engaged?

1.8 How is management assured that all the relevant (and specific) requirements, timings and obligations are appropriately and accurately incorporated into the contract?

1.9 Are all contracts subject to management authorisation (and if so, how is this evidenced)?

1.10 What steps are taken to ensure that contracts are legally enforceable and correctly enacted?

1.11 When applicable, how does management ensure that all the possible European and international legal implications are satisfactorily addressed?

1.12 What measures are in place to protect contract documentation from loss, damage, destruction or theft?

2 Detailed Issues

2.1 How does management prevent the disruption and possible additional costs associated with utilising an inappropriate form of contract?

2.2 Are standard forms of contract ever utilised, and if so are they confirmed as offering the optimum remedy?

2.3 How does management assess the contractual requirements for a given project or scenario?

2.4 Are contracts subject to review by appropriately qualified legal experts (and what is the evidence for this)?

2.5 What steps are in place to ensure that documentation errors are effectively and promptly detected prior to the relevant contract being enacted?

2.6 What specifically prevents unauthorised or invalid contract relationships being formalised?

2.7 Where necessary, how does management ensure that contract negotiations are proficiently and adequately conducted?

PERFORMANCE MONITORING

All contracts are created for a purpose, and they will only exist where an individual or organisation has identified and justified a particular need, perhaps expressed through a number of objectives, criteria or targets. To achieve the identified objectives, the project and contract must be monitored for progress according to plan. In this section we take account of the issues for the establishment and operation of a performance monitoring environment.

Control Objectives for Performance Monitoring

> (a) To ensure that all the relevant contracting and business-related objectives are fulfilled.
>
> (b) To ensure that the contract is successfully completed on time and within budget.
>
> (c) To ensure that quality, technical and workmanship targets are met.
>
> (d) To ensure that key stages and milestones are identified and achieved.
>
> (e) To enable the monitoring and assessment of contractor and consultant performances against their contractual obligations.
>
> (f) To ensure that all contractual obligations are correctly discharged.
>
> (g) To ensure that all key contract events are promptly identified and reacted to.
>
> (h) To aid the effective management of the contract or project.
>
> (i) To enable the assessment of the relevance and effectiveness of the contracting management environment as the basis for identifying weaknesses to address subsequently.
>
> (j) To ensure that any apparent problems can be dealt with promptly and effectively.
>
> (k) To ensure that remedy or redress is promptly sought wherever relevant.

Risk and Control Issues for Performance Monitoring

1 Key Issues

1.1 How is management made aware of contract progress and the achievement of key stages and the underlying objectives?

1.2 What measures alert management if the contract or project is not going to be completed on time or within budget?

1.3 Would management be advised promptly of problems or delays (and how is this evidenced)?

1.4 How does management monitor that quality, technical and workmanship standards are being achieved?

1.5 How does management assess objectively the performance of a contractor or consultant during a contract (and how would management be alerted to shortcomings, delays or other problems)?

1.6 What measures ensure that all contract obligations are being appropriately achieved?

1.7 What measures ensure that management would be made aware of the following possible contract events:

- extensions of time
- contractual claims or contractor disputes
- requirement for design changes or modifications
- problems with providing adequate resources?

1.8 How does management ensure the accuracy and reliability of performance information and reporting?

1.9 Where weaknesses, problems or shortcomings are apparent, how does management ensure that such data is complete and that appropriate corrective action has been taken in each case?

2 Detailed Issues

2.1 Has action been taken to identify accurately all the key and critical stages of the contract, so that progress can be subsequently monitored?

2.2 Have realistic budgets been established for the contract (and constituent stages) to enable subsequent comparisons with actual costs?

2.3 Would management be alerted to shortfalls in anticipated quality or workmanship standards?

2.4 What specific measures are in place to ensure that all reported problems, delays, etc. are actually followed up and effectively addressed?

2.5 Where performance shortfalls have a contractual implication, how does management ensure that the appropriate contract remedy is applied and concluded?

2.6 Are performance shortcomings and related administrative problems noted as the basis for subsequently revising and improving the quality of the contract management environment?

VALUING WORK FOR INTERIM PAYMENTS

Where a contract is set to run over a prolonged period (such as for a building or civil engineering project) the contract terms may specify the circumstances for interim or staged payments. This section considers the related objectives and issues.

Control Objectives for Valuing Work for Interim Payments

> (a) To ensure that payments are made only for work actually completed and goods and services received.

(b) To ensure that payments are made only where goods and services are to the required standard and quality.

(c) To ensure that all payments are subject to suitable prior authorisation.

(d) To ensure that payments relate only to contracted activities.

(e) To ensure that work completed is accurately measured and correctly calculated using the defined methods and prices.

(f) To ensure that work completed or goods received are adequately supported by documentation in accordance with contract conditions.

(g) To ensure that accounts are accurately settled within the timescales stipulated within the contract.

(h) To ensure that all nonstandard charges (e.g. for variations) are valid and supported.

(i) To ensure that, where applicable, the correct value of retention is calculated and applied to interim accounts.

Risk and Control Issues for Valuing Work for Interim Payments

1 Key Issues

1.1 What measures ensure that all interim accounts are valid and relate to work actually completed and goods received?

1.2 What specific measures would prevent payments being made for work that is substandard or incomplete?

1.3 Are all payments subject to prior authorisation (and what is the evidence for this)?

1.4 How does management ensure that all contractual obligations have been met before any payments are made to contractors?

1.5 How is management assured that chargeable work has been correctly measured in accordance with the methods defined in the contract?

1.6 What measures are in place to ensure that interim accounts are accurately calculated and that the prices used are valid and agreed?

1.7 Whenever applicable, how does management ensure that interim accounts are settled within the timescales defined in the contract?

1.8 How does management ensure that all nonstandard charges and costs are valid, authorised and correctly supported by appropriate documentation (prior to settlement)?

1.9 What measures provide assurance that retention values are accurately calculated and applied to interim accounts?

2 Detailed Issues

2.1 What specific measures would detect invalid charges for substandard or incomplete goods/services?

2.2 How does management ensure that all goods and services are provided to the defined quality and workmanship standards?

2.3 Are interim accounts correctly supported by documentary evidence, and is this examined and confirmed as correct prior to account settlement?

2.4 What measures would prevent the settlement of duplicated accounts or charges for previously costed work elements?

2.5 What specific measures would detect pricing or invoice compilation errors?

2.6 Is the calculation of retention values confirmed as being in accordance with the relevant contract conditions?

CONTRACTOR'S FINAL ACCOUNT

Upon completion of a contracted activity, the contractors will submit their final account. This may be the only account rendered or it may be preceded by previous interim accounts (as discussed in the previous section). The employer will wish to ensure the accuracy and relevance of the account, and to confirm that the effects of prior payments, outstanding claims and retained values have been accurately accounted for.

Control Objectives for Contractor's Final Account

(a) To ensure that only valid, accurate and authorised accounts are paid.

(b) To ensure that accounts relate only to work actually completed or goods/services provided to the required standard.

(c) To ensure that all accounts are costed in accordance with the measurement methods and prices contained in the contract.

(d) To ensure that the contractor has met all contract obligations prior to account settlement.

(e) To ensure that previous (interim) account payments have been correctly taken into account.

(f) To ensure that retention values have been accurately calculated and applied.

(g) To ensure that price fluctuations have been correctly calculated in accordance with the agreed formula base.

(h) To ensure that the values of any outstanding contractual claims are valid and have been accurately incorporated.

(i) To ensure that charges in respect of variations or modifications are valid, authorised and correctly calculated.

(j) To ensure that, where applicable, values of liquidated damages are correctly incorporated.

(k) To ensure that all taxation matters are correctly addressed.

(l) To ensure that any agreed damages due to the organisation have been deducted.

(m) To ensure that all the key contract events reflected in the account are adequately supported by documentation.

(n) To ensure that the amount is settled within any agreed period stipulated in the contract.

Risk and Control Issues for Contractor's Final Account

1 Key Issues

1.1 How does the organisation confirm that all accounts are valid and accurate before settlement?

1.2 Are all contract accounts subject to formal authorisation prior to payment (and how is this evidenced)?

1.3 How does management ensure that goods and services reflected in the contractor's accounts have actually been provided?

1.4 How does management ensure that the contractor's accounts are correctly costed in accordance with the contract conditions?

1.5 How does management ensure that the contractor has satisfactorily met all contract obligations prior to settlement of accounts?

1.6 What measures are in place to ensure that retention and maintenance values are correctly calculated and withheld from the final account?

1.7 Where applicable, how does management ensure that price fluctuations during the course of the contract period have been accurately adjusted on the accounts in accordance with the agreed fluctuation formula?

1.8 What measures would ensure that the values of agreed contractual claims and damages due to the organisation have been correctly adjusted on the accounts?

1.9 How does management ensure that the charges for variations and modifications are valid, accurate and relate only to agreed and authorised changes?

1.10 What measures are in place to confirm the accuracy and validity of VAT and other taxation calculations?

1.11 How does management ensure that all contractors' accounts are settled within the periods stipulated in the relevant contracts?

2 Detailed Issues

2.1 How are account queries, errors and irregularities identified, brought to the attention of the contractor and satisfactorily resolved?

2.2 What specific measures would prevent the payment of any unauthorised or invalid contractor's account?

2.3 Are all elements of contractors' accounts examined for their validity and accuracy prior to payment (and how are these checks evidenced)?

2.4 How is management assured that all the relevant goods and services meet the required quality and workmanship standards before account settlement (and what action is taken on the costs relating to any substandard elements)?

2.5 What action is taken to confirm the correct application of the agreed work measurement method?

2.6 How does management verify that the accounts are based on the agreed prices contained in the contract?

2.7 Are all the key account elements supported by accurate and reliable documentation (i.e. as a means to confirm the validity and accuracy of charges)?

2.8 Would the failure of the contractor to meet all contract obligations result in a suitable adjustment being applied to the account (where this is permitted under the terms of the contract)?

2.9 How does management confirm that previous (interim) account payments have been correctly taken into account in the final account balance?

2.10 Where retention (or maintenance) values have been deducted, what measures will ensure that these values are eventually paid over to the contractor at the appropriate time?

2.11 How would disputes arising from the final account be fairly and objectively resolved?

2.12 How does management confirm the accuracy of price fluctuation adjustments (e.g. are all such entries confirmed using a formula model)?

2.13 How does management ensure that the values of a contractor's claims added to the account are valid, authorised and correctly calculated?

2.14 What specific measures would prevent the duplicated settlement of a contractor's claims?

2.15 How does management ensure that any liquidated damage liability is identified and adjusted on the account (and how is this accurately calculated)?

2.16 What steps are taken to code accurately and enter the contractor's account on to the accounting system?

2.17 Are all key contract events (e.g. staged completions, variations, deliveries) adequately supported by accurate and complete documentary trails?

REVIEW OF PROJECT OUTTURN AND PERFORMANCE

Where a project (contracted or otherwise) has run its course, it can be beneficial to conduct a post-completion review of the project, primarily to ensure that all the objectives established at the outset have actually been achieved. Additionally, where the organisation is regularly involved in conducting such projects, it can also be useful to examine how the project progressed and the extent to which the contract/project management framework contributed to the process. There may be important administrative and control issues arising from such a post-completion review which can lead to the subsequent improvement and refinement of relevant procedures so that future projects can be more effectively managed.

Control Objectives for Review of Project Outturn and Performance

(a) To ensure that all the contract and project objectives were actually achieved.

(b) To ensure that all aspects of the contract and the contractor's performance are reviewed against expectations, requirements and standards.

(c) To ensure that the contract management procedures and policies are reviewed so that they can be progressively improved.

(d) To ensure that all contract obligations have been satisfactorily met.

(e) To ensure that the contract was completed on time and within budget, and to note reasons for failures and shortcomings.

(f) To ensure that the accounting and management information systems are assessed for their accuracy, efficiency and reliability.

(g) To ensure that all key contract events were effectively and efficiently handled.

(h) To ensure that all key contract events were supported by adequate and accurate documentary trails.

(i) To ensure that all nonstandard events (e.g. variations and extensions of time) were suitably assessed, justified, and authorised.

(j) To ensure that all the relevant legal and regulatory issues were satisfactorily addressed and that the most appropriate form of contract was applied in the circumstances.

(k) To ensure that the performance of contractors and consultants are fully assessed.

(l) To ensure the organisation's resources and staff are reviewed in light of their performance during the contract, so that administrative improvements can be made.

(m) To ensure that all conclusions and action points are reported, agreed by senior management and subsequently authorised.

(n) To ensure that any outstanding contractual obligations are identified and resolved.

(o) To ensure that staff training and development needs are identified and addressed.

Risk and Control Issues for Review of Project Outturn and Performance

1 Key Issues

1.1 How does management confirm that all the contract objectives were fully achieved?

1.2 How does management accurately assess how a contract was conducted as a means of identifying problems and shortcomings for their attention?

1.3 How does management obtain assurance that existing contract management procedures and practices are valid, authorised, justified, effective, and are being correctly complied with?

1.4 How is management assured that contracts are completed on time and within budget (and what action do they take in the event of a shortfall)?

1.5 Does management assess the quality, accuracy, efficiency and reliability of accounting and management information systems as the basis for their decision making?

1.6 Does management undertake an assessment of the accuracy and completeness of the contract documentation system?

1.7 How does management obtain the assurance that all nonstandard contract events were authorised, justified and fulfilled?

1.8 Does management confirm the acceptability and relevance of the chosen form of contract?

1.9 How does management confirm that all the relevant legal and regulatory issues were appropriately addressed?

1.10 Is the performance of contractors (and consultants) assessed against the defined expectations (especially where they may be considered for involvement in future contracts)?

1.11 How does management ensure that the organisation's staff and resources were efficiently utilised (and how would shortcomings and problems be addressed)?

1.12 What measures would highlight potential staff training and development needs (and how would these be addressed)?

1.13 How does management ensure that all shortcomings, problems and potential improvements will be highlighted and appropriately addressed so that future contracts are more efficiently, securely and effectively administered?

1.14 How does management ensure that all outstanding contractual obligations would be identified and acted on?

2 Detailed Issues

2.1 What measures would ensure that any failed objectives or obligations would be identified and addressed (and is there evidence that corrective action has been agreed and taken)?

2.2 How does management ensure that all outstanding contractor obligations are identified and effectively followed up?

2.3 Are existing procedures reviewed for their relevance and contribution to efficiency and control?

2.4 How does management identify redundant, unnecessary or costly procedures (and what action is generally taken to continually improve the quality of procedures and policies)?

2.5 How does management ensure that project reviews are objectively and independently conducted (as a means of improving their potential value)?

2.6 How does management ensure that all the necessary and prescribed authorisations are in place and valid?

2.7 What specific measures would prevent unauthorised, fraudulent or invalid contracting activities or events?

2.8 Does management positively confirm that the chosen form of contract was the appropriate and optimum solution in the circumstances?

2.9 Are outstanding legal issues assessed by a suitably qualified person, so that they can be addressed and resolved in future?

2.10 Where lists of approved contractors are maintained, what measures ensure that these records are accurately updated with the results of actual contract performance reviews?

2.11 What specific measures would prevent the re-engagement of unsatisfactory contractors (i.e. based on a review of their performance during previous contracts)?

2.12 Is senior management informed of the results of the contract/project review, and how are action points confirmed as being satisfactorily addressed?

NOTE

1. For more detail on wider contract auditing see Chambers, A. D. and Rand, G. (1997) *Auditing Contracts*. Management Audit, www.management-audit.com.

15
Auditing Operations and Resource Management

INTRODUCTION

In this chapter we consider the operational auditing dimensions of production and manufacturing as being representative of operations in general. Although we have chosen to focus our discussion on matters relevant to production and manufacturing, there are, of course, other types of activities that could legitimately form the basis of an organisation's primary operations. For example, either the provision of a specific service to customers or retailing.

While accepting that this chapter is deliberately focused, there are many points in common between one type of operation and another. For example, they normally involve the following aspects:

- identifying an underlying requirement and endeavouring to cost-effectively exploit it;
- ensuring that suitable and adequate resources (human and material) are brought together at the right time and place to fulfil the identified requirements;
- ensuring that the operation is conducted safely, economically, efficiently, effectively, to the required standard, and in accordance with any prevailing regulations and laws; and so on.

Consult other chapters for discussion of related issues (refer to the Contents and the Index). For instance, just-in-time (JIT) management, which may be applied by management to operations and production, is looked at in Chapter 9.

First we shall consider the systems and functions that are likely to constitute this area of activity. Secondly, we shall examine each of these component functions and highlight the relative control objectives and the risk and control issues (divided into key issues and detailed issues) arising from the various constituent activities.

SYSTEM/FUNCTION COMPONENTS OF A PRODUCTION/ MANUFACTURING ENVIRONMENT

We have chosen to use an essentially functional approach to define the production and manufacturing audit universe, which gives us the following possible breakdown of the key functions, systems or activities:

- planning and production control
- facilities, plant and equipment
- personnel
- materials and energy
- quality control
- safety
- environmental issues
- law and regulatory compliance
- maintenance.

The subject of just-in-time management techniques is not specifically addressed in this chapter, but see Chapter 9.

CONTROL OBJECTIVES AND RISK AND CONTROL ISSUES

We shall now examine the control objectives and the related risk and control issues for each of the production/manufacturing areas listed above. This data can be used within the format of the Standard Audit Programme Guides (SAPGs) looked at in Chapter 3. To save space we have stripped out the format and focused on the objectives to be stated and the questions to be asked and have not presented them within the SAPG format.

PLANNING AND PRODUCTION CONTROL

Here we are generally concerned with matters of planning and multi-discipline coordination so as to contribute to the efficient and economic use of production facilities.

Control Objectives for Planning and Production Control

> (a) To ensure that production and manufacturing requirements are accurately determined, authorised, effectively communicated and suitably planned for.

(b) To ensure that adequate facilities and resources are made available at the appropriate time in order to meet the agreed production and manufacturing obligations.

(c) To ensure that the required quantity of products is manufactured to the required quality standards.

(d) To ensure that the actions of all affected departments and functions are adequately coordinated to achieve the defined objectives.

(e) To ensure that production resources and facilities are efficiently utilised and that waste is avoided/minimised.

(f) To ensure that the necessary production equipment is fully operational and operated efficiently.

(g) To ensure that production staff are suitably trained and experienced in order to maximise their contribution.

(h) To ensure that production downtime is minimised, suitably monitored and reacted to.

(i) To ensure that all materials, resources and finished goods are accurately accounted for.

(j) To ensure that production activities are effectively monitored, reported to management and shortfalls and problems are promptly detected and resolved.

(k) To ensure that all relevant legislation, health and safety and other regulations are complied with.

(l) To ensure that actual production plant efficiency and performance are adequately monitored for management information and action.

Risk and Control Issues for Planning and Production Control

1 Key Issues

1.1 How does management ensure that the production and manufacturing requirements are accurately defined and suitably authorised?

1.2 What mechanisms ensure that authorised production/manufacturing requirements are effectively communicated to all affected parties, and that suitable plans are agreed and implemented to meet the defined obligations?

1.3 What processes ensure that all the required resources and facilities (e.g. materials, staff, machines, knowledge) are available to meet the required production obligations?

1.4 How are actual progress and use of production facilities effectively monitored and problems, shortfalls and delays promptly detected and corrected?

1.5 What measures ensure that the required quantity of products is actually manufactured and accounted for?

1.6 How does management ensure that the items produced conform to the required quality standards, and that defect rates are effectively monitored?

1.7 What measures does management take to minimise and avoid disruption of production caused by machine breakdown, poorly experienced staff, and absence of raw materials and components?

1.8 Is the utilisation of all resources (materials and workforce) fully accounted for and would waste be identified promptly and appropriate action taken? (How is this evidenced?)

1.9 Is management kept informed of overall production performance and efficiency, and what evidence is there of corrective action being taken to address shortcomings, etc.?

1.10 What mechanisms ensure that compliance with all the prevailing legislation and regulations is confirmed?

2 Detailed Issues

2.1 Are all amendments to customer orders, production requirements, forecasts, etc. promptly and accurately identified and reported in order to modify the relevant production activities?

2.2 What measures are in place to ensure that adequate and accurate information flows are established for all affected parties?

2.3 How would uneconomic or unrealistic production runs be prevented?

2.4 How would unauthorised production activity be prevented or identified?

2.5 How does management ascertain that the practical manufacturing implications of new product lines have been identified, assessed and planned for?

2.6 Are plant utilisation records maintained and would surplus capacity be identified and reacted to?

2.7 How does management ensure that the layout of the production line maximises efficiency and avoids unnecessary movements and processes?

2.8 What processes ensure the correct flow of raw materials to the production area?

2.9 Are materials and components adequately protected from loss and damage in the production areas?

2.10 What steps are taken to avoid/minimise machine failures and downtime?

2.11 Is downtime recorded, attributed and effectively monitored by management (and how is this evidenced)?

2.12 What mechanisms ensure that the skills of the workforce are adequately maintained in line with the current requirements?

2.13 Are staff skills suitably balanced to provide adequate cover during holidays, etc.?

2.14 Would production delays be promptly detected?

2.15 Are all finished goods accounted for and trailed into the stock control system?

2.16 Are all damaged, spoilt, scrap and rejected items identified, authorised and accounted for?

2.17 How can management be assured that all production activities are accurately costed and that reliable product costings are generated?

2.18 Would uneconomic products/production runs be prevented or promptly detected?

2.19 Are machine utilisation and performance statistics accurately produced, circulated and reacted to?

2.20 Are employee productivity levels effectively monitored?

2.21 Does management periodically evaluate the adequacy of production facilities?

2.22 How does management confirm compliance with all the relevant heath and safety regulations?

2.23 How does management remain aware of the relevant regulations and keep up to date?

2.24 How would violations of regulations be detected?

2.25 Have realistic and workable contingency and disaster plans been established, and are they regularly tested for their effectiveness?

2.26 How is the accuracy of data input from other systems (e.g. sales orders, planning) confirmed?

2.27 How is the accuracy of data output to other systems (e.g. time recording to payroll, product accounting) confirmed?

FACILITIES, PLANT AND EQUIPMENT

This section addresses the requirement to provide adequate resources to facilitate the production processes, and to take proper account of them. Matters relative to the acquisition, installation and maintenance of plant and equipment are included. In addition, accounting aspects together with health and safety considerations are incorporated.

Control Objectives for Facilities, Plant and Equipment

(a) To ensure that appropriate and sufficient facilities, plant and equipment are provided in order to support the achievement of defined business objectives.

(b) To ensure that buildings provide adequate, efficient and well laid out working spaces complete with all the necessary services.

(c) To ensure that plant and equipment are properly maintained in working order, operated correctly by sufficiently trained staff and in accordance with the manufacturers' directions and recommended loadings.

(d) To ensure that the production area is logically and safely laid out in order to maximise operational efficiency.

(e) To ensure that machinery and equipment is correctly installed, configured, calibrated, tested and maintained in order to avoid the disruption of the production processes.

(f) To ensure that the necessary ancillary equipment (e.g. cranes, conveyor systems, environmental systems) are provided and fully operational.

(g) To ensure that machine loadings and performance are recorded and monitored in order to achieve the optimum safe utilisation of plant.

(h) To ensure that all plant and equipment is adequately identified and accounted for.

(i) To ensure that all usage, operational and overhead costs are accurately identified and reflected in the accounts.

(j) To ensure that all plant, equipment and facilities are adequately protected from loss, damage and deterioration.

(k) To ensure that plant and equipment requirements are monitored in accordance with current and future trends, and that acquisition of new equipment is appropriately assessed and authorised.

(l) To ensure that all the relevant health and safety issues and regulations are satisfactorily addressed.

(m) To ensure that disposals and transfers of plant and equipment are justified, authorised and correctly reflected in the accounts.

(n) To ensure that staff facilities (e.g. washrooms) are adequate and of an appropriate quality.

Risk and Control Issues for Facilities, Plant and Equipment

1 Key Issues

1.1 How does management ensure that production facilities, plant and equipment are (and will remain) adequate to fulfil the defined business and operational needs?

1.2 How would facility and equipment shortcomings or surpluses be promptly identified and addressed?

1.3 What measures are in place to ensure the optimum efficiency of the production facility layout, and how are problems identified and resolved?

1.4 What steps are in place to ensure that equipment is operated correctly, appropriately maintained and effectively utilised?

1.5 How is management made aware of production downtime caused by failure of or problems with plant and equipment, and what action is taken to avoid and minimise such disruptions?

1.6 How is all plant and equipment appropriately accounted for and correctly reflected in the accounts?

1.7 Are all acquisitions and disposals of plant and equipment subject to adequate prior assessment and authorisation, and how is this evidenced?

1.8 What measures are in place to ensure that all the relevant usage, operational and overhead costs associated with the production facilities are identified and correctly accounted for?

1.9 How does management ensure that all the relevant prevailing health and safety regulations are fully complied with?

2 Detailed Issues

2.1 How does management accurately and reliably assess the production facility, plant and equipment requirements, and ensure that future needs are both identified and planned for?

2.2 How does management avoid both shortfalls and excesses of facilities and equipment?

2.3 Has management prepared and tested contingency arrangements in the event of a major disruption to production facilities (e.g. a serious fire)?

2.4 Has appropriate, adequate and current insurance cover been provided?

2.5 Does the production facility layout allow for the logical flow of goods and avoid unnecessary handling, etc.?

2.6 Are facilities maintained in an orderly and clean manner, and have all potential dangers and debris been removed?

2.7 How do the facilities conform to the requirements of the relevant regulations?

2.8 How does management monitor that the appropriate environmental systems (e.g. heating, lighting, air conditioning) are operating correctly, efficiently and in accordance with defined standards?

2.9 Have sufficient and appropriate staff facilities been provided and do they comply with relevant regulations and standards?

2.10 Have safe and realistic working loads been determined for production plant and equipment, and how does management ensure that actual operations conform with the required levels?

2.11 Has management implemented an ongoing programme of equipment maintenance that complies with the manufacturer's recommendations, and how do they monitor that the programme is correctly conducted?

2.12 How does management ensure that all equipment is correctly installed, configured and calibrated?

2.13 Is downtime recorded at an individual machine level, and would problems with specific equipment be actively pursued with the manufacturers (e.g. through service and warranty arrangements)?

2.14 Are standard operating procedures defined and documented for all production equipment?

2.15 How are all relevant staff made aware of the correct, standard and safe methods of operation, and how is their compliance monitored?

2.16 Are measures in place to detect and resolve instances of the inappropriate or unsafe operation of equipment?

2.17 What mechanisms ensure that production staff are appropriately and adequately trained to perform their duties efficiently and safely?

2.18 Would breaches of the defined safety codes be identified and reacted to?

2.19 Is sufficient ancillary equipment (e.g. conveyors, cranes, handling devices, specialist tools) provided and maintained?

2.20 Have accurate and appropriate performance monitoring facilities been established, and what evidence is there that the data is reviewed and actioned by management?

2.21 How does management confirm that all the production assets (e.g. plant and equipment) recorded in the accounts are valid and available for use?

2.22 What mechanisms prevent the unauthorised or premature disposal of plant and equipment?

2.23 What precautions are taken to prevent loss of, damage to, or deterioration of plant and equipment?

2.24 Would failures to comply with health and safety regulations be detected so that appropriate action could be taken?

2.25 How is the accuracy of data input from other systems (e.g. production planning) confirmed?

2.26 How is the accuracy of data output to other systems (e.g. fixed assets) confirmed?

PERSONNEL

Irrespective of the sophistication of the available facilities and equipment, the success or otherwise of a production process will inevitably be dependent on the extent and quality of the human resources. Unless staff are suitably experienced, trained, organised, supervised and equipped, there is the attendant danger that the overall process will be uneconomic or technically deficient. Our focus here is on production personnel issues; the wider implications of personnel and training are dealt with in Chapter 15.

Control Objectives for Personnel

(a) To ensure that adequate and appropriately trained staff are provided in order to fulfil the current and future production objectives.

(b) To ensure that production staff are appropriately organised, experienced and qualified to satisfactorily address the production objectives.

(c) To ensure that staff resources are efficiently and cost-effectively employed.

(d) To ensure that staff performance is effectively monitored and shortcomings are detected and addressed.

(e) To ensure that production staff are adequately supervised so that the work is undertaken in the relevant timescale and to the required standard.

(f) To ensure that nonproductive time is minimised.

(g) To ensure that all hours worked are correctly recorded, costed and accounted for.

(h) To ensure that employees on hourly rates are paid, at the correct rate, only for hours actually worked.

(i) To ensure that production employees are provided with relevant and sufficient equipment, tools, clothing, etc. to enable them effectively and safely to discharge their responsibilities.

(j) To ensure that all production employees (including temporary and casual staff) are stable, reliable and confirmed as suitably experienced prior to engagement.

(k) To ensure that staff turnover and absenteeism are monitored and minimised.

(l) To ensure that communication between management and staff is effectively handled and aims to foster good labour relations.

Risk and Control Issues for Personnel

1 Key Issues

1.1 What mechanisms are in place to ensure that production staffing requirements are accurately determined and procured?

1.2 How does management ensure that the required production demands will be met through the provision of sufficient staff?

1.3 How is management assured that the production workforce is appropriately and sufficiently skilled to meet the production objectives?

1.4 How does management ensure that staff resources are efficiently and cost-effectively utilised?

1.5 What mechanisms are in place to monitor production staff performance, and are shortcomings identified and suitably dealt with?

1.6 What processes ensure that goods are produced within the defined timescales and to the required quality standards?

1.7 What steps are taken to ensure that hours worked are correctly recorded and accounted for?

1.8 How does management ensure that hourly paid employees are paid only for true productive time?

1.9 How does management ensure that the workforce is adequately trained to meet the production demands and targets?

1.10 How is the engagement of unsuitable, unstable and poorly experienced staff prevented?

1.11 What steps are taken to foster and maintain good labour relations with the production employees and their representatives, and are changes in conditions and practices adequately communicated, discussed and agreed?

2 Detailed Issues

2.1 How are the current and future production staffing requirements determined, and how can management be assured of the accuracy and reliability of these data?

2.2 Are the skill requirements for production staff accurately determined and how are these data used to ensure that the workforce skills are adequately maintained?

2.3 Are staff suitably skilled to enable the effective coverage of absences, holiday periods, etc.?

2.4 What mechanisms prevent undue levels of unproductive time (e.g. during retooling)?

2.5 Are staff and supervisors appropriately organised and structured to facilitate the allocation of responsibilities and adequate lines of communication?

2.6 Are all staff aware of their explicit responsibilities, and how is this achieved?

2.7 Would surplus or underused staff resources be promptly identified and re-deployed?

2.8 Would failures to meet timescale and/or quality targets be promptly identified, and how is this evidenced?

2.9 How is management assured that all the required resources are made available at the appropriate time so as to avoid/minimise nonproductive time?

2.10 What measures ensure that hourly paid staff are paid only for the hours actually worked and at the appropriate rate?

2.11 What mechanisms ensure that overtime payments are valid, authorised and correctly accounted for through the payroll and accounting systems?

2.12 What measures prevent the fraudulent manipulation of time sheets?

2.13 Does management ensure that evening and night shifts are adequately supervised?

2.14 How does management ensure that all the required equipment, tools, safety devices, etc. are provided, and that staff comply with the prevailing health and safety regulations?

2.15 Are the previous employment records of staff confirmed as correct and satisfactory prior to engagement, and would shortcomings be adequately identified?

2.16 Is staff turnover a problem, and what measures are in place to monitor and minimise turnover of employees?

2.17 Is management monitoring absenteeism and taking appropriate action against persistent offenders or where production objectives are being adversely affected?

2.18 How is the accuracy of data input from other systems (e.g. production planning) confirmed?

2.19 How is the accuracy of data output to other systems (e.g. payroll, product accounting) confirmed?

MATERIALS AND ENERGY

The efficiency of the production process relies partly on the availability of the right components in the right place at the right time. If the organisation is to avoid both the unnecessary costs of holding excess stocks and the disruptions caused by inadequate levels of available material, effective stock resourcing and allocation mechanisms need to be established. Chapter 17 incorporates separate sections on related subjects such as stock control, and warehousing and storage.

This chapter also incorporates issues relative to the use of energy, especially the application of an economically viable energy strategy, so that costs are contained and waste is avoided.

Control Objectives for Materials and Energy

(a) To ensure that adequate supplies of the appropriate materials are available at the correct time to support production requirements.

(b) To avoid or minimise any disruptions caused by an inadequate flow of materials through the production facility.

(c) To ensure that all materials are protected from damage and in a suitable condition for production purposes.

(d) To ensure that all materials are fully accounted for.

(e) To ensure that the organisation has an energy strategy covering such aspects as preferred fuel types, adequate usage monitoring, economic use of energy and an awareness of realistic conservation measures.

(f) To ensure that energy consumption is monitored and action is taken to contain energy costs and avoid waste.

(g) To ensure that energy is efficiently used.

(h) To ensure that optimum terms are obtained from the most appropriate energy suppliers.

(i) To ensure that all energy costs are monitored and authorised for payment.

(j) To provide an ongoing awareness of energy conservation methods and to promote a positive attitude to energy matters.

Risk and Control Issues for Materials and Energy

1 Key Issues

1.1 How does management ensure that adequate supplies of all the appropriate materials will be available at the correct time to support production and manufacturing requirements?

1.2 What measures ensure that shortfalls in supplies or delays in the availability of materials will be promptly detected and effectively reacted to?

1.3 How are all materials accounted for (from procurement, through delivery to eventual usage)?

1.4 Has management established a strategy or procedure to ensure that the most appropriate form of energy is utilised and that usage costs are adequately monitored (and what evidence is there that the current strategy is being complied with)?

1.5 How does management ensure that energy supplies are obtained from appropriate suppliers at the optimum cost?

1.6 What measures are in place to monitor energy usage and identify waste and inefficiencies?

1.7 What measures are in place to ensure that payments for energy costs are valid, accurate and suitably authorised?

1.8 Are alternative sources of energy and improvements in energy usage considered on an ongoing basis as a means of improving efficiency, conserving energy and reducing the associated costs?

2 Detailed Issues

2.1 How are supplies of materials coordinated in order to ensure that appropriate and adequate supplies are maintained?

2.2 Are changes in the production plans adequately communicated to the purchasing, stock control and other affected functions in order to ensure that the appropriate inventory levels are maintained?

2.3 What measures prevent materials from being damaged or lost in the production area(s)?

2.4 Are effective measures in place to ensure that substandard or damaged materials are promptly identified and appropriate corrective action is taken?

2.5 Would losses of materials (for example, through pilferage) be detected and effectively reacted to?

2.6 Where realistic alternative energy types/sources exist, how can management be certain that the most appropriate type/source is utilised?

2.7 What measures are in place to ensure that energy is efficiently consumed and that waste is avoided?

2.8 How are the accounts received for fuel and energy correctly quantified and priced (and how is this evidenced)?

2.9 How does management ensure that all equipment is operating efficiently and that excessive energy consumption is prevented?

2.10 Are measures in place to monitor energy usage and costs against expectations, and are unusual variations adequately followed up?

2.11 Does management monitor energy consumption and costs for each key building or facility?

2.12 What checks are in place to ensure that all the relevant control equipment is correctly and appropriately configured to safely contain energy usage within the optimum ranges?

2.13 Where alternative sources exist, how does management ensure that they obtain the best terms for energy?

2.14 Are projects designed to improve the efficiency of energy consumption fully appraised, cost justified and suitably authorised?

2.15 Are measures in place to ensure that staff are adequately aware of and trained in the efficient use of energy?

2.16 How does management ensure that all the relevant safety factors are satisfactorily addressed?

2.17 Are measures in place to ensure appropriate compliance with all the required statutory obligations?

2.18 How is the accuracy of data input from other systems (e.g. stock control) confirmed?

2.19 How is the accuracy of data output to other systems (e.g. energy accounts payable) confirmed?

QUALITY CONTROL

At a mechanical level, adopting a quality approach to production involves the definition and subsequent monitoring of appropriate standards, thus ensuring that they are both achieved and monitored for their relevance on an ongoing basis. However, it is also crucial that the affected management and staff are suitably committed to the driving quality ethos.

Chapter 9 includes a section on total quality management, which discusses the wider implications of adopting a quality-oriented approach throughout the organisation.

Control Objectives for Quality Control

(a) To ensure that the required quality standards are defined, monitored and complied with.

(b) To ensure that the production methods required to achieve the prevailing quality standards are adequately defined and communicated.

(c) To ensure that both materials received and goods produced are to the required standard.

(d) To avoid the additional costs, wasted resources and erosion of the organisation's reputation associated with the production of poor quality goods.

(e) To ensure that any relevant statutory and industry quality regulations are satisfactorily addressed.

(f) To ensure that effective testing and inspection methods are defined and implemented.

(g) To ensure that production output is appropriately inspected and tested to ensure the maintenance of quality standards.

(h) To ensure that any quality problems are promptly identified, reported, evaluated and resolved.

(i) To ensure that management is kept informed of defect rates and the implications of quality problems.

Risk and Control Issues for Quality Control

1 Key Issues

1.1 Have quality specifications been established for materials, components and finished items, and what form do they take?

1.2 How does management ensure that the defined quality standards are being cost-effectively achieved?

1.3 What measures are in place to identify quality problems or shortcomings and how can management be certain that all such problems are promptly and effectively resolved?

1.4 What measures prevent substandard and poor-quality items from reaching end customers?

1.5 What mechanisms are in place to ensure compliance with any prevailing statutory or industry-level quality standards?

1.6 How does management ensure that the established quality assurance, inspection and testing arrangements are justified and effective?

2 Detailed Issues

2.1 Are quality considerations built into the product design and development processes in order to ensure that they can adequately be addressed in subsequent production runs?

2.2 Are measures in place to confirm the quality specification of materials received from outside suppliers at the time of delivery?

2.3 Is prompt action taken to reject substandard supplies and arrange replacement stocks?

2.4 What measures are in place to assess potential suppliers for their competence and commitment to quality?

2.5 Have quality specifications been defined, authorised and formally documented, and how can management be sure that the current and valid specifications are in use?

2.6 Where achievement of the defined quality standards is dependent on the correct application of a specific production process or method, have such methods been adequately recorded, tested and communicated to all affected parties?

2.7 What mechanisms are in place to achieve an up-to-date awareness of all relevant regulatory quality standards?

2.8 What measures prevent the production, circulation and marketing of substandard items?

2.9 Are the required testing and inspection programmes defined (e.g. in respect of sample sizes, the nature of tests, tolerance limits)?

2.10 What checks are in place to ensure that the defined testing and inspection programmes are being correctly applied?

2.11 Where appropriate, are the organisation's testing processes operated to all the required regulatory standards (and how is this evidenced)?

2.12 How does management ensure that the testing and inspection staff are adequately skilled and experienced to perform their duties?

2.13 Where necessary, are the organisation's quality testing facilities certified by the relevant regulatory/industry bodies?

2.14 Is management kept regularly informed of detected defect rates and the action taken to correct shortcomings, etc.?

2.15 How is the accuracy of data input from other systems (e.g. product development) confirmed?

2.16 How is the accuracy of data output to other systems (e.g. industry regulation and compliance) confirmed?

SAFETY

Management will need to ensure that employees are adequately protected from potentially hazardous processes, equipment and substances. This presupposes that management is fully aware of all the potential risks so that appropriate steps can be taken to address them. The adopted approach to safety issues will need to incorporate the provision (and maintenance) of appropriate equipment as well as suitable staff training in the use of such facilities. In the production environment many of the safety issues will be the subject of specific regulations and legislation, and management will therefore need to ensure ongoing compliance. The broader aspects of health and safety are also addressed in Chapters 18 and 20.

Control Objectives for Safety

(a) To ensure that a comprehensive, approved and documented safety policy is established and complied with.

(b) To ensure that all the safety factors relevant to the production facility have been identified and satisfactorily addressed.

(c) To ensure that all the necessary safety equipment is provided and maintained in operational order.

(d) To ensure that all the relevant prevailing legislation and regulations are being fully complied with.

(e) To ensure that all staff are fully aware of the workplace risk, how to use correctly the safety equipment and protect themselves.

(f) To ensure that machinery and equipment are safely installed, effectively maintained and fitted with protective guards when necessary.

(g) To provide adequate and operative fire prevention and protection facilities.

(h) To ensure that building evacuation procedures and drills are established and regularly tested.

(i) To provide adequate and appropriate first aid and medical facilities.

(j) To ensure that all accidents and incidents are promptly reported and addressed.

(k) To ensure that adequate hygiene and cleaning standards are maintained.

(l) To ensure that hazardous materials are correctly and safely stored.

(m) To ensure that all the required certifications are obtained from regulatory bodies.

Risk and Control Issues for Safety

1 Key Issues

1.1 Has an authorised and documented health and safety policy been developed and implemented, and is it maintained and kept up to date?

1.2 How does management monitor, identify and adequately address all the health and safety risks and hazards within the production facility?

1.3 What measures are in place to monitor full and ongoing compliance with all the relevant legislation and regulations?

1.4 What processes ensure that all staff are fully aware of workplace risks and how to use safety equipment correctly and adequately protect themselves?

1.5 Are appropriate and safe methods used to move materials and goods around the production area, and are staff suitably instructed in the correct lifting and carrying techniques in order to avoid injury?

1.6 What measures ensure that appropriate and sufficient safety equipment has been provided, and that it remains in working order?

1.7 What checks are made to ensure that all machinery is correctly installed and maintained in safe working order?

1.8 Are all relevant machines fitted with effective and operational guards, safety cut-outs, etc.?

1.9 Have sufficient and effective fire prevention and protection systems been provided, and is there evidence that they are regularly tested?

1.10 Have adequate first aid and medical facilities (equipment and personnel) been provided, and are supplies replenished when used?

1.11 What steps are taken to ensure that all incidents and accidents are promptly reported and appropriately dealt with?

1.12 Are adequate hygiene and cleanliness standards established, and what measures ensure that the required standards are maintained?

1.13 How does management ensure that adequate and appropriate insurance cover is provided and maintained?

1.14 Have adequate and appropriate procedures been defined for the storage, movement and handling of hazardous materials (and how is compliance confirmed)?

1.15 Where it is essential for continued operations, what mechanisms ensure that all the required regulatory inspections are conducted at the relevant time and that the appropriate certification is obtained?

2 Detailed Issues

2.1 Has management undertaken a risk assessment of health and safety implications throughout the organisation in order to identify the risks and ensure that they are addressed?

2.2 How does management maintain an up-to-date awareness of all the relevant health and safety regulations?

2.3 Are all staff adequately trained in safety matters, including the use of relevant equipment and clothing (and how can management be certain that all the relevant staff actually receive the appropriate training)?

2.4 Are staff progressively tested on their level of understanding of safety measures in order to identify further training needs?

2.5 How does management ensure that appropriate and adequate lifting and materials handling equipment is provided?

2.6 Are building evacuation, fire and security drills regularly conducted and assessed for effectiveness?

2.7 What measures ensure that all access points and traffic areas are kept clear of obstructions?

2.8 Are adequate fire alarms installed, tested and maintained (and would faults be detected promptly)?

2.9 What processes ensure that the records of incidents and accidents are fully and correctly maintained in accordance with any regulatory requirements?

2.10 Are sufficient and suitably trained first aid and medical personnel available, and how are they promptly summoned to an incident?

2.11 Are medical staff suitably trained and equipped to cope with industry or process-specific incidents (e.g. chemical spillage, high voltage shocks)?

2.12 In the event of an emergency, how can management be sure that all staff and visitors will be accounted for?

2.13 Are transitory safety risks (such as trailing power leads, or wet floors due to cleaning) adequately avoided and addressed?

2.14 What measures prevent the accumulation of waste materials, combustible materials, etc. in working areas?

2.15 What processes ensure that all the required certificates and licences are obtained to enable the lawful operation of the production facilities?

2.16 What measures ensure that any failures to fully comply with the regulatory requirements are promptly identified and effectively dealt with?

2.17 What mechanisms prevent unauthorised access to hazardous materials?

2.18 How is accuracy of data input from other systems (e.g. risk management) confirmed?

2.19 How is the accuracy of data output to other systems (e.g. the staff training records) confirmed?

ENVIRONMENTAL ISSUES

Our focus here is on the environmental implications of production processes, but we also aim to encompass the issues relative to product design as well as those relating to the production processes themselves. The selection of environmentally friendly or renewable materials may be an issue, particularly when viewed against the background of increased customer concern for the general environment. Sector-specific or national regulations may apply, especially in the area of materials disposal, and management will need to be assured about compliance. All these areas underpin the relevance of establishing an overall environmental polity for the organisation, so that management and staff are fully aware of their responsibilities.

Chapter 21 examines the broader implications of environmental interactions against a background of increasing concern with and awareness of environmental issues.

Control Objectives for Environmental Issues

> (a) To provide an authorised and documented policy on environment issues as a framework for conducting production activities.

(b) To minimise the impact of production activities on the environment.

(c) To ensure that the organisation's products are environmentally friendly.

(d) To ensure that waste is minimised and properly disposed of.

(e) To avoid pollution and environmental contamination.

(f) To assess, on an ongoing basis, the environmental impacts of production and define the requirements to be adhered to.

(g) To ensure that alternative and potentially environmentally friendly processes and technologies are considered and implemented where justified.

(h) To minimise/avoid the use of scarce materials and nonrenewable energy sources.

(i) To ensure that harmful or hazardous materials and waste products are safely and responsibly transported and disposed of.

(j) To ensure that all environmental legislation and regulations are fully complied with.

(k) To avoid adverse impacts upon the organisation's reputation and image.

(l) To ensure that environmental issues are subject to monitoring and management.

Risk and Control Issues for Environmental Issues

1 Key Issues

1.1 Has an approved and documented environment policy been established for the production facility?

1.2 What measures ensure that the principles of the environmental policy are complied with, and how would noncompliance be promptly detected?

1.3 Have the production processes and activities been assessed for their environmental impacts (and how is the necessary corrective action evidenced)?

1.4 How does management ensure that all the relevant environmental legislation and regulations are fully complied with, thus avoiding penalties and adverse effects on the organisation's public image?

1.5 How does management monitor that all waste products are correctly and safely treated, discharged or disposed of?

1.6 What measures prevent the pollution and contamination of the environment?

1.7 Are the organisation's products assessed for "environmental friendliness" (e.g. impact during production/use, potential to be recycled, safe disposal at end of product life, restricted use of scarce resources)?

1.8 Has management actively considered alternative and less environmentally harmful production processes?

1.9 Are measures in place to ensure that all environmental impacts are identified, monitored and effectively managed (and what is the evidence for this)?

2 Detailed Issues

2.1 Is the environmental policy supported by the commitment of senior management and a suitable staff training/awareness programme?

2.2 Are all projects to reduce the impact of production activities on the environment subject to a full feasibility and cost appraisal, before being authorised?

2.3 Is the assessment of environmental impacts kept up to date in order that management action is relevant and targeted?

2.4 Has a responsibility for environmental management been defined and allocated?

2.5 What measures ensure that all waste products are identified, assessed for their environmental impact and appropriately treated/processed?

2.6 Are all discharges of waste products subject to monitoring and permitted within the prevailing regulations (and how would non compliance be detected)?

2.7 How does management ensure that all waste product treatment processes are operating correctly and efficiently?

2.8 What measures ensure that management would be made aware of all accidental and unintentional spillages of potentially harmful materials?

2.9 Are contingency plans and resources in place to deal effectively with the likely range of environmental accidents?

2.10 How does management confirm that waste disposal sites and operators are appropriately licensed to handle the specific by-products generated by the organisation?

2.11 Is management considering utilising alternatives to hazardous or scarce materials as a means of reducing the environmental impacts?

2.12 Are the potential long-term environmental liabilities adequately assessed for both newly acquired sites and those being disposed of?

2.13 Are environmental impact audits regularly conducted by appropriately experienced personnel and are their findings and recommendations effectively followed up?

2.14 Does the design and development of new products take into account the potential environmental impact of production, and what measures ensure that such impacts are minimised and contained?

2.15 How is the accuracy of data input from other systems (e.g. new product development or design) confirmed?

2.16 How is the accuracy of data output to other systems (e.g. industry regulation and compliance) confirmed?

LAW AND REGULATORY COMPLIANCE

The scope in this section takes into account local, national and sector-specific regulatory issues, encompassing such matters as awareness, ensuring ongoing compliance, and thus avoiding the adverse impacts of non compliance.

Control Objectives for Law and Regulatory Compliance

(a) To ensure that management and staff maintain an accurate awareness of all relevant legislation and regulations.

(b) To ensure full compliance with the prevailing legislation and regulations.

(c) To ensure that business operations are reviewed and assessed for legal and regulatory implications.

(d) To ensure that specific responsibility for addressing the relevant requirements is defined and allocated.

(e) To take the legislative and regulatory requirements into account when planning change.

(f) To prevent and minimise penalties and litigation arising from non compliance.

(g) To seek reliable professional advice on legal matters in order to select the optimum solutions.

Risk and Control Issues for Law and Regulatory Compliance

1 Key Issues

1.1 How does management ensure full awareness of all the relevant legal and regulatory implications for the production facility?

1.2 What measures are in place to ensure that all the relevant legislation and regulations are correctly complied with?

1.3 Would management be promptly made aware of any failure to comply or breaches of regulations, and how is this evidenced?

1.4 What mechanisms ensure that all staff are suitably aware of their responsibilities for legal and regulatory matters?

1.5 Does management take the legal and regulatory implications into account when considering or planning changes within the production environment?

1.6 Does management have access to reliable sources of professional legal advice when necessary?

1.7 What steps would be taken to minimise the extent of penalties, litigation cost and adverse impacts on the organisation's image and reputation in the event of a serious breach of regulations?

2 Detailed Issues

2.1 Has the production facility/environment been fully assessed for all the relevant legal and regulatory implications as the basis for defining the compliance requirements?

2.2 How does management maintain awareness of new and changed legal and regulatory requirements, and how is this evidenced?

2.3 Are any forms of independent inspection undertaken as a means of further ensuring the necessary compliance?

2.4 Are the relevant regulatory and legal requirements correctly incorporated into operating procedures and policies (and are they maintained and kept up to date)?

2.5 Are measures in place to address the specific regulations for the following areas:

- employment
- hours of work
- working conditions
- safety
- facilities
- equipment?

2.6 How is the accuracy of data input from other systems (e.g. the legal department) confirmed?

2.7 How is the accuracy of data output to other systems (e.g. staff training records) confirmed?

MAINTENANCE

Continuity is the keyword here; ensuring that production processes are not unduly disrupted by equipment failure due to any inadequacies in the maintenance of same. Beyond the cost implications of production disruption, management would also seek to ensure that the organisation's investment in plant and machinery is protected through adequate and regular maintenance, and that serious and potentially costly faults are minimised.

Control Objectives for Maintenance

(a) To ensure that all production equipment and machinery is cost-effectively maintained in working order.

(b) To prevent/minimise any disruption to production caused by the failure of equipment, plant and machinery.

(c) To define and implement a structured and planned approach to preventive maintenance in order to ensure that all relevant devices are regularly inspected and serviced.

(d) To ensure that adequate and appropriately skilled maintenance staff are employed to fulfil the defined maintenance obligations.

(e) To provide a prompt and effective response to emergency maintenance problems during working hours.

(f) To ensure that preventive maintenance work is conducted at a time to avoid undue disruption of production processes.

(g) To ensure that the maintenance programme does not contravene any current supplier/manufacturer warranties and service conditions.

(h) To ensure that all maintenance work is conducted to the required standard and complies with any prevailing safety regulations.

(i) To ensure that the performance of external maintenance contractors is monitored and confirmed as being effective and acceptable.

(j) To ensure that all maintenance costs are accurately identified, justified, recorded, authorised and accounted for.

(k) To ensure that all spares and materials used during maintenance are correctly accounted for.

(l) To ensure that maintenance costs are adequately monitored and that the appropriate action is taken with regard to troublesome or costly pieces of production machinery.

Risk and Control Issues for Maintenance

1 Key Issues

1.1 What measures are in place to ensure that all production equipment and machinery is maintained in working order?

1.2 Has management defined, documented and implemented a suitable maintenance plan which identifies the servicing needs for all key equipment?

1.3 How is management assured that all the intended maintenance work is correctly conducted?

1.4 How does management ensure that adequate and appropriately skilled maintenance staff are provided?

1.5 What mechanisms minimise the disruptions caused by the failure of machinery during production runs?

1.6 When appropriate, are external suppliers and maintenance contractors used to conduct regular servicing and emergency repairs (and is their performance monitored for effectiveness and value for money)?

1.7 Are all machines and equipment maintained to the required standard (and how is this evidenced)?

1.8 How are all maintenance costs (labour and materials) accurately identified, justified, authorised and correctly accounted for?

1.9 Is regular and accurate information on maintenance costs and machine performance provided, and what action is taken by management in respect of persistently faulty equipment?

1.10 Is management made aware of the need to replace or upgrade production equipment, and what is the evidence that such replacements are fully examined, justified and authorised to proceed?

2 Detailed Issues

2.1 Are machine failures and operational problems promptly reported to the appropriate staff to enable effective action to be taken?

2.2 What measures prevent equipment being overlooked for maintenance purposes?

2.3 Are maintenance requirements documented and differentiated between items to be serviced by internal staff and external contractors/suppliers?

2.4 Is a preventive maintenance plan documented and in place, and how can management be sure that it is adhered to?

2.5 Is equipment under the supplier's warranty adequately identified so that all maintenance is handled by the supplier or the manufacturer?

2.6 What measures prevent unauthorised or unqualified staff from tampering with or servicing production equipment?

2.7 Is preventive maintenance conducted out of normal working hours (or during re-tooling or production set-up periods) in order to avoid any undue disruption of production processes?

2.8 Is the performance of key pieces of equipment subject to effective monitoring so that potentially disruptive faults can be anticipated and countered?

2.9 Are accurate and up-to-date servicing records maintained for each piece of key production equipment?

2.10 Are effective and workable contingency arrangements in place (and tested) in the event of the failure of a key piece of machinery?

2.11 How does management ensure that any devices used in continuous manufacturing processes are operating correctly and receive the necessary maintenance attention?

2.12 Are all claims against suppliers for persistently faulty equipment effectively pursued and compensation sought?

2.13 Are maintenance staff suitably trained to deal with the range of production equipment in place, and how is this confirmed?

2.14 Are maintenance staff resources adequate to ensure appropriately skilled coverage during holiday periods, etc.?

2.15 Are out-of-hours maintenance activities suitably justified and authorised?

2.16 Are maintenance activities (both internally and externally resourced) subject to monitoring for justification and performance purposes?

2.17 How would management be made aware of any unnecessary or unjustified activities?

2.18 Does management conduct appraisals of the performance of external service contractors and take remedial action when necessary?

2.19 What measures ensure that claims are pursued against external maintenance contractors in the event of unsatisfactory or delayed service provision?

2.20 Where safety and other regulatory implications apply, how can management be certain that the required maintenance standards are achieved?

2.21 What mechanisms ensure that relevant production equipment is correctly calibrated, configured and operating at the optimum level recommended by the manufacturer?

2.22 Are purchase orders for spare parts and maintenance consumables suitably justified, authorised and accounted for?

2.23 Are stocks of maintenance parts accounted for and regularly verified (and what prevents pilferage and other losses occurring)?

2.24 How is the accuracy of data input from other systems (e.g. external contractors' charges from the accounts payable system) confirmed?

2.25 How is the accuracy of data output to other systems (e.g. overtime hours worked by the maintenance team for payroll calculation purposes) confirmed?

16
Auditing Marketing and Sales

INTRODUCTION

In this chapter we consider the operational auditing dimensions of the marketing and sales functions.

SYSTEM/FUNCTION COMPONENTS OF THE MARKETING AND SALES FUNCTIONS

We have chosen to use an essentially *functional* approach to define the marketing and sales audit universe, which gives us the following possible breakdown of the key functions, systems or activities, further subdivided between marketing and sales and after sales support:

Marketing and sales:

- product development
- market research
- promotion and advertising
- pricing and discount policies
- sales management
- sales performance and monitoring
- distributors[1]
- relationship with parent company
- agents
- order processing.

After sales support:

- warranty arrangements
- maintenance and servicing
- spare parts and supply.

In common with other chapters in this book, the component activities/functions noted for the given subject area are closely interconnected, and should not be viewed in isolation, as there inevitably will be synergy and information flow between the separate elements. The points of interconnection should be of particular concern (to auditors and management alike) as they can represent changes of managerial responsibility and jurisdiction, which often results in reduced control effectiveness at the interface.

GENERAL COMMENTS

The specific marketing stance taken by an organisation will be relative to its particular industry, and also strongly determined by wider economic and general market influences, such as:

- increasing price competition;
- the increasing role and importance of customer service quality;
- the level of general competition;
- the implications of consolidation of the competition (i.e. into fewer and larger market players);
- the globalisation of competitors and markets;
- the need to improve products and service quality.

Customer focus is seen as increasingly important and many organisations have oriented their marketing approach accordingly, perhaps to the extent of viewing their customers as assets, through the use of such techniques as MCSA (managing customers as strategic assets).

Although we have opted to adopt a functional approach to marketing, there is a trend to move away from a centralised marketing approach (typified by a specialist department serving the whole organisation) to a *line marketing* orientation, which devolves marketing responsibilities to line management for a given product, range or segment. The reasoning behind this move is to achieve improved synergy and integration between the marketing activities and the day-to-day decisions taken in a wider business management context. In other words, marketing is being moved closer to the front line. In tandem with this change, marketing can become a more generalised and widespread thread running through the organisation so that it becomes "everyone's business".

The functional components we have identified can be used in any marketing situation, but the devolution of marketing responsibility may result in audit coverage being spread across a number of areas of influence where an organisation has many discrete products or segments.

CONTROL OBJECTIVES AND RISK AND CONTROL ISSUES

We shall now examine the control objectives and the related risk and control issues (divided into key issues and detailed issues) for each of the marketing, sales and after sales support areas listed above. This data can be used within the format of

PRODUCT DEVELOPMENT

This subject area is predominantly about the future cost-effective positioning of product lines in association with the driving strategic direction of the organisation and taking into account the implications of external market and economic forces. Where product developments are justified, appropriate, realistic and suitable, coordinated plans will be required to support the development process and bring the product to the market on time and at the right price.

Chapter 19 contains a section on product development from a research and development viewpoint. Chapter 12 includes a related section on product/project accounting.

Control Objectives for Product Development

(a) To ensure that new and existing products are developed in accordance with market factors and the strategic objectives of the organisation.

(b) To ensure that product lines do not become prematurely obsolete.

(c) To ensure that all product developments are fully assessed in relation to the potential market, estimated production costs and selling price.

(d) To ensure that all product development projects are suitably authorised to proceed.

(e) To ensure that the design assessment and product specification processes are adequate and address matters of quality and performance.

(f) To ensure that the product development is timed so that market and competitive advantages are optimised.

(g) To ensure that the resources required to undertake the development are accurately identified, costed, justified and authorised.

(h) To ensure that the activities of all the afflicted functions (e.g. production, advertising, quality control and sales team) are coordinated in order to achieve the defined objectives.

(i) To ensure that the eventual product is adequately and appropriately protected from exploitation by others (e.g. through the use of patents).

(j) To ensure that all information about the organisation's product developments remains confidential.

(k) To ensure that the progress of the development project is adequately monitored by management and appropriate changes are applied when necessary and authorised.

(l) To ensure that all the actual development costs are correctly identified and monitored against the established budgets.

(m) To ensure that all significant project variations or problems are promptly reported to management for corrective action.

(n) To ensure that the product is thoroughly tested throughout the development and subject to appropriate consumer testing prior to launch.

(o) To ensure that the market launch of new or modified products is adequately planned and monitored.

(p) To ensure that the initial sales performance of new products is closely monitored.

(q) To ensure that shortfalls in sales performance are promptly detected and reacted to.

(r) To ensure that the objectives and performance criteria established at the outset of the development are actually achieved.

Risk and Control Issues for Product Development

1 Key Issues

1.1 Has management defined and authorised strategic business objectives, and what measures are in place to ensure that all product developments comply with these targets?

1.2 Has management established, authorised and implemented documented procedures for the development and evolution of all product ranges?

1.3 What checks are in place to monitor that product plans remain adequate, appropriate, viable, etc.?

1.4 How does management ensure that all product development projects are valid and authorised?

1.5 What mechanisms ensure that the product design and specification stages are effectively conducted so as to avoid problems and repercussions during later development stages (e.g. production or cost implications)?

1.6 Are all the appropriate and relevant recognised quality and performance standards adequately addressed in the product development process?

1.7 What forms of market research are undertaken, and how can management be sure that the target product has a viable market?

1.8 How are all the relevant issues addressed to ensure the most appropriate launch of the eventual product?

1.9 What processes ensure that all the resources required to undertake the development are accurately identified, costed, justified and authorised?

1.10 Are all product developments subject to adequate project management in order to cater for the following aspects:

- adequate coordination of all affected functions to ensure achievement of development objectives
- definition of key stages of the project and the ongoing monitoring of actual progress against target
- authorisation and control of all project resources and costs?

1.11 What measures ensure that new or modified products are subject to extensive, adequate and appropriate testing (including any sector-specific or specialist product testing requirements)?

1.12 What processes ensure that the launch of new products is adequately planned for and coordinated (e.g. in terms of supporting promotion, adequacy of stocks)?

1.13 Are actual sales of new products adequately monitored in order to ensure that the overall business objectives are achieved?

2 Detailed Issues

2.1 What mechanisms prevent the investigation or development of a product outside the defined and authorised strategic parameters of the business?

2.2 Has management defined and authorised product development plans with the intention of extending and prolonging the life of existing products and introducing viable new lines?

2.3 How does management ensure that its product plans remain relevant, up to date and in step with customer needs and market developments?

2.4 Are product developments geared to a price-driven market, and what measures does management take to ensure that the costing criteria are accurate?

2.5 Is appropriate account taken of competitor analysis and are critical marketing timing considerations identified and planned for?

2.6 How does management ensure that all the affected functions are adequately consulted during the product development?

2.7 How would all the implications of a new product reliably be identified and planned for?

2.8 How does management ensure that product details and development plans and business development strategies remain confidential?

2.9 What steps are taken to protect product designs, related production techniques and technologies from exploitation by others?

2.10 Are key staff involved in product development subject to fidelity bonding or commercial confidentiality clauses in their employment contracts?

2.11 How confident is management that problems, shortcomings, cost overruns, etc. would be promptly detected and reported?

2.12 Have adequate arrangements been made to provide management with regular, accurate and relevant project information?

2.13 Where appropriate, are products subject to testing under recognised trade, national or international quality/standards schemes?

2.14 Upon product launch, how does management ensure that all the necessary promotional activities are coordinated?

2.15 What measures are in place to provide adequate stocks of new products upon launch?

2.16 What mechanisms ensure that all affected staff (e.g. sales, servicing, customer enquiries clerks, etc.) are suitably trained to respond effectively to customers' requirements?

2.17 What procedures ensure that management is promptly made aware of sales and performance shortfalls?

2.18 How is the accuracy of data input from other systems (e.g. market research or planning) confirmed?

2.19 How is the accuracy of data output to other systems (e.g. production control, sales management) confirmed?

MARKET RESEARCH

To keep the marketing direction of the organisation pertinently focused, it is critical that an accurate and up-to-date awareness of customer and market expectations is maintained. Where it is justified, the use of market research techniques can provide the necessary marketing intelligence to reinforce or influence the marketing strategy. In this section, we consider the implications of market research for the business and seek to ensure that such techniques are cost-effectively and efficiently applied.

Control Objectives for Market Research

(a) To ensure that the organisation remains aware of the needs of their target customers.

> (b) To ensure that all product development, marketing and sales activities are based on accurate determinations of the prevailing economic, market and customer trends.
>
> (c) To ensure that market research activities are accurately costed, justified and authorised.
>
> (d) To ensure that the organisation is kept informed about competitor products and activities.
>
> (e) To ensure that promotional and advertising activities are appropriately targeted as a means to ensure value for money and effectiveness.
>
> (f) To identify potential new markets or opportunities to differentiate products and services.
>
> (g) To ensure that the organisation's products and services match the market expectation in respect of quality, price and performance.
>
> (h) To ensure that customer complaints and product returns are appropriately analysed as the basis for taking corrective action.
>
> (i) To maintain a database of market intelligence relevant to the operating sector to support effective decision making.

Risk and Control Issues for Market Research

1 Key Issues

1.1 How does management maintain an accurate and up-to-date awareness of market trends, customer needs and competitor activities as the basis for their own planning and decision making?

1.2 What steps are taken to ensure that customer requirements are identified and effectively addressed?

1.3 How does management correlate market research findings with product development, promotional and sales activities?

1.4 Are all market research activities accurately costed, and justified as being worthwhile and authorised?

1.5 How does management assess that promotional activities and advertising are appropriately targeted and offer value for money?

1.6 How does management identify potential new markets or opportunities to differentiate their products?

1.7 What measures ensure that products continue to match the required performance, quality and price criteria?

1.8 Are new and prototype products/services realistically market tested prior to full launch, and how are the results utilised?

1.9 How is management assured that market research data is accurate and reliable?

2 Detailed Issues

2.1 Are suitably skilled and experienced marketing staff employed to conduct or direct market research activities?

2.2 How does management ensure that external market research agencies and consultants are reliable, qualified and cost-effective?

2.3 Is the performance of market research activities reviewed and assessed for effectiveness (over a suitable period)?

2.4 Are macroeconomic events, general sector trends and other market influences taken into account by management and what assurances are there that interpretations of such factors are accurate?

2.5 Does management conduct a comprehensive competitor analysis as the basis for determining the appropriate tactical responses?

2.6 Are customer complaints and comments recorded, assessed and used to define the necessary corrective action?

2.7 How is the accuracy of data input from other systems (e.g. sales performance, financial reporting) confirmed?

2.8 How is the accuracy of data output to other systems (e.g. planning function, promotion and advertising) confirmed?

PROMOTION AND ADVERTISING

Setting the appropriate tone and approach for advertising and promotion can be seen as a crucial requirement given the high costs normally associated with these processes. It is debatable whether they are, in truth, arts or sciences—much depends on the study and interpretation of human expectation, susceptibility and desire. In this section, we consider the key business-related issues, incorporating those relating to the engagement and use of external specialists in the field.

Control Objectives for Promotion and Advertising

(a) To ensure that a planned approach (perhaps by product type) to promotion and advertising is agreed, authorised and implemented.

(b) To ensure that promotional and advertising budgets are agreed, authorised and adhered to.

(c) To ensure that advertising activity is of an appropriate type, sufficient in quantity, adequately targeted at the relevant market, represents value for money, and is monitored for effectiveness.

(d) To ensure that the engagement and utilisation of external advertising agencies and consultants is accurately costed, justified and authorised.

(e) To ensure that the organisation pays for only confirmed advertising activities.

(f) To ensure that advertising and promotional budgets allocated to external agencies are authorised and confirmed as used for the defined purpose.

(g) To ensure that the expenditure of promotional budgets is accurately accounted for and reflected in the accounts.

(h) To ensure that budgets for individual promotions are agreed, authorised and monitored.

(i) To ensure that the advertising and promotional plans and strategy are kept confidential and are protected from unauthorised access.

(j) To ensure that promotional literature (e.g. point of sale materials, leaflets, price lists) is accurate, lawful and that sufficient supplies have been obtained.

(k) To ensure that promotions are lawful, fairly conducted, active for a defined but limited period, and that adequate resources are allocated.

(l) To ensure that promotional staff are adequately trained so as to project a positive and informed image.

(m) To ensure that promotional items (e.g. gifts exchanged for coupons, redeemable vouchers) and merchandising stocks are accounted for.

(n) To ensure that staff and agents are prevented from taking part in, and benefiting from, promotional activities.

(o) To ensure that advertising and promotional budgets passed over to agents, etc. are accounted for and used only for the prescribed purpose.

(p) To ensure that sponsorship deals are justified, authorised and subject to a written agreement which defines the fees payable and the type and level of service(s) to be provided in exchange.

(q) To ensure that all promotional and advertising activities are reviewed and appropriately amended on an ongoing basis.

Risk and Control Issues for Promotion and Advertising

1 Key Issues

1.1 Has a planned approach to advertising and promotion been agreed, authorised and implemented?

1.2 How does management ensure that advertising and promotional expenditure is adequately targeted, budgeted, effectively used and fully accounted for?

1.3 What mechanisms prevent expenditure on unauthorised advertising and promotional schemes?

1.4 Is the engagement of external advertising agencies, creative consultants and marketing companies subject to adequate assessment, justification and authorisation?

1.5 How does management verify that the organisation is paying only for actual advertising and promotional activities?

1.6 What measures ensure that all advertising and promotional activities are lawful, accurate and project a positive corporate image?

1.7 Are budgets established and is actual expenditure monitored against budget?

1.8 What precautions prevent unauthorised access to or leakage of advertising and promotional plans?

1.9 How does management ensure that promotional activities are adequately defined, authorised, proficiently conducted and adequately resourced?

1.10 What measures ensure that sales, marketing and promotional staff are well informed about the products and present a positive corporate image?

1.11 Are all sponsorship deals subject to a written agreement, and are they monitored to confirm that all the prescribed obligations have been satisfactorily discharged?

2 Detailed Issues

2.1 What processes prevent the operation of unauthorised advertising and promotional activities?

2.2 Does management measure and monitor the effectiveness of advertising and promotional activities?

2.3 Are the merits of alternative advertising media, coverage frequency, etc. explored in order to implement the optimum approach?

2.4 How does management know that the adopted approach is adequate and effective?

2.5 If a specific advertising agency or consultant is hired, is management sure that alternatives would not offer improved service and value for money?

2.6 What measures are in place to prevent payments being made for invalid advertising and promotional services?

2.7 Are external agencies held accountable for all expenditure on the organisation's behalf?

2.8 What monitoring processes ensure that allocated budgets are being correctly and appropriately utilised?

2.9 What measures ensure that all promotional and advertising literature is accurate, up to date, lawful and correctly utilised?

2.10 Are all promotional and merchandising stocks securely held, used only for the defined purpose, regularly verified, and fully accounted for?

2.11 How does management verify that all advertising and promotional expenditure is correctly reflected in the accounts?

2.12 How are staff and agents prevented from taking part in or benefiting from promotional schemes?

2.13 How are potential sponsorship arrangements assessed and judged to be worthwhile?

2.14 Are all sponsorship arrangements authorised and subject to a written agreement?

2.15 Are all the obligations of sponsorship clearly defined (for all parties) and monitored for full compliance?

2.16 How does management determine the "value" and benefits of sponsorship and related promotional activities?

2.17 How are agents assessed for their stability, reliability, suitability, etc.?

2.18 How is accuracy of data input from other systems (e.g. sales performance and monitoring) confirmed?

2.19 How is the accuracy of data output to other systems (e.g. planning, product development) confirmed?

PRICING AND DISCOUNT POLICIES

When an organisation establishes its pricing policy it needs to ensure that all the internal and external economic and market-related factors have been duly considered and incorporated; otherwise there is the danger that the product or service will fail in the real world. This section explores the related accounting, marketplace and business strategy issues.

Chapter 12 includes an examination of the issues surrounding the related subject of product/project accounting.

Control Objectives for Pricing and Discount Policies

(a) To ensure that pricing and discount structures are authorised and documented.

(b) To ensure that pricing levels are competitive, profitable, and adequately cover the underlying costs.

(c) To ensure that an awareness of market trends, competitor pricing, etc. is maintained to enable the appropriate commercial response.

(d) To ensure that authorised prices and discounts are correctly applied to invoices.

(e) To ensure that changes to prices and discounts are authorised and correctly implemented.

(f) To ensure that accurate and reliable records of costs are maintained in support of determining the pricing policy.

(g) To provide adequate costing information as a means of identifying the potential for cost savings, etc.

(h) To ensure that the effects of taxation and duty are taken into account when setting prices.

(i) To ensure that, when applicable, geographic differentials and the effects of cyclical sales patterns are taken into account when determining variations to the pricing policy.

(j) To ensure that pricing structures accord with the relevant distributor, agent, retailer chain and are competitive at each stage.

(k) To ensure that government, national and international pricing restrictions are taken into account when applicable.

Risk and Control Issues for Pricing and Discount Policies

1 Key Issues

1.1 Have documented pricing and discount policies been authorised and implemented (and are they based on established profit margins, etc.)?

1.2 What steps are taken to ensure that prices remain competitive, profitable and sustainable?

1.3 How is management assured that the correct prices and discounts are always applied to invoices (and what mechanisms are in place to detect and report any unauthorised variations)?

1.4 How does management confirm that product costing information is accurate, complete and reliable as the basis for determining prices?

1.5 What measures ensure that changes to prices and discount structures are justified, authorised and correctly applied?

1.6 Does management take into account the effects of taxation (e.g. VAT or sales tax), duty and any prevailing price constraints when determining pricing levels?

2 Detailed Issues

2.1 How does management ensure that the most appropriate form of product costing is applied?

2.2 How does management maintain an accurate awareness of market trends, competitor prices, etc. as determinants of pricing policy?

2.3 Are the required profit levels and returns realistically established?

2.4 What processes link individual customers to the correct pricing and discount structure, so as to ensure the accurate calculation of invoices?

2.5 What parameters govern the eligibility for discounts, and what mechanisms ensure that they are correctly applied?

2.6 What steps are taken to protect commercially sensitive pricing information from unauthorised access and leakage?

2.7 Does management take into account the potential for geographic differentiation in pricing policy, and if so what assurances are there that the variations are correctly applied to invoices?

2.8 Where the sales of a product are affected by cyclical patterns, does the pricing structure vary in relation to demand (and is this process duly authorised)?

2.9 Where prices vary according to cyclical sales patterns, how does management ensure that the correct price is applied?

2.10 What measures prevent the set-up and application of invalid or unauthorised prices and discounts?

2.11 How does management verify that the prevailing pricing structure complies with any national or international pricing regulations?

2.12 How is the accuracy of data input from other systems (e.g. product costing) confirmed?

2.13 How is the accuracy of data output to other systems (e.g. accounts receivable or advertising and promotion) confirmed?

SALES MANAGEMENT

How best to organise, target and utilise the sales force resources are the key points here. On the one hand we are concerned with the development of a clear overall strategy for achieving the desired sales levels, but on the other hand there is a need to contain the costs of seeking out suitable and stable customers and maintaining their ongoing interest in the organisation's products and services.

Control Objectives for Sales Management

(a) To ensure that realistic sales strategies and quotas are developed, authorised, implemented and monitored.

(b) To ensure that customers and potential customers are identified and pursued.

(c) To ensure that accurate and up-to-date customer and sales activity data is obtained and maintained in support of sales activities and reporting.

(d) To ensure that adequate and appropriately trained sales staff are provided.

(e) To ensure that sales staff are adequately managed to maximise their performance and attain the defined sales quotas.

(f) To ensure that workable sales territories are established and suitably staffed.

(g) To ensure that sales staff operate within the defined and authorised company policies (e.g. for prices, discounts, credit rating, etc.).

(h) To ensure that new customers are confirmed as being bona fide, financially stable, etc. prior to a trading relationship being established.

(i) To ensure that order data is accurately captured and subsequently processed.

(j) To ensure that sales staff expenses, commissions, bonuses, etc. are valid, correctly calculated and authorised.

(k) To ensure that the costs associated with maintaining the sales force are accurately identified, authorised, accounted for and monitored against performance.

(l) To ensure that delinquent sales accounts and customers are pursued.

(m) To ensure that customer enquiries and complaints are recorded and adequately followed up.

(n) To ensure that all the requirements of export sales are correctly addressed.

(o) To ensure that sales staff account for all trade samples. etc.

Risk and Control Issues for Sales Management

1 Key Issues

1.1 Are sales activities conducted in accordance with defined and authorised strategies and quotas?

1.2 What measures are in place to ensure that current and potential customers are identified and that customer data is accurately maintained and kept up to date?

1.3 How does management ensure that adequate (and justifiable) sales staff are provided and that they are suitably trained and knowledgeable about the company products?

1.4 How are sales staff workloads allocated (e.g. through defined territories or specific customer allocations) and how does management measure and monitor performance (e.g. for leads and confirmed sales)?

1.5 What mechanisms ensure that all orders fully comply with company policies on

- prices
- discounts
- credit ratings and limits, etc.

1.6 What measures are applied to ensure that customers are financially stable and reliable (and what prevents the acceptance of unsuitable customers)?

1.7 How are individual customer credit limits determined and are they subject to a higher level of authority prior to orders being accepted?

1.8 How does management confirm that all order data is accurately captured, conforms to company policies, and is accurately reflected through delivery and invoice accounting?

1.9 What mechanisms are in place to confirm the accuracy and validity of sales staff expenses, commissions, bonuses, etc.?

1.10 Is management made aware of the actual costs associated with maintaining the sales force, and is this data related to budgets and required levels of sales activities as a means of determining the effectiveness of sales activities?

1.11 Are sales staff engaged in following up delinquent accounts and resolving customer complaints (and how is management assured that such actions are effectively conducted)?

1.12 How does management verify that all the administrative and regulatory requirements of export sales are correctly fulfilled?

2 Detailed Issues

2.1 Upon what basis have sales quotas and targets been produced (and are they realistic and reliable)?

2.2 How are sales quotas rolled down to the sales team?

2.3 What levels of authority would be applied to amendments of the sales strategy and quotas (and how is this authority evidenced)?

2.4 Are product development, marketing, promotional and advertising activities coordinated to support actively sales staff activities?

2.5 How is the success (or otherwise) of the defined strategy measured, and how are changes agreed and implemented?

2.6 Have mechanisms been established to reliably identify potential customers and marketing opportunities?

2.7 How is customer and sales lead data protected from unauthorised access and amendments (and how is management assured that it remains up to date and relevant)?

2.8 What checks are in place to ensure that data on sales activities (e.g. leads, confirmed orders) is accurate?

2.9 Would management promptly be made aware of unproductive or under-achieving sales staff?

2.10 What mechanisms prevent the establishment of unauthorised, unlawful or uneconomic trading terms with a customer?

2.11 How does management ensure that adequate time is allowed for sales staff to implement major changes in sales policy?

2.12 How does management ensure that all sales staff are suitably experienced and demonstrate an accurate knowledge of company products and trading terms?

2.13 What measures are in place to ensure that all sales leads are captured, trailed and accounted for?

2.14 Are sales leads and transactions reported through the agents' network accurately captured, in compliance with the prevailing terms, and taken into account when allocating commission payments?

2.15 Have authorised procedures been established and applied for determining and operating credit and trading limits?

2.16 What mechanisms prevent established credit and trading limits being exceeded?

2.17 Is the acceptance of new customers (or increased limits for existing customers) subject to suitable authorisation (and how is this evidenced)?

2.18 What measures prevent the acceptance of orders where prices and/or discounts are outside the authorised range?

2.19 What measures does management take to avoid losses associated with trading with financially unsuitable customers?

2.20 Are all orders accounted for?

2.21 Have standard rates for sales staff expenses (mileage charges, hotel accommodation, subsistence, entertaining, etc.) been agreed, authorised and implemented?

2.22 What mechanisms prevent the payment of sales staff expenses claims that fall outside of the authorised rates?

2.23 Are sales staff expense claims subject to scrutiny for validity and accuracy (and are they authorised for settlement)?

2.24 Are sales territories and staff journeys optimised in relation to their operational base, so as to contain travel and overnight accommodation costs?

2.25 What steps are taken to verify that payments of sales commission and bonus are accurate, based on actual sales achievements, correctly calculated and authorised?

2.26 What mechanisms prevent the payment of invalid or unauthorised expenses, commissions and bonuses?

2.27 Are established expense rates, commission and bonuses subject to regular review, justification and authorised amendment?

2.28 How does management maintain an awareness of all customer complaints/comments, and what checks are in place to ensure that such queries are effectively dealt with?

2.29 What mechanisms are in place to detect failures to comply with all the prevailing export sales regulations?

2.30 Are sales staff held to account for all product samples, demonstration products and merchandising stocks in their possession (and would shortfalls be promptly detected and followed up)?

2.31 How is the accuracy of data input from other systems (e.g. planning or pricing policy) confirmed?

2.32 How is the accuracy of data output to other systems (e.g. order processing or petty cash reimbursement) confirmed?

SALES PERFORMANCE AND MONITORING

The overall development, production, pricing, promotion and marketing strategies associated with a given product or service will interface with the real world through a comparison between forecast and actual sales performance levels. The initial determination of sales forecasts needs to be both realistic and accurate. The actual performance of the sales force (in terms of both sales achievement and operating costs) will require accurate ongoing monitoring against the predicted targets, in order that management are provided with up-to-date and reliable data to support their decision making. It will also be necessary to evaluate whether an adequate and suitably trained sales force is provided and maintained in relation to the performance requirements.

Control Objectives for Sales Performance and Monitoring

> (a) To ensure that realistic and accurate sales forecasts, targets and quotas are calculated, authorised and implemented.
>
> (b) To ensure that accurate sales performance data is obtained and monitored against the authorised targets.
>
> (c) To ensure that the performance of the sales function is subject to ongoing monitoring and that any shortcomings are satisfactorily addressed.
>
> (d) To ensure that the organisation's marketing and performance objectives are met.
>
> (e) To ensure that adequate sales staff are engaged and effectively managed to maximise their performance and achieve the defined quotas.
>
> (f) To ensure that sales staff are suitably trained to adequately represent the company and its products.
>
> (g) To ensure that significant fluctuations in margins, sales volumes and revenue generation are accurately reported to management.
>
> (h) To ensure that the sales function operating costs are justified in relation to performance achievements.

Risk and Control Issues for Sales Performance and Monitoring

1 Key Issues

1.1 How does management ensure that projected sales targets are accurately and realistically determined?

1.2 Is the establishment of sales targets/quotas and any subsequent amendment subject to suitable authorisation (and how is this evidenced)?

1.3 Does management maintain adequate records of historical sales trends, volumes, etc. as the basis for sales planning (and how can they be sure of the accuracy and validity of such data)?

1.4 How does management ensure that all actual sales data is accurately and completely captured?

1.5 Is management provided with accurate and up-to-date sales performance statistics?

1.6 What action is taken to detect and react promptly to sales performance shortcomings, etc.?

1.7 How does management determine and justify the staffing establishment of the sales function so as to avoid under or over-staffing?

1.8 How does management ensure that sales staff are adequately trained and knowledgeable about company products and terms of business?

2 Detailed Issues

2.1 Are up-to-date sales forecasts (by product where applicable) available that reflect the following elements:
- unit volumes
- revenue levels?

2.2 What factors are taken into account when determining the sales forecasts and targets?

2.3 How does management confirm that the data and methods used to generate sales forecasts are accurate and reliable?

2.4 How does management ensure that sales quotas are accurately rolled down to members of the sales team?

2.5 Are actual sales figures differentiated between in-house sales force, agents, distributors, etc. (and is each group separately monitored for performance and achievement of objectives)?

2.6 Is account taken of market trends and the potential for securing increases in market share?

2.7 Is the underlying sales strategy and generated forecast subject to ongoing review and modification (and how are amendments authorised)?

2.8 Are all actual sales activities accurately captured and incorporated into the appropriate information system?

2.9 What mechanisms protect the sales data from unauthorised access and amendment?

2.10 How does management ensure that sales returns, cancelled orders, rejected orders, discounts and allowances are all correctly and accurately reflected in the sales performance statistics?

2.11 Where sales performance is related to staff rewards (e.g. commissions), what mechanisms ensure that the calculation and payment of such rewards is correct and not based on inaccurate or manipulated data?

2.12 Would management be made aware of deviations from established margins?

2.13 Would management be made aware of unproductive or under-achieving sales staff?

2.14 Is "sales performance" assessed in any of the following ways, and if so how are variations reported and reacted to:
- selling costs as a percentage of total sales
- sales personnel remuneration and other costs as a percentage of total sales

- agent sales and commissions as a percentage of total sales
- discounts given as a proportion of total sales
- call success rates and average cost?

2.15 How is accuracy of data input from other systems (e.g. order processing or accounts receivable) confirmed?

2.16 How is the accuracy of data output to other systems (e.g. payroll or management information system) confirmed?

DISTRIBUTORS

The use of external distributors may offer an organisation competitive, strategic or economic advantages. For example, using an established external distribution infrastructure, avoids the substantial costs associated with the development of an internal distribution system. In this section we take into consideration the relevant internal and customer-related issues, with the underlying objective of seeking the most advantageous, efficient and cost-effective distribution solution.

The following material on distributors is duplicated in Chapter 17, which takes a broader view of the overall subject of distribution.

Control Objectives for Distributors

(a) To ensure that the use of distributors offers the organisation competitive or strategic advantage.

(b) To ensure that customers' needs are best served by a distribution arrangement.

(c) To ensure that external distributors are appropriately qualified, suitably resourced, financially stable and provide a cost-effective and efficient service.

(d) To ensure that engagement of external distributors is subject to adequate assessment, justification and authorisation.

(e) To ensure that all arrangements with external distributors are the subject of a suitable and enforceable legal agreement.

(f) To ensure that responsibility for advertising and promotion of company products is clearly defined and that appropriate budgets are authorised and established.

(g) To ensure that territories and geographic operational areas are clearly defined so that there is no conflict with other distributors or with company direct selling operations.

(h) To ensure that customer enquiries and orders are routed accordingly and that the distributor is responsible for accurately fulfilling the order.

(i) To ensure that all aspects of distributor performance are monitored and reacted to when necessary.

(j) To ensure that all payments to external distributors (e.g. fees or commissions) are valid and authorised.

(k) To ensure that external distributors have sufficient, suitable and secure storage facilities, and are adequately insured.

(l) To ensure that external distributors are capable of installing and appropriately configuring company products when applicable.

(m) To ensure that stocks of company products held by distributors are fully accounted for, verified and correctly invoiced.

(n) To ensure that distributors are not subject to conflicts of interest with either their own or a competitor's product.

(o) To ensure that any settlements due from the distributor are correctly accounted for.

(p) To ensure, where necessary, that distributors are proficient in the maintenance and after sales servicing of company products.

(q) To ensure that all the relevant legislation and regulations are fully complied with.

(r) To ensure that distributors project a positive image of the company.

Risk and Control Issues for Distributors

1 Key Issues

1.1 In the determination of the agreed sales policy, have the benefits of indirect versus direct sales organisations been fully assessed?

1.2 Has management determined the competitive or strategic advantages of entering into a distributed sales arrangement, e.g.:
- access to new or overseas markets
- greater market penetration
- benefiting from an established infrastructure?

1.3 How does management assess the proficiency of potential and current distributors, and what checks are in place to ensure that the end customer is receiving a suitable and high-quality service?

1.4 What measures are in place to assess the financial stability and suitability of distributors?

1.5 Are all distribution arrangements adequately assessed, authorised and subject to a suitable legal agreement?

1.6 Are geographic distribution areas clearly established, and how does management ensure that there are no conflicts with existing distributors and direct sales activities?

1.7 What mechanisms prevent an association with a distributor involved in marketing similar products (e.g. either the distributor's own or from a competitor)?

1.8 How does management ensure that responsibilities for related costs (e.g. advertising, promotion, staff training, etc.) are clearly defined, and authorised where necessary?

1.9 How does management monitor the performance of distributors, and what action is taken with those performing below expectations?

1.10 Have the prices for the organisation's products been agreed, authorised and defined in writing, and what measures ensure that accounts are accurately produced?

1.11 What steps are taken to ensure that invoices for goods supplied to distributors are promptly and fully paid on time?

1.12 When appropriate, are fees or commissions due to distributors accurately calculated and authorised?

1.13 How does management determine that the distributor (and the distributor's staff) are sufficiently skilled to promote, install and maintain the organisation's products (and how are shortcomings identified and addressed)?

1.14 Does management confirm that the distributor's storage facilities are adequate and secure, and that all company goods held are adequately protected and covered by the distributor's insurance?

1.15 How does management ensure that all the relevant prevailing legislation and regulations are fully complied with (and has specific responsibility or liability been clearly allocated)?

2 Detailed Issues

2.1 Are all alternative sales approaches (including the use of distributors) subject to full assessment?

2.2 How does management justify the use of distributor arrangements?

2.3 Are distributors used solely for selling-on company products, or are they also involved in any of the following variations:

- adding value through modification or incorporation
- providing full training and support to end customers
- installing and maintaining products, etc.?

2.4 Are the costs of establishing new or overseas markets using direct selling techniques compared to the use of distributors?

2.5 How does management accurately assess the technical ability, resources, staff proficiency and facilities of distributors?

2.6 What mechanisms prevent an arrangement being made with an unsuitable, financially unstable, poorly resourced or technically deficient distributor?

2.7 Are all distributor arrangements subject to suitable authority, and how is this evidenced?

2.8 Are all initial distributor arrangements subject to a satisfactory probationary period?

2.9 Does management have the right of access to the distributor's records?

2.10 How does management decide the nature of distribution arrangements to establish (e.g. "exclusive" or "sole"), and how is conflict with any direct sales activity avoided?

2.11 Who is responsible for funding local advertising and product promotion (if this is the organisation, how is management assured that budget limits are adhered to and the expenditure is valid and represents value for money)?

2.12 Is the organisation responsible for training the distributor's staff in respect of company products (and is there a financial limit applied and enforced on such expenditure)?

2.13 How are agreed performance criteria established and monitored (and would management promptly be made aware of shortcomings, etc.)?

2.14 What measures are in place to prevent incorrect prices and terms being invoiced to the distributors?

2.15 Are all supplies forwarded to distributors fully accounted for, regularly verified and securely held?

2.16 Are claims lodged for company products stolen or damaged while in the distributor's care?

2.17 What measures ensure that all relevant customer enquiries and orders are routed to the correct distributor?

2.18 How does management verify that any fees or commissions due to distributors are valid and accurately calculated and paid?

2.19 Does management periodically review all the costs associated with maintaining the distribution network as a means of justifying the approach in comparison to other techniques?

2.20 How does management ensure that all the regulatory requirements of export sales and movements of stocks to overseas distributors are fully complied with?

2.21 Is the distributor authorised to use company trade marks in the promotion and advertising of products, and how does management confirm that such marks are properly used for the agreed purposes?

2.22 How is the accuracy of data input from other systems (e.g. pricing policy or product development) confirmed?

2.23 How is the accuracy of data output to other systems (e.g. order processing, after sales support) confirmed?

RELATIONSHIP WITH THE PARENT COMPANY

Taking a marketing and sales standpoint, we are concerned here with the efficacy (or otherwise) of the relationship established between the parent company and any overseas (or satellite) operations. For example, there may be the need to take account of local taxation implications so that the relationship is specifically established to optimise the taxation conditions. Other significant aspects, such as foreign exchange issues or local regulations may also require management attention.

Control Objectives for Relationship with the Parent Company

(a) To ensure that the establishment and operation of overseas and satellite activities are adequately assessed in order to optimise the fiscal, legal and operational factors.

(b) To ensure that the financial and funding arrangements made for overseas/satellite operations legally optimise the taxation advantages for the parent company.

(c) To ensure that the set-up conditions of subsidiary operations are suitably authorised.

(d) To ensure that local economic and currency factors are accurately monitored and reacted to.

(e) To ensure that management maintains an accurate awareness of all the relevant, fiscal, legal and political factors which could affect overseas and satellite operations as the basis for effective decision making.

(f) To ensure that the parent organisation adequately monitors all subsidiary, overseas and satellite operations for their effectiveness, performance, contribution, stability, etc.

(g) To ensure that suitably experienced and trustworthy local management are engaged in order to sustain operations and achieve strategic business objectives.

(h) To ensure that the parent organisation provides sufficient and appropriate support and resources.

AUDITING MARKETING AND SALES

> (i) To ensure that adequate and effective lines of communication are established between the subsidiary and parent organisations.
>
> (j) To ensure that accurate, reliable and appropriate management information is generated and circulated to parent company management.
>
> (k) To ensure that local legislation and regulations are fully complied with.
>
> (l) To generally protect and safeguard company assets and investments in subsidiary, overseas and satellite operations.

Risk and Control Issues for Relationship with the Parent Company

1 Key Issues

1.1 How does management confirm that all the relevant fiscal, legal and operational factors have been satisfactorily assessed and addressed?

1.2 How does management maintain an accurate awareness of all the relevant factors (legal, fiscal, etc.) which could affect the subsidiary operation?

1.3 How does management ensure that the establishment and operation of subsidiary activities is optimised for the benefit of the parent company and supports the achievement of business objectives?

1.4 Are all subsidiary operations based on agreed and authorised criteria, and what measures prevent the establishment of unsuitable or unauthorised conditions?

1.5 What steps does management take to ensure that local managers and staff are of the appropriate calibre and are capable of effectively handling the relevant operations?

1.6 How does management satisfy itself that it has taken all the possible (and legal) precautions to protect the parent company from penalty or other adverse consequence?

1.7 What steps are taken to ensure that adequate and accurate management information is provided to support effective decision making, etc. (and would management promptly be made aware of significant events or problems)?

1.8 What mechanisms ensure that all the relevant and prevailing legislation and regulations are fully complied with?

2 Detailed Issues

2.1 Are the relevant overseas, subsidiary and satellite operations subject to formal (perhaps legally binding) and authorised agreements (and if so, how does management ensure ongoing compliance)?

2.2 What steps does management take to optimise the taxation implications of overseas and subsidiary operations?

2.3 How does management remain adequately aware of the key taxation and other fiscal factors that could affect specific operations?

2.4 Are investments in subsidiary operations subject to adequate prior assessment by suitably experienced individuals, and how are such investments protected?

2.5 What mechanisms would prevent parent company investment and involvement in potentially unprofitable or commercially unstable subsidiary ventures?

2.6 In areas where there are known potential risks, are the investment and activity levels restricted (perhaps initially) so as to contain any adverse impact?

2.7 How does management check that all arrangements are within the prevailing law and regulations in the target country?

2.8 Are currency exchange rates (and any possible currency restrictions) adequately monitored, and how are the necessary actions authorised and legally implemented?

2.9 Has management access to appropriate legal and fiscal expertise to support their decisions and actions, and how is the accuracy and reliability of such advice ensured?

2.10 Have contingency plans been defined in the event of an emergency befalling the subsidiary operation (e.g. political instability)?

2.11 How does management ensure that the organisation's quality and performance standards are maintained by subsidiary operations, and how would they be made aware of related failures?

2.12 How is the accuracy of data input from other systems (e.g. from legal department or risk assessment) confirmed?

2.13 How is the accuracy of data output to other systems (e.g. management information) confirmed?

AGENTS

If there are notable commercial advantages in the engagement of external agents to promote the company's products and services, the organisation will need to ensure that such relationships are established only with financially stable, reliable, suitably experienced and adequately resourced entities.

Control Objectives for Agents

(a) To ensure that the use of agents offers the organisation either competitive or strategic advantage.

(b) To ensure that customers' needs are best served by an agency arrangement,

(c) To ensure that external agents are appropriately qualified, suitably resourced, financially stable and provide a cost-effective and efficient service.

(d) To ensure that engagement of external agents is subject to adequate assessment, justification and authorisation.

(e) To ensure that all arrangements with external agents are the subject of suitable and enforceable legal agreement.

(f) To ensure that responsibility for advertising and promotion of company products is clearly defined and that appropriate budgets are authorised and established.

(g) To ensure that territories and geographic operational areas are clearly defined so that there is no conflict with other agents or company direct selling operations.

(h) To ensure that all aspects of agency performance are monitored and reacted to when necessary.

(i) To ensure that all payments to external agents (e.g. fees or commissions) are valid and authorised.

(j) To ensure that stocks of company products held by agents are fully accounted for, verified and correctly invoiced.

(k) To ensure that agents are not subject to conflicts of interest with either their own or a competitor's product.

(l) To ensure that all the relevant legislation and regulations are fully complied with.

(m) To ensure that agents project a positive image of the company and its products.

Risk and Control Issues for Agents

1 Key Issues

1.1 In the determination of the agreed sales policy, have the benefits of agencies versus direct sales operations been fully assessed?

1.2 Has management determined the competitive and strategic advantages of entering into an agency arrangement, i.e.:

- access to new or overseas markets

- greater market penetration
- benefiting from an established infrastructure?

1.3 How does management assess the proficiency of potential and current agents?

1.4 What measures are in place to assess the financial stability and suitability of agents?

1.5 Are all agency arrangements adequately assessed, authorised and subject to a suitable legal agreement?

1.6 Are geographic areas of operation clearly established, and how does management ensure that there are no conflicts with existing agents, distributors or direct sales activities?

1.7 What mechanisms prevent an association with an agent involved in marketing similar products (e.g. the distributor's own or from a competitor)?

1.8 How does management ensure that responsibilities for related costs (advertising, promotion, staff training, etc.) are clearly defined, and authorised where necessary?

1.9 How does management monitor the performance of agents, and what action is taken with those performing below expectations?

1.10 Are fees or commissions due to agents accurately calculated and authorised?

1.11 How does management assess that the agent (and the agent's staff) are sufficiently skilled to promote the organisation's products (and how are shortcomings identified and addressed)?

1.12 How does management ensure that all the relevant prevailing legislation and regulations are fully complied with (and has specific responsibility or liability been clearly allocated)?

2 Detailed Issues

2.1 Are all alternative sales approaches (including the use of agents or distributors) subject to full assessment?

2.2 How does management justify the use of agents?

2.3 Are agents used solely for selling-on company products, or are they also involved in any of the following variations:

- adding value through modification or incorporation
- providing full training and support to end-customers
- installing and maintaining products?

2.4 Are the costs of establishing new or overseas markets using direct selling techniques or distributors compared to the use of agents?

2.5 How does management accurately assess the technical ability, resources, staff proficiency and facilities of its agents?

2.6 What mechanisms prevent an arrangement being made with an unsuitable, financially unstable, poorly resourced or technically deficient agent?

2.7 Are all agency arrangements subject to suitable authority, and how is this evidenced?

2.8 Are all initial agency arrangements subject to a satisfactory probationary period?

2.9 Does management have the right of access to the agent's records?

2.10 Who is responsible for funding local advertising and product promotion (if this is the organisation, how does management ensure that budget limits are adhered to and the expenditure is valid and represents value for money)?

2.11 Is the organisation responsible for training the agent's staff in respect of company products (and is there a financial limit applied and enforced on such expenditure)?

2.12 How are agreed performance criteria established and monitored (and would management promptly be made aware of shortcomings, etc.)?

2.13 How does management check that all relevant customer enquiries and orders are routed to the correct agent?

2.14 How does management ensure that all fees or commissions due to agents are valid and accurately calculated and paid?

2.15 Does management periodically review all the costs associated with maintaining the agency network as a means of justifying the approach in comparison to other techniques?

2.16 Are agents authorised to use company trade marks in the promotion and advertising of products, and how does management confirm that such marks are properly used for the agreed purposes?

2.17 How is the accuracy of data input from other systems (e.g. pricing policy) confirmed?

2.18 How is the accuracy of data output to other systems (order processing or sales performance) confirmed?

ORDER PROCESSING

Sales orders may be generated in a number of ways (e.g. through a dedicated internal sales force, external agents, telephone sales enquiries). Irrespective of how they are generated, the organisation's management will need to be assured that all orders are accounted for and efficiently processed. However, there will be the attendant requirement to ensure that customers are (and remain) suitable, financially stable and that they operate within the confines of realistic credit limits so as to contain any financial exposures. This section is concerned with all these issues; however, the related aspects for the effective operation of an accounts receivable system are addressed in detail within a separate section of Chapter 12.

Control Objectives for Order Processing

(a) To ensure that all valid orders are correctly identified, accounted for and processed in accordance with the organisation's policies and procedures.

(b) To ensure that official orders are accepted only from bona fide, authorised and suitable customers.

(c) To ensure that orders are accepted only for creditworthy customers with sufficient available credit limits.

(d) To ensure that new customers are properly assessed and authorised for set-up with an appropriate credit limit.

(e) To ensure that the determination and amendment of credit limits is appropriately authorised.

(f) To ensure that effective credit control is exercised to ensure that customers' accounts are promptly followed up and payments obtained.

(g) To ensure that all order details are accurately captured for subsequent processing purposes.

(h) To ensure that all affected functions are coordinated so that the order is promptly and efficiently fulfilled.

(i) To ensure that orders are promptly and accurately acknowledged.

(j) To ensure that delivery and any other special customer requirements are identified and appropriately addressed.

(k) To ensure that all orders are promptly fulfilled, delivered and confirmed as received.

(l) To ensure that invoices are raised against all fulfilled orders and accounted for within the accounts receivable system and accounts.

(m) To ensure that the correct terms, prices and discounts are reflected on subsequent invoices,

(n) To ensure that key data (product prices, order records, etc.) are adequately protected from unauthorised access and amendment.

(o) To ensure that export orders are handled in accordance with all the prevailing regulations.

(p) To ensure that all the current laws and regulations are correctly and fully observed.

Risk and Control Issues for Order Processing

1 Key Issues

1.1 What measures ensure that all orders (from all possible sources) are correctly identified, logged, reviewed, authorised to proceed, and accounted for?

1.2 What measures prevent the acceptance of orders based on invalid or unauthorised terms and conditions (e.g. those outside the defined company policies)?

1.3 What measures are applied to ensure that only orders from established, authorised, bona fide customers are accepted?

1.4 What mechanisms prevent the acceptance and processing of orders from customers who have an outstanding/overdue balance on their account or insufficient authorised credit remaining?

1.5 How does management assess new customers for their financial stability and suitability, etc. (and what measures prevent the acceptance of inappropriate customers)?

1.6 Are all new customers and the setting of their initial credit limits subject to suitable authorities?

1.7 How is management assured that credit limits are strictly observed and amended only when suitably authorised?

1.8 What measures ensure the accurate capture of order data?

1.9 What mechanisms ensure the appropriate coordination of the following functions in the correct and prompt processing of customer orders:

- sales
- production
- stock control
- export department
- accounts receivable
- credit control
- despatch/distribution
- after sales support?

1.10 What measures ensure that all orders are acknowledged and efficiently fulfilled?

1.11 How is management assured that accurate invoices are raised and accounted for within the accounts receivable system?

1.12 How does management ensure that all export orders are correctly processed and handled in accordance with all the prevailing regulations?

1.13 What measures are in place to ensure that all the relevant legislation and regulations are correctly observed?

2 Detailed Issues

2.1 Have authorised and documented policies been established for the following:
- new customer acceptance
- setting credit limits
- credit control
- pricing and discounting
- standard terms/conditions
- export sales procedures?

2.2 How is compliance with all the authorised policies assured?

2.3 Are accurate and reliable records of authorised existing customers maintained, and how are they protected from unauthorised access and invalid amendments?

2.4 What form of assessment and verification is applied to new or potential customers to confirm their acceptability?

2.5 What measures prevent the set-up of a customer record when the required assessment and credit checks have not been applied?

2.6 Are procedures in place governing the determination and amendment of credit and trading limits, and how is management sure that they are always correctly complied with?

2.7 What mechanisms prevent the acceptance of an order where the customer has previous accounts overdue for payment?

2.8 Are measures in place to identify and cater for any special customer requirements (e.g. specific delivery dates, modified specification)?

2.9 What measures are in place to identify accurately the status of all orders and highlight those outstanding for delivery?

2.10 What processes identify and accordingly progress outstanding orders?

2.11 Are all deliveries accurately recorded and documented as either received or rejected (in whole or in part)?

2.12 What procedures link orders delivered to the accurate generation of the relevant invoices?

2.13 What mechanisms ensure that the correct, appropriate and authorised details (prices, discounts, quantities, terms, etc.) are reflected on invoices?

2.14 What processes prevent the delivery of an order without the generation of the relevant invoice?

2.15 What measures protect key data (prices, discounts, order records, invoice records, etc.) from unauthorised access and amendment?

2.16 Are all invoices correctly and accurately accounted for on the customer's debtors accounting record?

2.17 What measures ensure that all invoices are promptly despatched to customers?

2.18 In order to prevent staff malpractice and fraud, are key duties adequately segregated?

2.19 Is management provided with adequate, accurate and timely management information about orders received and in progress, etc.?

2.20 How is the accuracy of data input from other systems (e.g. agencies or stock control) confirmed?

2.21 How is the accuracy of data output to other systems (e.g. distribution or accounts receivable) confirmed?

WARRANTY ARRANGEMENTS

Control Objectives for Warranty Arrangements

(a) To ensure that after sales support and warranty arrangements are defined, documented and authorised for all products.

(b) To ensure that customers are accurately advised of the conditions of the organisation's warranty arrangements.

(c) To ensure that liabilities for warranties are accurately recorded and maintained as the basis for validating requests and claims.

(d) To ensure that customers are provided with an adequate timely, and cost-effective after sales warranty service.

(e) To ensure that all warranty requests are valid and eligible.

(f) To ensure that authorised charges are applied for after sales service and support outside the warranty period.

(g) To ensure that all the costs associated with the provision of warranty services are identified, accounted for and monitored.

(h) To ensure that all warranty requests, claims and action taken are accurately recorded.

(i) To ensure that the underlying causes of warranty problems are identified, monitored and reported to the affected function (design, quality control, production, etc.).

(j) To ensure that adequate and appropriate resources are provided to support the required service levels.

(k) To ensure that problems caused by external factors (e.g. the supply of substandard components) are identified and appropriately followed up with suppliers and contractors.

(l) To ensure that all consumer and warranty legislation and regulations are fully complied with.

(m) To ensure that the establishment of extended warranty schemes is adequately assessed, justified, authorised and appropriately implemented.

(n) To ensure that the charges made for out-of-warranty and extended warranty work are adequate to cover the costs.

(o) To ensure that ongoing product development and research contributes to increasingly reliable and quality products in order to further reduce or to contain after sales and warranty liabilities.

Risk and Control Issues for Warranty Arrangements

1 Key Issues

1.1 Are all after sales support and warranty arrangements authorised, documented and adequately communicated to eligible customers?

1.2 How does management check that the existing warranty arrangements fully comply with all the prevailing consumer and general legislation and regulations?

1.3 How does the organisation's warranty and after sales conditions compare with both those applicable within the sector/industry and those offered by competitors?

1.4 How does management verify that all warranty requests, claims and enquiries relate to valid customers with products still within the applicable warranty period?

1.5 What mechanisms prevent the servicing and follow-up of products that fall outside the warranty arrangements or period of eligibility?

1.6 Are all warranty requests/claims accurately recorded, accounted for and confirmed as satisfactorily addressed?

1.7 What measures are in place to ensure that the appropriate charges for work outside the warranty arrangements are applied and fully paid by the relevant customers?

1.8 What mechanisms ensure that the charges made for out-of-warranty work are sufficient to cover the actual costs?

1.9 Are steps taken to accurately identify, account for and monitor all the costs associated with the provision of warranty and after sales support?

1.10 Has management taken effective action to identify the underlying causes of service problems as the means of taking remedial action (e.g. with suppliers, contractors or internal departments)?

1.11 Where applicable, is the establishment of extended warranty schemes subject to adequate assessment, justification, and authorisation (and are such schemes adequately monitored for effectiveness and profit contribution)?

2 Detailed Issues

2.1 What mechanisms prevent or detect the operation of an unauthorised or illegal warranty scheme?

2.2 How does management confirm that the established warranty policy is complied with?

2.3 Have adequate steps been taken to record all the relevant sales as a basis for validating warranty claims?

2.4 What steps ensure that all warranty and service requests are promptly and effectively dealt with?

2.5 Are warranty and servicing performance statistics circulated to management for monitoring purposes, and would shortfalls, delays and problems be detected and resolved?

2.6 What prevents servicing work being conducted outside the warranty period where no charge is made to the customer?

2.7 How does management ensure that service personnel are engaged only on official workloads?

2.8 Would management be alerted to unpaid charges for servicing work?

2.9 Does management regularly monitor the costs associated with warranty activities and take action either to reduce costs or to improve efficiencies?

2.10 Are warranty and after sales support resources subject to ongoing monitoring by management, and what is the evidence that corrective action is being taken when necessary?

2.11 How is the accuracy of data input from other systems (e.g. sales order and customer data) confirmed?

2.12 How is the accuracy of data output to other systems (e.g. accounts receivable for recovering servicing costs from customers) confirmed?

MAINTENANCE AND SERVICING

Control Objectives for Maintenance and Servicing

(a) To ensure that an authorised product maintenance and servicing system is documented and established to support customers and discharge the organisation's liabilities.

(b) To ensure that all service requests are validated and classified as either chargeable or nonchargeable (e.g. within warranty).

(c) To ensure that all service requests are accurately logged, recorded, allocated and subsequently confirmed as completed.

(d) To ensure that adequate staff, stock and other resources are made available to support an efficient and cost-effective service.

(e) To ensure that servicing staff are adequately trained and appropriately equipped to conduct their duties effectively.

(f) To ensure that all the costs associated with the provision of maintenance and servicing facilities are identified, accounted for, authorised and monitored.

(g) To ensure that the performance and cost-effectiveness of the maintenance and servicing facilities are subject to ongoing monitoring and management.

(h) To ensure that alternative methods of providing maintenance and servicing (e.g. contracting out to an external service organisation) are considered and kept under review.

(i) To ensure that the customers are charged for servicing work at the recognised rate.

(j) To ensure that debtors accounts for servicing activities are accurately established and maintained.

(k) To ensure that outstanding debtor accounts are actively pursued and paid.

(l) To ensure that the hours worked by all service engineers and maintenance staff (including travelling) are accurately recorded, accounted for and charged out when necessary.

(m) To ensure that the usage of all spares and parts is valid, authorised, accurately accounted for and costed.

(n) To ensure that faulty or substandard components are referred to the suppliers for replacement or credit.

(o) To ensure that accurate data is obtained on fault histories and recurrent problems as the basis for continually improving the product.

Risk and Control Issues for Maintenance and Servicing

1 Key Issues

1.1 Has management established an authorised maintenance and servicing policy which defines the conditions, charges and performance criteria?

1.2 How does management check that servicing activities fully comply with the documented policy?

1.3 How does management ascertain that all maintenance and service requests relate to valid customers?

1.4 What mechanisms prevent the servicing of products for nonregistered or invalid customers?

1.5 Are measures in place to record accurately all service requests and differentiate between those within and outside warranty as the basis for determining the charging arrangements?

1.6 What measures ensure that all service calls are promptly allocated to an engineer and regularly progressed until completion is confirmed?

1.7 Are outstanding or particularly problematic service calls adequately identified and progressed to the customer's satisfaction?

1.8 Has management established service level criteria which are subject to performance monitoring and follow-up?

1.9 How does management ensure that adequate and appropriately trained staff, materials, servicing equipment and all other resources are made available to fulfil the obligations and workload?

1.10 Are all the costs associated with the provision of maintenance and servicing accurately identified, accounted for, authorised, and monitored?

1.11 What mechanisms ensure that all valid customer charges (labour and materials) are accurately applied and pursued for settlement?

1.12 Are all service debtor accounts accurately reflected and accounted for in the accounts receivable system?

1.13 What mechanisms ensure that the charges made for out-of-warranty work are sufficient to cover the actual costs of provision?

1.14 Is management provided with accurate data on the actual labour and material costs incurred?

1.15 How does management monitor that spare parts are utilised for only bona fide purposes and are fully accounted for (including periodic verification)?

2 Detailed Issues

2.1 Have adequate steps been taken to record all the relevant sales as a basis for validating service requests?

2.2 How is management assured that all service requests are promptly and effectively dealt with?

2.3 Are servicing performance statistics produced and circulated to management for monitoring purposes, and would shortfalls, delays and problems be detected and resolved?

2.4 What mechanisms prevent servicing work being conducted outside the warranty period where no charge is made to the customer?

2.5 How would management be alerted to potential staff training needs?

2.6 Has adequate and operational servicing equipment been provided?

2.7 How does management confirm that the present servicing arrangements are the best option (and are alternatives assessed)?

2.8 How does management verify that servicing personnel are engaged only on official workloads?

2.9 What measures ensure that the correct labour rates and component costs are reflected on customer invoices?

2.10 Where faults or recurring problems appear to be related to externally sourced components, is management taking action to seek redress from the supplier?

2.11 How does management monitor that all the relevant legislation and regulations are being complied with?

2.12 How is the accuracy of data input from other systems (e.g. sales records and component costings) confirmed?

2.13 How is the accuracy of data output to other systems (e.g. accounts receivable) confirmed?

SPARE PARTS AND SUPPLY

Control Objectives for Spare Parts and Supply

(a) To ensure that adequate stacks of spare parts are maintained to support customer requirements and future servicing requirements.

(b) To ensure that all stock issues movements are valid, authorised and accounted for.

(c) To ensure that under-stocking, over-stocking and obsolete holdings are avoided.

(d) To ensure that spares can be cost-effectively produced or purchased in good time to support requirements.

(e) To ensure that stocks are accurately valued and periodically verified.

(f) To ensure that re-order levels are accurately determined and effectively used to avoid out-of-stock situations.

> (g) To ensure that spares used for warranty and other nonchargeable work are identified and costed.
>
> (h) To ensure that chargeable spares are invoiced to customers at authorised prices.
>
> (i) To ensure that persistent faults relating to components are accurately identified and followed up with the production function or the relevant external supplier.

Risk and Control Issues for Spare Parts and Supply

1 Key Issues

1.1 What measures ensure that stocking levels of spare parts are accurately and cost-effectively determined in order to support anticipated demands?

1.2 What mechanisms prevent under or over-stocking of spare parts?

1.3 What processes ensure that all stock movements are valid, authorised and correctly accounted for?

1.4 Are re-order levels realistically set and effectively used to trigger the required (and authorised) production or purchase?

1.5 Are all production runs and purchase orders suitably authorised and optimised for quantity and price (e.g. how are uneconomic requests avoided)?

1.6 How does management ensure that stocks of spares are accurately and appropriately valued in the accounts (and how can they be sure that the stocks actually exist)?

1.7 Are all the costs associated with the usage of spare parts accurately identified, accounted for and effectively monitored against expectations?

1.8 Are spare part costs for chargeable (e.g. non warranty) work validated, accounted for, and recovered from customers (and what measures prevent the unauthorised or invalid usage of components)?

1.9 What steps are in place to ensure that persistent component faults or problems are promptly identified, verified and appropriately followed up?

2 Detailed Issues

2.1 Has management defined, documented and authorised a policy governing the permitted use of spares, and how do they ensure that it is fully complied with?

2.2 What is the applied policy on supplying components for discontinued products, and how is the accumulation of obsolete spares avoided?

2.3 What measures prevent the unauthorised usage or pilferage of spares (and would such events be capable of detection)?

2.4 Are accurate sales records maintained to support decision making about potential spares stock requirements (and if so, how does management ensure the accuracy of such data over time)?

2.5 Are the relevant stock records subject to periodic and effective verification, and how are variances and anomalies reported and resolved?

2.6 Are production and supplier lead times accurately identified and taken into account when determining re-order levels for spares?

2.7 How does management ensure that the cost of components recovered from customers continues to reflect accurately their true cost and the required margins?

2.8 What measures prevent unauthorised access to and unauthorised amendment of stock and costing records?

2.9 Would potential design or performance weaknesses promptly be detected and resolved?

2.10 How is the accuracy of data input from other systems (e.g. the warranty customer records) confirmed?

2.11 How is the accuracy of data output to other systems (e.g. accounts receivable for chargeable spares or the stock control system) confirmed?

NOTE

1. The use of distributors may represent an important component in the adopted marketing strategy. In Chapter 17 we examine the broader operational implications of distribution, including the use of external distributors. For convenience, we have duplicated the detailed material addressing *distributors* in both this chapter and Chapter 17.

17
Auditing Distribution

INTRODUCTION

In this chapter we consider the subject of distribution, and the related subjects of stock control, and warehousing and storage. Our discussion of distribution incorporates two logical areas: general distribution principles and utilisation of external distributors.

Consult other chapters for discussion of related issues—see the Contents and the Index. For instance, just-in-time (JIT) management, which may be applied by management to distribution, is discussed in Chapter 9.

SYSTEM/FUNCTION COMPONENTS OF DISTRIBUTION

We have used an essentially *functional* approach to define the distribution audit universe, which gives us the following possible breakdown of the key functions, systems or activities:

- distribution, transport and logistics
- distributors
- stock control
- warehousing and storage.

The distribution methods employed will vary between organisations, for example they may include:

- indirect shipment through a network of strategically located warehouses
- direct shipment from the production unit using in-house transport
- via third-party distributors and/or haulage contractors.

The objectives and risk issue questions provided in this chapter are deliberately wide-ranging and take into consideration the variations noted above; as a result they will require editing prior to use so that the points covered more closely follow the actual scenario encountered by the auditor.

CONTROL OBJECTIVES AND RISK AND CONTROL ISSUES

We shall now examine the control objectives and risk and control issues (divided into key issues and detailed issues) for each of the distribution areas listed above. This data can be used within the Standard Audit Programme Guides (SAPGs) looked at in Chapter 3. To save space we have concentrated on the objectives to be stated and the questions to be asked and have not presented them within the SAPG format.

DISTRIBUTION, TRANSPORT AND LOGISTICS

In an attempt to apply the optimum distribution and transport solution, the use of both in-house resources and external contractors may need to be considered. The following objectives and risk and control issues cover points relevant to both these potential situations. Where there is an established in-house transport function, additional factors are noted covering areas such as the maintenance of the vehicle fleet, ensuring compliance with all the prevailing laws and regulations, and economic planning of delivery runs.

Control Objectives for Distribution, Transport and Logistics

(a) To ensure that an adequate, appropriate, efficient and cost-effective distribution and transport infrastructure is provided to meet the needs of customers.

(b) To ensure that goods are distributed and delivered in the most efficient manner.

(c) To ensure that stock is located in the optimum position to fulfil the anticipated demands and to avoid localised shortages.

(d) To ensure that only correctly constituted and valid consignments are actioned and accurately reflected in the accounts.

(e) To ensure that the appropriate goods in the relevant quantities are delivered on time.

(f) To ensure that goods are adequately protected from loss and damage during intermediate storage and transit.

(g) To ensure that contracts with external distributors and haulage contractors are suitable and authorised.

(h) To ensure that external distribution and transport contractors are paid at the agreed rate for work actually done.

(i) To ensure that the performance and cost-effectiveness of external contractors are monitored as a means of ensuring that they offer the appropriate quality and value for money.

(j) To ensure that exports and all overseas consignments are correctly handled, documented and comply with the relevant regulations.

(k) To ensure that an adequate number of appropriate delivery vehicles are provided and operated cost-effectively.

(l) To ensure that the most efficient and cost-effective means of delivery is used.

(m) To ensure that the delivery demands are adequately and accurately determined and planned for.

(n) To ensure that delivery journeys/runs are sufficiently and economically planned so as to avoid delays and excess mileages, etc.

(o) To ensure that transport facilities are operated legally and in accordance with the prevailing regulations for drivers and vehicles.

(p) To ensure that the correct type and quantity of goods are safely loaded and that the relevant materials handling devices are provided.

(q) To ensure that deliveries are agreed and signed for, and that any discrepancies are identified, documented, investigated and resolved.

(r) To ensure that adequate and appropriate insurance cover is provided for goods while in store and transit.

Risk and Control Issues for Distribution, Transport and Logistics

1 Key Issues

1.1 How does management assess that the distribution facilities in place are adequate, efficient and able to cater for current and future demands?

1.2 Is there adequate and timely liaison and information flow between the sales, production, stock control, distribution and transport functions in order to ensure that customer demands are fulfilled?

1.3 How does management ensure that the most appropriate, efficient and cost-effective distribution and transport options are used?

1.4 How is management certain that only correctly constituted and valid consignments are actioned, and that they are accurately reflected in the relevant accounting systems?

1.5 Are all external distribution and transport contract arrangements appropriate, authorised and regularly monitored for quality, performance and value for money?

1.6 How does management ensure that external contractors' charges are valid and authorised, and what mechanisms prevent the payment of invalid or erroneous charges?

1.7 Are adequate precautions taken to protect goods in intermediate storage and transit from damage and loss?

1.8 How does management verify that all deliveries are undertaken in the required timescale and agreed and signed for?

1.9 Are all delivery discrepancies identified, documented, investigated and resolved (and how is this evidenced)?

1.10 How does management ensure that the delivery vehicle fleet is appropriate, adequate and is operated efficiently and legally?

2 Detailed Issues

2.1 Are accurate and appropriate delivery schedules prepared as the basis for loading, distribution and delivery (and how would errors be prevented)?

2.2 Are distribution and transport facilities provided on a stable and planned basis in line with the anticipated demands?

2.3 How does management maintain an awareness of the alternative distribution and transport options as a means to ensure that the optimum solution is applied?

2.4 Are distribution depots and intermediate storage facilities located in accordance with the organisation's trading patterns and customer base?

2.5 Would management be able to detect any underused, surplus or redundant storage facilities?

2.6 How does management check that the flow of goods from production through sales to the customer is accurately anticipated and planned for, so that the customer's requirements are efficiently fulfilled?

2.7 Are all stocks and movements of goods adequately tracked and trailed in order to determine their whereabouts?

2.8 Are distribution stocks accurately organised and identified so that orders can be efficiently prepared for despatch and all items accounted for?

2.9 Are all stock movements supported by authorised documentation and what processes ensure that all movements are correctly reflected in the accounting system for the appropriate accounting period?

2.10 What processes ensure that the correct type and quantity of goods are prepared for despatch?

2.11 What mechanisms prevent shortages of goods or unreasonable order backlogs at the distribution centres?

2.12 What processes prevent the despatch of incorrect or false consignments?

2.13 What processes ensure that goods are stored and delivered in saleable and good condition?

2.14 How is the financial stability, suitability and reliability of external distribution and transport contractors evaluated and confirmed?

2.15 How is management made aware of poor external contractor performance?

2.16 What prevents the acceptance of false, invalid or unauthorised distribution and transport charges from external contractors?

2.17 Are individual consignments assessed for the optimum delivery method, and how can management be sure that delivery costs are contained?

2.18 Would late, delayed or missing deliveries be detected and appropriate action taken?

2.19 Are all goods damaged in transit accurately identified, investigated and action taken to promptly despatch suitable replacements?

2.20 Are all export and overseas consignments correctly documented in accordance with customs and export regulations?

2.21 Are export and overseas consignments despatched by the most efficient and economic means?

2.22 Are the additional costs of overseas deliveries recovered?

2.23 How does management verify that the delivery vehicle fleet is suitable and efficiently utilised?

2.24 Are transport fleet operating costs monitored and reacted to?

2.25 What mechanisms prevent uneconomic and poorly planned delivery journeys?

2.26 How does management ensure that the vehicle fleet is operated in accordance with the prevailing laws and regulations (including conforming with required driving periods, distances and rest periods)?

2.27 Are all transport drivers suitably qualified, experienced and licensed?

2.28 Are vehicles loaded logically and efficiently in accordance with the scheduled delivery run?

2.29 Are goods loaded safely on delivery vehicles and have the appropriate loading devices been supplied to unload safely at the destination without damaging the goods?

2.30 Are drivers held to account for all the goods loaded on their vehicles and delivered to customers?

2.31 Are vehicles and goods in transit covered by adequate, suitable and current insurance provision?

2.32 Are goods held in distribution and intermediate stores covered by appropriate and current insurance?

2.33 How is the accuracy of data input from other systems (e.g. sales orders) confirmed?

2.34 How is the accuracy of data output to other systems (e.g. stock control) confirmed?

DISTRIBUTORS

It may be more viable for the organisation to outsource the distribution of its products through an established and stable contractor, and thereby take advantage of an existing infrastructure. This option will also avoid funds being tied up in the in-house development and running of such activities, and therefore enable their more effective application elsewhere. However, this requires the careful selection of a suitable and financially stable contractor with the necessary resources to fulfil both the organisation's requirements and any existing workloads to the required standards.

The points noted below are also listed in Chapter 16 as part of the consideration of the use of distributors in the development of a strategic approach to marketing.

Control Objectives for Distributors

(a) To ensure that the use of distributors offers the organisation either competitive or strategic advantage.

(b) To ensure that customers' needs are best served by a distribution arrangement.

(c) To ensure that external distributors are appropriately qualified, suitably resourced, financially stable and provide a cost-effective and efficient service.

(d) To ensure that engagement of external distributors is subject to adequate assessment, justification and authorisation.

(e) To ensure that all arrangements with external distributors are the subject of a suitable and enforceable legal agreement.

(f) To ensure that responsibility for advertising and promotion of company products is clearly defined and that appropriate budgets are authorised and established.

(g) To ensure that territories and geographic operational areas are clearly defined so that there is no conflict with other distributors or with company direct selling operations.

(h) To ensure that customer enquiries and orders are routed accordingly and that the distributor is responsible for accurately fulfilling the order.

(i) To ensure that all aspects of distributor performance are monitored and reacted to when necessary.

(j) To ensure that all payments to external distributors (e.g. fees or commissions) are valid and authorised.

(k) To ensure that external distributors have sufficient, suitable and secure storage facilities, and are adequately insured.

(l) To ensure that external distributors are capable of installing and appropriately configuring company products when applicable.

(m) To ensure that stocks of company products held by distributors are fully accounted for, verified and correctly invoiced.

(n) To ensure that distributors are not subject to conflicts of interest with either their own or a competitor's product.

(o) To ensure that any settlements due from the distributor are correctly accounted for.

(p) To ensure, where necessary, that distributors are proficient in the maintenance and after sales servicing of company products.

(q) To ensure that all the relevant legislation and regulations are fully complied with.

(r) To ensure that distributors project a positive image of the company.

Risk and Control Issues for Distributors

1 Key Issues

1.1 In the determination of the agreed sales policy, have the benefits of indirect versus direct sales organisations been fully assessed?

1.2 Has management determined the competitive or strategic advantages of entering into a distributed sales arrangement, e.g.:
- access to new or overseas markets
- greater market penetration
- benefiting from an established infrastructure?

1.3 How does management assess the proficiency of potential and current distributors, and what checks are in place to ensure that the end customer is receiving a suitable and high-quality service?

1.4 What measures are in place to assess the financial stability and suitability of distributors?

1.5 Are all distribution arrangements adequately assessed, authorised and subject to a suitable legal agreement?

1.6 Are geographic distribution areas clearly established, and how does management ensure that there are no conflicts with existing distributors and direct sales activities?

1.7 What mechanisms prevent an association with a distributor involved in marketing similar products (e.g. either the distributor's own or from a competitor)?

1.8 How does management ensure that responsibilities for related costs (advertising, promotion, staff training, etc.) are clearly defined, and authorised where necessary?

1.9 How does management monitor the performance of distributors, and what action is taken with those performing below expectations?

1.10 Have the prices for the organisation's products been agreed, authorised and defined in writing, and what measures ensure that accounts are accurately produced?

1.11 What steps are taken to ensure that invoices for goods supplied to distributors are promptly and fully paid on time?

1.12 When appropriate, are fees or commissions due to distributors accurately calculated and authorised?

1.13 How does management determine that the distributor (and the distributor's staff) are sufficiently skilled to promote, install and maintain the organisation's products (and how are shortcomings identified and addressed)?

1.14 Does management confirm that the distributor's storage facilities are adequate and secure, and that all company goods held are adequately protected and covered by the distributor's insurance?

1.15 How does management ensure that all the relevant prevailing legislation and regulations are fully complied with (and has specific responsibility or liability been clearly allocated)?

2 Detailed Issues

2.1 Are all alternative sales approaches (including the use of distributors) subject to full assessment?

2.2 How does management justify the use of distributor arrangements?

2.3 Are distributors used solely for selling-on company products, or are they also involved in any of the following variations:

- adding value through modification or incorporation
- providing full training and support to end customers
- installing and maintaining products, etc.?

2.4 Are the costs of establishing new or overseas markets using direct selling techniques compared to the use of distributors?

2.5 How does management accurately assess the technical ability, resources, staff proficiency and facilities of distributors?

2.6 What mechanisms prevent an arrangement being made with an unsuitable, financially unstable, poorly resourced or technically deficient distributor?

2.7 Are all distributor arrangements subject to suitable authority, and how is this evidenced?

2.8 Are all initial distributor arrangements subject to a satisfactory probationary period?

2.9 Does management have the right of access to the distributor's records?

2.10 How does management decide the nature of distribution arrangements to establish (e.g. "exclusive", "sole"), and how is conflict with any direct sales activity avoided?

2.11 Who is responsible for funding local advertising and product promotion (if this is the organisation, how is management assured that budget limits are adhered to and the expenditure is valid and represents value for money)?

2.12 Is the organisation responsible for training the distributor's staff in respect of company products (and is there a financial limit applied and enforced on such expenditure)?

2.13 How are agreed performance criteria established and monitored (and would management be promptly made aware of shortcomings, etc.)?

2.14 What measures are in place to prevent incorrect prices and terms being invoiced to the distributors?

2.15 Are all supplies forwarded to distributors fully accounted for, regularly verified and securely held?

2.16 Are claims lodged for company products stolen or damaged while in the distributor's care?

2.17 What measures ensure that all relevant customer enquiries and orders are routed to the correct distributor?

2.18 How does management ensure that any fees or commissions due to distributors are valid and accurately calculated and paid?

2.19 Does management periodically review all the costs associated with maintaining the distribution network as a means of justifying the approach in comparison to other techniques?

2.20 How does management ensure that all the regulatory requirements of export sales and movements of stocks to overseas distributors are fully complied with?

2.21 Is the distributor authorised to use company trade marks in the promotion and advertising of products, and how does management confirm that such marks are properly used for the agreed purposes?

2.22 How is the accuracy of data input from other systems (e.g. pricing policy, product development) confirmed?

2.23 How is the accuracy of data output to other systems (e.g. order processing, after sales support) confirmed?

STOCK CONTROL

Effective and accurate stock control is important in maintaining the adequacy of supplies to sales and/or production activities. See also the following related sections of other chapters:

- Chapter 12 contains a section on the subject of inventories.
- Chapter 14 features the implications for the interface between the receipt of goods and the accurate updating of stock control records.
- Chapter 15 includes a discrete section on the subject of materials and energy, which has connotations for accurate stock control.

Control Objectives for Stock Control

(a) To ensure that adequate and appropriate stocks are held to meet the demands of sales and production.

(b) To avoid overstocking.

(c) To ensure that all stock movements are valid, authorised, correctly processed, accounted for and accurately reflected in the accounts.

(d) To ensure stocks are securely and appropriately stored in order to prevent loss, theft, deterioration or misappropriation of stock items.

(e) To ensure that stock records are accurately maintained, adequately protected from unauthorised access, and regularly verified.

> (f) To ensure that stock discrepancies are promptly highlighted, investigated and resolved.
>
> (g) To ensure that stock write-offs, scrap and other disposals are justified, authorised and correctly handled.
>
> (h) To ensure that stock levels are monitored in order to detect and react to replenishment requirements, obsolete and slow-moving items.
>
> (i) To ensure that all stockholdings are traceable to a known storage location.
>
> (j) To ensure that management is provided with accurate and timely information on stock levels and usage.
>
> (k) To ensure that liaison between the stock control function and other relevant activities (e.g. sales and production) is sufficient to achieve the organisation's objectives.

Risk and Control Issues for Stock Control

1 Key Issues

1.1 Have authorised and documented stock control policies and procedures been implemented, and how is management sure that they are fully complied with?

1.2 How does management determine the current and future stock requirements, and what checks are in place to monitor that actual stock levels can accurately meet sales and production demands?

1.3 Is management made aware of overstocking and stock shortages, and how are remedial actions evidenced?

1.4 What measures ensure that all stock movements are valid, authorised, correctly processed and accounted for?

1.5 What mechanisms prevent the acceptance and processing of invalid or unauthorised stock movements?

1.6 What measures are in place for storing stock securely?

1.7 What processes ensure that stock valuations are accurate and correctly reflected in the inventory and accounting records?

1.8 What mechanisms prevent the manipulation, distortion or falsifying of stock records?

1.9 How does management verify that all stock adjustments, write-offs and scrap disposals are justified, authorised and correctly processed?

1.10 How would management promptly be made aware of slow-moving and potentially obsolete stock items?

2 Detailed Issues

2.1 Are processes in place which ensure that adequate information is provided to facilitate adequate stock planning to achieve business objectives?

2.2 Have suitably trained and experienced stock control staff and management been provided?

2.3 What prevents the overstocking of items?

2.4 How are stocks maintained at the optimum level, taking into account such factors as supplier or production lead time, etc.?

2.5 Are raw materials, items in production and finished goods discretely identified, physically tracked and correctly reflected in the accounts?

2.6 Is management promptly alerted to low stock levels, and how are responses evidenced and monitored?

2.7 Are all stock movements and adjustments supported by documentation and trailed?

2.8 Are all damaged items and those returned from customers, etc. accurately identified and appropriately returned for credit?

2.9 Is it possible to verify the validity of stock sales through to the accounts receivable system?

2.10 Is it possible to verify all stock movements to the production facility and agree stock inputs to the output of finished goods?

2.11 Are stock issues of raw materials promptly actioned and the associated items moved into the production area to minimise workflow disruptions?

2.12 What are the procedures for authorising and accounting for all stock issues?

2.13 What processes ensure that stock items are used in rotation so that items do not deteriorate?

2.14 How does management ensure that all stock deliveries (including those made directly to production or sales locations) are identified, confirmed as correct and duly accounted for?

2.15 How is management certain that the appropriate accounting treatment is applied to stock items (i.e. fixed or current assets, write-off to revenue, appropriate timing, etc.)?

2.16 What measures prevent the theft or misappropriation of stock items?

2.17 Is stolen or damaged stock reported to the police (where appropriate) and claimed against the insurers?

2.18 What checks are in place to ensure that all stock movements are accurately reflected on the stock control/inventory records?

2.19 Are stock records adequately protected from unauthorised or false entries?

2.20 Are the stock records subject to regular verification; if so, how often and how is this evidenced?

2.21 How does management ensure that all stock items are subject to reliable verification and that the valuations contained in the published accounts are complete and accurate?

2.22 How does management ensure that the prices used to evaluate stockholdings are valid, accurate and up to date?

2.23 What mechanisms ensure that all stocktaking variances are accurately recorded, reported to management, investigated and resolved?

2.24 Is adequate authorisation applied and evidenced in support of all stocktaking adjustments?

2.25 Are adequate and secure stock storage facilities provided in order to prevent deterioration of items and losses due to theft?

2.26 Can the precise storage locations of all stock items promptly be determined?

2.27 Are stock write-offs, disposals, etc. authorised at the appropriate level and how is this evidenced?

2.28 What measures ensure that the best price is obtained for stock disposals (i.e. for scrap) and are such transactions authorised and the relevant proceeds confirmed?

2.29 How is accuracy of all data input from other systems (e.g. purchasing) confirmed?

2.30 How is the accuracy of data output to other systems (e.g. product costing, accounts receivable) confirmed?

2.31 How is the accuracy and integrity of the stock system records assured, and what measures prevent unauthorised access to the stock data?

2.32 How does management confirm that management information extracted from the stock system is accurate, timely and complete?

WAREHOUSING AND STORAGE

This section examines a number of interrelated issues which should aim to support the provision of goods at the right place, at the right time and in good condition. The requirements also have linkages with choosing the optimum location(s) for warehousing and ensuring that goods are safely and securely stored. There may also be health and safety implications wherever hazardous materials are stored.

Control Objectives for Warehousing and Storage

(a) To ensure that materials, goods and products are adequately and securely stored in order to facilitate their prompt identification and despatch.

(b) To ensure that sufficient storage space is available and the layout of storage facilities is suitable to meet the operational requirements of the organisation.

(c) To ensure that goods are effectively stored in order to provide an efficient service to customers and internal users.

(d) To ensure that the optimum warehouse locations are utilised to maximise the efficiency of distribution to customers, etc.

(e) To ensure that all goods are adequately protected from damage, deterioration and loss, in order that they remain in optimum condition for use.

(f) To ensure that all stock movements are valid, authorised and properly executed.

(g) To ensure that goods are stored safely.

(h) To ensure that staff are appropriately trained in the handling of goods in order to avoid damage to the goods and injury to staff.

(i) To provide adequate and serviceable materials handling devices as an aid to efficiency and cost-effectiveness.

(j) To ensure that hazardous items are safely stored.

(k) To ensure that all relevant regulations and legislation are complied with.

(l) To ensure that stocks are used in rotation.

(m) To ensure that adequate and relevant insurance cover is provided for both the stocks and storage facilities.

Risk and Control Issues for Warehousing and Storage

1 Key Issues

1.1 How is management made aware of the current and future storage capacity requirements, and what is the evidence of effective planning to meet the identified demands?

1.2 How does management decide where to locate warehouses, and is adequate account taken of the relevant logistical, transport and customer service considerations?

1.3 Are the storage locations (i.e. bins or bays) adequately identified to enable the prompt location of stock units?

1.4 Are storage facilities adequate to protect goods from damage or deterioration?

1.5 What mechanisms are in place to ensure that all stocks are adequately protected from theft and pilferage?

1.6 What measures are in place to prevent unauthorised access to the storage areas?

1.7 How does management verify that all movements of stock are valid, authorised and correctly executed?

1.8 Are goods (especially hazardous materials) stored safely and in accordance with established regulations and good practice, and how is management assured that this is the case?

1.9 Are staff adequately trained in the various materials handling techniques, and how does management confirm this?

1.10 Is the efficiency of the storage facility enhanced with the use of appropriate handling devices (trolleys, pallets, forklift trucks, cranes, etc.) and how is management assured that all such devices are serviceable and contributing to the overall cost-effectiveness of the operation?

1.11 How does management ensure that all the relevant regulations and legislation are being complied with?

1.12 What mechanisms ensure that adequate, up-to-date and relevant insurance cover is in place for both the stocks and the storage facilities?

2 Detailed Issues

2.1 Is space allocated in order to cope with peak loads rather than normal or minimum requirements?

2.2 Has management provided spare storage capacity as a contingency to cater for expansion, etc. (and how was this accurately determined)?

2.3 Is space usage monitored and action taken to avoid wasted or excess space?

2.4 Are raw materials, goods and finished goods appropriately segregated?

2.5 How does management avoid excess storage space and aim to contain the costs of providing storage facilities?

2.6 Are fast-moving items accurately identified and conveniently located for efficient handling?

2.7 Are items adequately trailed to all the relevant storage locations?

2.8 Are stocks used in rotation (as appropriate) in order to avoid the build-up of older or outdated items?

2.9 Is there sufficient space between storage locations to enable effective and safe access, the use of handling equipment, and the safe evacuation of the building in case of emergency?

2.10 How does management ensure that production and sales requirements are promptly and accurately advised to the warehouse?

2.11 Have specific responsibilities for the warehouse operation been allocated (and does this include maintaining an awareness of current materials handling trends and relevant regulations)?

2.12 Are packaging, storage and handling techniques adequate to protect the goods from damage and deterioration?

2.13 Are damaged items promptly identified and appropriate action taken (and how is this evidenced)?

2.14 Are the appropriate environmental conditions (i.e. air conditioning, humidity and temperature) provided and maintained at the required level?

2.15 Are storage areas well lit for safety and security purposes?

2.16 What physical and other security measures are in place to protect goods and personnel, and are they regularly tested for effectiveness?

2.17 Are adequate and operational intruder alarm systems installed and regularly tested?

2.18 Are adequate and operational fire prevention, protection and containment facilities provided, and are they regularly tested and maintained?

2.19 Would the fire containment systems (e.g. sprinklers, foam inlets) cause significant damage to stocks?

2.20 What measures prevent staff pilferage of stock items?

2.21 Are adequate staff provided to meet the operational demands of the organisation, and how does management determine and maintain the staffing requirements?

2.22 Are staff aware of the required and safe handling techniques, and how is this confirmed?

2.23 Has management provided adequate and suitable protective equipment and clothing for staff, and how is its use confirmed?

2.24 What checks are in place to ensure that goods are stacked and stored safely?

2.25 Are sufficient and adequate facilities provided for moving heavy items, and are staff aware of the correct use of such facilities?

2.26 Are delicate items adequately protected during storage and when being moved?

2.27 How is the accuracy of data input from other systems (e.g. stock control or sales order processing) confirmed?

2.28 How is data output to other systems (e.g. distribution) confirmed?

18
Auditing Human Resources

INTRODUCTION

In this chapter we consider the operational auditing dimensions of human resource management.

SYSTEM/FUNCTION COMPONENTS OF THE PERSONNEL FUNCTION

Adopting an essentially functional approach to define the human resource management audit universe results in the following possible breakdown of the key functions, systems or activities. The first item listed is intended to be a general and top level review of the overall human resources function and touches on each of the other noted components in summary terms, whereas the other components tackle the given subjects in considerably more depth.

- human resources department
- recruitment
- manpower and succession planning
- staff training and development
- welfare
- pension scheme (and other benefits)
- health insurance
- staff appraisal and disciplinary matters
- health and safety
- labour relations
- company vehicles.

CONTROL OBJECTIVES AND RISK AND CONTROL ISSUES

We shall now examine the control objectives and risk and control issues (divided into key issues and detailed issues) for each of the personnel functions listed above.

This data can be used within the Standard Audit Programme Guides (SAPGs) looked at in Chapter 3. To save space we have concentrated on the objectives to be stated and the questions to be asked and have not presented them within the SAPG format.

HUMAN RESOURCES DEPARTMENT

Personnel are likely to represent the largest proportion of operating costs for an organisation. Furthermore, the performance of (and the contribution made by) employees is normally crucial to the success or otherwise of the entity. Management is responsible for ensuring that adequate numbers of suitably experienced, trained and motivated employees are provided in support of the organisation's objectives. In organisations of any size, the application of agreed employment policies and practices are normally administered by the human resources (or personnel) department.

The objectives and risk/control issues that follow in this particular section are concerned with the set-up and ongoing operation of a human resources (HR) function with defined responsibilities for such elements as recruitment, training and management development, staff appraisal schemes and labour relations.

The programme of risk and control issues noted below could be used for a high level review of the HR function so that the top level findings can be used, by the internal auditor, as pointers to those specific constituent areas which may require subsequent in-depth examination.

Control Objectives for the Human Resources Department

(a) To ensure that adequate and suitably experienced staff are recruited and provided in order that the organisation's business objectives are achieved.

(b) To ensure that policies which support the recruitment, retention, training and development, performance appraisal, remuneration, welfare, disciplining and employment termination of the personnel are developed, implemented and monitored.

(c) To ensure that all the prevailing employment and employee legislation and regulations are fully complied with.

(d) To ensure that the organisation's remuneration and benefits remain competitive and relative to the industry standards.

(e) To ensure that staff are adequately trained to perform their duties and that their skills and abilities are developed and maintained in accordance with the current and future business operational requirements.

(f) To foster positive labour relations at all levels and to avoid disruptive disputes.

> (g) To ensure that personnel turnover and absenteeism are monitored, maintained at acceptable levels, and problems are promptly reacted to.
>
> (h) To ensure that staff recruitment is suitably authorised in accordance with the operational demands of the business and cost-effectively conducted.
>
> (i) To ensure that staff performance is monitored and the necessary remedial action is taken.
>
> (j) To ensure that adequate personnel records are maintained and protected from unauthorised access.
>
> (k) To provide information and a cost-effective and professional service to management on all human resource matters.

Risk and Control Issues for the Human Resources Department

1 Key Issues

1.1 How does management ensure that there will be adequate and suitably skilled staff available now and in the future, to ensure the achievement of their business objectives?

1.2 Have documented policies been established for staff recruitment, training, remuneration, performance appraisal and disciplinary matters?

1.3 What measures are in place to prevent the engagement of staff on terms outside the prevailing policies, terms and conditions?

1.4 What measures ensure that all staff recruitment is authorised and that only suitably skilled persons are employed?

1.5 How is ongoing compliance with all the prevailing employment regulations and laws confirmed, and would failure to comply be promptly detected?

1.6 What measures ensure that salaries, benefits and all other terms and conditions remain competitive and realistic in relation to the sector and national norms?

1.7 How does management ensure that skill requirements are identified and staff are adequately trained and developed to meet the demands of the business?

1.8 What measures ensure that good labour relations are maintained and costly disputes are avoided?

1.9 Is management made aware of absenteeism and staff turnover levels, and what action is taken in the event of increased or unacceptable levels?

1.10 How does management monitor staff performance to check it is at the appropriate level and proficiency, and what action is taken to identify and correct any shortfalls?

1.11 Is there a documented disciplinary and grievance procedure in place, and does it conform to the necessary regulations?

1.12 What measures are in place to ensure that human resource staff maintain an accurate and up-to-date awareness of all the relevant regulations and professional practices (and is line management also kept informed)?

1.13 How does management ensure that all staff are made aware of their responsibilities and entitlements under the prevailing personnel policies?

1.14 How does management verify that the personnel records are up to date, accurate and adequately protected from unauthorised use and access?

2 Detailed Issues

2.1 How are the current and future staffing levels and skills geared to the needs of the strategic plans for the organisation?

2.2 How is over-staffing avoided?

2.3 What actions ensure that there are always adequate numbers of suitably experienced and trained staff available to meet the organisation's needs?

2.4 What measures prevent the build-up of inappropriately skilled or inadequately qualified staff?

2.5 How does the organisation avoid the high costs associated with staff redundancies?

2.6 How are the various documented personnel policies and standards maintained and kept up to date and relevant?

2.7 Have standard pay/salary scales been established, and what prevents the engagement and set-up of an employee on nonstandard rates and conditions?

2.8 Are the official salary scales accurately maintained and amended only when authorised?

2.9 Who is responsible for determining remuneration and benefits packages and how is management authorisation for these evidenced?

2.10 What measures ensure that salary reviews are suitably authorised, accurately calculated and correctly applied to the payroll?

2.11 Are all new positions independently evaluated in respect of grade, applicable salary, special conditions, etc., and how is this process evidenced?

2.12 What measures prevent the establishment of an unauthorised or nongraded position?

2.13 Has management agreed and defined the required staffing establishment levels, and are these used to verify all recruitment activity?

2.14 Are all positions supported by an authorised and up-to-date job description or specification?

2.15 Is recruitment driven, in every case, by the requirements of an authorised job description?

2.16 How are high recruitment costs avoided (for example, unreasonable recruitment consultancy commissions)?

2.17 Are recruitment activities suitably targeted?

2.18 Are temporary or short-term staffing requirements accurately identified and authorised?

2.19 Are candidates for temporary positions suitably assessed?

2.20 How does management avoid the engagement of unsuitable staff, those with a previous poor employment/attendance record, or those with unconfirmed qualifications?

2.21 How does management make sure that training resources are appropriately targeted in accordance with need?

2.22 How does management monitor that the available training resources are appropriate, up to date and effective?

2.23 How does management ensure that individuals' training needs are being accurately identified and effectively addressed?

2.24 How are staff and management kept aware of current employment regulations and their relevant responsibilities?

2.25 Have adequate sources of employment and human resource information been established for the use of staff and management?

2.26 If management failed to comply with relevant employment legislation, would the transgression be capable of prompt detection?

2.27 Have adequate channels of communication been established to enable the prompt identification and reporting of potential staffing problems?

2.28 Is management provided with accurate, reliable and regular information on such matters as staffing levels, days lost due to sickness, absenteeism, etc., and is it obliged to take corrective action when necessary?

2.29 Are staff kept sufficiently aware of changes and developments which affect them?

2.30 What measures ensure that staff who perform below the required standard are accurately identified?

2.31 Have suitable and lawful mechanisms been provided to enable staff to bring their concerns and grievances to the attention of management as the basis for a fair and full review?

2.32 Has management provided the necessary facilities to deal sympathetically and effectively with employee problems and personal matters, taking into account any relevant local regulations?

2.33 What processes ensure that all staff leavers are correctly dealt with (i.e. paid all their entitlements, removed from the payroll, company property recovered, other benefits discontinued, etc.)?

2.34 What mechanisms ensure that staff dismissed for disciplinary reasons are correctly and lawfully treated?

2.35 What prevents the unauthorised access to or use of personnel data, and would violations be detected and reacted to?

2.36 Does the personnel data maintained by the organisation conform to the requirements of any relevant legislation?

2.37 How can management be assured that the current practices conform to the relevant equal opportunities and anti-discrimination regulations?

2.38 How is the accuracy of data input from other systems confirmed?

2.39 How is the accuracy of personnel data output to other systems confirmed?

RECRUITMENT

Identifying and engaging the right person for the job can be an expensive process, especially where the vacancy is a specialist one and external recruitment agencies are involved. Recruitment is initially about the accurate identification of a justified need and then selecting the most effective and cost-effective methods to fulfil the requirement.

Control Objectives for Recruitment

(a) To ensure that appropriately experienced and stable staff are recruited to meet the organisation's business and operational objectives.

(b) To ensure that a structured, targeted, and cost-effective approach to recruitment is adopted.

(c) To ensure that all recruitment and appointments are suitably authorised.

(d) To ensure that recruitment activities comply with current legislation and regulations.

(e) To ensure that new employees are engaged in compliance with the prevailing remuneration and conditions policies.

(f) To ensure that all positions are suitably evaluated and that the key recruitment criteria are identified.

> (g) To ensure that candidates are evaluated against the job specification and adequately screened to confirm their previous employment and educational record.
>
> (h) To ensure that personnel and employment records are correctly established and accurately maintained in accordance with any applicable legislation.
>
> (i) To ensure that valid and correct employment contracts are agreed, signed and retained.

Risk and Control Issues for Recruitment

1 Key Issues

1.1 Have documented recruitment policies and procedures been established, and how is management assured that they are up to date and complied with?

1.2 Have standard remuneration scales and employment conditions been implemented, and would management be made aware of staff engagements which fall outside these standards?

1.3 How is management certain that all staff recruitment and appointments are warranted and authorised?

1.4 What processes ensure that the requirements of a particular position are clearly established as the basis for evaluating subsequent applicants?

1.5 How does management ensure that the most appropriate and cost-effective method of recruitment is used, and that excessive recruitment costs are avoided?

1.6 What steps are taken to confirm the previous employment record and educational qualifications of candidates, and what prevents the engagement of someone with an invalid or unsuitable record?

1.7 How does management monitor that all the prevailing employment and engagement legislation and regulations are being correctly observed?

1.8 Are all staff engagements supported by a valid, accurate, agreed and signed contract of employment, and what prevents staff being engaged without a contract being in force?

1.9 What measures ensure that new employees are correctly set up on the payroll and that their salary rate is valid for the position?

1.10 How does management check that accurate, complete and up-to-date personnel records are maintained which conform to any relevant laws and regulations?

1.11 Are personnel and employment records adequately protected from unauthorised access and use?

2 Detailed Issues

2.1 How are recruitment requirements identified and are they all subject to suitable authorisation (and how is this evidenced)?

2.2 What prevents an unauthorised position being filled?

2.3 Are all new positions and replacements subject to assessment and management authority?

2.4 Are all positions supported by an up-to-date job description and specification?

2.5 How can management be certain that recruitment is directed by the requirements of the job description or specification?

2.6 Is a planned approach adopted for recruitment which defines the optimum method(s) to be used?

2.7 Is the recruitment method agreed with the relevant manager and an overall budget established (for advertising, use of agencies, etc.)?

2.8 Is recruitment advertising appropriately directed (i.e. to relevant journals and locations)?

2.9 How does management verify that recruitment costs (including advertising and external agency fees) are valid, authorised and within budget?

2.10 Are recruitment efforts suitably targeted and are internal candidates sought and considered?

2.11 Are the established job criteria (salary range, preferred age range, etc.) realistic and current in relation to the local employment conditions?

2.12 Where recruitment activities are either protracted or unsuccessful, is management consulted and a revised approach agreed?

2.13 Is recruitment performance monitored by management and is there evidence of the corrective action taken?

2.14 Are all those concerned with recruitment suitably aware of the implications of all the prevailing recruitment and employment legislation and regulations (and how is this evidenced)?

2.15 What processes would detect actual or potential infringements of the prevailing employment legislation?

2.16 How is management assured that prevailing equal opportunity and anti-discrimination laws are being complied with?

2.17 Are applicant/staff complaints about the recruitment process promptly and effectively dealt with in accordance with the current law?

2.18 Are references obtained and checked for validity, etc.?

2.19 Are claimed educational and vocational qualifications verified, and how are anomalies followed up?

2.20 Are interviews professionally conducted by suitably experienced personnel and are interview objectives established as the basis for the conduct of the interview?

2.21 Are standard rates established for interview expenses and are claims checked for validity and suitably authorised for payment?

2.22 How are interview expense payments outside the standard rates prevented?

2.23 Where specific skills are required, are candidates adequately tested and evaluated prior to engagement?

2.24 Are candidates required to undergo a medical examination as a condition of employment (e.g. for acceptance into the company health insurance scheme), and how is management assured that unsuitable candidates are identified?

2.25 Are applications efficiently dealt with and are rejected candidates informed?

2.26 Are accurate records maintained of all applicants (including current employees)?

2.27 How does management ensure that all offers of employment are valid, accurate and lawful?

2.28 Are all offers of employment accounted for and are acceptances correctly acknowledged and processed?

2.29 Are the contents of employment contracts verified for accuracy before release, and how would errors be prevented?

2.30 Are all employment contracts accounted for, and how can management be certain that all contracts are signed and in force?

2.31 Are new staff made aware of all relevant conditions of employment, operational practices, safety regulations, etc., and how is this evidenced?

2.32 Are suitable arrangements made for new employees (e.g. issue of security cards, induction or safety training)?

2.33 Would inaccurate or incomplete personnel/employment records be detected and what action is taken to correct such records?

2.34 Is management information generated from the personnel and employment records accurate, reliable, timely and appropriate?

2.35 How is the accuracy of data input from other systems (e.g. manpower planning) confirmed?

2.36 How is the accuracy of data output to other systems (e.g. payroll) confirmed?

MANPOWER AND SUCCESSION PLANNING

Nothing is ever static in business, and the general ability of the organisation to pre-empt anticipated change and adequately plan for its consequences can be a fundamental matter of survival. This can be particularly true where staff are concerned. Even setting aside the effects of natural levels of staff turnover, any company will need to ensure that the workforce is capable of meeting both the current and foreseeable demands. Changes in staffing skills may, for example, be required as a consequence of introducing new technology or the effects of external market influences.

This section aims to explore the issues arising from the need to ensure that future staff skill demands are planned for and accordingly met. In a dynamic employment situation, staff will be promoted and move into other areas of the organisation, and there should be mechanisms in place to ensure that other employees are suitably groomed and waiting in the wings to move into the vacated positions. Where the vacant roles are especially critical, the need to plan for the succession is even more vital.

Control Objectives for Manpower and Succession Planning

(a) To ensure that sufficient and suitable staff are provided now and in the future so that corporate objectives are achieved.

(b) To determine a staffing policy which takes into account the need to adapt to both internal and external changes.

(c) To ensure that recruitment and staff allocation activities are coordinated to ensure the optimum staffing level and to avoid over-staffing.

(d) To ensure that the workforce is adequately and appropriately skilled to meet the ongoing business and operational demands.

(e) To ensure that staff training and development are coordinated to provide an adequate reserve of experienced staff.

(f) To ensure that staffing levels and costs are contained within defined limits.

(g) To ensure that any need to reduce staffing levels is determined in good time so that the appropriate implications can be evaluated and suitable consultations/arrangements made.

Risk and Control Issues for Manpower and Succession Planning

1 Key Issues

1.1 Has management implemented a structured approach to manpower and succession planning?

1.2 Have the implications of the mid to long-term strategic business objectives of the organisation been appropriately taken into account when considering the manpower and succession requirements?

1.3 In determining the ongoing staffing requirements, has management taken appropriate account of technical, social and economic influences?

1.4 Has a suitable staffing policy been established, and are line management fully aware of the requirements?

1.5 Are all recruitment and/or staff reduction activities undertaken in accordance with the manpower plan, and how is this evidenced?

1.6 Have current and future skill requirements been accurately identified, and what action is being taken to ensure that staff are appropriately developed and trained to meet the requirements?

1.7 What measures prevent the recruitment of staff outside the established levels?

1.8 Are unavoidable staff reductions adequately planned for (including appropriate staff communication, assessment, counselling and redundancy arrangements, etc.)?

2 Detailed Issues

2.1 What measures are in place to ensure that manpower and succession plans are up to date, relevant and attainable?

2.2 How does management monitor that all the necessary implications of their business plans have been taken into account when undertaking staff planning?

2.3 Are all new or revised business activities reviewed in the context of their implications for manpower requirements?

2.4 What measures prevent the necessity for urgent or emergency recruitment of temporary staff?

2.5 Does the manpower plan contain accurate and up-to-date financial implications, and are these correctly reflected in the budgeting system?

2.6 How does management remain fully aware of all the potential influences on staffing, recruitment, training, etc.?

2.7 Have effective measures been established to ensure that there is an adequate reserve of trained staff for both key executive replacement and to cover natural wastage?

2.8 Have the objectives of the manpower and succession processes been adequately communicated to affected management personnel, and are they aware of their relevant responsibilities?

2.9 Are training and staff development strategies/plans positively linked to the projected manpower requirements, so that unnecessary or wasteful training is avoided?

2.10 Is management undertaking ongoing monitoring of the actual staffing situation in relation to the planned requirements, and is appropriate action being taken to correct deviations, etc.?

2.11 Are staff subject to regular performance and skill appraisals as a means of determining the current status of staff proficiency?

2.12 Where the manpower and succession plans contain confidential or sensitive data, are adequate precautions taken to prevent unauthorised access or leakage?

2.13 When significant staff reductions are foreseen, are adequate procedures and plans established to ensure that staff transfers, redundancies, etc. are appropriately, legally and sympathetically handled?

2.14 How is the accuracy of data input from other systems confirmed?

2.15 How is the accuracy of data output to other systems confirmed?

STAFF TRAINING AND DEVELOPMENT

Staff need to be suitably trained to discharge their responsibilities effectively and efficiently. The cost of providing adequate training can be high and management will need to ensure that precious training resources are targeted to the areas of the greatest need. Where an organisation is going through far-reaching changes, staff training may be an essential ingredient in the achievement of the related objectives. In the points that follow, the need for an agreed and justified policy on training is regarded as a key requirement as a point of reference for all the related activities. The importance of monitoring the effects of training is also emphasised.

Control Objectives for Staff Training and Development

(a) To ensure that training and staff development resources are accurately targeted in order to maximise their effects and avoid wasteful activity.

(b) To ensure that employees are adequately trained to enable them to discharge their responsibilities effectively.

(c) To ensure that the skills of the workforce are maintained at the appropriate level and in line with the business objectives of the organisation.

(d) To motivate staff and increase their commitment by providing suitable personal and skill development facilities.

(e) To anticipate the future skill needs of the business and ensure that relevant training is planned for.

> (f) To provide adequate and appropriate training facilities and resources on a cost-effective basis.
>
> (g) To maximise the benefits available from government or trade training schemes and subsidies.
>
> (h) To consider the use of training and staff development as means to gain a competitive advantage.

Risk and Control Issues for Staff Training and Development

1 Key Issues

1.1 Has management defined, documented and implemented a training policy which incorporates training programmes and timetables, required standards of skill proficiency, training methods to be used, authority limits for training expenditure, and so on?

1.2 How is management assured that all training and staff development activities are justified, authorised and appropriately targeted?

1.3 Is expenditure on training and development subject to budgetary control, and what prevents unauthorised or unnecessary training activities from taking place?

1.4 Has management determined the required skill and knowledge base for the workforce and implemented a planned training approach to ensuring that the employees remain competent and able to discharge their duties?

1.5 How is management certain of identifying and suitably addressing individual training and development needs?

1.6 Are training activities actively monitored for their effectiveness, so that deficiencies can be recognised and remedied?

1.7 How does management ensure that the most suitable and cost-effective training methods and resources are used?

1.8 Are the costs of training and staff development offset, whenever possible, by obtaining government or trade-related training subsidies?

1.9 Is training conducted to a suitable trade or nationally recognised standard?

1.10 Whenever possible, does management consider the use of training in order to gain a competitive or strategic advantage?

2 Detailed Issues

2.1 Are all new employees promptly provided with adequate induction training to inform them about the organisation and its aims?

2.2 Are all relevant employees provided with a personal training and development plan, and how does management ensure that the established objectives are met?

2.3 Are future skill requirements anticipated and adequately planned for, and how is this evidenced?

2.4 How are the development and training needs of individual employees identified, justified and fulfilled?

2.5 How is a training requirement justified and authorised?

2.6 How does management ensure that all training requirements are addressed?

2.7 What mechanisms prevent unauthorised or unjustified training activities?

2.8 What procedures are established for the review and authorisation of training and support for relevant professional qualifications, and how is the authorisation evidenced?

2.9 Are clear procedures available which define the extent to which the organisation will contribute to the fees for relevant professional qualification training?

2.10 Are staff who pursue relevant professional qualifications entitled to study leave and how is this controlled?

2.11 Are all specialist training requirements identified and addressed in order that key business processes and activities are protected?

2.12 Does management allow sufficient time to address the recognised training needs?

2.13 How does management monitor that training activity is (and remains) effective?

2.14 Are training staff kept abreast of the available and relevant training techniques and methods, and are they in a position to recommend the optimum form?

2.15 Are training methods, tools and facilities regularly reviewed for their relevance and effectiveness?

2.16 Is the use of external training facilities subject to adequate prior assessment and authorisation, and how is this evidenced?

2.17 How does management ensure that the organisation receives value for money in respect of training?

2.18 Whenever possible, is training conducted to a recognised standard?

2.19 Are there mechanisms in place to identify employees with a high development potential?

2.20 Are senior and key employees further motivated by the establishment and implementation of personal development programmes, and are such regimes monitored for their effectiveness and contribution to retaining key staff?

2.21 Does management take full advantage of any available government or trade-related training subsidies or grants?

2.22 Has management considered the role of training to improve the appeal of the organisation's products or services (for example, through improved customer advice and support)?

2.23 How is the accuracy of data input from other systems (e.g. staff appraisal scores) confirmed?

2.24 How is the accuracy of data output to other systems (e.g. personnel records) confirmed?

WELFARE

Individual organisations will take different views of staff welfare, and not all will provide all the facilities hinted at in the section that follows, as they can be seen as costly options.

Control Objectives for Welfare

(a) To ensure that adequate provision is made for the protection of staff from injury or death in the course of their duties.

(b) To ensure that appropriate and relevant employer's liability insurance cover is provided in accordance with the prevailing legal requirements.

(c) To motivate staff, to maintain staff morale, and improve their working conditions by providing, as appropriate, refreshment facilities, medical services, sporting and recreational facilities, transport facilities to/from sites, crèche facilities, staff shops/discounts, etc.

(d) To ensure that all staff welfare facilities are provided on an authorised and cost-effective basis.

(e) To ensure that only eligible employees benefit from welfare and other general facilities.

(f) To ensure that all goods and stock associated with welfare activities are adequately accounted for.

(g) To ensure that both unauthorised access to and abuse of staff welfare facilities are prevented.

(h) To ensure that the costs associated with the provision of welfare and fringe benefits are contained within budget.

Risk and Control Issues for Welfare

1 Key Issues

1.1 Has management defined, agreed, documented and implemented a policy and procedures on the provision of and eligibility for staff welfare facilities?

1.2 What does management do to provide adequate facilities to protect staff from injury or death in the course of their duties?

1.3 Are all relevant staff made aware of the specific health and safety regulations?

1.4 How does management confirm that the organisation is correctly complying with all the relevant health, safety and insurance requirements and regulations?

1.5 Are all accidents and incidents recorded and reported (in accordance with the prevailing regulations)?

1.6 Are all staff welfare facilities subject to suitable authorisation and management monitoring?

1.7 What measures prevent the use of staff facilities by outsiders and unauthorised employees?

1.8 How does management verify that all assets, goods and stock associated with staff welfare facilities are secure and accounted for?

1.9 Are staff welfare facilities operated within the agreed budgets, and are variances reported to management and acted upon?

2 Detailed Issues

2.1 What does management do to ensure that all the required staff protection and safety facilities are provided to the relevant standards?

2.2 Are staff fully aware of their responsibilities with respect to their well-being?

2.3 Are security facilities at company buildings and sites adequate?

2.4 Are staff who are involved in hazardous or potentially dangerous activities (such as transporting large amounts of cash) suitably trained and protected?

2.5 How does management confirm that insurance cover is appropriate, sufficient and currently in force?

2.6 Are all claims processed against the company insurance policies suitably documented, verified and pursued?

2.7 Are staff made aware of the available facilities and their eligibility to use them?

2.8 How does management justify and authorise staff welfare facilities?

2.9 Are staff welfare facilities monitored for usage and their contribution to staff motivation and morale (and are underused or ineffective facilities withdrawn)?

2.10 How does management verify that the organisation is providing all the facilities required by local or national regulations and laws?

2.11 Are all the costs associated with the provision of welfare facilities accounted for and compared to the relevant budgets for management action?

2.12 How does management prevent unofficial, illegal or unauthorised activities?

2.13 Are club membership fees correctly accounted for?

2.14 Are company subsidies (e.g. for staff canteen or site transport) accounted for, within the agreed budget and suitably authorised?

2.15 Are suitably experienced or qualified staff provided (e.g. for medical services) and appropriate regulations (e.g. licensing arrangements) fully observed?

2.16 Are independent staff counsellors available to confidentially assist staff with their personal problems and concerns?

2.17 Are welfare facilities withdrawn from individual employees in proven cases of abuse or malpractice?

2.18 Are employees asked to prove their identity when using company facilities, and how is this achieved?

2.19 How are ex-employees or outsiders prevented from benefiting from welfare facilities?

2.20 How is accuracy of data input from other systems (e.g. from personnel records or payroll) confirmed?

2.21 How is the accuracy of data output to other systems (e.g. to payroll) confirmed?

PERFORMANCE-RELATED COMPENSATION, PENSION SCHEMES (AND OTHER BENEFITS)

The ethical administration of pension schemes has become a high-profile issue in the UK following the well-publicised Maxwell situation, where pension funds were supposedly used to prop up an ailing business empire. The improper use of the Maxwell pension scheme funds led to pension payments to thousands of pensioners being put in jeopardy. This case raised issues about the prudent management and trusteeship of pension funds, which often represent very large sums. More recently, the challenge has been the adequacy of funding of pension schemes, leading to the withdrawal of many defined benefit schemes, at least for new staff, and their substitution by defined contribution schemes where the final benefit risk is largely transferred from the employer to the staff.

In addition to the issues surrounding pension schemes, this section also considers other systems provided for the benefit of employees and directors, such as employee share schemes, share option schemes and profit-related pay (PRP) schemes. The noted control objectives and key issues cover all the above mentioned types of schemes; the detailed issues are subdivided into the various schemes.

Control Objectives for Performance-related Compensation, Pension Schemes (and Other Benefits)

(a) To ensure that pensions schemes are correctly established and operated in accordance with the prevailing legislation and good practice, so as to protect members' interests and safeguard the funds.

(b) To ensure that the scheme is suitably authorised and subject to a suitable trust deed if required.

(c) To ensure that pension funds are kept completely separate from company funds and fully accounted for.

(d) To ensure that membership eligibility rules are established and that only bona fide employees are accepted as members in accord with the membership rules.

(e) To ensure that the prescribed investment and funding policy is followed in all transactions, and periodically reviewed in order to remain pertinent.

(f) To ensure that all contributions (employee and employer) are accurately calculated, recorded, deducted, paid over and fully accounted for.

(g) To ensure that trustees (and management) are kept regularly informed of the performance and status of the fund.

(h) To ensure that the accumulated funds are adequate in order to meet the projected pension and benefits demands.

(i) To ensure that the fund is subject to external audit scrutiny and that any recommendations are appropriately followed up.

(j) To ensure that members are kept informed of their accrued pensions rights and other benefits.

(k) To ensure that all death in service and lump sum claims are validated and handled in accordance with the prevailing legislation and tax regulations.

(l) To ensure that pension payments are correctly calculated, accounted for and only paid over to bona fide pensioners.

(m) To ensure that refunds of contributions are valid, permissible under the law and fully accounted for.

(n) To ensure that transfers to/from other pension schemes are correctly valued and accounted for.

(o) To provide suitably experienced and qualified staff to administer the scheme and respond efficiently to members' enquiries. etc.

> (p) To ensure that any employee share, share option or profit-related pay schemes are correctly established, comply with the relevant legislation, are fully accountable and are only operated for the benefit of bona fide and eligible members.

Risk and Control Issues for Performance-related Compensation, Pension Schemes (and Other Benefits)

1 Key Issues

1.1 How does management ensure that the pension scheme is correctly established and operated, and complies with the current legislation and good practice?

1.2 Is the scheme in its current form authorised by management and supported by documented procedures, rules and a suitable trust deed (if applicable)?

1.3 Would any failure to comply with either the established rules or prevailing legislation be promptly detected?

1.4 How do management and trustees confirm that all pension funds are kept strictly separate from company activities and remain fully accounted for?

1.5 What mechanisms prevent unauthorised or ineligible employees becoming members of the pension scheme?

1.6 Has the preferred investment policy and strategy been defined, agreed and documented, and how are management and trustees assured that it is always followed in investment transactions?

1.7 How are members, management and trustees assured that all pension contributions are valid, correctly calculated, deducted, paid over and accounted for?

1.8 What processes would detect anomalies or irregularities in respect of contribution accountability, and how is any corrective action evidenced?

1.9 Are management and trustees regularly supplied with accurate, timely and relevant information on the scheme in order to discharge their responsibilities?

1.10 Is the fund subject to regular scrutiny by suitably qualified external auditors (or any other regulatory bodies), and are their recommendations and observations adequately followed up?

1.11 Are there processes in place to ensure that all payments from the fund are valid, authorised, correctly calculated, paid over to bona fide persons and fully accounted for?

1.12 How does management ensure that the operations of any other schemes (e.g. employee shares, share options, profit-related pay) fully comply with the current legislation and tax regulations, and are fully accounted for?

1.13 Are all aspects of all the organisation's performance-related pay schemes aligned with the long-term interests of the organisation and its owners?

2 Detailed Issues

Pensions

2.1 Are the pension administrators and trustees kept fully aware of the current legislation and good practice affecting the operation of pension schemes, and how is this evidenced?

2.2 Has the establishment and ongoing operation of the pension scheme been subject to appropriate authorisation?

2.3 Has senior management sanctioned the extent of the company contributions to the scheme, the costs of operation, the methods of funding and the membership rules?

2.4 Are adequate and up-to-date pension scheme rules and procedures in place, and made available to scheme members and potential members?

2.5 Has a suitable trust deed been established for the scheme, and does it define:
- the nature and purpose of the scheme
- the names of the trustees
- the rules for appointing trustees
- the trustees' terms of reference
- the method of funding the scheme
- investment policy
- benefits and conditions of membership
- the reporting and auditing requirements?

2.6 How are management and members assured that the requirements of the trust deed are complied with?

2.7 Do the nomination and election processes for trustees comply with the regulations and good practice, and are the appointed trustees suitably experienced and do they adequately represent the interest of scheme members?

2.8 Are trustees and/or the scheme administrators held accountable for their actions, and have their responsibilities and duties been clearly defined?

2.9 Are separate bank accounts and fund accounts maintained for the operation of the fund, and is there adequate segregation from company funds and activities?

2.10 Are all investment transactions authorised and confirmed as being in accordance with the documented investment policy and aims of the scheme, and what prevents the processing of invalid or unauthorised transactions?

2.11 How are members and potential scheme members confirmed as being eligible for membership, and how are all eligible members identified at the appropriate time?

2.12 Are all contributions (employee and employer) calculated in accordance with the rules of the scheme?

2.13 What prevents the level of individual members' contributions exceeding any statutory or regulatory limits?

2.14 Are all additional voluntary contributions (AVCs) in accordance with the prevailing regulations and scheme rules, and correctly accounted for?

2.15 Are all scheme contributions accounted for within the fund, and what prevents the incorrect calculation and deduction of contributions?

2.16 Are all staff leavers identified and correctly notified of their options under the pension scheme, and what processes prevent incorrect or invalid advice/data being provided?

2.17 How are all contribution refunds confirmed as being valid, accurate, within the scheme rules and in compliance with current legislation?

2.18 Are all contribution refunds correctly calculated, accounted for, trailed and confirmed as paid only to bona fide members?

2.19 How do trustees, members and management ensure that the accumulated fund is sufficient to meet the projected pension demand, and how can they be confident that the current fund valuation is accurate and realistic?

2.20 Are trustees kept informed of the fund performance in order that they can appropriately discharge their responsibilities to members?

2.21 What evidence is there that appropriate action is taken by trustees to respond to investment or fund concerns?

2.22 Are trustees obliged to meet regularly and are minutes of their meetings and details of the authorised actions appropriately maintained?

2.23 Are audited accounts provided to members on a regular basis?

2.24 Are all members' queries and concerns about the fund and its administration recorded and confirmed as being adequately (and independently) dealt with?

2.25 Are the conditions under which the organisation can declare a contribution holiday clearly defined and subject to adequate review and authorisation?

2.26 Are regular statements of their entitlements provided to members, and how is the accuracy and validity of this data confirmed?

2.27 How are death-in-service payments confirmed as being valid, authorised, correctly calculated and paid over to bona fide beneficiaries?

2.28 What mechanisms prevent pension department staff, trustees and management from misappropriating members' funds?

2.29 How are tax-free lump sum payments confirmed as being valid, correctly calculated in accordance with the relevant regulations, and accounted for?

2.30 Are all members approaching retirement identified and correctly advised of their pension valuations?

2.31 What measures are in place to prevent pension payments being made to invalid persons?

2.32 How are trustees and pension administrators made aware of all pensioner deaths so that the payments of pension benefit are accordingly ceased or correctly routed to eligible and valid dependants, and how is this documented?

2.33 Are all transfers from other schemes accurately assessed for their eligibility, confirmed value, and the relative value in the target scheme?

2.34 Are the best interests of the members taken into account when transfers to and from the scheme are being considered, and how are members assured that they are receiving accurate and appropriate information and guidance?

2.35 How are all transfers into and from the pension fund accounted for, authorised and trailed?

2.36 Are pension administration staff suitably experienced and qualified?

2.37 How are surplus scheme funds identified and dealt with, and is the action taken authorised and confirmed to be within the law and in the best interests of scheme members?

2.38 How is accuracy of data input from other systems (e.g. payroll and bank accounts) confirmed?

2.39 How is the accuracy of data output to other systems (e.g. accounting systems) confirmed?

2.40 What mechanisms prevent the unauthorised access to and misuse of pension scheme and membership data?

2.41 Are pension administration and any external fund costs authorised and monitored by management?

Employee Share Schemes

2.42 Has management authorised the scheme and ensured that it conforms to the prevailing legislation and regulations?

2.43 Have the scheme rules been defined, agreed and documented?

2.44 How is membership eligibility confirmed and what prevents the acceptance of invalid members?

2.45 Are staff leavers accurately identified, correctly notified of their options under the scheme, correctly processed and removed?

2.46 Are staff share holdings held in trust for the prescribed period and are all holdings accurately identified and accounted for?

2.47 How are the periodic allocation of shares calculated and the individual allocations recorded and accounted for?

2.48 Are appropriate individual share holdings transferred from the trust to personal ownership at the correct time (as determined by the current regulations)?

2.49 Are all scheme and individual share holdings correctly registered (and are accurate holding certificates issued in good time)?

2.50 How does management ensure that all dividends due on scheme and individual holdings are accurately calculated and paid over to bona fide shareholders?

2.51 Are all ownership transfers of scheme/individual holdings (i.e. upon the death of the employee) confirmed as valid, authorised and accounted for?

2.52 How is accuracy of data input from other systems confirmed?

2.53 How is the accuracy of data output to other systems confirmed?

2.54 What mechanisms prevent the unauthorised access to and misuse of scheme and membership data?

Share Option Scheme

2.55 Has management authorised the scheme and ensured that it conforms to the prevailing legislation and regulations?

2.56 Have the scheme rules been defined, agreed and documented, and how is compliance with them confirmed?

2.57 How is membership eligibility confirmed and what prevents the acceptance of invalid members?

2.58 How is the accuracy and validity of the option allocations confirmed?

2.59 Is the accuracy of scheme data confirmed?

2.60 When members wish to exercise their rights to purchase shares from the scheme, are their requests validated to the rules and confirmed as complying with the current taxation regulations?

2.61 Are members' payments for shares confirmed as being correct, recorded and fully accounted for?

2.62 Are all shares purchased by members from the scheme subsequently correctly registered and the appropriate ownership documentation issued?

2.63 Are members leaving the scheme or the organisation correctly advised as to their rights and liabilities?

2.64 How is accuracy of data input from other systems confirmed?

2.65 How is the accuracy of data output to other systems confirmed?

2.66 What mechanisms prevent the unauthorised access to and misuse of scheme and membership data?

Profit Related Pay

2.67 Has management authorised the scheme and ensured that it conforms to the prevailing legislation and regulations?

2.68 Have the scheme rules been defined, agreed and documented, and how is compliance with them confirmed?

2.69 How is membership eligibility confirmed and what prevents the acceptance of invalid members?

2.70 What checks are in place to confirm that all entitlements are correctly calculated, disbursed and accounted for?

2.71 What processes ensure that only eligible staff partake in the scheme and what prevents unauthorised and ineligible participation?

2.72 Are payments under the scheme authorised by management, and how is this evidenced?

2.73 Is the scheme subject to management review as to its effectiveness?

2.74 How is accuracy of data input from other systems confirmed?

2.75 How is the accuracy of data output to other systems confirmed?

2.76 What mechanisms prevent the unauthorised access to and misuse of scheme and membership data?

2.77 Has care been taken to ensure that the scheme avoids perversely incentivising staff to take excessive risks?

2.78 Are performance-related rewards made in a combination of forms (cash, shares, share options, etc.) that weight the incentive effect towards the long-term health of the organisation?

2.79 Are performance-related awards deferred appropriately until the medium to long-term impact of the executive's performance can be reliably assessed?

2.80 Are there appropriate clawback arrangements in place if performance-related awards turn out to have been misjudged, and are these applied in practice?

2.81 Are staff contracts such that the organisation avoids contractual commitments which are counter-productive to the best interests of the organisation, including its public reputation and the interests of its shareholders?

2.82 Are there clear criteria established in advance to determine performance-related rewards, and are these rigorously applied so that the awards are not automatic and are not made if specified performance is not achieved?

2.83 Are "rewards for failure" avoided?

HEALTH INSURANCE

Many employers will provide health insurance cover for their employees (with eligibility perhaps linked to a qualifying job grade, or following a probationary employment period). This section examines the issues emerging from such schemes, and includes points relevant to both externally sourced and in-house funded schemes.

Control Objectives for Health Insurance

> (a) To provide an authorised and cost-effective health insurance scheme for eligible staff.
>
> (b) To ensure that only eligible staff become members of the scheme.
>
> (c) To ensure that premiums paid by the company are correctly calculated, authorised, relative to actual membership, accounted for and are competitive.
>
> (d) To ensure that any additional contributions made by employees are correctly calculated, received and paid over to the scheme.
>
> (e) To ensure that the provision of the scheme fully complies with all the relevant legislation and taxation regulations.
>
> (f) To ensure that claims against the scheme are correctly routed and dealt with.
>
> (g) To prevent the processing of invalid or excessive claims so as to contain the operating costs to the organisation.
>
> (h) To ensure that management periodically reviews the performance and costs of the scheme so as to ensure that it continues to represent good value for money.

Risk and Control Issues for Health Insurance

1 Key Issues

1.1 Has the scheme been suitably authorised and the costs justified and negotiated on the best terms?

1.2 Have appropriate membership eligibility rules been established, and are only eligible employees accepted for membership at the appropriate time?

1.3 How does management make sure that the operation of the scheme complies with all the relevant legislation and current taxation regulations?

1.4 How are the organisation's premiums calculated, and does this process represent the actual level/type of membership?

1.5 How does management ensure that the premiums represent good value for money and that they are competitive (e.g. are they subject to review by management upon renewal)?

1.6 Are all premium payments authorised, recorded and adequately accounted for?

1.7 Are all scheme claims assessed for validity and recorded as passed over to the scheme providers?

1.8 Are excessive or invalid claims identified and prevented from being processed?

2 Detailed Issues

2.1 What processes prevent the acceptance of unauthorised, ineligible, invalid or high risk scheme members?

2.2 Has the responsibility for administering the scheme been allocated?

2.3 Have realistic and economic benefit limits been established (as a means to contain the premium costs), and are members fully aware of any such limits to scheme coverage?

2.4 Is the scheme arranged with a recognised, stable and reliable provider?

2.5 Is the performance of the scheme provider monitored and regularly assessed for value for money, etc.?

2.6 How does management ensure that any available company taxation advantages of the scheme are appropriately and legally exploited?

2.7 When applicable, are the individual members' personal benefit taxation liabilities accurately recorded and reported to the relevant authorities (e.g. as for P11D returns in the UK)?

2.8 How does management verify that the premiums paid by the organisation are accurately based on the actual scheme membership (excluding staff leavers)?

2.9 Are additional premiums to be paid directly by members correctly calculated, deducted, paid over and accounted for?

2.10 How is accuracy of data input from other systems (e.g. human resources or payroll) confirmed?

2.11 How is the accuracy of data output to other systems (e.g. general ledger) confirmed?

STAFF APPRAISAL AND DISCIPLINARY MATTERS

Staff motivation can be aided by the setting (either globally or individually) of performance and personal development targets, against which actual achievement is subsequently measured. In some formal schemes, the achievement success of employees may be linked to rewards (for example, the extent of the annual pay review). Alongside these elements is the need to identify the training and development requirements of individuals so that costly training resources can effectively be targeted and staff skill levels suitably maintained in step with the current environmental factors.

This section also addresses staff disciplinary matters and the need to establish formal complaints and disciplinary procedures.

Control Objectives for Staff Appraisal and Disciplinary Matters

(a) To ensure that staff performance is monitored and regularly appraised so that employee contributions are maximised.

(b) To ensure that the staff appraisal system is authorised by management and that the scheme is supported by realistic and workable procedures.

(c) To ensure that management and staff are fully aware of the aims of the system and their role in the process.

(d) To ensure that staff are aware of their responsibilities and have determined measurable goals and objectives to achieve.

(e) To ensure that the achievement of personal goals and objectives is monitored and reasons for non achievement identified and reviewed.

(f) To link performance and personal achievement to the reward structure.

(g) To ensure that personal training and development needs are assessed and addressed.

(h) To ensure that the appraisal process is fair, unbiased and gives employees the opportunity to comment on and agree their obligations and performance standards.

(i) To ensure that staff with consistently poor performance records are detected and dealt with accordingly.

(j) To ensure that all appraisal and disciplinary schemes operate within the confines of the prevailing employment legislation.

(k) To ensure that matters of absenteeism and misconduct are formally dealt with.

(l) To provide facilities to enable staff to bring their problems and concerns to the attention of management without fear of retribution.

(m) To provide a formal complaints and disciplinary procedure, incorporating escalation procedures, rights of appeal and representation, and defined disciplinary stages (letters of warning, withdrawal of privileges, dismissal, etc.).

Risk and Control Issues for Staff Appraisal and Disciplinary Matters

1 Key Issues

1.1 How does management confirm that staff are performing at the appropriate level and standard?

1.2 Has management authorised and established a staff appraisal system supported by documented procedures?

1.3 Does the staff appraisal scheme have the commitment of senior management, and are staff and management aware of their roles in the process?

1.4 Are staff performances assessed against realistic and measurable factors and objectives, and how are these recorded?

1.5 Is line management adequately trained and briefed for their role and responsibilities in the appraisal scheme?

1.6 Are individuals' performances regularly assessed against their defined goals and objectives, and are failures to achieve the desired standard examined to determine the underlying reasons?

1.7 Are performance shortcomings used as the basis for determining and agreeing the personal training and development needs of staff?

1.8 How does management ensure that staff training and development needs are satisfactorily and cost-effectively addressed?

1.9 Have formal, authorised and documented disciplinary procedures been established, and how is compliance assured?

1.10 Do all staff appraisal and disciplinary procedures comply with the current and relevant employment legislation, and how is compliance confirmed?

1.11 Is management assured that cases of persistent absenteeism or serious misconduct would be detected and appropriately dealt with?

1.12 In dealing with disciplinary matters, are the rights of employees adequately catered for?

2 Detailed Issues

2.1 Are all staff made aware of their responsibilities and the scope of their position?

2.2 Is line management adequately trained to consistently and fairly conduct appraisal interviews and assessments?

2.3 Is adequate account taken of employees' views and comments?

2.4 Does the system cater for the comments of management above the level of appraiser as a means of quality control?

2.5 How does management monitor that the appraisal scoring method is consistent and reliable?

2.6 Is the appraisal scheme used in a positive context as the basis for improving and developing staff, rather than in a punitive context?

2.7 Does the appraisal system enable the detection of exceptional or high performing employees who could be groomed for promotion?

2.8 Where appraisal results/scores are used as a basis for pay reviews, how can management be certain that the scores are valid and not manipulated?

2.9 Are employees required to signify their agreement to the recorded goals and objectives?

2.10 What mechanisms are in place to detect poor performance on the job?

2.11 Are regular staff, department, team or quality circle meetings encouraged in order to promote a positive attitude towards performance and contribution?

2.12 Do staff have access to alternative independent channels of communication for their problems and concerns, and the right formally to escalate their grievances (and is the relevant procedure formalised)?

2.13 Are employees' rights to have trade union, staff association or legal representation at disciplinary hearings complied with?

2.14 What steps does the organisation take to avoid the escalation of disciplinary disputes to public industrial tribunals?

2.15 What processes ensure that all the stages of the disciplinary procedure are conducted in compliance with the relevant legislation?

2.16 How is the accuracy of data input from other systems (e.g. attendance records or performance statistics) confirmed?

2.17 How is the accuracy of data output to other systems (e.g. personnel records) confirmed?

HEALTH AND SAFETY

Health and safety matters will range from general (perhaps even common sense) measures that will normally apply to every employer through to those which are specifically relative to the sector or operations of the organisation. In either case, there is an obligation on employers to ensure that all the required health and safety issues are satisfactorily addressed. Management will need to be assured that all the relevant and prevailing regulations are being complied with. Additionally, it is crucial that staff are fully aware of their responsibilities and are suitably trained in the use of any required safety equipment.

This section also touches on general security matters. Chapter 20 also features the following points about health and safety in the context of providing a suitably safe environment for staff and visitors as a part of ensuring their overall security.

Control Objectives for Health and Safety

(a) To ensure that risk assessment identifies all potential health and safety implications as the basis for rectifying exposures.

(b) To ensure that all health and safety matters are addressed for the protection of staff, visitors and customers.

(c) To ensure the relevant legislation and regulations are fully complied with.

(d) To ensure that all staff are fully aware of workplace risks, how to use safety equipment and protect themselves.

(e) To ensure that adequate safety equipment and training are provided.

(f) To ensure that machinery and equipment is effectively maintained, safely installed and protected where necessary.

(g) To provide adequate and operative fire prevention and protection facilities.

(h) To ensure that building evacuation drills are effective and regularly tested.

(i) To provide adequate security measures for the protection of staff and visitors.

(j) To ensure that all accidents and incidents are promptly reported.

(k) To ensure that appropriate, sufficient and current insurance cover is in place.

(l) To provide adequate first aid and medical facilities.

(m) To ensure that adequate hygiene and cleaning standards are maintained.

(n) To ensure that hazardous materials are correctly and safely stored.

(o) To ensure that all required certifications are obtained from regulatory bodies.

Risk and Control Issues for Health and Safety

1 Key Issues

1.1 How does management verify that they have identified and adequately addressed all health and safety risks and hazards within the organisation?

1.2 Has an authorised and documented health and safety policy been developed and implemented, and is it maintained up to date?

1.3 How does management confirm compliance with all the relevant legislation and regulations?

1.4 What processes ensure that staff are fully aware of workplace risks and how properly to use safety equipment and protect themselves?

1.5 Has sufficient and appropriate safety equipment (e.g. fire extinguishers, protective clothing) been provided, and what measures ensure that it all remains in working order and effective?

1.6 Have sufficient and effective fire prevention and protection systems been provided, and are they regularly tested?

1.7 Are adequate security measures in place to restrict access to facilities and protect staff and equipment from attack?

1.8 What steps are in place to ensure that all incidents and accidents are reported and appropriately dealt with?

1.9 Have adequate first aid and medical facilities (equipment and personnel) been provided, and are supplies replenished when used?

1.10 Are adequate hygiene and cleanliness standards established, and what mechanisms ensure that the required standards are maintained?

1.11 How does management provide and maintain adequate and appropriate insurance cover?

1.12 What mechanisms ensure that all the required regulatory inspections are conducted and that the appropriate regulatory certification is obtained?

1.13 How does management ensure that all hazardous materials are safely, correctly and securely stored?

2 Detailed Issues

2.1 Has management undertaken a risk assessment of health and safety implications throughout the organisation in order to identify the risks and ensure that they are addressed?

2.2 Has a health and safety policy been introduced, and have specific responsibilities for safety issues been allocated?

2.3 What mechanisms prevent non compliance with the prevailing health and safety regulations?

2.4 How does management maintain an up-to-date awareness of all the relevant health and safety regulations?

2.5 Are all staff adequately trained in safety matters, including use of equipment and clothing (and how can management be certain that all the relevant staff actually receive the appropriate training)?

2.6 Are staff progressively tested on their level of understanding of safety measures in order to identify further training needs?

2.7 How does management monitor that all the relevant safety equipment is maintained in working order?

2.8 Are all relevant machines fitted with guards, safety cut-outs, etc. to the required standard?

2.9 How does management monitor that all computer equipment conforms to the required standards (e.g. screen radiation levels)?

2.10 Are building evacuation, fire and security drills regularly conducted and assessed for effectiveness?

2.11 Are adequate fire alarms and security systems installed, tested and maintained (and would faults be detected promptly)?

2.12 How does management monitor that all building environmental systems (heating, lighting, air conditioning, etc.) are working correctly and to the required legal standards?

2.13 What mechanisms prevent unauthorised access to buildings and facilities?

2.14 Are the relevant staff (receptionists, door guards, post room staff, etc.) aware of the action required in the event of a bomb alert, an attack on the building, a suspicious package, and so on?

2.15 What processes ensure that the records of incidents and accidents are fully and correctly maintained in accordance with any regulatory requirements?

2.16 Are sufficient and suitably trained first aid and medical personnel available, and how can they promptly be summoned to an incident?

2.17 In the event of an emergency, how does management account for all visitors?

2.18 Are transitory safety risks (such as trailing power leads, wet floors due to cleaning) adequately addressed?

2.19 What does management do to maintain sufficient insurance cover in the event of the organisation being sued for negligence with regard to health and safety conditions?

2.20 What processes ensure that insurance cover is renewed, on time and at the appropriate level?

2.21 What processes ensure that all the required certificates and licences are obtained to enable the lawful operation of facilities?

2.22 What mechanisms prevent unauthorised access to hazardous materials?

2.23 How is accuracy of data input from other systems (e.g. human resources) confirmed?

2.24 How is the accuracy of data output to other systems (e.g. estates management) confirmed?

LABOUR RELATIONS

In larger organisations, this can be a vital area. Wherever there is a sizeable (perhaps specially skilled) workforce, it is obviously important that disruptions to such aspects as production, customer service, etc. are minimised through prompt and effective action. Dealing effectively and fairly with workforce concerns (perhaps involving trades union representation) calls for great skill and diplomacy. In the following section we incorporate pre-emptive points such as establishing effective channels of communication with staff and ensuring that all staff are kept informed of significant change and developments.

Control Objectives for Labour Relations

(a) To ensure that good labour relations are developed and maintained in order that operations and processes are not interrupted.

(b) To avoid the disruption of services to customers.

(c) To avoid costly disputes and adverse impact on the organisation's public image and reputation.

(d) To ensure that the company policy on labour relations is suitably authorised and complied with.

(e) To ensure that labour relations and negotiations are handled in accordance with the requirements of the prevailing legislation.

(f) To secure the trust and involvement of employees as a means of effectively managing change and business development.

(g) To ensure, where applicable, that relationships and negotiations with trade unions, staff associations, etc. are appropriately handled.

(h) To enable the prompt identification and rectification of potential labour problems.

Risk and Control Issues for Labour Relations

1 Key Issues

1.1 Has the organisation developed, agreed, authorised and documented a labour relations policy?

1.2 Has the basis for communicating with the workforce and their representatives been clearly established, endorsed and communicated?

1.3 How does management ensure that the organisation's labour relations policy and associated procedures fully comply with the prevailing legislation and regulations?

1.4 How does management make sure that all the requirements of the labour relations policy are complied with?

1.5 What measures are in place to avoid or cater for the disruptions and impacts of labour relation problems?

1.6 How is management sure that it would detect potential labour relations problems and be able to react promptly?

1.7 Have suitably experienced and qualified staff, familiar with negotiation and other relevant techniques, been employed and allocated the responsibility for dealing with labour relations?

1.8 Are staff (and their officially recognised representatives) actively involved in the development of the business and instances of major change?

1.9 How does management ensure that the balance of power between the organisation and staff representation is maintained?

2 Detailed Issues

2.1 Has management established effective channels of communication between themselves and the workforce (including trade unions and staff associations when applicable)?

2.2 Has management allocated a defined responsibility for handling public and media relations in the event of a labour dispute?

2.3 How does/would management protect the organisation's public image and corporate reputation during any labour dispute?

2.4 Have procedures been established which define the framework for negotiating change, pay reviews, etc., and how is management assured that all such procedures are being complied with?

2.5 Has management recognised the role of arbitration in the settlement of disputes and agreed a formal arbitration procedure with other affected parties?

2.6 Has adequate provision been made to enable staff to communicate their views to management (i.e. through staff meetings, works committees or board representation)?

2.7 Is there a formal agreement in place addressing the recognition of nominated trade unions and other representative bodies?

2.8 How is the accuracy of data input from other systems (e.g. manpower and succession planning) confirmed?

2.9 How is data output to other systems (e.g. personnel system) confirmed?

COMPANY VEHICLES

The determination of corporate company vehicle policy often resides with the human resources function, and they may even control the allocation of vehicles to staff based on the agreed policy. Although the day-to-day administration of the fleet may rest with an appropriately skilled transport function, we have intentionally included all the issues relating to company vehicles in this section.

Control Objectives for Company Vehicles

> (a) To ensure that an authorised vehicle policy is established and adhered to.
>
> (b) To ensure that vehicles are allocated to and used only by authorised and eligible staff for defined purposes.
>
> (c) To ensure that vehicles of the appropriate type are acquired at the optimum cost.
>
> (d) To ensure that all vehicle acquisitions are authorised.
>
> (e) To ensure that vehicles are operated legally and comply with all the relevant regulations.
>
> (f) To ensure that vehicles are adequately and economically maintained and operated.
>
> (g) To ensure that all vehicle expenditure is justified and authorised.
>
> (h) To ensure that vehicles are disposed of at the optimum time and price.
>
> (i) To ensure that vehicles are maintained in accordance with the warranty conditions.
>
> (j) To ensure that all accidents and damage are reported, claimed via the insurers and satisfactorily settled.
>
> (k) To ensure that all fuel costs are valid, authorised and accounted for.
>
> (l) To ensure that all vehicle costs are correctly identified, authorised and accounted for.
>
> (m) To ensure that vehicles used to deliver and distribute goods are suitably licensed and conform to the relevant regulations.
>
> (n) To ensure that suitably qualified and experienced staff are employed to administer the vehicle fleet.

Risk and Control Issues for Company Vehicles

1 Key Issues

1.1 Has a suitable company vehicle policy been developed, authorised and implemented?

1.2 What mechanisms are in place to ensure that all company vehicle purchases and allocations are authorised, in accordance with the policy, and correctly treated in the accounts?

1.3 What processes ensure that all vehicles are operated legally and in accordance with all the relevant regulations?

1.4 How does management verify that all vehicle operating costs are justified, correct, authorised and accounted for in the accounts?

1.5 What mechanisms ensure that all vehicles are regularly and adequately maintained in accordance with the warranty conditions?

1.6 What are the procedures to ensure that vehicles are disposed of at the optimum time and price, and that all disposal proceeds are correctly accounted for?

1.7 Are all accidents involving company vehicles correctly reported, processed and settled through the insurers?

1.8 How does management exercise control over fuel costs, so that only justified, appropriate and authorised fuel costs are accounted for?

2 Detailed Issues

2.1 Does the prevailing vehicle policy adequately define the authorised vehicle types and applicable staff categories?

2.2 What mechanisms prevent the acquisition of an unauthorised vehicle type?

2.3 If vehicle price limits are established, how are purchases exceeding the limit prevented?

2.4 How does management ensure that vehicles are purchased at the best negotiated prices?

2.5 Are vehicles purchased only from reputable dealers/agents, and what mechanisms prevent dealings with unauthorised suppliers?

2.6 Are appropriate discounted terms arranged with manufacturers in the event of quantity purchases?

2.7 How are all vehicle purchases authorised, and what prevents an invalid transaction being processed?

2.8 Are all new vehicles subject to inspection and would faulty or damaged vehicles be detected and rejected?

2.9 How can management be certain that all vehicle purchase costs are accurately identified and correctly accounted for (i.e. in the fixed assets records)?

2.10 Has an authorised company vehicle depreciation policy been implemented, and does it follow normal accounting practice or fiscal legislation?

2.11 Has an adequate vehicle fleet administration department been established, with suitably qualified and experienced staff?

2.12 How are all legal and regulatory matters dealt with (road fund licences, adequate insurance cover, vehicle roadworthiness, legal emission levels, etc.)?

2.13 Would failures to comply with legal and regulatory requirements be promptly detected and rectified?

2.14 How does management monitor that all company vehicle drivers are (and remain) correctly licensed and eligible (including heavy goods vehicle and specialist vehicle drivers)?

2.15 What mechanisms ensure that goods vehicle drivers are operating in accordance with the prevailing legislation (including permitted driving hours, correct utilisation of tachographs, etc.)?

2.16 Are drivers made fully aware of their responsibilities for vehicles allocated to them and made to sign for the vehicle in good condition upon allocation?

2.17 Are all company vehicles correctly and adequately insured, and are drivers aware of their responsibilities in the event of an accident?

2.18 Are company vehicles adequately protected against theft?

2.19 What checks are in place to monitor that vehicles are serviced and maintained in accordance with the manufacturers' recommendations and relevant warranty conditions?

2.20 What mechanisms ensure that all valid warranty claims are identified, processed and settled?

2.21 How does management verify that all vehicle maintenance and repair costs are justified and authorised?

2.22 What controls prevent non company vehicle costs being accepted and processed?

2.23 Are all company vehicles traceable to a named driver and location?

2.24 Does the vehicle administration system alert management to forthcoming events and actions (e.g. renewal of taxation)?

2.25 Would management be able promptly to identify unusually high vehicle servicing costs for an individual vehicle?

2.26 Is regular and accurate vehicle fleet management information provided, and how is follow-up action to reported anomalies evidenced?

2.27 Is the system capable of highlighting vehicles that are either approaching their disposal date or have excessive associated costs?

2.28 Are all maintenance and repairs conducted only by suitably qualified and authorised suppliers to the necessary standard (and how is the standard confirmed)?

2.29 Have emergency and out-of-hours breakdown facilities been cost-effectively provided, and are the relative costs monitored?

2.30 Has management established an authorised policy for vehicle fuel costs, and what prevents unauthorised or invalid fuel costs being met by the company (e.g. for private journeys)?

2.31 Are company fuel cards issued only to authorised employees, and what mechanisms prevent their misuse?

2.32 Are fuel costs reported, adequately monitored and followed up by management?

2.33 What is the procedure for reporting accidents?

2.34 What steps are in place to ensure that all accident damage is suitably inspected and assessed for repair cost in order that actual costs are reasonable and authorised?

2.35 How does management confirm that all accident repair costs are justified, authorised and reclaimed from insurers whenever possible?

2.36 Are accident claims adequately monitored to ensure prompt and appropriate settlement?

2.37 How does management verify that vehicle insurance arrangements are appropriate, legal, and offer good value for money?

2.38 How are vehicles for disposal identified, and is the basis for disposal at the optimum time for the company and the resale market?

2.39 How does management ensure that the company receives a fair market price for vehicle disposals?

2.40 Are all vehicles assessed for their likely disposal value and monitored to ensure that the actual proceeds are reasonable?

2.41 Has management established authorised disposal methods for company vehicles (e.g. via car auctions, dealers, staff sales) and how can they be sure that only authorised disposal outlets are used?

2.42 How is management certain that all vehicle disposal proceeds are correctly identified and fully accounted for?

2.43 Are management made aware of the value of disposal proceeds against the written-down value of the vehicle in the company books, and would unfavourable variances be promptly highlighted?

2.44 Are disposal proceeds subject to management authority and monitoring, and how is this evidenced?

2.45 How are all vehicle write-offs justified and suitably authorised, and what prevents the unauthorised write-off of a vehicle?

2.46 How is the accuracy of data input from other systems (e.g. authorised drivers from the personnel records) confirmed?

2.47 How is accuracy of data output to other systems (e.g. vehicle disposals to the fixed asset system, or servicing costs to the accounts payable system) confirmed?

19

Auditing Research and Development

INTRODUCTION

In this chapter we consider research and development (R&D).

Ethics

Before looking at the individual functions of R&D, we'll look briefly at a subject of growing importance within research and development—ethics.

Ethics is a theme never far away from the contents of this book. For instance, Chapter 21 considers environmental ethics issues.

SYSTEM/FUNCTION COMPONENTS OF RESEARCH AND DEVELOPMENT

We have chosen to use an essentially *functional* approach to define the research and development audit universe, which gives us the following possible breakdown of the key functions, systems or activities:

- product development
- project appraisal and monitoring
- plant and equipment
- development
- project management
- legal and regulatory issues.

CONTROL OBJECTIVES AND RISK AND CONTROL ISSUES

We shall now examine the control objectives and risk and control issues (divided into key issues and detailed issues) for each of the research and development functions listed above. This data can be used within the Standard Audit Programme Guides (SAPGs) looked at in Chapter 3. To save space we have concentrated on the objectives to be stated and the questions to be asked and have not presented these within the SAPG format.

The data supplied in the following sections are deliberately general and broad in nature, so that they can be related to a range of possible organisational scenarios. However, in practice, all manner of specific industry or sector factors may apply and these should then be suitably incorporated into the data. Conversely, some of the issues raised may not apply (either in organisational or national terms) and these can accordingly be disregarded. The overall aim of the supplied data is to provide a general awareness of the likely elements for each activity.

PRODUCT DEVELOPMENT

Organisations will need to define the future strategy for their products and allocate appropriate resources to support their objectives in this area. This section examines such objectives from the research and development viewpoint, where such R&D activities are handled in-house. This stance presupposes that the relevant organisation has the requisite facilities, resources and expertise to conduct an R&D exercise, and therefore we exclude the considerations applicable to the set-up of an R&D facility.

See also the points discussed in Chapter 16 under the heading "Product Development", which refer to the ongoing development of new and improved products as a vital part of an overall marketing policy and plan.

Control Objectives for Product Development

(a) To ensure that new and existing products are researched and developed in accordance with market factors and the defined strategic objectives of the organisation.

(b) To ensure that all product developments are fully assessed in relation to the potential market, estimated production costs and selling price.

(c) To ensure that R&D resources are adequate and targeted on those areas with the greatest potential for the organisation.

(d) To ensure that R&D facilities, resources and costs are commensurate with the planned activities.

(e) To ensure that management maintains an accurate and up-to-date awareness of current technological trends and their potential application for the organisation.

(f) To ensure that an adequate level of general/speculative research is undertaken to enable the organisation to achieve a technological advantage over its competitors.

(g) To ensure that the resources required to undertake research and development are accurately identified, costed, justified and authorised.

(h) To ensure that all product development and research projects are suitably assessed and authorised to proceed.

(i) To ensure that the design assessment, feasibility and product specification processes are adequate and address matters of quality and performance.

(j) To ensure that the research activity, theories, specifications, drawings, technology, and the eventual products are adequately protected from exploitation by others.

(k) To ensure that research and development activities do not, in themselves, violate existing patents and copyrights.

(l) To ensure that the use of external research and specialist facilities is subject to assessment, authorisation, monitoring, and effective levels of security.

(m) To ensure that specialist staff are recruited, appropriately trained, and retained for the benefit of the organisation.

(n) To ensure that all information about the organisation's product developments and research programme remains confidential.

(o) To ensure that all the actual development costs are correctly identified and monitored against the established budgets.

(p) To ensure that the progress of all research and development projects is adequately monitored by management and appropriate changes are applied when necessary and authorised.

(q) To ensure that adequate, appropriate and legally required levels of testing are conducted and evidenced.

(r) To ensure that all significant project variations or problems are promptly reported to management for corrective action.

(s) To ensure that the objectives and performance criteria established at the outset of the development are actually achieved.

(t) To ensure that all the relevant legal and regulatory requirements are met.

(u) To ensure that the market launch of new or modified products is adequately planned, appropriately timed to maximise the market impact, coordinated between the affected functions, and monitored.

Risk and Control Issues for Product Development

1 Key Issues

1.1 Has management defined and authorised strategic business objectives, and what checks are in place to ensure that all product developments and research activities comply with these targets?

1.2 Has management established, authorised and implemented documented procedures for the development and evolution of all product ranges?

1.3 How does management keep product plans adequate, appropriate, viable, etc.?

1.4 How is management sure that all product development projects are valid, justified and authorised?

1.5 What processes govern the direction of research activities in order to ensure that attention is focused on those projects with the greatest potential benefit and implications for the organisation?

1.6 Have an R&D strategy and plan been developed, documented and authorised, and what steps are taken to monitor progress and achievements?

1.7 How does management ensure that R&D resources are justified, adequate and relative to the planned activities?

1.8 How does management maintain an accurate and up-to-date awareness of all current technologies, innovations, etc. with a potential impact for the organisation?

1.9 Beyond the specific product development projects, is the organisation sufficiently active in general and sector-related speculative research in order that a technological advantage is maintained over competitors and industry entrants?

1.10 What processes ensure that all the resources required to undertake the development are accurately identified, costed, justified and authorised?

1.11 What measures ensure that clear (and authorised) objectives and targets are established for each project (and is their achievement monitored and confirmed)?

1.12 How is management assured that the design assessment, feasibility and specification processes are adequate and satisfactorily address quality, performance and regulatory standards?

1.13 What measures are taken for adequate protection of research activities, intellectual property, specifications and all research plans and data from exploitation by others or unauthorised exposure?

1.14 How does management ensure that research activities do not violate existing patents and copyrights?

1.15 Are all product developments subject to adequate project management in order to cater for the following aspects:

- adequate coordination of all affected functions to ensure achievement of development objectives
- definition of key stages of the project and the ongoing monitoring of actual progress against target
- authorisation and control of all project resources and costs?

1.16 What steps does management take to retain the skills and knowledge of key specialist staff, and prevent others benefiting from the individual's expertise?

1.17 What measures ensure that new or modified products are subject to extensive, adequate and appropriate testing (including any sector-specific, legally required or specialist product testing requirements)?

2 Detailed Issues

2.1 What mechanisms prevent the investigation or development of a product outside the defined and authorised strategic parameters of the business?

2.2 Has management defined and authorised product development plans with the intention of extending and prolonging the life of existing products and introducing viable new lines?

2.3 How does management ensure that its product plans remain relevant, up to date and in step with customer needs and market developments?

2.4 Is appropriate account taken of competitor analysis and are critical marketing timing considerations identified and planned for in the research programme?

2.5 What measures are in place to ensure that crucial costs and selling price targets are identified and monitored for achievement throughout the project?

2.6 How does management ensure that research projects, product details, development plans and business development strategies remain confidential?

2.7 What measures would prevent unauthorised research and development costs?

2.8 When applicable, does the organisation take appropriate advantage of available government and research grants (and what measures ensure that eligibility for such schemes is maintained)?

2.9 Are all appropriate technologies, processes and techniques developed by the organisation adequately protected (at the most appropriate time) from exploitation by others (and how can this be assured)?

2.10 Are key staff involved in product development subject to fidelity bonding or commercial confidentiality clauses in their employment contracts?

2.11 What steps does management take to ensure that adequate numbers of specialist staff are recruited and that their skill levels are maintained through authorised training, etc.?

2.12 If relevant expertise or specialist knowledge exists outside the organisation, how does management ensure that the engagement of such external specialists is justified, authorised, accurately costed, and that progress is monitored?

2.13 What measures ensure that external consultants will not exploit and/or pass on details of the research they are conducting on the organisation's behalf?

2.14 How does management ensure that problems, shortcomings, cost overruns, etc. would promptly be detected and reported?

2.15 What processes ensure that all R&D costs are identified, accounted for, and reflected in the corporate accounts?

2.16 What mechanisms ensure the correct accounting treatment of R&D costs and the recovery of related taxation benefits whenever applicable?

2.17 Have adequate arrangements been made to provide management with regular, accurate and relevant project information (progress, costs versus budgets, failures to achieve deadlines, technical problems, etc.)?

2.18 Where appropriate, are products subject to testing under recognised trade, national or international quality/standards schemes?

2.19 Prior to commercial launch, how does management know that products are subject to the appropriate licensing by government or trade regulators?

2.20 Upon launch of the product, how does management ensure that adequate plans are in place to address such matters as:

- adequacy of stocks
- provision of staff training
- launch timing to maximise the market impact
- coordination of all affected functions, etc.?

2.21 How is the accuracy of data input from other systems (e.g. market research or planning) confirmed?

2.22 How is the accuracy of data output to other systems (e.g. production control, sales management, etc.) confirmed?

PROJECT APPRAISAL AND MONITORING

Here we examine the issues surrounding the identification of potential projects, the appraisal of R&D projects leading to their justification and authorisation to proceed, and the general monitoring of costs and progress against those planned for and approved.

Control Objectives for Project Appraisal and Monitoring

(a) To ensure that all research and development activities are in accordance with the defined and authorised strategic objectives of the organisation.

(b) To ensure that all R&D projects are fully assessed in respect of technical implications, product potential, equipment and tooling costs, timescale, research costs, production costs, selling price, and so on.

(c) To ensure that project appraisals are effectively conducted in order to assure management as to the value and justification of the project under review.

(d) To provide (where justified) a formal, documented and authorised project appraisal procedure and ensure compliance.

(e) To recommend to management those projects that should be implemented and to obtain management authorisation to proceed.

(f) To ensure that the appraisal process identifies and accurately costs the R&D resources required to fulfil the project.

(g) To ensure that the key project stages and deliverables are identified and monitored for achievement.

(h) To ensure that key responsibilities are defined and allocated.

(i) To ensure that an appropriate project management framework is defined and established.

(j) To ensure that budgets are established and monitored against actual expenditure and efforts.

(k) To ensure that the progress of the research and development project is adequately monitored and that shortcomings, variations, etc. are promptly identified and dealt with.

(l) To ensure that all the key stages and project objectives are met on time and within budget.

(m) To ensure that management is provided with adequate, timely and accurate information on project progress, costs, etc.

(n) To ensure that all the relevant legal and regulatory requirements are identified, monitored and fulfilled.

Risk and Control Issues for Project Appraisal and Monitoring

1 Key Issues

1.1 Has management defined and authorised strategic business objectives, and how can they be sure that all R&D activities comply with these targets?

1.2 Have formal, documented and authorised project appraisal procedures been defined and implemented (and if so, how is compliance with them ensured)?

1.3 How does management verify that all R&D activities are valid, justified and authorised (and what mechanisms prevent unauthorised activities)?

1.4 Are all R&D projects subject to adequate appraisals incorporating the following factors:

- technical implications
- product and market potential
- research costs
- equipment and tooling costs
- estimated production costs
- project timescale
- specialist requirements, etc.?

1.5 How does management make sure that the appraisal staff will conduct the assessment in an objective, considered and professional manner?

1.6 How does management signify their authorisation to proceed with an R&D project, and what prevents the initiation of an unauthorised project?

1.7 Does the appraisal process identify and cost all the R&D resources required to fulfil the project?

1.8 What measures ensure that clear (and authorised) objectives, key stages, targets and deliverables are identified and established for each R&D project?

1.9 What mechanisms ensure that the project budgets, and all the factors noted in point 1.4 above, are adequately monitored and achieved?

1.10 What measures ensure that all key responsibilities are defined, allocated and monitored?

1.11 Would management promptly be made aware of project progress shortcomings, problems and delays, and what measures ensure that objectives are met on time and within budget?

2 Detailed Issues

2.1 Are all R&D project costs subject to effective accounting and budgetary control (and would significant variations promptly be brought to management's attention)?

2.2 Are all the management information requirements identified and addressed (and how can the accuracy and reliability of such data be assured)?

2.3 Is overall responsibility for managing and coordinating the project allocated, and is the nominated individual charged with the appropriate authority to achieve the defined objectives?

2.4 Has a formal, documented and appropriate project management framework been established to progress and monitor the project?

2.5 Have steps been taken to consult with and coordinate the action of all the affected functions so that the project objectives and timescales are satisfactorily achieved?

2.6 Are all costs outside the authorised budgets subject to prior justification and special authority?

2.7 What measures ensure that all the relevant legal and regulatory requirements are identified and appropriately addressed?

2.8 How is accuracy of data input from other systems (e.g. corporate planning or industry regulation) confirmed?

2.9 How is accuracy of data output to other systems (e.g. budgetary control) confirmed?

PLANT AND EQUIPMENT

R&D projects often require the acquisition or manufacture of specialised pieces of equipment (such as test or calibration devices). In this section we consider the procurement, accounting treatment, installation, usage, maintenance and eventual disposal of such R&D equipment.

Control Objectives for Plant and Equipment

(a) To ensure that all R&D plant and equipment requirements are accurately identified, justified and authorised.

(b) To ensure that appropriate resources are made available in order to support project activities and meet the defined R&D objectives.

(c) To ensure that R&D equipment and associated costs are commensurate with planned activities.

(d) To ensure that R&D assets are accurately identified, recorded, correctly accounted for, suitably valued and periodically verified.

(e) To ensure that all R&D equipment costs are accurately identified, authorised and allocated to related projects, etc.

(f) To ensure that R&D and specialist equipment is adequately maintained in full working order and accurately calibrated.

(g) To ensure that redundant, underused, surplus or obsolete equipment is promptly identified and authorised for appropriate disposal.

(h) To ensure that staff have the relevant skills to correctly use R&D and specialist equipment.

Risk and Control Issues for Plant and Equipment

1 Key Issues

1.1 How are R&D plant and equipment requirements defined, and is the acquisition of such equipment subject to formal prior justification and authorisation (and if so, how is this evidenced)?

1.2 What mechanisms prevent the unauthorised procurement of R&D equipment outwith the project budget?

1.3 How does management ensure that equipment is obtained using the most advantageous funding method (i.e. purchase, leasing, etc.)?

1.4 What measures ensure that all R&D assets are accurately identified, recorded in the accounts and correctly valued?

1.5 What mechanisms ensure that the correct and appropriate accounting treatment is applied to R&D assets?

1.6 Does management take adequate steps periodically to confirm the existence and valuation of all R&D assets (and would untraced or incorrectly valued items be identified and investigated)?

1.7 Are all R&D equipment costs (i.e. acquisition, supply of consumables and ongoing maintenance) identified, accounted for and accurately allocated to specific R&D projects?

1.8 How does management monitor that all R&D equipment is appropriately and regularly maintained in working order (and are the associated costs authorised and accounted for)?

1.9 What steps does management take to avoid the accumulation of underused, redundant or obsolete items of R&D equipment?

1.10 What measures ensure that surplus items of R&D equipment are authorised for disposal and that the relevant proceeds are maximised and accounted for?

1.11 How does management monitor that specialist equipment is being correctly used by research staff in order to support the validity of research and development activities?

2 Detailed Issues

2.1 How does management verify that decisions to obtain R&D equipment are appropriately related to the significance, length and perceived value of projects (e.g. are those high-value items required for short-term projects leased or hired, rather than being purchased outright)?

2.2 Can all R&D assets be promptly traced and located at any time?

2.3 Are orders and invoices for all R&D equipment authorised at the appropriate level?

2.4 How does management verify that the values of R&D equipment reflected in the company accounts are accurate, up to date and verified?

2.5 Are write-offs of R&D assets subject to specific authorisation, and how is this evidenced?

2.6 What measures ensure that items of long-term R&D plant are correctly treated as fixed assets and appropriately depreciated over an acceptable period?

2.7 Are R&D equipment requirements for specific projects justified and authorised as part of the overall project appraisal process?

2.8 Are project equipment budgets authorised, established, effectively monitored, and followed up when necessary (and how are investigations of variances evidenced)?

2.9 What steps are taken to ensure that specialist equipment is correctly installed and calibrated?

2.10 What measures prevent the unauthorised disposal of R&D equipment?

2.11 How are all disposal proceeds identified and accounted for?

2.12 How does management ensure that the best prices are obtained against equipment disposals (and are such arrangements authorised)?

2.13 How is the accuracy of data input from other systems (e.g. project appraisal) confirmed?

2.14 How is the accuracy of data output to other systems (e.g. fixed assets or project accounting) confirmed?

DEVELOPMENT PROJECT MANAGEMENT

Here we consider the management and progress of an R&D project from the point of authorisation to its ultimate completion. On the way, aspects such as cost and progress monitoring, the provision of adequate and accurate project information, and the achievement of defined objectives are considered. See also Chapter 12, which has a section on "Product/Project Accounting".

Control Objectives for Development Project Management

> (a) To ensure that all R&D projects are effectively managed so that the objectives and key criteria established at the outset of the project are cost-effectively and efficiently achieved.

(b) To ensure that all the resources required to undertake research and development projects are accurately identified, costed, justified, authorised and provided.

(c) To ensure that project management responsibilities and accountabilities are defined and allocated.

(d) To ensure that all the actual project costs are correctly identified, accounted for and monitored against the established budgets.

(e) To ensure that the progress of all projects is adequately monitored by management and that appropriate changes are authorised and applied when necessary.

(f) To ensure that adequate, accurate and timely management information is provided.

(g) To ensure that adequate, appropriate and legally required levels of testing are conducted and evidenced.

(h) To ensure that all the relevant legal and regulatory requirements are correctly addressed.

Risk and Control Issues for Development Project Management

1 Key Issues

1.1 Have formal project management procedures been defined, authorised and implemented (and if so, how is management assured that the procedures are adhered to)?

1.2 Has management defined and authorised the project objectives, and how can they be sure that these will be achieved?

1.3 Have key project targets and deliverables been identified, and are they subject to ongoing monitoring throughout the project?

1.4 What processes ensure that all the required project resources are accurately identified, costed, justified, authorised and provided?

1.5 What measures are in place to ensure that adequate and suitable staff resources are made available for the duration of the project (and have any training requirements been satisfactorily addressed)?

1.6 Have management responsibilities been formally allocated to named individuals, and how do they report on their progress, etc.?

1.7 How is management assured that all project costs are correctly accounted for and monitored against the defined budgets?

1.8 Are all R&D projects subject to adequate ongoing management in order to cater for the following aspects:

- adequate coordination of all the affected functions to ensure achievement of the project objectives
- definition of key stages of the project and the ongoing monitoring of actual progress against targets and budgets
- authorisation and control of all project resources and costs?

1.9 What steps are taken to ensure that adequate, timely, accurate and relevant project information is generated and circulated to management?

1.10 What measures are in place to ensure that any project problems, shortcomings or budget problems would promptly be identified and reported for action?

1.11 How does management keep abreast of all the relevant legal and regulatory requirements, and ensure appropriate compliance is attained?

2 Detailed Issues

2.1 Have accurate and realistic timing and cost targets been set for projects?

2.2 What measures prevent unauthorised project expenditure or activities, and how would management be made aware of them?

2.3 Have sufficiently detailed budgets been established, and are they subject to ongoing monitoring against actual costs?

2.4 What processes ensure that all R&D costs are identified and correctly reflected in the project and company accounts?

2.5 Have adequate arrangements been made to provide management with regular, accurate and relevant project information (such as progress, actual costs versus budgets, failures to achieve deadlines, technical problems)?

2.6 Have quality and performance targets been established, and what measures ensure that they are cost-effectively achieved?

2.7 If project objectives prove to be impossible or unreasonably expensive to achieve, are they reviewed by senior management so that either expenditure limits are authorised for amendment or the objectives are amended?

2.8 Who has the authority to abandon an unsuccessful project, and what measures are in place to fully assess the impact of such a decision?

2.9 How does management monitor that products and technologies under development are adequately and appropriately tested?

2.10 Where necessary, are product testing programmes related to the achievement of recognised national, regulatory or legally required standards?

2.11 How are the conclusions and outcomes of R&D projects presented and converted into the related production processes, and are they subject to formal commercial and financial assessment before proceeding?

2.12 How is the accuracy of data input from other systems (e.g. budgetary control and project control system) confirmed?

2.13 How is the accuracy of data output to other systems (e.g. project accounting) confirmed?

LEGAL AND REGULATORY ISSUES

Many industries (e.g. pharmaceuticals and chemicals) are governed by an array of legal and regulatory conditions. This segment takes account of the need to ensure that any legal and/or regulatory requirements are accurately identified and effectively addressed as part of the overall R&D environment. Also included are aspects such as protecting research activities (e.g. through patents), ensuring that new R&D projects do not violate existing patents and copyrights, and identifying possible sources of external funding for R&D.

Control Objectives for Legal and Regulatory Issues

(a) To ensure that all the relevant and prevailing legal and regulatory issues are identified, addressed and complied with.

(b) To ensure that defined quality, performance and testing standards are achieved.

(c) To ensure that all research activity, theories, specification, drawings, technologies and products are adequately protected from exploitation by others.

(d) To ensure that research and development activities do not, in themselves, violate existing patents and copyrights.

(e) To ensure that projects comply with the conditions of any grant funding schemes.

(f) To ensure that all processes utilised during the R&D project fully comply with the relevant health and safety standards.

(g) To ensure that, when appropriate, project facilities and products obtain the necessary certifications.

Risk and Control Issues for Legal and Regulatory Issues

1 Key Issues

1.1 How does management verify that all the relevant and prevailing legal and regulatory issues have been accurately identified and planned for?

1.2 What mechanisms are in place to prevent liabilities for legal penalties and related commercial and reputation implications?

1.3 Has management identified and addressed all the industry quality, safety, testing and performance standards, and have the relevant certifications and accreditations been obtained?

1.4 Have the resource and cost implications of compliance been accurately determined and authorised?

1.5 What measures are taken to protect adequately research activities, intellectual property, specifications, technologies, innovations and data from exploitation by others and unauthorised exposure?

1.6 How does management ensure that research activities do not violate existing patents and copyrights?

1.7 Does management fully investigate the possibility of offsetting R&D costs by identifying and applying for available government and trade research funding grants?

1.8 What steps are taken to ensure that the project remains eligible to receive grant funding and that amounts due are received, correctly applied, and accounted for?

1.9 Does management ensure that all projects are assessed for health and safety implications as the basis for providing all the required precautions, equipment and staff training?

1.10 How is management confident that any failure to comply with relevant laws and regulations would be promptly identified for action?

2 Detailed Issues

2.1 Are the costs associated with regulatory and legal compliance accurately identified, authorised, accounted for and monitored against budget?

2.2 Does management take appropriate and prompt action to protect the various aspects of in-house research by filing patent applications?

2.3 How does management ensure that the level of legal protection obtained for R&D activities is sufficient (e.g. are overseas patents required and justified)?

2.4 What precautions are in place to prevent unauthorised access, copying or manipulation of R&D project materials?

2.5 How does management ensure that adequate investigations are conducted into existing third-party research activities, patents and published materials which may present legal implications for the proposed R&D project?

2.6 How does management maintain an accurate awareness of all the potential sources of grant funding?

2.7 What steps are taken to ensure that grant income is fully accounted for and only used for the defined purposes?

2.8 How does management ensure that the maximum benefit is derived from grant income?

2.9 When considering applications for grants, are all the implications assessed (e.g. stipulations that the resultant research must be published for general use)?

2.10 Where products have to be officially registered before being marketed, what steps are taken to minimise the possibility of failure?

2.11 When applicable and commercially acceptable, are the benefits of jointly funded research projects fully assessed and authorised?

2.12 How is the accuracy of data input from other systems confirmed?

2.13 How is the accuracy of data output to other systems (e.g. industry regulation) confirmed?

20
Auditing Security

INTRODUCTION

In this chapter we shall examine security matters within a typical organisation. This subject is, as you would expect, primarily concerned with the protection of property, premises and persons so that the business can continue to be conducted without disruption or material loss. However, when considering the broader implications of security, account should also be taken of matters beyond the physical—for example, of less tangible elements such as corporate data or intellectual property.

Protection processes aim to avoid theft of and/or damage to property and premises owned or used by the organisation. Where an organisation is involved in trading, the loss of or damage to stock not only represents an unwanted disruption, but may actually result in an inability to continue operating.

So that management can take appropriate, adequate and cost-effective steps to prevent or contain such disruptions, it will be necessary for them to take a realistic view of their situation from a risk assessment standpoint. Without obtaining an accurate assessment of the inherent risks, management cannot expect to react accordingly and cost-effectively. Indeed, one of the essential elements of any effective control environment is the practice of risk assessment (see Chapters 6 and 7). Most areas of operational risk can be offset by the provision of suitable and cost-effective insurance and we shall also be looking at the arrangements for insurance cover.

Although this subject area is normally focused on those physical and preventive measures that guard against unauthorised access and unrestricted movement within company premises, there are related safety aspects that also need to be taken into consideration. These range from the obvious fire prevention and detection systems to more explicit situations where the very operations themselves have significant safety implications. For example, the storage and use of hazardous chemicals or the dangers associated with a large-scale industrial process. Beyond the practical dimensions associated with these subjects and the physical dangers they can present, there are likely to be stringent regulatory and legislative requirements that will need to be addressed. Accordingly, management will have to actively demonstrate that the appropriate action has been taken and that the prevailing laws have been complied with.

In the context of protecting employees we also set out control objectives and risks and control issues for the subject of health and safety; this is also covered in the chapter on human resource management, Chapter 18.

As with most fundamental elements of business operations, the topics of security and health and safety should ideally be the subject of a formal and documented corporate policy, so that all affected parties are aware of their responsibilities and the required actions.

CONTROL OBJECTIVES AND RISK AND CONTROL ISSUES

We shall now examine the control objectives and the related risk and control issues (divided into key issues and detailed issues) for each of the following activity areas:

- security
- health and safety
- insurance.

This data can be used within the Standard Audit Programme Guides (SAPGs) looked at in Chapter 3. To save space we have concentrated on the objectives to be stated and the questions to be asked and have not presented them within the SAPG format.

SECURITY

Control Objectives for Security

(a) To ensure that adequate and appropriate security measures are in place in order to protect assets, persons and business activities.

(b) To ensure that company property is adequately protected from theft, loss and damage.

(c) To ensure that risks are appropriately assessed as the basis for providing effective counter-measures.

(d) To ensure that the costs associated with security measures are accurately determined, justified and authorised.

(e) To ensure that adequate., trustworthy and appropriately trained security staff are provided.

(f) To ensure that adequate and operational security and fire alarms systems are provided, tested and maintained.

(g) To ensure that staff are aware of their responsibilities in respect of security (i.e. personal and company property).

> (h) To ensure that adequate emergency and evacuation drills are defined and regularly tested for their effectiveness.
>
> (i) To prevent unauthorised access to company premises and to account for the movement and access of all visitors.

Risk and Control Issues for Security

1 Key Issues

1.1 What measures are in place to prevent the following:
- unauthorised access to company premises
- theft of company property from premises
- damage and disruption caused by vandalism, burglary and other security threats?

1.2 Have potential risks and security threats been adequately defined and assessed?

1.3 Are authorised and documented security policies in place (e.g. for controlling access to premises by visitors), and how is management assured that the procedures are adhered to?

1.4 How does management monitor that security measures are effective and in line with changing situations?

1.5 What measures are applied to ensure that security staff are suitably trained, appropriately experienced and trustworthy?

1.6 What processes ensure that security, intruder and fire alarm systems are adequate, operative, suitably maintained and tested?

1.7 How are staff made aware of their security and personal safety responsibilities (and how does management ensure that staff awareness of such matters is adequately maintained)?

1.8 Have documented procedures and instructions been implemented for emergency drills, building evacuations and contingency arrangements (and how is their effectiveness assessed)?

1.9 How does management accurately identify the costs associated with all security measures, and are these subject to effective authorisation and monitoring?

2. Detailed Issues

2.1 How does management ascertain that current security measures relate to and address the potential risks?

2.2 Are all operational and physical changes adequately assessed for their impact on the security arrangements (and how is this review process evidenced)?

2.3 How does management ensure that only staff and suitably authorised visitors gain access to company premises?

2.4 What security precautions are taken to prevent unauthorised access to especially sensitive or critical facilities (e.g. main computer installation or cash handling areas)?

2.5 Are the staff employed in sensitive areas subject to appropriate pre-employment checks and/or fidelity bonding (where this is justified)?

2.6 How can bona fide employees be reliably identified by security personnel and other employees?

2.7 What measures are in place to identify and trail all keys to company premises?

2.8 How are building and office keys allocated to employees, and what measures prevent unauthorised staff, past employees and other persons gaining access to company keys?

2.9 What steps are in place to ensure that all keys and other access devices are recovered from employees leaving the company?

2.10 How are staff made aware of their responsibilities for security?

2.11 What measures are in place to prevent the unauthorised removal of company property and goods from the premises?

2.12 What measures are in place to identify and effectively deal with suspicious or unattended packages on company premises?

2.13 Are reception and security staff aware of the required action to take in the event of a bomb threat, physical assault on the building, etc.?

2.14 Are fire and security alarms systems regularly tested and any faults reported and dealt with?

2.15 What security measures are taken out of normal office/operational hours (and are they justified)?

2.16 Are documented procedures in place in the event of a fire, and are all staff and visitors accounted for?

2.17 Are procedures in place to summon the relevant emergency services (fire, police or ambulance)?

2.18 How does management ensure that existing security and related safety matters fully comply with the prevailing laws, by-laws and regulations?

2.19 Have all company premises been assessed by the appropriate external agency and confirmed or certified as being of an appropriate standard (and if not, are all shortcomings adequately dealt with)?

2.20 Would management be made aware of uneconomic or unjustified security measures?

2.21 Are costs associated with security incidents accurately determined and claimed via the insurers whenever appropriate?

2.22 What specific access arrangements are made for visiting consultants, tradesmen, representatives and contractors (and how is their access restricted to the relevant areas)?

2.23 How is the accuracy of data input from other systems (e.g. staff recruitment) confirmed?

2.24 How is the accuracy of data output to other systems confirmed?

HEALTH AND SAFETY

Health and safety matters will range from general (perhaps even common sense) measures that will normally apply to every employer through to those which are specifically relative to the sector or operations of the organisation. In either case, there is an obligation on employers to ensure that all the required health and safety issues are satisfactorily addressed. Management will need to be assured that all the relevant and prevailing regulations are being complied with. Additionally, it is crucial that staff are fully aware of their responsibilities and are suitably trained in the use of any required safety equipment.

Control Objectives for Health and Safety

(a) To ensure that risk assessment identifies all potential health and safety implications as the basis for rectifying exposures.

(b) To ensure that all health and safety matters are addressed for the protection of staff, visitors and customers.

(c) To ensure the relevant legislation and regulations are fully complied with.

(d) To ensure that all staff are fully aware of workplace risks, how to use safety equipment and protect themselves.

(e) To ensure that adequate safety equipment and training are provided.

(f) To ensure that machinery and equipment is effectively maintained, safely installed and protected where necessary.

(g) To provide adequate and operative fire prevention and protection facilities.

(h) To ensure that building evacuation drills are effective and regularly tested.

(i) To provide adequate security measures for the protection of staff and visitors.

(j) To ensure that all accidents and incidents are promptly reported.

> (k) To ensure that appropriate, sufficient and current insurance cover is in place.
>
> (l) To provide adequate first aid and medical facilities.
>
> (m) To ensure that adequate hygiene and cleaning standards are maintained.
>
> (n) To ensure that hazardous materials are correctly and safely stored.
>
> (o) To ensure that all required certifications are obtained from regulatory bodies.

Risk and Control Issues for Health and Safety

1 Key Issues

1.1 How does management verify that it has identified and adequately addressed all health and safety risks and hazards within the organisation?

1.2 Has an authorised and documented health and safety policy been developed and implemented, and is it kept up to date?

1.3 How does management confirm compliance with all the relevant legislation and regulations?

1.4 What processes ensure that staff are fully aware of workplace risks and how properly to use safety equipment and protect themselves?

1.5 Has sufficient and appropriate safety equipment (e.g. fire extinguishers, protective clothing) been provided, and what measures ensure that it all remains in working order and effective?

1.6 Have sufficient and effective fire prevention and protection systems been provided, and are they regularly tested?

1.7 Are adequate security measures in place to restrict access to facilities and protect staff and equipment from attack?

1.8 What steps are in place to ensure that all incidents and accidents are reported and appropriately dealt with?

1.9 Have adequate first aid and medical facilities (equipment and personnel) been provided, and are supplies replenished when used?

1.10 Are adequate hygiene and cleanliness standards established, and what mechanisms ensure that the required standards are maintained?

1.11 How does management provide and maintain adequate and appropriate insurance cover?

1.12 What mechanisms ensure that all the required regulatory inspections are conducted and that the appropriate regulatory certification is obtained?

1.13 How does management ensure that all hazardous materials are safely, correctly and securely stored?

2 Detailed Issues

2.1 Has management undertaken a risk assessment of health and safety implications throughout the organisation in order to identify the risks and ensure that they are addressed?

2.2 Has a health and safety policy been introduced, and have specific responsibilities for safety issues been allocated?

2.3 What mechanisms prevent non compliance with the prevailing health and safety regulations?

2.4 How does management maintain an up-to-date awareness of all the relevant health and safety regulations?

2.5 Are all staff adequately trained in safety matters, including use of equipment and clothing (and how can management be certain that all the relevant staff actually receive the appropriate training)?

2.6 Are staff progressively tested on their level of understanding of safety measures in order to identify further training needs?

2.7 How does management monitor that all the relevant safety equipment is maintained in working order?

2.8 Are all relevant machines fitted with guards, safety cut-outs, etc. to the required standard?

2.9 How does management monitor that all computer equipment conforms to the required standards (e.g. screen radiation levels)?

2.10 Are building evacuation, fire and security drills regularly conducted and assessed for effectiveness?

2.11 Are adequate fire alarms and security systems installed, tested and maintained (and would faults be detected promptly)?

2.12 How does management monitor that all building environmental systems (heating, lighting, air conditioning, etc.) are working correctly and to the required legal standards?

2.13 What mechanisms prevent unauthorised access to buildings and facilities?

2.14 Are the relevant staff (receptionists, door guards, post room staff, etc.) aware of the action required in the event of a bomb alert, an attack on the building, a suspicious package, and so on?

2.15 What processes ensure that the records of incidents and accidents are fully and correctly maintained in accordance with any regulatory requirements?

2.16 Are sufficient and suitably trained first aid and medical personnel available, and how can they promptly be summoned to an incident?

2.17 In the event of an emergency, how does management account for all visitors?

2.18 Are transitory safety risks (such as trailing power leads, wet floors due to cleaning) adequately addressed?

2.19 What does management do to maintain sufficient insurance cover in the event of the organisation being sued for negligence with regard to health and safety conditions?

2.20 What processes ensure that insurance cover is renewed, on time and at the appropriate level?

2.21 What processes ensure that all the required certificates and licences are obtained to enable the lawful operation of facilities?

2.22 What mechanisms prevent unauthorised access to hazardous materials?

2.23 How is accuracy of data input from other systems (e.g. human resources) confirmed?

2.24 How is the accuracy of data output to other systems (e.g. estates management) confirmed?

INSURANCE

Control Objectives for Insurance

(a) To ensure that all relevant business and operational risks are accurately assessed as the basis for providing adequate and appropriate insurance cover.

(b) To ensure that prevailing insurance cover would remove, reduce or minimise risk exposures as appropriate.

(c) To ensure that insurance cover arrangements are justified and authorised.

(d) To ensure that insurance costs represent value for money and are competitive, effectively monitored and contained.

(e) To ensure that insurance arrangements are made through competent, reliable and stable brokers/companies.

(f) To ensure that insurance cover is renewed when appropriate and remains current.

(g) To ensure that claims are reviewed, agreed and authorised prior to release.

(h) To ensure that insurance claims are valid, correctly costed and pursued with the insurers until settled.

(i) To ensure that insurance claims are controlled to prevent excessive levels and the potential for increased premiums.

> (j) To ensure that insurance arrangements comply with all the applicable legal and regulatory requirements.
>
> (k) To ensure that measures designed to reduce risks and related insurance costs are assessed, justified and authorised.

Risk and Control Issues for Insurance

1 Key Issues

1.1 How does management ensure that all insurable risks are identified, assessed and adequately covered?

1.2 What processes ensure that the levels and types of insurance cover are appropriate and adequate?

1.3 Are insurance arrangements subject to prior authority, and what mechanisms prevent the establishment of invalid, unauthorised or unnecessary insurance arrangements?

1.4 How does management ensure that insurance costs are competitive and represent value for money?

1.5 What processes ensure that all insurance arrangements are arranged with suitable and reliable insurance institutions?

1.6 How does management verify that the required insurance cover is current and in force?

1.7 Are insurance claims subject to appropriate assessment and authority prior to submission?

1.8 How does management ensure that all insurance claims are appropriately costed and eventually settled?

1.9 How does management ensure that suitable insurance cover is obtained for all areas where it is required by law (e.g. for employer's liability and motor vehicles)?

1.10 What measures are in place to monitor and assess methods of reducing risks and their impact on insurance costs?

2. Detailed Issues

2.1 Are new or modified business operations adequately assessed for their inherent risks, and how can management be certain that the prevailing insurance arrangements remain suitable and adequate?

2.2 What mechanisms prevent the continuation of unwanted, uneconomic or unwarranted insurance arrangements?

2.3 Is current insurance cover available for the following areas (as applicable):
- employer's liability
- third party
- buildings/premises
- equipment/plant
- key assets
- IT equipment
- vehicles
- interruption/loss of business
- stocks?

2.4 Are payments of all insurance premiums (including renewals) suitably authorised?

2.5 Are insurance renewal premiums subject to review and authorisation?

2.6 What mechanisms prevent the automatic renewal of insurance premiums where the cover is no longer valid or required?

2.7 Are brokers' fees subject to authorisation prior to payment?

2.8 What mechanisms prevent the arrangement of insurance cover with unreliable or financially unstable insurance companies?

2.9 Are small or uneconomic claims prevented in order to avoid the potential for increased renewal premiums?

2.10 Are all claims based on realistic, accurate and legitimate cost data?

2.11 Are policy documents scrutinised for inappropriate conditions or unreasonable exclusion clauses (and what action would be taken in such instances)?

2.12 What measures ensure that the proceeds from all insurance claims are identified and correctly accounted for?

2.13 Are certificates of insurance obtained, securely stored and/or displayed when required by the prevailing regulations?

2.14 Are adequate, accurate and up-to-date records of all current insurance policies maintained?

2.15 How does management ensure that the status of all insurance cover can be promptly and accurately determined?

2.16 What processes ensure that all the prevailing laws and regulations are fully complied with?

2.17 How is the accuracy of data input from other systems (e.g. risk assessment or fixed assets) confirmed?

2.18 How is the accuracy of data output to other systems (e.g. to the general ledger) confirmed?

21
Auditing Environmental Responsibility

INTRODUCTION

All businesses interact with the wider environment, whether through the procurement of materials, the impact of manufacturing processes or the disposal of waste products, and in other ways.

In recent years there has been a growing global recognition that the physical environment needs to be protected from damage. The planet is being viewed as a total mechanism with finite resources, a limited capability to regenerate and a ceiling to its ability to cope with consequential pollution levels. This raising of environmental awareness has taken place not only at a general public level, but has been increasingly supported by emerging scientific evidence. Past industrialisation has had an enormous impact on the land, water and air.

Environmental protection legislation is now in force, but there is still a great deal that individual businesses can do to ease the impact of their operations on the environment and perhaps make financial savings as well. In the public consciousness it is no longer acceptable for businesses to be reactive in relation to environmental impacts; instead, they are encouraged to adopt a proactive stance in their attitudes and deeds. Indeed, it could be said that it is in the best interests of the wider business community to ensure that the business impact on the environment does not jeopardise future opportunities for sustained growth; and "green" technologies are increasingly providing new commercial opportunities.

Public awareness about environmental matters has also undergone a drastic change and personal initiatives (such as recycling) have emerged rather hesitantly, only to be converted into mandatory compliance obligations. Some organisations have exploited the currency of environmental matters and now deliberately project a more caring and concerned image to their potential customers.

Environmental responsibility can be good for business. The greening of business and other elements of corporate social responsibility are increasingly driving the market, rather than being viewed as antipathetic to the economic bottom line. Companies that show responsibility in these matters are likely to command a premium on their share price. Ethical investment funds are now a significant force in driving this agenda.

Even that arch doyen of the free market, Milton Friedman, acknowledged the imperative to abide by laws and regulations, but his dictum now seems passé:

There is one and only one social responsibility of business—to use its resources and engage in activities designed to increase its profits, so long as it stays within the rules of the game.

While laws, regulations and voluntary codes of conduct in this area are becoming even more widespread, demanding and important, it is also becoming more readily appreciated that companies should actively pursue the "triple bottom line"[1] (environmental, social and economic) if they are to best serve the interests of their shareholders and other stakeholders.

There is a stronger appreciation that the interests of other stakeholders are important if the interests of the owners are to be safeguarded. UK law is now reflecting this. The 2006 UK Companies Act has for the first time codified the duties of directors which had previously been dependent upon common law and case law. One of these codified duties, known as "the enlightened shareholder value duty", requires directors to make decisions having regard to social responsibility issues.[2] Arguably, UK law is therefore now moving the UK company from the traditional Anglo-Saxon free market model of the company more towards the European social market model of the company.

Later in this chapter we examine the European Commission's Eco-Management and Audit Scheme and we will note that one of its requirements is for a company-wide environmental policy to be established. The principle of "the polluter pays" is now widely recognised as the foundation for both formal regulation and individual environmental action programmes. It underpins the emergence of carbon trading legislation. This premise has motivated companies to find alternative business strategies which take due account of environmental concerns. In some high-profile industries (such as mineral extraction and chemicals) the potential costs associated with the aftermath of an environmental disaster are considerable. This, together with the public relations and other longer-term implications for the survival of the business, has encouraged organisations to take their environmental responsibilities very seriously. Many companies have instigated product recycling programmes as recognition of their ongoing responsibility for the environmental impact of their products. In the motor industry, a notable percentage of the materials used in new vehicles should be recyclable. In the office equipment market, companies have established programmes that let users return their office equipment and printer cartridges etc. for recycling.

When considering the environmental impact of the business, a wide range of factors should be examined for their environmental implications, for example the following questions may be applicable:

- Are more environmentally friendly materials available? (i.e. naturally sustainable)?
- Can we use renewable energy sources? Can we use less material?

- Can the choice of materials influence the useful life of the product or improve the opportunities for eventual recycling?
- Can we make savings by recovering and reusing materials?
- Can we adequately protect the product with less packaging material?
- How can waste be minimised?
- How can we protect and conserve surrounding land?

In this chapter, we will look at the emergence of environmental management standards and how they can be applied. The environmental management and audit framework will be examined and the possible role of internal auditors discussed. The chapter concludes with an example audit programme for conducting a high level review of environmental issues within an organisation.

This programme includes control objectives and risk/control issues in the form of key questions.

ENVIRONMENTAL AUDITING

Responsibility for environmental management spans the organisation and is not necessarily the sole preserve of one specialist function. In many respects the broader issues of environmental responsibility (and accountability) are matters of organisational culture. In some industries (such as petrochemicals), operations that are likely to have an environmental impact are already governed by combinations of industry best practice and specific laws and regulations.

THE EMERGENCE OF ENVIRONMENTAL CONCERNS

The emergence of environmental regulations and increased general awareness was first most apparent in the developed industrial nations. Economic reality in the developing world has limited the necessary investment in alternative environmentally friendly technologies and methods. New techniques of material extraction and production may have higher associated costs which are very challenging for developing nations to underwrite. While the future of the planet depends in part on the environmental responsibility of emerging nations, it is not unfair for them to point out that it was the developed nations who caused the problem and who must not only put their own houses in order but also resource the adoption of green technologies by the emerging nations of the world.

Initial warnings of the consequences of environmental damage were particularly noticeable in the 1960s, especially in relation to the widespread use of chemical pesticides. Although environmental concerns were initially seen as marginal matters that were the province of a few dedicated activists and scientists, the spread of general interest in the environment, underpinned by a number of well-publicised disasters and expanding scientific findings, soon reached a point when positive action was being demanded of governments.

In the United States, the US Environmental Protection Agency published (in 1969) an outline approach to environmental auditing which coincided with the passing of the National Environmental Policy Act, which required that the environmental impacts of major projects be properly assessed and addressed.

There were early parallel and equally significant developments in environmental awareness elsewhere in the world, for example in Japan where very demanding and rigorously policed pollution control criteria were established early on.

EMAS—THE EUROPEAN ECO-MANAGEMENT AND AUDIT SCHEME

The intention of EMAS[6] is to recognise and reward organisations that go beyond minimum legal compliance and continuously improve their environmental performance. In addition, it is a requirement of the scheme that participating organisations regularly produce a public environmental statement that reports on their environmental performance. It is this voluntary publication of environmental information, whose accuracy and reliability has been independently checked by an environmental verifier, that gives EMAS and those organisations that participate enhanced credibility and recognition.

Since the 1980s a large number of EU Directives on environmental issues have been introduced.[3]

EMAS originally came about by an EC Council Regulation,[4] enacted in 1993, which allowed "voluntary participation by companies in the industrial sector in a Community eco-management and audit scheme" (EMAS). As an EU Regulation it was directly applicable to all member states. The contents of this document were supported by other separately developed standards, such as BS 7750 and, more recently, BS 8555 and ISO 14001.[5] European Regulation 1836/93 was replaced by Council Regulation 761/01.

The EMAS initiative established by this European law was essentially a voluntary scheme introduced in April 1995 and supported by the UK government.[6] The scheme is primarily targeted at industrial sites located within Europe, but in the UK the scheme has been extended to include local authorities. EMAS is supported by standards such as BS 8555 in the UK and the ISO 14000 series. The underlying long-term aim of EMAS is to continuously improve environmental performance with benefits accruing for both the organisation and the environment.

Participation in EMAS is site-based, but multi-site organisations can obviously apply the mechanism to all their locations. Organisations seeking involvement in EMAS will need to address each of the following requirements at each site:

1. Establish a company-wide **environmental policy**, which incorporates the environmental priorities, a commitment to continuous improvement and acknowledges compliance with the relevant environmental regulations. Any such policy should be documented and ratified by senior management. In order to maintain its relevance, the policy should periodically be reviewed and modified if necessary—amendments should be officially authorised by senior management.

2. Undertake an **environment review** incorporating an analysis of all inputs, processes and outputs for the site. Use this data to catalogue the environmental impacts and issues for management attention. This stage should be broad-based and take account of such areas as energy, materials, noise control, waste avoidance and waste disposal. It is also crucial to identify any regulations or laws that apply to the site and to confirm that they are being fully complied with.

3. Using the previous two stages as a guide and structural framework, create an **environmental programme** which documents the targets, objectives and goals for the site in question and the measures to be taken in order to achieve them.

4. Develop an **environmental management** system which incorporates the necessary operating procedures and controls to achieve the successful implementation of both the environmental policy and environmental programme. This process is likely to generate changes in operations, procedures, staff responsibilities, etc. The requirements of a standard such as BS 7750 (for environmental management systems) can be applied at this stage, or you can opt to develop your own.

5. Having defined and officially documented your environmental policies and practices, it is now necessary to enter the **environmental audit cycle** so that the actual performance is compared to the standards and objectives. This level of environmental audit is an *internal* review and is aimed at identifying any specific changes in order either to confirm compliance with the required practices or to generally improve the efficiency or effectiveness of same. The frequency of the audit cycle at this stage will vary in relation to the underlying levels of risk and the nature of activities; however, such a review must take place at least every three years. It is possible initially to register the organisation under EMAS at stage 2 (the environmental review) assuming that stage 4 (the environmental management system) is operational, and prior to undertaking the audit review. However, the intended audit process should be described and subsequently carried out.

6. Following the audit review (and every year thereafter) the organisation should prepare an **environmental statement** for each site, which is intended for publication. The aim here is to reassure the public and others that the environmental impacts associated with the site are fully understood and subject to ongoing management attention. Where related plans and objectives have been defined (or previously set), the statement should make reference to the progress achieved.

7. At the end of each cycle, the following elements must be verified by an accredited and independent environmental verifier in a formal validation process:

- the environment statement produced at stage 6 above
- the environmental policy (stage 1)
- the environmental programme (stage 3)
- the environmental management system (stage 4)
- the environmental audit procedure (stage 5).

Of course, if the relevant component systems are certified to BS 7750 they will meet the EMAS requirements.

Those organisations that have been successful in achieving (and maintaining) registration under EMAS have the right to use the official scheme symbol in correspondence and company reports.

LINKING ENVIRONMENTAL ISSUES TO CORPORATE STRATEGY AND SECURING BENEFITS

To address environmental issues effectively, they need to be woven into the business strategy and direction of the organisation. The relative issues cannot be regarded as elements to "bolt on" to the organisation, but they must be treated as fundamental to the day-to-day business. The cynical may say that the marketing and public relations imagery projected by a business entity in relation to the environment need only be skin deep, but here we are more concerned with ingrained, realistic and responsible processes which make an effective contribution to the environment and at the same time generate tangible benefits for the organisation, such as:

- potential for cost savings (e.g. recycling materials, less waste)
- lower costs achieved through improved production processes
- improved usage of energy (i.e. possible reduction in consumption)
- potential savings in packaging, storage and transportation costs
- the creation of new technologies, product lines and/or new markets
- effective marketing exploitation of the current public concerns over the environment
- securing competitive advantages through improved performance
- avoidance of potential environmental liabilities (i.e. fines, clean-up costs and punitive insurance premiums)
- improved relationships with customers, investors, insurers, the media, regulators, and so on.

Before any of the benefits can be achieved, an organisation must accurately determine the current environmental impact of its business as the basis for moving forward and applying effective change and improvements. A structured and methodical approach is therefore required, especially if compliance with the relevant standards is to be achieved.

Of course, when developing a corporate strategy, the environmental issues do not stand alone, but rather sit alongside the principal business considerations (such as financial and operational performance, efficiency, risk implications, and so on). The environmentally aware dimensions may be secondary in nature—for example, the conversion of waste by-product into a useful new product. In addition to both the general business and internally relevant factors which are likely to influence corporate direction, account also needs to be taken of the views of interested external parties (for example, customers, shareholders, local communities).

In establishing a strategy which takes account of environmental matters, the organisation will wish to formalise aspects of its related approach so that all concerned are aware of the objectives and their responsibilities. One process of this output is the development of written environmental policies and/or codes of practice.

ENVIRONMENTAL ASSESSMENT AND AUDITING SYSTEM CONSIDERATIONS

Here we are initially concerned with the operation of an *internal* environment audit system, which in larger organisations is likely to be operated by a specialist function within the organisation as distinct from any internal audit review of the overall environmental approach applied by the business. We also initially exclude here the use of the term *environmental audit* in the context of verification audits conducted by accredited verifiers.

The EMAS framework and British as well as international standards (as discussed earlier) can be applied as recognised and well-defined models that address the spirit of the relevant EU Directive.

In order to take account of all the possible environmental consequences of the business, management and auditors alike will need to consider the organisation's products and services on a "cradle to grave" or "lifecycle" basis. This approach, which can point up those areas of significant environmental concern, assesses the implications at each stage of the product lifecycle spanning from creation through to destruction, for instance:

- research and development
- design and performance criteria
- selection and sourcing of raw materials
- methods of production
- waste materials, emissions, discharges, etc. during production
- the use of energy
- product packaging
- methods of distribution
- environmental impacts generated by using or applying the product
- implications for the eventual disposal (or recycling) of the used product.

The nature of the business and its operations will dictate the type(s) of environmental audits that are applied. For example, they may focus on the audit of:

- current (or projected) production methods
- the use of energy
- the extent of any potential liabilities related to either the acquisition or divesture of specific activities
- the determination of safety and/or health risks
- compliance with all the prevailing industry regulations
- the effectiveness of the prevailing environmental management system
- pollution prevention measures
- a particular product or service.

The scale of each audit may also vary—for example, the review may either span the whole organisation, a specific area of activity or particular physical site.

The frequency of audit reviews may represent the last factor in the equation of planned coverage; for instance, a cyclical approach within a total timescale (i.e. annually) may be appropriate, or alternatively circumstances may require a special one-off review to be conducted.

There is some implied synergy between the approach adopted for the development of an environmental assessment/audit strategy and that relevant to the formation of a total quality management (TQM) culture. Both require high levels of employee commitment, effective communication and the encouragement of a culture underpinned by continuous improvement. Furthermore, there are structural similarities between TQM standards and those applicable to environmental systems—for example, the requirements for verification assessment carried by accredited bodies and the use of similar system management structures.

The development of a corporate approach to environmental management takes time and considerable resources. Given that each business will have unique and specific requirements, it is likely that external expertise may have to be sought during the emergence of the overall strategy and programme.

THE ROLE OF INTERNAL AUDIT

Internal auditors are increasingly becoming involved in providing assurance to senior management and to boards on external aspects of governance, which includes the accountability of the board to external stakeholders, for instance in the annual report and accounts. Many companies are now publishing sustainability reports, either as a section within their Annual Report and Accounts, or as a separate report. When a company's published sustainability assertions are subject to an audit by independent environmental auditors, which is a requirement of EMAS, there may be less need for internal audit to provide assurance to management and the board on the reliability of their sustainability assertions.

Where a company's sustainability assertions are not subject to independent attestation by environmental auditors, it is likely that management and the board will need to depend upon internal audit for assurance that their assertions are soundly based. Whether or not the company reports on sustainability matters, and whether or not their report is independently audited, there is an important role for internal audit to advise the board and management on the adequacy of the company's governance, risk management and internal control processes for the sustainability purposes. We discussed these processes in Chapters 4, 5 and 6 respectively. Potential sustainability internal audit engagements will be considered along with all other possible internal audit engagements for inclusion in the future plan of audit engagements, having regard to relative risk. In today's world it is unlikely that sustainability matters will be assessed by the chief audit executive as being of low risk. Where there is a specialist environmental team within the organisation, internal audit will assess the extent to which reliance can be placed on that team's work when determining the internal audit approach. But, clearly, management and the board will need assurance on the extent to which they can rely on the work product of that specialist environmental team.

EXAMPLE PROGRAMME

In this section we have provided an example of a high level programme for the review of environmental issues within an organisation. The format follows that adopted in earlier chapters and features control objectives and risk/control issues (divided into key issues and detailed issues) in the form of relevant questions. This data can be used within the Standard Audit Programme Guides (SAPGs) looked at in Chapter 3. To save space we have not presented the information within the SAPG format.

Control Objectives for Environmental Issues

> (a) To provide an authorised and documented policy on environment issues as a framework for responsibly conducting related business activities.
>
> (b) To minimise the impact of the organisation's activities on the environment.
>
> (c) To ensure that the organisation's products are environmentally friendly.
>
> (d) To ensure that waste is minimised and properly disposed of.
>
> (e) To avoid pollution and environmental contamination.
>
> (f) To assess, on an ongoing basis, the environmental impacts of business operations and define the requirements to be adhered to.
>
> (g) To ensure that alternative and potentially environmentally friendly processes and technologies are considered and implemented where justified.
>
> (h) To minimise or avoid the use of scarce materials and nonrenewable energy sources.
>
> (i) To ensure that harmful or hazardous materials and waste products are safely and responsibly transported and disposed of.
>
> (j) To ensure that all environmental legislation and regulations are fully complied with.
>
> (k) To avoid adverse impacts on the organisation's reputation and image.
>
> (l) To ensure that environmental issues are subject to monitoring and management.

Risk and Control Issues for Environmental Issues

1 Key Issues

1.1 Has an approved and documented environment policy been established which defines the required approach for business operations?

1.2 What measures ensure that the principles of the environmental policy are complied with, and how would non compliance be promptly detected?

1.3 Have production processes and other business activities been assessed for their environmental impacts (and how is the necessary corrective action evidenced)?

1.4 How does management ensure that all the relevant environmental legislation and regulations are fully complied with, thus avoiding penalties and adverse effects on the organisation's public image?

1.5 How does management ensure that all waste products are correctly and safely treated, discharged or disposed of?

1.6 What measures prevent the pollution and contamination of the environment?

1.7 Are the organisation's products assessed for "environmental friendliness" (e.g. impact during production/use, potential to be recycled, safe disposal at end of product life, restricted use of scarce resources)?

1.8 Has management actively considered alternative and less environmentally harmful production/business processes?

1.9 Are measures in place to ensure that all environmental impacts are identified, monitored and effectively managed (and what is the evidence for this)?

1.10 Has management established a "recycling" policy and if so, how is compliance confirmed?

1.11 Have the full costs of adopting an environmental approach to the business been accurately identified, justified and authorised (and are they subject to monitoring and review)?

2 Detailed Issues

2.1 Is the environmental policy supported by the commitment of senior management and a suitable staff training/awareness programme?

2.2 Are all projects to reduce the impact of business activities on the environment subject to a full feasibility and cost appraisal, before being authorised?

2.3 Is the assessment of environmental impacts kept up to date so that management action is relevant and targeted?

2.4 Where required, have measurements of environmental impact (e.g. water discharge, fume extraction, waste materials) been established (and are they checked for accuracy)?

2.5 How does management make certain that it remains aware of all the relevant environmental legislation and regulations?

2.6 Has a responsibility for environmental management been defined and allocated?

2.7 What measures ensure that all waste products are identified, assessed for their environmental impact, and appropriately treated/processed?

2.8 Are all discharges of waste products subject to monitoring and permitted within the prevailing regulations (and how would non compliance be detected)?

2.9 How does management ensure that all waste product treatment processes are operating correctly and efficiently?

2.10 Would management be made aware of all accidental and unintentional spillages of potentially harmful materials?

2.11 Are contingency plans and resources in place to deal effectively with the likely range of environmental accidents?

2.12 How does management check that waste disposal sites and operators are appropriately licensed to handle the specific by-products generated by the organisation?

2.13 Whenever necessary, is management considering utilising alternatives to hazardous or scarce materials as a means of reducing the environmental impacts?

2.14 Are the potential long-term environmental liabilities adequately assessed for both newly acquired sites and those being disposed of?

2.15 Are environmental impact audits regularly conducted by appropriately experienced personnel and are their findings and recommendations effectively followed up?

2.16 Does the design and development of new products take into account the potential environmental impact of production, and what measures ensure that such impacts are minimised and contained?

2.17 Are the operating costs of any "recycling" programmes monitored, and are such programmes assessed for their effectiveness?

2.18 How does management verify that the adopted environmental approach is justified (on either cost or company image grounds)?

2.19 Has management reviewed the type of packaging in use as the basis for adopting alternatives with a reduced environmental impact?

2.20 In the event of an environmental problem, are mechanisms in place to deal effectively with media and public relations, so that the reputation of the organisation will be protected?

2.21 How is the accuracy of data input from other systems (e.g. new product development or design) confirmed?

2.22 How is the accuracy of data output to other systems (e.g. industry regulation and compliance) confirmed?

NOTES

1. A triple bottom line (TBL or 3BL) approach commits the organisation to work for social, economic and environmental benefits, sometimes termed "people, planet, and profit". The goal is sustainability. The phrase was coined for Shell by SustainAbility. Patrick Geddes, the 20th century urbanist, had earlier introduced notion of "folk, work and place". The *Global Reporting Initiative* (GRI) has developed guidelines that enable organisations to quantify and report comparably these matters.
2. The 2006 Companies Act for the first time codifies in a statutory statement the general duties of directors, including a new "enlightened shareholder value" duty, with effect from 1 October 2008, to:

act in the way he considers, in good faith, would be most likely to promote the success of the company for the benefit of the members as a whole [i.e. shareholders] ... having regard to:
- the longer term
- the interests of the company's employees
- the need to foster the company's business relationships with suppliers, customers and others
- the environment
- the impact of operations on the wider community
- the desirability of the company maintaining a reputation for high standards of business conduct and the need to act fairly between members of the company
- (not exhaustive).

The Act therefore introduces new social responsibility factors. This has become known as the "enlightened shareholder value" duty, broadly replacing the old fiduciary duty to act in the company's best interests. It is a single duty rather than separate duties in relation to each of the parties listed.

The statutory statement sets out a director's seven general duties as:
1. to act within the company's powers;
2. to promote the success of the company for the benefit of its members as a whole, and in doing so have regard (*inter alia*) to specified matters;
3. to exercise independent judgement;
4. to exercise reasonable care, skill and diligence (as would be expected of a reasonably diligent person carrying out the functions of the director, as well as based on the director's actual knowledge, skill and experience);
5. to avoid conflicts of interest;
6. not to accept benefits from third parties;
7. to declare interests in a proposed transaction or arrangement with the company.

These general duties are, as before, owed to the company. They apply to directors, shadow directors and, in certain cases, to former directors—executive or nonexecutive.

Note that the traditional "subjective" standard of skill and care has been replaced by a new objective standard which assesses an individual director's conduct against the knowledge, skill and experience that may reasonably be expected of a person carrying out the director's functions.

In addition to the new codification of directors' duties, the 2006 UK Companies Act includes a new statutory basis for a shareholder to take action against directors by means of the new extended right for shareholders to sue directors, known as "derivative action". The codified "derivative claims" provisions make the criteria and procedure for minority shareholders to make a claim in the name of the company clearer, but include protections to ensure that unmeritorious suits are quickly dismissed with costs falling to the person bringing the claim. Protections include that before the shareholder(s) is allowed to proceed with an action the shareholder(s) will be required first to establish as prima facie case of breach and, second, to satisfy the court that the alleged conduct was inconsistent with the director's fundamental duty to act in a way which "promotes the success of his company"; and the court will be expected to take into account whether the petitioning shareholder(s) is acting in good faith, whether the conduct has been authorised or ratified by the company and any views expressed by "independent" shareholders. A director will only be liable to the company (or its shareholders on behalf of the company) if the company can demonstrate that it has suffered loss as a result of the breach.

The rules on directors' duties apply to all companies—large and small, private and public.

The effect of this is that it is now very important that the board decision-making process pays due attention to this newly-formalised framework, and that the fact that it has done so is properly recorded. This will be especially important in larger companies with large numbers of shareholders.

3. See Ledgerwood, G., Street, E. and Therivel, R. (1992) *The Environmental Audit and Business Strategy*. Pitman/Financial Times, London, Appendix B for a very comprehensive analysis of early, related EU legislation.
4. No. 1836/93 dated 29 June 1993—Published in L168 Volume 36 of the *Official Journal of the European Communities*.
5. British Standard BS 8555 (full title: Guide to the phased implementation of an environmental management system including the use of environmental performance evaluation) published in April 2003 encompasses the six phase achievement criteria utilised in the IEMA Acorn Scheme. This standard links Environmental Management Systems (ISO 14001) and Environmental Performance Evaluation (ISO 14031), providing for focused training, auditing and implementation at each level and supports relationships between suppliers and customers. BS 8555 describes how to implement a generic environmental management system and can be used as a route towards ISO 14001 and EMAS. The standard's inclusion of ISO 14031 allows the development of tasks focusing on indicators that add value and are driven by company needs, e.g. Turnover, competitive advantage, views of interested parties. The environmental performance focus of BS 8555 is valuable within the supply chain and concentrates on:

   - Delivery of measurable benefits for participants
   - Delivery of performance data for internal/external reporting.

6. Maximum credibility and competitive advantage. Further details of EMAS in the UK can be obtained from The Institute of Environmental Management and Assessment, St Nicholas House, 70 Newport, Lincoln, LN1 3DP, Tel: +44 (0)1522 540069, Fax: +44 (0)1522 540090, Email: info@iema.net. Further information for the UK is available from emas@iema.net. The EU website is at http://ec.europa.eu/environment/emas/ and an EMAS toolkit for small and medium sized businesses (SMEs) is at http://ec.europa.eu/environment/emas/toolkit/.

Part III:
Auditing Information Technology

22
Auditing Information Technology

INTRODUCTION

In this section, which contains separate chapters for each principal topic, we consider the audit review of information technology (IT) activities. This section is not intended to be a technical manual for computer or IT auditors; rather, it approaches IT activities from business and operational viewpoints, the objectives being to consider the key issues and identify optimum actions.

Much has changed in the IT environment since the first edition of this book was published. Hardware, memory and electronic storage have become cheaper, faster and more reliable. Alongside the technical developments, organisations have become even more dependent upon information technology to support and innovate their activities and operations. Indeed, many have implemented initiatives that wholly depend on IT, such as trading on the Internet.

We have included in this section some additional topical areas, such as Information Management, Records Management and Knowledge Management. Although acknowledging that these topics have a scope wider than information technology, dealing as they do with all forms of records, including paper documents, it is more likely that the majority of organisations will be primarily supported by electronic records; hence the inclusion of the related topics within this section.

The international importance of Data Protection and Freedom of Information issues is explored in considerable depth in Chapters 44 and 45. Appendices 3 and 4 provide the details of international legislation and regulation, by country, for Data Protection and Freedom of Information respectively. We hope this data provides a useful reference point and a gauge of the progress achieved internationally as well as identifying those nations who would appear to be lagging behind.

There has been a conscious effort to avoid any overtly technical or confusing management terminology throughout this section, but some is inevitable. Definitions are provided in Appendix 5.

Before examining, in some detail, each of the various IT activities, we continue with a discussion of current and emerging international standards with implications for information technology and the use of electronic records.

INTRODUCTION TO RECOGNISED STANDARDS RELATED TO INFORMATION TECHNOLOGY AND RELATED TOPICS

Here we describe the various internationally recognised standards that relate to information technology and linked activities.

Becoming accredited under any of the standards is a matter for the organisation to decide upon. In some sectors such accreditation is a necessary part of operating. There are obviously cost and resource implications associated with full accreditation; however, these standards do reflect a body of best practice and their adoption will contribute to the stability and resilience of IT-related activities.

Many of the control and best practice issues associated with these various standards are considered in the following discrete chapters of this section.

Additional information about the noted standards can be obtained from either the British Standards Institution (BSI) or the ISO, the contacts details for which are noted below, where copies of the standards can also be ordered:

BSI

Global site: www.bsi-global.com

Please note that the BSI has a number of other national sites in the local languages, all of which can be accessed from the Global home page.

Mail: BSI, 389 Chiswick High Road, London, W4 4AL, United Kingdom

Email: cservices@bsigroup.com

ISO

ISO web: www.iso.org/iso/home.htm

Mail: International Organization for Standardization (ISO), 1, ch. de la Voie-Creuse, Case postale 56. CH-1211 Geneva 20, Switzerland

The ISO/IEC 27000 Series of Standards

The development of the ISO 27000 (or ISO 27K) group of standards is based upon the earlier work of the United Kingdom's Government Department of Trade and Industry (DTI) and the British Standards Institute which resulted, in 1995, in the publication of the BS 7799 Code for Information Security Management.

The second part of BS 7799 was published in 1999 and dealt with Information Security Management Systems. BS 7799 became, in turn ISO 17799 and was then reworked into the ISO/IEC 27000 series of international standards. ISO/IEC standards are the joint work of the International Organisation for Standardisation (ISO) and the International Electrotechnical Commission (IEC).

The BERR survey of Information Security Breaches in UK companies, published in 2008[1] indicated that 11 % of the surveyed companies had implemented BS 7799 or ISO 27001, as compared with 5 % as at 2002. However the same survey noted that 79 % of the surveyed companies were not aware of the contents of these standards.

The ISO/IEC 27000 series of standards is still being developed, with the following individual standards either in place or in development:

Reference/Status	Comments
ISO/IEC 27000: 2009	*Introduction to the ISMS (ISO/IEC 27000) family of standards.*
(Published April 2009)	This document, which is suitable for all types of organisation, provides an overview of information security management systems (ISMS) and defines related terms.
ISO/IEC 27001:2005	*Information Technology—Security Techniques—Information Security Management Systems—Requirements.*
(Published October 2005)	This standard is based upon BS 7799—Part 2.
	This standard has the objective to *"provide a model of establishing, implementing, operating, monitoring, reviewing, maintaining and improving an Information Security Management System"*.
	"The design and implementation of an organisation's ISMS is influenced by their needs and objectives, security requirements, the process employed and the size and structure of the organisation."
ISO/IEC 27002:2007	*Code of Practice for Information Security Management.*
	This standard started life as BS 7799—Part 1, after which it became ISO/IEC 17799.
(Published July 2007)	This standard started life as BS 7799—Part 1, after which it became ISO/IEC 17799.
	This standard has 12 main sections:
	1. Risk Assessment
	2. Security Policy—management direction
	3. Organisation of information security—governance of information security
	4. Asset management—inventory and classification of information assets

Reference/Status	Comments
	5. Human resources security—security aspects for employees joining, moving within and leaving an organisation
	6. Physical and environmental security—protection of computer facilities
	7. Communications and operations management—management of technical security controls in systems and networks
	8. Access control—restriction of access rights to networks, systems, applications, functions and data
	9. Information systems acquisition, development and maintenance—building security into systems
	10. Information security incident management—anticipating and responding appropriately to information security breaches
	11. Business continuity management—protecting, maintaining and recovering business-critical processes and systems
	12. Compliance—ensuring compliance with information security policies, standards, laws and regulations.
	Each of the sections has a set of related best practice controls related to objectives. Please note that this standard has directly equivalent national standards in the following countries:
	Australia, Brazil, Czech Republic, Denmark, Estonia, Japan, Lithuania, Netherlands, New Zealand, Poland, Peru, Spain, Sweden, Turkey, UK, Uruguay and Russia.
ISO/IEC 27003	*ISMS Implementation Guidance.*
In preparation as at 2009, expected to be published by early 2010.	The suggested title, to be confirmed, is *Information Technology—Security techniques, Information security management system implementation guidelines.*
ISO/IEC 27004	*A Standard for Information Security Management Measurements.*
In preparation as at 2009, expected to be published by early 2010.	This document will relate to ISMS measurement and metrics with the intention of assisting organisations establishing the effectiveness of their ISMS mechanisms.

Reference/Status	Comments
ISO/IEC 27005: 2008	*Information Security Risk Management.*
(Published 2008)	This standard is interesting as it neither provides nor recommends a specific risk methodology but rather provides guidelines. This approach may be appropriate as each sector and organisation will vary in terms of its potential risk impacts and their operational relevance.
ISO/IEC 27006; 2007	*Information Technology—Security Techniques. Requirements for bodies providing audit and certification of information security management systems.*
(Published 2006)	A guide to the certification and registrations process for the ISO/IEC 27001 standard.
ISO/IEC 27007 **In preparation.**	A guideline for ISMS auditing (focusing on the management system).
ISO/IEC 27008 **In preparation. Publication expected in November 2011.**	A guideline for ISMS auditing (focusing on the security controls).
ISO/IEC 27010 **In preparation.**	*Information Security Management for Inter-Sector Communications.*
ISO/IEC 27011 **In preparation**	*Information Security Management Guidelines for Telecommunications Organisations Based on ISO/IEC 27002.*
ISO/IEC 27012 **Speculative**	Believed likely to relate to ISMS guidance for e-government.
ISO/IEC 27013 **In preparation**	Guidance on the integrated implementation of ISO/IEC 20000-1 and ISO/IEC 27001.
	NB: ISO/IEC 20000-1 (formerly known as BS 15000/BS 15000) is the world's first standard for IT service management. The standard specifies a set of interrelated management processes, and is based heavily upon the ITIL (IT Infrastructure Library) framework.

Reference/Status	Comments
ISO/IEC 27014	Information Security Governance Framework
In preparation	
ISO/IEC 27015	ISMS Guidance for Financial Services Organisations
In preparation	
ISO/IEC 27031	Specifications for ICT Readiness for Business Continuity
In preparation	
ISO/IEC 27032	Guidelines for Cyber Security with an ISMS
In preparation	
ISO/IEC 27033	Multipart standard for IT Network Security within an ISMS.
In preparation	Will replace ISO/IEC 16028:2006
ISO/IEC 27034	Guidelines for Application Security within an ISMS
In preparation	
ISO/IEC 27035	Guidelines of the classification of security incident management within an ISMS
In preparation	
ISO/IEC 27799: 2008	*Health Informatics—Information Security Management in Health Using ISO/IEC 27002.*
(Published 2008)	*Health sector-specific ISMS implementation guide.*
ISO/IEC 27809: 2007	*Health Informatics—Measures for Ensuring Patient Safety of Health Software.*
(Published 2007)	

ISO 15489 Information and Documentation—Records Management

This ISO standard relates to the effective management of any organisation's records irrespective of their type and form (i.e. encompasses both paper-based and electronic forms). The standard adopts a cradle to grave approach to records ranging from the creation of a record, through its use and maintenance, to the eventual disposal or destruction.

The availability of accurate and reliable records is essential for any operation and any disruption of the efficient access to them can result in wasted resources. The time spent is seeking lost or misplaced records and information is wasted resource as well as being frustrating at the time. Alternatively, excessive or unnecessary records can clog a system and again lead to inefficiencies and wasted resources.

We examine the specific issues related to Records Management in Chapter 29, but ISO 15489 provides best practice guidance.

The standard is in two parts, both published in 2001, as follows:

15489- 1 Information & Documentation—Records Management—General

The first part illustrates a framework for records-keeping and notes the related benefits and regulatory considerations. It also covers the key process of record creation (including capture of information), form and structure, storage, retention, access, etc. IT is divided into the following sections:

1. Scope
2. Normative references
3. Terms and definitions
4. Benefits of Records Management
5. Regulatory environment
6. Policy and responsibilities
7. Records Management requirements
8. Design and implementation of a records systems
9. Records Management processes and controls
10. Monitoring and auditing
11. Training

15489- 2 Information & Documentation—Records Management—Guidelines

Part 2 augments Part 1 with practical and detailed guidance and is divided into the following sections:

1. Scope
2. Policies and responsibilities
3. Strategies, design and implementation
4. Records processes and controls
5. Monitoring and auditing
6. Training

Emerging Standards and Best Practice for Knowledge Management

We will be exploring the issues surrounding Knowledge Management in Chapter 30. Knowledge Management (KM) has its foundation in the private sector but is of equal importance to the public sector. Royal Dutch Shell have defined Knowledge Management as "the capabilities by which communities within an organisation capture the knowledge that is critical to them constantly improve it and make it available in the most effective manner to those people who need it, so that they can exploit it creatively to add value as a normal part of their work".

The development of an appropriate international standard for Knowledge Management is still in the pipeline. However the BSI has produced the following guidance publications on the subject:

PAS 2001:2001 *Knowledge Management—A Guide to Good Practice*, Published July 2001 by BSI—ISBN 0 580 38412 8

PD 7500:2003 *Knowledge Management—Vocabulary*, Published April 2003 by BSI—ISBN 0 580 3340 X

PF 7501:2003 *Managing Culture and Knowledge—Guide to Good Practice,* Published May 2003 by BSI—ISBN 0 580 433341 8

PD 7502:2003 *Knowledge Management—Guide to Measurements in Knowledge Management,* Published July 2003 by BSI—ISBN 0 580 33342 6

PD 7503:2003 *Introduction to Knowledge Management in Construction*, Published June 2003 by BSI—ISBN 0 580 33343 4

PD 7504:2005 *Knowledge Management in the Public Sector—A Guide to Good Practice.* Published October 2005 by BSI—ISBN 0 580 46528 4

PD 7505:2005 *Skills for Knowledge Management—A Guide to Good Practice.* Published October 2005 by BSI—ISBN 0 580 46527 6

PD 7506:2005 *Linking Knowledge Management with other Organisational Functions and Disciplines. A Guide to Good Practice.* Published September 2005 by BSI—ISBN 0 580 46526 8

SYSTEM/FUNCTION COMPONENTS OF INFORMATION TECHNOLOGY AND MANAGEMENT

We have elected to use an essentially broad and *functional* approach to define the information technology and management auditing universe, which gives us the following possible breakdown of the key functions, systems or activities, each of which will be the subject of a discrete chapter within this section.

- IT Strategic Planning
- IT Organisation
- IT Policy Framework
- Information Asset Register*
- Capacity Management
- Information Management (IM)*
- Records Management (RM)*
- Knowledge Management (KM)*
- IT sites and Infrastructure (including physical security)
- Processing Operations
- Back-up and Media Management

- Removable Media
- System and Operating Software (including Patch Management)
- System Access Control (or logical security)
- Personal Computers (including laptops and PDAs)
- Remote Working
- Email
- Internet Usage
- Software Maintenance (including change management)
- Networks
- Databases
- Data Protection
- Freedom of Information
- Data Transfer and Sharing (Standards and Protocol Guidelines)
- Legal Responsibilities
- Facilities Management
- System Development
- Software Selection
- Contingency Planning
- Human Resources information security
- Monitoring and Logging
- Information Security incidents
- Data Retention and Disposal
- Electronic Data Interchange (EDI)
- Viruses
- User Support
- BACS (i.e. automated cash/funds transfer)
- Spreadsheet design and good practice
- IT Health Checks
- IT Accounting.

The above listing of activities and functions is deliberately pitched to take account of a potentially wide range of possible IT scenarios. For example, some of the items are more akin to traditional IT operations, whereas other aspects are geared to the contemporary business use of networks, servers and personal computers. This broad-brush approach is intended to enable auditors to identify and extract those elements that match their own organisation's use of IT. We should not become too transfixed by the definition of this list of activities, as they will rarely operate in complete isolation from each other—for example, IT strategic planning outputs may have direct relevance to system developments or the expansion of local area networks. The degree of relevance and importance of the noted components will vary in each organisation. In addition, the level and degree of implementation of certain methods and aspects will also vary, largely in relation to the nature of the organisation and the prevailing information culture.

Those items marked with an asterisk (*) are relevant to the wider aspects of information and knowledge that, although including electronic records, should also encompass information and records in any form. Their inclusion within this IT chapter is justified on the grounds that by far the majority of organisations will have a preponderance of electronic records, albeit that some of the subsequently discussed issues can, in fact, relate to any form or media.

CONTROL OBJECTIVES AND RISK AND CONTROL ISSUES

In the following chapters (23 to 62) we will examine the control objectives and the related risk and control issues (divided into key issues and detailed issues) for each of the information technology and management activity areas listed above. This data can be used within the format of the Standard Audit Programme Guides (SAPGs) looked at in Chapter 3. To save space we have concentrated on the objectives to be stated and the questions to be asked and have not presented them within the SAPG format.

NOTE

1. *2008 Information Security Breaches Survey*, Department for Business, Enterprise and Regulatory Reform (2008), www.berr.gov.uk.

23
IT Strategic Planning

Here we are primarily concerned with planning for the use of IT in the organisation so as to ensure that the business objectives and operational requirements are effectively met. There are many possible choices for IT-based business solutions, and selecting the most appropriate can be both difficult and crucial for the business. There is the medium-term danger that the organisation will become locked into a quickly outdated and inflexible IT environment which fails to deliver any commercial or competitive advantages.

Applying formal strategic planning techniques to the operational use of IT will normally concentrate on the key business requirements and the objectives set by management as part of their wider long-term planning. Against these targets, goals and objectives it is then usual to map the existing use of IT to support the business, highlighting any high value and data-related activities that could be improved by the use of IT-based methods. The key output of any IT strategy exercise is an action plan designed to take the organisation forward from the current IT scenario to the future environment. If the output represents extensive change, the action plan is likely to be a staged programme which may include such elements as:

- acquiring and moving over to new hardware or software platforms (e.g. replacing legacy systems with more contemporary solutions);
- improving or extending the data communications infrastructure (e.g. installing local and wide area networks, dedicated communication lines, etc.);
- improving or upgrading existing application systems (e.g. extending the types of data held or extending the processing functionality);
- commissioning new application software to support business activities (e.g. the internal or external development of software);
- introducing new or improved IT development and management techniques to contribute to efficiency and cost-effectiveness (e.g. the use of formal system development methodologies or the introduction of a revised user support system);
- implementing a training plan in order to ensure that IT staff skill levels are maintained up to date.

Not all the changes generated through the IT strategy process will necessarily be hardware or software-related; there may be a case for introducing new or revised techniques which aid the efficiency of the IT function.

The approach adopted for conducting an IT strategy plan will, of course, depend on the scale and type of the underlying organisation and the current level of IT involvement. For example, larger organisations may be able to justify an in-house software development team to create and support their business-specific application systems, whereas the norm may be to engage external software developers to tailor an existing standard system or to build a new one.

Whatever forms the recommended action plans take, the key point is that they must be justified in business terms and deliver tangible benefits, efficiencies or enhanced facilities. There is no place for IT for ITs sake, otherwise the IT tail starts to wag the business dog!

Control Objectives for IT Strategic Planning

(a) To ensure that the IT facilities and services support both the strategic objectives of the business and the maintenance of competitive advantage.

(b) To ensure that the use of IT throughout the organisation is adequately planned and geared to the underlying business needs.

(c) To ensure that investments in IT facilities are justified and represent value for money.

(d) To ensure that a stable, reliable and secure IT environment is provided to support the business.

(e) To ensure that both the current and anticipated requirements of the business are appropriately served by the IT facilities.

(f) To ensure that adequate and appropriately skilled personnel are provided to support the achievement of established objectives.

(g) To ensure that the IT environment incorporates appropriate and justifiable hardware, software, methods, facilities and tools to support the business.

(h) To ensure that the information needs of the business are best served by current and planned systems.

(i) To ensure that a suitable planning methodology is utilised in order to accurately identify underlying requirements and convert them into action plans.

(j) To ensure that only justified and authorised systems are developed and maintained.

(k) To ensure that all IT projects and acquisitions are authorised and in accord with the established planning objectives.

(l) To ensure that cost-effective and optimum solutions are applied.

(m) To ensure that IT-related costs are accurately identified and contained within budgeted limits.

Risk and Control Issues for IT Strategic Planning

1 Key Issues

1.1 How does management ensure that the provision of all IT hardware, software, methods and resources remains in step with the strategic direction of the business and the achievement of competitive advantages, etc.?

1.2 What action does management take to identify and review possible ways of achieving competitive advantage through the application of IT?

1.3 How is management certain that the use of IT facilities best serves the organisation and that unnecessary, inadequate or outdated systems and methods are identified and avoided?

1.4 Has management established a mechanism to ensure that both current and future business needs will be appropriately supported by the use of IT (and how is this evidenced)?

1.5 How does management ensure that the information needs of the business are adequately served?

1.6 What processes ensure that the IT facilities remain relevant and in step with business changes and developments?

1.7 What measures are in place to ensure that all IT costs and investments are in step with the agreed plans and appropriately authorised?

1.8 What mechanisms prevent the acquisition and development of unauthorised systems and facilities (i.e. those outside the agreed direction)?

2 Detailed Issues

2.1 How is management certain that the key business objectives are identified as the basis for accurate IT planning (and what checks are in place to ensure that the objectives remain up to date)?

2.2 How does management ensure that IT planning takes account of current and emerging technical trends as the basis for assessing potential benefits?

2.3 How does management monitor that potential IT projects and facilities are adequately assessed, justified and authorised?

2.4 Has management established a range of agreed and documented policies to support the application of IT throughout the organisation, and to ensure that the objectives of the business are adequately addressed?

2.5 How does management ensure that all IT facilities support a stable, reliable and secure environment (and what checks are in place to establish that key suppliers are stable)?

2.6 What mechanisms ensure that agreed changes to the business operations and objectives are promptly identified and assessed for their impact upon the IT facilities?

2.7 How does management ensure that adequate and appropriately skilled IT staff are available to support the current and anticipated needs?

2.8 How does management ensure that the impacts of adopting specific IT hardware, software, methods and facilities are identified, assessed and adequately planned for?

2.9 Have the data needs of the business been identified as the basis for both current and future systems (and how is redundant or duplicate data avoided)?

2.10 What mechanisms ensure that all new systems and amendments to existing ones are justified and authorised?

2.11 How is the commitment of senior management to the defined IT strategy evidenced?

2.12 How does management ensure that all affected staff are aware of the requirements of the IT strategy and their responsibilities?

2.13 Are all potential systems and IT environmental changes subject to a formal feasibility assessment, justification and approval processes?

2.14 What procedures ensure that all the IT-related costs are accurately identified, monitored and contained?

2.15 Are all amendments to the IT strategy formally reviewed and authorised (and how is this evidenced)?

2.16 How does management ensure that all affected parties (users, system owners, etc.) are adequately consulted and involved in the IT planning process?

2.17 What measures ensure that only accurate and reliable data is used in the IT planning process?

2.18 How is commercially sensitive or confidential information used in the planning process protected from leakage or misuse?

24
IT Organisation

This chapter targets the organisational structure of an in-house IT function. In practice, such functions vary considerably in size and operational scope, so there is no "one style and size fits all" model. The organisation will need to consider the primary purposes of the IT function and how they are to be delivered. Once completed, the key factors can be defined in agreed and authorised policies, such as:

- optimum organisational structure
- terms of reference for the IT function
- service level agreements
- definition of roles and responsibilities (i.e. job descriptions)
- required operational and technical standards, etc.

Control Objectives for IT Organisation

> (a) To ensure that an appropriate and efficient organisational structure is established for the IT function.
>
> (b) To ensure that responsibilities and accountabilities are defined, agreed and allocated.
>
> (c) To ensure that adequate and appropriate IT resources and skills are provided to support the business.
>
> (d) To ensure that an appropriate framework of operating standards, procedures and policies is established, adhered to, maintained and kept up to date,
>
> (e) To ensure that the required levels and standards of IT service provision are established, agreed and can be observed.
>
> (f) To ensure that key duties are appropriately segregated in order to protect the integrity of operations, systems and data.

> (g) To ensure that skill requirements are identified and met through ongoing training and staff development.
>
> (h) To ensure the accuracy and security of user application systems and data.
>
> (i) To ensure that the continuity of operations can be maintained in the event of a disaster or failure.
>
> (j) To ensure that effective channels of communication are provided and that staff remain aware of the required performance, quality and service objectives.

Risk and Control Issues for IT Organisation

1 Key Issues

1.1 Has management adequately defined the organisational structure and responsibilities of the IT function (and how is this kept up to date and relevant)?

1.2 How are management assured that the IT function organisational structure is best placed to support the operation and objectives of the business?

1.3 Have the organisational structure and specific responsibilities been formally agreed and authorised (and how is this evidenced)?

1.4 What mechanisms ensure that agreed responsibilities and accountabilities are accurately and effectively communicated to the IT staff?

1.5 How does management ensure that sufficient levels of IT resource (including suitably skilled staff) are provided to support the current and future needs of the business?

1.6 What steps does management take to ensure that the skills of the IT staff remain relevant and up to date?

1.7 Has a framework of authorised and documented operating standards, procedures and policies been established and implemented?

1.8 How does management ensure that the established standards, procedures and policies are effectively complied with?

1.9 How does management monitor that the required and necessary levels of IT service provision are being appropriately delivered?

1.10 How does management prevent the potential for staff fraud or malpractice in order to protect the integrity of systems and data?

1.11 What steps have been taken to ensure that IT operational facilities are capable of prompt and effective recovery in the event of a disaster or major failure?

1.12 What measures are in place to ensure that operational systems are secure and that operations are correctly conducted?

2 Detailed Issues

2.1 Have formal terms of reference for the IT function been agreed, documented and authorised?

2.2 Have the organisational structure and staffing establishment level been ratified and authorised by senior management (and how is this evidenced)?

2.3 Are changes to the organisational structure and establishment levels formally reviewed, documented and authorised?

2.4 How does management ensure that business objectives and plans are appropriately converted into action plans?

2.5 Has management established monitoring processes to ensure that defined responsibilities, standards and performance objectives are being appropriately met?

2.6 Have agreed budgets been established for the IT function and are they subject to regular and effective monitoring by management?

2.7 What measures ensure that all the required procedures, standards and policies are kept up to date?

2.8 Are changes to procedures and policies subject to management authorisation (and how is this evidenced)?

2.9 How is IT management sure that the level of service provision is adequate and appropriate, and what mechanisms are in place to ensure that users' requirements are identified and addressed?

2.10 How does management ensure that agreed levels of staff training and development resource are effectively targeted in order to avoid waste?

2.11 Has management taken action to prevent important skills being restricted to a limited number of individual employees?

2.12 How does management confirm that the measures in place to aid recovery from disaster or failure remain effective, up to date, and relevant?

2.13 What specific policies or procedures have been established to ensure that processing operations are correctly conducted and that data is adequately protected from corruption, loss or destruction?

2.14 Has management taken steps to ensure that cost-effective and appropriate industry standards and practices are applied in the IT function (i.e. the use of a recognised system development methodology or appropriate programming standards)?

2.15 What mechanisms ensure that adequate lines of communication are established (and used) with system users and owners?

2.16 How does IT management maintain an up-to-date awareness of the current business objectives and requirements?

25
IT Policy Framework

A framework of pragmatic policies surrounding the use and control of IT and information-related facilities should fundamentally guide staff on what to do and, just as importantly, what not to do. Creating such documented guidance is not at the top of everyone's list of tasks, but the process can set the cultural tone and clearly state the objectives that have to be achieved and the risks that have to be avoided or mitigated. In the public sector such policies may be mandatory and also serve to advise the public of the organisation's commitment to good practice.

Each sector and organisation will have its own drivers for creating an IT Policy environment and the specific optimum Policy components will vary. In a later chapter we consider the development of an encompassing Information Management Environment that operates within the relevant legislative and regulatory framework. The following diagram (Figure 25.1) illustrates the documented components of such an environment. The listing of documents is deliberately comprehensive and not all the noted elements will be relevant in every instance.

Taking the elements featured in the following diagram, the table in Appendix 6 briefly describes the purpose of each. The items in the table marked with an asterisk (*) indicate topics which will be covered in greater detail in subsequent chapters of this section. The entries in bold text in Appendix 6 are regarded as key documents in any IT situation.

Many of the noted elements feature as required aspects of the associated ISO/IEC standards and would form part of a mandatory requirement for accreditation purposes.

In the development of IT-related policies, procedures and guidance, organisations should avoid a "tick in the box" mentality, which only gives lip service to the related subjects. Having a policy in place, however comprehensive or detailed, will not guarantee compliance unless it is appropriately promoted within the organisation and supported by effective training, guidance and compliance monitoring.

When considering the development of policies and procedures it should be made clear that information, data, records and media could refer to any form, for example:

- hardcopy data output
- handwritten notes
- physical files of documents

PREVAILING LEGISLATION, REGULATIONS AND STANDARDS	
INFORMATION MANAGEMENT ENVIRONMENT AND CULTURE	
INFORMATION MANAGEMENT POLICY	
IT SECURITY POLICY	**OTHER POLICIES**

Supported by:
• Policy or Mandatory Guidance on:
 	
  • Communications and Operation Management
  • Computer, Telephone and Desk Use
  • Email*
  • Human Resources Information Security Standards
  • Information Protection
  • Incident Management
  • Internet Acceptable Usage*
  • IT Access*
  • IT Infrastructure Security*
  • Legal Responsibilities*
  • Remote Working*
  • Removable Media*
  • Software (selection and development)*
 	
• Change Management Policy (including Patch Management)*
• Anti-virus Update Policy
• Capacity Management Policy*
• Back-up Procedures*
• Business Continuity Plan*
• Disaster Recovery Plan*
• Information Asset Register*
	• Data Protection Policy*
	• Freedom of Information Policy*
	• Publication Scheme
	• Physical Security Policy*
	• Records Management* Policy
	• Knowledge Management* Policy
	• Data Quality Policy
	• Data Transfer and Sharing Standards and Protocol Guidelines*
	• Protective Marking Scheme Guidance
	• Roles and Responsibilities Guidance*
	• Record Retention & Disposal Guidelines*

Figure 25.1 Documented Components of Information Management Environment

- electronic records
- spreadsheet or work processing files
- magnetic media (tape, video tape or disks)
- optical media (CD and DVD)
- film
- photographs or negatives
- plans or drawings
- speech recordings.

Additionally, policies should be targeted not only at employees, but temporary staff, contractors and any agents working on behalf of the organisation. In particular instances it may be necessary to include special or specific groups in the target audience, where they will have a justified and authorised need to use information resources; an example could be elected members of local authorities or bodies, who are not classified as employees.

Policies need to be "owned" by an appropriate manager or officer, who is responsible for ongoing maintenance, periodic review and update of the document. In a more formal management environment, policies may have to be ratified at a senior level prior to their introduction.

Having a policy in place is only the beginning. Employees and other affected parties need to be aware of the contents and the implications for them during the course of their duties. Policies need to be clear and unambiguous and easily accessible, for example from a library of official policies maintained on the organisation's Intranet site. Only the latest and agreed form of the policies and associated documents should be made available, with one definitive access point. Where necessary, support training should be provided for staff to reinforce the key messages and clearly state the key responsibilities arising from the policy or guidance.

The matter of ensuring the required level of understanding of policies and procedures is a more subjective process, but refresher training and periodic reminders delivered through the email system or the corporate Intranet can serve this purpose. Staff and others utilising IT facilities should, in some way, acknowledge that they have read and understood the key policies and understood the associated implications. In larger organisations this can be an onerous task and some organisations have opted to provide a warning message at the point of logging on to the corporate networks to the effect that any user proceeding with the log on, usually signified by clicking on an OK button, has read and understood their responsibilities for adhering to the prevailing policies and procedures. The downside to such a mechanism is that it becomes second nature just to click the OK button without necessarily having taken the time to truly understand the current rules and obligations. Hence the need for appropriate points of reference and support training.

Lastly, policies have a given shelf life and activities, external and internal influences and change all have a potential bearing on the currency and relevance of policies and procedures. As part of the version control of key corporate documentation, a set cycle of policy revision should be considered so that, for example, policy documents are reviewed by their "owners" every two years and updated, ratified and promoted accordingly.

Control Objectives for IT Policy Framework

(a) To ensure that the appropriate policy and procedural framework is in place to provide secure and reliable IT facilities in order to support the organisation's operational and administrative requirements.

(b) To develop, agree and ratify a range of appropriate best practice policies suited to the specific utilisation of IT by the organisation.

(c) To ensure that policies (and related procedural processes) are "owned" by a named manager or officer, who is responsible for promoting, supporting and maintaining the allocated policies.

(d) To ensure that all policies are ratified and formally agreed by senior management as a means of ensuring that they are seen as significant parts of the culture and management oversight of the organisation.

(e) To ensure that policies incorporate any sector-specific issues and best practice exemplars.

(f) To ensure that any legislative or regulatory obligations are included in the relevant policies.

(g) To ensure that policies define how the related key activities will be monitored and managed.

(h) To ensure that the policies (and supporting materials) clearly state what is, in turn, acceptable or unacceptable action or behaviour.

(i) To ensure that policies include, where appropriate, the potential implications of a failure to comply, including employee sanctions.

(j) To provide, where appropriate, documented practical guidance and procedures to support the objectives and principles contained within the various IT policies.

(k) To ensure that general and specific roles and responsibilities are clearly defined within the policies.

(l) To ensure that all policies are periodically reviewed and maintained up to date.

(m) To ensure that policies and the obligations they contain are suitably promoted within the organisation.

(n) To ensure that policies are accessible by all employees as sources of reference.

(o) To ensure that policy awareness is supported by appropriately targeted training.

(p) To ensure that there are reliable methods in place to monitor policy compliance and promptly detect non compliance or breaches of information security.

Risk and Control Issues for IT Policy Framework

1 Key Issues

1.1 Has management established a suitable overarching policy and procedural culture in relation to information and information technology?

1.2 Have management acted to identify all of the required IT related policies, and how is this demonstrated?

1.3 Has management established and demonstrated the principle of "ownership" for policies and procedures? If so, how can employees reliably discover which manager is responsible for which policy?

1.4 Is there a defined official route and process for management to review, agree and ratify corporate IT policies and procedures? If so, how is this evidenced and trailed?

1.5 When creating (or reviewing) IT-related policies and procedures, how does management ensure that all the relevant sector-specific, legislative, regulatory and best practice issues are incorporated?

1.6 Does management take steps to ensure that policies are lawful and enforceable if necessary?

1.7 Has management ensured that the implications of non compliance with legislative or regulatory requirements are defined in the relevant policies?

1.8 Are the policies explicit in terms of the roles and responsibilities of staff?

1.9 How does management ensure that policy compliance is monitored? How would management be alerted to instances of non compliance or a potential breach of information security?

1.10 Are steps taken to ensure that policies and procedures contain clear guidance on what is either acceptable or unacceptable action or behaviour by staff?

1.11 Has management taken effective steps to promote policies and raise staff awareness of the associated issues? Consider how this is evidenced.

1.12 What steps have been taken to ensure that all current policies and procedures are accessible by all staff?

1.13 Has management taken adequate action to support policies with clear documented guidance that is freely accessible by employees?

1.14 How are training needs in relation to policies and procedures (new or amended) identified and addressed?

1.15 Has management established a defined timetable and process for the periodic review of all IT-related policies? Is such action evidenced by the currency of the version dates on extant policies and documents?

1.16 How, in practice, would management be made aware of a policy or procedure that is overdue for review?

2 Detailed Issues

2.1 How have senior management ensured that corporate policies are seen as an essential part of the organisation's management framework?

2.2 How does management ensure that only agreed and ratified policies are circulated for access by employees? How would the presence of outdated or unofficial policies be detected?

2.3 How can employees efficiently establish the status and currency of a policy or procedure and whether its content applies to them?

2.4 What measures are in place to prevent outdated policies being accessed by staff?

2.5 Are staff made aware of the explicit legislative and regulatory compliance issues and the implications for them in the event of non compliance?

2.6 Is there clear guidance provided to staff on what actions would be regarded as unacceptable and the sanctions that could be applied?

2.7 How does management ensure that all target IT users (not just employees) are suitably aware of policy contents and requirements?

2.8 Would it be possible for an employee (or other IT user) to evade the policy awareness processes and claim ignorance of the associated requirements?

2.9 Have specific policy obligations and responsibilities been appropriately incorporated into job descriptions?

2.10 How does management ensure that it is fully aware of issues and changes that could impinge on policy content and trigger a review? In addition, what processes are in place to signify the identification, review and incorporation of such issues and changes?

2.11 How would staff be aware of the training and support available to support IT-related policies?

2.12 Does management monitor the take up of policy training and ensure that steps are taken to ensure that the required messages are effectively and adequately delivered across the organisation?

26
Information Asset Register

To begin, there is a need to define the different types of asset that relate to IT and Information Management, as follows:

- All IT equipment, owned by the organisation, is regarded as **hardware assets** and treated, for accounting purposes, as fixed assets (further comment on the issues relating to fixed assets can be found in Chapter 12).
- All software, owned or licensed by the organisation, is regarded as a **software asset**, and will likely be treated as revenue expenditure.
- The final category of **information assets** includes the contents of:
  - databases
  - electronic records, files and documents
  - paper records and files
  - mailboxes
  - data files
  - drawings
  - configuration files
  - photographs, and so on.

Although all the noted categories of asset need to be accounted for and controlled, this chapter focuses on **information assets** which, although not represented in financial accounting terms, are usually of great operational value to an organisation and without which the organisation may cease to function or exist. However, consider how many organisations, both public and private, actually make the effort to identify, record and truly manage their information assets. In one sense, information can become such a recognised, familiar and commonplace part of the organisation that its continued presence and sustainability can be taken for granted.

To paraphrase a well-known observation, it may be true that "if we only knew all the information we had, we could do a lot better". From the audit and review standpoint, the appropriate phrase might be "if you don't know what information you have, how can you be sure that you are treating it appropriately?" In either case, there can be value in identifying existing sets of information as the basis for either singly or collectively:

- ensuring the accuracy and integrity of information;
- identifying opportunities to develop and enhance information and its uses;
- identifying gaps in current information sets;
- using information in innovative and positive ways;
- maximising the use of information to the benefit of the organisation;
- adequately protecting information from loss or disruption;
- ensuring that security measures in place are appropriate and proportional to the type and value of the information being protected;
- identifying personal or sensitive information (for example, in a Data Protection context) as a means of ensuring appropriate compliance;
- identifying information that is either exempt from or applicable to disclosure under the prevailing Freedom of Information regime;
- ensuring that information is obtained, used, disclosed and disposed of in accordance with the relevant laws and regulations;
- identifying any redundant, unused or unnecessary information;
- ensuring that the organisation is not exposed to risks and liabilities;
- enabling information to be classified according to its sensitivity (for example in relation to the categories of a Protective Marking Scheme).

It is critical that the responsibility for the operation and oversight of creating and maintaining an Information Asset Register or Inventory should be allocated to a specific individual (such as a project manager), even though some of the required constituent tasks may be devolved to others. In more formal conditions or where the creation of a register or inventory is for a large and complex organisation, a formally managed project may be necessary with a detailed project plan, key milestones and the associated senior management monitoring of progress and costs, etc.

In order to encompass the above noted activities and aspects, it would be necessary to create some form of comprehensive record of all the relevant information assets within the organisation. However, this process needs to be established on a pragmatic and achievable basis so as to constrain the range of potential asset targets. On the one hand, the range of assets could drill down to lower levels (such as spreadsheet files) or copies or subsets of data that may have secondary uses, but it would be a long-winded and onerous task just to identify this level of detail let alone catalogue it. Additionally, it is doubtful whether such a level of detail would generate any significant benefits. The corollary of this detailed identification is one that is at a too high a level and that fails to provide sufficient depth to reflect the underlying security and management issues. In order for the process to be achievable and manageable, some form of cut-off limit is required that allows for all the active key and primary information sets to be identified.

Having established a workable scope to the process of identifying information assets, the types of data required to be collected and the means of capturing and recording the data will need to be determined.

When determining the data that needs to be collected about information assets, it can be said that it may fall into one of two categories; firstly essential elements such as the form and format of the data (for example, physical handwritten index cards, electronic data in a relational database or electronic records with the customer number as the index key, and so on); secondly, additional data fields that may serve another administrative or analysis function beyond the essentials required for the operation of the Information Asset Register (for example, details of the number of user licences in place, identifying the files required for a system rebuild, and so on).

The following data fields are suggested as the basis for an Information Asset Register or inventory. Some of the fields lend themselves to being in the form of codes and others could be automatically completed based on entries in other fields or in accord with the rules held in a macro or automated process:

- **Name** of information or data set.
- **Dates** of creation of initial entry or when the asset became operationally active.
- Register or inventory **reference** number.
- **Status** of asset (for example, in live operational use or under review for replacement by Project X).
- Category, code or indicator for the **sensitivity of the data** asset (this element could directly relate to the classifications used with a Protective Marking Scheme (PMS) or be tailored so as to reflect whether the data was of a personal or sensitive nature and related to any Data Protection legislation. In any event it should clearly determine how the data should be treated in terms of access protection, disclosure protection and disposal.)
- **Freedom of Information status** (this field could be used, in association with a formal Publication Scheme, to indicate whether the data can be released under the conditions of freedom of information, right to information or access to information legislation. NB: If the data is encoded as exempt from public disclosure the next data field should record the reason for withholding its release.)
- **FoI exemption** (for example, if the data are officially categorised as Confidential or where the release of the data could be prejudicial to the public or national interest).
- Category, code or description of **asset contents** (i.e. Primary Retail Customer Database).
- Category, code or description of **use of asset** (i.e. to validate eligibility for trade discount).
- Related **application system or software environment** (i.e. the system with which the data is used; for example, Spectrum Accounts V3, Microsoft Excel™, Vista™, etc.).
- **Directorate or Department** (i.e. the area of the organisation where the asset is primarily used. This aspect can be recorded in a number of ways so as to better match the organisational structure of a specific entity).
- **System Owner** (i.e. the senior employee in the area where the data is primarily used).
- **Data Owner** (i.e. this may be the same person or officer as the System Owner, but it relates to the individual who has the most influence and active oversight role for data entry, accuracy and integrity).
- Category or code relating to the **level of security to be applied** to the data (for example, High, Medium or Low. NB: The application of this code could be automatically derived by taking into account some of the other data fields below.)
- **Usage level** (e.g. High, Medium or Low in terms of activities).

- **Frequency of update** (for example encoded for real time, 24/7, daily, weekly, etc. as best suits the organisation).
- **Method of update** (for example, authorised users, online, offline, system administrator only, and so on).
- **Form** (i.e. physical card index arranged in account number sequence or electronic file).
- **Technical Format** (i.e. sequential flat file with comma separated variables with a total length of 256 characters sorted by account number or relational database confirming to an unmodified application supplier design). If either the form or format are no longer capable of being supported (due to media or software obsolescence), consideration should be given to the sustainability of the records in terms of ongoing digital preservation.
- **Location** (this field could address a number of requirements, for example it could simply hold the physical location of a set of physical files (e.g. Accounts Department Archive) or indicate the "systematic" location details (for example, active database in the live version of Proteus Accounts on shared server Y).
- **Total number of records.**
- Total number of **live records**.
- Total number of **dormant records** (also include how such records are identified, for example by adding an asterisk to the account number).
- **Date last amended** (plus name of editor and reason for change).
- **Retention period** (this factor may be defined by either legislation or regulation, which in turn may apply further conditions on the method of archiving, long-term storage and access).
- **Disposal method** (this field should indicate the method to be applied to disposing of the data. This is likely to depend on a combination of other factors on the register, such as the sensitivity of data or whether it is of a personal nature. The coding of this field should be simple and clear, for example, Cross-cut shred all documents, Confidential Disposal or Irreversible Destruction of electronic media and so on.)
- **Controls in place** (this field could be used to note, in summary form, the nature of the key controls in place to protect data, such as access controls that restrict user access, the daily back-up of data files, controlling access to a physical record storage area through the use of key cards and so on).
- **Gaps in controls** (it is possible that during the course of compiling the register or subsequently reviewing the contents, some gaps in control are detected. Details of such gaps and the related risks could be recorded in this area together with any planned corrective action in a specified timescale. Any significant residue risks should be formally assessed and considered for entry on to the corporate risk register for monitoring purposes.)
- **Comments** field to accommodate additional notes (ideally data stamped).

There are various collection methods that could be applied, including for example:

- A centrally-driven information gathering exercise using consistent methods of enquiry and capture. (Although this method is the most time-consuming and costly to apply, it should deliver accurate and consistent outcomes); or

- A self assessment approach whereby system owners or administrators gather the data for their area(s) of responsibility using some form of standard pro forma. (This approach would require some degree of coordinated quality control to ensure data accuracy and consistency.)

The key control elements at this stage are to ensure that the collection of data is complete and consistent across all of the organisation's functions. Some form of cross-checking or quality control should be applied, perhaps centrally, prior to the collected data being accepted for the purpose of creating the Information Asset Register.

In addition the options for the recording of data about information assets could include, for example:

- gathering and holding the information asset data on paper, using a standard format, which would severely limit the subsequent analysis and interrogation of the records and would be prone to damage or loss;
- gathering the data on paper for subsequent transcription onto a suitable electronic system, which could introduce interpretation and transcription errors;
- gathering the data electronically (perhaps online) through an intermediary system for later upload to the eventual asset register or inventory. This method could incorporate some form of data validation and completeness checking to contribute to data accuracy; or
- direct entry of the data into the register or inventory system, although access and use of the system will have to be limited in the case of those entering data so as not to compromise the integrity of the overall register. For example, data entry users should be limited to accessing only that area of the system that relates to their department, service or function and actively prevent them from accessing other data and facilities.

Whatever the methods employed to gather and record the data about information assets, the register should be periodically reviewed and maintained up to date. Ideally there should be processes in place to alert the nominated register manager to any changes in information records. Such changes will include, but not be limited to:

- the introduction of new information sets or systems;
- the modification or expansion of existing information sets;
- the withdrawal from use of data sets due to, for example, the redundancy of an application system or the cessation of an operational service;
- changes in any of the characteristics recorded on the register, for example, the inclusion of personal data in the information set, a change of Protective Marking Scheme categorisation, or the transfer of data to a different storage format.

As part of the wider Information Management Environment, the asset register forms a critical part of enabling the identification of key information assets and determining whether they are being adequately managed, maintained, exploited and protected.

If an organisation has the intention of systematically ensuring the adequacy of its Information Management Environment, the data contained within the Information Asset Register should support the current status for key and critical information assets. It can also be used by internal audit as a means of assessing relative risks and targeting audit resources in to reviewing areas of potential risk and/or assessing whether the status and other conditions recorded on the register are accurate and justified. Finally, and taking into account, where applicable, the activities of internal audit and others who independently review the Information Asset Register, senior management can use the register in their consideration of the effectiveness of information and corporate governance.

In summary, the register or inventory of information assets is a major and key component in the overall Information Management Environment, by being the consolidated repository of details of the key data sets used and managed by the organisation. As such, it is a platform upon which other aspects of the Information Management Environment can be built and developed, for example, as a means of supporting the legitimacy of protecting and disclosing data.

Control Objectives for Information Asset Register

(a) To ensure that management take the steps necessary to assess the benefits of creating an Information Asset Register or inventory and, if proven justified, to allocate adequate resources for its creation and ongoing maintenance.

(b) To ensure that there is ownership of the register or inventory at both a senior management (e.g. board) level and across the organisation.

(c) To ensure that day-to-day responsibility for the creation and ongoing maintenance of the register or inventory is allocated to a nominated person, manager or officer.

(d) To ensure that, where appropriate, the creation of an Information Asset Register or inventory is regarded as a project to be managed using formal project planning and management method and led by a suitably experienced project manager.

(e) To ensure that the register provides senior management with the ability to accurately consider the impacts of their decisions on the organisation's information assets and to support effective decision making and planning.

(f) To ensure that senior management utilise the facility of an Information Asset Register to aid their assessment of information governance and corporate governance.

(g) To ensure that all information assets are accurately identified as the basis for their effective management and protection.

(h) To ensure that the data specification for the register is robust, practical and provides the necessary reporting and monitoring functionality.

(i) To ensure that the application system or software environment hosting the register is robust, proven, fit for purpose and adequately secure. This should include the application of any IT procurement procedures aimed at assessing the financial stability of the supplier and the technical quality of the system itself.

(j) To ensure that the optimum method of data collection is used to accurately populate the register. This should include the validation of data (either manually or by some automated means) and some form of data quality control process.

(k) To ensure that all information assets are correctly categorised and codified so as to accurately reflect their significance, degree of sensitivity and operational importance to the organisation.

(l) To ensure that only authorised and appropriate amendments are applied to the register; and that only authorised users have access to the register system.

(m) To ensure information security measures are proportional to the value and sensitivity of the data.

(n) To facilitate the efficient identification of personal data sets that should be managed in accordance with the prevailing Data Protection legislation and/or regulations should be specifically codified and identifiable.

(o) To ensure that the register provides clear indications of the data that can be publicly disclosed, for example under the prevailing Freedom of Information legislation or an approved Publication Scheme.

(p) To ensure that management take the action necessary to ensure that all staff are made aware of the register, its various purposes and its use as a reference point for determining when information can and cannot be released due to either being defined, as appropriate in each specific case, as publicly accessible, personal or lawfully exempt.

(q) To ensure that there is the ability to readily detect situations which could have an impact on the contents of the register (for example, the expansion of an existing system or the removal from service of a legacy system) and to promptly reflect such changes on the register.

(r) To ensure that an Information Asset Register or inventory is accurately maintained and periodically reviewed.

(s) To ensure that any gaps in controls exercised over information assets are promptly identified and action taken to improve control to an adequate level.

Risk and Control Issues for Information Asset Register

1 Key Issues

1.1 What steps has management taken to assess the justification and purpose of an Information Asset Register or inventory, and how is this evidenced?

1.2 What is the evidence for senior management buy-in to and ownership of the Information Asset Register and its supporting concepts?

1.3 Have management identified the possible uses and potential benefits of the register in relation to effective decision making, comprehensive planning, compliance with Data Protection and Freedom of Information regulations, information governance and corporate governance? Is there documented evidence of this assessment?

1.4 Has a senior manager been allocated the overall responsibility for the creation and ongoing maintenance of the register? (If so, have the relevant responsibilities been made clear and documented, for example in the manager's job description?).

1.5 Has management taken adequate steps to positively promote the register to all staff and is the awareness of employees at an appropriate level in terms of the implications of the register for their duties and their related responsibilities?

1.6 Have management considered treating the development of the register as a discrete project that would be subject to formal project planning and management methods? If not, how do they envisage the process being handled?

1.7 If necessary, has a suitably experienced and knowledgeable project manager been appointed and been given documented terms of reference and responsibilities?

1.8 Has management ensured that all of their needs will be adequately supported by the identification of all the required data fields and the analysis functionality of the host system?

1.9 How has management ensured that the codification, categorisation and classification of register entries are suitably robust, comprehensive, workable and effective?

1.10 How has management ensured that the most appropriate system has been adopted to host the register?

1.11 How will management ensure that the register contents will be complete, accurate and reliable, and will be maintained in that condition on an ongoing basis?

1.12 How can management be assured that all the current sets of information have been identified, assessed for inclusion on the register and then recorded within it?

1.13 What mechanisms would prevent unauthorised access to and/or amendment of the contents of the register?

1.14 How is the current and ongoing accuracy and completeness of the register assured?

1.15 How would management be made aware of any incomplete, corrupted or inaccurate register data?

1.16 Has management defined and promoted a clear basis for determining the required level of security measures for each of the categorisations of information contained within the register?

1.17 Has management ensured that the register will enable the prompt, accurate and complete identification of information sets that have either Data Protection and/or Freedom of Information implications?

1.18 How can management be sure that the data contained within the register will not allow a breach of information security to occur?

1.19 How does management ensure that gaps in controls in relation to information security and management are identified and appropriately addressed?

2 Detailed Issues

2.1 Have management provided adequate guidance and support material for staff so that the purpose and use of the Information Asset Register is sufficiently clear?

2.2 Has management made adequate arrangements for all staff to have read only access to the register so as to support employees in determining the appropriate action to take with regard to information?

2.3 Has appropriate and sufficient training and supporting documentation been provided and can it be readily accessed by staff?

2.4 Have the implications and resource requirements of the register exercise been accurately determined?

2.5 If the creation of the register is to be formally managed, has a comprehensive plan been created that reflects key milestones, inter-dependencies and practical target timescales?

2.6 Has management taken adequate steps to assess the stability and suitability of the selected host application for the register and to ensure the financial stability and reliability of the system supplier? (For example, have formal procurement processes been applied including the development of functional and technical requirement specifications?)

2.7 Have management established a process by which only authorised users will be able to update or amend the register?

2.8 Does the register provide adequate information to enable staff to discern when information can and cannot be publicly disclosed?

27
Capacity Management

It is obviously essential that capacity of the IT service keeps pace with the demands placed upon it both currently and in the future. In order to be sufficiently forewarned and prepared there should be a firm linkage between the long-term operational and service area planning process and the development and maintenance of the IT Strategy or Strategic Plan as discussed in Chapter 23.

IT capacity management will likely embrace a number of components of the IT infrastructure including, but not necessarily limited to:

- network performance (speed and bandwidth)
- electronic storage (devices for holding and maintaining electronic records)
- processing ability (the capacity to efficiently perform processing).

As for the development of an IT strategic plan, capacity planning can be based on clearly understanding the current situation, assessing the various capacity impacts of known forthcoming changes (for example taking on a new service or activity), evaluating what needs to be done in order to meet the changed demands and then developing a planned and authorised approach to implementing the required changes.

As with any other aspect of an organisation, change will inevitably happen and must be, whenever possible, planned for and coordinated. Despite aiming for a smooth and well managed change utopia, sudden and drastic change is often necessary, for example to take advantage of new business opportunities or to limit the impacts of a recession. Although capacity should avoid over-egging the IT pudding, there is some merit in ensuring that there is sufficient contingency in order to cope with unplanned peaks in demand and to cushion the introduction of new aspects prior to obtaining all the required target capacity. However, as always, cost is a factor here and the costs of providing increased capacity need to be taken into account in any financial modelling of new or speculative ventures and weighed against the overall benefits.

The ongoing monitoring and assessment of IT capacities should ideally be defined with an agreed Capacity Management Policy and Plan.

Control Objectives for Capacity Management

> (a) To ensure that the various IT capacities remain at an optimum level in order to support the organisation currently and in the future.
>
> (b) To ensure that IT capacities are economically provided and to avoid unnecessary or excessive provision costs.
>
> (c) To ensure that any proposed changes in operations or service provision are appropriately planned for and assessed in terms of potential IT capacity impacts.
>
> (d) To ensure that IT management are engaged in the high-level organisation planning process so that they can assess and plan for the IT implications.
>
> (e) To avoid the disruption or failure of operations or service provision due to a lack of available IT capacities.
>
> (f) To avoid sudden or unplanned operational changes that could adversely impact upon IT capacities.

Risk and Control Issues for Capacity Management

1 Key Issues

1.1 What action does IT management take to ensure that IT capacities (of all relevant types) are sufficient for the current and future needs of the organisation?

1.2 How does IT management avoid wasteful, excessive or unnecessary capacity expansion?

1.3 How does IT management monitor capacity performance?

1.4 By what means would IT management be alerted to potential capacity shortcomings?

1.5 How can IT management be sure that they remain aware of all long-term organisation plans?

1.6 How does IT management ensure that there is sufficient time to implement capacity changes between being made aware of the need to change and the instigation of the related organisational changes?

1.7 How does senior management ensure that IT capacity changes offer value for money and are justified?

1.8 How does IT management calculate the various capacity contingency levels and how do they ensure that such calculations are realistic?

2 Detailed Issues

2.1 Are the cost implications of changes in IT capacity calculated and taken into account when considering new operations, services or functions?

2.2 Are IT capacity arrangements defined within an agreed and ratified Capacity Planning Policy?

28
Information Management (IM)

Information in combination with employees, finance, products, technologies etc. represents the valued assets of an organisation. Without accurate, complete, up-to-date and reliable information, an organisation would struggle to exist if not completely fail. As was noted in Chapter 26 above, corporate information has a true value and is deserving of careful husbandry and protection in order to deliver benefits.

Information Management (IM) has a wide-ranging influence over an organisation's management and governance of the information assets it uses. In addition to good practice, the Information Management Environment should also address legal or regulatory implications and ensure the security and appropriate protection of information. The effort and resources involved in implementing an effective IM environment should not be underestimated, although the actual impacts will vary and are likely to be lessened in organisations where good practices in relation to information and IT have previously been in place. However, many organisations may face the development of the IM environment either from scratch or in a culture that has previously been somewhat fragmented or lacking a corporate focus.

It is usual to have in place an Information Management Policy and such a policy should contain the necessary principles so that all information assets will be:

- accurate, up-to-date and comprehensive for the purpose they are intended;
- accessible and readily usable;
- managed and governed by a set of rules that all staff understand and apply;
- kept safe and secure;
- compliant with the prevailing legislation, regulations, recognised standards and the organisation's policies and procedures;
- effectively managed as records and be described, stored, archived and disposed of in an organised, managed and regulated manner;
- created and stored in a manner that, although providing appropriate protection, enables them to be shared with Data Subjects, across the organisation and, where authorised, with strategic partners and external bodies;

- regularly evaluated to ensure they support the organisation's objectives, service delivery commitments, corporate planning and decision making and the effective management of employees, assets, resources and technologies.

In summary, Information Management (and its associated policy) provides the overall structure and cultural tone for the organisation's collection, utilisation, storage, sharing, protection, disclosure and disposal of information assets.

Organisations will use information in a variety of ways, including, but not limited to:

- collecting information about people, businesses and organisations (e.g. customers, debtors and regulatory authorities);
- using information to provide services (e.g. transactions, case information, specifications);
- using information for planning purposes (e.g. previous sales trends, levels of market penetration and financial budgeting);
- developing the organisation and its services (e.g. financial assessment of possible new ventures);
- sharing information internally and externally (e.g. moving data between service areas to support more coherent service provision or passing employee income data to national taxation authorities);
- supporting decision making and administration (e.g. assessment of business expansion or controlling creditor payments);
- collecting and using information about staff (e.g. attendance records, establishment budgeting and training requirements);
- managing financial records (e.g. asset management, liabilities or project costs).

The policy approach to Information Management (IM) should include the following commitments:

- To manage and organise information assets to support the objectives and aims of the organisation, service provision and delivery, decision making and effective administration of operations, assets and resources.
- To manage information held as records in a regulated way (please refer to Chapter 29 on Records Management for further details).
- To ensure that data, information and knowledge are readily available to authorised users in a form that is understandable.
- To ensure that information assets are accurate, accessible, complete, appropriately organised and managed in compliance with good practice, prevailing regulations and recognised standards.
- To ensure that the sharing and transfer of information is lawful, authorised and subject to appropriate protection from loss, unauthorised access or disclosure and corruption (please refer to Chapter 46 on Data Transfer and Sharing for further details).
- To ensure that personal and sensitive data is protected so as to maintain its confidentiality (please refer to Chapter 44 on Data Protection for further details).

From the management and employee viewpoint, Information Management requires them to think about the information and related systems used in their sections, functions and departments and to consider the following key questions:

- How is the information gathered, stored, used, disclosed and disposed of?
- Have specific responsibilities for these activities been clearly allocated?
- In what ways would the disclosure of information be either illegal or inappropriate?
- Is there an appropriate level of knowledge and understanding about the lawful and secure use of information?
- Are there any possible improvements that should be considered and introduced in respect of protecting and controlling information?
- How do we ensure the accuracy and overall integrity of information?
- Is there effective control exercised over access to information?
- Is information protected from unauthorised access and who within the organisation is actually authorised to view the department's information?

The following key aspects of IM are provided together with comments on how they can be supported within an organisation. In many instances, these components should also be the subject of a specific policy underpinned by supporting procedures and employee guidance materials. A mapping of the policy linkages to the noted aspects is provided later in this chapter. In addition, the key policy areas are the subject of separate chapters within this section.

Accessibility

- Ethos of openness and transparency limited, as necessary, by matters of privacy, confidentiality and any legislative on regulatory stipulations.
- Information may be shared across the organisation in order to provide improved and coordinated services.
- Access to information will be granted in relationship to its categorisation or determination under privacy rules or those of a Protective Marking Scheme.

Accuracy

- Validation of information at the point of acquisition.
- Verification of information against other proven sources.
- Automatic validation checks applied within application systems to detect and trap possible errors or omissions.

Compliance

- Ensuring that employees have an appropriate awareness of compliance issues.
- Provision of specific and detailed supporting guidance on key compliance areas such as Data Protection and Freedom of Information.
- Establishing a system of policies to support the overall IM environment.

Information Sharing

- Where information can be lawfully shared within and outwith the organisation it will be stored and organised to facilitate the shared access.
- Information will be shared in accordance with the conditions of prevailing laws, regulations, internal policies and information categorisation schemes so as to protect personal and sensitive information from unauthorised use or disclosure.
- Information will be shared, as is appropriate, for the prevention or detection of fraud.
- Information will be shared with national government departments, agencies and bodies as required by law or regulation (for example, with the taxation authorities or law enforcement agencies).
- Information sharing with partners or other external parties must always be justified, agreed and subject to a formal and documented information sharing agreement between all parties that includes, *inter alia*, procedures for encryption, access security and secure disposal.

Monitoring and Evaluation

- Departments, functions and service areas of the organisation should undertake ongoing monitoring of the use of information as a means of ensuring that it continues to be lawful, supportive of the organisation's objectives and is accurate and fit for purpose.
- Management should take remedial action in the event that information becomes inaccurate, unreliable or otherwise corrupted.
- Management should ensure that the internal and external sharing of their information is lawful, doesn't contravene privacy and security considerations and is appropriately justified.

Records Management (RM)

- A ratified Records Management Policy should be in place and staff should be aware of its implications and their responsibilities.
- Information resources will be created and managed as records in accordance with a defined set of rules.
- Information records will only be gathered and used for valid and authorised purposes.
- Records will be retained for operational purposes and in accordance with any prevailing legislative or regulatory requirements.
- Redundant records will be disposed of in prescribed and secure ways that take account of the nature and sensitivity of the contents.
- There will be mechanisms in place that prevent the accidental or premature disposal of records.

Roles and Responsibilities

- Staff and other authorised users of information should be aware of all the policy and procedural requirements, especially areas where there are specific responsibilities involved.
- Management will be responsible for ensuring compliance with the prevailing policies and procedures, and should also be monitoring for any actual or suspected failures to comply.
- Training and supporting guidance will be provided.

Security and Safety

- An IT Security Policy will be in place and available to all employees.
- The IT Security Policy will be supported, where necessary, by other specific policies, guidance documentation and training resources.
- All employees will be required to understand their responsibilities under the various policies and to comply accordingly.
- Managers will ensure that the various policies are deployed and implemented in their departments, services and functions.
- Employees will specifically take steps to protect their user identities and associated passwords from unauthorised use.
- Employees will be aware of how to treat and handle personal and sensitive data (in any forms, including verbal information) and the limits of their own authority to access, view and disclose such information.

Further information on matters of Information and IT Security can be obtained from:

- The Institute of Information Security Professionals (IISP)
  - Mail: 83 Victoria Street, London, SW1H 0HW
  - Web: www.instisp.org
  - Email: info@instisp.com
- The Information Security Awareness Forum (ISAF)
  - Web: www.theisaf.org
- The Information Security Forum (ISF)
  - Web: www.securityforum.org
- The Information System Security Association (ISSA)
  - Mail: ISSA Inc. 9220 SW Barbur Blvd #119-333 Portland, OR 97219
  - Web: www.issa.org
- The International Information Systems Security Certification Consortium (ISC)
  - Web: www.isc2.org
  - Mail:

- (ISC) Americas, 1964 Gallows Road, Suite 210, Vienna, Virginia, 22182, USA
- (ISC) EMEA, Winchester House, 259–269 Old Marylebone Road, London NW1 5RA
- (ISC) Asia-Pacific, Unit A, 10/F, BOCG Insurance Tower, No. 134–136 Des Voeux Road, Central Hong Kong
- (ISC) Japan, Kamiyacho Prime Place, 3FL 4-1-17 Toranomon Minato-ku, Tokyo 105-0001 Japan

Standards

- The organisation will define and apply the appropriate and recognised standards to all aspects of IM.
- All employees should be made aware of the implications of such standards in respect of their work activities.
- Employees will apply corporate standards in the use of documents, all means of communication (internal and external) and promotional materials.
- Where necessary, training in the application of standards will be provided.
- Management will ensure that any defined standards are applied.

Up to Date Information

- All departments, service areas and functions will ensure that their information is maintained up to date.
- There will be processes in place to ensure the timely update of records and the detection of any shortfall in applying such amendments.

Usability

- Information assets will be created and maintained in a form that is usable by all of the intended users and recipients.
- Information assets will be in a format and language that supports the needs of the end-user.
- The means of delivering information will be diverse as a means of enabling the appropriate exposure.
- If information has to be provided in support of complex regulatory requirements, it should be supported by supplementary information that simply explains the terminology and issues.

Knowledge Management

- A formal Knowledge Management Policy and process will be created, when appropriate, as a means of ensuring that key corporate knowledge is identified, captured, shared and beneficially exploited. See Chapter 30 for further details of Knowledge Management.

The following table maps the potential interrelationships between the above noted aspects of the Information Management Environment and the supporting policies and guidance that should be considered for development and implementation. The presence of a symbol (▲) indicates that such a relationship exists and that the relevant practical aspects will need, at least, to be considered. The following mapping is a comprehensive one and adopts an all-embracing and liberal view of the associated relationships. In practice, a specific organisation, by virtue of its sector, type, regulatory obligations and size, may generate a less demanding mapping.

Policy or guidance document	Accessibility	Accuracy	Compliance	Information Sharing	Monitoring & Evaluation	Records Management	Roles and Responsibilities	Security and Safety	Standards	Up to Date	Usability	Knowledge Management
Information Management Policy	▲	▲	▲	▲	▲	▲	▲	▲	▲	▲	▲	▲
IT Security Policy	▲	▲	▲	▲	▲	▲	▲	▲	▲	▲	▲	
Communications and Operations Management	▲	▲	▲	▲	▲	▲	▲	▲	▲	▲	▲	
Computer, Telephone and Desk Use	▲	▲	▲	▲		▲	▲	▲	▲			
Email		▲	▲	▲	▲	▲	▲	▲	▲		▲	
Human Resources Information Security Standards	▲	▲	▲	▲	▲	▲	▲	▲	▲	▲	▲	
Information Protection	▲	▲	▲	▲	▲	▲	▲	▲	▲	▲		▲
Incident Management	▲	▲	▲	▲	▲	▲	▲	▲	▲	▲	▲	
Internet (Acceptable Usage)	▲		▲	▲	▲	▲	▲	▲	▲			▲
IT Access	▲	▲	▲	▲	▲	▲	▲	▲	▲	▲	▲	▲
IT Infrastructure Security	▲	▲	▲	▲	▲	▲	▲	▲	▲	▲	▲	
Legal Responsibilities	▲	▲	▲	▲	▲	▲	▲	▲	▲	▲	▲	▲
Remote Working	▲	▲	▲	▲	▲	▲	▲	▲	▲	▲	▲	
Removable Media		▲	▲	▲	▲		▲	▲	▲			
Software	▲	▲	▲		▲	▲	▲	▲	▲	▲		
Change & Patch Management		▲	▲		▲		▲	▲	▲	▲		
Anti-Virus Update	▲	▲	▲	▲	▲	▲	▲	▲	▲	▲	▲	
Capacity Planning	▲				▲	▲	▲	▲	▲	▲	▲	

Policy or guidance document	Accessibility	Accuracy	Compliance	Information Sharing	Monitoring & Evaluation	Records Management	Roles and Responsibilities	Security and Safety	Standards	Up to Date	Usability	Knowledge Management
Back-up Procedures	▲	▲	▲		▲	▲	▲	▲	▲	▲	▲	
Business Continuity Plan	▲	▲	▲	▲	▲	▲	▲	▲	▲	▲	▲	▲
Disaster Recovery Plan	▲	▲	▲		▲	▲	▲	▲	▲	▲		
Information Asset Register	▲	▲	▲	▲	▲	▲	▲	▲	▲	▲		▲
Data Protection Policy	▲	▲	▲	▲	▲	▲	▲	▲	▲	▲	▲	▲
Freedom of Information Policy (FoI)	▲	▲	▲	▲	▲	▲	▲	▲	▲	▲	▲	
Publication Scheme	▲	▲	▲	▲	▲		▲	▲	▲	▲	▲	
Physical Security Policy	▲	▲	▲	▲	▲	▲	▲	▲	▲	▲	▲	
Records Management Policy	▲	▲	▲	▲	▲	▲	▲	▲	▲	▲	▲	▲
Knowledge Management Policy		▲		▲		▲	▲	▲	▲	▲	▲	▲
Data Quality Policy		▲	▲	▲	▲	▲	▲		▲	▲	▲	▲
Data Transfer and Sharing Standards & Protocol	▲	▲	▲	▲	▲	▲	▲	▲	▲	▲	▲	▲
Protective Marking Scheme		▲	▲	▲	▲	▲	▲	▲	▲	▲	▲	▲
Roles and Responsibilities	▲	▲	▲	▲	▲	▲	▲	▲	▲	▲	▲	▲
Record Retention & Disposal		▲	▲		▲	▲	▲	▲	▲	▲	▲	

Control Objectives for Information Management

(a) To ensure that all the organisation's information assets have been accurately identified as the basis for applying effective Information Management.

(b) To ensure that information is effectively managed and exploited.

(c) To ensure that the creation and use of corporate information is geared to the overall objectives and commitments of the organisation.

(d) To ensure that there is a sufficiently defined and robust policy and procedural framework in place for the application of best practice Information Management.

(e) To ensure the IM Policy and procedural requirements have been adequately promoted.

(f) To ensure that there is sufficient senior management buy in to the concepts of IM.

(g) To ensure that an appropriate IM culture is developed across the organisation and that all employees have a sufficient awareness of the key issues and their responsibilities for IM.

(h) To ensure that the IM environment fully meets with any legislative, regulatory or standard requirements.

(i) To ensure that the organisation and storage of information is both accessible to authorised users and adequately protected from loss, corruption or inappropriate disclosure.

(j) To ensure that data is only transferred or shared when it is lawful to do so and for defined and justifiable purposes.

(k) To ensure that the sharing of data with external parties is only permitted in authorised situations and bound by the terms of a formal signed Information Sharing Agreement that defines the expectations in relation to usage, storage, access control, security, additional distribution and eventual disposal.

(l) To ensure that key information assets that are utilised in the creation and management of knowledge are identified and protected.

Risk and Control Issues for Information Management

1 Key Issues

1.1 How are management assured that they have identified the key information assets upon which the continued operation of the organisation depends?

1.2 What steps have been taken to ensure that information assets will be effectively managed and exploited?

1.3 What steps have management taken to ensure the accuracy, integrity and security of information assets?

1.4 How can senior management be assured that management of information across the organisation will adequately support the corporate objectives?

1.5 What steps have management taken to establish clear rules that have to be applied to information?

1.6 How can management be assured that, through its use of information, the organisation will be and remain compliant with all the prevailing legislation, regulations and standards?

1.7 How does management ensure that any control failures within the Information Management Environment will be promptly detected and targeted for remedial action?

1.8 Has management established key criteria and a structured approach for the implementation and operation of a suitable IM environment?

1.9 What mechanisms are in place to ensure that the organisation's approach to Information Management remains up to date and reflects either international, national or sector-specific best practice?

1.10 What steps have been taken to ensure that information is only transferred between internal operational units and functions when it is justified and lawful?

1.11 How can management be assured that all transfers of information outside of the organisation are justified, authorised and the subject of documented agreements? In addition how would they either prevent or detect breaches of associated procedures?

1.12 By what means does management ensure that only authorised users with a proven operational need can access the required information?

2 Detailed Issues

2.1 How are staff expected to be aware of the policy, procedural and regulatory requirements related to Information Management?

2.2 How does management ensure that staff are adequately aware of their responsibilities for Information Management?

2.3 How does management ensure that the policy and procedural components of the IM environment are maintained up to date?

2.4 What proactive measures have been taken to raise the profile of IM across the organisation and are they sufficient to create the necessary cultural tone?

2.5 Have staff been suitably advised of the circumstances when it is either acceptable or unacceptable to share or transfer information with other parts of the organisation or with external parties?

2.6 How would management be made aware of any breaches of the rules in relation to either the internal or external transfer of data?

2.7 Are there clear guidelines on the conditions that need to be met before information can be transferred outside of the organisation to a third party?

29
Records Management (RM)

The majority of organisations will accept that, alongside employees and other assets, information plays a key role in sustaining operations, maintaining control of administration and offering alternative ways of doing business. Information can come in many forms and the effective management of records can contribute to efficiencies, sound decision making and due accountability.

In the context of Records Management, a record is defined as being any information held by an organisation irrespective of the medium, including, but not necessarily limited to, the following:

- Electronic records (e.g. within an application system or in the form of Microsoft Word™ or Excel™ document files)
- Paper files (including handwritten documents and forms)
- Reports and printouts
- Microfiche and microfilm
- Plans and maps
- Drawings
- Emails
- Photographs
- Audio-visual materials.

As noted in Chapter 25 on Policies, a ratified Records Management Policy augmented by appropriate employee guidance materials should be in place and contain appropriate objectives and outlines of the related measures that the organisation will have in place to meet those objectives.

It is crucial that employees are suitably aware of their responsibilities in relation to Records Management and the wider Information Management Environment. However, in relation to Records Management obligations, the following standard model could be adapted and applied to suit most types of organisations:

- Board members, Executive Directors and senior managers have a collective responsibility for defining, managing and monitoring the organisation's Records Management Policy and its obligations. In addition, each Executive Director will

be responsible for ensuring that the Records Management Policy is duly applied within their own directorates.
- Ideally, a specific Executive Director should be allocated overall responsibilities for the Information Management Environment and the Records Management Policy. However, the day-to-day management can be devolved to a member of that Director's team.
- Specific managers or officers should be allocated responsibilities for:
  - administering the organisation's Publication Scheme (if relevant);
  - Data Protection matters, including the administration of requests to access personal information, arranging for incorrect data to be corrected and handling any complaints relating to the organisation's Data Protection arrangements or processes;
  - Freedom of Information matters, including the administration of requests for information, adjudicating on interpretations of exempt information and dealing with associated complaints.
- At an operational level, System Owners, nominated Information Stewards (or Champions) and System Administrators should have defined responsibilities relating to the accuracy, integrity and security of records.
- Section or Service Managers are responsible for the effective management of their own records and ensuring that staff are appropriately aware of their Records Management obligations.
- All of the organisation's employees with any working interface with records have an underlying duty to ensure the accuracy, integrity and security of the records that they access or use in the course of their activities.

Although legislation, regulations and standards in relation to Records Management issues will vary between nations and sectors, it is essential that all the specific implications are identified and adequately addressed. As a demonstration of the potential complexity of such regulatory frameworks, taking the UK public sector as an example, the following legislation, regulations and standards could all have a bearing on the Records Management approach for a UK local government authority:

Legislation

- Data Protection Act 1998
- Freedom of Information Act 2000
- Human Rights Act 1998
- Electronic Communications Act 2000
- Local Government Act 1972
- Local Government Act 1974
- Local Government (Records) Act 1962
- Limitation Act 1980
- Public Records Act 1958 and 1967
- Local Government (Access to Information) Act 1985
- Public Interest Disclosure Act.

Regulation

- The Environmental Information Regulations 2004
- The Re-Use of Public Sector Information Regulations 2005
- Telecommunications (Lawful Business Practice) (Interception of Communications) Regulations 2000.

Standards

- BS 4783—Storage, transportation and maintenance of media for use in data processing and information storage
- BS 5454—Recommendations for the storage and exhibition of archival documents
- BS 7799/ISO 17799—Code of practice for information security management
- BS/ISO 27001—Specification for Information Security Management Systems
- BS/ISO 15489—Information and Documentation—Records Management
- BSI DISC PD0008—Code of practice for legal admissibility and evidential weight of information stored on electronic document management systems
- BSI DISC PD0010—Principles of Good Practice for Information Management
- BSI DISC PD 0012—Guide to the practical implications of the Data Protection Act 1998
- Records Management Society of Great Britain—Retention Guidelines for Local Authorities 2003:1
- Requirements issued by the National Archives for Electronic Records Management Systems
- The Lord Chancellor's Code of Practice on the Management of Records under Section 46 of the Freedom of Information Act 2000 (November 2002)
- Guidance on "proper arrangements" for archives, issued by the Office of the Deputy Prime Minister (ODPM), responsibility for which was transferred to Communities and Local Government in May 2006
- Functional Requirements and Testing of Electronic Records Management Systems issued by the Public Record Office in 1999.

Although in Chapters 44 and 45 we look, in some detail, at the international legislation for both Data Protection and Freedom of Information, it is not possible for this volume to identify and explore the varying national Records Management regimes that could apply. Auditors and others involved in reviewing Records Management arrangements are advised to obtain a comprehensive and clear grounding in all the legal and regulatory factors applicable in their country and operational sector.

In summary terms, the following logical stages of a record lifecycle illustrate the key elements of a Records Management environment:

Record Creation

- An organisation should have in place adequate systems for documenting its various activities that also take into account any legislative or regulatory implications (for example as apply to the maintenance of lawful accounting records).

- Only official and recognised records should be created and used (for example, employees should not create their own supplementary or parallel records).
- Records should be created on the basis of an accurate, reliable and lawful source (including necessary and appropriate mechanisms to cross-check or validate gathered information).
- Each record or information asset set should be recorded on the organisation's Information Asset Register or inventory and be classified, categorised or coded in accordance with its relative level of sensitivity, as a means to ensure that the appropriate level of security and management is applied in accordance with the organisation's procedures (for example as would relate to personal data as defined within Data Protection law).
- Records should be arranged in a record keeping system that supports the prompt and easy retrieval of information to support operations and administration, but that also provides adequate protection from unauthorised access, loss or damage.
- Taken as a whole, the set or grouping of records should enable (as perhaps demanded by local regulatory requirements) their audit or forensic examination by authorised individuals, the protection of the organisation's legal and other rights and those of the organisation's clients and other persons affected by its actions, and ensure the authenticity of the records so that they can be a credible and authoritative source for legal evidence.

Record Keeping

- Once again, the existence of an Information Asset Register can greatly support the overall management of records. The register will reflect what records are held, in what form they are accessible and their relationship to the organisation's functions and operations.
- In order to effectively manage records and, for example, to enable the efficient appraisal of the implications for records in the event of a proposed change of use of the records, the associated record keeping systems should also be described in terms of metadata (i.e. data about data that includes descriptive and technical documentation relating to the record system).
- There should be rules defined for the referencing, titling, indexing and, if relevant, the protective security marking of records. It is essential that employees utilising such records are appropriately aware of such rules and use them to condition how the records are used, disclosed and disposed of.
- Procedures should be in place and applied that ensure and support the currency, accuracy and completeness of records.

Access to Records

- Physical and logical access to records should be determined by each employee's "need to know" and relate to the requirements of their defined duties.
- Physical security measures (such as code controlled doors, secure storage areas and locked file stores) should be combined with logical security measures (such as user ID and password access controls on computer application systems) to

restrict access to authorised personnel only and to actively prevent unauthorised access.
- The precise mapping of an authorised user's access to records should be tailored to their working requirements and omit any areas or functions that would compromise control or circumvent any necessary separation of duties.
- The prevailing Data Protection legislation will need to be complied with in relation to personal data and reflected in terms of data collection, accuracy, protection from unauthorised disclosure, access by Data Subjects and secure disposal.
- The prevailing Freedom of Information (Right to Information or Access to Information) Regulations will also influence and direct the access arrangements applied to specific records systems.

Record Maintenance

- Records may have to be in place for considerable lengths of time (for example mortgage or trust fund records) and action should be taken so that they can be sustained for the required period in an accessible form. (For an overview of some of the issues surrounding digital preservation, please refer to the following section of this chapter headed "Additional Considerations for Electronic Records".)
- The ongoing accuracy of records will be affected by, among other factors, how they are updated and amended over time. Amendments applied to records should be justified, accurate, complete and, where necessary, authorised. The control implications of maintaining the overall integrity of records over time are linked to the access arrangements and the security of the processing of amending transactions, whether the latter is either manually or systematically applied.
- Records should be stored in an environment that both provides adequate security and the appropriate environmental conditions to support their continued existence. For example, paper-based records should be adequately protected from the effects of damp, water incursion, extreme temperatures, vermin infestation and fading relating to the use of poor quality paper. Electronic records also require appropriate environmental conditions that will vary in relation to the form of media involved, for example magnetic media should be protected from strong electromagnetic fields, excessive heat or water incursion. (The subject of media handling is more comprehensively reviewed in Chapter 33.) Overall, the security and protection measures should also facilitate the permitted degree of access so that operations are not disrupted.
- The contents of the agreed Retention and Disposal procedures have to be applied to the maintenance of records, especially where there are specific, legally enforceable retention periods in place. Records that are no longer required for current purposes should be identified, suitably catalogued and withdrawn to a secure storage facility. Consideration should also be given to any residual requirement to occasionally access the removed records and how this can be accommodated.
- Critical and key records that are essential for the operation and continued existence of the organisation should be identifiable from the Information Asset Register. The contingency and recovery arrangements for such records should be incorporated into the organisation's documented recovery plans.

Record Disclosure

- Although the various measures described under "Access to Records" above should restrict access to authorised users only, they don't necessarily prevent subsequent or related disclosure incidents. For example, a physical file may be in the possession of an authorised user but could be left unattended on a desk so that anyone passing by could view the contents; alternatively an authorised user of a computer application system will be granted access to a record that could also be viewed on an unattended PC screen by a passing and unauthorised person. However, the unauthorised and inappropriate disclosure of information contained within records can happen in other internal and external circumstances, for example how does an authorised user know that a work colleague who is requesting access to a secure record actually has the right to access that information; or what measures would prevent an opportunist being able to access the organisation's data on a misplaced or lost CD?
- The occurrence of unauthorised disclosure of information takes on greater significance when it relates to personal information that can be specifically related to a Data Subject. (NB: This situation has actually happened to one of the authors of this book, when their former public sector employer passed over a printout containing the author's name, address, national insurance number, bank account number and the details of actual payments made, to their payroll contractor who, in turn, managed to lose custody of the document which was then found at the side of a road by the Police.) In this and other such situations where there has been a breach of the required degree of protective security and personal data has been exposed in a way that could have resulted in an unauthorised disclosure, there may be legal, image and reputation implications for the organisation holding the data (i.e. the Data Controller). We consider the prevention, detection and handling of information security incidents within Chapter 54.

Record Disposal

- Records will reach a point in their lifecycle when they are no longer required to support an organisation's needs. In addition, their age may have also exceeded any legally prescribed retention period. In either case, they will be eligible for disposal.
- Disposal of records can take a number of forms, including:
  - The transfer of a paper records to an archive storage facility in a manner that would still allow ad hoc access if that proved necessary;
  - The transfer of records that have a significance, regulatory status or a level of public interest to a recognised formal local or national archive (e.g. as could apply to selected public body records);
  - The archiving of electronic records retaining their original format and media context;
  - The destruction of electronic records by physically and irreversibly erasing and dismantling the storage media making it completely unusable, unreadable and incapable of being reconstituted.

- The disposal of records should be formally managed so that they are accurately identified, assessed as being appropriate for disposal, assessed for their contents and the association with any security implications related to the method of their disposal, appropriately isolated and stored pending disposal and during any necessary transport or movement, clearly authorised for disposal and, finally, actually disposed of in the appropriate and prescribed manner.
- When records are being considered for disposal, public bodies need to make an assessment of whether or not it is likely that the information the records contain will be requested under the prevailing Freedom of Information (or equivalent) regulations.
- Each operational area of an organisation should have in place documented processes for the assessment, authorisation and appropriate form of disposal of unwanted records.
- Ideally there should be a process for detecting when records (including those that have been archived or removed from current and active record systems) are approaching the end of their obliged retention period, so that they can be assessed and authorised for permanent disposal.
- A record should be maintained of the destruction of the organisation's records that incorporates a description of the affected records, the date of disposal, the method of disposal and the required authorisation.
- Physical records that contain sensitive or personal data should be physically destroyed in a way that makes the outputs unreadable. For example cross-cut shredding using accredited shredders operated by approved and, where appropriate, licensed contractors in secure conditions. (Also refer to Chapter 55 on Data Retention and Disposal.)

Additional Considerations for Electronic Records

- Although the primary record management issues for electronic records are the same as those for the management of any record, the means by which they are addressed are markedly different in the electronic environment. For example, the organisation of fields and component data, the methods for relating different elements of the electronic record and the trailing of activities carried out on the record.
- There is an additional dimension of significance relating to the capturing and recording of the details of electronic records onto an Information Assets Register or inventory; for example in terms of the future upgrade path for the records or their ability to be easily adapted over time to meet changing operational demands. Such special differences will need to be captured in the form of metadata and supporting systems documentation so that such records can be managed now and in the future.
- The grouping and arrangement of records in an electronic context needs careful consideration in relation to ease, efficiency and speed of access and the ongoing integrity.
- The security of electronic records is achieved by various means embedded within application systems and database management systems and these

mechanisms need to be understood and documented as they may, for example, have implications for proposed future changes and developments.
- The ongoing and future accessibility and use of electronic records poses some interesting problems related to the rapid changes in the IT world that render equipment and media redundant. If critical records are going to be required for the foreseeable future, how can the organisation be sure that the technical means to maintain them will still be available say five years from now? Industry standard application systems will often go through a number of evolutionary changes over time, changing and adopting according to, for example, changes in hardware and software platforms, the methods and costs of storage and the associated availability of expanding functionality and interoperability. We further examine the thorny and important subject of Digital Preservation below.
- Electronic records demand forms of disposal and erasure that are significantly different than those employed for physical records. For example, deleting an electronic record or a file on a PC doesn't necessarily remove all trace of it, and it is possible to resurrect previously deleted files, a process that is often used in the forensic recovery of unsuitable image files, for example in the prosecution of child pornography cases.
- Electronic records rarely exist in an operational vacuum and often co-exist with manual records in a mixed environment that requires cross-referencing or relationships to be established between the electronic and the manual portions of the records. In many instances, the electronic record may reflect the whole or part of its physical counterpart, but in a form that offers more opportunities for effective analysis of additional processing and control.
- The increasing use of Electronic Document Management Systems (EDMS) is potentially pointing towards a future where physical documents may be the exception. An Electronic Document Management System can be defined as a computer system or suite of programs designed to store and track electronic documents and other media. The features of EDMS vary but are likely to contain a combination of the following attributes:
  - scanning of physical documents into an electronic form;
  - migrating existing electronic documents into a standard form handled by the EDMS;
  - storage, tracking and retrieval of electronic documents;
  - recording metadata for each document (perhaps by type) to facilitate the correct classification, routing and storage of the record;
  - additional indexing of documents to associate them with particular customers, suppliers, clients, and so on;
  - powerful search facilities that support the identification of documents and related records with common indices;
  - connecting, interfacing and relating documents to and from other application systems (including standard tools such as email and word processing) (NB: this is often a problematic area given the available range of document formats in existence, however standards such as ODMA (Open Document Management API) can support the transfer and mobility of files);
  - taking the previously described step a stage further, it is possible to interface the EDMS with third party systems, such as for payments to a regular supplier

through the creditor system or the electronic transmission of invoice charges for services rendered;
- Workflow management facilities that route and track a document through a logical step-by-step process route. Workflow systems are very powerful in that they can direct documents to the appropriate employee or department, keep tabs on progress as it passes through processing stages, enforce any required electronic authorisation processes and report on the actual performance times of tasks against pre-set targets. However, in order to reap all the benefits of such workflow facilities a considerable amount of prior work analysis and set-up time is required;
- Version control mechanisms that aim to ensure the evolution of a document or record and its final emergence as the definitive version;
- Multilevelled security features to manage authorised access and to prevent inappropriate disclosure.

What is Digital Preservation and Why is it so Important?

The term "digital preservation" relates to the technical, cultural and strategic issues surrounding the ongoing preservation of records of all types in digital form, including electronic records used by organisations, public bodies and ordinary citizens across the world. A problem arises in relation to the pace of technological developments that often leave once dominant electronic devices, media and formats behind to the point that they disappear from the market place and anyone with associated media containing their life's work is suddenly left high and dry. Consider the following mainstream examples of once familiar but now fading or redundant technologies:

- 45 or 78rpm single records and 33rpm albums
- Stereo 8™ (8 track tape cartridges)
- 8", 5.25" and 3.5" floppy disks
- Compact Cassette™ (audio tape cassettes)
- Sony Betamax™ Philip Video 2000™ or VHS™ video tape formats.

The above examples have faded with differing timescales, some protracted and others swift and decisive (perhaps following a major marketing failure). Beyond the realms of the motivated specialist or hobbyist, their use is very sparse and will be further pressured in the future as residual stocks become exhausted and existing recorded examples become too impaired or fragile to be used. It is impossible to conceive that any will be produced again as the justification for doing so would be difficult to conceive and the associated production costs for small quantities would be prohibitive.

The specific parallel situation in relation to information technology and Records Management goes a step further in that as well as redundant hardware (such as outdated back-up tape formats) there is also the matter of the software used to create and handle data files, much of which was platform-specific. Examples would include operating environments such as CP/M™, DPP™, ICL-VME™ and MS-DOS™. Even if equipment and the necessary software can be tracked down, supplier support probably dried up a long time ago. Because of its "pure" form when compared to analogue means of recording, digital was seen, perhaps falsely, as an enduring foundation upon which to base an ever-increasing range of products and technologies both in the business and retail markets. For example, Compact Discs™ (CD) and their variants were originally launched with promises of being virtually indestructible but these claims have been proven untrue with some formats deteriorating within a relatively short timescale.

In addition to the technical and availability issues relating to types of formats and media, there are the vulnerabilities of digital formats to also take into consideration. Magnetic media and some optical media are susceptible to loss, damage or destruction often because they are intrinsically fragile. High humidity, heat, airborne contaminants, exposure to dampness or electromagnetic energy can all impair the condition of media and render them useless.

One short-term approach involves the progressive copying or recoding of key electronic records (either still in use, back-up copies or archived versions) from a fading format onto a contemporary one. This approach is often referred to as a refreshment cycle and has associated cost and resource implications. However, there is always the spectre that the new chosen technology itself has a short life span.

There are also potential legal implications associated with an inability to preserve records held in redundant formats, such as:

- possible infringement of intellectual property rights (IPR) if data and software code is copied or changed through recoding and recording;
- public bodies may be required to retain records and be penalised if they fail (for example, UK local authorities are obliged to retain records in accordance with the various Public Records Acts);
- statutory requirements to retain data will also affect business organisations, for example in relation to the retention of accounting records for a prescribed time period that may well exceed the period for which the records can remain technically accessible; and
- privacy and confidentiality implications relating to personal data will also need to be considered.

Many of the international efforts to secure the preservation of digital records are being driven by national archive organisations and well-respected libraries across the globe. There is obviously great emphasis being placed on the preservation of unique or historically significant national digital records. However, all organisations are potentially affected by the relentless march of technical innovation and should be identifying any of their records which are potentially exposed to this vulnerability as the basis for taking appropriate remedial action in the form of a long-term preservation strategy.

Selected Organisations Active in the Field of Digital Preservation

- In the UK, the Digital Preservation Coalition (DPC) is a not-for-profit organisation with the objective of raising awareness of digital preservation issues.

- Mail: Digital Preservation Coalition, Innovation Centre, York Science Park, Heslington, York, YO10 5DG.
- Web: www.dpconline.org
- NESTOR ("<u>N</u>etwork of <u>E</u>xpertise in long-term <u>ST</u>Orage and long-term availability of digital <u>R</u>esources in Germany") is a German network of expertise in long-term digital preservation (Kompetenznetzwerk Langzeitarchivierung)
  - Mail: NESTOR Project Manager (Natascha Schumann) Deutsche Nationalbibliothek, Nestor Kompetenznetzwerk, Adickesallee 1, D-60322 Frankfurt am Main
  - Email: n.schumann@d-nb.de
  - Web: www.langzeitarchivierung.de
- In the UK, the Joint Information Systems Committee (JISC) supports educational and research establishments in the use of digital technologies and has an involvement in digital preservation matters.
  - Mail: (London) JISC Office, Brettenham House (South Entrance), 5 Lancaster Place, London, WC2E 7EN
  - Mail: (Bristol) JISC Office, University of Bristol, 3rd Floor, Beacon House, Queens Road, Bristol, BS8 1QU
  - Web: www.jisc.ac.uk
  - Email: info@jisc.ac.uk
- In the US, the National Digital Information Infrastructure and Preservation Program (NDIIPP) at the Library of Congress offers leadership and guidance on matters relating to the digital preservation.
  - Mail: 101 Independence Avenue, SE Washington, DC 20540-1300.
  - Web: www.digitalpreservation.gov
- In Australia, the National Library of Australia operates the Preserving Access to Digital Information (PADI) initiative, which aims, *inter alia*, to provide information and facilitate guidelines for the preservation of access to digital information.
  - Mail: PADI Coordinator, Web Archiving and Digital Preservation Branch, National Library of Australia, Canberra ACT 2000.
  - Web: www.nla.gov.au/padi
  - Email: padi@nla.gov.au
- In the Netherlands, the e-Depot initiative by the National Library of the Netherlands (Koninklijke Bibliotheek) supports research and development into maintaining the integrity of digital objects.
  - Mail: Digital Preservation Project, Koninklijke Bibliotheek, Prins Willem-Alexanderhof 5, 2595 BE Den Haag
  - Web: www.kb.nl
- Also in the Netherlands is the Digital Longevity Department of the Dutch National Archives which aims to ensure that Dutch government digital information is sustainable, properly managed and can be preserved in an authentic and reusable manner for the long term.
  - Mail: Postbus 90520, 2509 LM Den Haag
  - Web: www.digitaleduurzaamheid.nl
  - Email: testbed@nationaalarchief.nl

- In Europe, the Digital Preservation Europe (DPE) initiative continues the earlier work of ERPANET.
  - Mail: DPE, HATII, George Service House, 11 University Gardens, University of Glasgow, G12 8QJ, Scotland
  - Web: www.digitalpreservationeurope.eu
- The International Research on Permanent Authentic Records in Electronic Systems (InterPARES) project is a three-stage project now in its final stage that is due to be completed by 2012. The current research is termed as TEAM (Theoretical Elaborations into Archival Management) in relation to digital systems in small and medium-sized archival organisations. The international alliance associated with the project has representatives from Africa, Belgium, Brazil, Canada, Catalonia, China, Colombia, Ireland, Italy, Korea, Malaysia, Mexico, Netherlands, Norway, Singapore, Turkey and the United Kingdom.
  - Mail: The InterPARES Project, School of Library, Archival & Information Studies, The University of British Columbia, 470-1961 East Mall, Vancouver, BC V6T 1Z1, Canada
  - Web: www.interpares.org
  - Email: information@interpares.org
- The PLANETS Project is a Europe-focused exercise to deliver a sustainable framework to enable the long-term preservation of digital content.
  - Web: www.planets-project.eu
  - Email: info@planets-project.eu

Control Objectives for Records Management

> (a) To ensure that the organisation will create and capture accurate, complete, authentic and reliable records which demonstrate evidence, accountability and information for decisions and activities.
>
> (b) To ensure that records are efficiently and effectively maintained in order to meet the organisation's operational and administrative requirements.
>
> (c) Ensuring that records that are no longer required are disposed of in an appropriate and secure manner in accordance with the agreed Retention and Disposal procedures.
>
> (d) To prevent the premature or accidental disposal of records.
>
> (e) To protect the interests of Data Subjects and comply with the requirements of the Data Protection legislation.
>
> (f) To ensure the provision of appropriate and effective security to protect vital records from accidental or unauthorised access, loss, alteration, destruction or leakage.
>
> (g) To ensure that records remain readily accessible to those who are authorised to view and use them.

(h) To maintain (where appropriate) a Publication Scheme that provides permitted information to members of the public and others.

(i) To facilitate access to permitted information as defined within either the Data Protection or Freedom of Information legislation (and taking into account any lawful exemptions from disclosure).

(j) Ensuring that appropriate arrangements are in place for the prompt recovery of records and operations in the event of an unplanned event occurring.

(k) To ensure compliance with all the prevailing legislation, regulations, required standards and government directives.

(l) To ensure the preservation of records of permanent interest.

(m) To ensure that digital records are reviewed in respect of their ongoing sustainability.

(n) To ensure that all employees are aware of the importance of Information Management and Records Management and especially of their areas of responsibility through the provision of appropriate guidance and training, including upon induction to the organisation.

Risk and Control Issues for Records Management

1 Key Issues

1.1 What steps have been taken to comprehensively identify and document the organisation's records, especially those that are critical to support operations and the existence of the organisation?

1.2 How can management be assured that all records are suitably managed?

1.3 What mechanisms are in place to ensure that actions and decisions are supported by adequate records?

1.4 How does management ensure that only officially sanctioned records are created and used?

1.5 How does management ensure that records are created and maintained in accordance with all relevant and prevailing laws, regulations and standards? (Specifically, have records or systems containing personal data been appropriately registered under the prevailing Data Protection regulations and how is the registration maintained up to date?)

1.6 How does management ensure that records are created on the basis of accurate and reliable sources?

1.7 Has management taken action to appropriately classify, categorise or codify records so that they can be managed and protected in relation to their significance, sensitivity, legal obligations, etc? In addition, are the details of any subsequent changes or amendments to the format and structure of records captured and updated on the central record or register?

1.8 How can management be sure that records are retained and arranged in a form that optimises access and retrieval?

1.9 What actions are prescribed and in place to ensure the efficient and adequate referencing, indexing and security marking of records?

1.10 How would employees be made aware of the various rules and conditions applicable to records and the actions they are required or permitted to take?

1.11 What methods are used to ensure the accuracy and completeness of records?

1.12 How does management control the access to records (both manual and electronic) so as to protect them from loss, corruption of unauthorised access, amendment or disclosure?

1.13 Has management defined processes to ensure the ongoing accuracy of records?

1.14 Has management introduced measures designed to limit access to records (both manual and electronic) to authorised users only?

1.15 How have staff been advised of situations where it is either acceptable or unacceptable to disclose information contained with the organisation's records?

1.16 What action has management taken to ensure that employees are sufficiently aware of the requirements of any prevailing Data Protection or freedom of information regulations?

1.17 How does management ensure that the extant security measures are proportional and relative to the significance and sensitivity of records?

1.18 What steps have been taken to identify and track physical files removed from records storage systems? In addition, how would managers be able to promptly locate and retrieve removed records?

1.19 Has management taken action so that employees are made aware of the needs to protect their system access IDs and passwords?

1.20 Have management put in place clear guidance on the acceptable distribution of copies of physical and electronic records?

1.21 What steps have been taken to ensure that records remain sustainable and accessible over the period they are either required for use or to be retained for legislative purposes?

1.22 How does management ensure that records are only correctly updated with appropriate and authorised amendments?

1.23 What processes are in place to protect records from loss or disruption? Is there the potential to fall back to saved or parallel versions of records?

1.24 How can management be assured that the back-up of records is sufficient and fit for purpose?

1.25 How does management ensure that physical records are stored or archived in appropriate environmental conditions that would prevent their loss, damage or deterioration?

1.26 Has management taken action to create, document and test adequate business contingency and disaster recovery plans that incorporate the actions necessary to promptly locate and make available (at least) the critical records?

1.27 How can management be assured that adequate measures are in place in the event that primary sets of records are lost or completely destroyed?

1.28 How does management ensure that the contents of the organisation's records are only appropriately and lawfully disclosed?

1.29 How are records eligible for disposal identified and what specific mechanisms would prevent the accidental or premature disposal of records?

1.30 How does management ensure that records are retained for legally defined periods?

1.31 How are closed, dormant or redundant records identified and signified?

1.32 How does management ensure that physical records are disposed of in a manner that makes them totally unreadable and unusable?

1.33 What processes are in place to completely and irreversibly destroy electronic records and the media containing them?

1.34 How does management identify and deal with records of related interest that justify the transfer of them to a formal archival repository?

2 Detailed Issues

2.1 Has management established clear procedures and guidance relating to Records Management?

2.2 What action has been taken to ensure that employees are aware of the requirements associated with both Information Management and Records Management and fully understand their related responsibilities?

2.3 What steps have been taken to ensure that employees are fully aware of their specific record management responsibilities in relation to applicable laws and regulations?

2.4 How would management be alerted to the existence and use of unofficial or unauthorised records?

2.5 How would management be made aware of breaches of legislative or regulatory requirements relating to Records Management?

2.6 What would alert management to the presence of inaccurate or unreliable records?

2.7 How can management be assured that the process of identifying and categorising records takes account of all key records and specific characteristics?

2.8 How would potentially inefficient or inappropriate forms of record keeping be highlighted?

2.9 What measures ensure that relevant record sets can be readily audited or otherwise reviewed as required by prevailing laws and regulations?

2.10 Has management taken action to create and maintain meaningful metadata relating to the organisation's records?

2.11 What mechanisms are in place to detect the absence of a given record or any overall failure to maintain a complete record set?

2.12 How is management alerted in the event of unauthorised attempts to access records?

2.13 How are employees to know in what circumstances it is either acceptable or unacceptable to disclose information held within records? In addition, are the boundaries of such disclosures precise enough to enable employees to be clear about internal disclosures to colleagues across the organisation?

2.14 How does management ensure that employees are conversant with how to deal with requests for information under either the Data Protection or Freedom of Information regulations? In addition, are employees provided with guidance on how to differentiate between these two types of request?

2.15 What specific measures are in place to prevent unauthorised persons gaining access to records or areas where such records are held?

2.16 How does management ensure that physical security measures designed to protect records are always applied?

2.17 Does management undertake periodic reviews and assessments of security measures associated with records, identify any potential weaknesses and take action to resolve them?

2.18 Are keys, access control cards and other access devices recorded, controlled and promptly recovered from employees who leave the organisation or are suspected of a breach of discipline?

2.19 Are physical access codes regularly changed?

2.20 Has management promoted a "clear desk" policy and if so, is compliance periodically verified?

2.21 Are staff aware of the action they are required to take if their access devices or access passwords have been lost, stolen, misplaced or otherwise compromised?

2.22 Has management put in place procedures to ensure that robust access passwords are used, have to be regularly changed and need to be protected from misuse?

2.23 Have employees been advised of the requirements to protect copies of records, including printouts and reports?

2.24 Have standards layouts been defined for the content structure of physical files? If so, how is the use of the required structure enforced?

2.25 Has management ensured that key transactions are adequately trailed from the source of the information to the related records (e.g. where a physical document record is used to create or amend a related electronic record)?

2.26 Have long-term records been assessed for their ability to be sustained? In addition, have vulnerabilities been identified and adequately addressed?

2.27 Has management taken action to ensure the digital preservation of electronic records including the availability of the supporting hardware devices and software environments?

2.28 How would management be alerted to any failure to take the required back-up copies of electronic records?

2.29 Does management periodically review the adequacy of back-up and recovery processes, and test them for their continued integrity? If not, how does management get assurance that the organisation could survive an unplanned disruption or event?

2.30 Are physical records periodically inspected for any signs of physical deterioration or damage? In addition, are the environmental conditions for physical records subject to monitoring?

2.31 Has management prepared contingency arrangements for the location and storage of physical records in the event of an unplanned or disruptive event?

2.32 How can management be sure that any contingency or recovery measures related to records will actually operate correctly?

2.33 How would it be possible to retrospectively determine what records have been disposed of and the method of disposal applied?

2.34 In course of being disposed of, is it ensured that records continue to be subject to appropriate levels of physical and logical protection from loss, theft and unauthorised access?

2.35 How would management be made aware of the premature, accidental or unauthorised disposal or destruction of records?

2.36 Is the disposal of records adequately supported by documentation?

2.37 Are only recognised, trusted, secure and appropriately accredited contractors used to dispose of physical records?

2.38 What measures explicitly prevent the reuse or passing on of electronic media that does contain or has contained any form of the organisation's records?

2.39 What measures are in place to prevent the disposal or destruction of records that could either have local or national significance or be in the public interest, and that should be appropriately archived and preserved?

30
Knowledge Management (KM)

Although Knowledge Management (KM) is an approach and methodology with a history stemming from the private sector it can readily apply to the public sector and a wide range of types of organisation. There are a number of different recognised KM methodologies and many high-profile consultancy firms have their own house approach to the subject. This chapter will deal with the generic issues rather than any one commercial or academic method.

Firstly, we consider what KM relates to and then move on to identify some key aspects of a Knowledge Management environment.

KM is the creation of an environment that encourages knowledge to be created, acquired, shared, learned, enhanced and organised in a way that benefits an organisation and its various relationships. To assist in the later discussion of KM issues, Figure 30.1 below provides definitions of data, information and knowledge and their differences will hopefully set the scene with some simple examples of each and how they evolve.

It can be seen that knowledge is created from a mixture of information, experience and insight and that KM is the systematic and effective gathering, harnessing and exploitation of such knowledge. In order to be of use, Knowledge Management processes should include the recognition, capture and communication of such elements as good practice, collective intelligence and the outcomes of previous situations.

An organisation's management should not assume that it knows all it needs to know and that every instance of useful knowledge has necessarily been identified and harnessed.

There are a number of potential benefits associated with effective Knowledge Management, including:

- improving performance by making better use of the knowledge possessed by employees;
- avoiding future mistakes;
- harnessing proven and relevant knowledge from other internal and external sources;

Term	Description	Example
Data	Data is akin to raw material or facts, values and statistics that can be analysed, combined and used to provide information. A single data item, taken out of context, has no meaning. However, it can be essential and of value in the generation of information.	11,250 and 9,500 10% and 13.7%
Information	Information can be created by combining data and human interpretation. Data is given context and meaning when information is generated. There are various possible forms of information, for example in documents and records in a structured form or in people's heads without any necessary structure.	11,250 is the current reading of the revolutions per minute of the engine of the motorcycle I am riding. 9,500 is the recommended maximum number of revolutions per minute recommended for the engine of this motorcycle. 10% is the price increase of raw materials that I budgeted for in the next six months' production. 13.7% is the actual price increase of raw materials that will be charged with immediate effect.
Knowledge	By making use of the information and adding the effects of human experience, expertise, prior examples, capacities and decision making etc. can create knowledge. Knowledge is linked to understanding and action (i.e. know-how). Knowledge enables processes to move on and evolve.	If I continue to maintain the current actual level of engine revolutions I will either ruin the engine, face a large repair bill or have a crash in which I may be severely injured. I have decided to stop the bike. Unless I make economies elsewhere in producing my new products or obtain a cheaper alternative source of materials, I will make a loss and put the future of my business and its employees at risk.

Figure 30.1 Definitions of data, information and knowledge

- ensuring that the right information is provided in the right context, to the right person, at the right time for the right purpose (although this seemingly simple concept is more difficult to achieve in practice); and
- highlighting inefficiencies or duplicated efforts.

In the same way that information assets are significant to an organisation, knowledge assets, if well managed and exploited, can provide a useful competitive edge or operational advantage. The information sources for Knowledge Management are diverse and not purely related to electronic forms; for example, they could include:

- documents
- case files
- industry sector research and reports

- central government departments and websites
- professional or trade bodies.

However, the most common location of knowledge is in the employee's head and one of the objectives of effective Knowledge Management is to engender the effective and appropriate communication and sharing of employee knowledge and experience.

Before moving on to consider the Knowledge Management Lifecycle, we should consider the two widely recognised forms of knowledge, Explicit and Tacit, which can be defined as follows:

- **Explicit Knowledge** is the knowledge that has been captured somewhere, for example in documents or a database. It is knowledge that has, through some process, been laid down, and put into a re-usable format, so that other people or systems can work with it.
- **Tacit Knowledge** is personal knowledge that includes skills, insight and judgement. It is rooted in experience, ideals and values, and is more difficult to capture in explicit form. For individuals, tacit knowledge is evidenced through the know-how they demonstrate. For example, a surveyor will have an instinct for believing that a set of measurements are either right or wrong based on similar previous situations.

Tacit knowledge may not be documented but accrued by an individual over time. Within departments the ways things are done are not always written down in detail but rather grow over time through people working together and sharing tacit knowledge.

It is possible for knowledge to move between the two types noted above. For example, tacit knowledge can be shared and documented to become explicit. The reverse is also true in that explicit knowledge can enhance or improve existing tacit knowledge. In addition, it is possible for two sets of knowledge to be combined to form a new set of knowledge. However, the potential for the successful management of all of these mechanisms requires an appropriate and open KM culture.

In a manner similar to records within a Records Management Environment, knowledge has a natural lifecycle the stages of which can be described as follows:

- Firstly knowledge must be **created** and this can happen either within or outside of the organisation. The creation of knowledge may involve the interpretation of data, the application of personal experience, the merging of information sources, and so on.
- Once captured, knowledge can then be recorded and **stored** somewhere so that it is accessible for others to find and use.
- Those who need the specific knowledge must then be able to **find** out where it is, when they need it, by searching in the right places or by asking the right people. This activity requires the supporting infrastructure to be effective.
- The knowledge is then **acquired** by individuals and this can also include the gaining of additional insight from other colleagues or through documented sources. Once again the ability to acquire knowledge can be linked to the Knowledge Management facilities in place.

- The knowledge can then be put to **use** or applied towards some productive or beneficial purpose.
- Having been used, perhaps repeatedly or in a variety of ways, the user will **learn** what worked well and not so well as a result of applying the knowledge gained. These good and bad experiences can then be used as significant inputs to further considerations of the knowledge creation and distribution process so that they can improve over time.
- Once the learning process is complete there is a natural feedback connection to modify the create stage of the lifecycle.

The concept of learning in the above cycle is a key contributor to the effective management of knowledge. Without a learning component, the cycle is devoid of knowledge and defaults to being a simple information delivery process. We will examine some of the key issues related to the above noted lifecycle elements later in this chapter.

Most organisations have employees with a vast pool of experience, expertise and knowledge, all of which are brought to bear on the provision of a full range of services and operations. Very often when an experienced employee leaves an organisation, their pool of experience and knowledge is lost to the organisation. In addition, there is always a risk that the organisation can become too reliant upon the skills and knowledge of individual employees. Knowledge Management is also about managing organisations in ways to mitigate these risks and to ensure that accrued knowledge is retained (in the so-called "corporate memory") so that it can be used in the future.

Possible Existing KM Elements

An organisation is likely to have existing methods of gathering, recording, communicating and using knowledge, for example:

Gathering

External sources could include:

- Peer group interchange (through informal and formal sector-related groups)
- Advice and guidance from professional bodies
- Specialist legal advice
- Central government departments and websites
- Research institutions and bodies
- Universities and other educational or study bodies
- Externally commissioned research
- Reliable Internet sources.

Internal sources could include:

- Existing databases
- Internal reports

- Information analysis
- Management information
- Procedural documentation
- Process specifications.

Recording

Knowledge recording can be achieved in a number of ways, for example:

- In hardcopy documents and files
- Scanned or facsimile documents
- Databases
- Electronic files (including word processor documents, spreadsheets, reports, notes and emails)
- In a person's memory
- On shared file servers
- In the form of performance "dashboards"
- Placement on the corporate Intranet.

The method of knowledge recording and storage will have attendant benefits and some disadvantages in terms of ease of access, understanding and communication. Retrieval of knowledge is critical to accruing any of the associated benefits. It isn't only knowledge held in employees' memories that can be difficult to access; the structure and dispersed ways in which electronic files are distributed, copied and stored can make identifying the latest or definitive version difficult.

Communication

There are many ways in which knowledge can be communicated, as per the selected examples given below. However, very often the first time an item of knowledge is imparted this happens verbally, from the person who created it. Any form of communicating knowledge is likely to have strengths and weaknesses relating to matters of access, coverage, interpretation and effectiveness.

- Cascading a knowledge message through a management hierarchy
- Team meetings and briefings
- Management meetings or committees
- Contacts at conferences
- Peer groups
- Policy plans
- Gained through external education activities
- Whole organisation or tailored email updates, news items, etc.
- Training sessions
- E-learning systems
- Placement on the corporate Intranet site
- Discussions within departments between colleagues
- Dialogue between departments and functions.

Use

The way in which a nugget of knowledge can be used is potentially the most fragmented stage in that it is not only dependent upon the previous gathering, recording and communication phases but is strongly reliant upon the means by which a department or function generally considers and assimilates knowledge. This latter factor is, in turn, conditioned by more subjective dynamics such as the prevailing management style, the motivation of employees and how information normally flows through and within the section.

In adjudging the ability to get the right information to the right person, the existing organisational structure will play a leading role. However, giving a nominated employee the responsibility of seeking and relaying knowledge can be an effective option, especially in highly complex or technical areas of operation.

The following checklists for the key aspects of the Knowledge Management Lifecycle summarise some additional key points for consideration.

Create

- Encourage employees and team members to share information on how they dealt with particular cases, events or incidents.
- Encourage specialist and knowledgeable employees to communicate and record their knowledge for others to access.
- Record key learning points arising from discussion at meetings, training events, etc.
- Consider involvement in a form of learning network either within or outside of the organisation. (For example, in the UK local government sector, the concept of Communities of Practice (CoPs) is in place which facilitates the sharing of ideas, experience and good practice. An online CoP will link a network of members with common interests or problems. The Improvement and Development Agency (IDeA) has developed an online platform that enables users to set up a new CoP or join an existing one for a related sector and topic. Further details can be found at www.communities.idea.gov.uk.)
- Formal and informal exchanges of information between organisations operating in the same sector can be a useful source of knowledge.
- Organisations or associated interest groups often undertake or commission benchmarking research that can stimulate revised thinking about a policy, approach or method.
- If an organisation is planning to embark on a new project or to wander into uncharted territory, the concept of "peer assist" may be worth considering. The process entails the partnering of those seeking assistance with an individual "peer" or group of peers who have experience and knowledge in the relevant area. Further information on the concept of "peer assist" can be obtained from the IDeA website www.idea.gov.uk.
- It is relatively easy to fall into working in a silo and not necessarily having the time or inclination to take a view of the bigger picture across other areas of the organisation. There should be encouragement for employees to work

collaboratively with colleagues and share learning and experience. However, due consideration for matters of confidentiality should always take precedence before imparting information, however informally it is done.
- Documenting operational procedures can be a way of initially capturing aspects of knowledge.

Store

- Develop, document and publicise an approach to recording and storing knowledge that ideally spans the organisation. Having created the store of knowledge, make sure it is easy to locate and use. One method of enabling wide access is to place the store on either an organisation-wide or shared file server. This will allow access to be controlled if it is either necessary or commercially expedient.
- In making knowledge available ensure that version control mechanisms are applied together with the removal of outdated versions from circulation. In addition give electronic files clear and appropriate file names that incorporate the relevant date or period covered.

Find

- Consider the implementation of a directory of internal and external knowledge sources that is both indexed in a logical way and capable of being searched electronically.
- Employees should be able to promptly and efficiently locate existing and relevant knowledge.
- Knowledge facilities and sources should be openly promoted to employees.
- Ensure that the contents of corporate Intranet sites are maintained up to date, with responsibilities for maintaining such sites being allocated to a nominated employee or officer.
- They may be skill implications associated with the analysis, extraction and interpretation of knowledge. Core competencies should be developed to enable employees to confidently and efficiently use IT tools to find, create, use and share knowledge.

Acquire

- Where knowledge can be derived from an existing application system or a set of electronic records, the provision of effective and user-friendly interrogation, analysis and reporting tools should be considered. In addition, users should be suitably trained to apply best practice to the use of such tools.
- Where employees can extract knowledge from application systems into a more user-friendly and flexible environment, such as a spreadsheet, it is essential that the employee has the appropriate skills to organise, sort and manipulate the data in a way that protects the integrity and accuracy of the results, especially if they are intended for use as management information or to support decision making.

Learn

- Post-implementation reviews of projects and activities can be used to identify what went well and what problems there were. The outcomes of the review should be documented and accessed when similar exercises are being planned. More significant systematic shortcomings should be dealt with as a priority and guidance and procedures updated accordingly.
- If an employee is approaching a subject, activity or discipline for the first time, encourage them to contact someone who is (or has in the past) been involved in similar situations. Unless it would be inappropriate for any reason, contact with such experienced personnel outside of the organisation should also be considered.

What Needs to Generally Happen in Practice?

- The approach to managing an organisation's knowledge will be dependent upon the type of organisation and the environment in which it operates. The key objectives of a Knowledge Management environment need to be supported by an agreed and ratified Knowledge Management Policy as a part of a wider and interlocking range of policy documents that collectively support the development of an Information Management Environment.
- It is necessary to understand why the organisation needs to manage its knowledge, and then consider what knowledge is critical to success and also who has the knowledge. Then management can begin to address the question of "how do we do it?" The following checklists of why, what, who and how-related questions provide a taste of some of the relevant considerations.

Why?

- Why does the organisation need to get better at learning from experience, sharing good practice across boundaries and managing its knowledge?
- What could the organisation do better?
- Is knowledge leaking out of the organisation when staff leave?
- Is the organisation overly dependent upon a few key and knowledgeable individuals?
- Are projects and new programmes of work built on existing good practice?

What?

- What knowledge is truly critical to the effectiveness of the organisation?
- Where are the strengths and the gaps that need to be filled?

Who?

- Who has unique knowledge?
- What would be the cost to the organisation of the loss of this knowledge?

- How does the organisation stand under the "lottery test"? That is, if an individual or a whole team "win the lottery" and leave could new staff easily pick up the reins and the operation survive?

How?

- How are we going to develop the systems, processes and behaviours we need to manage our knowledge more effectively?
- How might staff better find, use and create knowledge?
- How might staff better share and manage knowledge, both internally and externally?
- Have previous reviews identified any areas for improvement where managing knowledge more effectively would make a difference?
- With regards to its vision, has any part of the organisation articulated how improved performance and value will derive from managing existing knowledge?
- Are there any examples of matrix or partnership working that draw upon the use and sharing of knowledge?
- Are staff coached and trained in Information and Knowledge Management?
- Does the organisation's culture encourage the exchange of knowledge and learning from activities and projects?
- Does the organisation have any existing roles dedicated to acquiring, managing and coordinating knowledge?
- Does the organisation have a clear view of its key knowledge assets and systems in place to protect them?
- Has the organisation implemented systematic processes for gathering, organising, indexing and making accessible its knowledge assets?
- Has the organisation employed any informal mechanisms to gather and mobilise its tacit knowledge, for example, post-implementation reviews, staff community groups, master classes or networking events?
- Does the organisation convert its working experience into improved processes and services?
- Do tools exist within the organisation that have further potential for knowledge organisation and access?

Control Objectives for Knowledge Management

(a) To ensure that existing knowledge assets are identified and effectively managed.

(b) To ensure that other sources of knowledge of interest to the organisation are identified, assessed and, if appropriate, harnessed and exploited.

(c) To obtain the commitment and buy-in of senior management to the concepts and mechanisms of Knowledge Management.

(d) To ensure that management is clear about which aspects of knowledge are critical to the success and effectiveness of the organisation.

(e) To create an environment and culture in which knowledge is valued and effectively managed for the benefit of the organisation, its employees and partners.

(f) To ensure that staff are suitably aware of the value of Knowledge Management and are able to apply sound Knowledge Management methods in the course of their work.

(g) To ensure that, where appropriate, specific responsibilities for gathering, storing and communicating knowledge are allocated to nominated employees.

(h) To provide mechanisms and processes to support the KM environment and optimise the use of knowledge.

(i) To ensure that tacit knowledge held by employees is sought, recorded and appropriately shared.

(j) To avoid key knowledge escaping the organisation when employees leave.

(k) To avoid the organisation becoming overly dependent upon the skills of specific individuals.

(l) To ensure that recording and storage of knowledge facilitates ease of access and retrieval.

(m) To apply a formal post-implementation review process to projects and activities so that lessons can be learned for the future.

(n) To ensure that knowledge is appropriately and efficiently communicated in the right form to the right people.

(o) To ensure that the organisation's approach to Knowledge Management is monitored and subject to periodic review.

Risk and Control Issues for Knowledge Management

1 Key Issues

1.1 What action has management taken to ensure that the organisation recognises the importance and value of knowledge and of its effective management?

1.2 What steps have been taken to set the appropriate cultural tone for Knowledge Management (and how is this evidenced)?

1.3 How is management assured that there is sufficient senior-level buy-in to the concepts and practices of Knowledge Management?

1.4 What steps have been taken to promote and support a Knowledge Management environment and culture to all employees? In addition, has the effectiveness of such promotion been assessed?

1.5 What steps have been taken to identify the types of knowledge that are of most significance and importance to the organisation?

1.6 How is responsibility for KM matters allocated?

1.7 Have existing knowledge assets been identified and recorded?

1.8 How does the organisation go about identifying and assessing additional potential sources of knowledge?

1.9 How has management addressed the need to protect the organisation from the leakage of knowledge when employees leave?

1.10 What active steps have been taken to capture and record elements of tacit knowledge?

1.11 What mechanisms have been provided to facilitate the efficient identification and retrieval of knowledge assets?

1.12 How can management be assured that the communication of knowledge assets is effective and prompt?

1.13 Have steps been taken so that the organisation learns from past activities and projects and thus avoids previous pitfalls and problems, whilst being able to recognise positive outcomes and apply them in future as required?

1.14 How does management ensure that the Knowledge Management environment and supporting processes remains relevant and effective over time?

2 Detailed Issues

2.1 Has a specific Executive Director (or equivalent) been given overall responsibility for Knowledge Management?

2.2 Have the board (or equivalent senior management) supported the KM initiative and ratified an appropriate KM Policy supported by a strategy/plan for implementation and supporting guidance.

2.3 Have sufficient training and support resources been made available to employees to enable them to understand and apply effective KM within their duties? In addition, what evidence is there that the deployment of such resources has been effective?

2.4 Is there a culture of encouraging internal and external communication in the pursuit of knowledge?

2.5 Are staff encouraged to seek out potential external sources of knowledge and to become involved in appropriate external groups?

2.6 How does management prevent or deal with instances of over-dependence on specific employees?

2.7 Are employees appropriately aware of where and how to access corporate knowledge assets?

2.8 Have employees been trained in the proficient use of data interrogation, extract and analysis tools?

2.9 Is it clear who has the responsibility for communicating knowledge, especially newly acquired forms?

2.10 Are employees encouraged to share examples of good practice and their experiences?

31

IT Sites and Infrastructure (Including Physical Security)

Here we are principally concerned with the provision of an adequate and secure IT facility, where equipment, operations and data are protected from damage, disruption or loss.

IT management will have specific responsibilities for ensuring the protection of centralised parts of the IT infrastructure, such as server rooms, network communications equipment and the physical network. However, there is also a wider responsibility placed on all employees to ensure that physical security measures are actually correctly applied in practice.

The related policies in place will vary between organisations but may include specific IT Infrastructure Security requirements and a corporate Physical Security Policy which, in turn, is supported by specific staff guidance. These related issues are briefly discussed here; however the key IT Site and Infrastructure objectives and issues follow later in this chapter.

An example Physical Security Policy may contain the following key elements:

- The commitment, usually in the form of a policy statement, from senior management to the protection of staff, customers, visitors from harm or injury.
- A similar commitment to adequately protecting the premises, physical assets and information assets from damage, loss, destruction or disruption.
- The top-level definition of what action(s) the organisation will take to address the physical security needs.
- Defining the various roles and responsibilities for physical security (i.e. Fire Officer, Health and Safety Advisor, Security Manager, etc.).
- A series of principles and standards that will be applied by all affected employees to support the policy statement; these may include, but not be restricted to:
  - the use of industry standard security devices (i.e. locks, alarms, etc.);
  - the reporting, recording, review and monitoring of all actual or potential security incidents;
  - those situations when Police assistance will be sought;
  - the proportionate and lawful use of CCTV surveillance;

- the arrangement of appropriate and proportionate insurance cover;
- only engaging external security services or personnel who comply with the appropriate professional standards (for example, in the UK, those organisations who are licensed by the Security Industry Authority (SIA) and apply their defined standards. British Standard BS 7499 relates to Static Site Guarding and Mobile Patrol Services—Code of Practice).

The remaining contents of the Physical Security Policy may break down the requirements into specific areas:

Perimeters and External Environs

- Fences or barriers need to be adequate and maintained in good order.
- Provision of adequate external lighting.
- Consideration of lines of sight to and from the premises.
- Avoiding areas where individuals could lurk unseen.
- Clear and well lit pathways and routes (for example to and from car parks).
- The use of CCTV where appropriate, lawful and in accord with any prevailing standards of use.

Buildings

- Buildings are well constructed to recognised standards and well maintained.
- Points of entry are protected (via locks or controlled access mechanisms).
- Keys and other barrier access devices are controlled, registered, periodically verified and recovered when the employee leaves the organisation.
- Secure storage of unallocated keys.
- Consideration and justification of intruder alarms.
- Compliance with the prevailing health and safety regulations including the Fire Code.
- Appropriate and lawful signage inside and outside the premises.
- Emergency lighting facilities.
- Safe, tidy and clean condition of all areas.

Access Control

- Control access to staff only areas.
- The controlled issue and use of access key cards (and other such devices).
- Access codes (i.e. on door locks) to be changed periodically and when an employee leaves the organisation.
- Staff should wear or carry official identity cards.
- Staff alertness to strangers in the building and the need to challenge them for their identity.
- Registering all visitors and ensuring that they are met and accompanied at times during their visit.
- Vacant, unattended or dormant premises adequately secured against entry.

Personal Safety

- Minimise potential hazards.
- Where appropriate, issue Personal Protective Equipment (PPE) to employees and ensure that they are aware of the correct use of all such equipment.
- Provision and maintenance of adequate First Aid facilities and the appointment of Qualified First Aiders.
- Ensuring that employees know what to do in the event of an emergency (i.e. fire, bomb threat or physical attack).

Property and Assets

- Physically securing IT equipment in place.
- Identity marking the organisation's assets and maintaining an up-to-date assets register which is periodically verified.
- Guidance on the secure use of company vehicles including the necessary measures to deploy when transporting IT equipment or information assets.

Dealing with Emergencies

- Having in place documented plans in the event of various emergency scenarios (e.g. fire, bomb threat, suspicious packages, physical attacks, terrorism, etc.).
- Periodic testing of such plans and their ongoing improvement.
- Allocating specific responsibilities.
- Ensuring that staff know what to do.
- Calmly and effectively dealing with visitors and customers on site at the time.

Control Objectives for IT Sites and Infrastructure

(a) To provide a sure and reliable environment for all IT activities.

(b) To ensure that all IT facilities are adequately protected from damage, loss or disruption.

(c) To ensure that adequate plans are in place to deal effectively with emergencies.

(d) To ensure that appropriate and reliable environmental and physical conditions are provided and maintained.

(e) To prevent unauthorised access to the IT facility.

(f) To ensure that risks are assessed and IT facilities are adequately and appropriately insured.

(g) To ensure that staff maintain an up-to-date awareness of their responsibilities for security and safety.

(h) To ensure that buildings, persons and property are effectively protected from fire.

Risk and Control Issues for IT Sites and Infrastructure

1 Key Issues

1.1 What general steps does management take to identify and address the potential risks in respect of the IT facility?

1.2 How does management ensure that all IT sites are secure and adequately protected from unauthorised access?

1.3 How does management take due regard of the location of the IT facility and the potential hazards?

1.4 What specific measures are in place to further restrict access to the main computer room or processing facility (and how does management ensure that the measures are effective)?

1.5 What measures are in place both to prevent and to detect the unauthorised removal of IT equipment?

1.6 Have steps been taken during the design and construction of the IT facility to ensure that water, power and fuel are stored and routed so as to avoid any adverse impact due to leakage, short circuit, etc.?

1.7 Have adequate physical security and fire prevention systems been installed (and how does management ensure that they remain operational, appropriate, and effective)?

1.8 How does management ensure that adequate and effective plans and procedures are in place to deal with emergencies, disasters, bomb threats, attacks on the building, etc.?

1.9 Are regular emergency, fire and contingency drills conducted as a means of evaluating the effectiveness of the prevailing measures?

1.10 How does management ensure that staff are sufficiently aware of their responsibilities in respect of fire detection/prevention, and emergency evacuation drills, etc.?

1.11 How does management verify that all the environmental requirements (such as air conditioning, temperature and humidity) have been identified, provided and maintained?

1.12 How is management assured that adequate and appropriate levels of insurance cover are in place for the IT facilities?

2 Detailed Issues

2.1 What measures are in place to protect the IT installation from staff malpractice?

2.2 How are existing access control measures tested for effectiveness?

2.3 How does management ensure that staff access control measures are kept up to date?

2.4 What specific measures are in place to control access by visitors, delivery staff, etc.?

2.5 What measures are in place to deal with out-of-hours access?

2.6 Are "high risk" or sensitive areas provided with additional access measures?

2.7 Have specific security and storage needs been effectively addressed (i.e. media library)?

2.8 Are computer room staff aware of the actions to be taken in the event of an emergency (i.e. the correct power-down procedure)?

2.9 Have adequate fire detection systems been installed (and how does management ensure that they remain operational and effective)?

2.10 Does the design of the building adequately support the containment of fire (i.e. provision of fire doors, sealed conduits, and fire-proof barriers, etc.)?

2.11 Have suitable and lawful fire containment systems (e.g. sprinklers or gas-smothering facilities) been installed?

2.12 Does the air-conditioning system shut off automatically in the event of a fire being detected?

2.13 Has management consulted with the local fire fighting service when determining the necessary precautions and facilities?

2.14 How does management monitor that appropriate steps are taken to protect the well-being and safety of staff and visitors?

2.15 What measures ensure that the relevant and correct temperature and humidity are maintained for the IT facilities?

2.16 Where necessary or justified, have back-up or secondary environmental systems been provided?

2.17 Have facilities been provided to address the loss or disruption of the power supply?

2.18 Does the prevailing insurance cover address the potential for the following categories of risk?

- material damage (e.g. to buildings, hardware, etc.)
- consequences of the damage (e.g. disruption of business operations, loss of data, etc.)
- risks to and from personnel or third parties (e.g. injury liability or staff negligence/fraud).

32
Processing Operations

The contents of this chapter are designed so that they can be applied to a variety of different processing situations. For example, the traditional batch oriented methods normally associated with centralised systems or the more direct (and usually more informal) entry of data into freestanding or networked personal computers.

Irrespective of the hardware platform in use, the auditor will mainly be concerned with matters of data accuracy, validity, authorisation and completeness. These factors are linked not only to matters of access control, but are also dependent on the use of the authorised and valid versions of computer programs. Beyond these points, it is probable that there will be performance considerations to take account of; for example, is the output data available on time for its use in other interfaced systems and for circulation to staff in order to support their activities?

Control Objectives for Processing Operations

> (a) To ensure that all processing is valid, authorised and accurate.
>
> (b) To ensure that data is protected from unauthorised access and use.
>
> (c) To ensure that the required service levels are achieved in support of the business objectives.
>
> (d) To ensure that only authorised and tested programs are used.
>
> (e) To ensure that only accurate, complete and timely data is provided.
>
> (f) To ensure that IT processing facilities are operated at optimum performance/ efficiency without jeopardising system integrity and reliability.

Risk and Control Issues for Processing Operations

1 Key Issues

1.1 What general measures are in place to ensure that processing activity is valid, accurate and authorised?

1.2 What specific measures prevent unauthorised transactions and/or system amendments being applied?

1.3 How can management be assured that data is accurate, complete, authorised and reliable?

1.4 How is commercially sensitive or confidential data protected from unauthorised access or leakage?

1.5 What measures ensure that only authorised and tested versions of programs are utilised?

1.6 How would management promptly be made aware of any abnormal processing activity?

1.7 What steps are in place to prevent development staff directly accessing the live production environment?

1.8 How does management monitor that the skills of the operating and technical support staff are kept up to date and relevant?

1.9 How does management ensure that the mainframe and distributed systems are operated at optimum efficiency (and that facility overloads are prevented)?

1.10 What measures prevent unauthorised usage of mainframe (or equivalent) facilities?

1.11 How does management check that the operating system is efficiently configured and that adequately skilled staff are available to maintain and/or rebuild the system in the event of major failure?

1.12 Have adequate steps been taken to ensure that all key hardware is regularly and appropriately maintained in order to avoid unnecessary disruption of services, etc.?

1.13 What measures ensure that the use of job control language (JCL) or system control language (SCL) is optimised and that inefficient or inappropriate tasks are not loaded?

1.14 Is access to the JCL and SCL facilities adequately restricted in order to avoid unauthorised amendments?

1.15 What steps are in place to ensure that all the necessary processing stages are correctly applied in the appropriate sequence?

1.16 What measures ensure that processing is conducted in accordance with the business requirements and within the required timescales?

1.17 What steps ensure that only authorised, accurate and appropriate data is loaded for access by users?

1.18 Have management defined the required service provision levels, and what measures ensure that the agreed performance criteria are achieved?

2 Detailed Issues

2.1 How would management promptly be made aware of any corrupt or inaccurate data?

2.2 What specific steps would prevent the loading and use of unauthorised and untested programs or system amendments?

2.3 What measures are in place to assess and promptly deal with processing problems and delays?

2.4 What measures are in place to confirm positively the accuracy and completeness of processing operations?

2.5 What measures prevent the delivery or provision of inaccurate output to users?

2.6 Are contingency measures in place to restore promptly disrupted services?

2.7 How does management ensure that access to and use of utility programs is valid, appropriate and trailed?

2.8 Are the actions of operations staff capable of being identified and trailed (and are they made accountable for their actions)?

2.9 Are the activity logs routinely reviewed in order to ensure that unauthorised activities would be detected?

2.10 What specific measures prevent the application of inefficient or invalid JCL or SCL?

2.11 What steps are in place to ensure that all general processing operations are conducted in the correct sequence and at the relevant time?

2.12 What measures ensure that only the correct data files are loaded, and that invalid files are detected?

2.13 What measures prevent the premature overwriting or erasure of data files?

2.14 What measures would enable the continuation of processing activities if key data or a program was lost or destroyed?

2.15 Has management provided adequate operational procedures and policies in order to ensure that operating staff are fully aware of their responsibilities?

2.16 What steps are taken with urgent or nonstandard processing jobs in order to prevent the disruption of mainstream processing?

2.17 What measures prevent unauthorised access to confidential data output, and how is such data securely distributed to authorised users?

33

Back-up and Media Management

In this chapter we examine the issues relating to protection of data through adequate back-up, and also include details of the related practices of secure storage and media handling.

Paying attention to the back-up and secure storage of data is often (falsely!) seen as a chore which can be left to another day. It is all too easy to overlook the real value of operational and business data and not take adequate precautions to protect it should a problem occur with the computer, the application system or the physical environment. The situation is exacerbated by the widespread use of personal computers (PCs) in business, where the option to take the necessary precautions with data is usually left to the discretion of the user. The formal data handling and security techniques that emerged from mainframe installations over the years do not readily translate into the more informal and open world of the PC. In addition, unless the responsibility for data and system back-up is clearly defined and complied with, it is all too easy for end-users to assume that someone else is securing their systems.

The move to server-based applications often results in centrally located server rooms (or server farms for larger installations) and this type of controlled environment lends itself to the back-up being conducted by IT staff in accordance with an agreed timescale and rota. This relieves the end-user of having to address back-up issues.

When media reaches the end of its life or becomes faulty, care should be exercised over its secure disposal. Although it is often assumed that the deletion of a file removes all trace of it, this is untrue in most cases and there are means to resurrect previously deleted files. In order to be completely sure that data contained on media, irrespective of its type and format, remains inaccessible to unauthorised users and protected from inappropriate disclosure, the media will need to be irreversibly destroyed or rendered unusable. Issues relating to the disposal of data, records and media are more fully discussed in Chapter 55 (Data Retention and Disposal).

Control Objectives for Back-up and Media Management

(a) To ensure that critical systems and data are adequately and frequently backed up to protect the business operations and integrity of the organisation,

(b) To provide the means to recover promptly and accurately from system failure or invalid processing situations.

(c) To ensure that the organisation's data is adequately protected from loss, damage and leakage.

(d) To ensure that all corporate data is safeguarded and retained.

(e) To ensure that retained data remains in a usable and accessible form.

(f) To ensure that the organisation is capable of complying with the prevailing data retention legislation and regulations.

(g) To ensure that data storage facilities provide the appropriate environmental conditions to prevent deterioration or damage to media.

(h) To ensure that media staff are appropriately skilled in media handling techniques.

(i) To ensure that all media and data are accurately identified, trailed and accounted for.

(j) To ensure that media and data are not prematurely disposed of or destroyed.

(k) To prevent the infection of media and systems with viruses.

(l) To ensure that users are made aware of their responsibilities with regard to the back-up and protection of PC data.

(m) To ensure that only the correct data are used for processing operations.

(n) To ensure that faulty or defective media are identified, replaced and disposed of by a means that makes them unusable.

(o) To prevent the unauthorised use of media and data.

Risk and Control Issues for Back-up and Media Management

1 Key Issues

1.1 How does management ensure that all the key systems and data are effectively protected in the event of a failure or breakdown in order to avoid disruption to business operations and requirements?

1.2 How are management assured that systems and data files are appropriately backed up at the right time?

1.3 What checks are in place to monitor that the prescribed data (and system) back-up routines are being correctly applied in practice?

1.4 How does management ensure that the current data back-up and recovery procedures are adequate so that systems could be restored promptly and accurately?

1.5 What measures ensure that all data and system back-ups are securely stored and adequately protected from damage, loss or deterioration?

1.6 What steps are in place to protect key elements of corporate data in the event of a major systems failure or disaster befalling the IT facility?

1.7 What measures ensure that all key data and system back-ups can be accurately and promptly identified and traced?

1.8 How does management ascertain that the organisation is correctly complying with all the prevailing and relevant data retention legislation and regulations (i.e. for accounting and financial data)?

1.9 What measures ensure that long-term back-up media remain readable and usable?

1.10 What measures ensure that only the correct and valid data and systems files are used in processing activities?

1.11 What specific measures prevent the premature erasure, disposal or reuse of back-up media?

1.12 What measures are in place to prevent and/or detect the virus infection of media and the spreading of that infection throughout the corporate systems?

2 Detailed Issues

2.1 Has management established an agreed back-up procedure which defines, among other things, the following elements:
- back-up frequency
- number of copies
- retention period?

2.2 How does management ensure that the back-up procedures remain appropriate in relation to changing business requirements, etc.?

2.3 What measures are in place to detect any failure to undertake a prescribed back-up at the appropriate time?

2.4 How is management sure that systems and data could be promptly recovered from back-up copies (i.e. has the recovery process been tested to prove its effectiveness)?

2.5 How does management check that end-users are applying adequate data back-up routines in order to protect their PC-based activities?

2.6 Does management ensure that all key back-ups are regularly accounted for?

2.7 Where are the back-up storage facilities located (and does this location afford appropriate protection in the event of a disaster, such as a fire, affecting the main IT facility)?

2.8 How is the disposal of outdated or unwanted media controlled so that valid items are not destroyed or overwritten?

2.9 Are the staff involved in media handling suitably trained in handling and transporting techniques in order to protect corporate data and systems?

2.10 Have adequate copies of key data been provided in case one copy becomes damaged or unreadable?

2.11 What measures ensure that virus infections are promptly detected, contained and effectively dealt with?

2.12 What specific measures prevent the transfer of virus-infected media to third parties (such as suppliers or customers)?

2.13 How would unauthorised access to or use of back-up media be prevented (or detected)?

34
Removable Media

In this chapter we discuss the risks associated with the use of removable media devices, such as USB memory sticks, data CDs and DVDs and portable external hard drives. Such removable devices are often involved in high profile breaches of information security. Although the devices offer the user convenience and portability, those very attributes expose the media to possible loss, theft or misuse. Reported incidents include the loss or theft of memory sticks or CDs containing customer or client data, the leaving of such items in public places such as a train or airport waiting area and the lack of measures to prevent or control access to the contents (i.e. no password protection or encryption).

In a 2008 survey of UK companies[1] it was noted that 78 % of those companies that had computers stolen did not encrypt hard discs. In addition, the survey revealed that 67 % of the companies did nothing to prevent confidential data leaving on USB sticks, etc., and only 11 % used the technical configuration of PCs to either prevent the use of removable devices or restrict their use to authorised devices only.

Whether or not removable media are an appropriate and secure means of holding data and information will depend, in part, upon the nature of the organisation and the types of data which it handles. For example, where the data is deemed personal, sensitive or confidential, the organisation may completely ban the use of removable media devices so as to minimise the opportunities for the loss, theft or unlawful exposure of the associated data or information assets.

In order to ensure that employees are appropriately aware of their responsibilities for the secure use of removable media, the organisation may consider the implementation of a ratified Removable Media Policy or procedure which contains some or all of the following conditions and requirements:

- A clear definition of removable media devices covered by the policy and its requirements, for example:
  - Data CDs
  - Data DVDs
  - Optical disks
  - External, removable or portable hard drives
  - USB memory sticks (also known as pen drives or flash drives)
  - SD (and similar) memory cards

- Embedded microchips (for example those within mobile phones or PDAs)
- Digital cameras
- Cassettes
- Audio recording formats.

- Restrict usage of removable media devices to those specified, approved and supplied by the organisation.
- The withdrawal of all corporate removable devices and the procurement of devices that do not have either the physical or logical ability to support removable devices (i.e. using the "Thin Client" approach).
- The explicit prohibition of the employee's own devices in association with official duties and the organisation's IT hardware and facilities.
- Only procuring and providing approved forms of devices.
- Limiting the use of removable media devices to a restricted type and number of employees.
- Controlling the issue and recovery of the organisation's devices.
- Only using removable media to supplement the primary version of the associated data and never allowing the removable version to become the primary or dependent version.
- The use of a recognised standard and form of encryption on all devices.
- The use of password protection on all devices to a required standard (including strength of password and regular enforced password changes).
- Applying adequate security measures to protect the device at all times, including during times away from the official premises.
- Where appropriate, enable the logging of events involving the copying or downloading of files to and from removable devices (NB: this measure could be linked to the disabling of software and hardware to prevent such actions).
- The prompt reporting, logging and investigation of any actual or suspected breaches of information security related to the use or loss of removable devices.
- Prohibiting the use of removable media devices to pass over data or information to external parties, partners or organisations.
- The prompt and effective removal of data and files from permitted removal media devices immediately after use (so as to reduce downstream opportunities for unauthorised loss or disclosure of data).
- The return and irreversible destruction of damaged or faulty removable media devices.
- Protection of removable media devices from virus infection or malicious software (and their onward transmission or dispersal).

Control Objectives for Removable Media

(a) To ensure that the use of removable media devices is appropriate, sanctioned and protects the organisation from data loss, theft or authorised disclosure.

(b) To ensure that all employees are aware of required, appropriate and secure use of removable media devices and of their specific responsibilities for data security.

(c) To avoid the loss, theft and/or subsequent misuse of data and information held on removable media devices.

(d) To prevent the infection of removable media devices with viruses and other malicious software and the associated onward transmission and dispersal of infected files.

(e) To ensure that management are fully aware of any actual or suspected information security incidents relating to removable media devices as a means to take appropriate action to prevent or limit any possible future reoccurrence.

Risk and Control Issues for Removable Media

1 Key Issues

1.1 How has management assessed and mitigated the risks associated with the use of removable media devices?

1.2 How does management prevent the unsafe or unauthorised use of removable media devices?

1.3 How has management ensured that all employees are aware of the organisation's attitude and stance towards the use of removable media devices?

1.4 How would management be made aware of the use (including unauthorised use) of removable media devices?

1.5 What active measures are in place to prevent the loss, theft and misuse of data held on removable devices?

1.6 What measures are in place to alert management to related information security incidents?

1.7 How does management ensure that authorised media devices are accounted for?

1.8 What measures are in place to prevent, detect and deal with the infection of media with viruses or other forms of malicious software?

1.9 What measures would prevent data and information from being accessed or retrieved from media that has been disposed of?

2 Detailed Issues

2.1 What specific measures would prevent unauthorised access to or use of information on lost, stolen or misplaced removable media devices?

2.2 What specific measures are applied to the protection of personal, sensitive or confidential data held on removable devices?

2.3 How would management be made aware of authorised use of removable media devices?

2.4 Have steps been taken to prevent, restrict or detect the use of an employee's own removable media devices?

2.5 What measures ensure that only suitable and reliable devices are procured and in use?

2.6 How does management ensure that only recognised and reliable forms of data encryption are applied?

2.7 How is the consistent use of data encryption and/or password protection of data enforced?

2.8 How would management be made aware of lost, stolen or misplaced media devices?

2.9 How does management prevent the onward transmission or dispersal of virus infections and other malicious software?

NOTE

1. *2008 Information Security Breaches Survey*, Department for Business, Enterprise and Regulatory Reform (2008), www.berr.gov.uk.

35
System and Operating Software (Including Patch Management)

This chapter is concerned with the category of software which is fundamental to the operation of computers. System and operating software will determine how the computer basically handles data, stores files, etc. In the more familiar personal computer environment, operating system software examples would be Microsoft Windows™, XP™ and Vista™ or Apple Corporation's MAC™ environment.

PC users who use the Windows™ environment will probably be aware that there are many configuration options provided and that it can take some time to settle upon the particular set-up which most suits their needs. Windows™ has the benefit of being fairly user-friendly, once you have understood the jargon and the range of possibilities. The available options have the potential to affect the speed and efficiency of operations, the appearance of the screens, and the range of options offered to users. However, operating systems for networking and server environments are normally much more complex and usually require considerable expertise in their configuration and use.

This chapter is not intended to be technically oriented, but concentrates on the business and operational implications of systems and operating software. The commercially available operating systems are normally the subject of dedicated technical books which explore the depths of their complexity for the benefit of system managers and other IT specialists. Indeed there are such texts specifically designed for internal auditors' including those produced by The Institute of Internal Auditors (IIA).

A key factor with any system or operating software is maintaining it up to date with bug fixes, security patches and official upgrades from the supplier. Such requirements will equally apply to PCs, other hardware platforms and network software environments. Failing to maintain the software up to date could expose the organisation to unauthorised intrusion or infection by viruses, malware or spyware.

The various types of updating can be defined as follows:

- **Patch or Fix** – Relates to software designed to enhance performance or address previously known programming bugs.
- **Driver** – Drivers are used by operating systems to support the operation of hardware devices, such as printers or scanners. Hardware manufacturers and software suppliers will often release enhanced or more reliable drivers over time. Applying the latest driver may have performance and efficiency benefits for users or solve previous problems and errors.
- **Service Pack or Service Release** – This category relates to the grouping or bundling of a number of patches and/or updates necessary to bring the software to a recognised level of release (for example from Version 1.0 to Version 1.1).
- **Update** – Updates are usually related to either additional or improved software functionality that may take the software up to the next full version. (NB: When software is newly released it may be version 1.0. Any patches or fixes to that version may generate versions 1.1, 1.2, 1.2.1 and so on. However, when a new or enhanced version is released it could be noted as being version 2.0 which, in turn, will be progressively patched or fixed and referred to as 2.1, 2.2 etc.)
- **Build or Version** – As noted above, progressive versions of software can be noted by the use of logical sequential version numbering. The higher the version number, the more developed the software should be and it should be expected to be more reliable and have fewer problems.

Suppliers' approaches to charging for updates will vary. However it is usual for the patches and fixes within a main version of software to be supplied without additional cost to the user so long as the user has an appropriate maintenance agreement in place, which is normally subject to an annual charge relating to a set percentage of the original licence cost of the software. For example, patches to Version 3 of a product, named progressively as V3.1, V3.2 etc, will be provided free of additional costs (other than those involved in their deployment by the user).

Where a supplier creates a new build or version of the product (say from Version 3 to Version 4) which is substantially different (and hopefully better and more reliable) from the previous version, it is usual for the user to have to pay a proportional fee. Software contracts and agreements will vary and the specific terms and conditions should be clearly identified and monitored. In some instances, suppliers will, after a suitable period, withdraw their support for a given version of their product, which may force the issue of accepting an upgrade, whether or not it represents any advantage for the user. In general terms, the organisation would benefit from having a planned and documented approach to the migration and upgrade of all the software it uses. Even though a new software version may be available, the pros and cons of adopting the new version should be assessed, not least in terms of the cost and resource implications.

In relation to software designed to protect the IT environment from viruses, malware, spyware or other malicious software, it is normal for the definitions required to enable the detection of all possible threats to be regularly provided, perhaps on a subscription basis, as part of the software agreement.

In relation to operating and system software these maintenance processes can be collectively termed as "Patch Management" and the following key issues specifically apply:

- There should be a clearly defined approach to the management of software upgrades and patching so that these are controlled, assessed for operational and cost impacts, justified, adequately tested and appropriately applied.
- Patch Management should ideally be centrally controlled and applied, and not left to individual users or system owners to undertake.
- The creation and maintenance of an accurate and current inventory of components that could be subject to patching or upgrade (hardware and software). Such an inventory will enable the assessment of the impact of a forthcoming change so it can be managed appropriately.
- Responsibility for Patch Management across the organisation should be clearly allocated (for example to a nominated Patch Administrator).
- Patch Management can be related to the information contained within a formal Configuration Management Database (CMDB) or a network topology mapping. In any event, it will be necessary to identify the totality of devices etc. that need to be kept updated in terms of systems and operating software.
- Access to accurate and reliable sources of information about new patch releases, driver updates, virus definition updates, and so on should be in place. (NB: Supplier product maintenance websites often facilitate automated email messages to registered users whenever new patches are available for use. Such messages may also incorporate an indication of the urgency of applying the patch.)
- The following implications of Patch Management will apply in most instances:
  - **Costs** – In the form of subscriptions, software maintenance charges and possibly acquiring a new (or later) version of the product.
  - **Resources** – The resource impact will obviously depend on the size of the organisation and the complexity of its IT environment. Where it is necessary to test and "manually" deploy patches etc., the impacts on staffing associated with keeping the environment updated should be considered. Even if the patches are automatically deployed (for example in the upgrading of the Microsoft Windows™ environment), there will still be a need to monitor and manage the associated processes.
  - **Time** – In terms of maintaining the required level of awareness of patching for all aspects of the organisation's IT environment and the effective testing and deployment.
- The creation and application of a planned approach to the testing and deployment of patches.
- Consider whether there is a need to obtain prior formal management authority to apply the amendment.
- Ensuring that Patch Management staff are appropriately trained.
- Consider the optimum timing for the deployment so as to avoid or minimise operational disruptions (and to allow for the reversal of the deployment in the event of any problems arising).

- Consider whether automated deployment would be the preferred method and how the deployment would otherwise be managed.
- Ensure that any deployment failures are detected and dealt with (for example if some PCs were not either switched on or connected to the network at the time of an automated deployment. This situation can be subsequently automatically detected by software designed to check and verify the version of software in place.)
- Testing of the patch prior to deployment within a separate testing environment that mirrors the characteristics of the live environment. The testing should obviously include aspects that the patch is said to address, but other general functionality should also be evaluated.
- The requirements for deploying patches will vary according to the nature of the software being amended and the sequence of processes that need to be followed.
- Ensure that it is possible to roll back the software in the event of any problems arising.
- Following the deployment, continue to monitor the environment and be alert to any adverse or unexpected implications.
- Ensure that the central inventory is updated with the details and extent of the deployment.

Control Objectives for System and Operating Software

(a) To ensure that only authorised and reliable systems and operating software are used in order to provide a stable basis for data processing operations.

(b) To ensure that the configuration of the systems/operating software supports the efficient running of systems.

(c) To ensure that the operating system prevents unauthorised access to systems, data and facilities.

(d) To ensure that adequate and appropriately skilled staff are available to maintain the systems/operating software.

(e) To ensure that all configuration changes or software amendments applied to the operating software are valid, authorised and fully tested prior to implementation.

(f) To ensure that the use of privilege user or high-level facilities is valid, authorised, and suitably trailed.

(g) To ensure that the operating systems for personal computers are appropriately configured for maximum performance and integrity.

(h) To ensure that personal computer operating systems are adequately protected from unauthorised tampering.

> (i) To ensure that the capability to recover from a major systems failure is maintained and periodically tested.
>
> (j) To ensure that error conditions, etc. are appropriately logged and followed up.
>
> (k) To ensure that the use of powerful utility and diagnostic software is controlled and monitored in order to prevent disruption of services or corruption of data and systems.

Risk and Control Issues for System and Operating Software

1 Key Issues

1.1 What measures ensure that only recognised, reliable, industry standard, and correctly configured operating systems are used throughout the organisation?

1.2 How does management ensure that the various operating systems are appropriately configured to support the efficient and secure running of systems?

1.3 What measures prevent unauthorised access to and amendment of operating systems and systems software?

1.4 Are all systems software upgrades and fixes adequately assessed, tested and authorised prior to application to the live environment?

1.5 How does management monitor that the efficiency and performance of the operating system is optimised?

1.6 Are systems and operating software facilities effectively configured and established so that unauthorised access to data and systems is prevented (or at least detected)?

1.7 What is the procedure to ensure that full recovery from a major systems failure can be achieved promptly (i.e. the ability to quickly and correctly rebuild the operating environment)?

1.8 How does management ensure that adequate and appropriately skilled staff are available to maintain operating and systems software?

1.9 Are abnormal or unauthorised events promptly and independently brought to the attention of management for action?

1.10 Is access to "privilege user" facilities adequately restricted and trailed?

1.11 Has management established adequate and appropriate levels of operating system journals in order to maintain an accurate awareness of system usage and operating efficiency?

1.12 How does management ensure that all personal computers throughout the organisation are appropriately and consistently configured?

1.13 What measures prevent users from applying unauthorised or inappropriate amendments to PC configurations?

2 Detailed Issues

2.1 How does management ensure that the organisation is using the most appropriate operating systems to support their requirements?

2.2 Would management promptly be made aware of the use of unauthorised or unsuitable operating systems?

2.3 What measures prevent the inappropriate or disruptive configuration of operating/systems software?

2.4 Do access facilities reflect both the operational requirements of the organisation and protect users' data?

2.5 Are up-to-date records maintained which reflect the current and authorised condition and configuration of operating systems?

2.6 What measures prevent the application of invalid, unsuitable or unauthorised amendments to the operating system?

2.7 How does management verify that all operating system amendments are fully and effectively tested prior to update in the live environment?

2.8 How is the performance of the operating system monitored (and would this process enable the prompt detection of potential problems)?

2.9 Who has the responsibility and authority to amend the "workmix"?

2.10 How is management made aware of error conditions, abnormal events or the use of "privilege user" facilities?

2.11 Is access to utility and diagnostic facilities suitably restricted and trailed?

2.12 How does management check that all job control language (JCL) or systems control language (SCL) instructions are valid, authorised and tested prior to introduction to the live environment?

2.13 What specific measures prevent the introduction and use of unauthorised or unreliable PC operating systems?

2.14 What measures prevent PC users from introducing unauthorised operating systems by rebooting from a system disk placed in the floppy disk drive?

2.15 Would the measures in place enable the detection of unauthorised amendments to PC operating systems?

36
System Access Control (Logical Security)

Access Control is also known as Logical Security and is often a key and critical proactive component in the protection of data and systems from unauthorised use. The most common form of access control is the use of a unique user identity and an associated password. However, in more demanding security environments, this basic approach can be augmented by additional biometric methods such as iris, finger print or voice recognition.

Access to data, information and systems is normally based on the individual employee's "need to know". Access to application system functionality can be precisely tailored to the specific needs of a user so that unnecessary, sensitive or other areas that are not commensurate with the individual's role can be barred. In operational terms such precision in mapping system access can support segregation of key duties as a means of, for example, preventing fraudulent or inappropriate activities. Selected users, such as those acting as System Administrators, will often be granted access to higher system functions and facilities that widely affect the way in which the system operates; such access should be restricted and, in the case of critical systems, subject to logging and monitoring.

Access control may work, in practice, at more than one level. For example, one user ID and password may grant access to the corporate network and a further ID and password is required to use a specific application system or access a secure file server.

Management should consider the creation of an IT Access Policy supported by unambiguous guidance for all staff that addresses the following key components:

- Clear definition of who is affected by the Policy (i.e. all employees, contractors, temporary workers and agents of the organisation).
- A controlled process for the set up of new users based on appropriate authorisation.
- Only applying authorised and necessary changes to existing access rights.
- Users should be reminded that actions attempted or taken using their user IDs will be logged so as to clearly indicate who did what and when.

- The prompt disabling of access rights when an employee either leaves the organisation or is suspended from duty.
- Regular verification of active users to ensure that they are still relevant and appropriate.
- The application of password standards incorporating minimum length, the use and combination of upper and lower case, numbers and other characters leading to the creation of "strong passwords" that are more difficult to second guess.
- Ensuring that staff protect their passwords from loss, theft or unauthorised use. This includes not writing them down, never using the "remember password" facility and not sharing passwords with colleagues.
- Users should not attempt to access systems or data to which they are not entitled.
- Password changes should ideally be periodically automatically forced by the system or operating systems (as appropriate).
- The reuse or recycling of previous passwords should be prevented.
- The password should be obscured on the screen as it is typed in (for example using asterisks).
- The number of unsuccessful attempts to access the network or systems should be limited and result in the user account being locked, the incident being logged for monitoring and follow-up purposes.
- External connections to the organisation's networks need to be subject to additional access control measures to prevent unauthorised or malicious access. In practice, such measures include the use of two-factor authentication using the usual password and an additional element such as a standard key card attached to the device. (NB: Remote Working is the subject of Chapter 38.)

Control Objectives for System Access Control

(a) To ensure that systems and data are secure from unauthorised access and usage.

(b) To prevent disruption of the business caused by unauthorised access to computing facilities.

(c) To ensure that data are adequately protected from unauthorised amendment, loss or leakage.

(d) To ensure that all system usage is recorded and accounted for.

(e) To ensure that potential breaches of access security are promptly detected and reacted to.

(f) To ensure that staff are aware of their responsibilities for protecting company systems and data.

(g) To ensure that access passwords are of an acceptable standard and kept confidential.

(h) To ensure that access rights and associated records are kept up to date.

Risk and Control Issues for System Access Control

1 Key Issues

1.1 Has management established a policy of system and data ownership whereby users take responsibility for their systems and data?

1.2 What measures are in place to ensure that data and systems are effectively protected from unauthorised access and/or amendments?

1.3 How is system usage identified (and charged for, where necessary)?

1.4 What measures ensure that the access control arrangements are kept up to date and relevant to the underlying business needs?

1.5 Who controls the granting of access rights, and how does management check that this operation is correctly conducted?

1.6 How does management monitor that staff are fully aware of their responsibilities with regard to data and system security?

1.7 How does management ensure that user access passwords are effective and are protected from leakage and misuse?

1.8 What specific measures prevent the casual use of terminals (and personal computers) left switched on and unattended?

1.9 How does management ensure that users access systems on a strictly "need to know" basis?

2 Detailed Issues

2.1 How are valid access rights to systems and data determined?

2.2 What mechanisms ensure that leavers and those changing position are appropriately amended on the access system(s)?

2.3 Are the established access rights periodically checked for accuracy and relevance (with outdated entries being removed or edited)?

2.4 Will attempted security breaches or violations be promptly detected and reported to management for action?

2.5 What additional measures are in place to ensure that high-level or privilege access rights are effectively controlled and that relevant actions are trailed (and authorised)?

2.6 Has management established that attempted security breaches are staff disciplinary offences?

2.7 Are access arrangements subject to periodic review and assessment (and how is this evidenced)?

2.8 Have standards been established for passwords (minimum length, regular changing, avoidance of obvious or previously used words, etc.)?

2.9 If password standards have been established, how is management certain that they are complied with?

2.10 How are initial passwords communicated to the relevant user, and what measures ensure that the password remains secure in transit?

37

Personal Computers (Including Laptops and PDAs)

The business (and personal) use of computers has mushroomed in popularity and society's reliance upon computers for social, business and cultural purposes is becoming progressively dominant.

As at the end of 2008[1] there were said to an estimated 1.19 billion personal computers (PCs) in use across the world, although the accurate determination of the actual figure is both difficult and the subject of some dispute. The reported figures for the top 15 countries are as follows (see Figure 37.1) and collectively they account for 72 % of the total world ownership of PCs. It has been suggested that a world level of 2 billion will be reached by 2014.

PCs are approachable, easy to use, increasingly reliable and ever more powerful. When linked together through networks they become even more flexible and enable the sharing and exchange of data. They have also been responsible for changing working methods. PCs do, however, have some downsides.

The very ease of approach afforded by the PC presents problems of security, access control, and so on. The growth in an organisation's reliance upon PCs can be insidious, and unless sensible security and usage methods are concurrently introduced, exposure to real risks will follow. In this chapter we consider the primary concerns of PC usage in a business environment.

Organisations often choose to define the boundaries of the permitted use of personal computers in the form of a PC Acceptable Use Policy or Procedure, including the following points:
- Prohibiting the use of PC resources for the purposes of fraud, theft or dishonesty.
- Limiting the use of the PC for private or non work purposes.
- Prohibiting the downloading, loading, storage and execution of software which is not work-related.

Position	Country	PCs in Use at end of 2008 (Millions)	World Share
1.	United States	264.10	22.19 %
2.	China	98.67	8.29 %
3.	Japan	86.22	7.24 %
4.	Germany	61.96	5.21 %
5.	United Kingdom	47.04	3.95 %
6.	France	43.11	3.62 %
7.	Russia	36.42	3.06 %
8.	Italy	35.69	3.00 %
9.	South Korea	34.87	2.93 %
10.	Brazil	33.30	2.80 %
11.	India	32.03	2.69 %
12.	Canada	27.63	2.32 %
13.	Mexico	19.13	1.61 %
14.	Australia	17.01	1.43 %
15.	Spain	16.71	1.40 %
	Total of Top 15:	853.89	71.74 %
	Worldwide Total	1190.10	

Figure 37.1 PC ownership—top 15 countries

- Prohibiting the loading, storage and execution of software that is neither officially sanctioned for use for work purposes, acquired through approved procurement processes, the subject of a valid program licence held by the organisation, nor which has been checked for virus or malware infection.
- Prohibiting the use of a corporate PC for matters related to a private business or venture.
- Not copying software and data that are the licensed or direct property of the organisation and for which the organisation is the legal copyright owner.
- Storing, processing and printing data for any non work purpose.
- Email facilities must only be used in accord with the prevailing Email Policy (see Chapter 39 on Email for further details).
- Internet usage must be in compliance with the prevailing Internet Usage Policy (see Chapter 40 on Internet Usage for further details).
- Requiring employees to perform their duties and use the PC in accord with the relevant laws and regulations (for example, in the UK this could include: The Freedom of Information Act 2000; The Data Protection Act 1998; The Human Rights Act 1998; The Electronic Communications Act 2000; The Regulation of Investigatory Powers Act 2000; The Copyright Designs and Patents Act 1988 and The Computer Misuse Act 1990).

Control Objectives for Personal Computers

(a) To ensure that personal computers are consistently and securely used throughout the organisation as a means of contributing to efficiency and the achievement of business objectives.

(b) To ensure that the use of all personal computers is justified and authorised.

(c) To ensure that only suitable industry standard personal computers are acquired from stable and reliable suppliers capable of providing the required support.

(d) To ensure that all personal computers and ancillary equipment are effectively protected from loss, theft or damage.

(e) To ensure that staff are suitably trained in the effective and efficient use of personal computing facilities.

(f) To ensure that only authorised and licensed versions of software are used throughout the organisation.

(g) To ensure that all PC equipment is correctly installed and appropriately configured.

(h) To prevent unauthorised configuration and software amendments being applied.

(i) To ensure that only authorised users are granted access to PC facilities.

(j) To ensure that the organisation conforms to the prevailing software licensing conditions.

(k) To prevent the unauthorised copying and theft of PC software and data.

(l) To prevent the loading of unauthorised software.

(m) To ensure compliance with the requirements of the Data Protection legislation.

(n) To ensure that business disruption caused by hardware failure is minimised.

(o) To prevent the infection of PC equipment and other IT facilities with viruses, and to deal promptly and effectively with any suspected or actual infection.

Risk and Control Issues for Personal Computers

1 Key Issues

1.1 How does management ensure that personal computing supports the objectives of the IT strategic plan?

1.2 How does management ensure that PC facilities are justified and contribute to business efficiency and/or the achievement of corporate objectives?

1.3 What measures are in place to ensure that personal computers are consistently and securely used throughout the organisation?

1.4 How does management ensure that suitable personal computers are obtained from reliable suppliers and that they meet the relevant performance and facility requirements?

1.5 Does management take effective steps to ensure that PC hardware is of an appropriate (and recognised) type and quality, and is capable of future expansion?

1.6 What steps are taken to protect PC hardware from theft, damage or misuse?

1.7 How does management ensure that only authorised and appropriate software is loaded onto personal computers (and what specifically prevents users from loading their own software files)?

1.8 What measures prevent users from applying unauthorised or inappropriate configuration amendments which could adversely affect performance and reliability?

1.9 How is the unauthorised use of personal computers and the relevant data prevented?

1.10 How are staff adequately trained in the correct and efficient use of PC facilities and specific software applications?

1.11 What steps does management take to ensure that the requirements of the prevailing Data Protection legislation are fully complied with?

1.12 What measures are in place to prevent undue disruption in the event of hardware failure?

1.13 What measures protect personal computers from virus infections?

1.14 What measures prevent users from making unauthorised copies of licensed software and sensitive data files?

1.15 What measures prevent users from circumventing access and operating system controls?

2 Detailed Issues

2.1 What measures ensure that only justified and authorised PC equipment is acquired (and how is the authorisation evidenced)?

2.2 How are staff made aware of their responsibility for accurate and appropriate usage of PC facilities?

2.3 Are all personal computers of an acceptable industry standard (and is the acquisition of nonstandard items subject to suitable authorisation)?

2.4 How does management ensure that PC suppliers are capable of providing an effective support and maintenance service?

2.5 What mechanisms ensure that the most appropriate method of financing PC acquisition is used in the circumstances?

2.6 How is the unauthorised movement or removal of PC equipment prevented?

2.7 How does management monitor that the number of software packages used throughout the organisation conforms to the licences held?

2.8 How is management made aware of the use of unlicensed or pirated software systems?

2.9 What measures prevent users from applying unauthorised or inappropriate software updates (and how can management be assured that the use of software is consistent throughout the organisation)?

2.10 How does management ensure that only authorised and valid users can gain access to corporate systems and data?

2.11 Would attempted access violations or system security breaches be promptly and effectively detected and reported?

2.12 What measures are in place to ensure that system/data access rights are kept up to date and are relevant to operational needs?

2.13 Are staff made aware of the need to regularly back up and securely store their data (and how does management ensure that such precautions are actually taken)?

2.14 How is management assured that back-up and other precautionary measures are effective (for example are system recovery processes periodically tested for their effectiveness)?

2.15 Are all hardware and software upgrades applied only by suitably trained and authorised staff (and how is this confirmed)?

2.16 Would virus infections be promptly identified, and what arrangements are in place to deal effectively with such infections?

2.17 What measures would prevent the uncontrolled spread of virus infections (e.g. through local area networks)?

NOTE

1. Contained within a press release dated 14 January 2009 from Computer Industry Almanac Inc. www.c-i-a.com.

38

Remote Working

This chapter considers the issues relating to the control of users remotely accessing an organisation's networks and computer systems. This will include employees who are travelling for their job, those who work from home or at other remote sites and any authorised partner or contractor with a justifiable need to remotely access central systems and data.

An Information Security Breaches Survey, conducted on behalf of the UK Government Department for Business, Enterprise and Regulatory Reform (BERR) and published in 2008,[1] advised that of the UK companies surveyed:

- 54 % allow their employees access to their systems remotely;
- 84 % restrict which staff can access systems remotely and/or what systems they are allowed to access;
- 53 % require the use of additional passwords over and above the normal network sign-on;
- 9 % apply strong authentication (for example using tokens, smart cards or biometric verification);
- 44 % utilise a Virtual Private Network (VPN).

The organisation's requirements, expectations and control measures can be set out in a ratified Remote Working Policy or procedure, the contents of which may include the following:

- Defining the scope of the Policy/procedure in terms of employees, contractors, partners, etc. as is deemed operationally appropriate. It may also be necessary to specify any post or role or circumstances where it would not be acceptable for remote access rights to be granted.
- A definition of the relevant access devices to which the Policy relates, such as:
  - Personal computers (irrespective of ownership)
  - Laptop computers
  - Tablet PCs
  - Personal Digital Assistants (PDA)
  - Mobile phones
  - Wireless devices.

- Establishing the ground rules for assessing, justifying and authorising an employee's need to work remotely and for providing the associated facilities.
- Clearly defining the organisation's ownership of all equipment provided to the employee for the purpose of remote working; and the associated right of access for maintenance or recovery purposes.
- Ensuring that all equipment is of an acceptable technical standard and incorporates the necessary technology to support secure connection to the required standard (e.g. as would apply in the case of accessing the UK Government's secure networks).
- It may be preferable to exclude the use of any of the employee's own equipment, not only for matters of technical quality and reliability but also to avoid any compensation implications if the equipment has to be replaced.
- The necessary equipment should only be installed by the organisation's IT experts or nominated contractors in a manner and form that ensures compliance with any required technical standards, etc.
- The provision of application and access software should be tailored to the legitimate operational needs of the individual users, with any unwanted or unnecessary applications being removed or disabled.
- Appropriate and licensed software applications (including any specialised communications software) will be provided, loaded and configured by the organisation.
- Applying, as appropriate, suitable and proven encryption to all remote access and transmissions (in both directions).
- Ensuring that the organisation's anti-virus and malware software is loaded and capable of being maintained up to date.
- Undertaking periodic software audits in order to confirm compliance with the organisation's policies and procedures.
- Avoiding the storage of key data on the remote hardware (e.g. C: Drive) and ensuring that it is held on secured central servers whenever possible.
- To ensure the correct and appropriate use of removable media devices in accord with the prevailing Removable Media Policy or procedure.
- Clearly defining the employee's responsibilities, including:
    - to take care of the organisation's equipment and protecting it from damage, loss or theft at all times (including when in transit or in use at remote locations);
    - not to leave equipment on open view (including in vehicles or other sites, such as customer's offices);
    - if possible to use a separate and secure area of the home for work purposes that can be locked when not in use;
    - to log off, switch off or otherwise disable computers when they are left unattended (even at home);
    - to prevent information (especially personal data) from being viewed or accessed by unauthorised persons (e.g. including house visitors and potentially unauthorised employees at other locations);
    - to protect any access or authentication devices, removable media devices or hardcopy information from loss or theft (e.g. storing them separately from the PC).

- not to amend any system or software configuration parameters;
- not to install, download or load any non work software onto the organisation's computer, including screensavers;
- not to attach or install any unauthorised hardware or devices;
- to protect corporate information and have due regard for the correct and lawful handling, storage and disclosure of personal or sensitive data. (NB: It may be necessary to prohibit the remote access to and use of any data within higher security and protective marking classifications.)
- to ensure that any waste or unwanted hardcopy information is completely destroyed (e.g. by cross-cut shredding);
- not to make unofficial copies of any corporate data and not to load or use (for any purpose) such information on the employee's own computer or storage hardware;
- to report any faults or suspected information security breaches immediately to the central IT Helpdesk;
- to define any limits on the use of the hardware for personal purposes (for example, prohibiting the use in respect of an external business activity);
- to ensure that other family members and visitors do not use the supplied computer equipment and software in any circumstances;
- not to take the equipment outside of the country unless specifically authorised to do so;
- to otherwise comply with all the extant IT and Information Management policies and procedures issued by the organisation.

Control Objectives for Remote Working

(a) To ensure that remote access is only granted to and provided for use by authorised users (including non employees) and in justified circumstances.

(b) To ensure that the technical basis for remotely accessing the organisation's systems and data are sufficiently robust and reliable in order to protect such information assets from loss, unauthorised access or unlawful disclosure.

(c) To ensure that the basis for providing remote access to IT facilities is clearly defined together with the employee's specific responsibilities.

(d) To ensure that the non work use of the provided facilities is clearly defined and enforced.

(e) To effectively protect systems and data and to retain their accuracy and integrity.

(f) To provide and install adequate, robust and industry standard hardware and supporting devices and to maintain them in working order.

(g) To ensure that adequate physical security measures are in place to protect the hardware, software and hardcopy information from theft, loss, damage or corruption.

(h) To ensure that appropriate and licensed software is provided and correctly configured for secure and efficient use.

(i) To ensure that log-on processes are appropriately secure and operate in accord with any prevailing required technical standards.

(j) To actively prevent the loading or use of unauthorised software or code.

(k) To prevent the interception or other misuse of network transactions and data flow.

(l) To ensure that the storage and back-up of data is suitably robust, including protecting the storage devices from loss or theft.

(m) To ensure that all aspects of remote working are conducted lawfully and comply with the current documented policies and procedures.

Risk and Control Issues for Remote Working

1 Key Issues

1.1 What steps are taken to effectively access, justify and authorise instances of remote access to the organisation's systems and data?

1.2 How are management assured that the remote access equipment and software are sufficiently robust in order to protect corporate information assets?

1.3 How can management be sure that employees and others who have been granted remote access facilities know and understand their specific information security and other responsibilities?

1.4 What measures are applied to ensure the identity and validity of remote access attempts?

1.5 How can management be assured that network transmissions to and from authorised remote devices are not intercepted or accessed?

1.6 How would management be alerted to any suspected or actual information security breaches relating to remote access facilities?

2 Detailed Issues

2.1 Have management clearly defined the criteria to be considered when assessing and justifying requests for remote access?

2.2 What measures would actively prevent opportunist, organised or coordinated attempts to gain unauthorised remote access to the organisation's systems and data?

2.3 Can management be sure that any attempted unauthorised remote access attempts would be promptly identified and followed up?

2.4 What steps have management taken to prevent the loading and use of unauthorised software and code on remote computer equipment?

2.5 Has management defined and applied suitable and effective physical security measures?

2.6 How does management ensure that staff and others with remote access operate in accordance with the prevailing policies and procedures?

2.7 What specifically would prevent users from either opting out of the procedural requirements or implying that they were not aware of them?

2.8 Is there the capability to promptly shut down or close off remote access functionality in the event of a concerted effort to gain access to systems and data? (If so, how would such an attack be detected?).

2.9 Does management monitor the remote access activity (both authorised and attempted)?

2.10 How is the organisation protected in the event that the remote equipment malfunctions with the result that remotely held data is either lost or corrupted?

2.11 How would management be alerted to any unauthorised changes to the configuration parameters on remotely located computers?

2.12 What is in place to ensure a prompt response to hardware and software faults reported by employees working remotely? (NB: Conceivably, this could happen at some considerable distance from the central IT facilities and any disruption could have notable operational implications.)

NOTE

1. *2008 Information Security Breaches Survey*, Department for Business, Enterprise and Regulatory Reform (2008), www.berr.gov.uk.

39
Email

Email Marketing Reports is an Austrian-based organisation providing information on the commercial and marketing uses for email. The organisation estimates[1] that globally some 247 billion emails are sent every day and that in the time it takes you to read this sentence some 20 million new emails have entered the global system. The Radicati Group Inc. is a California-based technology market research firm and they suggest[2] that the number of emails created each day is likely to nearly double to some 507 billion by 2013. In addition Radicati advise that some 81 % of all email traffic in 2009 will be spam.

Love it or loathe it, email has developed into a vital communication resource for organisations, whether as a marketing tool to reach countless potential customers or as an effective and fast way of communicating with colleagues within the organisation or with contacts and customers outside of it.

However, it is as an unnecessary diversion and a waste of resources and time that email is truly supreme. Reading and responding to private or other non work emails can eat into productive time. In addition, an email can carry malicious code in attachments, facilitate the fast but unauthorised distribution and disclosure of information and be the platform for all manner of inappropriate behaviour.

In this chapter we focus on the corporate use of email and the suggested measures for the control, monitoring and management of email usage by an organisation's staff. Although there are undoubtedly creative and effective ways of using emails in a marketing sense, this aspect of their use is not addressed here.

Emails form part of the organisation's records and in most legislative environments have the same status as any other form of written communication. For example, emails within the UK public sector can be provided in response to a Freedom of Information request and are not exempt from the requirements of the Data Protection Act 1998 if they contain personal or sensitive information.

The BERR Information Security Breaches Survey of UK companies in 2008[3] contained the following summary findings in relation to email usage and management:

Of the companies surveyed:

- 97 % filtered their incoming email for spam
- 95 % scanned incoming email for viruses

- 94% quarantined suspicious email attachments
- 9% had fake (phishing) emails sent asking their customers for data
- 84% **do not** scan outgoing emails for confidential data
- 33% noted that email messages to and from main business partners can be encrypted
- 26% scan email content for inappropriate content (for example profanity).

Email is not necessarily a secure means of communication. Emails sent between users within an organisation should be secure as they are routed through a closed (and hopefully protected) network. When emails are sent outside of the organisation, over public networks, they could be intercepted or lost. In addition, they could leave a trail and a copy on the public system. Because of these insecurities, the use of more robust and secure networks may be justified for the handling of personal, sensitive or restricted information.

In order to prevent high levels of unnecessary email usage and protect itself from harm, an organisation could consider the publication of an Email Usage Policy, which can also be called an Acceptable Usage Policy. The purpose of such a policy would be to:

- Provide clear guidance to employees (and other authorised email users) on the appropriate use of corporate email systems.
- Point out the implications of and issues relating to the use of email.
- Define the standards that must be maintained.
- Indicate how email systems will be monitored and managed.
- Define the consequences of the inappropriate use of email.

The following detailed points are suggested for inclusion in an Email Usage Policy or procedure:

- Definition of scope (i.e. all users, including non employees and any emails sent from or received into the organisation's email system).
- Noting that the primary reason for providing email facilities is to support the conduct of official business and operations.
- Access to email facilities will be granted as and when it is necessary in order that employees can fulfil their duties.
- Any use (or attempted use) of email facilities by employees who have not been granted official access would be regarded as a disciplinary offence.
- In some organisations there may be more than one official email system, for example in the public sector, where the use of more secure (perhaps Government-operated) email networks are mandatory for communicating confidential or secret information. Eligibility for access to such secure systems may require more specific and security-centric controls.
- The use of non work email accounts for the conduct and support of official business should be prohibited.
- Emails are to be considered part of the organisation's official records and subject to the same security, protection, handling and disclosure requirements as apply to any other form of record.
- The legal status of emails should be clearly determined in each national situation relevant to the organisation.

- All official emails (and especially those going outside of the organisation) should bear a suitable disclaimer covering the following:
    - A warning that the email is intended for the named addressee only and that it should not be copied, used or disclosed by anyone else.
    - If the email has been received, in error, by anyone else they should be requested to contact the sender immediately.
    - A warning that the email traffic may be subject to lawful monitoring and that the organisation reserves the right to monitor both sent and received emails.
    - A warning that the email contents and any file attached are confidential and solely intended for the use of the named addressee.
    - A warning that, where appropriate, the contents of the email may be disclosed under the prevailing Data Protection and/or Freedom of Information legislation or regulations.
    - If any of the email contents or attachments are defined as being personal, confidential or otherwise of a sensitive nature, the lawful limitations of using, protecting and disclosing the information it contains should be clearly defined.
- In the UK, it is permissible, in very precisely defined circumstances and in accordance with the Regulation of Investigatory Powers Act 2000, to monitor, intercept and use emails in the investigation of suspected fraud or malpractice. If the organisation intends to maintain its legal right to access emails in this way, it should make this clear and that it will only do so in lawful ways and with due regard to the privacy rights of the individuals involved.
- Unless a user had given explicit consent for their emails to be accessed, such access could be deemed as unlawful and/or an infringement of the user's right to privacy (for example, under the convention of the UK Human Rights Act). Such consent may be necessary if a user is going to be absent, perhaps through illness, for a long period and there is a proven operational justification for gaining access to their email account. It is essential, in order to avoid any legal implications, that such access is documented and authorised.
- Monitoring of emails may also be required as a means of assessing compliance with the various defined acceptable conditions of use.
- Management should establish a mechanism for users to report actual or suspected abuses of the email facilities without prejudice or the need for their identity to be revealed (unless it is deemed necessary in any related legal or disciplinary action).
- Users should be advised that although they may have deleted an email from their inbox or sent box, it is likely that a copy still exists within the email system archive and logs.
- The extent of the permitted private use of corporate email should be made clear (including the total prohibition of such use where it is justified). The conditions for private use could include, but may not be limited to, the following:
    - Personal use of emails should only be outside of working hours (including lunch breaks) and should not impede or adversely affect operations or business.
    - The use of corporate emails for personal commercial purposes may be prohibited.

- Outgoing personal emails should be clearly marked as such and contain a standard form of disclaimer making it clear that the contents are not an official communication from the organisation and that the organisation accepts no responsibility in connection with the email.
- The forwarding of material that has been clearly classified as confidential should not be permitted.
- In their use and possible forwarding of personal email contents, employees should take care to avoid the infringement of copyright or intellectual property rights.
- Users should be aware that the storing and archiving of emails would include any personal details contained within personal emails and that they must accept the associated risks.

• Emails containing sensitive or restricted information should be clearly marked as such and treated accordingly. (NB: Email systems may have the ability to electronically tag emails as being confidential or of high importance.)

• All official emails should conform to a standard format, which should ideally include:

- a standard form of signature that incorporates the sender's full name, their job title, department or function, telephone and other contact details and the agreed form of corporate identity (i.e. logo, crest or approved graphics);
- the use of standard and agreed fonts, point sizes and colours so as to present a consistent and clear corporate identity in email communications;
- a meaningful subject line;
- although potentially less formal than traditional letters and other official communications, email standards and the use of language should not reflect badly on the organisation or its image and reputation.

• Employees should be given guidance on other aspects of the appropriate use of email, such as:

- regularly check incoming emails and promptly responding;
- target the more critical and urgent emails;
- only copy in people who really need to receive a copy;
- make sure that any attachments are in a format that the user is likely to be able to open and use;
- do not use email as a weapon of office politics and not sending an email in anger, haste or frustration as you may subsequently regret it;
- exercise caution when providing your office email address to others especially on the Internet;
- be alert to carefully handling and responding to emails from unfamiliar or unexpected sources (particularly if personal information is being requested);
- don't use emails as a substitute for potentially difficult face-to-face meetings or to provoke confrontations;
- avoid using capitals as it can be interpreted as shouting by some recipients;
- take care with emails from senders or organisations you either don't recognise or that look suspicious;

- seek advice from the IT Helpdesk if you have any concerns about an incoming email or attachments;
- don't open attachments from unexpected sources until you have separately checked that they are legitimate.
- if you receive unsolicited email attachments, check that the sender is bona fide before opening the attachments;
- users must not attempt to circumvent the anti-virus systems or to knowingly transmit any email or attachment that they know to be infected or contain any form of malicious code. This form of behaviour is likely to be regarded as gross misconduct;
- junk and spam mail should be stopped by filtering software, but any that get through the net should be deleted without being opened and the details passed on to the IT Helpdesk;
- never reply to spam emails;
- attachments may contain malicious code that could infect PCs and the corporate network and systems, so any suspicious emails should be left unopened and referred to the IT Helpdesk for removal and quarantine;
- consider setting the Out of Office Assistant whenever you are going to be absent from the office (the Out of Office message should include alternative points of contact and an indication of when you will return to the office);
- regularly review the contents of your email folders and delete any outdated or unwanted items, especially those with large attachments. Be aware of the prevailing email storage limits for your account and manage the contents accordingly;
- avoid attaching very large files to emails and be aware of any size limits applied by the system. For example, if a file can be accessed by the recipient from a shared drive, email the file location details rather than a copy of the file;
- if users suspect others of abusing the email facilities, they should be encouraged to report their concerns without prejudice.
- under no circumstances should corporate email facilities be used for the following, some of which may be regarded as matters of gross misconduct or liable to criminal prosecution:
  - to create and distribute any unsuitable material or comments that could reflect badly on the organisation, its image and reputation;
  - to create, communicate, forward or distribute inappropriate material that could be regarded as obscene, defamatory, indecent, unlawful, etc.;
  - to create and communicate material that could cause annoyance, inconvenience, stress, needless anxiety or could be abusive, threatening, bullying or harassing to others;
  - to create and communicate material that is discriminatory or encourages discrimination on grounds of race, ethnicity, gender, disability, political affiliation, sexual orientation or religious belief;
  - to transmit or distribute material where doing so is an infringement of copyright or intellectual property rights;

- where the transmission results in a waste of staff time, disruption of the work of colleagues, adverse effects on the network capacity and performance or service denial to other users;
- the use of defamatory, impolite, offensive, profane, condescending, demeaning, abusive, overtly or unfairly critical language. This includes content that has been disguised by the use of replacement symbols to mask unsuitable words and phrases;
- the further distribution of what was originally a private communication on to others without the express consent of the other originating party or parties;
- any content that relates to unacceptable topics in a work situation such as threats, the promotion of violence, the conduct of unlawful or fraudulent activities, gambling or gaming, unsavoury, offensive or sexually explicit jokes;
- do not respond to or forward chain letter emails.

Control Objectives for Email

(a) To ensure that corporate email facilities are reliable and efficient.

(b) To ensure that the permitted use of email is clearly defined for all users.

(c) To prevent wastage of resources, operational disruption or other adverse effects generated by the inappropriate use of email.

(d) To ensure that consistent standards are applied to the format and content of official emails.

(e) To retain and protect email records as part of the organisation's official documentation.

(f) To prevent the disruptions caused by spam email and emails containing viruses or other malicious code.

(g) To ensure that the use of email is lawful and complies with the prevailing regulations.

(h) To ensure that personal or sensitive information contained within emails or attachments is appropriately protected from loss or inappropriate disclosure.

(i) To ensure that any highly sensitive or restricted information is only emailed using recognised and approved secure networks.

(j) To prevent the interception of corporate emails by unauthorised persons.

> (k) To ensure that access to employee's email accounts, in exceptional circumstances, is lawful and granted with the explicit permission of the employee concerned.
>
> (l) To monitor email usage as a means of determining any excessive usage or abuse of the permitted levels of activity.

Risk and Control Issues for Email

1 Key Issues

1.1 What steps have management taken to define and apply clear standards and processes relating to the efficient use of corporate email facilities?

1.2 How would management be made aware of failures to comply with the corporate email standards?

1.3 What measures are in place to protect email records as part of the official documentation of the organisation?

1.4 How can management be sure that any potential disruptions caused by viruses, malware, spyware or other malicious code are effectively avoided, detected and dealt with?

1.5 Has management taken adequate measures to ensure the lawful use of emails?

1.6 How would management be made aware of the inappropriate or unlawful circulation or disclosure of personal, sensitive or restricted information via email?

1.7 Have appropriate measures been established to ensure that highly sensitive or restricted information is only contained within emails sent over designated secure networks and circuits?

1.8 How can management be assured that email traffic cannot be intercepted at any stage in the transmission process?

1.9 How are instances where it is necessary to access an employee's email account authorised and handled in a lawful manner?

2 Detailed Issues

2.1 How can management be sure that the emails being sent outside of the organisation are reflecting a suitable corporate image?

2.2 How is management assured that emails are responded to efficiently and, where appropriate, within specified time constraints?

2.3 How can management be sure that all staff are duly aware of their responsibilities for the appropriate, ethical and lawful use of email?

2.4 Has management verified the legal status of emails in the context of those countries in which it operates?

2.5 Has management established and communicated clear disciplinary and other sanctions that would apply in cases of email abuse or related gross misconduct?

2.6 What processes have been put in place to effectively detect and investigate instances of actual or suspected email abuse?

2.7 How would management be made aware of any interception of emails?

2.8 How does management ensure that appropriate (and lawful) disclaimers are attached to every corporate email?

NOTES

1. Via their website (www.email-marketing-reports.com) as at October 2009.
2. Via their website (www.radicati.com) as at October 2009.
3. *2008 Information Security Breaches Survey*, Department for Business, Enterprise and Regulatory Reform (2008), www.berr.gov.uk.

40
Internet Usage

The Internet, alongside the internal combustion engine, the telephone, radio and television, is arguably one of the most powerful instruments of cultural and social change that has ever been created.

From the early days of its development pedigree in the 1960s when engineers and software specialists were aiming to provide the ability to simply enable networking between physically separate networks; through the development of early examples of the concept which led to the linking of two US academic sites via the ARPANET in 1969; the creation of various transmission protocols such as the TCP/IP (transmission control protocol/internet protocol); the development of mainly government and military networks such as MILNET and NIPRNET in the 1970s and 1980s; the first recognised use of the term Internet in late 1974; the initially limited levels of take-up with examples including CERN between 1984 and 1988; the Internet has latterly expanded rapidly across the globe to embrace governmental, commercial and private users alike.

The power of the Internet to drive the open availability of information, open up alternative ways of communicating and socialising, establish new ways of doing business and to cross cultural barriers has been hugely influential. The relentless march of the Internet has been fuelled and supported by the coincidental availability of cheaper and more reliable hardware devices, increased inter-connectivity and the spreading development of broadband, fibre-optic and other high speed transmission platforms.

In the great scheme of technological and social developments in the last and current centuries, the Internet has been conceived, created, developed, widely launched and has expanded at a prodigious if not unprecedented rate in a comparatively short period. As the following graph illustrates, the number of Internet users worldwide has risen from an estimate of a mere 18 million in 1995 to an estimated total of just under 1.7 billion in 2009. The 2009 level represents 24.7% of the world's population. The expansion of users within the period between 2000 (361 million) and 2009 represents a growth rate of some 362%.

As previously noted the Internet is fast becoming an essential platform for commercial organisations to conduct business and promote themselves and for government and other public bodies to interface with citizens for the provision of services or the imparting of information. Whilst recognising that the use of the Internet

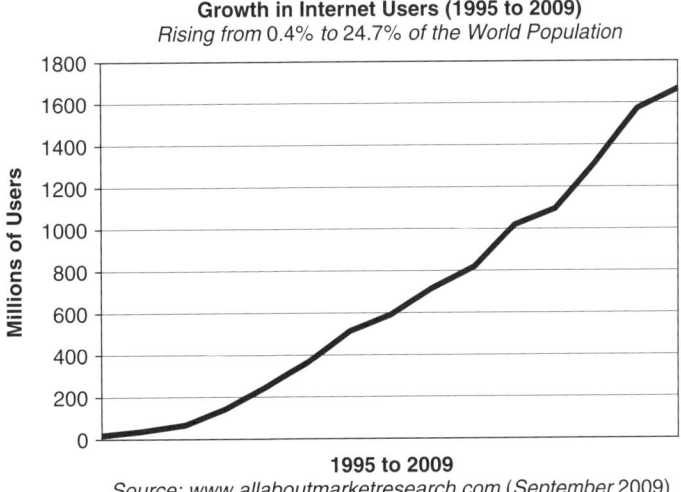

Figure 40.1 Growth in Internet usage 1995–2009

has notable business and marketing benefits (together with some associated risks), in this chapter we concentrate on the auditing issues surrounding the use of the Internet from an employee perspective in terms of what is and is not acceptable usage.

The foundation for the suggested approach is that although the Internet can be useful as a research source and enable the networking of users with common interests and concerns, it can also become an addictive and time-wasting activity that distracts users from their given duties and could, in the more extreme situations, involve unlawful or unacceptable activities with potentially serious implications for the organisation.

In the 2008 BERR survey of UK companies,[1] the following findings were noted in relation to the companies surveyed:

- 48% had an Acceptable Internet Usage policy in place **and** required staff to acknowledge that they have read it before they are granted Internet access.
- 21% had an Acceptable Usage policy in place **but did not** require staff to acknowledge that they have read it.
- 24% reported that they restricted Internet access to some staff only.
- 38% blocked access to inappropriate websites.
- 48% logged and monitored web access.
- 35% of the surveyed companies had no controls in place over staff use of instant messaging.

The creation and circulation of a formal Internet Acceptable Usage Policy (or procedure) will clearly establish the ground rules for employees and support the appropriate and lawful use of the Internet. The following key aspects should be considered for inclusion into such a Policy, but the extent to which they are relevant will be dependent upon the size and nature of the organisation and the legislative framework in which it operates.

Internet Acceptable Usage Policy—Suggested Contents

- Define the scope of the Policy in terms of who it relates to, the primary purposes for which Internet access is granted, and on what basis such access is granted.
- In addition to containing the limits and responsibilities placed upon individual users of the corporate Internet facilities, the Policy should also define the responsibilities allocated to line management to monitor Internet usage in their areas to ensure that it complies with the terms of the Policy, is relevant to the conduct of business and is not excessive.
- Employee Internet access may be granted for a number of reasons, for example to enable staff to keep up to date with sector or business trends and activities, to support work-related research or to conduct authorised electronic commerce on behalf of the organisation. The scope of an individual's Internet activities will need to be clearly defined and communicated so there is no leeway for misinterpretation.
- The following issues relate to an employee's permitted work-related use of the Internet:
  - Employees should be reminded to stay focused during work-related Internet use and avoid being sidetracked or distracted.
  - Only material that is necessary for work purposes should be either downloaded or printed off.
  - Although potentially useful, the Internet does contain some dubious material in terms of its accuracy and reliability. Accordingly employees should be advised to restrict their activity to known, approved, recognised or well established websites. Users should check the reliability, accuracy and currency of information before they or others rely upon it for operational or decision-making purposes.
  - News groups and discussion boards can be a useful source of work-related research, however the following issues should be taken into consideration:
    - Users may spend a large amount of time and effort in locating suitable sites and extracting what they need. The benefits of using such sites need to be realistically weighed against the downsides, including the amount of time that will have to be spent.
    - Newsgroups, etc. may contain links to other sites, which may be of an unacceptable or inappropriate nature.
    - Accessing non work-related or social networking groups and boards should not be permitted.
    - Care must be taken in respect of online discussions that may relate to politically sensitive, controversial or provocative issues. Users should be cautious in expressing purely personal opinions that they know do not align with the organisation's viewpoint. The organisations represented by participants may be discernable and so off-the-cuff remarks may be unwittingly associated with the organisation by inference.
    - Public forums can be accessed by anyone, so users should not impart any corporate information that is, in any way, restricted, sensitive, personal or confidential.

- The terms and conditions of an employee's personal use of the Internet should be determined and clearly communicated, for example:
  - Whether personal use is at the discretion of management.
  - The times during which personal use is permitted (i.e. during lunch breaks or only in the employee's own time) and not permitted (i.e. during core working periods).
  - The employee's responsibility for any of their actions, personal transactions and activities on the Internet. (NB: It may be necessary to obtain a signed declaration from the employee that absolves the organisation from any liability arising from their employee's personal use of the Internet.)
  - There needs to be a clear distinction drawn between those permitted transactions being made on behalf of the organisation and those that are strictly personal to the employee. This distinction should be abundantly clear when transactions are entered into.
  - Goods and services ordered for personal use via the Internet should not be delivered to any of the organisation's premises.
  - All personal use of the Internet must comply with the contents of the prevailing Internet Acceptable Usage Policy and the failure to comply may result in disciplinary action being taken.
  - Employees should be advised that their Internet usage may be monitored, both in terms of extent and the nature of the sites visited. In addition, the organisation may take proactive steps to prevent or bar access to sites of an unacceptable nature and that such blocked events will be logged and monitored.
  - Employees should protect their Internet user ID and password and, on no account, should they share or divulge these details to anyone else.
  - They should be reminded that all Internet activity is logged against the relevant user ID.
- The Policy should clearly define all those Internet activities and sites that the employee is prohibited from accessing. The organisation may take proactive steps to block access to such sites. The prohibitions could include, but are not necessarily limited to, the following sites and activities:
  - Adult, sexually explicit or obscene issues
  - Criminal, fraudulent or anti-social behaviour
  - Offensive, tasteless or objectionable issues
  - Topics related to intolerance, extremist views, hatred, violence, weapons, terrorism, bomb making or incitement
  - Drugs, illegal substances, alcohol or tobacco
  - Gaming, betting, gambling or money-making ventures
  - Spyware, malware, viruses, malicious code, hacking, phishing, cyber crime or cyber terrorism
  - Downloading of any kind (including video, images, audio, software and ring tones) or accessing media streaming sites
  - Personal advertising, dating, social networking, personal messaging, text messaging, paging and chat rooms (especially where these operate in real time and could utilise or disrupt corporate communications capacity)
  - Host sites for personal email services

- Sites provided as hyperlinks within Spam emails
- Sites related to the operation of a personal or private business.
- Specific guidance on the potential legal implications of accessing certain materials should be stressed to users, for example, in the UK this will include:
  - The creation, downloading, uploading, display, storage distribution or accessing (via the Internet) of sites that contain pornography or other unsuitable materials that could be deemed as being illegal, obscene or offensive. (NB: There is understandable public concern over child pornography, possession of which is a criminal offence in the UK. Accordingly any detected incidents involving such material should be treated seriously and referred to the Police.)

Control Objectives for Internet Usage

(a) To ensure that usage of the Internet is appropriate, is a beneficial contribution to the organisation and does not adversely affect either employee performance or operational capacities.

(b) To ensure that the permitted work and personal uses of the Internet are clearly defined and communicated.

(c) To ensure that all employees are made aware of their responsibilities and obligations in relation to the appropriate use of the Internet for both work and personal purposes.

(d) To ensure that employees have clear guidance on the types of Internet activities that they are prohibited from accessing together with details of the sanctions and disciplinary action that the organisation may choose to take in the event of breach of the defined conditions.

(e) To ensure that the usage of the Internet is always lawful and appropriate.

(f) To ensure that the organisation's systems and data are adequately protected from virus infections, malware, spyware and other forms of malicious code.

(g) To ensure that Internet usage is monitored for either excessive or inappropriate activity.

(h) To ensure that personal, confidential or restricted information is protected from unauthorised disclosure via the Internet.

Risk and Control Issues for Internet Usage

1 Key Issues

1.1 Has management a clear view of the legal and regulatory implications of Internet use in all of the national legal regimes in which it operates?

1.2 How does management ensure that all Internet activities comply with the prevailing legal and regulatory requirements?

1.3 How does management ensure that Internet usage is productive and beneficial?

1.4 What mechanisms are in place to detect and react to excessive or abnormal levels of Internet usage?

1.5 How does management ensure that employee use of the Internet is clearly defined and controlled?

1.6 What action has been taken to actively prevent employees from accessing unsuitable or unlawful sites and material?

1.7 What mechanisms would prevent unauthorised employee access to the Internet using the organisation's facilities?

1.8 What measures would prevent the infection of corporate systems and data with viruses, malware, spyware and malicious code?

1.9 Has the organisation established a clear linkage between breaches of Internet conditions and the employee disciplinary processes?

1.10 What steps have been taken to prevent the unauthorised disclosure of personal, sensitive, confidential or restricted corporate information via the Internet?

1.11 How is the download of unauthorised files from the Internet prevented?

1.12 Has a protocol been established to deal with serious unlawful Internet activities, including how they should be investigated and in what circumstances the law enforcement agencies would be involved?

2 Detailed Issues

2.1 How would management maintain an ongoing awareness of all the legal and regulatory obligations relating to Internet use?

2.2 How would management be made aware of any actual or suspected breaches of legal and regulatory requirements?

2.3 How would management be made aware of or alerted to wasteful or inefficient use of the Internet?

2.4 Has action been taken to define how employee access to the Internet is to be assessed, justified and authorised?

2.5 Are employees required to acknowledge and signify that they fully understand the requirements of corporate and personal use of the Internet? In addition, does this process incorporate a declaration supporting the acceptance of any liabilities related to personal use of the Internet?

2.6 How would management be alerted to actual or suspected attacks using viruses and any type of malicious code? In addition, have documented actions been put in place to efficiently and effectively deal with such incidents?

2.7 Has management established clear guidance on the implications for employees found to have breached the prevailing Internet usage policy or conditions?

2.8 Has management ensured that its human resources and disciplinary procedures will adequately support the investigation of serious legal breaches through to criminal proceedings?

NOTE

1. *2008 Information Security Breaches Survey*, Department for Business, Enterprise and Regulatory Reform (2008), www.berr.gov.uk.

41

Software Maintenance (Including Change Management)

Our focus here is on applications system software and its maintenance and amendment. Where a system has a critical role in the business operations, management will need to be assured that it can continue to operate in a secure and reliable manner. From time to time, it may be necessary to apply amendments to the functionality and operational aspects of the programs, and in order for the overall integrity of the system to be maintained, such modifications will need to be applied proficiently and tested thoroughly prior to live use.

The application of software amendments and updates can be undertaken either by in-house system development staff, or by external software companies where a standard "off-the-shelf" application system is involved.

Change Management processes, designed to ensure the effective and controlled migration to updated or new software versions, have much in common with the principles previously described in relation to Patch Management within Chapter 35. These points are not repeated here, but it is suggested that readers become familiar with the previous comments and take them into account when considering the contents of this chapter. The primary difference between the two scenarios relates to matters of scale in that changes to an operating system are likely to affect a large number of devices and users, whereas application software updates can be more contained, albeit potentially more complex and with direct implications for specific operations, services or functions.

It is in the organisation's interests to ensure that business or operation-critical systems are maintained up to date with the latest proven versions of the software when this is justified. The process of change control should take into account the following issues:

- The change process and the steps that must be followed should be formally documented.

- The nature of the change and its business rationale and implications should be defined and assessed in order to justify proceeding with the amendment.
- A form of impact assessment should be conducted which includes such factors as operational impacts, risks, security implications, implied functional changes and so on.
- A documented approach to testing the changed software in a separate test environment prior to implementation in the live environment.
- A form of authorisation to proceed should be incorporated.
- It is vital that all affected parties are involved in the change process including system owners, users and operational managers. In addition means of effective communication should be established and used.
- It is possible that the change or migration could involve representatives of the software supplier or developer and in such situations all the preconditions and the role to be performed by the supplier will need to be identified and planned so that their resources are efficiently and cost-effectively managed from the organisation's standpoint.
- The overall process should be documented in the form of a structured plan which also incorporates how the process can be safely aborted and rolled back if this becomes necessary.
- At the conclusion of the process (hopefully successfully achieved) there should be a formal sign-off from the system owner.
- The completed change process should be capable of being trailed and subsequently audited.

Control Objectives for Software Maintenance

> (a) To ensure that systems are capable of being maintained in order to prolong their useful life and continue to serve the business.
>
> (b) To ensure that all system amendments are justified and authorised.
>
> (c) To ensure that system amendments are comprehensively and independently tested prior to being correctly applied in the live environment.
>
> (d) To ensure that only authorised and tested amendments are applied.
>
> (e) To ensure that systems are adequately documented so that they can be effectively maintained.
>
> (f) To ensure that the various versions of programs are accurately identified so that only the authorised versions can be used.
>
> (g) To ensure that the systems documentation is appropriately updated following software amendments.
>
> (h) To ensure that live programs are strictly separated from those under development, and that movements between the live and development environments are adequately controlled.

> (i) To ensure that the live program library only contains valid and authorised versions of current programs.
>
> (j) To ensure that personal computer application software is correctly updated with officially recognised upgrades and fixes.
>
> (k) To ensure that facilities are in place to deal effectively with emergency program fixes.

Risk and Control Issues for Software Maintenance

1 Key Issues

    1.1 Are all key systems adequately documented to a defined standard so as to ensure that they can be maintained effectively?

    1.2 What steps ensure that software amendments are accurately defined, justified and authorised?

    1.3 What steps ensure that all software amendments and corrections are fully and satisfactorily tested before being introduced into live use?

    1.4 Are all software amendments appropriately coded and valid for the purpose?

    1.5 What procedures ensure that only authorised and current versions of programs are used in the live production environment?

    1.6 What measures ensure that all amendments are suitably specified and documented to the required standard?

    1.7 What mechanisms ensure that live programs and those under development are kept strictly separate?

    1.8 What checks are in place to monitor the validity of the contents of the live and production program libraries?

    1.9 What procedures ensure that personal computers are correctly updated with only official and appropriate software upgrades and fixes?

    1.10 Has management established effective routines to deal with emergency (i.e. out-of-hours) program fixes without jeopardising system integrity or business operations?

2 Detailed Issues

    2.1 What mechanisms ensure that all systems are suitably documented and that the records are updated whenever an amendment is applied?

    2.2 What measures ensure that all proposed software amendments are appropriately specified to the satisfaction of users?

2.3 What specific measures prevent the application of unauthorised or invalid system amendments to the live environment?

2.4 What is the documentary evidence for the comprehensive testing of software amendments (and does this have to be reviewed and authorised by management prior to acceptance of the amendment)?

2.5 What measures ensure that additional functionality (perhaps with a fraudulent or malicious intent) is not incorporated into software fixes?

2.6 How does management ensure that all programming is conducted in accordance with best practice and to the required standard?

2.7 Are the contents of the various program libraries periodically checked to ensure that only valid items are held?

2.8 What measures prevent the unauthorised transfer of programs between the development and live program libraries?

2.9 How is the testing of programs and amendments defined (and what prevents the application of ineffective or inadequate levels of testing)?

2.10 How does management ensure that the versions of personal computer applications used throughout the organisation are consistent (i.e. would invalid or outdated versions be promptly identified)?

42
Networks

Data communication technology has undergone a period of rapid and explosive development in recent years, with notable gains in transmission speeds and the interconnectivity of systems, including the growing use of wireless and fibre-optic network technologies. Organisations will use variations of the networking theme to achieve the effective (and secure) sharing and communication of business data.

Local area networks (LANs) are now commonplace and larger geographic areas of data communication coverage can be achieved by using wide area networks (WANs), metropolitan area networks (MANs) or Global Area Networks (GANs). Where it can be justified, organisations may have their own Virtual Private Networks (VPNs). Educational establishments have their own network type referred to a Campus Area Network (CAN).

The growing use of fibre-optic systems and the development of dedicated communication networks are pushing us inexorably towards a global networking future. This is especially true given such associated trends as decentralisation of operations, truly global operations, the use of Internet-based technologies and the reducing costs of communications.

Although we use the term LAN throughout the following contents, the business-oriented issues noted within this chapter can be generally applied in any network communications environment. The underlying control and risk principles can equally be applied to WANs, MANs, etc. We have deliberately avoided a technically driven approach.

The 2008 UK Government survey of UK companies[1] noted that of the surveyed companies:

- 97% have a broadband connection to the Internet.
- 93% have a corporate website.
- 42% use a wireless network and 94% of those encrypt their wireless network transmissions.
- 17% use Voice over IP telephony.
- 97% protect their website with a firewall.
- 98% have software that scans for the presence of spyware.
- 14% use strong (i.e. multifactor) authentication.
- 13% had detected unauthorised outsiders within their network.

Responsibility for the management and maintenance of corporate networks should be clearly allocated with specific key duties being contained in the related job descriptions. It is preferable to segregate network management responsibilities from those related to either computer operations or system development as a means of contributing to the overall integrity of computer facilities.

The network architecture and topography should ideally be documented as part of the overall system documentation. Given the complexity of networks, the documentation should also include details of the hardware and software components together with the agreed configuration parameters. All the documentation should be maintained up to date as a means of providing a degree of resilience in the event that key and knowledgeable network staff leave the organisation.

The risks associated with widespread use of networking technologies include the potential for transmissions to be intercepted and misused. One counter measure may be the application of encryption to a recognised technical standard. Encryption is an essential aspect of wireless networking.

There is a trend, especially in the public sector, to create closed and highly secure networks that use leading edge software and methodologies. It may be a condition of use that the participating organisations have to comply with a set of mandatory standards. In the UK an example would be the Government Connect Secure Extranet (GCSx) which is designed to handle the secure transfer of data between government departments, local authorities and other public bodies. (Further details can be obtained from Government Connect website: www.govconnect.gov.uk.)

Control Objectives for Networks

(a) To ensure that appropriate, justified and authorised network facilities are provided to support the business.

(b) To ensure that local area network facilities are secure and adequately protected from unauthorised access and tampering.

(c) To ensure that the optimum networking solution is applied in the circumstances.

(d) To ensure that adequate account is taken of future expansion needs.

(e) To ensure that systems and data are adequately protected from unauthorised use.

(f) To ensure that network installations are suitably planned and implemented.

(g) To ensure that only recognised and industry standard network hardware and software are used.

(h) To ensure the integrity and reliability of the network system software.

(i) To ensure that the required performance and response criteria are achieved.

(j) To ensure that file and system servers, gateway PCs and other network equipment are protected from unauthorised access and tampering.

(k) To ensure that supervisor and other high-level user facilities are protected from unauthorised usage.

(l) To ensure that network support staff are adequately and appropriately skilled to support the network operations.

(m) To ensure that external (i.e. dial-up) access to the network facilities is valid and authorised.

(n) To ensure that adequate and effective contingency and recovery plans are in place to enable the controlled and prompt recovery of service in the event of a major failure, etc.

Risk and Control Issues for Networks

1 Key Issues

1.1 How does management ensure that LAN requirements are fully assessed, justified, and accord with the needs of the business and the IT strategic plan?

1.2 Are performance and service availability requirements accurately identified as the basis for determining the optimum networking solution(s)?

1.3 How does management take due account of predicted future needs when planning and providing LAN facilities?

1.4 What specific measures prevent unauthorised access to the networking facilities, and protect user systems and data from invalid access and usage?

1.5 How is management assured of the integrity of the network system software and its contribution to general data and system security?

1.6 How are file and system servers, gateway PCs and other LAN hardware protected from unauthorised access, tampering, etc.?

1.7 How are supervisor and other high-level user facilities protected from unauthorised usage?

1.8 Has management made adequate arrangements to ensure that network support staff are suitably skilled?

1.9 How does management ensure that effective plans have been established to support the prompt recovery of critical LAN systems following a major failure or disaster?

2 Detailed Issues

2.1 What specific measures prevent the unauthorised introduction or updating of LAN facilities?

2.2 How does management ensure that the defined performance and response requirements are being consistently achieved in practice?

2.3 How does management monitor that planned LAN development keeps pace with the needs of the business?

2.4 Has management established a planned approach to the expansion of the LAN in step with anticipated business growth?

2.5 Who is responsible for defining access rights and how does management ensure that such rights do not jeopardise the integrity of systems and data?

2.6 How are access rights accurately maintained up to date?

2.7 Are measures in place to ensure that only industry standard LAN hardware is acquired from stable and proven suppliers (who are capable of providing ongoing support and maintenance)?

2.8 What steps are taken to ensure that all LAN software is reliable and proven?

2.9 What checks are in place to ensure that the LAN software is correctly, appropriately and efficiently configured?

2.10 What specific measures are in place to prevent unauthorised external access to the LAN (i.e. through dial-up services)?

2.11 How is management made aware of invalid amendments to the configuration of LAN hardware and software?

2.12 Are unusual (or potentially damaging) events prevented, logged or reported?

2.13 What measures prevent users from applying unnecessary and invalid amendments to LAN hardware and software configurations?

2.14 Are LAN recovery plans periodically tested for their effectiveness (and how is this evidenced)?

NOTE

1. *2008 Information Security Breaches Survey*, Department for Business, Enterprise and Regulatory Reform (2008), www.berr.gov.uk.

43
Databases

This chapter relates to use of database techniques to support an organisation's operations and administration. Many of the formal system analysis and development techniques are built around a data-driven approach, where the information needs of the relevant organisation are accurately established as the foundations for the development and operation of all the related business and operational systems. Normally, the data approach is typified by data modelling and database techniques, which aim to reduce (or eliminate) instances of data duplication and redundancy through the creation of a fundamental relational database schema.

From the management standpoint, it is important that the chosen data structure and the database management system used to contain and manipulate information are secure, reliable and provide accurate information to support the organisation's needs. There also needs to be some consideration of the future flexibility of the data structure.

Control Objectives for Databases

(a) To ensure that the information needs of the organisation are appropriately reflected and addressed in the data structure.

(b) To ensure that the most suitable, reliable, secure and flexible database system is established.

(c) To ensure that users embrace the concept of system and data ownership,

(d) To ensure that data are adequately protected from unauthorised access, amendments, usage and leakage.

(e) To ensure that the database system and the data it contains are accurately set up and maintained.

(f) To ensure that the ongoing integrity of the database is maintained.

(g) To ensure that all subsequent amendments to the database form and structure are valid and authorised.

> (h) To ensure that suitably skilled staff are available to support the operation and maintenance of the database.
>
> (i) To ensure that the database is resilient and can be promptly and fully recovered in the event of a major failure or disaster.
>
> (j) To ensure that the data are regularly and appropriately backed up to protect the business operations.
>
> (k) To ensure that users are appropriately trained in the use of ancillary database facilities (such as query languages) so that they are efficiently and effectively used.
>
> (l) To ensure that all systems developments and amendments fully take into account the implications for the database structure and system.
>
> (m) To avoid the holding and processing of duplicated or redundant data.

Risk and Control Issues for Databases

1 Key Issues

1.1 How does management ensure that the data needs of the organisation are accurately identified and reflected in current systems and databases?

1.2 How has management ensured that appropriate, secure, reliable and flexible database management systems are in place and maintained?

1.3 How can management be assured that appropriate control is exercised over systems and data ownership and the determination of access rights?

1.4 How are data protected from unauthorised access and amendments?

1.5 What measures ensure that the initial set-up of the database structure is relevant, accurate and reflects the agreed corporate data requirements?

1.6 How is the ongoing integrity of the database structure and contents assured?

1.7 Are all subsequent amendments to the database structure and contents subject to authorisation, and what measures prevent unauthorised structural amendments?

1.8 What steps does management take to ensure that sufficiently skilled staff are available to support the operation and maintenance of the database?

1.9 What specific measures ensure that the database can promptly and accurately be rebuilt in the event of a major failure?

1.10 Are adequate and effective database back-up precautions taken?

1.11 How does management ensure that query languages are efficiently and appropriately used (and that enquiries are neither excessive nor over demanding on systems resources)?

1.12 What measures ensure that all system developments and amendments conform to the agreed structure and contents of the database system?

2 Detailed Issues

2.1 Has the required data structure been documented and formally authorised (and how is this evidenced)?

2.2 What measures are in place to prevent the holding (and processing) of redundant or duplicated data items?

2.3 How does management verify that the chosen database supplier is stable, reliable and capable of providing ongoing support?

2.4 Does the selected database management system conform to recognised industry standards?

2.5 Has the capacity and flexibility of the database system been assessed in light of anticipated growth (and has the ability to meet future demands been confirmed)?

2.6 Are users/system owners held responsible for defining and authorising access rights?

2.7 How does management monitor that the access rights to data and systems are accurately kept up to date?

2.8 Are the database rebuilding procedures subject to periodic testing as a means of assessing their effectiveness?

2.9 Is the database backed up at the appropriate frequency (and are the back-up media tested for readability)?

2.10 How is management made aware of attempts to violate access arrangements or other unusual database activities?

44
Data Protection

The principles of Data Protection, initially prevalent and made subject to legislation across the European Union, have now reached further across the globe. The level and nature of worldwide Data Protection regimes vary from the complete absence of even the basic principles, through voluntary regulations all the way up to binding legislative requirements and a supporting infrastructure of authorities to oversee the operation of the law and to ensure compliance.

Appendix 3 contains the results of detailed research specially conducted for this book into the state of play with Data Protection measures in 175 countries. The information provided includes the specific legislation or regulations, the status as at September 2009, the key dates of enactment or coming into effect, details of the national or regional oversight authorities or bodies, together with their mail, web and email contact details. In some instances, we have provided the title of the legislation/regulation and the name of the key contact point in the local language. Many of the websites contained in the Appendix have versions in languages other than the local one(s), including a large number with English versions.

With the emergence and growth of the global economy and the flow of data between organisations and businesses located in different countries and states, it is essential that the owners and primary users of personal or sensitive data are aware of the underlying principles and legislative requirements in place in nations to which they intend to transfer such data. It is highly likely that the providing organisation will have a duty of care under their legislation to ensure that any data they transfer outside of their national boundaries will be adequately protected from loss, insecure disposal or unauthorised disclosure.

It could be said that all Data Protection legislation principles are formalised common sense. However, a business registered under the UK Data Protection Act 1998, will need to ensure that the principles are effectively applied throughout the organisation. This is partly a matter of clear communication of staff responsibilities, underpinned by defined procedures which are capable of being monitored for compliance.

It would be a mammoth task, and well beyond the scope of this book, to cover all the variations of the implications of Data Protection that apply across the world.

Accordingly, the remaining contents of this chapter primarily relate to a combination of the generally accepted definitions and tenets of Data Protection and the specific legislative requirements contained within the UK Data Protection Act 1998. Readers will need to obtain an accurate picture of the Data Protection framework in their own country.

The passing of the original UK Data Protection Act 1984, was set against an underlying problem with the unscrupulous trade in personal information as operated by some (albeit a minority of) organisations and individuals who use devious means to obtain data. In specific circumstances, these activities were not regulated by the Data Protection Act 1984, and therefore prosecution under that Act was ruled out. In order to address this problem, three new criminal offences were incorporated into the Criminal Justice and Public Order Act 1994, which came into effect on 3 February 1995.

It is now an offence "for a person to procure the disclosure of personal information to him, where he knows or has reason to believe that he is not a person to whom the data user is registered to disclose the data". Guidance issued by the then Data Protection Registrar goes on to say: "In cases where either bribery or deception is used, it may be fairly clear that the person obtaining the data in that way has good reason to believe that the organisation approached would not, in normal circumstances, authorise the disclosure in question. If this is the case, then the person seeking the data is likely to have committed a criminal offence."

The other two new offences created by the amendments "relate to the sale, or offering for sale (including advertising for sale) of personal data (or information extracted from such data) procured in the manner described above". Internal auditors should be aware of these amendments to the UK legislation when considering reviews of Data Protection measures.

The UK Data Protection legislation was updated as the Data Protection Act 1998 which came into effect on 1 March 2000. The Act provided for the replacement of the original Data Protection Registrar with the Information Commissioner. Details on the Commissioner's roles, guidance and interpretation in relation to the Act can be found at the website of the Information Commissioner's Office (www.ico.gov.uk).

The remainder of this chapter is relative to the UK Data Protection Act 1998; however it should provide coverage of the essential elements of Data Protection applicable in other legal environments. In the context of the UK Act, the following terminology is used:

- The **Data Controller** relates to the person or organisation controlling the contents and use of the data (i.e. in most cases the organisation).
- **Data Subject** relates to the individual who is the subject of the personal data (the Act grants rights to Data Subjects to gain access to the data stored about them and also requires that any errors in the data be corrected. In some circumstances, the Data Subject may have a right to compensation for damages or distress caused).
- **Personal Data** is information relating to a living individual the identity of whom can be discerned from that information (or from that and other information in the possession of the Data Controller).

- **Sensitive Data** is any information about a living individual (Data Subject) relating to his or her:
  - racial or ethnic origins
  - religious beliefs or other beliefs of a similar nature
  - political opinion
  - membership of a trades union
  - physical or mental health or condition
  - sexual life
  - the commission or alleged commission by them of an offence
  - proceedings for any offence committed or alleged to have been committed by them, the disposal of such proceedings or the sentence of any Court in such proceedings.
- **Notification** is the term used to describe the registration of the details of a Data Controller's use of personal information including to whom it will be disclosed and whether or not it will be disclosed to a recipient outside of the UK.

As for other aspects of IT management and oversight, the organisation's objectives, obligations and control measures can be contained within a ratified Data Protection Policy, the suggested contents of which could include:

- A **policy statement** that reflects the organisation's commitment to comply with the prevailing legislation, for example:

The organisation regards the lawful and correct treatment of personal information as an essential component of its operations and as a means of maintaining the confidence of those with whom it carries out business. The organisation will ensure that it will treat personal information lawfully and correctly, including accurately maintaining its notification to the Information Commissioner. In addition, it will establish formal processes for efficiently dealing with requests from Data Subjects to obtain the personal information that the organisation holds about them and enable them to promptly amend any inaccuracies. The organisation fully endorses and will adhere to the Principles of Data Protection and all the other obligations of the Data Protection Act 1998.

- An overview of the key operational issues relating to Data Protection and in particular to the eight Data Protection Principles contained within the Act (details and implications of which will be discussed subsequently).
- An overview of the corporate and specifically allocated responsibilities, including:
  - Overall senior management responsibility for the appropriate application of the Act across the organisation.
  - A nominated Data Protection Officer responsible for maintaining an up-to-date and accurate notification to the Information Commissioner.
  - The general responsibility of all employees to comply with the requirements of the Act.

The UK Data Protection Act 1998 is based upon eight Data Protection Principles that were originally defined for the 1984 version of the Act, of which the details are as follows (Figure 44.1):

Data Protection Principle	Additional Comments
1. Personal data shall be processed fairly and lawfully and, in particular, shall not be processed unless at least one of the conditions in Schedule 2 is met (see table below) and in the case of sensitive personal data, at least one of the conditions in Schedule 3 is also met (see table below).	Data would not be obtained and processed fairly and lawfully if the person was deceived about the purpose for which it was gathered. If the organisation is regularly involved in gathering personal data for operational or service provision purposes, for example on application forms, then it should consider including a standard paragraph (or "fair obtaining" statement) on such documents that define why the information is required, how it will be used, if it is to be disclosed outside of the organisation and seeking the applicant's acceptance of these conditions. Such statements should be conspicuously placed. If personal information is collected either by telephone or during face-to-face interviews, the employee should clearly explain why the information is required and how it will be used. A standard text should be considered for this purpose in order to ensure consistency.
2. Personal data shall be obtained only for one or more specified and lawful purposes, and shall not be further processed in any manner incompatible with that purpose or those purposes.	This principle does not put any constraints on the purposes for which personal data is used except that they should be lawful; it merely requires that the purposes be clearly defined and notified/registered with the Information Commissioner. Once data has been collected for certain defined purposes it should not then be used for other purposes. It is incumbent upon Data Controllers to ensure that the notification to the Information Commissioner is kept up to date with the effects of any new or amended types or uses of personal data. However, it is common practice for organisations to notify on a very broad basis so that minor changes in operations should not require a substantive amendment to the notification.
3. Personal data shall be adequate, relevant and not excessive in relation to the purpose or purposes for which they are processed.	Data Controllers are not able to collect data "for the sake of it" or in case "it might come in handy". The personal data held should be sufficient to operate the relevant system or support the operational need.
4. Personal data shall be accurate and, where necessary, kept up to date.	The principle requires Data Controllers to take steps and implement measures to ensure the accuracy and integrity of data that they hold and to keep it up to date. Data Controllers can be held liable for damages and compensation payable to Data Subjects if inaccurate data causes harm or distress to them. It is also an offence to knowingly or recklessly enter or hold inaccurate data.

(*continued*)

Data Protection Principle	Additional Comments
5. Personal data processed for any purpose or purposes shall not be kept longer than is necessary for that purpose or those purposes.	This principle implies that data should be destroyed once it has served the purpose for which it was collected. The basic requirement is not to hold data for indefinite periods and it will be necessary to justify the period for which personal data is kept. It is important to remember that some types of data (such as financial records) have to be retained for periods specified by legislation or regulation and such requirements have a priority when considering the deletion or destruction of records. The organisation may have in place Record Retention and Disposal Guidelines which include the periods for which certain types of records must be retained. (The retention and disposal of records is discussed in Chapter 33).
6. Personal data shall be processed in accordance with the rights of the Data Subjects under the Act.	The Data Subjects' rights include: To have his/her personal data processed fairly and lawfully; To be given (following a written request and the payment of a fee) a description of all the personal data that is being processed and being told the purposes of the processing and the sources and disclosures of such personal data; To give notice, in writing, to the Data Controller to stop or not to begin processing personal data on the grounds that it will cause damage or distress. If the Data Controller fails to comply, the Data Subject can apply to the Court for a decision; To stop processing for direct marketing; Not to have decisions taken by a Data Controller which affect him/her and which are based solely on automatic decision making; To apply to a Court for rectification, blocking, erasure or destruction of personal data if it is inaccurate; and To receive compensation if he/she suffers damage by reason of any contravention by the Data Controller of any requirement of the Data Protection Act.
7. Appropriate technical and organisational measures shall be taken against the unauthorised or unlawful processing of personal	This principle places on Data Controllers an obligation to take reasonable security measures to ensure that the data cannot be lost, accessed or tampered with by unauthorised persons.

Data Protection Principle	Additional Comments
data and against accidental loss or destruction of, or damage to, personal data.	Access to an organisation's computer systems and data is normally granted on a "need to know basis" that ensures that staff only have access to the information they need to perform their duties and responsibilities.
8. Personal data shall not be transmitted to a country or territory outside the European Economic Area unless that country or territory ensures an adequate level of protection for the rights and freedoms of Data Subjects in relation to the processing of personal data.	This principle may not universally apply to all organisations, but those engaged in international business may have the need to transfer or share data with suppliers, customers or partners. As can be seen in Appendix 3, the level of Data Protection varies between countries and states, so the onus is on the Data Controller to ensure that any personal data being moved into any country will be adequately protected. We consider the wider issues for sharing and transferring data in a later section of this chapter. Although it should be very unlikely to be necessary to place personal information on the organisation's website, doing so will potentially disclose the information across the globe without any barriers. One example of this would be the placing of details of staff on a corporate web page with some biographical information, the use of which must be cleared beforehand with the Data Subject and a written consent obtained.

Schedule 2 Conditions (the general conditions)
Processing may not take place unless one of the following criteria are met: • The Data Subject has given his consent to the processing; • To perform a contract to which the Data Subject is a party or the taking of steps at the request of the Data Subject with a view to entering into a contract; • The processing is necessary for compliance with any legal obligation to which the Data Controller is subject, other than an obligation imposed by contract; • The processing is necessary in order to protect the vital interests of the Data Subject; • The processing is necessary to carry out public functions (such as the administration of justice, the exercise of any functions conferred on any person by or under any enactment, the exercise of any functions of the Crown, a Minister of the Crown or a government department or the exercise of any other function of a public nature exercised in the public interest by any person); • The processing is necessary for the purposes of the legitimate interests pursued by the Data Controller unless it is prejudicial to the interests of the individual.

(continued)

Schedule 3 Conditions (Sensitive Data)
The Data Protection Act contains the category of Sensitive Data. In order to process Sensitive Data, one or more of the following Schedule 3 conditions must be met: • The Data Subject has given his/her explicit consent to the processing of the personal data; • The processing is necessary for the purposes of exercising or performing any right or obligation which is conferred or imposed by law on the Data Controller in connection with employment; • The processing is necessary to protect the vital interests of the Data Subject where consent cannot be given or withheld; • The processing is carried out by certain (specified) nonprofit bodies about their members; • The information contained in the personal data has been made public as a result of steps deliberately taken by the Data Subject; • The processing is necessary for the purpose of, or in connection with, any legal proceedings, or the purpose of obtaining legal advice or is otherwise necessary for the purposes of establishing, exercising or defending legal rights; • The processing is necessary to carry out public functions (such as the administration of justice, the exercise of any functions conferred on any person by or under any enactment, the exercise of any functions of the Crown, a Minister of the Crown or a government department or the exercise of any other function of a public nature exercised in the public interest by any person); • The processing is necessary for medical purposes and is undertaken by a health professional or a person who in the circumstances owes a duty of confidentiality which is equivalent to that which would arise if that person were a health professional; or • The processing consists of information as to the racial or ethnic origin where it is necessary for the purpose of identifying or keeping under review the existence or absence of equality or opportunity or treatment between persons of different racial or ethnic origins, with a view to enabling such equality to be promoted or maintained; and is carried out with appropriate safeguards for the rights and freedoms of Data Subjects.

Figure 44.1 Eight Data Protection principles

A key Data Protection issue for any organisation is how they ensure that any disclosure of personal data is lawful and appropriate. In one respect disclosure can be prescribed by other laws or regulations (for example in the UK to HMRC (Revenue and Customs), the Benefits Agency or the Department of Work and Pensions), although the concern is that employees do not unduly disclose personal information in the course of their work to an unauthorised person. In practice, disclosure can be in the form of printed information, an electronic document or file, via email or even verbally in a telephone conversation. One measure for preventing such incidents is ensuring that all employees collecting, using, updating, storing or disclosing personal data are fully aware of their responsibilities under the Data Protection legislation through the provision of adequate training and supporting guidance materials. The following are some key messages relating to Data Protection to impart to employees:

- Every employee has an underlying duty to ensure that personal data, accessed and used in the course of their duties, is appropriately and confidentially treated.

Most employees are also Data Subjects and would want their own personal data adequately protected.
- Keep the eight Data Protection principles in mind and clearly understand the requirements for compliance.
- Be alert to the means by which personal data could be unwittingly or unintentionally disclosed, for example:
  - in a telephone conversation
  - viewed on an unattended PC screen
  - a document or file left exposed on a desktop
  - any information read (or overheard) by an unauthorised person is classified as unauthorised disclosure.
- Take account of the workplace in terms of how it may facilitate unauthorised disclosure of information. For example, consider the following points:
  - Is personal information left lying around on view?
  - Is the area secure so as to prevent the presence of unauthorised persons?
  - Is it an area open to visitors or members of the public, where information could be read from exposed PC screens?
  - Are PCs logged off when not in use or left unattended?
- Be clear about who, within and outside of the organisation, has a valid, legitimate and authorised right to view data. Don't assume that a work colleague has the same rights of access as you.
- Telephone, fax and email are not secure means of communication.
- Employees can be held liable if they fail to apply or knowingly disregard the required Data Protection measures.
- *Never* share or reveal system user IDs or passwords with others and do *not* accept the offer to use someone else's ID and password.
- Do *not* write passwords down or have them on post-it notes by the computer.
- Apply the measures contained within the organisation's IT Security Policy and other guidelines, such as creating strong passwords that are more difficult to determine.
- Users should never attempt to gain access to information to which they are not entitled.
- Log out of application systems or use the locked screensaver facility on your PC to avoid unauthorised use of your computer or the viewing of information on the screen.
- Don't just provide, copy or pass on personal information without clearly establishing that the recipient is appropriately authorised to view and handle such data. If in doubt about the other person's right to access or view data that is your responsibility, then politely decline their request and seek further advice from your line manager. Remember, you could be liable in the event of an unauthorised disclosure of information.
- Be especially wary of persons purporting to be the Data Subject and asking to see their own information. Unless they are known through prior contact or their identity has been reliably confirmed, *do not* pass over any information as this could be a breach of the DPA requirements. Any requests from Data Subjects to

view their own information or that include mention of the Data Protection Act should be routed to the person nominated to deal with such requests so that a consistent and appropriate approach can be applied that adequately protects the organisation from failing to comply.
- Be aware that although Data Subjects are, under the Act, entitled to see the information held about them by the Data Controller, there are certain exceptions to this, for example:
  - Where a criminal offence is suspected and the supply of information could prejudice the investigation.
  - Where there is the possibility of causing harm to a third party.
- Take particular care when removing files from the usual workplace.
- In order to ensure that the organisation's notification to the Information Commissioner is maintained up to date, the Data Protection Officer should be consulted when any of the following situations apply:
  - Making changes to the use of a computer or manual system that uses personal data.
  - Reuse of personal data for another or new purpose.
  - Setting up a new system.
  - Introducing a new or revised document for the collection of personal data.
- Safeguard computer printouts and manual records against disclosure to unauthorised persons.
- Adopt a "clear desk" approach by securing hardcopy personal information when it is not being used.
- Only dispose of confidential documents by cross-cut shredding.
- Be aware that there are individuals who will try and trick employees into giving out personal information to which they are not entitled and which they may use for their own personal gain or benefit.
- Carry out reasonable prior checks before giving out personal information to someone making a request for information via the telephone or email.
- Make sure that records are promptly updated and accurate.

Data Subject Access Requests

One of the specific rights granted to Data Subjects under UK law is that, upon making a written request and paying a fee (if deemed necessary by the Data Controller and within any prescribed limits), they can be given a description of all their personal data being processed by the Data Controller, details of the purposes for holding the information and the sources and disclosures of such data. This information must be provided in an intelligible form with interpretations provided for any codes or abbreviations used in the data.

Organisations will need to establish a process for dealing with requests from Data Subjects. Standard forms may be used to record the relevant details and a nominated officer (usually the Data Protection Officer) should handle the requests and oversee the collection of the data from all of the relevant internal departments and functions. The request administration process should also include the setting, charging and accounting of related charges.

The UK law stipulates that the Data Controller has 40 days in which to respond to the request, but this period only begins once the organisation is satisfied that the application is correct and excludes any prior time spent clarifying the request etc.

The Data Subject has the right to give notice in writing to the Data Controller to stop or not begin processing their personal data on the grounds that it will cause damage or distress. If the Data Controller fails to comply, the Data Subject can apply to the Court for a decision. If any employee receives any such communication from a Data Subject, they should refer the matter immediately to either their line manager or the Data Protection Officer and not deal with it themselves due to the potential legal implications of failing to react accordingly.

The Data Subject can refer matters of process to the Information Commissioner who has the power to apply sanctions upon the Data Controller.

If the personal data held by the Data Controller is proven to be inaccurate or out of date, the Data Subject has the right to apply to the Court for the rectification, blocking, erasure or destruction of personal data.

If Data Subject suffers damage by reason of any contravention by the Data Controller of any requirement of the Act, then he/she has the right to receive compensation.

Control Objectives for Data Protection

(a) To ensure compliance with the prevailing Data Protection legislation.

(b) To ensure that staff are aware of their responsibilities in respect of the Data Protection regulations.

(c) To ensure that the organisation's Data Protection registration is accurate and maintained up to date.

(d) To ensure that Data Protection implications are appropriately addressed for all system developments and amendments.

(e) To ensure that enquiries from Data Subjects are promptly, efficiently and accurately dealt with.

(f) To ensure that data errors are promptly corrected.

Risk and Control Issues for Data Protection

1 Key Issues

1.1 How does management ensure that all the prevailing Data Protection requirements are cost-effectively complied with (and how is such compliance evidenced)?

1.2 What steps has management taken to ensure that all affected staff are made aware of their responsibilities under the prevailing Data Protection legislation?

1.3 What measures ensure that the organisation's registration details remain accurate and up to date (e.g. for new systems and business activities)?

1.4 How does management ensure that Data Protection implications are appropriately considered for all systems under development (or where significant amendments are being applied)?

1.5 What systems are in place to ensure that all enquiries from Data Subjects are promptly identified and auctioned?

1.6 What processes ensure that data errors are promptly and appropriately corrected?

2 Detailed Issues

2.1 How does management maintain staff awareness of Data Protection issues and their correct treatment?

2.2 Has the responsibility for periodically confirming the accuracy of the organisation's Data Protection registration been allocated?

2.3 How is management assured that personal data is obtained fairly and lawfully?

2.4 How is management assured that personal data is only held for the required purpose?

2.5 How is management assured that personal data is disseminated in accordance with the registration?

2.6 How is management assured that personal data is accurate and up to date?

2.7 What measures are in place to ensure that unwanted, surplus or obsolete personal data is erased?

2.8 How is personal data restricted to authorised users only?

2.9 What procedures avoid unauthorised amendment of data?

2.10 How does management ensure that data is protected from accidental loss, leakage or destruction?

2.11 How does management confirm that printed or filmed personal data is securely disposed of?

2.12 How is management assured that all Data Subject enquiries are accounted for?

# 45

Freedom of Information

Freedom of Information (also referred to as a "right to information" or "to access official information") usually relates to a citizen's right to request and obtain information from the Government (and its agencies) and other public bodies and institutions. The same access rights can also be applied to the press and other media and can be seen, in part, to reflect the tone and openness of the relevant Government.

As a concept, Freedom of Information (FoI) is now an established part of the US public sector, and has spread around the globe, although Sweden can hold claim to the earliest legislative form of freedom of information in a section of the 1766 Constitution that states "all government documents are public in the absence of a statute that expressly regulates otherwise". This early example also contains a form of the caveat that is still often used as a limiting factor to restrict the nature of information that can be publicly released. This sort of "get out" clause can provide that certain classifications of information can be legitimately related to matters of national security or interest, indeed most extant Freedom of Information legislation reflects such justified limitations. However, although it is laudable to have a legislative right to access information, it can be quite another thing to actually obtain the information sought. Excessive bureaucracy or the lack of coordination and structure of public records can, in practice, frustrate or even prevent access attempts. This scenario could be seen, albeit cynically, as having ticked the "FoI legislation in place" box without necessarily ensuring (or indeed having the will to ensure) the provision of an effective supporting administrative framework.

Freedom of Information, however it may be legislated or regulated, has implications for public bodies in most nations and states; this chapter examines the key issues based on the UK Freedom of Information Act 2000 which came into force on 1 January 2005 and is modelled on broader European-based principles reflected across member states of the European Union.

In preparation for creating this chapter, extensive research was conducted into the existence of FoI legislation or regulation across the world. Appendix 4 contains the results of this research relating to 183 countries or states, including the details of any specific FoI legislation (either in place or in the pipeline) and the contact details for either the overseeing authority or other relevant national or nongovernmental organisations.

The type and extent of rights revealed by the research varied considerably, ranging from potentially vague references, that could be interpreted in a number of ways, in national constitutions through to comprehensive definitions of rights in robust laws overseen by independent authorities. The UK has no written constitution but does have FoI legislation overseen by the same Information Commissioner who deals with Data Protection; whereas the Republic of South Africa, uniquely we believe, extends the right of access to information to include not only that held by the State but by "another person" which is interpreted as meaning private organisations and individuals.

It should be noted that all 47 member states of the Council of Europe are parties to the European Convention on Human Rights (ECHR), Article 10 of which includes a right to "receive and impart information".

It could perhaps be expected that closed or restricted regimes would limit their citizen's right to access information, although there are a few surprises contained in the results that appear to contradict this view. However, the overall impression is that the international move to increased openness and transparency in government and public administration is increasing in both pace and intent.

The following guidance and discussion is based upon the UK Freedom of Information Act 2000 and readers with interests outside of the UK are advised to verify the specific and relevant national FoI implications that fits their own situation.

The development of a documented Freedom of Information Policy should be considered as a clear statement of the organisation's obligation to the legislation and the intention to provide the required access to its records. The Policy could include the following attributes:

- A Policy Statement to the effect that:

  - The organisation will enable access to the information that it holds subject to the conditions and exemptions which are prescribed by statute.
  - The organisation will provide the information requested unless it is exempted from disclosure.
  - The organisation will inform any applicant who requests information whether or not the organisation holds it and communicate it to the applicant unless the disclosure is exempt from inspection and, where appropriate, public interest in maintaining any applicable exemption outweighs the public interest in its disclosure.

- In many instances, UK public bodies, such as local authorities, are obliged to maintain a Publication Scheme which defines what information can be made available to the public (or indeed the media). The information types and formats detailed under the Publication Scheme are accordingly seen as being automatically available under the auspices of the FoI Act.

- Details of how the organisation will provide advice and assistance to applicants making requests for information and also how it will deal with such requests, including details of the following:

  - The form that requests should take (i.e. in writing, perhaps using a standard pro forma).

- The key contact for FoI matters (often a nominated Freedom of Information Officer).
- The processes necessary to clarify and refine information requests so that they can be efficiently dealt with.
- The organisation's response to potentially vexatious applications (as defined within the Act).
- The timescale in which the organisation will deal with FoI requests (normally 20 working days but this may be subject to variation if the request is complex, requires detailed analysis or preparation and/or if there is a need to refer the matter to a third party as would apply if personal data was involved and where a consent may have to be obtained).
- The fees that will be charged (in accord with the regulations and any relevant Codes of Practice).
- How the organisation will deal with requests that it cannot process but that relate to another public body (this could include advising the applicant of the situation and, where appropriate, transferring the request to the other relevant public body).
- How the organisation will consider the public interest associated with the request and decide, on that basis, whether the information can be provided in the requested form.
- The various situations where the organisation may justifiably refuse the request (usually related to specific exclusions from disclosure or excessive costs or efforts relating to the extraction and preparation of the information).

- Organisations should register and monitor all FoI requests. Local authorities in the UK are required to maintain a public record of all requests for information under the FoI Act.
- The Policy should include details of how complaints relating to the organisation's FoI processes will be handled. This is likely to include an overview of the organisation's general complaints procedure and its various escalation levels. All complaints should be recorded and effectively managed. Ultimately, the applicant can refer complaints that he/she feels have not been satisfactorily resolved by the organisation to the Information Commissioner who may, at his discretion, investigate and comment upon the matter.
- It follows that the organisation should have in place a suitable process for identifying FoI requests and efficiently dealing with them within the prescribed timescales. The FoI request handling process should take account of the following:

    - Prompt identification and appropriate routing of FoI requests.
    - The clear allocation of responsibilities for dealing with FoI requests and the promotion of this and the required process to all staff across the organisation. In addition, the organisation should publicise its Freedom of Information Policy and process to the public, for example via the public website.
    - Capturing all the required information relating to the request, including:

        - Name of person/organisation making the request.
        - Address and contact details for correspondence.

- A clear description of the information being sought (including the level of analysis or summarisation, the period to be covered or any scoping factors such as geographic areas or value ranges).
- Preferences relating to the form and format required (for example, electronic files such as documents or spreadsheets, copies of documents etc.).
- Any special needs such as supplying the information in a particular language or in a larger font to aid the visually impaired.
- The provision of adequate facilities so that the organisation can provide assistance to applicants in the preparation of their request.
- Identifying the internal source(s) of the requested information and liaising with other employees in the affected area(s) to coordinate the provision of the required information in the necessary form within the relevant timescale.
- A prompt determination of whether or not the organisation holds the requested information and advising the applicant of whether or not their request can be fulfilled (including the referral of the request to any other public body).
- The maintenance of a register of all FoI requests which is up to date, publicly available and open to scrutiny.
- Providing the means to record and track the progress of requests and their fulfilment.
- Consideration of the timescale required to respond, taking into account matters of data availability and the complexities of obtaining and refining the requested information.
- Advising applicants whether or not the information can be or will be supplied within the usual 20-working-day period stipulated in the Act and providing a realistic and achievable alternative timescale.
- The rigorous assessment of all requests and determining whether the information should be defined as either an exception, an absolute exemption or a qualified exemption, including the application of the public interest test where necessary. (NB: Definitions of Absolute and Qualified Exemptions are provided later in this chapter.)
- The prompt advising of applicants as to why their request is being refused.
- The setting and application of lawful charges that are proportional to the effort required to fulfil the FoI request. The applicant should be promptly advised of the fee that will be levied in their case and given the opportunity, *inter alia*, to refine their request as a means of reducing the associated costs.
- To record when and how the request was fulfilled.
- To facilitate the effective and objective assessment of complaints received in relation to the organisation's handling of FoI requests and advising applicants of the available complaint routes open to them (including the organisation's own complaints procedure and the situations in which the matter can be referred to the Information Commissioner).

In order that the organisation's handling and administration of its FoI obligations are effective and efficient, it is essential that employees are aware of the implications of FoI and what they should do in the course of their duties. Specific FoI training should be considered for staff supported by freely available support guidance. The following points should be included in any staff guidance:

- A clear explanation of FoI terminology, including:

  - The **Right to Know** is the right, under the UK FoI Act, to request information held by public authorities.
  - A **Publication Scheme** details all the information that the organisation routinely or proactively makes available. Managers should keep the contents of the Publication Scheme under review and advise the officer charged with maintaining the Scheme of any required changes.
  - The **Request for Information (or RFI)** is the term used to refer to any FOI request submitted by an individual or organisation. Anyone can request information under the Act regardless of their age, location or nationality. Members of the press and other media will request information when preparing an article or media report. Students may make requests to aid their course work or dissertations.
  - The right of access to information is subject to a number of defined **Exceptions and Exemptions**, the latter being further subdivided into defined **Absolute Exemptions** and **Qualified Exemptions**.[1] Where information falls under an Absolute Exemption, the harm to the public interest that would result from its disclosure is already established, for example, in relation to personal information (as defined under the Data Protection Act), or if disclosure would result in an actionable breach of confidence. If it is believed that the requested information is covered by a qualified exemption or an exception, the public interest test must be applied.
  - The **Public Interest Test** should be used where either a qualified exemption or an exception applies. In such cases, the information may be withheld only if the public authority considers that the public interest in withholding the information is greater than the public interest in disclosing it.

- A brief overview of the legislation and its key implications for the organisation and employees.
- Under the UK Act it is not necessary for applicants to specify why they want the requested information and there is no right granted to the organisation to request or be informed of a reason.
- The range of types of information that can be legitimately requested under the UK FoI Act is very broad and includes emails, letters, minutes of meetings, plans, internal reports, leaflets, photographs, research materials, drawings, case notes, video or sound recording, etc.
- The information requested may either be in its original form (for example, specific supplier invoices or outgoing letters) or in summary form (for example, an analysis or summary).
- Staff should be made aware of any other form of information request that the organisation may receive and how to identify them; for example, UK local authorities also have to deal with requests for information relating to the environment

in a manner defined within the Environmental Information Regulations 2004 (EIR). However the most likely requests for information will apply to either the Data Protection Act 1998 or the Freedom of Information Act 2000; the following simple guidance should be provided to staff to aid their differentiation of these two types of request and how to deal with them:

- FoI relates to the right to request *official information held by the Government (and its agencies) and public bodies*, and applies to members of the public, customers or clients of public bodies and agencies and media organisations and representatives. The UK FoI Act explicitly exempts the publication or release of personal data. FoI requests should be routed to the nominated Freedom of Information Officer for assessment and fulfilment; whereas
- The UK Data Protection Act 1998 gives *rights to individuals to gain access to information about themselves* (so-called Personal Data) and enables them to request sight of all the data that *any organisation (public or private)* holds about them and to be informed of the purposes for which the information is required. Data Protection requests are normally referred to the organisation's nominated Data Protection Officer for assessment and action. For further details of the issues relating to Data Protection, please refer Chapter 44.
- Employees need to be alert to the possibility that a FoI request may be either vexatious or time wasting. The Act does not specify any limit to the number of requests that an individual or organisation can make. However, section 14 of the Act states that a public authority can reserve the right to refuse requests. Such a refusal may be on grounds of repeated requests being made for the same information by the same person or where the intent of the request is to disrupt the authority's operations in some way (for example requesting information that it would be extremely difficult or costly to generate and involving the diversion of significant resources). Decisions to refuse a request should only be made by the nominated Freedom of Information Officer and, where necessary, taking into account the view of the organisation's legal advisor.

Control Objectives for Freedom of Information

> (a) To ensure that senior management has an accurate, comprehensive and up-to-date understanding of the organisation's FoI obligations.
>
> (b) To ensure that responsibilities for the oversight of FoI and dealing with FoI requests are clearly allocated to a nominated officer.
>
> (c) To ensure that the organisation is fully compliant with all the requirements of the prevailing Freedom of Information legislation and regulations.
>
> (d) To ensure that there is an adequate process in place to accurately and lawfully determine when information is either an exception, absolute exemption or a qualified exemption and to treat such information appropriately.

- (e) To ensure that personal information, or that which is exempt from public disclosure, is not inadvertently or otherwise publicly released under FoI.

- (f) To ensure that the organisation is adequately prepared to deal correctly and efficiently with all FoI requests.

- (g) To ensure that all employees are adequately conversant with the requirements of the FoI legislation and are clear about their own specific responsibilities.

- (h) To ensure that the organisation has established a Publication Scheme (as may be mandatory within their sector) and that it is up to date and complete.

- (i) To ensure that appropriate, proportionate and lawful fees are charged for processing and providing requested information under FoI.

- (j) To provide an accurate and complete record of all FoI requests received (irrespective of whether or not they were refused) to enable performance monitoring, effective management and (where required by regulation) public scrutiny of FoI activities.

- (k) To ensure that vexatious or disruptive FoI requests are promptly identified and effectively dealt with.

Risk and Control Issues for Freedom of Information

1 Key Issues

1.1 How can management be assured that all the implications of the extant FoI legislation and regulations have been identified and adequately addressed in terms of processes and measures? In addition, how is this evidenced?

1.2 How can management be assured that the organisation is fully compliant with the FoI law and regulations? In addition, how would any instances of non compliance be detected and dealt with?

1.3 What action has management taken to promote its FoI obligations to its customers, clients and employees?

1.4 Has the organisation defined and promoted the importance of FoI to all employees and provided them with appropriate and adequate training and guidance materials? How is this evidenced?

1.5 How are staff made aware of their specific and general responsibilities for FoI?

1.6 How does management ensure that staff are adequately trained in respect of FoI?

1.7 What measures are in place to specifically prevent the release of information that is either an exception or exemption under the FoI legislation or where the public interest test, if applied, would adjudge the release as being prejudicial?

1.8 What facilities have been provided to support and advise applicants in the preparation of their requests?

1.9 How can management be assured that applicants are kept informed of the status and progress of their request and are specifically advised of any exceptional aspects of their request that could delay or otherwise affect its fulfilment?

1.10 How does management ensure that any required Publication Scheme is maintained up to date, is accurate and publicly accessible?

1.11 Has management appropriately determined a scale of fees that is lawful and reflects the level of effort and cost implications for the organisation? In addition, is the scale of fees periodically reviewed in light of changes in costs, etc.?

1.12 How is it ensured that the correct fee is always charged and actually received prior to the information being released?

1.13 Is management able to promptly determine the progress and status of each FoI request and to monitor the overall FoI workload effectively?

1.14 What specific mechanisms would detect potentially vexatious or disruptive FoI requests?

2 Detailed Issues

2.1 What steps has management taken to formally document its commitment to FoI and the measures necessary to be compliant and to provide an appropriate level of service in handling FoI requests?

2.2 How would management be made aware of any changes to the FoI legislation or its regulation and delivery within their sector?

2.3 Has management made adequate provision for applicants to readily identify how they should correctly make their FoI request?

2.4 How does management ensure that FoI requests are promptly identified and correctly routed?

2.5 Are actions taken to accurately determine the effort required and the costs involved to fulfil a FoI request and to ensure that an appropriate charge is made that is both lawful and goes some way to meet the organisation's costs?

2.6 Are employees able to efficiently and accurately differentiate between FoI and Data Protection requests and to deal with them appropriately?

2.7 How does management ensure that all FoI requests are processed and fulfilled in the prescribed timescale? In addition, are exceptional requests evaluated and the applicant advised of any deviations away from the prescribed 20-working-day period?

2.8 How can management be sure that FoI requests relating to other public bodies are identified and correctly referred on? In addition, how is the applicant kept informed of the action being taken?

NOTE

1. Further details of FoI Absolute and Qualified Exemptions are available from the Information Commissioner's Office website: www.ico.gov.uk.

46

Data Transfer and Sharing (Standards and Protocol)

In the course of normal operations, any organisation will use data of all kinds and, as appropriate, transfer or share such data either within the organisation (between departments) or externally to, for example, suppliers, outsource contractors, central government departments, other public or regulatory bodies and partners.

Overarching any operationally expedient movement, transfer or sharing of data, an organisation is likely to have a number of standard obligations in respect of the use, disclosure and security of the data it uses. For example, the prevailing Data Protection legislation will define how personal data can be lawfully disclosed and national financial and taxation bodies will require information on employee earnings, tax payments and other statutory deductions.

To set the scene for the rest of this chapter, it will be useful to define the following types of transfer or sharing of data:

- As mentioned above, there will be **mandatory, regulatory and statutory** movements of data outside of the organisation.
- **Day-to-day** processes and operations may involve the standard exchange of data between departments and functions within the organisation. These types of **fixed standard types of data transfers** are likely to be well established and, possibly, defined within operational procedures. In addition, the system owner should define how the data can be used and by whom, and these elements will then drive the permitted and authorised use of the data concerned.
- Beyond the established and routine movement of data within an organisation, there could be other **ad hoc internal requests** for information.
- The last and potentially most concerning category relates to the **regular transfer or sharing of data with external parties**, such as partners, contractors, peer groups, industry bodies, and so on.

Although, we will touch later, albeit lightly, upon the key issues relating to ad hoc internal requests for data, it is the specific category of regular external transfers and sharing that the remainder of this chapter mainly concentrates upon, because the other noted forms are usually more systematic, structured, established and controlled.

In considering any type of data transfer or sharing there are a number of consistent elements or dimensions that will need to be taken into account as befit each specific scenario:

Media and Means of Transfer.

- The appropriate media, form and means used to facilitate will depend on a number of issues, including:
  - Whether the transfer is internal or external
  - What is the most appropriate means, taking into account the security implications, for example:
    - Physical transfer of documents or files
    - Email content or attachments
    - Electronic documents and files (word processor, spreadsheet or database formats)
    - Online transmission over a secure network
    - Portable media (CD, DVD, memory sticks or data tapes)
    - National mail services (Recorded or Special Delivery)
    - Courier
    - Verbally
    - Via Fax
    - Via the internal mail service.
- Level of permitted access to data (disclosure rules)
  - Does the transfer follow the "need to know" principle of disclosure?
  - Is the recipient duly authorised to receive, view and use the data?
  - Have the legal implications been considered?
  - Is disclosure only permitted if other specific conditions will be applied?

Level of explicit detail of data.

- What is the level of data being requested, transferred and shared, for example:
  - Complete sets of data (i.e. all records and full details)
  - Partial records (i.e. all records but with some fields omitted)
  - Individual transactions or records
  - Extracted full records (i.e. a subset of data with all fields)
  - Extracted limited records (i.e. a subset of data with selected fields)
  - Depersonalised records (i.e. with the personal identifiers removed or encoded)
  - Summarised, aggregated or analysed data (possibly eliminating the ability to identify individuals resulting in higher level statistics)
  - Are there defined and required standards of security relevant to each of the above levels of detail, rising in stringency the more detailed, complete and explicit the data becomes?

- Exemptions and exceptions
  - Are there any prevailing legal, public interest or commercial limitations relating to the disclosure of the data?
  - Is the data of a personal or confidential nature?
- Legal and Regulatory Implications
  - Have all the legal and regulatory obligations been identified and met?
  - Would the sharing of the data be a breach of regulations?
- Security implications and standards
  - Physical security measures over documents and media, including periods when in transit
  - Encryption to a recognised standard
  - Password protection
  - Only entrust the physical transfer of information to known employees or representatives.
- Custody of data
  - Have the responsibilities of custody and related security measures been defined and understood by all parties?
- Permitted uses of data
  - Have clear rules been established over both the permitted and prohibited use of data?
- Eventual disposal or destruction of data
  - It is clear to all parties how long the data may have to be kept?
  - How is the secure and appropriate disposal of data after use to be handled and does the process take account of the relative sensitivity and detail levels of the data?

Ad Hoc Internal Requests to Transfer or Share Information

Employees may receive ad hoc requests (via the telephone, face-to-face, via email, memo or fax) from others purporting to be employees of the organisation. It must not be automatically assumed that the person requesting is either *bona fide* or actually authorised to handle, view or use the requested data. The following general points should be taken into account in such ad hoc situations:

- Confirm the identity of the person requesting the data.
- Obtain management consent to share the data if it is safe, appropriate and feasible to do so.
- Confirm the reason why the information is required.
- Be fully satisfied that it is necessary to share the requested data.
- Be fully satisfied that you are able to share and that there are no legal impediments to doing so.

- Don't share more information than is necessary.
- Inform the recipient if any of the information is potentially inaccurate or unreliable.
- Ensure that the information is shared safely and securely.
- Be clear with the recipients how the information will be used.
- Ensure that all parties are aware of their responsibilities and obligations.
- Ensure that the recipient has adequate security and Data Protection arrangements in place before data is provided.
- Be clear that the data will be disposed of securely after use.
- Record what information is shared, when, with whom and why.

Sharing Information with or Transferring Information to External Organisations and Partners

The regular transfer to and sharing of data with external organisations and partners should be more formally based than the internal equivalents. As we will explore later in this chapter, it is advised that all external data transfers and sharing be the subject of a suitable Information Sharing Agreement (ISA), the recommended minimum contents of which we will note later.

Generally, what should be expected of external organisations and partners? The following examples are offered as a baseline for any such arrangement:

- There is a reasonable expectation that any partners to a data transfer or sharing arrangement will act lawfully, honestly and in accordance with all the conditions contained within any signed Information Sharing Agreement (ISA).
- Where there is a requirement for the parties to an ISA to comply with a specific technical or regulatory standard or condition, the details of these should be clearly expressed within the ISA so that there is no possible avoidance of the need to comply.
- Any risks associated with the sharing, transfer and subsequent use of organisation's data should be clearly allocated in a balanced way that reflects the issues that could arise and who would be likely to be primarily responsible for creating and managing them. The aim is to ensure that the organisation should not be unduly exposed to risks and any associated liabilities and in order for this to be so, any draft ISA documentation should be reviewed and agreed by the organisation's legal representative.
- All partners should be expected to adhere to the requirements of the Data Protection legislation. In addition, all partners should declare that they have current, up-to-date and relevant registrations under the relevant Data Protection laws that specifically permit the uses and disclosures required in relation to the specific ISA.
- There should be ongoing and open communication between the parties during the operation of the ISA so that problems, issues and revisions can be promptly brought to general attention and effectively managed; this is especially important in respect of data quality so that any detected errors or shortcomings can be resolved as a matter of urgency.

- The ISA should allow for the periodic review of long-running arrangements so that circumstantial, regulatory and legislative changes can be taken into account and the ISA reset to reflect them.
- Where appropriate to the scale and length of the sharing arrangements, a representative user group should be considered so as to provide advice, ongoing monitoring, feedback on various issues and matters of compliance, etc. The group should report back to the members of the partnership so that any significant issues can be escalated if necessary.
- Where appropriate and in proportion to the nature of the data involved and the relative risks associated with the data transfer/sharing partnership, consideration should be given to incorporating, within the ISA, the rights of partners to involve their internal audit function in the objective review of the operation of the scheme, the security and Data Protection measures in place and to provide assurance in relation to the compliance issues.
- Where the supplying organisation has a Protective Marking Scheme, the documents and information being supplied should be appropriately marked. In ad-dition, all other parties to the ISA should be made aware of the suitable security and other measures necessary in relation to the relevant Protective Marking classification.
- The recipient(s) of data should have adequate and effective physical and logical security arrangements in place.
- It is desirable that all parties to the ISA should conform to the requirements of ISO 27002 (formerly called ISO 17799) and the emerging ISO 27001. ISO 27002 is a code of practice for information security. It is recognised that full compliance and accreditation under these schemes may not be possible for some partners or affordable by others, but partners should aim to comply with the principles contained within the standards.
- As a minimum requirement, all partners should have ratified Information Security, Data Protection and other relevant Policies in place that are actively promoted and applied throughout their organisations.
- Partners should have confidentiality policies and associated statements covering all affected staff including those who are permanent, temporary, voluntary, contract, students on placements, etc.

Information Sharing Agreements (ISA)

It is strongly recommended that all data transfer and sharing arrangements with external parties should be the subject of a formally documented Information Sharing Agreement (ISA) or Protocol. This section provides guidance on the required contents for such an agreement.

Legal and Statutory Framework

It will be necessary, in each case, to identify all the legislative and regulatory implications affecting the data transfer, for example in the UK this would likely include The Data Protection Act 1998, The Freedom of Information Act 2000, The

Human Rights Act 1998 and the Common Law Duty of Confidence. Any such implications should be clearly and lawfully incorporated into the ISA.

When entering into wider data sharing or transfer initiatives it is possible that a suggested form of agreement will be presented to the organisation as the basis for the relationship. In such circumstances or when drawing up a new Information Sharing Agreement, appropriate legal advice should be sought to prevent any exposure to any unreasonable requirements or potential liabilities.

The actual content and form of an ISA will depend on a range of factors that reflect the nature and scale of the data sharing situation; however the following can be considered as a *de minimis* level of good practice content:

- Details of all the parties to the agreement and any specific differences in their roles and responsibilities.
- The purpose of the data sharing, including any objectives to be achieved and how they will be measured, reported, monitored and managed.
- Details of any relevant prevailing legislation or regulation should be defined together with any specific obligations that are contained therein.
- The period of the agreement, including any dates for periodic review or renewal of the arrangements.
- Named key contacts within all of the participating organisations.
- Details of the information to be provided including indications of whether the data set is to be complete, extracted, truncated and/or depersonalised. A determination of whether any of the supplied information could be termed confidential and the details of any specific measures required to protect it from misuse, leakage, etc.
- The format and form in which the data is to be provided.
- A determination of whether any of the supplied data is either personal data or sensitive data (per the prevailing Data Protection legislation and regulations). If so:
  - Include assurances that the appropriate consent to disclose was obtained by the relevant Data Controller.
  - Insert a clause to the effect that "it is the responsibility of all parties to this information sharing agreement to ensure that they are properly registered to exchange information as required by the prevailing Data Protection law and that they will adhere to the eight defined Data Protection principles".
  - Include a further clause to the effect that "the extent of any personal information disclosed will be limited to that which is relevant to the purpose or purposes for which the information was requested and shared only with appropriate parties".
  - The details of any known potential secondary disclosure of information which, if applicable, should be the subject of specific limiting conditions.
- Frequency of data provision or update.
- The information security arrangements to be applied (i.e. encryption, the method of transfer (via secure network), personal collection, etc.).
- The security obligations of the recipient organisation(s) including:
  - Ensuring that their employees are able to access the provided data in accordance with the principle of "need to know";

- Ensuring that it is a condition of employment that employees will abide by their rules and policies in relation to the protection and use of confidential information and that any failure, by an individual, to adhere to the prevailing rules will be dealt with as a disciplinary offence.
- Ensuring that their employees are appropriately trained so that they understand their responsibilities for confidentiality and privacy;
- Providing adequate physical and logical security arrangements;
- Ensuring that the data is only retained for a period necessary to fulfil the defined requirements and purpose and that it will be securely and irreversibly destroyed upon completion of the task;
- Ensuring that all parties are promptly informed of any loss of data or other breaches of security and are subsequently kept informed of the ongoing investigations, conclusions and outcomes.

- Comments on the quality of the supplied data (including the measures taken to ensure such quality), whether there are any potential deficiencies in the data quality and the requirement to advise if any data errors are noted so as to enable prompt correction.
- Incorporate appropriate disclaimers, such as "Data providers will not be liable for any financial or other costs incurred by other parties to the agreement as a result of any information being wrongly disclosed by another party to the agreement or as a result of any negligent act or omission by another party to the agreement".
- Defining a process for dealing with complaints from Data Subjects.
- Arrangements for collectively reviewing the Information Sharing Agreement and updating it in line with emerging best practice and technical improvements, etc.

Control Objectives for Data Transfer and Sharing

(a) To ensure that all transfers and sharing of data are lawful and appropriate.

(b) To ensure that all employees are aware of the appropriate situations where they are permitted to share or transfer data either internally or externally.

(c) To ensure that personal, sensitive, protected, restricted and confidential data is appropriately identified, secured and dealt with.

(d) To ensure that the conditions and processes relating to the day-to-day and established internal transfer, sharing and movement of data are incorporated into documented procedures.

(e) To ensure that the optimum and secure means and media are used to transport data.

> (f) To ensure that all parties to external sharing arrangements are clear about their respective responsibilities and obligations.
>
> (g) To ensure that all external transfers of data are the subject of an agreed, signed and binding Information Sharing Agreement.

Risk and Control Issues for Data Transfer and Sharing

1 Key Issues

1.1 What action has management taken to ensure that all internal and external transfers and sharing of data is appropriate and lawful?

1.2 How is management assured that all employees are appropriately aware of the circumstances when data can and cannot be transferred or shared? In addition, how is this evidenced?

1.3 How does management ensure that all external recipients of corporate data will comply with good practice and the required standards?

1.4 What specific actions are taken to ensure that all external transfers of data will be compliant with the prevailing Data Protection requirements?

1.5 How does management go about evaluating, justifying and authorising potential data transfer or sharing arrangements?

1.6 What action is taken to recognise, minimise or negate any risks associated with the transfer of data outside of the organisation?

1.7 How can management be sure that external partners have in place all the required mechanisms to handle, store, use, secure and dispose of data transferred to them?

1.8 Has a clear view of required levels of security and custodial care for all categories of data been established, and if so how is compliance assured?

1.9 What specific measures would prevent unauthorised access to data in the event the relevant files or media were either lost, stolen or misplaced?

1.10 What processes would ensure that the most appropriate form of ISA is applied in every case?

2 Detailed Issues

2.1 How would management be made aware of any unlawful or inappropriate transfer or sharing of corporate data?

2.2 How is employee understanding of the issues surrounding appropriate practices for data transfers evaluated and tested?

2.3 What specific measures would prevent an employee from either intentionally or unintentionally releasing data to an authorised party?

2.4 What would specifically prevent the establishment of an unauthorised transfer of data?

2.5 What specific measures would prevent the data supplied to an external party from being either abused or used beyond the legitimate purpose?

2.6 How can management be sure that supplied information is securely and appropriately destroyed or disposed of after it has fulfilled its purpose?

2.7 What mechanisms would prevent the use of an unsuitable or unbalanced form of ISA?

2.8 What measures would prevent the establishment of an external transfer or sharing of data in the absence of an agreed ISA?

2.9 How does management ensure that all ISAs are ratified and formally signed off by all parties?

2.10 Can management be sure that the other parties have sufficient and appropriate forms of indemnity in the event of the organisation's data being compromised by others?

47
Legal Responsibilities

There is an increasing pattern of legislative and regulatory involvement in matters related to IT and information in general. Although where it grants and protects personal rights or ensures fair and secure treatment of information, such control is seen as a positive force, it can place an additional strain on an organisation that is then compelled to jump through a succession of variously sized hoops in order to be compliant and avoid any adverse financial, operational or reputation impacts.

This is not the appropriate place to go into great detail about all the possible national, regional, industry or sector-specific variations for legal and regulatory matters relating to IT and information; indeed it would be a dubious and taxing exercise for any single volume. However, we are more concerned with the generic requirement for any organisation to be sufficiently aware of all its specific legal and regulatory requirements (in relation to matters of IT and Information Management) as a firm basis for effectively dealing with them and avoiding the associated downsides.

For the purposes of illustration, the following table (Figure 47.1) incorporates (hopefully all of) the legislation and regulation that affect a local government authority in the UK (relative to information).

Control Objectives for Legal Responsibilities

> (a) To ensure that the organisation takes due account of all relevant legal and regulatory requirements pertaining to its use and management of information and information technology.
>
> (b) To ensure comprehensive compliance with all legislative and regulatory requirements relating to information and information technology matters.
>
> (c) To proactively avoid or mitigate any risks or adverse impacts associated with breaches of relevant laws and regulations.

Legislation or Regulation	IT and Information Aspects Affected
The Freedom of Information Act 2000	Public access to public sector information
The Human Rights Act 1998	Right to privacy and confidentiality
The Electronic Communications Act 2000	Cryptography, electronic signatures
The Regulation of Investigatory Powers Act 2000	Covert monitoring of performance through metric data; monitoring of Internet activity filtration of email content or access to email account
The Data Protection Act 1998	Protection and use of personal information
The Copyright Designs and Patents Act 1988	Software piracy, music downloads, theft of corporate data
The Computer Misuse Act 1990	Hacking and unauthorised access
Local Government Acts 1972 and 1974	Records Management
Local Government (Records) Act 1962	Records Management
Local Government (Access to Records) Act 1985	Records Management
Public Records Acts 1958 and 1967	Records Management
Public Interest Disclosure Act	Records Management
Obscene Publications Act 1959 and 1964	Defines the types of material that it is unlawful to possess, publish, sell or make available
The Environmental Information Regulations 2004	Public access to information relating to the environment
The Re-use of Public Sector Information Regulations 2005	The local authority's ability to sell certain data sets for commercial gain
Telecommunications (Lawful Business Practice) (Interception of Communications) Regulations 2000	Accessing communications systems or hacking in
Limitation Act 1980	Defines the various periods of limitation for various legal processes

Figure 47.1 Legislation and regulations affecting local government authorities

Risk and Control Issues for Legal Responsibilities

1 Key Issues

1.1 How is management assured that they possess a comprehensive and up-to-date knowledge of all the IT and information laws and regulations that relate to the organisation?

1.2 What steps have been taken to ensure that all compliance issues have been identified?

1.3 What mechanisms are in place to ensure that actual compliance to the required level is achieved in practice?

1.4 How would management be alerted to actual or suspected legal or regulatory breaches?

2 Detailed Issues

2.1 How are staff expected to be aware of all the legal and regulatory issues in relation to IT and information? How is this evidenced?

2.2 Is there any independent assessment of the level of understanding and compliance with legislative and regulatory issues?

48
Facilities Management

The trend for outsourcing extends to IT activities, especially where an organisation wishes to concentrate its internal resources upon the key operational and business activities that it is best placed to handle. The outsourcing of IT activities is normally referred to as facilities management (FM), where an external organisation takes over the day-to-day running of such functions as centralised computer operations, system development or system maintenance. In some instances, this transfer of responsibility includes the transfer of the employing organisation's former staff in the relative area.

The application of facilities management solutions can remove the onerous and often costly need for the organisation to maintain specialist staff skills and equipment. This off-loading can free resources and funding which can be concentrated on more worthwhile activities; for example, the development of new products and services designed to enhance the continued efficiency and survival of the organisation.

The engagement of an FM contractor should be preceded by an accurate determination of the relevant IT service requirements including consideration of service levels, required quality standards, etc.

Control Objectives for Facilities Management

(a) To ensure that the IT requirements are accurately determined and the optimum solution is adopted.

(b) To ensure that the use of facilities management solutions is fully assessed, justified and authorised as part of the strategic direction for IT.

(c) To ensure that the required service levels and performance criteria are accurately determined and addressed by the FM contractor.

(d) To ensure that the selected FM contractor is stable, reliable and capable of delivering the required services.

(e) To ensure that the contractual arrangements accurately and appropriately define the respective responsibilities, rights and liabilities.

(f) To ensure that adequate and effective security will be exercised over the organisation's systems and data in order to protect its business operations.

(g) To ensure that the ownership of hardware, software, systems and data is clearly defined.

(h) To ensure that cost and performance measures are monitored against targets and that prompt action is taken in the event of shortfalls, etc.

(i) To ensure that adequate and proven contingency and disaster recovery arrangements are in place to protect the ongoing business operations.

(j) To ensure that all transactions and processing are accurately trailed and accounted for.

(k) To ensure that any proposed operational changes or developments are subject to prior mutual agreement and authorisation.

(l) To ensure that adequate operational and quality standards are in place.

(m) To ensure that any migration to third party FM arrangements is adequately planned for and implemented.

Risk and Control Issues for Facilities Management

1 Key Issues

1.1 How has management determined that the use of FM services is appropriate and justified?

1.2 How is management sure that the optimum FM solution has been selected?

1.3 Is the use of FM services subject to formal authorisation (and how is this evidenced)?

1.4 How does management ensure that the required levels of service and cost saving are accurately identified, addressed and achieved?

1.5 How is management assured that the selected FM contractor is stable, reliable and fully capable of providing the required service(s)?

1.6 Have all the relevant responsibilities, rights and liabilities been fairly allocated between the parties and accurately reflected in the contractual documents?

1.7 How can management be assured that adequate and effective security will be exercised over company systems and data?

1.8 Has management clearly established the ownership of hardware, general software and specific company systems?

1.9 How does management ensure that cost and performance targets are actually achieved?

1.10 Has management confirmed that adequate (and regularly tested) contingency plans are in place to protect ongoing processing and service provision?

1.11 Are measures in place to ensure that all new systems or process amendments are subject to prior agreement, authorisation and effective testing?

1.12 Is the FM contractor responsible for ensuring that all processing is subject to accurate and adequate trailing?

1.13 How does management ensure that the migration to FM services is adequately planned and implemented in order to minimise disruption, etc.?

2 Detailed Issues

2.1 Have all the viable alternatives to FM been fully assessed?

2.2 What measures prevent the unauthorised establishment or amendment of FM arrangements?

2.3 How does management monitor that the selected FM contractor operates to recognised and appropriate quality and performance standards (and are such standards defined in the contractual documents)?

2.4 What specific measures prevent unauthorised amendment of (or access to) the organisation's systems and data?

2.5 What measures ensure that any cost or performance shortcomings are promptly identified and effectively reacted to?

2.6 How does management ensure that the required service levels are actually achieved?

49

System Development

Beyond the common generic types of business systems (e.g. payroll, general ledger, word processing), organisations will often have the need for very specific types of computer application system to support their particular business and operational needs. For example, a hotel will require a room booking, allocation and billing system, and a local government authority may require a property rental or housing repairs system.

A requirement to develop a new application can be addressed in a number of ways, for example using an in-house system development team, adapting an existing application or by going out to tender to a number of external software development companies. The maintenance of a dedicated in-house development team can be expensive, partly because it is necessary to maintain the staff skill levels in a constantly evolving technical environment. In either case, the costs of such system developments may represent a considerable investment for the organisation. Development projects should be fully appraised, justified and subject to proficient project management techniques with defined testing stages, so that the output system is seen to be reliable, secure and robust.

The following points are designed so that they can be applied in a variety of different development scenarios.

Control Objectives for System Development

> (a) To ensure that all systems developments are authorised and in accord with the IT strategic objectives.
>
> (b) To ensure that all developments are assessed and justified on business, cost and benefit grounds.
>
> (c) To ensure that an adequate structured and secure systems development environment is provided and maintained.
>
> (d) To ensure that adequate and appropriately skilled development staff are provided to support the creation and maintenance of reliable systems.

(e) To ensure that systems are developed to a stable and recognised standard.

(f) To ensure that users are adequately represented in the realistic and accurate definition of functional requirements.

(g) To ensure that systems are secure and offer suitable protection of data and business interests.

(h) To ensure that development projects are effectively managed and are delivered on time and within budget.

(i) To ensure that all systems are fully and satisfactorily tested prior to live use.

(j) To ensure that systems are accurately and appropriately documented in order to support their ongoing maintenance.

(k) To ensure that systems are effectively implemented and all considerations and impacts are appropriately taken into account.

(l) To ensure that the required benefits and performance requirements are actually achieved.

Risk and Control Issues for System Development

1 Key Issues

1.1 Has management established the authorised strategic direction for information technology within the organisation, and are all systems developments authorised in relation to this agreed strategy?

1.2 How does management ensure that all systems developments are justified and authorised (i.e. on cost, business or benefit grounds)?

1.3 What steps has management taken to provide a secure and stable environment for the development of systems (i.e. the provision of recognised development methodologies and standards)?

1.4 How can management ensure that only stable, reliable and secure systems are developed?

1.5 What measures ensure that the relevant staff skills are acquired and maintained to support the creation of appropriate systems?

1.6 What measures ensure that accurate and appropriate system requirements and functional specifications are used as the basis for developments?

1.7 How does management ensure that delivered systems provide adequate protection of data from misuse and unauthorised access?

1.8 What action is taken to ensure that development projects are efficiently managed and delivered on time and within budget?

1.9 How does management verify that delivered systems conform to the agreed requirements and are free from errors?

1.10 What measures are in place to document systems accurately and comprehensively so that they can be maintained efficiently?

1.11 How does management identify all the implications and impacts of systems under development and plan for their successful and smooth introduction?

1.12 Are all developments monitored and reviewed after completion to ensure that all the anticipated benefits (i.e. cost savings or performance improvements) are actually achieved?

2 Detailed Issues

2.1 What specific measures would prevent the development of unauthorised or inappropriate IT systems?

2.2 Are developments that involve the acquisition of new hardware platforms, development tools or skills subject to appropriate prior assessment and authorisation (and how is this evidenced)?

2.3 Are all major system developments subject to formal feasibility study, financial assessment and/or authorisation?

2.4 What measures ensure that systems are developed to an acceptable quality?

2.5 How does management ensure that system specifications take sufficient account of the users?

2.6 Are documented system specifications provided as the basis for all development projects (and are they subject to formal prior authorisation)?

2.7 Has management established a data security and access policy, and if so how is this enforced during systems development projects?

2.8 How does management ensure that program coding is of an acceptable quality and satisfactorily addresses the authorised requirements?

2.9 Are all development projects related to authorised budget and targets, and how does management ensure that projects are delivered within the agreed limits?

2.10 How is management made aware of project delays and shortfalls, and is this done promptly?

2.11 Does management ensure that all new systems are fully tested to the satisfaction of users prior to live usage (and if so, how is this evidenced)?

2.12 Have system documentation standards been adopted, and if so how is compliance assured?

2.13 Where external resources are used in a development project, how does management ensure that all the required quality, specification and performance issues are satisfactorily addressed?

50
Software Selection

This chapter contrasts with the previous one in that it is concerned with the selection of software solutions from outside contractors and this normally relates to fairly general types of computer system (e.g. a stock control system) rather than the specialised system requirements normally addressed by either bespoke or substantially modified developments.

In opting to source software externally, management will be looking to ensure that the suppliers are stable, reliable and capable of satisfying their needs.

Control Objectives for Software Selection

> (a) To ensure that the acquisition of software is justified, authorised and accords with the agreed IT strategic direction.
>
> (b) To ensure that all software is reliable, secure, flexible, and adequately supported.
>
> (c) To ensure that software suppliers are stable and able to provide ongoing product support.
>
> (d) To ensure that all impacts and costs associated with the acquisition of software are accurately identified and addressed.
>
> (e) To ensure that the optimum software solution is selected.
>
> (f) To ensure that staff are adequately trained and supported in the efficient use of software.

Risk and Control Issues for Software Selection

1 Key Issues

1.1 Are all software acquisitions subject to formal assessment, justification and authorisation (and how is this evidenced)?

1.2 How does management ensure that acquired software conforms to the agreed IT strategy and established platforms, etc.?

1.3 How does management ensure that only reliable, proven and secure software products are acquired?

1.4 How does management confirm that the optimum software solution is selected (and are all possible solutions examined)?

1.5 What steps does management take to confirm the stability and reliability of potential software suppliers?

1.6 How does management confirm that software suppliers are capable of providing suitable product support (including implementation and staff training where necessary)?

1.7 Upon what basis are market solutions sought (i.e. are requirement specifications used to assess software suitability)?

1.8 How does management ensure that all the costs and implications of software acquisition are assessed and authorised?

1.9 Are software products subject to formalised testing and the achievement of satisfactory results prior to purchase being authorised?

1.10 Does management ensure that adequate user support facilities (including documentation and training) are provided in order to maximise the benefits of the system?

1.11 What measures ensure that the implementation of the new software is adequately planned for and that appropriate resources are made available?

2 Detailed Issues

2.1 What specific measures prevent the acquisition of unauthorised and poor quality software packages?

2.2 Is due account taken of the market position and reputation of the software supplier?

2.3 Are existing users contacted for their comments about the software prior to acquisition?

2.4 How does management ensure that software products have a demonstrable upgrade path relevant to the platforms used within the organisation?

2.5 Are the costs of future product upgrades and staff training accurately assessed prior to purchase?

2.6 If changes or enhancements to the standard product are deemed necessary, are they and the associated costs subject to prior justification and authorisation (and how is this evidenced)?

2.7 Are performance shortcomings (in actual use) detected and resolved?

51

Contingency Planning

As an organisation's dependence on IT grows, the development of suitable contingency arrangements in the event of major incidents can become vital to ensure the ongoing operation or survival of the organisation. The contingency solution chosen will, in part, depend on the extent and degree of risks associated with major IT-related failures.

The UK Government's 2008 survey of UK companies[1] reported that 48% of disaster recovery plans had not been tested in the last year and that 52% of the surveyed companies did not carry out any formal security risk assessment.

Control Objectives for Contingency Planning

> (a) To ensure that adequate and effective contingency plans have been established to support the prompt recovery of crucial IT facilities in the event of major failure or disaster.
>
> (b) To ensure the survival of the business and to minimise the implications of a major IT failure.
>
> (c) To ensure that all the potential risks to the IT facility are identified and assessed in preparation of the contingency plans.
>
> (d) To ensure the optimum contingency arrangements are selected and cost-effectively provided.
>
> (e) To ensure that an authorised and documented disaster recovery plan is created, kept up to date, and securely stored.
>
> (f) To ensure that the recovery plan is periodically tested for its relevance and effectiveness.
>
> (g) To ensure that all internal and external parties to the recovery process are fully aware of their responsibilities and commitments.

> (h) To ensure that appropriate liaison is maintained with external parties (i.e. insurers, emergency services, suppliers, etc.).
>
> (i) To ensure that both the damaged and recovery sites are secure and that IT systems are securely operated in support of the business.
>
> (j) To ensure that systems and procedures are adequately and accurately documented to aid the recovery process.
>
> (k) To ensure that public and media relations would be addressed effectively during an emergency in order to minimise adverse publicity and business implications.

Risk and Control Issues for Contingency Planning

1 Key Issues

1.1 What measures are in place to prevent, avoid or minimise the potential for a disaster befalling the IT facility?

1.2 Has management given formal consideration to the potential for an IT-related disaster, the relevant risks and the implications for the business operations?

1.3 What action has management taken to plan for dealing with the effects of a major failure or disaster affecting the IT installation?

1.4 How is management assured that the prescribed contingency arrangements would lead to the prompt and effective recovery of IT services?

1.5 How can management be certain that the current contingency arrangements are the most appropriate and cost-effective in the circumstances?

1.6 How does management ensure that the recovery arrangements remain up to date?

1.7 How is management certain that all affected parties (internal and external) are fully aware of their responsibilities and commitments in the event of a disaster?

1.8 Has the recovery plan been formally documented (and if so, how are the copies protected from loss or damage so that they would remain accessible in the event of a disaster)?

1.9 What measures would ensure that systems and data could promptly be rebuilt (and is this capability regularly tested)?

1.10 Has provision been made to deal effectively with media and public relations in the event of a disaster, so that the image and reputation of the business is appropriately maintained?

2 Detailed Issues

2.1 Have matters of physical security, fire prevention, detection and control within the IT installation been effectively addressed in order to reduce the possibility of a disaster?

2.2 Has management taken steps to identify the most vulnerable and crucial aspects of the IT and business operations?

2.3 What measures have been taken to ensure that IT facilities would promptly be re-established?

2.4 Has management identified the minimum level of IT service required in order to maintain business operations (and the means to ensure that this level can be reinstated and/or maintained)?

2.5 Has management accurately determined the critical timescale following a disaster, during which IT services must be recovered in order for the business to survive?

2.6 Has management authorised a recovery plan and fully documented the related actions and responsibilities?

2.7 How does management ensure that this documented plan is accurately kept up to date?

2.8 Were all the possible recovery and contingency options assessed and costed as the basis for selecting the optimum solution?

2.9 Has management sought and obtained commitments in writing from key suppliers and contractors as to their level of response in the event of an IT-related disaster (and are these kept up to date)?

2.10 Has the recovery plan been subject to regular and realistic testing in order to confirm that it remains appropriate?

2.11 How is management assured that adequate and appropriate insurance cover is in place to address both the direct losses and the business impacts of an IT-related disaster?

2.12 Are up-to-date copies of the recovery plan and all other system and procedural documentation securely stored and accessible?

NOTE

1. *2008 Information Security Breaches Survey*, Department for Business, Enterprise and Regulatory Reform (2008), www.berr.gov.uk.

52
Human Resources Information Security

In this chapter we consider the various issues relating to the checking and vetting of potential IT users and those involved in dealing with information, so as to ensure that they can be suitably authorised to access data and systems.

We focus upon the processes that should be followed prior to employing an individual and/or granting that person access to corporate information and systems. In addition to obvious and standard human resources pre-employment checks, we also consider what prior training and preparation may be necessary for all new employees.

This lead-in to the induction process should ensure that new staff are appropriately aware of what they can and can't do in relation to their use of IT facilities and the organisation's information assets and thus contribute to the secure use of such assets.

The overall objective is to ensure that only appropriate and trustworthy staff are engaged and only suitably vetted users are permitted access to information.

There is a natural chain of top-level events associated with the supporting processes, as follows:

- Prior to granting access to information, checks will be conducted to ensure that the individual is suitable to access the organisation's information and IT systems. Any individual who, for whatever reason, fails to jump this primary hurdle should not be allowed to continue with their application to join the organisation
- Prior to and during the period when the user is granted access to information and systems, they will be appropriately trained, guided, mentored and monitored for levels of understanding of the prescribed methods for the secure use of information and associated systems. (NB: Some of the supporting training can either be provided prior to the employee taking up his/her full duties, as part of an induction period or on-the-job.) During this stage, the access rights can be assessed against the employee's progress and level of understanding.
- During the term of their employment, employees' access rights may have to be amended in line with any changes of duty or responsibilities. (This aspect should be catered for during the normal management processes in place to control access to systems.)

- When the employee either decides to leave the organisation, is the subject of any disciplinary action or suspected of misconduct, their access rights should be terminated in a controlled and systematic way.

The following detailed points will need to be taken into account during the overall process described above:

Role Related Access Rights

The prior determination, in consultation with the relevant system owner(s), of the specific access rights to be granted for all the potential roles.

Responsibilities for Creating New Users, Amending and Disabling Access Rights

The clear allocation of responsibilities for:

- Promptly advising IT of new users and the required access rights for the user's role;
- Obtaining the required authority for setting up, amending or disabling a user's access rights;
- Promptly advising IT of the need to amend access rights;
- Promptly advising IT of the need to disable or withdraw access rights (perhaps in urgent situations where malpractice is either suspected or detected);
- Actually applying the set-up, amendment and deletion of user access rights;
- Ongoing monitoring to ensure that users and their access rights are accurately maintained up to date and in association with the user's current duties.

Defining a User's Information Security Responsibilities

- This level of definition will be driven by the maturity of the organisation's Information Management and IT security environment and how it is defined in extant policies, procedures, standards, etc.
- Once agreed, for a specific role or a range of roles, the responsibilities should be formally adopted within the relevant job descriptions or contracts of employment, so that the potential employee is aware, before commencing their duties, of their specific and general responsibilities for IT and information security.
- In any event, there should be a formal process for the user to signify their understanding and acceptance of the requirements. This formality may be preceded by training or access to the relevant policies and supporting guidance.

User Screening

- Prior to confirming the employment of an individual, the relevant pre-engagement and background verification checks should be conducted, including, as appropriate:
  - The level of checks to be performed should be pre-determined and proportionate to the role in question and any associated risks to the organisation.

- Any checks made must be lawful and have regard for any standing regulations, codes of conduct of statements of ethics.
- The verification checks may include, but are not necessarily limited to, the following. Some of the items listed may be relevant to potential users of higher classifications of information, those who will be authorised to access secure networks and databases or to conduct system administration tasks:
  - Verification of the applicant's recent and contiguous employment history for a specified minimum period;
  - Obtaining two satisfactory employment references for the last two positions held;
  - Obtaining a satisfactory personal or character reference from a suitable and reliable source;
  - Checking the accuracy and completeness of the contents of the application form;
  - Sighting evidence of the claimed academic and professional qualifications (and confirming their currency);
  - Confirming the applicant's eligibility and right to work in the country without limitations;
  - Verifying the identity of the candidate against a passport, national identity document or other reliable source that incorporates a photograph;
  - Verification of nationality and immigration status;
  - Sight of:
    1. A national driving licence
    2. Birth certificate
    3. Proof of residence
  - Obtaining formal Government Security Clearance
  - Verification of Criminal Record
- In the UK, it is acceptable practice in the public sector or where an employee will have some interaction with children, vulnerable adults or sizeable amounts of cash, to conduct a Criminal Records Bureau (CRB) check. These CRB checks should detect whether anyone has a notable criminal record or any history of paedophilia or sexual crimes. The necessity to carry out such checks will be in proportion to the anticipated role of the applicant. That the information supplied by the candidate will be used as the basis for such a check must be brought to the candidate's attention and their consent formally obtained. In addition, application forms may contain specific questions about unspent prior convictions and the CRB check will also determine if such declared information is accurate.
- The organisation may deem it necessary to obtain the applicant's signature on a Confidentiality Statement to the effect that they understand the nature and sensitivity of the information they will access and use, that they will not use any information for unauthorised purposes and that they must return or destroy any information when their employment terminates.

- The organisation should consider the provision of training and supporting materials covering the relevant aspects of IT and information security and management. In addition, it should be management's responsibility to ensure that staff are adequately trained and especially aware of any legal or regulatory issues related to their use of information and systems.

As can be seen above, many of these processes and stages are likely to be performed outwith the operational department and the IT section, so it is important that the whole process is suitably orchestrated and coordinated in order to be effective and efficient. It is also important that the Human Resources service has in place the appropriate and lawful recruitment policies to support the objectives of information and IT security. The end result should be the engagement and employment of trustworthy, honest and reliable employees who understand their responsibilities and obligations relating to information and IT systems.

Control Objectives for Human Resources Information Security

(a) To ensure that the standard access rights for each employee position are agreed and defined as the basis for subsequent user administration.

(b) To ensure that granted access rights are always provided on the agreed and authorised basis.

(c) To ensure that the set-up, amendment, disabling or removal of access rights is only undertaken when suitably authorised.

(d) To ensure that the actual creation and amendment of access rights is independently administered.

(e) To ensure that current users and their allocated access rights are periodically reviewed to verify the accuracy and currency of access arrangements.

(f) To ensure that only suitably qualified, honest, reliable and trustworthy employees are engaged and granted access to systems and information.

(g) To ensure that the employee's responsibilities and obligations for IT and information security are clearly established, acknowledged and accepted by the employee.

(h) To ensure that comprehensive training and support materials are provided in order that employees have the knowledge necessary to protect and lawfully use the organisation's information assets.

(i) To ensure that access rights are removed or disabled at the point when an employee leaves the organisation.

(j) To ensure the prompt removal or suppression of all access rights of any employee who is either suspected of or is proven to have been engaged in malpractice, etc.

Risk and Control Issues for Human Resources Information Security

1 Key Issues

1.1 What steps are taken to ensure that all users have access rights commensurate with their roles and duties?

1.2 How can management be assured that all users are actually set up with the agreed access rights?

1.3 Has management established an independent process for the administration and maintenance of all users and their access rights? In addition, is the accuracy and status of such rights periodically verified?

1.4 What measures are taken to confirm the honesty, integrity and trustworthiness of potential employees?

1.5 What measures are in place to confirm the accuracy of claimed education and professional qualifications?

1.6 What measures are applied to prevent the engagement of an employee who does not have the right to work?

1.7 What action is taken to ensure that new employees are adequately aware of all their responsibilities and obligations in respect of IT and information security? How is this evidenced?

1.8 How can management be certain that any employee either suspected of or proven to have been engaged in acts of malpractice has had their access rights promptly removed or disabled?

2 Detailed Issues

2.1 How would management be made aware of any users with nonstandard, unauthorised or inappropriate access rights?

2.2 What mechanisms are in place to ensure that all changes to defined access rights are suitably authorised?

2.3 How would management be alerted to any users who have left the organisation but still have live access rights?

2.4 How can management be sure that the identity and validity of employees is assured?

2.5 What measures are applied to ensure that the organisation is in compliance with all the legislative and regulatory requirements relating to the recruitment, vetting and engagement of its employees?

2.6 What specific precautions would prevent the engagement of an employee with an unsuitable criminal record?

2.7 Have effective mechanisms for training, guiding and supporting employees in respect of IT and information security matters been established and applied? In addition, what process specifically ensures that such action is actually applied in every case?

53
Monitoring and Logging

The monitoring and logging of IT systems and the actions of employees normally fall into one of the following categories:

- Activity logging within application systems (i.e. specific transactions logged against the relevant user ID and time/date stamped).
- Logging (within applications, operating systems or network software systems) of higher level system administration activities (i.e. amending standing data parameters, setting up new users or amending access rights).
- Operating system logging of basic operations or actions (i.e. file copying, file deletion or sending files to a printer).
- Proactive monitoring in order to detect or prevent an event (i.e. checking for infected email attachments, prevention of access to unsuitable Internet sites or monitoring employee performance through the collection of metrics related to activities and the time taken to complete them).
- In the wider context, beyond the monitoring of systematic events, the monitoring and measurement of compliance with the Information Security Policy and other policies, procedures, laws, regulations and standards should also be considered. This can be done in a number of ways, such as:
  - utilising software that detects, records and reports actual or attempted security violations;
  - the logging of unusual events as determined by being outwith defined parameters; and
  - independent review and assessment of security procedures and processes (e.g. by internal audit, external security specialists or senior management).

The organisation is advised to have a defined and documented approach to monitoring and logging which takes into account the likely associated risks, the IT resource implications, the need to ensure compliance with policies and procedures, and matters of the legality of such monitoring.

Logging activities in most application and operating software can often be at a very low level of functionality and so it is necessary to assess and determine the optimum level required in each case. This process of setting the level of required monitoring should be undertaken alongside a realistic assessment of the risks and impacts that could apply if the logged or monitored action or event were to materialise. (For example, if the sales tax rate is inadvertently amended so as to be unlawful; a key archive file is deleted; or an employee is attempting to gain access to an unsuitable Internet site).

Logging, if at too low a level, can be very resource hungry and lead to the accumulation of large log files (that perhaps will only be rarely examined) that take up storage capacity. In addition, the process of extensive logging may have adverse impacts on system performance and reaction times, thus impinging on operations. One key issue in setting the right logging level is how likely it is that you will need to use that logged data. This consideration will vary in relation to the type of system involved and the situations you are attempting to identify or isolate. For example, systems constructed around relational database technologies will often log each amendment of a record so that, if necessary in the event of an incident occurring, the data can be rolled back or forward to realign the database; in such systems, the suppression of the logging activity could jeopardise the ability to recover from a problem event.

If possible, and to avoid undue resource or performance impacts, logging should be tailored to a range of specified exceptions. If this defined extraction of events of interest were linked to the generation of appropriately periodic reports, management monitoring and oversight could be applied.

IT logs are often referred to as Audit Logs and it is suggested that these are retained for at least six months before being removed. This period should be ample enough for most operational purposes; however, the level of normal management scrutiny and monitoring applied should also be taken into account when defining the shelf life of system logs.

Access to the logs must be protected from unauthorised access that could result in recorded information being altered or deleted. System administrators must be prevented from erasing or deactivating logs of their own activity.

As a minimum audit logs should contain the following information:

- System identity
- User ID
- Successful/Unsuccessful login
- Successful/Unsuccessful logoff
- Unauthorised application access
- Changes to system configurations
- Use of privileged accounts (e.g. account management, policy changes, device configuration).

Automated logs can be supplemented by the maintenance of documented manual logs in some instances, for example the action undertaken by IT Operational Staff or Operators. This type of manual log may include the recording of such events as:

- Back-up timings and details of exchange of backup tape
- System event start and finish times and who was involved
- System errors (nature of error, date, time) and corrective action taken.

These operations logs, which it is suggested should be retained for at least six months, can be used as the basis of periodic checks applied by the IT Security Officer so as to ensure that the correct procedures are being followed and appropriate actions have been taken.

The logging, recording and reporting of events or conditions will only be effective if there is sufficient and effective management review and reaction in place. The follow-up of reported anomalies should be part of the normal management activities.

Control Objectives for Monitoring and Logging

> (a) To ensure that appropriate and effective levels of system activity and event logging are agreed and applied.
>
> (b) To ensure the prompt and adequate reaction to logged events that are unexpected, unusual, suspicious, harmful or noncompliant with extant regulations, policies or procedures.

Risk and Control Issues for Monitoring and Logging

Key Issues

1.1 What steps have been taken to identify and assess the inherent systematic logging and monitoring capabilities of systems?

1.2 How is management assured that appropriate and adequate logging and monitoring is in place?

1.3 How is management assured that all the identified logging and monitoring is actually applied?

1.4 How would management be alerted to the temporary or permanent disabling of logging processes?

1.5 How can management be sure that archived log files are retained for the specified period?

1.6 What measures would actively prevent the unauthorised amendment of or tampering with log files? In addition, how would management be alerted to such unauthorised events?

1.7 By what means would management be alerted to possible breaches of IT and information security requirements as evidenced by logged activities?

Detailed Issues

2.1 What steps have been taken to ensure the setting, agreement and application of optimum levels of logging and monitoring? In addition, how is this evidenced?

2.2 What measures would prevent (or at worst detect) the premature deletion of log files? In addition, how would management be made aware of such situations?

2.3 Is the performance of systems monitored so that any undue degradation caused by excessive levels of logging will be detected?

2.4 How can management be assured that sufficient levels of detail are being recorded in the logs to facilitate effective follow-up or investigations?

2.5 Where appropriate, how does management ensure that manual logs of IT events are accurate, up to date and complete?

2.6 How are staff and managers expected to monitor logs and take appropriate action?

54

Information Security Incidents

Information security incidents can take many forms, for example: unauthorised access to systems and data; hacking into systems; the corruption of data through the use of viruses or malware; unauthorised disclosure of data; failure to securely dispose of information; the loss or theft of information assets; breaches of confidentiality, and so on. There is no realistic ability to construct a guaranteed 100 % secure IT and information environment as so many variables are involved including the sometimes irrational and unpredictable behaviour of human beings.

Other specific IT chapters in this section cover the types of IT and information security and management measures that will either mitigate against incidents occurring or limit their adverse impacts. Accordingly, this chapter avoids repeating the details of the preventative and detective controls and focuses upon awareness of incidents, their effective management and monitoring.

We start by providing some indications of the level of incidents and the degree to which companies in the UK are taking steps to prevent and detect breaches. Then we provide some real life examples of breaches as reported in the UK media and as compiled in the United States. Finally in this chapter, we provide some guidance relating to the set-up and operation of an information security incident reporting system.

UK Survey Results on IT/Information Security Incidents and Actions

The 2008 BERR survey of UK companies[1] noted that of the companies surveyed:

- 56 % logged and responded to security incidents.
- 63 % had contingency plans for dealing with possible security breaches.
- 34 % had specialist insurance policies covering damage suffered from cybercrime or viruses.
- 45 % had a security incident.
- 23 % had an accidental security incident.
- 35 % had a malicious security incident.
- 26 % had a serious incident.

- 6% had suffered a confidentiality breach.
- 9% had had customers impersonated (i.e. after identity theft).
- 10% of those companies that accepted payments through their website did not encrypt them.
- 38% of the worst incidents were caused externally (62% therefore being internally caused).
- 14% suffered infection by viruses or malicious software (where 84% of such incidents were associated with virus, worm or Trojan infection and 16% related to spyware).
- 16% reported staff misuse of information systems. The percentage of the total surveyed companies categorised the type of misuse as follows:
  - 14% misuse of web access
  - 7% misuse of email access
  - 2% unauthorised access to systems or data (i.e. using someone else's ID)
  - 1% breaching of Data Protection laws or regulations
  - 1% breach of confidentiality (i.e. intellectual property or customer data).
- 16% were attacked by an unauthorised outsider.
- 4% reported theft or fraud involving computers.
- 3% reported that the worst incident hadn't generated any media coverage but some customers had complained.
- 23% reported a system failure or data corruption.

UK Examples of IT/Information Security Incidents

The following actual IT security incidents were reported in the UK media and serve to illustrate the potential reputation and other more tangible impacts for organisations:

- In November 2007, Her Majesty's Revenue and Customs (HMRC) lost, in transit to the National Audit Office, a number of CDs containing the personal details of 25 million individuals (including their national insurance numbers and bank account details). The contents were password protected but not encrypted. The non appearance of the CDs was not promptly detected and reported to the HMRC.
- Also in November 2007, HMRC were involved in a further loss of data involving the records of 15 000 customers of a life insurance company that were being sent by the HMRC to the company using a third party courier. The unencrypted disk failed to arrive and has not been traced.
- A laptop belonging to Nationwide Building Society, which contained confidential customer information, was stolen from an employee's home in August 2006. The incident was investigated by the Financial Services Authority (FSA) who reported that Nationwide was not aware that confidential data was held on the computer and delayed investigating the situation until three weeks after the theft. The FSA imposed a fine of £1million.
- TJX Companies Inc, which operates discount retailing under a variety of trading names in the US, Canada and Europe (including TK Maxx in the UK), reported in

March 2007 that 45 million customer accounts had been compromised following hackers accessing the company's encrypted wireless LAN located in Minnesota. Details of accounts, credit and debit card transactions were affected.

US Examples of IT/Information Security Incidents

In the US, the Privacy Rights Clearinghouse[2] manages an excellent and very comprehensive Chronology of Breaches covering the period from 2005 to date, on its website: www.privacyrights.org. The listing focuses on data breaches across all sectors in the US and provides a useful insight into the various types of breaches and their impacts. We acknowledge the kind permission granted by the Privacy Rights Clearinghouse to provide the following more notable incidents that occurred in 2009:

- Network Solutions (July 2009)—Hackers accessed systems and compromised 573 000 credit and debit card transactions over a three-month period. The hackers planted malicious code which facilitated the interception of customer's personal and financial details.
- Cornell University (June 2009)—The potential unauthorized disclosure of the records of 45 000 current and former students, faculty and employees held on a computer that was stolen from the University.
- University of California (May 2009)—Hackers were able, over a period of months, to access and possibly steal some 160 000 records of current and former students, which contained Social Security Numbers and health insurance data.
- New York Police Department (February 2009)—A civilian employee of the Police Department's Pension Fund was accused of stealing eight data tapes from a back-up data warehouse after disabling the CCTV system. The tapes contained the personal details of 80 000 serving and retired Police officers.
- Arkansas Department of Information Systems/Information Vaulting Services (February 2009)—A computer tape containing personal details of 807 000 criminal background checks dating back to the mid-1990s went missing from the organisation's Data Protection vault.

Reporting and Management of IT/Information Security Incidents

The provision of an agreed and documented Information Security Incident Reporting and Management Policy or procedure should aim to provide a robust facility for identifying, reporting, recording, managing and dealing with any incident where the security and integrity of corporate systems and data has or could have been compromised. In addition to specific incidents, the reporting parameters could be extended so as to include the reporting, by any employee, of any possible information security weaknesses or shortcomings they have noticed.

Firstly there need to be suitable definitions for information security incidents and the means of their subsequent management.

An **information security incident** is an adverse event that has caused or has the potential to cause damage or harm to an organisation's information assets, operations, finances, reputation, customers, clients and employees. Incidents can include, but are not necessarily limited to, the following examples:

- Breaches of information and IT-related legislation and regulations.
- Breaches of the organisation's policies, procedures and codes of practice.
- The theft of information (irrespective of its form or format).
- The theft of corporate software (and any associated infringement of copyright and intellectual property rights).
- The illegal or inappropriate use of information assets.
- All attempts to gain unauthorised access to systems and/or information.
- Compromise or evasion of existing security control measures.
- Abuse of granted access rights.
- Unlawful or unauthorised activities relating to corporate information (i.e. in the pursuit of personal gains).
- The unlawful or unauthorised disclosure, sharing or transfer of information assets (e.g. including in hardcopy, electronically or verbally).
- Aiding, abetting, assisting or soliciting a third party to gain unauthorised access to systems and data.
- Deliberate introduction of viruses or other malware with intent to cause damage or disruption.
- Wilful or malicious changes applied to information assets (hardware, software and data) with the intention to cause damage, disruption, loss or adverse reputation impacts.
- Any methods that could mislead employees or customers into revealing their passwords, account numbers, key codes, etc. thus offering the potential to misuse related systems and data.

Information Security Incident Management relates to the identification of actual or suspected incidents, their effective containment, restoring the protection of all information assets, protecting the organisation's image and reputation and facilitating business continuity. The documented incident management procedure should incorporate, as appropriate, measures to address the following points:

- Speed is of the essence in containing and dealing effectively with incidents (for example to limit the effects of a possible virus infection or to counter the extent of unauthorised information disclosures).
- Employees should be instructed when faced with an actual or suspected incident to report it immediately to a central monitoring point such as an IT Helpdesk.
- If the incident involves personal data that may have been compromised, stolen or lost, the situation should also be reported to the nominated Data Protection Officer, who will need to be consulted throughout any investigations.
- The person initially detecting the incident should aim to capture as much relevant information as possible, for example:
  - any displayed error messages;
  - the noted effects of the problem;
  - what information or system may have been affected;
  - the circumstances leading up to and during the incident;

- whether the physical security measures were applied prior to and during the incident (e.g. doors and storage equipment securely locked and no unauthorised persons permitted in staff only areas);
- the actual or suspected involvement of others in the incident, and so on.

• The person receiving the notification of the incident should aim to capture all the key information that will subsequently aid the investigation and containment phases, for example:

- name, location, job title and telephone contact details of the person reporting the incident;
- date and time of the incident (or when it was detected or suspected);
- the location of the incident (e.g. a data storage location);
- a description of the equipment or information in question (e.g. form, format and extent);
- the type of information compromised (e.g. personal, restricted, confidential, financial, etc.);
- whether the compromising of the information puts anyone at risk or in danger;
- whether the incident risks the leakage or unlawful disclosure of personal information;
- whether electronic forms of compromised information were protected by logical security controls (i.e. file passwords or encryption);
- the asset inventory numbers of any stolen or lost hardware.

• All the incident information should be recorded, ideally in some form of electronic incident management system that facilitates trailing the grading, management, monitoring, escalation and resolution of incidents.

• Once logged, the appropriate employees or managers will need to be promptly informed of the incident and provided with all the captured information. One approach to ensuring the optimum routing of incidents would be to define the top-level categories of potential incidents and map them to key employees who normally have related responsibilities or specific knowledge to conduct the investigation. In especially complex incidents where a number of overlapping roles may apply, the overall approach should be coordinated by a suitably senior employee.

• The grading of incidents should support the escalation and associated level of management reporting required. Preprepared scenarios could include model risk assessments to aid the determination of the appropriate level of grading to apply and the key actions to apply.

• The type of incident may have image and reputation implications for the organisation. In such cases, handling enquiries from the press and other media or making official statements about the incident should only be undertaken by experienced and trained PR and Communications personnel. All other employees should be advised not to make any statements to the media but to refer any enquiries to the PR/Communications function.

• Those investigating and dealing with the incident should carefully analyse the situation and identify the potential implications and impacts.

- Depending on the seriousness and nature of the incident, it may be necessary to formally deploy the business continuity or disaster recovery plans.
- The collection of any related evidence needs to be undertaken carefully so as not to compromise or jeopardise any future disciplinary or legal action. The organisation's legal department or representative should be involved when appropriate and other guidance may be obtained from the internal audit function.
- If there are grounds for suspecting the incident is related to criminal behaviour, terrorist or coordinated attack, the decision to involve the Police (and any other relevant emergency services) should be made at the earliest opportunity by a senior manager. (NB: In some incidents, the involvement of the law enforcement services will be an obvious move, but for others, it may be better to get a more accurate picture of events before contacting them.)
- All the actions (proposed and applied) should be noted down as part of the incident documentation. In practice this may entail recording key facts and actions onto the electronic incident management system.
- There may be critical timing considerations to take into account and some means of establishing these and being alerted to them should be provided. For example the incident management system may have facilities to set and trigger event alarms or reminders (for example, to trigger the release of a press statement or to update senior management with the progress being made with resolving the incident).
- Where the involvement of employees is either suspected or proven, the organisation's disciplinary procedures should be applied, including where necessary referral of the matter to the Police for further criminal investigation and possible prosecution.
- In any event, the objectives must be to:
  - analyse the cause
  - determine the impacts and risks
  - contain the effects
  - determine a structured strategy to limit and resolve any impacts and problems
  - plan and apply the necessary corrective action
  - log progress and facilitate senior management monitoring of the situation
  - protect against any immediate repeat of the incident
  - protect the organisation's image and reputation
  - keep key staff informed
  - learn lessons from the incident and take the actions necessary to prevent a recurrence.

Control Objectives for Information Security Incidents

(a) To ensure that all employees are encouraged to be vigilant for actual or suspected information security incidents and to report them immediately.

(In addition, such vigilance should include the prompt reporting of any suspected weaknesses in the prevailing control measures.)

(b) To ensure that all actual or suspected information security incidents are promptly detected, registered and managed.

(c) To ensure the effective management of incidents and the minimising of adverse impacts.

(d) To ensure that senior management are kept informed of all significant information security incidents and the progress of investigations and remedial actions.

(e) To ensure that the organisation's image and reputation are adequately protected during and after any information-related incident.

(f) To ensure that recurrences of incidents is prevented.

(g) To ensure that information assets are adequately protected from loss, theft, corruption and unlawful or inappropriate disclosure.

(h) To ensure, when necessary, that law enforcement bodies are involved in the investigation of incidents.

(i) To ensure that any culpable employee involved in information security incidents is dealt with in accordance with the defined disciplinary procedures, including, where relevant, resultant dismissal and/or criminal prosecution.

(j) To ensure that adequate detective and preventative control measures are applied and updated in light of security incidents so as to improve their effectiveness.

Risk and Control Issues for Information Security Incidents

Key Issues

1.1 How can management be assured that employees will know how to promptly and appropriately detect and report information security incidents?

1.2 What measures are in place to promptly capture the essential details of either an actual or suspected information security incident? In addition, what is the evidence that they are or would be effective in practice?

1.3 How does management ensure that all information security incidents are reported and recorded?

1.4 How has management prepared for possible information security incidents and how they should be handled?

1.5 Have responsibilities for the recording and management oversight of incidents been clearly established?

1.6 What measures are in place to ensure that the effects and impacts of any incident are successfully contained?

1.7 How can management be sure that all of the risks associated with (various types of) incidents are identified, so that proportionate and effective actions can be taken?

1.8 How can management be assured that the involvement of the law enforcement authorities is activated when appropriate?

1.9 What measures ensure the correct, thorough and lawful investigation and securing of evidence?

1.10 Can management be sure that the prevailing human resources policies and procedures adequately cater for the investigation of employee malpractice or involvement in Information Management incidents?

1.11 What specific measures ensure that all press and media enquiries and statements are always handled by PR/Communication specialists?

1.12 By what means are senior management kept informed of the progress of incident management?

1.13 How does management ensure that all the necessary incident information is captured on a consistent basis?

1.14 What specific measures are in place to ensure that incidents involving personal or otherwise sensitive information are lawfully and effectively handled (so as to avoid breaching Data Protection or privacy obligations)?

1.15 Are there established processes for learning lessons from incidents and assessing how any recurrences could be avoided?

Detailed Issues

2.1 What steps has management taken to create a culture where potential or actual weaknesses and shortcomings in information security can be reported by any employee?

2.2 What specific measures would prevent employees from dealing, unofficially, with an incident themselves?

2.3 How have employees been advised of the required actions to be followed in the event of an incident occurring?

2.4 Have mechanisms been defined and applied that would prevent the uncontrolled spread of any infection or malware?

2.5 How are employees made aware of the requirements for the identification and gathering of forensic and other related evidence?

2.6 How are employees informed of the appropriate methods of dealing with press and media enquiries relating to information security incidents?

2.7 What measures would ensure that the most appropriate employees are involved in the investigation and resolution of information security incidents?

NOTES

1. *2008 Information Security Breaches Survey*, Department for Business, Enterprise and Regulatory Reform (2008), www.berr.gov.uk.
2. Privacy Rights Clearinghouse, 3100—5th Avenue, Suite B, San Diego, CA 92101.

55
Data Retention and Disposal

All records have a lifecycle, the end of which is normally marked by their lack of significance or redundancy from day-to-day use. The next steps will depend on the type of records, their format, the type of organisation, the historic significance of the records, whether or not there is any residual requirement to access them and the prevailing legal or regulatory requirements associated with the records or their use. Taking these factors into account the possible outcomes could include:

- Retention, in a useable condition, for any legally prescribed period.
- The permanent preservation in a suitable archive (including regional or national institutions).
- Relocation to a suitable long-term storage facility.
- Transfer to another format that potentially offers benefits in terms of sustainability.
- Disposal by any means.
- Irreversible destruction of sensitive materials.

The noted end-of-life options for records have a range of associated control issues not least in order to protect information from unauthorised disclosure. In this chapter, we discuss these issues and related measures.

Retention

For most organisations, the primary drivers for retaining records will be:

- The likelihood of records' ongoing use for reference purposes (and the anticipated frequency of such access).
- Whether or not they need to be held in a structured form to permit occasional access.
- Any legal or regulatory implications, such as defined periods of retention and the subsequent archiving requirements.
- The form and format (especially whether there are any required environmental conditions for their preservation).

- Issues relating to digital preservation (as previously discussed in Chapter 29).
- Security and protection implications (for example in relation to personal or restricted information).

Other organisations, notably those in the public sector, may also have to consider the significance of records in terms of their historical value or as parts of the public record. In such cases, there are normally well-established protocols for identifying such records and how they should be archived or relocated to recognised archives or institutions.

The key issue with retention is being able to efficiently determine the retention implications for any set or grouping of records. This ability is partly dependent on having initially identified all key sets of records and reflected their details on a suitable Information Assets Register or inventory. If an organisation hasn't accurately identified all of information assets, how can it ensure that all the related retention requirements are being met?

In UK local government bodies it is normal to document a Retention and Disposal Policy outlining the procedures for ensuring the lawful and appropriate long-term treatment of records. Such policies are normally underpinned by a detailed register which details, for each type of record, the period for which each should be retained, the necessary arrangements beyond that period and the required means of disposal or destruction.

The retention register, which could in practice, be an integral part of an Information Asset Register or inventory, will need to be maintained up to date with any regulatory or operational changes across the organisation. Both the Policy and Register should be periodically reviewed and amended as necessary.

The commitments contained in the register relating to records being retained for a given period will need to be supported in practice by procedures and measures designed to ensure compliance. Such measures will include, among other things, the active prevention of the premature disposal of records in any form and the provision of adequate and environmentally appropriate storage conditions.

The way in which archived or retained records are stored will have a direct bearing on the ease of access and future reference availability. For example, it may be necessary to hold documentary records in the same sequence that applied when they were in live use or files containing personal information may require enhanced levels of physical access security in order to prevent unauthorised disclosure.

All documents and electronic storage media are prone to deteriorate. In addition, the future viability of electronic records is linked to the continued availability of the related hardware and software facilities. The matter of digital preservation is further discussed in Chapter 29—Records Management.

Control should be exercised over the use, removal and return of retained records. For example, the logging of all files removed from storage that enables the identification of the employee removing the file and the date of its return. The loss or damage of any retained file should be treated as an information security incident and reported accordingly.

Each form of records will have associated environmental conditions required for their ongoing preservation. The conditions required to preserve paper records will differ from those related to microfilm or magnetic tape. In general terms, any of the following aspects of could apply:

- Authorised access only
- Humidity level
- Dampness (also linked to moulds that can accelerate decay)
- Temperature (for example, extreme cold can make microfilm and magnetic tape brittle and prone to breaking)
- Protection against damage or loss by fire (including the implications of the available methods of fire-fighting which may further damage records)
- Light levels (especially for paper records)
- Avoidance of electromagnetic fields (that can affect magnetic storage media)
- The age and acidity of paper documents (modern standard papers are prone to deteriorate faster than traditionally produced examples)
- Infestation by vermin or damaging insects
- The incursion of water or corrosive substances
- The suitability and robustness of storage devices
- Safety implications (such as permitted maximum stacking levels or amount of space between shelving). In addition the weight of stacked records could damage those contained in the lower levels.

Disposal

It is at the point of disposal that appropriate care needs to be taken in order to:

- prevent the premature destruction of records (in contravention of any legal or regulatory retention requirements);
- ensure that the method of disposal is lawful and satisfies the organisation's obligations for confidentiality, protection of privacy and the safeguarding of sensitive commercial knowledge;
- prevent the unlawful or inappropriate disclosure or leakage of information (for example, as would apply for personal or restricted information);
- prevent records being accessed, intercepted or used by unauthorised persons for inappropriate purposes;
- ensure that records are completely and irreversibly destroyed (for example, that electronic storage media are made unreadable and unusable).

The following examples of actual US cases of inappropriate disposal and retention of information are provided courtesy of the Privacy Rights Clearinghouse:[1]

- Binghampton University (March 2009)—Student payment data including personal information on students and parents, dating back ten years was being retained in a "haphazard and disorganised fashion" in unlocked cabinets and

units. The storage area was located adjacent to a heavily-used lecture hall and the door was not only unlocked but was taped open.
- Fulton County Board of Registration and Elections (May 2009)—Boxes found in a bin contained approximately 75 000 voter registration application cards and 24 000 precinct cards. The documents included personal data.

One method of destroying paper records is to shred them so that they can't be read or interpreted. However, these outcomes will only apply if the shredder used is of a suitable standard and uses a more effective form of shredding, such as cross-cut shredding that results in small pieces of paper rather than long thin strips. Disposal of records is often outsourced to specialist contractors and may involve the movement of records in their complete form to the contractor's premises where they may be stored for a period before being shredded, burned, etc.

As noted below there are standards in place for the secure destruction of confidential material and some national bodies that define and influence the security and disposal sectors. However, organisations should, when either engaging external contractors to dispose of records or undertaking the process in-house, ensure that the following aspects are satisfactorily addressed:

- The correct identification and isolation of records to be disposed of.
- Processes to ensure that the disposal is lawful and not in contravention of any defined retention requirements.
- Appropriate authorisation of all disposals.
- Accurate recording of the records being disposed, the methods used, those involved in undertaking the tasks and the dates of the key actions.
- The removal of the required records and their secure and stable packing (in order to prevent any loss and to protect against unauthorised access).
- Adequate physical security measures are applied within the organisation to protect records awaiting disposal.
- The conduct of in-house shredding (or other forms of destruction) within a secure area, using equipment of an appropriate standard and involving trustworthy employees.
- The use of trusted and professionally proficient external contractors (ideally registered with a recognised trade association and working to agreed standards).
- If the use of external contractors is a regular or ongoing requirement, the relationship should be formally reflected in an appropriate form of contract or agreement which incorporates the required standards of service, the prompt reporting of problems or potential breaches of information security and the means of redress in the event of a breach.
- Accounting for consignments of records when passed into the custody of the contractor, including obtaining signatures to support the movement.
- Prevention of loss, theft or leakage of records whilst in transit to the contractor's premises.
- Effective physical security measures at the contractor's premises to protect records awaiting destruction or in the process of being destroyed.

- The use, by the contractor, of methods and equipment of a sufficient standard to render the records unusable and/or illegible.
- In the case of magnetic or optical media that contains or has contained records or information, the devices should be completely and irreversibly destroyed.

Relevant Standards and Organisations

In relation to the disposal of information, the following recognised standards apply and the noted UK and US trade organisations are involved in the promotion and application of appropriate standards:

Standards

- BS EN 15713:2009 Secure Destruction of Confidential Material—Code of Practice, BSI (2009) ISBN 978 0 580 55195. This European standard replaces the earlier BS 8470:2006.
- In the UK, the Information Destruction Section of the British Security Industry Association (BSIA) supports BS EN 15713 and encourages its members to apply the relevant National Occupational Standards (NOS) created by Skills for Security which is a not-for-profit sector skills body created by employers to improve standards of professionalism. NOS course details and contact details as follows:

Relevant Organisations

- British Security Industry Association (BSIA)
  - Mail: BSIA, Kirkham House, John Comyn Drive, Worcester, WR3 7NS
  - Web: www.bsia.co.uk
- Skills for Security
  - Mail: NOS Suite: Information Destruction Operations Security House, Barbourne Road, Worcester, WR1 1RS
  - Web: www.skillsforsecurity.org.uk
  - Email: info@skillsforsecurity.org.uk
- In the United States, the National Association for Information Destruction (NAID) has a voluntary certification programme for its member companies. NAID is an international trade association for companies providing information destruction services with a mission to promote the information destruction industry and the standards and ethics of its member companies. International contact points for NAID are as follows:
  - Headquarters
    - Mail: 1951 W. Camelback Road, Suite 350, Phoenix, AZ 85015
    - Web: www.naidonline.org
    - Email: info@naidonline.org

- NAID—Canada
  - Mail: 301-250 The Esplanade, Toronto, M5A 1J2
  - Web: www.naidcanada.org
  - Email: info@naidcanada.org
- NAID—Europe
  - Mail: 287 Avenue Louise, 4th Fl. 1050 Brussels, Belgium
  - Web: www.naideurope.eu
  - Email: info@naideurope.eu
- NAID—Australasia
  - Web: www.naidaustralasia.org
  - Email: info@naidaustralasia.org

Control Objectives for Data Retention and Disposal

(a) To ensure that records are retained in an accessible and secure form to comply with all prevailing operational, legal and regulatory requirements.

(b) To actively prevent the premature, accidental or wilful destruction or loss of records.

(c) To ensure that any records required for historical, local, sector or national preservation and archiving are identified and appropriately treated.

(d) To ensure adequate and effective protection of retained records which contain personal or sensitive information.

(e) To ensure that the appropriate environment conditions are provided in order to protect records.

(f) To ensure that records for disposal are accurately identified and disposed of in a secure and appropriate manner.

Risk and Control Issues for Data Retention and Disposal

1 Key Issues

1.1 How is management assured that it is fully aware of all the required retention periods for the organisation's records?

1.2 How does management ensure that records that may require a lower level of ongoing access remain readily accessible?

1.3 How has management identified retained records containing personal, restricted, sensitive or confidential information and provided protection from unauthorised access, loss etc.?

1.4 What specific measures would prevent the premature, accidental or malicious destruction of records?

1.5 Has management identified all the relevant digital preservation issues and established a planned approach to maintaining the accessibility of affected records?

1.6 What steps have been taken to ensure that employees are adequately aware of their responsibilities and the general requirements for retention and disposal of records?

1.7 How is management assured that adequate measures are in place to address all the required security, storage and environmental implications as a means to ensure the ongoing preservation and availability of retained records?

1.8 How can management be sure that all retained records remain accounted for (including any that may have been temporarily removed)?

1.9 How are management assured that the methods of disposing of records are adequately secure, especially in respect of records that contain personal or sensitive information?

1.10 How does management ensure the integrity, security and professionalism of any external contractors used to dispose of records?

1.11 How can management be confident that records held in electronic, magnetic or optical forms are irreversibly destroyed?

2 Detailed Issues

2.1 By what means has management identified all the legal or regulatory implications associated with the retention and disposal of records and ensured the organisation is compliant?

2.2 What measures would prevent records from being identified as having specific retention and disposal requirements?

2.3 What measures are in place to prevent matters of digital preservation being overlooked for a set or range of electronic records?

2.4 How is the authorisation for either the retention or disposal of records evidenced?

2.5 What specific mechanisms would prevent the unauthorised treatment or destruction of records?

2.6 How can removed records be accurately traced to the employee using the record?

2.7 How would lost or damaged records be detected and followed up?

2.8 What measures are in place to ensure the secure and lawful in-house destruction of records?

2.9 How is the secure operation of external disposal arrangements defined and confirmed for all the key stages?

NOTE

1. Privacy Rights Clearinghouse, 3100—5th Avenue, Suite B, San Diego, CA 92101, www.privacyrights.org.

56
Electronic Data Interchange (EDI)

Electronic data interchange (EDI) has become a key technology for companies engaged in businesses where there are high levels of transactions regularly flowing between parties (e.g. electronic invoices moving between suppliers and customers). Industry standards have been established and the electronic transfer of data between entities is now commonplace with notable advantages, such as:
- accuracy and completeness of transaction data moved between parties
- reduction of errors caused by the previous need to re-key transactions
- removal of processing and postal delays.

Control Objectives for Electronic Data Interchange

(a) To ensure that the use of EDI is fully assessed, justified and authorised as part of the adopted IT and business strategies.

(b) To ensure that all the business and legal implications of using EDI are fully assessed and addressed.

(c) To ensure that the optimum EDI solution is identified and implemented.

(d) To ensure that relationships with suppliers and customers are not adversely affected by the introduction of EDI.

(e) To ensure that the chosen method and technology are secure and that traffic is suitably authenticated.

(f) To ensure that all transactions are confirmed as valid and reconciled.

(g) To ensure that data from feeder systems is accurate, complete and valid.

(h) To ensure that commercially sensitive data remains confidential.

(i) To ensure that the approval of the required regulatory body (i.e. HM Customs & Excise) is obtained as necessary for the chosen system.

(j) To ensure that all EDI systems are fully and satisfactorily tested before live use.

(k) To ensure that contingency plans are in place to provide emergency cover in the event of a failure or breakdown.

(l) To ensure that only recognised and reliable EDI systems and protocols are used.

(m) To ensure that the anticipated benefits and strategic advantages are actually achieved.

Risk and Control Issues for Electronic Data Interchange

1 Key Issues

1.1 Have the business and strategic advantages of using EDI been formally assessed, justified and authorised (and how is this evidenced)?

1.2 How has management assessed the business and operational implications of introducing EDI (and has its introduction been adequately planned for)?

1.3 Has management taken professional legal advice on the legal status of EDI transactions, and resolved any potential areas of concern?

1.4 What steps were taken to ensure that the optimum EDI solution was adopted?

1.5 How is management assured that suppliers and customers affected by the introduction of EDI are committed to the concept and prepared to accept this type of relationship?

1.6 How does management verify that the adopted EDI system is reliable and secure (and that transaction data is adequately protected)?

1.7 What measures ensure that all EDI transactions are accurate, valid and authorised?

1.8 What specific measures ensure that commercially sensitive data remains confidential and secure?

1.9 Where necessary, has management obtained the required approval of the appropriate regulatory body for the operation of the EDI system?

1.10 Was the EDI system fully tested to the satisfaction of users, prior to live use (and how can management be assured that the testing was suitably comprehensive)?

1.11 What measures are in place to enable the continuation of EDI services following a major systems failure or disaster (and how can management be assured that any disruption will be minimised)?

1.12 Has management reviewed the performance and benefits of the EDI system and confirmed the achievement of their initial objectives?

2 Detailed Issues

2.1 How is management assured that the chosen EDI system is stable, reliable and uses recognised protocols and standards?

2.2 How was the EDI system selected and was the ability of the suppliers to provide adequate support and maintenance taken into account?

2.3 Have the costs of introducing and using EDI systems been accurately identified, justified and authorised?

2.4 What specific measures prevent unauthorised access to (or usage of) EDI facilities?

2.5 What measures prevent both the transmission and receipt of unauthorised, duplicated or erroneous transactions?

2.6 How does management ensure that data extracted from feeder systems is accurate, complete and valid prior to EDI transmission?

2.7 Is all EDI data traffic satisfactorily reconciled between source and target systems?

2.8 Are the EDI contingency arrangements/plans regularly tested to ensure that they remain effective (and what is the evidence for this)?

57

Viruses

Although media hype can be said to have unduly raised the level of fear about the likelihood and effects of computer viruses within the business community, the actual effects of virus infection upon IT operations can still be very disruptive and costly to eradicate. The attendant dangers normally rise in proportion to the level of IT dependency and the associated devolvement of IT operational responsibility to end-users, who may be inexperienced in the methods of avoiding infection.

A key issue is ensuring that virus definitions are maintained up to date so as to counter the threats of emerging malicious software. Suppliers of anti-virus (and associated malware barriers) will constantly update the definition files of their systems and provide them, perhaps automatically online, to users who have subscribed to their update service. Once aware of a change in the definitions available, the organisation may automatically deploy the updates to all of its personal computers, servers and other devices.

Viruses can be found in email attachments and this form of viral distribution can be very effective unless emails are filtered for the presence of malware and employees are vigilant and aware of what to do if they receive an unsolicited email and attachment from an address they do not recognise.

The 2008 BERR survey of UK companies[1] reported that 14% of the surveyed companies suffered infection by viruses or malicious software (where 84% of such incidents were associated with virus, worm or Trojan infection and 16% related to Spyware).

The issues raised in this chapter can be modified and adapted to address a range of common flavours of malware, which can be said to have some degree of commonality in respect of the necessary objectives and implications.

Control Objectives for Viruses

(a) To ensure that all systems are adequately protected from virus infections.

(b) To ensure that the impact and disruption caused by virus infections is prevented and/or minimised.

> (c) To ensure that virus infections cannot be spread outside of the organisation (i.e. to customers or suppliers).
>
> (d) To ensure that staff are fully aware of their responsibilities in the avoidance of virus infections.
>
> (e) To ensure that only valid and authorised software is loaded onto company computers.
>
> (f) To ensure that adequate arrangements are in place to enable the prompt identification of virus infections.
>
> (g) To ensure that the company is able to achieve a complete recovery from virus infection.
>
> (h) To ensure that the measures in place keep pace with virus developments and remain effective.

Risk and Control Issues for Viruses

1 Key Issues

1.1 What measures are in place to prevent systems from becoming infected by viruses?

1.2 How are personal computers protected from virus infection?

1.3 What procedures are in place to ensure that management is promptly made aware of any virus infections?

1.4 What specific measures prevent the export of virus infections to suppliers or customers (e.g. via magnetic media or online services)?

1.5 How does management ensure that staff are adequately aware of their responsibilities for preventing viral infection (and what is the evidence for this)?

1.6 Have procedures been established that promptly isolate any suspected infection as a means of reducing the opportunity of it spreading?

1.7 Has management established a planned approach for dealing with infections, and how are they assured that this remains potentially effective?

2 Detailed Issues

2.1 What measures would detect infected media and/or prevent the loading of same?

2.2 What measures prevent the loading of unauthorised or pirated software?

2.3 How does management ensure that all magnetic media is free from infections?

2.4 In the event of an infection being detected, how does management ensure that it will not spread in an uncontrolled way?

2.5 What steps are in place to prevent the spreading of virus infections via the local area network or wide area network systems?

2.6 Do technical support staff have the necessary skills to identify, isolate and effectively deal with viral infections?

2.7 Are the procedures for dealing with infections subject to regular testing in order to confirm their effectiveness?

2.8 How does management ensure that measures for dealing with infections keep pace with both the virus developments and the evolution of corporate systems?

NOTE

1. *2008 Information Security Breaches Survey*, Department for Business, Enterprise and Regulatory Reform (2008), www.berr.gov.uk.

58
User Support

With increasing levels of IT responsibility being allocated to end-users, it is vital that adequate provision is made to support users and the systems they use. Where they have a problem with their computer or software, users need prompt and effective action to resolve the problem so that they can concentrate on their business responsibilities.

In this chapter the issues related to the provision of a centralised end-user support service are considered. However, a combination of user support mechanisms can be provided, such as contextual help systems, electronic guides or self assessment check lists.

Control Objectives for User Support

> (a) To provide adequate and effective user support services so as to ensure that IT facilities are consistently, correctly and securely used.
>
> (b) To ensure that hardware and software faults are promptly remedied and that business disruption is minimised.
>
> (c) To ensure that system availability complies with the prevailing service level agreements.
>
> (d) To ensure that end-users do not apply their own software and hardware solutions, which could result in damage and/or business disruption.

Risk and Control Issues for User Support

1 Key Issues

1.1 Has management taken steps to ensure that adequate and appropriate user support facilities are provided, as a means to ensure the consistent and secure use of IT facilities?

1.2 How does management ensure that adequate and sufficiently skilled support staff are available to provide an effective service (and how do they monitor the effectiveness of the service)?

1.3 Have clear reporting lines been established for hardware and software faults, and how does management ensure that all such problems are promptly and effectively dealt with?

1.4 Have service-level agreements been established, and how is management assured that such performance levels are being achieved?

1.5 What specific measures ensure that all user support enquiries/calls are logged, trailed and subsequently satisfactorily cleared?

1.6 What measures prevent end-users taking unauthorised action to investigate and rectify faults and problems?

2 Detailed Issues

2.1 Are all hardware and software faults logged and analysed?

2.2 What procedures ensure that faults referred out to external suppliers or engineers are promptly and cost-effectively dealt with?

2.3 How does management ensure that all charges from external suppliers and engineers for user support are correct and valid?

2.4 What mechanisms prevent reported faults from being disregarded or left unresolved?

2.5 Is the performance of the user support and fault service monitored (i.e. against defined service levels)?

2.6 How can management be assured that the skills of the user support staff remain compatible with the systems and hardware in use throughout the organisation?

2.7 Are sufficient copies of hardware and systems documentation available as reference sources (and what measures ensure that such documents are kept up to date)?

2.8 What measures ensure that user support staff do not breach either systems or data security facilities in the course of their duties?

59
BACS

Although we have chosen to title this chapter as being applicable to BACS (Bankers Automated Clearing Service), the following points can generally be applied to any system involving the electronic transfer of funds.

Control Objectives for BACS

> (a) To ensure that BACS facilities are only used for valid and authorised purposes.
>
> (b) To ensure that all BACS transactions are valid, accurate, trailed, reconciled and correctly accounted for.
>
> (c) To prevent staff fraud or malpractice.
>
> (d) To ensure that data rejections are promptly identified and correct.
>
> (e) To ensure the integrity of the BACS data conversion programs.
>
> (f) To ensure that data is submitted in accordance with the prevailing BACS processing timetables.
>
> (g) To ensure that all interfacing systems comply with the required transmission and format protocols.
>
> (h) To ensure that all BACS tapes and media are identified, securely stored and accounted for.
>
> (i) To ensure that transactions are protected from tampering prior to transmission.
>
> (j) To ensure that access to and use of BACSTEL electronic keys and passwords is adequately protected from unauthorised use.

Risk and Control Issues for BACS

1 Key Issues

1.1 What general measures has management established in order to ensure that only valid and authorised use is made of BACS facilities?

1.2 How does management ensure that all transactions destined for BACS transmission are accurate, complete, valid and authorised?

1.3 How does management ensure that all BACS activity is accounted for?

1.4 How does management verify that the programs used to prepare data for BACS processing are accurate and authorised for use?

1.5 What specific measures ensure that all BACS processing is conducted at the correct time and in accordance with the prevailing processing timetables and deadlines?

1.6 What mechanisms ensure that the relevant programs conform to the required BACS format and protocol standards?

1.7 Are all BACS tapes securely held, appropriately handled, and accounted for?

1.8 What general measures would prevent the unauthorised tampering with BACS data?

2 Detailed Issues

2.1 Has management documented the procedural requirements for BACS processing, and clearly allocated relevant responsibilities and accountabilities?

2.2 What measures actively prevent the introduction of invalid, fraudulent or unauthorised BACS transactions?

2.3 Would management be made aware of unusual or over-frequent transactions (prior to transmission)?

2.4 Is someone held responsible for ensuring the accuracy and completeness of BACS data prior to authorising the release of the relevant media?

2.5 What steps has management taken to prevent internal fraud through staff collusion?

2.6 Are all records of BACS activity reconciled to source (or target) systems?

2.7 How are data rejections handled so as to ensure their subsequent correct processing?

2.8 What measures prevent the submission of duplicated transactions through the BACS systems?

2.9 What mechanisms prevent the use of unauthorised programs in the preparation of BACS data?

2.10 Are all BACS service charges verified for accuracy and validity prior to payment?

60

Spreadsheet Design and Good Practice

Current spreadsheet software is easy to use, feature-rich and a familiar part of the PC environment. Spreadsheets are often (officially or unofficially) woven into the corporate information system. Because they are so approachable and easy to use, spreadsheets often evade any scrutiny during their development or live use. They may be rarely evaluated for their logic, resilience and reliability, which could place the organisation in a vulnerable position, especially if the knowledge of how a key spreadsheet operates solely resides in one employee's head.

This chapter aims to raise awareness of the potential adverse business impacts that the use of spreadsheets can represent, but first some high-profile examples of the consequences of spreadsheet errors and malpractice:[1]

- A missing minus sign caused Fidelity's Magellan Fund to overstate projected earnings by $ 2.6 billion and miss a promised dividend.
- A cut-and-paste error cost Trans Alta $ 24 million when it underbid on an electricity supply contract.
- Falsely linked spreadsheets permitted fraud totalling $ 700 million at the Allied Irish Bank.

Spreadsheets are prone to simple errors and oversights, and these include, for example:

- Overtyping of cells containing formulae (e.g. entering a fixed value over a calculation).
- Inserting new rows and columns and not amending related formulae;
- Inconsistencies in formulae (e.g. in a column or row).
- Inaccurate ranges of data used in formulae.
- Failing to cross-cast rows and columns as a means of proving accuracy.
- Failing to amend all formulae when constants or variables are changed.
- Confusion over the extent of formulae and how they interact, where a simple change in one part of the file can influence another area or calculation.
- Inappropriate mixing and use of units and frequencies.
- Putting function arguments in the wrong order.

- Failure to protect formulae cells from unauthorised amendment.
- Lack of control to prevent unauthorised access.
- Failure to use the correct data set in a regular cycle of use.
- Failure to fully understand the formulae in use.
- Undocumented changes applied.
- Failure to adequately test files before being put into live use.

There can be very real risks associated with the use of spreadsheets, especially where they form a significant part of the management information and decision-making processes and their development has been undertaken, perhaps in an informal way, by a single employee who may subsequently leave the organisation together with the key knowledge. There is a very fine dividing line between the use of spreadsheets to augment mainstream system information and a greater dependence being placed on spreadsheets when they become part of the mainstream system. This transformation can happen quite easily without necessarily being obvious. Taking source information out of its original context and into a spreadsheet environment can lead to undisciplined use, calculation and analysis resulting in dubious, unreliable or inaccurate outcomes, the knock-on effects of which can distort decision-making and management actions.

Inventory of Key Spreadsheets

In order to assess whether the organisation is unduly exposed to any spreadsheet risks, managers should consider undertaking an inventory so that the extent and nature of their use can be accurately determined and assessed. Key or operationally critical spreadsheets should be identified as information assets and be more formally recorded on the organisation's Information Asset Register or inventory. It is suggested that the following information should be captured for all critical or key spreadsheets:

- Filename of the spreadsheet
- File/Data Owner and Information Steward
- Author and/or person responsible for ongoing maintenance
- Date of introduction
- The part(s) of the organisation that use(s) the file
- An overview of its functionality and purpose
- Whether it is financial or operational in nature
- The magnitude of the spreadsheet (e.g. in financial terms or related to operational significance)
- Whether the file contains personal, sensitive, confidential or restricted information
- Any specific security features (such as access control or worksheet protection)
- When it was last amended
- Whether it has been documented
- Whether only a single copy or version is maintained or if copies are distributed potentially leading to numerous, perhaps different, versions being used across the organisation
- Any specific risk factors associated with either its use or its loss.

Assessing the Associated Risks

The following key questions should be considered when assessing the risks associated with either a particular spreadsheet or the general use of spreadsheets across the organisation:

- Who was involved in determining the logic and design?
- Was the design assessed, approved and signed off by the appropriate manager?
- Is the knowledge of the file structure documented or in the head of the designer?
- Were they tested thoroughly before being implemented (and what is the evidence for this)?
- Have they been constructed to recognised standards?
- How are they managed?
- How reliable are the calculations?
- How reliable are the generated results?
- Are they protected from either inadvertent or malicious amendments?

Only authorised spreadsheets should be developed and used, and managers should be aware of all the spreadsheets in use within their areas and take steps so that they can be confident that the files are reliable, accurate and capable of being adequately supported. Consequently, employees should not develop ad hoc spreadsheets on their own authority, especially where there is inter-relationship with other spreadsheets and a potential impact on operations and reporting.

Documenting Spreadsheets

Key or operationally critical spreadsheets should be treated in the same way as key application systems and be specified and documented so that ongoing maintenance and update can be based on a clear understanding of the structure and logic of the spreadsheet. The documentation should resemble that for the specification of a software application and, at least, define the following:

- The purpose of the spreadsheet.
- An assessment of how critical the sheet will be to the organisation.
- The owner and designer of the sheet.
- The filename of the sheet (and rules for amending the filename over time as different versions are created and used).
- How the sheet will be used and by whom (and where the operational copies will be stored).
- How the sheet will be constructed (including the separation of data, calculations and outputs).
- Any constants or standing data to be used in formulae (and how they are derived and appropriately amended when necessary).
- The basis of the calculations to be performed (including clear descriptions of complex formulae).
- Listings of all the formulae and macros.
- The nature and frequency of any update or usage activities which can be the basis of operating instructions or procedures (including the use of data and constants).

- The source of the data and how to ensure its validity.
- Details of any control or verification processes applied to maintain the accuracy and integrity of the sheet.
- How the file will be tested (cross-referenced to the results and outputs of such testing).
- How errors will be detected, trapped and reported (this could include limiting the contents of fields to agreed lists, regular use of Excel™'s Auditing Functions on the Tools toolbar or periodic reviews of the file conducted by a manager).
- Details of how the file should be amended and how changes should be documented, authorised and tested.
- Comments can be inserted into cells to describe the purpose of the cell, explain complex calculations or document user-defined functions and macros.

Examples of Good Practice

Spreadsheets are a powerful tool and have numerous features, many of which most users rarely use or are possibly completely unaware of. The level of the skills required to exploit and correctly use the available range of functionality should not be underestimated and it would be foolish to have someone attempt to design a complex and perhaps critical spreadsheet if it were their first experience of using the necessary functions and facilities.

Microsoft Excel™ is the currently recognised leader in the spreadsheet market and so some of the following aspects of good practice specifically relate to the Excel™ environment. The examples noted below should be considered in the appropriate circumstances as the means to provide greater assurance as to the stability, accuracy and reliability of internally developed spreadsheet solutions.

- Excel™ is a Flat File application and should be utilised as such; if a solution requires a relational database then use one.
- Create and circulate templates for common tasks incorporating the required format, formulae and macros, which can be used for future developments and ensure a degree of consistency.
- Avoid overcomplicated processes and try to break down complex chains into simpler more manageable ones.
- Assess and define how to use areas of the spreadsheet and the constituent worksheets to separate data, logic (i.e. formulae) and results (this will make maintenance easier as the three aspects will not be confused or intermixed).
- Attempt to keep all data on one worksheet and avoid breaking it down further over many worksheets.
- Use conditional formatting to highlight results as a warning.
- Ensure that data areas do not include blank rows as this can affect how Excel™ treats the blank areas (for example, the software may interpret the last blank row as the end of your data range).
- Data in the file should already be sorted in the most appropriate and efficient form (this can aid the speed of calculation, the presentation of results and avoid the need to resort data).

- Be wary of links to other spreadsheets or external data sources. Build in control value features that can be used to agree the output values of the source file to the input values in the target file.
- Avoid putting too much information in one cell when it would be more appropriate to place it in more than one (You can always combine them back later if required, but the reverse is not so easy.)
- Clearly label rows and columns to avoid ambiguity (making headings **Bold** assists Excel™ in identifying them as headings in functions such as Sort).
- Use dynamic ranges and give them meaningful names.
- Organise your worksheets vertically, limit the number of columns but have as many rows as necessary. For example, a formula should ideally only refer to the cells above it so the process flows from raw data at the top of the sheet to the final calculations at the bottom. A vertical design promotes a clearer flow of calculations and can aid the understanding and ongoing maintenance of the file.
- Macros should be carefully and thoroughly tested and incorporate the detection and reporting of errors. REM lines in the macro, which have no processing implications, can be used to insert comments and guidance notes.
- Consider the use of background colour and shading to highlight different areas of the sheet and to indicate where data can and cannot be entered. However, simple colour schemes are preferable to avoid turning the screen into a Technicolor nightmare.
- Incorporate protection of cells containing formulae or whole worksheets where necessary.
- Do not include variables (such as tax rates or number of months) as values in formulae but hold them as data elsewhere and include the appropriate cell reference within the associated formulae. This will aid maintenance and clearly segregate the key data elements from the formulae that use them.
- Ensure that the format and layout are clear and intuitive (avoid complex or confusing layouts and extravagant fonts, the need to re-enter data, etc.).
- Avoid applying "Text" formats to formulae cells.
- Ensure that formulae are consistently copied to the appropriate cell ranges (taking care over the appropriate use of "relative" and "absolute" cell references).
- Apply formats (for number type, etc.) just to the range in use and avoid formatting whole columns or rows (as Excel™ will assume you are using all the formatted cells and this may affect performance).
- Use pivot tables or charts to summarise data but ensure that they reflect all the required data ranges, especially after changes have been applied elsewhere in the file.
- Be aware that the following functions can adversely affect the speed of recalculation:
    - Array Functions (alternatives are Excel's™ Database Functions and Pivot Table features).
    - Sum product used for multiple condition summing or counting.
    - User-Defined Functions (or UDFs) (these need to be carefully constructed and will usually incorporate Excel's™ functions. They rarely operate at the same speed as the functions they contain. Creators of UDFs should be appropriately skilled in the use of Excel™ VBA (Microsoft Visual Basic for Applications™).

- Spreadsheet Lookup Functions (e.g. VLOOKUP) enable the extraction of data from tables of data and can consume processing resources if the command involves the examination of thousands of cells. This process can be made more efficient if used in combination with the Dynamic Range functions.
- Changes to spreadsheet files should be clearly determined and applied, so as to:
  - ensure that only valid, required, justified and authorised changes are applied.
  - ensure that all of the impacts and implications of the changes are identified and addressed.
  - ensure that changes are adequately reflected in the file documentation.
  - ensure that the nature and extent of the required testing is documented, planned, applied and the results assessed.
- Access to spreadsheets should, in line with the principle of "need to know", be restricted so that the update and maintenance of the file can be suitably controlled and its integrity maintained. Access measures should include an appropriate combination of the following:
  - Clearly allocating the responsibility for the maintenance of the file(s).
  - Placing the live versions of spreadsheet files in specific subdirectories, access to which is restricted to authorised users only.
  - Critical spreadsheet files should be protected by a password, which is subject to periodic change.
  - Staff who need to view spreadsheet data, but not to update it, should be given access to a "read only" version of the file.
  - Cell ranges and areas containing the logic and formulae should be protected (or locked) from unauthorised amendment.
- To protect file contents in the event of a PC or network failure the "autosave" or "autorecover" facilities should be turned on in operational use of the file.
- Operational versions of key spreadsheets should be backed up at an appropriate frequency and the copies securely stored. In addition, the spreadsheet documentation should also be copied and securely stored to aid any necessary recovery processes.
- Effective measures should be in place to prevent the unauthorised copying, proliferation and distribution of operational spreadsheets. Using an outdated or unofficially amended version of a spreadsheet could result in operational disruptions, wasted resources, additional costs, delays or an adverse impact on the organisation's image and reputation.
- Formal version control measures should be exercised over the maintenance and update of key spreadsheets and the version number and related date should be included in the file name, footer of any printed reports or clearly at the top of the worksheet.
- Employees should not forward copies of spreadsheets via email or otherwise make them available to colleagues, unless the recipient is known to be authorised

to view such information. Particular care should be taken when disclosing personal, sensitive or confidential information contained within spreadsheets.
- The structured testing of key spreadsheets should incorporate the following activities:
    - Documenting the rationale for the testing and defining how the testing will be conducted, including the use of test data (remembering to update test data as and when the operating conditions and the required functionality change over time).
    - The definition of the expected results and outputs (so they can be matched to the actual test outcomes).
    - Feeding back the testing outcomes and applying any necessary changes and updating the file documentation.
    - The scope and depth of spreadsheet testing should not be restricted to just the functions and attributes of the sheet that have been modified or updated, but rather should include the overall functionality and interaction of the file, as a means of ensuring the overall integrity of the file in live use.

Control Objectives for Spreadsheet Design and Good Practice

(a) To ensure that when spreadsheets are used, they are consistent and reliable.

(b) To ensure that spreadsheet data is accurate, complete and authorised to facilitate secure decision making.

(c) To ensure that best practice and secure techniques are used in the development of spreadsheet solutions.

(d) To ensure that staff involved in generating spreadsheets are appropriately skilled.

(e) To ensure that spreadsheets are given ongoing maintenance and support.

(f) To ensure that adequate and appropriate security is exercised over the access to key management spreadsheets.

(g) To ensure that spreadsheets are accurately specified and documented.

(h) To ensure that all key spreadsheets are comprehensively and satisfactorily tested prior to live use.

(i) To ensure that spreadsheets are protected from unauthorised amendment.

(j) To ensure that sensitive or confidential data is adequately protected.

Risk and Control Issues for Spreadsheet Design and Good Practice

1 Key Issues

1.1 How does management decide whether a spreadsheet is the most suitable form of data presentation and analysis in order to protect the integrity of decision making within the organisation?

1.2 What measures ensure that spreadsheet solutions are fit for the purpose, accurate, reliable and secure from unauthorised tampering?

1.3 What measures are in place to provide accurate guidance to spreadsheet developers as to best practice and methods?

1.4 Are spreadsheets subject to formal processes governing the following stages:

- specification
- determining the required logic testing
- documentation for maintenance purposes?

1.5 How does management ensure that critical spreadsheet models are adequately protected from unauthorised access?

1.6 How does management verify that the initial logic and construction of a spreadsheet remains constant?

1.7 What mechanisms ensure that all subsequent amendments and updates made to spreadsheets are valid, authorised and correctly applied?

2 Detailed Issues

2.1 How does management avoid the proliferation of inaccurate or unreliable spreadsheets which may undermine the quality of management data and decision making?

2.2 Has management established formal guidelines for the development of critical spreadsheet systems?

2.3 What steps has management taken to ensure that relevant staff are suitably trained in the use and development of spreadsheets?

2.4 Are spreadsheet developments documented so that they can be subsequently maintained and updated?

NOTE

1. Other examples of reported spreadsheet errors can be found on the European Spreadsheet Risks Interest Group (EuSpRIG) website: www.eusprig.org.

61
IT Health Checks

Organisations should consider undertaking periodic, at least annual, health checks of the overall IT environment. Such checks can be undertaken by staff within the IT section or function, but to achieve a more objective approach the use of suitably skilled internal audit personnel or specialist external consultants should also be considered.

In certain IT environments or sectors (e.g. the public sector), periodic independent assessments of such factors as IT Security are a mandatory requirement so as to confirm any required eligibility for the use of, for example, secure or dedicated networks or to access protected or restricted data sources.

Where an organisation has embraced a recognised IT standard, such as ISO 27001, and has either obtained or is seeking full accreditation, regular audits will need to be undertaken by authorised assessors to determine if the active measures remain effective and the required aspects of the relevant standards are being achieved.

In this chapter we focus on the conduct of periodic and general IT health checks irrespective of whether they are conducted by internal staff or by external experts. Such health checks may include, but are not necessarily restricted to, the following elements:

- Undertaking a full penetration test to determine any physical or logical security vulnerabilities.
- Creating a network summary that will identify all IP addressable devices as a means of confirming their validity.
- Verifying the currency and validity of live users and their respective access rights.
- Network analysis, including identifying and assessing any exploitable switches or gateways.
- Vulnerability analysis, including patch levels, poor passwords and services used.
- The currency and effectiveness of firewalls, virus and malware detection and prevention, spam filtration, etc.
- Assessing the state of readiness and preparedness for reacting to a serious incident or unplanned event.
- Assessing the required level(s) of achievement for any adopted (or aspired) standards and recognised benchmarks.

Any form of health check needs to be conducted in a comprehensive and structured way and result in the creation of an output report which highlights any areas of actual or potential weakness together with recommended actions.

Control Objectives for IT Health Checks

(a) To ensure that the appropriate form and scope of IT Health Checks are applied by suitably experienced and qualified personnel.

(b) To ensure the ongoing integrity and security of corporate IT facilities.

(c) To ensure that the control measures in place are, and will remain, adequate and effective.

(d) To ensure that any required legislative, regulatory or other standards are being achieved.

(e) To ensure the identification of any IT and information security or control weaknesses and their prompt and effective resolution.

Risk and Control Issues for IT Health Checks

1 Key Issues

1.1 How can management be certain that they are fully aware of all the potential IT risks and threats facing the organisation?

1.2 How can management be assured that the IT and information security measures in place are adequate and effective?

1.3 How would management be aware of any potential or actual shortcomings in relation to IT and information security?

1.4 By what means does management ensure that any IT health checks are conducted by suitably qualified and experienced personnel?

1.5 What steps have been taken to accurately identify all the measures and actions required in order to meet the full range of applicable standards across the organisation?

2 Detailed Issues

2.1 How does management determine which aspects of the IT environment are best suited to periodic assessment?

2.2 How does management ensure that appropriate external experts and specialists are engaged to conduct IT Health Checks?

2.3 How does management define the scope of IT Health Checks and how can they be sure that the scope is adequate and appropriate?

2.4 What specific mechanisms would prevent any required control improvements from being overlooked?

62
IT Accounting

Here we examine the issues arising from the need to account accurately for the various aspects of the IT environment. Of course, in practice the extent and range of such IT activities will vary enormously, and the level of specific accounting treatment will also differ in proportion. However, IT resources often represent considerable levels of investment that need to be monitored and controlled.

Control Objectives for IT Accounting

(a) To ensure that a documented and agreed accounting policy is created for the IT operations.

(b) To ensure that the cost and accounting structure accurately reflects the organisation and supports a meaningful accounts reporting system.

(c) To ensure that the accounts are accurate, complete and timely.

(d) To ensure that management information generated from the accounting system is accurate.

(e) To ensure that the accounting systems and practices fully comply with all the prevailing legislation and regulations.

(f) To ensure that all assets are correctly identified and accounted for.

(g) To ensure that reliable budget procedures are established, enabling the setting and monitoring of agreed budgets.

(h) To ensure that all accounting entries are authorised, valid and accurately processed within the correct accounting period.

(i) To ensure that all projects are accurately costed.

(j) To ensure that an accurate and fair basis is established for charging out IT facility usage to users.

Risk and Control Issues for IT Accounting

1 Key Issues

1.1 Has management agreed, documented and circulated an accounting policy for the IT function?

1.2 How does management verify that the adopted accounting structure accurately and appropriately reflects the IT operations and the information needs of management?

1.3 What measures ensure that the accounting data is accurate, complete, up to date and reliable?

1.4 How does management confirm that the accounting systems and surrounding practices fully comply with all the relevant accounting legislation and regulations?

1.5 What measures ensure that all assets are identified and correctly treated within the accounting system (additionally, are they regularly confirmed)?

1.6 Have agreed and authorised budgets been set for the IT function/operations?

1.7 How does management ensure that budgeted targets are achieved, and that variances are effectively reacted to?

1.8 How does management ensure that all accounting entries are valid, authorised and accurately processed within the relevant accounting period?

1.9 Have project accounting systems been established to enable actual costs to be accurately determined?

1.10 Have end-users been allocated responsibility for their IT related costs?

1.11 What measures have management taken to ensure that IT facility usage costs are fairly, accurately and completely accounted for and charged out to users where necessary?

2 Detailed Issues

2.1 What measures ensure that the agreed accounting policy is adhered to?

2.2 Would potential breaches of the prevailing accounting regulations be promptly identified and followed up?

2.3 What measures ensure that all the management information generated from the accounting system is accurate and reliable?

2.4 What prevents the unauthorised amendment of previously agreed budgets?

2.5 What prevents major actual versus budget variances from being disregarded?

2.6 What specific measures prevent the processing of unauthorised or invalid accounting entries?

2.7 What specific measures would detect incorrect account postings and duplicated transactions?

Appendix 1
Index to SAPGs on the Companion Website

These files are available on a password protected website accompanying this Handbook. The password protected website contains a Word format Standard Audit Programme Guide for each of the approximately two hundred business activities listed in this Appendix.

Those items marked with an asterisk (*) are relevant to the wider aspects of information and knowledge that, although including electronic records, should also encompass information and records in any form. Their inclusion within this IT set of SAPGs is justified on the grounds that by far the majority of organisations will have a preponderance of electronic records, albeit that some of the issues can, in fact, relate to any form or media.

SET	SAPG FILENAME REF.:
0. Tools	
Blank SAPG form for user to populate	SAPG_NEW
Standard audit programmes guides arranged by business processes	PROCESS
1. Management and Administration	
The Control Environment	0101
Organisation	0102
Management Information	0103
Planning	0104
Risk Management	0105
Legal Department	0106
Quality Management	0107
Estates Management and Facilities	0108

SET	SAPG FILENAME REF.:
Environmental Issues	0109
Insurance	0110
Security	0111
Capital Projects	0112
Industry Regulations and Compliance	0113
Media, Public and External Relations	0114
Company Secretarial Department	0115
2. Financial and Accounting	
Treasury	0201
Payroll	0202
Accounts Payable	0203
Accounts Receivable	0204
General Ledger / Management Accounts	0205
Fixed Assets (and capital charges)	0206
Budgeting and Monitoring	0207
Bank Accounts and Banking Arrangements	0208
VAT Accounting (where applicable)	0209
Taxation	0210
Inventories	0211
Product / Project Accounting	0212
Petty Cash and Expenses	0213
Financial Information and Reporting	0214
Investments	0215
3. Personnel and Human Resources	
Human Resources Department	0301
Recruitment	0302
Manpower and Succession Planning	0303
Staff Training and Development	0304
Welfare	0305
Performance-related Compensation, Pension Schemes (and Other Benefits)	0306
Health Insurance	0307
Staff Appraisal and Disciplinary Matters	0308
Health and Safety	0309

SET	SAPG FILENAME REF.:
Labour Relations	0310
Company Vehicles	0311
4. Procurement	
Purchasing	0401
5. Stock and Materials Handling	
Stock Control	0501
Warehousing / Storage	0502
Distribution, Transport and Logistics	0503
6. Production / Manufacturing	
Planning and Production Control	0601
Facilities, Plant and Equipment	0602
Personnel	0603
Materials and Energy	0604
Quality Control	0605
Safety	0606
Environmental Issues	0607
Law and Regulatory Compliance	0608
Maintenance	0609
7. Marketing and Sales	
Product Development	0701
Market Research	0702
Promotion and Advertising	0703
Pricing and Discount Policies	0704
Sales Management	0705
Sales Performance and Monitoring	0706
Distributors	0707
Relationship with Parent Company	0708
Agents	0709
Order Processing	0710
8. After Sales Support	
Warranty Arrangements	0801

SET	SAPG FILENAME REF.:
Maintenance and Servicing	0802
Spare Parts and Supply	0803
9. Research and Development	
Product Development	0901
Project Appraisal and Monitoring	0902
Plant and Equipment	0903
Development Project Management	0904
Legal and Regulatory Issues	0905
10. Information Technology	
IT Strategic Planning	1001
IT Organisation	1002
IT Policy Framework	1003
Information Asset Register*	1004
Capacity Management	1005
Information Management (IM)*	1006
Records Management (RM)*	1007
Knowledge Management (KM)*	1008
IT Sites and Infrastructure (including physical security)	1009
Processing Operations	1010
Back-up and Media Management	1011
Removable media	1012
System and Operating Software (including patch management)	1013
System Access Control (or logical security)	1014
Personal Computers (including laptops and PDAs)	1015
Remote Working	1016
Email	1017
Internet Usage	1018
Software Maintenance (including change management)	1019
Networks	1020
Databases	1021
Data Protection	1022
Freedom of Information	1023
Data Transfer and Sharing (Standards and Protocol Guidelines)	1024
Legal Responsibilities	1025

SET	SAPG FILENAME REF.:
Facilities Management	1026
System Development	1027
Software Selection	1028
Contingency Planning	1029
Human Resources information security	1030
Monitoring and Logging	1031
Information Security incidents	1032
Data Retention and Disposal	1033
Electronic Data Interchange (EDI) and the use of secure networks	1034
Viruses	1035
User Support	1036
BACS (i.e. automated cash/funds transfer)	1037
Spreadsheet Design and Good Practice	1038
IT Health Checks	1039
IT Accounting.	1040
11. Contracting	
Contract Management Environment	1101
Project Management Framework	1102
Project Assessment and Approval	1103
Engaging, Monitoring and Paying Consultants	1104
Design	1105
Assessing the Viability / Competence of Contractors	1106
Maintaining an Approved List of Contractors	1107
Tendering Procedures	1108
Contract & Tendering Documentation	1109
Insurance and Bonding	1110
Selection and Letting of Contracts	1111
Management Information and Reporting	1112
Performance Monitoring	1113
Arrangements for Sub-contractors and Suppliers	1114
Materials, Plant and Project Assets	1115
Valuing Work for Interim Payments	1116
Controlling Price Fluctuations	1117
Monitoring and Controlling Variations	1118
Extensions of Time	1119

SET	SAPG FILENAME REF.:
Controlling Contractual Claims	1120
Liquidations and Bankruptcies	1121
Contractor's Final Account	1122
Recovery of Damages	1123
Review of Project Outturn and Performance	1124
Maintenance Obligations	1125
12. Sector: Financial institutions	
Branch Security	1201
Branch Operations	1202
Management	1203
Treasury Dealing	1204
Investments—new accounts	1205
Investments—account maintenance	1206
Investments—account statements	1207
Secured Personal Loans	1208
Unsecured Loans	1209
Commercial Lending—new business	1210
Commercial Lending—account maintenance	1211
Cheque Accounts	1212
ATM Services	1214
Credit and Debit Cards	1215
New Mortgage Business	1216
Mortgage Account Maintenance	1217
Mortgage Arrears	1218
Mortgage Possessions and Sales	1219
Mortgage Mandates	1220
Mortgage Annual Statements	1221
Treasury Environment	1222
Staff Accounts	1223
Securities	1224
13. Sector: Health	
Purchaser Contracting	1301
Provider Contracting	1302
General Practitioner Fund Holding	1303

SET	SAPG FILENAME REF.:
Charitable Funds	1304
Use of Health Centres	1305
Private Patients	1306
Welfare Foods	1307
Residential Accommodation	1308
Joint Finance	1309
Residents' Monies	1310
Cashiers	1311
Family Health Service Authority	1312
Road Traffic Accidents	1313
Nursing Homes	1314
Trading Agencies	1315
Insurance Products	1316
Pharmacy Stores	1317
Risk Management	1318
Cash Collection—car parks	1319
Cash Collection—telephones	1320
Cash Collection—prescriptions	1321
Cash Collection—shops / restaurants	1322
Cash Collection—staff meals	1323
Cash Collection—vending machines	1324
Income Generation	1325
Staff Expenses	1326
Losses and Compensations	1327
14. Governance/Risk Management/Internal Control	
Internal Governance Processes	1401
The Board	1402
External Governance Processes	1403
Risk Management Processes	1404
Internal Control	1405
Control Self Assessment	1406
Internal Audit	1407

Appendix 2
Standard Audit Programme Guides

USE IN RELATION TO "BUSINESS PROCESSES"

A Word version of this appendix is to be found in the Tools directory of the material available on a password protected website accompanying this Handbook, with the filename "Process.doc". The password protected website contains a Word format Standard Audit Programme Guide for each of the approximately two hundred business activities listed in this Appendix.

The standard set of Standard Audit Programme Guides (SAPGs) is subdivided into a number of separate Activities or Systems, each of which is capable of free-standing audit use. However, most of these systems do not operate in complete isolation and have both potential and actual bearing upon other systems. For example, Purchasing activities have a positive connection with Accounts Payable, with the order data from the former having a payment implication for the latter. Whether or not the SAPGs are used in isolation is partly a matter for how audit management perceives their universe of discrete audit projects, but it is likely that the control effectiveness of these separate systems will be dependent upon the flow of data and materials to and from other systems.

On the final page of each SAPG we have provided a simple table which aims to plot the potential input and output interfaces with other systems. This table can be used to suggest which other systems may have to be reviewed to form a wider impression of control effectiveness. It is often at the point of interface between systems and activities where the controls are weakest. It is logical therefore that where there are doubts about the integrity of controls within the primary system, an examination of the knock-on effects within the related systems may be justified.

A "systems" approach can be supported by the use of individual SAPGs with the added flexibility of using a number of related system SAPGs in combinations to provide wider coverage and take into account related issues and implications. This flexibility lets the user establish the breadth of focus applicable to the specific scenario taking into account the audit findings relative to an SAPG system. However, there are further possible ways of combining individual SAPGs in order to reflect larger associations of related systems, activities or economic events. Such combinations may be referred to as Business Processes. In the attached analysis we have utilised six categories of Business Process, as follows:

Treasury

Revenue

Expenditure

Conversion

Financial Reporting

Corporate Framework

The first four process categories (which are defined below) are built around a range of related economic events which may in turn generate transactions and interactions with systems.

Treasury Process: This process incorporates those activities concerned with an organisation's capital funds. These activities may include, *inter alia*, definition of cash requirements, allocation of available cash to various operations, investment considerations and the outflow of cash to investors and creditors.

Revenue Process: This category is related to those activities that exchange the organisation's products and services for cash, and therefore include, *inter alia*, the following elements: credit granting, order entry, delivery/shipping, billing, accounts receivable and pursuing debtors.

Expenditure Process: This process could be defined to include those activities/systems that acquire goods, services, labour and property; pay for them; and classify, summarise and report what was acquired and what was paid.

Conversion Process: In this context, the term "conversion" relates to the utilisation and management of various resources (i.e. inventory stock, labour, etc.) in the process of creating the goods and services marketed by the organisation. The key issues in this cycle include accountability for the movement and usage of resources up to the point of supply which is then dealt with in the Revenue Process. Conversion Process activities include product accounting/costing, manufacturing control and stock management.

The fifth category (**Financial Reporting**) is not based upon the basic processing of transactions reflecting economic events, but concentrates upon the crucial consolidation and reporting of results to various interested parties (for example management, investors, regulatory and taxation authorities).

The last category (**Corporate Framework**) incorporates those activities concerned with the development and maintenance of effective management, strategic, infrastructure and control frameworks which should aim to give form to the underlying direction, structure and effectiveness of an organisation. This category can also include issues such as specific industry regulations and compliance.

It should be noted that there is likely to be selective interaction between the defined processes, for example the general management of cash is one of the key issues of the Treasury Process, but the Revenue Process is associated with cash receipts and the Expenditure Process will involve cash disbursements. In instances where a particular system or activity has a relevance to more than one of the named processes, we have differentiated between the Main (or primary) and Secondary relationships by the use of a large emboldened **M** and a regular S respectively on the attached analysis. This discrimination is intended to further assist users in selecting the appropriate combinations of SAPGs which can readily support the structural objectives of their adopted audit universe approach.

Activity/System	SAPG Ref.	Treasury Process	Revenue Process	Expenditure Process	Conversion Process	Financial Reporting	Corporate Framework
1. Management & Administration							
The Control Environment	0101						M
Organisation	0102				S		M
Management Information	0103					M	S
Planning	0104						M
Risk Management	0105	S	S	S	S		M
Legal Department	0106						M
Quality Management	0107				S		M
Estates Management & Facilities	0108			S	S		M
Environmental Issues	0109				S		M
Insurance	0110		S	S			M
Security	0111						M
Capital Projects	0112	M		S			S
Industry Regulations and Compliance	0113						M
Media, Public and External Relations	0114						M
Company Secretarial Department	0115					S	M

Activity/System	SAPG Ref.	Treasury Process	Revenue Process	Expenditure Process	Conversion Process	Financial Reporting	Corporate Framework
2. Financial and Accounting							
Treasury	0201	M				S	S
Payroll	0202	S		M		S	
Accounts Payable	0203	S		M		S	
Accounts Receivable	0204	S	M		S	S	
General Ledger/ Management Accounts	0205					M	S
Fixed Assets (and capital charges)	0206	S		M		S	
Budgeting and Monitoring	0207	S	S	S		S	M
Bank Accounts & Banking Arrangements	0208	M	S	S		S	S
VAT Accounting (where applicable)	0209		S	S		M	
Taxation	0210	S	S	S		M	S
Inventories	0211		S	S	S	M	
Product/Project Accounting	0212		S	S	S	M	M
Petty Cash & Expenses	0213			M		S	S
Financial Information and Reporting	0214	S	S	S	S	M	S
Investments	0215	M	S			S	S
3. Personnel							
Human Resources Department	0301			S	S		M
Recruitment	0302				S		M
Manpower & Succession Planning	0303				S		M

Activity/System	SAPG Ref.	Treasury Process	Revenue Process	Expenditure Process	Conversion Process	Financial Reporting	Corporate Framework
Staff Training and Development	0304			S	S		M
Welfare	0305			S			M
Performance-related Compensation, Pension Schemes (and Other Benefits)	0306			S		S	M
Health Insurance	0307			S			M
Staff Appraisal & Disciplinary Matters	0308						M
Health & Safety	0309						M
Labour Relations	0310						M
Company Vehicles	0311			S			M
4. Procurement							
Purchasing	0401	S		M	S	S	
5. Stock and Materials Handling							
Stock Control	0501		S	S	M	S	S
Warehousing/ Storage	0502		S	S	M	S	S
Distribution, Transport and Logistics	0503		M	S	S	S	S
6. Production/Manufacturing							
Planning & Production Control	0601			S	M		S
Facilities, Plant and Equipment	0602	S		S	M	S	S
Personnel	0603			S	M		S
Materials and Energy	0604			S	M		S

Activity/System	SAPG Ref.	Treasury Process	Revenue Process	Expenditure Process	Conversion Process	Financial Reporting	Corporate Framework
Quality Control	0605				S		M
Safety	0606				S		M
Environmental Issues	0607				S		S
Law and Regulatory Compliance	0608						M
Maintenance	0609			S	M		S
7. Marketing & Sales							
Product Development	0701	S	S	S	S		M
Market Research	0702		S				M
Promotion and Advertising	0703		S	S			M
Pricing and Discount Policies	0704		M		S		S
Sales Management	0705		M				
Sales Performance and Monitoring	0706		M			S	S
Distributors	0707		M				S
Relationship with Parent Company	0708	S	S	S		S	M
Agents	0709		M				S
Order Processing	0710		M			S	S
8. After Sales Support							
Warranty Arrangements	0801		M	S			S
Maintenance and Servicing	0802		M	S			S
Spare Parts and Supply	0803		M	S	S		S
9. Research and Development							
Product Development	0901	S	S	S	S		M

STANDARD AUDIT PROGRAMME GUIDES   725

Activity/System	SAPG Ref.	Treasury Process	Revenue Process	Expenditure Process	Conversion Process	Financial Reporting	Corporate Framework
Project Appraisal and Monitoring	0902	S	S	S	S		M
Plant and Equipment	0903	S		M	S		S
Development Project Management	0904			S	S		M
Legal and Regulatory Issues	0905				S	S	M
10. Information Technology							
IT Strategic Planning	1001		S	S			M
IT Organisation	1002				S		M
IT Policy Framework	1003		S	S			M
Information Asset Register	1004		S				M
Capacity Management	1005		S	S			M
Information Management (IM)	1006		S	S			M
Records Management (RM)	1007		S	S			M
Knowledge Management (KM)	1008		S	S	S		M
IT Sites and Infrastructure (including physical security)	1009			S			M
Processing Operations	1010	S	S	S	S	S	M
Back-up and Media Management	1011	S	S	S	S	S	M
Removable Media	1012						M

Activity/System	SAPG Ref.	Treasury Process	Revenue Process	Expenditure Process	Conversion Process	Financial Reporting	Corporate Framework
Systems/Operating Systems (including patch management)	1013						M
System Access Control (or logical security)	1014					S	M
Personal Computers (including laptops and PDAs)	1015						M
Remote Working	1016						M
Email	1017						M
Internet Usage	1018						M
Software Maintenance (including change management)	1019			S			M
Networks	1020						M
Databases	1021					S	M
Data Protection	1022					S	M
Freedom of Information	1023						M
Data Transfer & Sharing (Standards and Protocol Guidelines)	1024				S		M
Legal Responsibilities	1025						M
Facilities Management	1026	S		S			M
System Development	1027			S			M
Software Selection	1028						M
Contingency Planning	1029						M
Human Resources Information Security	1030						M

Activity/System	SAPG Ref.	Treasury Process	Revenue Process	Expenditure Process	Conversion Process	Financial Reporting	Corporate Framework
Monitoring and Logging	1031						M
Information Security Incidents	1032						M
Data Retention & Disposal	1033						M
Electronic Data Interchanges	1034	S	S	S	S	S	M
Viruses	1035						M
User Support	1036						M
BACS	1037	S		S		S	M
Spreadsheet Design & Good Practice	1038					S	M
IT Health Checks	1039						M
IT Accounting	1040					M	S
11. Contracting							
Contract Management Environment	1101	S	S	S		S	M
Project Management Framework	1102						M
Project Assessment and Approval	1103	S	S	S			M
Engaging, Monitoring & Paying Consultants	1104			S			M
Design	1105			S	S		M
Assessing the Viability/ Competence of Contractors	1106			S			M
Maintaining an Approved List of Contractors	1107			S			M
Tendering Procedures	1108	S		S			M

Activity/System	SAPG Ref.	Treasury Process	Revenue Process	Expenditure Process	Conversion Process	Financial Reporting	Corporate Framework
Contract & Tendering Documentation	1109						M
Insurance and Bonding	1110			S			M
Selection & Letting of Contracts	1111			S			M
Management Information & Reporting	1112					M	S
Performance Monitoring	1113		S	S		S	M
Arrangements for sub-contractors and suppliers	1114			S			M
Materials, Plant & Project Assets	1115	S		M		S	S
Valuing Work for Interim Payments	1116	S		M		S	S
Controlling Price Fluctuations	1117	S		M		S	S
Monitoring & Controlling Variations	1118			M			S
Extensions of Time	1119		S	S		S	M
Controlling Contractual Claims	1120	S	S			S	M
Liquidations & Bankruptcies	1121	S	S	S		S	M
Contractor's Final Account	1122	S		M		S	S
Recovery of Damages	1123		S	S		S	M
Review of Project Outturn & Performance	1124	S	S	S		S	M
Maintenance Obligations	1125			S			M

Appendix 3
International Data Protection Legislation

International progress with the development of legal support for Data Protection practices varies considerably. Member countries of the European Union have been obliged to take action and the legislation in these countries is at a more refined state of regulatory development than elsewhere. The following table contains details of the status of national Data Protection legislation listed alphabetically by country. This information was correct at the time of publication; however readers are advised to check the noted websites and contact points for the latest position.

Where your organisation is engaged in the regular international transfer of data, it will be important to ensure that the interests of local data subjects will be adequately and effectively protected in all the other affected target areas.

Country	Legislation	Status	Date Passed	Responsible Bodies/ Contacts/Comments
Afghanistan (Islamic Republic of Afghanistan).	No specific Data Protection legislation.	N/A	N/A	
Albania (Republic of Albania)	Act No. 8517 on the Protection of Personal Data	Enacted	1999	Republic of Albania People's Advocate. Web: avokatipopullit.gov.al Mail: Avokati i Popullit, Bulevardi "Zhan D'Ark", No. 2, Zip Code 1001, Tirana, ALBANIA Email: ap@avokatipopullit.gov.al

Country	Legislation	Status	Date Passed	Responsible Bodies/ Contacts/Comments
Algeria (People's Democratic Republic of Algeria)	No specific Data Protection legislation.	N/A	N/A	Article 39 of the Constitution of Algeria (Privacy, Secrecy of Communication): "(1) The private life and the honour of the citizen are inviolable and protected by the law. (2) The secrecy of private correspondence and communication, in any form, is guaranteed."
Andorra (Republic of Andorra)	Unable to establish	N/A	N/A	Andorran Agency of Data Protection (Agència Andorrana de Protecció de Dades) Web: apda.ad (in Catalan) Mail: c/ Prat de la Creu, 59-65 esc. A, planta 3, despatx 1-A AD500 Andorra la Vella-Principat d'Andorra Email: apda@apda.ad
Angola (Republic of Angola)	No specific Data Protection legislation.	N/A	N/A	
Argentina (Argentine Republic)	Data Protection Act of Argentina (Ley de Protección de los Datos Personales)	Enacted Regs	2000 2001	National Directorate for Personal Data Protection (Dirección Nacional de Protección de Datos Personales). Web: protecciondedatos.com.ar Web: habeasdata.org/Data-Protection-Act-Argentina-Law-25326 Web: jus.gov.ar/datospersonales Mail: Sarmiento 329 piso 5Â² Frente C.P.: C1041AAG
Armenia (Republic of Armenia)	The Law of the Republic of Armenia on Personal Data	Enacted Amended	2002 2006	There is no Armenian national data protection authority in place with appeals against the conditions of the law being heard in the courts.
Australia (Commonwealth of Australia)	Privacy Act 1988 Privacy Amendment (Private Sector) Act 2000	Enacted Amended	2001 2009	Office of the Privacy Commissioner. Web: privacy.gov.au/index.php Mail: GPO Box 5218 Sydney NSW 2001 Email: privacy@privacy.gov.au

Country	Legislation	Status	Date Passed	Responsible Bodies/ Contacts/Comments
Austria (Republic of Austria)	Data Protection Law (Datenschutzgesetz 2000—DSG 2000)	Enacted	2000	Austrian Data Protection Commission (Österreichischen Datenschutzkommission) Web: dsk.gv.at/site/6248/default.aspx Mail: Geschäftsstelle der Datenschutzkommission Hohenstaufengasse 3, 1010 Wien Email: dsk@dsk.gv.at
Azerbaijan (Republic of Azerbaijan)	Law of the Azerbaijan Republic on Data, Data Processing and Data Protection.	Enacted	1998	Unable to trace a national oversight authority for data protection.
Bahamas (The Commonwealth of The Bahamas)	Data Protection (Privacy of Personal Information) Act 2003	Enacted	2003	Data Protection Commissioner for the Bahamas. Web: bahamas.gov.bs/dataprotection Mail: P.O.Box N-3017 Nassau, Bahamas. Email: Dataprotection@bahamas.gov.bs
Bahrain (Kingdom of Bahrain)	No specific Data Protection legislation.	N/A	N/A	
Bangladesh (People's Republic of Bangladesh)	No specific Data Protection legislation.	N/A	N/A	
Barbados (Independent Continental Island-Nation)	Electronic Transaction Act (CAP3088)	Enacted	2001	Web: commerce.gov.bb/Legislation Mail: Ministry of Trade, Industry and Commerce, Reef Road, Fontabelle, St. Michael, Barbados Email: pscommerce@commerce.gov.bb
Belarus (Republic of Belarus)	There is no specific data protection in Belarus. Law Of The Republic Of Belarus "On Information, Informatization and Protection of information"	Unclear	1995	The 1995 Informisation Law does not contain any references to a data protection authority or commissioner. Web: e-belarus.org/docs/informationlawdraft.html

Country	Legislation	Status	Date Passed	Responsible Bodies/ Contacts/Comments
Belgium (Kingdom of Belgium)	Law of 8 December 1992 on the protection of privacy in relation to the processing of personal data (modified by the Law of 11 December 1998 transposing Directive 95/46/EC of 24 October 1995 of the European Parliament and the Council)(Privacy Law or Data Protection Act)	Enacted by Royal decree	2001	Commission for the Protection of Privacy (CPP) (Commission de la Protection de la vie privée) Web: privacycommission.be/en/ Mail: 139, rue Haute, 1000 Brussels Email: commission@ privacycommission.be
Belize (Formerly British Honduras)	No specific Data Protection legislation.	N/A	N/A	
Benin (Republic of Benin)	No specific Data Protection legislation.	N/A	N/A	
Bermuda (British Overseas Territory of Bermuda)	No specific Data Protection legislation. (See Comments)	N/A	N/A	Although Bermuda has not implemented any specific data protection legislation, Part VI s. 26 of the Electronic Transactions Act 1999 states: "Data protection (1) The Minister may make regulations prescribing standards for the processing of personal data whether or not the personal data originates inside Bermuda. (2) The regulations may provide for— (a) the voluntary registration and de-registration to the standards by data controllers and data processors; (b) the establishment of a register that is available for public inspection showing particulars of data controllers and data processors who have registered or de-registered to the standards and the dates thereof and the countries in respect of which the registration applies;

Country	Legislation	Status	Date Passed	Responsible Bodies/ Contacts/Comments
				(c) the application of the standards to those countries specified in the regulations; (d) different standards to be applied in respect of personal data originating from different countries."
Bhutan (Kingdom of Bhutan)	No specific Data Protection legislation.	N/A	N/A	
Bolivia (Plurinational State of Bolivia)	No specific Data Protection legislation.	N/A	N/A	
Bosnia and Herzegovina (Federal Democratic Republic of Bosnia and Herzegovina)	Law on the Protection of Personal Data	Enacted	2006	Agency for Identification Documents, Data Registers and Data Exchange of Bosnia and Herzegovina. (Agencija za identifikacijske dokumente, podatke evidenciju i razmjenu podataka Bosne i Hercegovine.) Web: iddeea.gov.ba Mail: Vuka Karadžića 6 Email: pr@cips.gov.ba
Botswana (Republic of Botswana)	No specific Data Protection legislation.	N/A	N/A	
Brazil (Federal Republic of Brazil)	No specific Data Protection legislation. (See Comments)	N/A	N/A	Bill reference 6891/02 was proposed in 2002 but there has been no subsequent progress with enacting legislation. Article 5 of the 1988 Constitution covers the right to privacy. Web: mre.gov.br Mail: Ministry of External Relations, Division of Science and Technology Itamaraty Palace Annex I - Room 403 70170-900 Brasilia - DP - Brazil
Brunei (State of Brunei)	No specific Data Protection legislation.	N/A	N/A	

Country	Legislation	Status	Date Passed	Responsible Bodies/ Contacts/Comments
Burkina Faso (Republic of Burkina Faso)	No specific Data Protection legislation.	N/A	N/A	Article 6 of the constitution of Burkina Faso: "The residence, the domicile, private and family life, secrecy of correspondence of every person are inviolable. It can only be affected according to the forms and in the cases specified by the law."
Bulgaria (Republic of Bulgaria)	Law for Protection of Personal Data (Закон за защита на личните данни)	Enacted Amended	2002 2004 2005 2006 2007	Commission for Personal Data Protection (Комисията за защита на личните данни) Web: cpdp.bg Mail: 15 Acad. Ivan Evstratiev Geshov Blvd, Sofia 1431 Email: kzld@cpdp.bg
Burma (Union of Myanmar)	No specific Data Protection legislation.	N/A	N/A	
Burundi (Republic of Burundi)	No specific Data Protection legislation.	N/A	N/A	
Cambodia (Kingdom of Cambodia)	No specific Data Protection legislation.	N/A	N/A	
Cameroon (Republic of Cameroon)	No specific Data Protection legislation.	N/A	N/A	The preamble to the 1996 Constitution of Cameroon states: "... the privacy of all correspondence is inviolate. No interference may be allowed except by virtue of decisions emanating from the Judicial Power."
Canada	Personal Information Protection and Electronic Documents Act (PIPEDA) and the Privacy Act	Royal Assent Enacted	2000 1983	**At a National level:** Office of the Privacy Commissioner of Canada (La commissaire à la protection de la vie privée du Canada) Web: priv.gc.ca Mail: 112 Kent Street, Place de Ville, Tower B, 3rd Floor, Ottawa, Ontario K1A 1H3, Canada Email: info@privcom.gc.ca

Country	Legislation	Status	Date Passed	Responsible Bodies/ Contacts/Comments
				At a Provincial level:
				Alberta
				Web: oipc.ab.ca
				Mail: Information and Privacy Commissioner of Alberta, 410, 9925—109 Street, Edmonton, Alberta T5K 2J8
				Email: ipcab@planet.eon.net
				British Columbia
				Web: oipc.bc.ca
				Mail: Information and Privacy Commissioner for British Columbia, P.O. Box 9038, Stn. Prov. Govt. 756 Fort Street, 3rd Floor, Victoria, British Columbia, V8V 1X4.
				Email: info@oipc.bc.ca
				Manitoba
				Web: ombudsman.mb.ca
				Mail: Office of the Ombudsman, 750—500 Postage Avenue, Winnipeg, Manitoba R3C 3X1
				Email: ombudsman@ombudsman.mb.ca
				New Brunswick
				Web: gnb.ca/0073
				Mail: Office of the Ombudsman, Sterling House, P.O. Box 6000, 767 New Brunswick Street, Fredericton, NB E3B 5H1
				Email: nbombud@gnb.ca
				Newfoundland & Labrador
				Web: opic.gov.nl.ca
				Mail: Office of the Information and Privacy Commissioner for Newfoundland and Labrador, 5th Floor, East Block, Confederation Building, P.O. Box 8700, St. Johns, NL A1B 4J6
				Email: opic@gov.nl.ca

Country	Legislation	Status	Date Passed	Responsible Bodies/ Contacts/Comments
				Northwest Territories
				Mail: Information and Privacy Commissioner of the Northwest Territories, 5018, 47th Street, Yellowknife, Northwest Territories X1A 2N2.
				Email: atippcom@theedge.ca
				Nova Scotia
				Web: gov.ns.ca/foiro
				Mail: Freedom of Information and Privacy Review Office, P.O. Box 181, Halifax, Nova Scotia, B3J 2M4
				Email: foipopro@gov.ns.ca
				Nunvut
				Web: info-privacy.nu.ca/en/home
				Mail: Information and Privacy Commissioner of Nunuvut, 5018, 47th Street, Yellowknife, Northwest Territories X1A 2N2.
				Email: atippcomm@theedge.ca
				Ontario
				Web: ipc.on.ca
				Mail: Information and Privacy Commissioner of Ontario, 2 Bloor Street East, Suite 1400, Toronto, Ontario M4W 1A8
				Email: info@ipc.on.ca
				Prince Edward Island
				Web: gov.re.ca
				Mail: Information and Privacy Commissioner of Prince Edward Island, J. Angus MacLean Building, 180 Richmond Street, P.O. Box 2000, Charlottetown, Prince Edward Island C1A 7N8
				Email: mismith@gov.pe.ca

Country	Legislation	Status	Date Passed	Responsible Bodies/ Contacts/Comments
				Quebec
				Web: cai.gouv.qc.ca/index-en.html
				Mail: **QUÉBEC CITY (Head Office)** Commission d'accès à l'information du QuébecBureau 1.10 575, rue Saint-Amable Québec (Québec) G1R 2G4
				MONTREAL Bureau 18.200 500, boul. René-Lévesque Ouest Montréal (Québec) H2Z 1W7
				Email: Cai.Communications@cai.gouv.qc.ca
				Saskatchewan
				Web: oipc.sk.ca
				Mail: Information and Privacy Commissioner of Saskatchewan, 503—1801 Hamilton Street, Regina, Saskatchewan S4P 4B4
				Email: gdickson@oipc.sk.ca
				Yukon
				Web: ombudsman.yk.ca
				Mail: Ombudsman and Information and Privacy Commissioner of the Yukon, 211 Main Street, Suite 200, P.O. Box 2703, Whitehorse, Yukon Territory Y1A 2C6
				Email: email.ombudsman@ombudsman.yk.ca
Cape Verde (Republic of Cape Verde)	No specific Data Protection legislation.	N/A	N/A	Articles 42 and 43 of the Constitution of Cape Verde (1992) state: Article 42 (Utilization of computerized means) 1. The utilization of computerized means for registration and treatment of data that are individually identifiable, relative to political, philosophical and ideological convictions or to religious faith, party or trade union affiliation and private life, shall be prohibited. 2. The law will regulate the protection of personal data stored in the computerized record, the conditions of access to the data banks, as well as the establishment and the use, by public or private authorities, of such data banks or computerized software.

Country	Legislation	Status	Date Passed	Responsible Bodies/ Contacts/Comments
				3. The access to the archives file, computerized records and data bases for information on personal data relative to third parties or the transfer of personal data from one computerized file to another belonging to different services or institutions shall not be allowed, except in cases laid out by law or by judicial decision.
				4. In no circumstance shall there be a sole national number ascribed to Capeverdean citizens.
				Article 43 (Habeas data)
				1. Habeas data shall be granted to every citizen to secure his knowledge of information stored in files, archive or computerized records concerning him, as well as to inform him of the objective of such information and to demand a correction or update of the data.
				2. The law will regulate the habeas data procedure.
Cayman Islands (British Overseas Territory of the Cayman Islands)	No specific Data Protection legislation. (See Comments)	N/A	N/A	Certain data protection rights are protected by: The Confidential Relationships (Preservation) Law 1995, The Computer Misuse Law 2000 and The Information and Communications Technology Authority Law 2004.
Central African Republic	No specific Data Protection legislation.	N/A	N/A	Article 13 of the Constitution of the Central African Republic (1995) states: "Privacy of correspondence as well as that of postal, electronic, telegraphic and telephonic communications are inviolable. Restrictions may only be prescribed for the above by application of a law."
Chad (Republic of Chad)	No specific Data Protection legislation.	N/A	N/A	Article 17 of the Constitution of Chad (1996) states: "The human person is sacred and inviolable. Each individual has the right to life, personal integrity, security, freedom, the protection of private life and possessions."
Chile (Republic of Chile)	Data Protection Law 1923	Enacted	1999	At present there is no data protection enforcement body. Enforcement is handled through the courts.

Country	Legislation	Status	Date Passed	Responsible Bodies/ Contacts/Comments
China (People's Republic of China)	No specific Data Protection legislation.	N/A	N/A	There is no single integrated data protection law in China at present. There have been moves to draft such a law but progress has been slow and the overall implementation timescale is unclear.
Colombia (Republic of Colombia)	No specific Data Protection legislation.	N/A	N/A	At the time of writing Colombia has no discrete data protection legislation in place. However, the Colombian Telecommunication Commission (CTC) advises that two data protection bills are currently pending approval in the Colombian Congress. The first bill (Bill No. 27/06 Senate—221/07 House of Representatives (05/06)) aims to specifically regulate personal data protection in Colombia. The other pending bill (Bill No. 112/2007) is intended to regulate the information society and create the National Spectrum Agency.
Comoros (Union of the Comoros)	No specific Data Protection legislation.	N/A	N/A	
Congo (Democratic Republic of the Congo—Congo-Kinshasa)	No specific Data Protection legislation.	N/A	N/A	
Congo (Republic of the Congo—Congo-Brazzaville)	No specific Data Protection legislation.	N/A	N/A	
Costa Rica (Republic of Costa Rica)	No specific Data Protection legislation.	N/A	N/A	At present there are three Bills being considered which have some data protection implications, as follows. However, none of the Bills require the set up of supervisory authorities but rather depend on matters being handled through the constitutional court. No. 14778(3) includes a mechanism for obtaining information held about a citizen by either the state or a private organisation. No. 14785 attempts to reform the Law of Constitutional Jurisdiction to add the habeas data procedure to the list of individual constitutional complaints accepted by the Constitutional Court.

Country	Legislation	Status	Date Passed	Responsible Bodies/ Contacts/Comments
				No. 15178 (9) is an attempt to implement a European-style data protection regime in Costa Rica
Croatia (Republic of Croatia)	The Act on Personal Data Protection (Official Gazette, No. 103/03)	Enacted	2003	Croatian Personal Data Protection Agency (Agencije za zaštitu osobnih podataka).
	The Amendments to the Act on Personal Data Protection (Official Gazette, No. 118/06)	Enacted	2006	Web: azop.hr/default.asp?jezik=2 Mail: Republike Austrije 25, 10000 Zagreb, Republic of Croatia Email: azop@azop.hr
	The Amendments to the Act on Personal Data Protection (Official Gazette, No. 41/08)	Enacted	2008	
Cuba (Republic of Cuba)	No specific Data Protection legislation.	N/A	N/A	
Cyprus (Republic of Cyprus)	Processing of Personal Data (Protection of the Individual) Law of 2001, its amendment (Law No. 37(I)/2003)	Enacted Amended	2001 2003	Office of the Commissioner for Personal Data Protection (Γραφείου Επιτρόπου Προστασίας Δεδομένων Προσωπικού Χαρακτήρα). Web: dataprotection.gov.cy Mail: 40, Th. Dervis Street CY - 1066 Nicosia Email: commissioner@ dataprotection.gov.cy
Czech Republic	Act 101 of April 4, 2000 on the Protection of Personal Data	Enacted	2000	The Office for Personal Data Protection (Úřad pro ochranu osobních údajů). Web: uoou.cz Mail: Pplk. Sochora 27, 170 00 Praha 7 Czech Republic Email: posta@uoou.cz
Denmark (Kingdom of Denmark)	The Act on Processing of Personal Data (Act No. 429 of 31 May 2000)	Enacted	2000	Danish Data Protection Agency (Datatilsynet) Web: datatilsynet.dk/english/ Mail: Datatilsynet, Borger Gade 28, 5 1300 Copenhagen. Email: dt@datatilsynet.dk

Country	Legislation	Status	Date Passed	Responsible Bodies/ Contacts/Comments
Djibouti (Republic of Djibouti)	No specific Data Protection legislation.	N/A	N/A	Article 13 of the Constitution of Djibouti states: "The secrecy of correspondence and all other means of communication shall be inviolable. This inviolability shall be subject only to such restrictions as are made applicable by law."
Dominican Republic	No specific Data Protection legislation.	N/A	N/A	
Ecuador (Republic of Ecuador)	No specific Data Protection legislation.	N/A	N/A	
Egypt (Arab Republic of Egypt)	No specific Data Protection legislation.	N/A	N/A	
El Salvador (Republic of El Salvador)	No specific Data Protection legislation.	N/A	N/A	
Equatorial Guinea (Republic of Equatorial Guinea)	No specific Data Protection legislation.	N/A	N/A	Item 13 of the Constitution of Equatorial Guinea includes: "Item 13: Every citizen shall enjoy the following rights and freedoms: g)—The inviolability of the home and the privacy of all correspondence."
Eritrea (State of Eritrea)	No specific Data Protection legislation.	N/A	N/A	Article 18 of the Constitution of Eritrea states: "1. Every person shall have the right to privacy."
Estonia (Republic of Estonia)	Personal Data Protection Act	Enacted	2003	The Data Protection Inspectorate (Andmekaitse Inspektsioon) Web: aki.ee/eng/ Mail: Andmekaitse Inspektsioon; Väike-Ameerika 19, Tallinn 10129 Email: viljar.peep@dp.gov.ee

Country	Legislation	Status	Date Passed	Responsible Bodies/ Contacts/Comments
Ethiopia (Federal Democratic Republic of Ethiopia)	No specific Data Protection legislation.	N/A	N/A	Article 26 of the Ethiopian Constitution (1994) states: "Right to Privacy Everyone has the right to privacy. This right shall include the right not to be subjected to searches of his home, person or property, or the seizure of any property under his personal possession. Everyone has the right to the inviolability of his notes and correspondence including postal letters, and communications made by means of telephone, telecommunications and electronic devices. Public officials shall respect and protect these rights. No restrictions may be placed on the enjoyment of such rights except in compelling circumstances and in accordance with specific laws whose purposes shall be the safeguarding of national security or public peace, the prevention of crimes or the protection of health, public morality or the rights and freedoms of others."
European Union	European Union Directive on Data Protection (Directive 95/46/EU).	Passed by EU Parl.	1995	The noted EU Directives are intended to provide a common basis for data protection and related matters across all member states. However, the stage of development of the national level legislation varies. Please refer to the entries for the EU member states for specific details. Web: ec.europa.eu/justice_home/fsj/privacy/
Fiji (Republic of the Fiji Islands)	No specific Data Protection legislation.	N/A	N/A	
Finland (Republic of Finland)	Personal Data Act (which replaced the Personal Data File Act of 1998)	Enacted	1999	The Office of the Data Protection Ombudsman (Tietosuojaval Tuutetun Toimisto) Web: tietosuoja.fi/1560.htm Mail: Office of the Data Protection Ombudsman, P.O. Box 315 FIN-00181 Helsinki, Finland. Email: tietosuoja@om.fi

Country	Legislation	Status	Date Passed	Responsible Bodies/ Contacts/Comments
France (French Republic)	Act N°78-17 of 6 January 1978 on Data Processing, Data Files and Individual Liberties (Loi N ° 78-17 du 6 Janvier 1978 relative à l'informatique, aux fichiers et aux libertés individuelles)	Enacted Amended	1978 2004	Data Protection Authority—The National Commission for Computing and Liberties (La Commission Nationale de l'Informatique et des Libertés (CNIL)) Web: cnil.fr/la-cnil Mail: Commission Nationale de l'Informatique et des Libertés 8, rue Vivienne, CS 30223 75083 Paris cedex 02 Email: hr@cnil.fr
Gabon (Gabonese Republic)	No specific Data Protection legislation.	N/A	N/A	Article 1 of the Constitution of Gabon (1997) includes: "6) The limits of the usage of information systems for the safeguard of man, the personal and familial privacy of persons, and the full exercise of their rights, shall be fixed by law."
Gambia (Republic of The Gambia)	No specific Data Protection legislation.	N/A	N/A	Section 23 of the Constitution of Gambia (2001) states: "Privacy (1) No person shall be subject to interference with the privacy of his or her home, correspondence or communications save as is in accordance with law and is necessary in a democratic society in the interests of national security, public safety or the economic well-being of the country, for the protection of health or morals, for the prevention of disorder or crime or for the protection of the rights and freedoms of others."
Georgia (Democratic Republic of Georgia)	No specific Data Protection legislation.	N/A	N/A	

Country	Legislation	Status	Date Passed	Responsible Bodies/ Contacts/Comments
Germany (Federal Republic of Germany)	Federal Data Protection Act (Bundesdaten-schutzgesetz (BDSG))	Enacted	2001	Federal Commissioner for Data Protection and Freedom of Information (Bundesbeauftragter für den Datenschutz und die Informationsfreiheit). Web: bfdi.bund.de/cln_118/EN Mail: Husarenstrasse 30 53117 Bonn Email: poststelle@bfdi.bund.de
Ghana (Republic of Ghana)	No specific Data Protection legislation.	N/A	N/A	Article 18 of the Constitution of Ghana (1992) states: "(2) No person shall be subjected to interference with the privacy of his home, property, correspondence or communication except in accordance with law and as may be necessary in a free and democratic society for public safety or the economic well-being of the country, for the protection of health or morals, for the prevention of disorder or crime or for the protection of the rights or freedoms of others."
Gibraltar (British Overseas Territory of Gibraltar)	The Data Protection Ordinance 2004	Enacted	2004	Data Protection Commissioner (operating within the Gibraltar Regulatory Authority (GRA)). Web: gra.gi Mail: Suite 603 Europort Email: info@gra.gi
Greece (Hellenic Republic)	Law 2472/1997 (Protection of Individuals with regard to the Processing of Personal Data)	Enacted	1997	Hellenic Data Protection Authority (HDPA) (Αρχής Προστασίας Δεδομένων Προσωπικού Χαρακτήρα) Web: dpa.gr
	Law 3471/2006 (Protection of personal data and privacy in the electronic telecommunications sector and amendment of Law 2472/1997).	Enacted	2006	Mail: Data Protection Authority Offices: Kifissias 1-3, PC 115 23 Ampelokipi Athens, Greece Email: contact@dpa.gr

Country	Legislation	Status	Date Passed	Responsible Bodies/ Contacts/Comments
Guatemala (Republic of Guatemala)	No specific Data Protection legislation.	N/A	N/A	
Guernsey States of Guernsey (Including the islands of: Alderney, Sark Herm, Jethou, Brecqhou and Lihou).	The Data Protection (Bailiwick of Guernsey) Law, 2001	Enacted	2002	The Data Protection Commissioner Web: gov.gg/ccm/navigation/home-department/data-protection-commissioner/ Mail: Data Protection Office, P.O. Box 642, Frances House, Sir William Place, St. Peter Port, Guernsey GY1 3JE, Channel Islands Email: dataprotection@gov.gg
Guinea (Republic of Guinea)	No specific Data Protection legislation.	N/A	N/A	
Guinea-Bissau (Republic of Guinea-Bissau)	No specific Data Protection legislation.	N/A	N/A	Article 48 of the Constitution of Guinea-Bissau states: "The state recognises the citizens' right to inviolability of domicile, correspondence and other means of private communication, except in cases expressly provided by the law in relation to criminal process."
Guyana (Co-operative Republic of Guyana)	No specific Data Protection legislation.	N/A	N/A	The following web link suggests that provision for Data Protection may be made in future. Web: mintic.gov.gy/legislation.html#consumer
Honduras (Republic of Honduras)	No specific Data Protection legislation.	N/A	N/A	
Hong Kong (Hong Kong Special Administrative Region)	Personal Data (Privacy) Ordinance	In force	1996	Privacy Commissioner for Personal Data (PCDP) Web: pcpd.org.hk Mail: 12/F, 248 Queen's Road East, Wanchai, Hong Kong Email: enquiry@pcpd.org.hk

Country	Legislation	Status	Date Passed	Responsible Bodies/ Contacts/Comments
Hungary (Republic of Hungary)	Act LXIII of 1992 on the Protection of Personal Data and the Disclosure of Information of Public Interest	Enacted Amended to align with EU	1992 1999	Parliamentary Commissioner for Data Protection and Freedom of Information (Országgyűlési biztosa az adatvédelmi és a tájékoztatás szabadságára vonatkozó) Web: obh.hu Mail: H-1051 Budapest, Nádor u. 22., Hungary Email: adatved@obh.hu
Iceland (Republic of Iceland)	Act on the Protection of Privacy as regards the Processing of Personal Data, No. 77/2000	Enacted	2000	Data Protection Authority (Skrifstofa Persónuverndar) Web: personuvernd.is Mail: Rauðarárstíg 10, 105 Reykjavík, Ísland Email: postur@personuvernd.is
India (Republic of India)	No specific legislation pertaining to data protection and privacy has been enacted in India but four components of a data protection and privacy regime do exist as follows: (a) Constitution of India (b) Judgments of the Supreme Court of India, articulating "protection of privacy" as one of the features of the Fundamental Rights [Article 21—Life and Liberty] (c) The Information Technology Act, 2000, and (d) The Indian Contract Act, 187	N/A	N/A	The Data Security Council for India (DSCI) is a self-regulatory organisation (SRO) that operates on a not-for-profit basis that is engaged in the development of best practices for Data Security and Data Privacy. Web: dsci.in Mail: Niryat Bhawan, 3rd Floor, Rao Tula Ram Marg, New Delhi—110057, India Email: info@dsci.in

Country	Legislation	Status	Date Passed	Responsible Bodies/ Contacts/Comments
Indonesia (Republic of Indonesia)	No specific Data Protection legislation (See Comments).	N/A	N/A	In 2008 a draft Electronic Information and Transaction Bill was issued and is still being considered. This Bill has only one section (section 28) to deal with the data protection which stipulates that data subjects must give "consent" before the "use" of any information containing personal data and privacy rights of that party, except in relation to public information that are no longer confidential. As regards regulatory oversight, no subsidiary regulation is mandated within the draft Bill.
Iran (Islamic Republic of Iran)	No specific Data Protection legislation.	N/A	N/A	
Iraq (Republic of Iraq).	No specific Data Protection legislation.	N/A	N/A	
Ireland (Eire) (Republic of Ireland—Eire)	Data Protection Act 1988. (The 1988 Act was amended by the Data Protection (Amendment) Act 2003)	Enacted Amended to align with EU	1998 2003	Data Protection Commissioner (An Coimisinéir Cosanta Sonraí). Web: //www.e/cln_118/EN/Home/ioner. dataprotection.ie Mail: Office of the Data Protection Commissioner. Canal House, Station Road, Portarlington, Co. Laois, Ireland. Email: info@dataprotection.ie
Isle of Man (Self-governing Crown Dependency)	Data Protection Act 2002	Enacted	2002	The Data Protection Supervisor Web: gov.im/odps/ Mail: P.O. Box 69, Douglas, Isle of Man IM99 1EQ, British Isles Email: enquiries@odps.gov.im
Israel (State of Israel)	Protection of Privacy Law 5741-1981 The Protection of Privacy Law (Amendment) 5745-1985	Enacted Amended	1981 1996 1985	Israeli Law, Information and Technology Authority is part of the Israel Ministry of Justice and incorporates the Database Registrar who oversees compliance with Law 5741-1981 Web: justice.gov.il

Country	Legislation	Status	Date Passed	Responsible Bodies/ Contacts/Comments
				Mail: The Government Campus 9th floor 125 Begin Rd. Tel Aviv
				Email: ILITA@justice.gov.il
Italy (Italian Republic)	Personal Data Protection Code (Legislative Decree no. 196) (Codice di protezione dei dati personali (D. Lgs. 196).)	Enacted	2004	Authority for the Protection of Personal Data (Garante per la Protezione dei Dati Personali). Web: garanteprivacy.it Mail: Piazza di Monte Citorio n. 121 00186 Roma Email: garante@garanteprivacy.it
Ivory Coast (Republic of Cote d'Ivoire)	No specific Data Protection legislation.	N/A	N/A	
Jamaica (Island Nation of Jamaica)	DRAFT—Data Protection Act 2005	Pending	N/A	The draft Data Protection Act is still being considered.
Japan	The Personalised Information Protection Law	Effective	2005	Ministry of Economy, Trade and Industry (METI) Web: Meti.go.jp/English/information/data/IT-policy/privacy soumu.go.jp/english/index.html Mail: Government Information Protection Office, Administrative Management Bureau, Ministry of Public Management Home Affairs Posts and Telecommunications 1-2 Kasumigaseki 2-chome, Chiyoda-ku, Tokyo 100-8926 Email: jyoho@soumu.go.jp
Jersey (Bailiwick of Jersey)	Data Protection (Jersey) Law 2005	Enacted	2005	The Data Protection Commissioner Web: dataprotection.gov.je Mail: Morier House, Halkett Place, St. Helier, Jersey JE1 1DD Email: dataproteciton@gov.je
Jordan (Hashemite Kingdom of Jordan)	No specific Data Protection legislation.	N/A	N/A	

Country	Legislation	Status	Date Passed	Responsible Bodies/ Contacts/Comments
Kenya (Republic of Kenya)	No specific Data Protection legislation.	N/A	N/A	
Kuwait (State of Kuwait)	No specific Data Protection legislation.	N/A	N/A	
Latvia (Republic of Latvia)	Personal Data Protection Law (Fizisko personu datu aizsardzības likums)	Adopted Amended	2000 2002 & 2006	Data State Inspectorate (Datu Valsts Inspekcija). Web: dvi.gov.lv/eng/ Mail: Riga, Blaumana 11/13 - 15, LV-1011, Latvia Email: info@dvi.gov.lv
Lebanon (Republic of Lebanon)	No specific Data Protection legislation.	N/A	N/A	
Lesotho (Kingdom of Lesotho)	No specific Data Protection legislation.	N/A	N/A	
Liberia (Republic of Liberia)	No specific Data Protection legislation.	N/A	N/A	
Libya (Socialist People's Libyan Arab Great Jamahiriya)	No specific Data Protection legislation.	N/A	N/A	
Liechtenstein (Principality of Liechtenstein)	Data Protection Act 2002 and relevant Ordinance on the Data Protection Act 2002.	Enacted	2002	Data Protection Authority (Datenschutzstelle) Web: dss.llv.li/ Mail: Postfach 684, 9490 Vaduz Email: info@dss.llv.li
Lithuania (Republic of Lithuania)	Law on Legal Protection of Personal Data	Enacted Amended	1996 2000 2002 2003	State Data Protection Inspectorate (Valstybinė duomenų apsaugos inspekcija). Web: ada.lt Mail: A. Juozapavičiaus str. 6 / Slucko str. 2 09310 Vilnius Lithuania Email: ada@ada.lt

Country	Legislation	Status	Date Passed	Responsible Bodies/ Contacts/Comments
Luxembourg (Grand Duchy of Luxembourg)	Data Protection Act (The Protection of Persons with regard to the Processing of Personal Data)	Enacted Amended	2002 2006 & 2007	National Commission for Data Protection (Commission Nationale pour la Protection des Données) Web: cnpd.lu Mail: 41, avenue de la gare L-1611 Luxembourg 4ième étage Email: info@cnpd.lu
Macedonia (Republic of Macedonia)	Law on Personal Data Protection	Enacted	2005	Directorate for Personal Data Protection (Дирекцијата за заштита на личните податоци) Web: dzlp.gov.mk/ Mail: St. Samoilova No.10 1000 Skopje Email: info@dzlp.gov.mk
Madagascar (Republic of Madagascar)	No specific Data Protection legislation.	N/A	N/A	
Malawi (Republic of Malawi)	No specific Data Protection legislation.	N/A	N/A	
Malaysia	DRAFT Personal Data Protection Bill	Pending, due for first reading in October 2009	TBA	Data Protection Commissioner (yet to be established pending the passing of legislation).
Mail (Republic of Mali)	No specific Data Protection legislation.	N/A	N/A	
Malta (Republic of Malta)	Data Protection Act 2001	Enacted	2001	Office of the Data Protection Commissioner Web: dataprotection.gov.mt Mail: 2, Airways House, High Street, Sliema SLM 16, Malta Email: commissioner.dataprotection@gov.mt

Country	Legislation	Status	Date Passed	Responsible Bodies/ Contacts/Comments
Mauritius (Republic of Mauritius)	Data Protection Act 2004	Enacted	2004	Data Protection Commissioner Web: dataprotection.gov.mu Mail: Data Protection Office, 6th Floor, New Government Centre, Port Louis, Republic of Mauritius Email: pmo-dpo@mail.gov.mu
Mexico (United Mexican States)	DRAFT Federal Personal Data Protection Bill 2001	Pending adoption	TBA	Federal Institute for Access to Public Information (Instituto Federal de Acceso a la Información Pública) Web: ifai.org.mx Mail: Av. México No. 151 Col. Del Carmen; Del. Coyoacán, México Distrito Federal C.P. 04100Tel Email: atencion@ifai.org.mx
Micronesia (Federated States of Micronesia)	No specific Data Protection legislation.	N/A	N/A	
Moldova (Republic of Moldova)	No specific Data Protection legislation (See Comments)	N/A	N/A	The modified Law on Copyright and Neighbouring Rights of 2003 stipulates for the protection of databases.
Monaco (Principality of Monaco)	Law No. 1.165 of 23 December 1993 regulating the processing of personal data. (Loi n° 1.165 du 23 décembre 1993 réglementant les traitements d'informations nominatives.)	Enacted Amended	1993 2008	Board of Control of personal information (Commission de Contrôle des Informations Nominatives) Web: ccin.mc Mail: Commission de Contrôle des Informations Nominatives, "Gildo Pastor Center", 7 rue du Gabian, MC 98000 Monaco Email: ccin@gouv.mc
Mongolia	No specific Data Protection legislation.	N/A	N/A	
Montenegro	The Law on Personal Data Protection for the Republic of Montenegro	Enacted In Force	2008 2009	Agency for Personal Data Protection
Morocco (Kingdom of Morocco)	No specific Data Protection legislation.	N/A	N/A	NB: In July 2009, the Moroccan Government indicated that it intended to establish a Commissioner for Protection of Personal Data (CNDP) supported by appropriate legislation.

Country	Legislation	Status	Date Passed	Responsible Bodies/ Contacts/Comments
Mozambique (Republic of Mozambique)	No specific Data Protection legislation.	N/A	N/A	
Namibia (Republic of Namibia)	No specific Data Protection legislation.	N/A	N/A	The status of the "The Use of Electronic Transactions and Communication Act" is unclear.
Nepal (Federal Democratic Republic of Nepal)	No specific Data Protection legislation.	N/A	N/A	
Netherlands (Kingdom of the Netherlands)	Personal Data Protection Act 2000 Exemption Decree DPA 2001	Enacted	2001	Data Protection Authority Web: dutchdpa.nl/ Mail: Postbus 93374 2509 AJ Den Haag Email: info@cbpweb.nl
New Zealand	The Privacy Act 1993—No 28 The Privacy Amendment Acts of 1993 and 1994	Enacted	1993	Privacy Commissioner (Te Mana Matapono Matatapu) Web: privacy.org.nz Mail: Auckland Office Level 13, WHK Gosling Chapman 51–53 Shortland Street PO Box 466, Auckland 1140 Mail: Wellington Office Level 4, Gen-i Tower 109-111 Featherston Street PO Box 10-094, Wellington 6143 Email: enquiries@privacy.org.nz
Nicaragua (Republic of Nicaragua)	No specific Data Protection legislation.	N/A	N/A	
Niger (Republic of Niger)	No specific Data Protection legislation.	N/A	N/A	
Nigeria (Federal Republic of Nigeria)	No specific Data Protection legislation.	N/A	N/A	
Norway (Kingdom of Norway)	Personal Data Act 2000 Regulations on the processing of personal data (Personal Data Regulations)	Enacted In force Enacted	2000 2001 2000	The Data Inspectorate (Datatilsynet) Web: datatilsynet.no Mail: P.O. Box 8177 Dep, N-0034 Oslo Email: postkasse@datatilsynet.no

Country	Legislation	Status	Date Passed	Responsible Bodies/ Contacts/Comments
Oman (Sultanate of Oman)	No specific Data Protection legislation.	N/A	N/A	
Pakistan (Islamic Republic of Pakistan)	DRAFT Foreign Data Safety and Protection Act 2004	Pending	N/A	The 2004 draft legislation was proposed by the then Information Technology Minister. Responsibility has subsequently been allocated to the Minister of IT ad Telecom.
Paraguay (Republic of Paraguay)	Data Protection Act (Regulation for Personal Data)	Passed	2000	Unable to trace definitive source of information.
Peru (Republic of Peru)	DRAFT Data Protection Bill (1999) (See Comments)	Uncertain	Unclear	The draft Data Protection Bill was introduced in September 1999 and was based upon examples of Data Protection legislation from Spain, Italy and Australia. A Data Protection Commissioner is also proposed. In 2002, a special commission was established to draft a new Data Protection Bill In August 2001, Peru enacted a data protection law specifically affecting private credit reporting agencies.
Philippines (Republic of the Philippines)	No specific Data Protection legislation.	N/A	N/A	
Poland (Republic of Poland)	Act of August 29, 1997 on the Protection of Personal Data	Enacted Updated 1999 & 2002	1997	Inspector General for Personal Data Protection (Generaly Inspektor Ochrony Danych Osobowych). Web: giodo.gov.pl Mail: Biuro Generalnego Inspektora Ochrony Danych Osobowych ul. Stawki 2 00-193 Warszawa Email: sekretariat@giodo.gov.pl
Portugal (Portuguese Republic)	Data Protection Act—Act 67/98 of 26 October (Lei 67/ 98—Lei da Protecção de Dados Pessoais)	Enacted	1998	National Commission for Protection of Computerised Personal Data (Comissão Nacional de Protecção de Dados Pessoais Informatizados). Web: cnpd.pt

Country	Legislation	Status	Date Passed	Responsible Bodies/ Contacts/Comments
				Mail: Comissão Nacional de Protecção de Dados, Rua de São Bento, 148, 3º 1200-821 Lisboa, Portugal
				Email: geral@cnpd.pt
Puerto Rico (The Commonwealth of Puerto Rico)	No specific Data Protection legislation.	N/A	N/A	
Qatar (State of Qatar)	No specific Data Protection legislation.	N/A	N/A	
Romania	Law No. 677/2001 on the Protection of Individuals with Regard to the Processing of Personal Data and the Free Movement of Such Data Amended by Law No. 682 in 2001	Enacted	2001	The National Supervisory Authority for Personal Data Processing. (Autoritatea Naţională de Supraveghere a Prelucrării Datelor cu Caracter Personal). Web: dataprotection.ro Mail: Str. Olari nr. 32 Sector 2, BUCUREŞTI Cod poştal 024057 Romania Email: anspdcp@dataprotection.ro
Russian Federation	Federal Act No. 24-FZ of the Russian Federation On Information. Informatization and Protection of Information	Enacted by the Duma	1995	Non-governmental website with related information: medialaw.ru
Rwanda (Republic of Rwanda)	No specific Data Protection legislation.	N/A	N/A	
San Marino (Republic of San Marino)	Regulating the Computerized Collection of Personal Data, Law No. 70 of May 23, 1995; revising Law No. 27 of March 1, 1983, amended by Law No. 70/95	Enacted Amended	1983 1995	

Country	Legislation	Status	Date Passed	Responsible Bodies/ Contacts/Comments
Saudi Arabia (Kingdom of Saudi Arabia)	No specific Data Protection legislation.	N/A	N/A	
Senegal (Republic of Senegal)	No specific Data Protection legislation.	N/A	N/A	
Serbia (The Republic of Serbia)	Law on Personal Data Protection	Enacted	2008	Commissioner for Information of Public Importance and Personal Data Protection. (Poverenik za informacije od javnog značaja i zaštitu podataka o ličnosti) Web: poverenik.org.rs Mail: 42, Svetozara Markovica str, Belgrade 11000
Seychelles (Republic of Seychelles)	Data Protection Act 2003	Unclear	Unclear	Data Protection Act 2003—unable to confirm if enacted etc.
Sierra Leone (Republic of Sierra Leone)	No specific Data Protection legislation.	N/A	N/A	
Singapore (Republic of Singapore)	No specific data protection law. However, there is a voluntary code of practice, for the private sector, operated by the National Trust Council under the name Trustsg. This scheme incorporates good Data Protection practice in respect of online transactions. "The E-Commerce Code for the Protection of Personal Information and Communications of Consumers of Internet Commerce"	N/A	N/A	In February 2002, the National Internet Advisory Committee (NIAC) released a draft "Model Data Protection Code for the Private Sector" which is modelled on internationally recognised standards. The Infocomm Development Authority of Singapore oversee the Trustsg scheme. Web: ida.gov.sg and trustsg.com.sg Mail: 8 Temasek Boulevard #14-00, Suntec Tower Three, Singapore 038988 Email: admin@trustsg.org.sg

Country	Legislation	Status	Date Passed	Responsible Bodies/ Contacts/Comments
Slovakia (Slovak Republic)	Act No. 52/1998 Coll. on Protection of Personal Data in Information Systems Act No. 428/2002 on Protection of Personal Data as amended by Act No. 602/2003	Enacted Amended	1998 2003	The Office for Personal Data Protection of the Slovak Republic (Úrad na ochranu osobných údajov SR). Web: dataprotection.gov.sk Mail: Úrad na ochranu osobných údajov Slovenskej republiky Odborárske námestie è. 3 817 60 Bratislava 15 Slovak republic Email: statny.dozor@pdp.gov.sk
Slovenia (Republic of Slovenia)	Personal Data Protection Act (RS No. 55/99) (Zakon o varstvu osebnih podatkov)	Enacted	1999	Information Commissioner (informacijski pooblascenec) Web: ip-rs.si Mail: Vošnjakova 1 p.p. 78 1001 Ljubljana Email: gp.ip@ip-rs.si
Somalia (Federal Republic of Somalia)	No specific Data Protection legislation.	N/A	N/A	
South Africa (Republic of South Africa)	No specific Data Protection legislation. (See Comments).	N/A	N/A	The Electronic Communication and Transaction (ECT) Law came into force in 2002. Chapter VIII (s. 51) of the Law relates to the scope of the protection of personal information, which in this case is restricted to electronic data transactions. (s. 52) defines some data protection principles. It is unclear how it is proposed to oversee and regulate compliance with the stated principles in the absence of a defined authority. Section 14 of the Constitution of the Republic of South Africa states: "Everyone has the right to privacy, which includes the right not to have d. the privacy of their communications infringed."

Country	Legislation	Status	Date Passed	Responsible Bodies/ Contacts/Comments
South Korea (Republic of South Korea)	The Act on Promotion of Utilization of Information and Communications Networks and Data Protection It is understood that more specific data protection legislation may be developed in the future.	Enacted	2001	Korea Information Security Agency (KISA) Web: kisa.or.kr Mail: Personal Data Protection Center, KISA, 78, Karak dong, Songpa-Gu Seoul 138-160, Korea
Spain (Kingdom of Spain)	Organic Law 15/1999 of 13 December on the Protection of Personal Data (LEY ORGÁNICA 15/1999, de 13 de diciembre, de Protección de Datos de Carácter Personal)	Enacted	1999	Spanish Data Protection Authority (AEPD) (Agencia Española de Protección de Datos) Web: agpd.es Mail: Agencia Española de Protección de datos, C/ Jorge Juan, 6 28001-Madrid Email: prensa@agpd.es
Sri Lanka (Democratic Socialist Republic of Sri Lanka)	No specific Data Protection legislation.	N/A	N/A	
Sudan (Republic of Sudan)	No specific Data Protection legislation.	N/A	N/A	Article 29 of the Constitution of the Republic of Sudan states: "All citizens are allowed freedom of communication and correspondence. Confidentiality is guaranteed and no communication or correspondence may be observed or recorded except as provided by law."
Swaziland (Kingdom of Swaziland)	No specific Data Protection legislation.	N/A	N/A	Chapter IV (c) of the Constitution of the Kingdom of Swaziland provides for the right to privacy of person and property.
Sweden (Kingdom of Sweden)	Personal Data Act (1998:204) (Personuppgiftslagen)	Enacted Enacted	1998 1998	Data Inspection Board (Datainspektionen). Web: datainspektionen.se

Country	Legislation	Status	Date Passed	Responsible Bodies/ Contacts/Comments
	Swedish Data Protection Ordinance (1998:1191)			Mail: Fleminggatan,14 9th Floor, Box 8114 SE-104 20 Stockholm Sweden Email: datainspektionen@ datainspektionen.se
Switzerland (Swiss Confederation)	Federal Act of 19 June 1992 on Data Protection (FADP) (Bundesgesetz vom 19. Juni 1992 über den Datenschutz (DSG))	Enacted Amended	1992 1999	Swiss Federal Data Protection Commissioner (Eidgenössischer Datenschutzbeauftragter). Web: edoeb.admin.ch Mail: Feldeggweg 1 CH - 3003 Bern Email: info@edsb.ch
Syria (Syrian Arab Republic)	No specific Data Protection legislation.	N/A	N/A	
Taiwan	Computer Processed Personal Data Protection Law 1995 (NB: this law only applies to public institutions)	Enacted	1995	There is no single oversight authority for the legislation, but action can be taken through the courts. Mail: Bureau of Legal Affairs, The Ministry of Justice, 130, Sec 1, Chung Ching South Road Taipei 100 Taiwan R.O.C. 100
Tanzania (United Republic of Tanzania)	No specific Data Protection legislation.	N/A	N/A	
Thailand (Kingdom of Thailand)	Official Information Act B.E. 2540 It is understood that a draft Data Protection Bill is in progress.	Enacted by the King	1997	Office of the Official Information Commissioner (OIC) Web: oic.thaigov.go.th Mail: Office of the Information Commission 2nd floor. The Prime Minister's Office Building Government House, Dusit Bangkok, Thailand 10300 Email: infothai@a-net.net.th
Togo (Togolese Republic)	No specific Data Protection legislation.	N/A	N/A	
Tonga (Kingdom of Tonga)	No specific Data Protection legislation.	N/A	N/A	
Trinidad and Tobago (Republic of Trinidad and Tobago)	Data Protection Bill 2009	In progress	TBA	The office of the Data Commissioner will be established once the legislation is enacted.

Country	Legislation	Status	Date Passed	Responsible Bodies/ Contacts/Comments
Tunisia (Republic of Tunisia)	Data Protection Act (Loi portant sur la Protection des Données à Caractère Personnel)	Enacted	2004	Web: jurisitetunisie.com
Turkey (Republic of Turkey)	No specific Data Protection legislation.	N/A	N/A	
Uganda (Republic of Uganda)	No specific Data Protection legislation.	N/A	N/A	Uganda does not have a Data Protection Authority.
Ukraine	Law on Information	Enacted Amended Amended	1992 2000 2002	The Law on Information (1992) establishes the general legal principles for receiving, using, distributing and keeping information, securing its protection and defends an individual and society against incorrect information.
	Law on Data Protection in Automatic Systems	Adopted Amended	1994 2004	The Law on Data Protection in Automatic Systems is aimed at establishing regulative principles concerning data protection in databases "under observance of property rights of Ukrainian citizens and legal entities to information and access to information". Web: kmu.gov.ua
United Arab Emirates (UAE)	Data Protection Law (DIFC Law No 1 of 2007)	Enacted	2007	Data Protection Administrator Web: dp.difc.ae Mail: The Data Protection Administrator, Dubai International Financial Centre Authority, Level 14, The Gate, PO Box 74777, Dubai, United Arab Emirates Email: administrator@dp.difc.ae
United Kingdom (United Kingdom of Great Britain and Northern Ireland)	Data Protection Act 1998	Enacted	2000	Information Commissioners Office Web: ico.gov.uk Mail: Information Commissioner's Office, Wycliffe House, Water Lane, Wilmslow, Cheshire SK9 5AF

Country	Legislation	Status	Date Passed	Responsible Bodies/ Contacts/Comments
				Tel: +44 (0)8456 30 60 60 or +44 (0)1625 54 57 45
				Regional Offices:
				Information Commissioner's Office—Scotland 93–95 Hanover Street Edinburgh EH2 1DJ Tel: 0131 301 5071 Email: scotland@ico.gsi.gov.uk
				Information Commissioner's Office—Wales Cambrian Buildings Mount Stuart Square Cardiff CF10 5FL Tel: 029 2044 8044 Email: wales@ico.gsi.gov.uk
				Information Commissioner's Office—Northern Ireland 51 Adelaide Street Belfast, BT2 8FE Tel: 028 9026 9380 Email: ni@ico.gsi.gov.uk
United States of America	There is no single federal data protection legislation in place. (See Comments for details of related legislation)	N/A	N/A	*Health Insurance Portability and Accountability Act of 1996 (HIPAA)*
				Organisation: US Department of Health and Human Services (HHS)
				Web: hhs.gov.ocr/hippa
				Mail: 200 Independence Avenue, SW Washington, D.C. 20201
				Organisation: Centers for Medicare & Medicaid Services (CMS)
				Web: cms.hhs.gov/hipaaGenInfo/
				Mail: 7500 Security Boulevard Baltimore, MD 21244
				The Financial Modernization Act of 1999 (also known as the Gramm-Leach-Bliley Act or GLB Act).
				Organisation: Federal Trade Commission
				Web: ftc.gov/privacy/privacyinitiatives/glbact.html
				Mail: Federal Trade Commission Consumer Response Center 600 Pennsylvania Avenue, NW Washington, DC 20580

Country	Legislation	Status	Date Passed	Responsible Bodies/ Contacts/Comments
				U.S. Safe Harbor
				(Scheme related to data transfers from the European Union to the U.S which requires compliance with defined privacy principles).
				Organisation: Export.gov
				Export.gov is managed by the U.S. Department of Commerce's International Trade Administration and involves the collaboration of nineteen other Federal Agencies.
				Web: export.gov/safeharbor/
				Children's Privacy and Protection Act of 1998 (COPPA)
				Organisation: U.S. Federal Trade Commission (FTC)
				Web: ftc.gov/privacy/coppafaqs.shtm
				Cable Communications Policy Act of 1984
				Organisation: U.S. Federal Communications Commission (FCC)
				Web: fcc.gov
				The Privacy Act of 1974
				Organisation: U.S. Department of Justice (DOJ)
				Web: usdoj.gov/opcl/ privacyact1974.htm
Uruguay (Eastern Republic of Uruguay)	Law No. 18,331 on the Protection of Personal Data (Ley N° 18.331 de Protección de Datos Personales y Acción de Habeas Data)	Enacted	2008	Regulatory Unit and Control of Personal Data (Unidad Reguladora y de Control de Datos Personales)
				Web: datospersonales.gub.uy
				Mail: Andes N° 1365 piso 8, Montevideo, Uruguay
Venezuela (Bolivarian Republic of Venezuela)	No specific Data Protection legislation.	N/A	N/A	

Country	Legislation	Status	Date Passed	Responsible Bodies/ Contacts/Comments
Vietnam (Socialist Republic of Vietnam)	No specific Data Protection legislation.	N/A	N/A	
Yemen (Republic of Yemen)	No specific Data Protection legislation.	N/A	N/A	
Zambia (Republic of Zambia)	No specific Data Protection legislation.	N/A	N/A	
Zimbabwe (Republic of Zimbabwe)	No specific Data Protection legislation.	N/A	N/A	

Appendix 4
International Freedom of Information Legislation

On the international stage, the degree to which countries address Freedom of Information issues varies considerably, as the following table illustrates. The rights of citizens to access and obtain official or government information can range from a general, and sometimes vague, right defined with the national constitution through to specific freedom of information legislation overseen by a nominated and independent authority, such as an Information or Privacy Commissioner.

All 47 member states of the Council of Europe are parties to the European Convention on Human Rights (ECHR or more formally known as the Convention for the Protection of Human Rights and Fundamental Freedoms), Article 10 of which relates to freedom of expression with the following basis and stipulations:

1. Everyone has the right to freedom of expression. This right shall include freedom to hold opinions and to receive and impart information and ideas without interference by public authority and regardless of frontiers. This article shall not prevent States from requiring the licensing of broadcasting, television or cinema enterprises.

2. The exercise of these freedoms, since it carries with it duties and responsibilities, may be subject to such formalities, conditions, restrictions or penalties as are prescribed by law and are necessary in a democratic society, in the interests of national security, territorial integrity or public safety, for the prevention of disorder or crime, for the protection of health or morals, for the protection of the reputation or rights of others, for preventing the disclosure of information received in confidence, or for maintaining the authority and impartiality of the judiciary.

The following table provides details, by country, of the state of play with national Freedom of Information rights and legislation. Where possible, sources of further information have been included.

Country	Legislation	Status	Date Passed	Comments
Afghanistan (Islamic Republic of Afghanistan)	No specific FoI legislation	N/A	N/A	The revised Constitution (2004), under Article 50, provides the following general rights of access to information: "(3) The citizens of Afghanistan have the right of access to the information from the government offices in accordance with the provisions of law. (4) This right has no limits, unless violation of the rights of the others."
Albania (Republic of Albania)	Law no. 8503, dated 30 June 1999, On the right to information over the official documents (Ligji nr. 8503, date 30.6.1999, Per të drejten e informimit per dokumentat zyrtare)	Enacted	1999	The Constitution (1998) guarantees the right of access to information in Article 23. The People's Advocate Web: avokatipopullit.gov.al Mail: Avokati i Popullit, Bulevardi "Zhan D'Ark", No. 2, Zip Code 1001, Tirana, Albania Email: ap@avokatipopullit.gov.al Member of the Council of Europe and party to the European Convention on Human Rights (ECHR)
Algeria (People's Democratic Republic of Algeria)	No specific FoI legislation	N/A	N/A	The Algerian Constitution (1996) has no specific right to access information.
Andorra (Republic of Andorra)	No specific FoI legislation	N/A	N/A	The Constitution (1993) has no specific right to access information. Member of the Council of Europe and party to the European Convention on Human Rights (ECHR)

Country	Legislation	Status	Date Passed	Comments
Angola (Republic of Angola)	Law of Access to Documents Held by Public Authorities (Law No. 11/02 on Access to Administrative Documents 2002)	Enacted	2002	Unable to trace an English translation of the Law, but a facsimile in Portuguese is available on the web at: privacyinternational.org/Countries/angola/foi-law02.doc The Constitution (1980) has no specific right to access information.
Antigua and Barbuda	Freedom of Information Act 2004	Enacted	2004	The Act requires the appointment of an Information Commissioner. Government website: ab.gov.ag
Argentina (Argentine Republic)	Regulation: The Access to Public Information Regulation (Acceso a la Informacion Publica)	Effective	2003	Web: mejordemocracia.gov.ar Email: info@mejordemocracia.gov.ar There are further Provincial-level FoI laws in place.
Armenia (Republic of Armenia)	The Law of the Republic of Armenia on Freedom of Information	Enacted	2003	The Freedom of Information Center of Armenia (FOICA) is a nongovernmental organisation formed in 2001. Web: foi.am Mail: /3 P. Buzand St., 4th floor, Yerevan, 0010, Republic of Armenia Email: foi@foi.am Member of the Council of Europe and party to the European Convention on Human Rights (ECHR)
Australia (Commonwealth of Australia)	Freedom of Information Act 1982	Enacted	1982	At a Federal level, the Commonwealth Ombudsman was appointed in 1977 and

Country	Legislation	Status	Date Passed	Comments
	NB: This Act operates at a Federal level and applies to all ministers, departments and public authorities. The following State and Territory FoI legislation is also in place: Australian Capital Territory—Freedom of Information Act 1989 New South Wales—Freedom of Information Act 1989 Northern Territory—Information Act 2003 Queensland—Freedom of Information Act 1992 South Australia—Freedom of Information Act 1991 Tasmania—Freedom of Information Act 1991 Victoria—Freedom of Information Act 1982 Western Australia—Freedom of Information Act 1992			subsequently took on the investigation of complaints about the actions and decisions taken by departments and agencies concerning requests for access to documents under the FoI Act. Web: ombudsman.gov.au Mail: GPO Box 442, Canberra ACT 2601 Email: ombudsman@ombudsman.gov.au The Commonwealth Ombudsman also has the following offices in Adelaide, Alice Springs, Brisbane, Darwin, Hobart, Melbourne, Perth and Sydney: Level 5, 50 Grenfell, Street, Adelaide SA5000 P.O. Box 2388, Alice Springs 0871 Level 17, 53 Albert Street, Brisbane Qld 4000 GPO Box 1344, Darwin NT 0801 GPO Box 960, Hobart TAS7001 P.O. Box 7444, St Kilda Road, Melbourne VIC 8004 P.O. Box Z5386, St George's Terrace, Perth WA 6831 P.O. Box K825, Haymarket NSW 1240

Country	Legislation	Status	Date Passed	Comments
Austria (Republic of Austria)	Federal Law on the Duty to Furnish Information (Auskunftspflicht Gesetz)	Enacted	1987	There are also FoI laws in place in the nine Austrian States including specific legislation relating to accessing information on the environment. The Austrian Ombudsman Board (Volksanwaltschaft) Web: volksanw.gv.at Mail: A-1015 Vienna, P.O. Box 20 Email: post@volksanwaltschaft.gv.at.gv.at Member of the Council of Europe and party to the European Convention on Human Rights (ECHR)
Azerbaijan (Republic of Azerbaijan)	Law of the Republic of Azerbaijan on the Right to Obtain Information	Enacted	2005	Article 50(1) of the Constitution states: "Everyone is free to look for, acquire, transfer, prepare and distribute information." Member of the Council of Europe and party to the European Convention on Human Rights (ECHR)
Bahamas (The Commonwealth of The Bahamas)	No specific FoI legislation	N/A	N/A	Section 23(1) of the Constitution (1973) contains a general right to receive and impart information, as follows: "Except with his consent, no person shall be hindered in the enjoyment of his freedom of expression, and for the purposes of this Article the said freedom includes freedom to hold opinions, to *receive and impart ideas and information without interference*, and freedom from interference with his correspondence."

Country	Legislation	Status	Date Passed	Comments
Bahrain (Kingdom of Bahrain)	No specific FoI legislation	N/A	N/A	The 2002 Constitution omits any specific right to access information.
Bangladesh (People's Republic of Bangladesh)	Right to Information Ordinance (No. 50 of 2008)	Issued	2008	The Right to Information (RTI) Ordinance is based on selected parts of the Indian Right to Information Act 2005. It will remain in effect until it is either approved or withdrawn by any subsequent Parliament.
Barbados (Independent Continental Island-Nation)	The Freedom of Information Bill has been proposed and is being considered.	Pending	N/A	Web: gov.bb. Email: freedomofinfobill@barbados.gov.bb The 1966 Constitution includes the following general rights to access information: "Article 20. 1. Except with his own consent, no person shall be hindered in the enjoyment of his freedom of expression, and for the purposes of this section the said freedom includes the freedom to hold opinions without interference, *freedom to receive ideas and information without interference, freedom to communicate ideas and information without interferences* and freedom from interference with his correspondence or other means of communication. 2. Nothing contained in or done under the authority of any law shall be held to be inconsistent with or in contravention of this section to the extent that the law in question makes provision—

Country	Legislation	Status	Date Passed	Comments
				a. that is reasonably required in the interests of defence, public safety, public order, public morality or public health; or
				b. that is reasonably required for the purpose of protecting the reputations, rights and freedoms of other persons or the private lives of persons concerned in legal proceedings, preventing the disclosure of information received in confidence, maintaining the authority and independence of the courts or regulating the administration or technical operation of telephony, telegraphy, posts, wireless broadcasting, television or other means of communication or regulating public exhibitions or public entertainments."
Belarus (Republic of Belarus)	No specific FoI legislation	N/A	N/A	Article 34 of the 1994 Constitution states: "(1) Citizens of the Republic of Belarus shall be *guaranteed the right to receive, store, and disseminate complete, reliable, and timely information on the activities of state bodies and public associations, on political, economic, and international life, and on the state of the environment.* (2) State bodies, public associations, and officials shall afford citizens of the Republic of Belarus an opportunity to familiarize themselves with material that affects their rights and legitimate interests."

Country	Legislation	Status	Date Passed	Comments
Belgium (Kingdom of Belgium)	Law on the right of access to administrative documents held by federal public authorities	Enacted Amended	1994 2000	Article 32 of the Belgian Constitution was amended in 1993 to incorporate a right of access to documents held by the government. Member of the Council of Europe and party to the European Convention on Human Rights (ECHR)
Belize (Formerly British Honduras)	Freedom of Information Act	Enacted	2000	Belize has an Ombudsman who acts as an independent Parliamentary Commissioner and can, under the FoI Act, consider complaints about accessing information. Mail: Office of the Ombudsman 60 Corner Douglas Jones & Castle Street, Belize City, Belize
Benin (Republic of Benin)	No specific FoI legislation	N/A	N/A	Article 8 of the 1990 Constitution states: "The human person is sacred and inviolable. The state has the absolute obligation to respect it and protect it. It shall guarantee him a full blossoming out. To that end, it shall assure to its citizens equal access to health, education, culture, *information*, vocational training, and employment."
Bermuda (British Overseas Territory of Bermuda)	No specific FoI legislation	N/A	N/A	Section 9 of the 1968 Constitution (under protection of freedom of expression) states: "1. Except with his consent, no person shall be hindered in the enjoyment of his freedom of expression, and for the purposes of this section the said freedom includes freedom to hold

Country	Legislation	Status	Date Passed	Comments
				opinions and *to receive and impart ideas and information without interference*, and freedom from interference with his correspondence."
Bhutan (Kingdom of Bhutan)	No specific FoI legislation	N/A	N/A	Article 7(3) of the 2008 Constitution states: "A Bhutanese citizen shall have the right to information."
Bolivia (Plurinational State of Bolivia)	No specific FoI legislation	N/A		Supreme Decree No. 28168, 2005 Following a constitutional referendum in 2009, a revised Constitution was enacted. Chapter 3, Section 1, Article 6 of this document states: "6. To access the information, interpret, analyze and communicate freely, individually or collectively."
Bosnia and Herzegovina (Federal Democratic Republic of Bosnia and Herzegovina)	Freedom of Access to Information Act Both of the federal entities (The Republika Srpska and the Federation of Bosnia & Herzegovina) respectively passed the following laws in 2001: Freedom of Access to Information Act for the Republika Srpska	Adopted by the Parliament Assembly	2000 2001	Under the legislation the Ombudsman is charged with dealing with any arising complaints and disputes. These duties are undertaken by different officers in the two federal entities as follows: 1) Ombudsman of the Federation of Bosnia and Herzegovina Unable to trace current contact details. 2) The Ombudsman of Republika Srpska—Human Rights Protector Web: ombudsmen.rs.ba/index_e.html

Country	Legislation	Status	Date Passed	Comments
	Freedom of Access to Information Act for the Federation of Bosnia & Herzegovina		2001	Mail: Kralja Alfonsa XIII br. 21, 78000 Banja Luka, Bosna i Hercegovina Email: ombudsman@blic.net The Center for Free Access to Information (CSpi) is an independent and nongovernment organisation to promote the Freedom of Access to Information Act throughout Bosnia and Herzegovina. Web: cspi.ba Mail: Sime Milutinovića S. 14, 71000 Sarajevo Bosnia and Herzegovina Email: info@cspi.ba Member of the Council of Europe and party to the European Convention on Human Rights (ECHR)
Botswana (Republic of Botswana)	No specific FoI legislation	N/A	N/A	The 1966 Constitution's only reference to rights of access to information is contained within Chapter 2, Section 12, as follows: "12. Protection of freedom of expression. (1) Except with his own consent, no person shall be hindered in the enjoyment of his freedom of expression, that is to say, freedom to hold opinions without interference, *freedom to receive ideas and information without interference, freedom to communicate ideas and information without*

Country	Legislation	Status	Date Passed	Comments
				interference (whether the communication be to the public generally or to any person or class of persons) and freedom from interference with his correspondence.

(2) Nothing contained in or done under the authority of any law shall be held to be inconsistent with or in contravention of this section to the extent that the law in question makes provision—

(a) that is reasonably required in the interests of defence, public safety, public order, public morality or public health; or

(b) that is reasonably required for the purpose of protecting the reputations, rights and freedoms of other persons or the private lives of persons concerned in legal proceedings, preventing the disclosure of information received in confidence, maintaining the authority and independence of the courts, regulating educational institutions in the interests of persons receiving instruction therein, or regulating the technical administration or the technical operation of telephony, telegraphy, posts, wireless, broadcasting or television; or

(c) that imposes restrictions upon public officers, employees of local government bodies, or teachers, and except so far as that provision or, as the case may be, the thing done under the authority thereof is shown not to be reasonably justifiable in a democratic society." |

Country	Legislation	Status	Date Passed	Comments
Brazil (Federal Republic of Brazil)	No specific FoI Law at present. A draft Bill on Freedom of Information was produced in 2005 and is currently still being considered by the Senate. (Also see the Comments column)	N/A	N/A	Article 5 XXXIII of the 1988 Brazilian Constitution states that: "all persons have the right to receive, from the public agencies, information of private interest to such persons, or of collective or general interest, which shall be provided within the period established by law, subject to liability, except for the information whose secrecy is essential to the security of society and of the State." However, there are no official mechanisms in place governing the manner of access to government information and the timetable to be followed.
Brunei (State of Brunei Darussalam)	No specific FoI legislation	N/A	N/A	The 1984 revision of the Constitution fails to define any specific rights relating to information.
Burkina Faso (Republic of Burkina Faso)	No specific FoI legislation	N/A	N/A	Article 8 of the 1991 Constitution provides a general right to information. However this is not put into any context of how this is either achieved or restricted.
Bulgaria (Republic of Bulgaria)	Access to Public Information Act	Enacted Being reviewed	2000 2008	There is also no independent oversight body in place to deal with disputes or complaints. However, access denials can be appealed to the regional court or the Supreme Administrative Court. The <u>Access to Information Programme (AIP) Foundation</u> is a nongovernmental organisation with a mission to facilitate implementation

Country	Legislation	Status	Date Passed	Comments
				of Article 41 of the Bulgarian Constitution which establishes the right of information:
				Web: aip-bg.org
				Mail: Access to Information Programme, Sofia, 1142 76, Vassil Levski Blvd. 3rd floor
				Email: office@aip-bg.org
				Member of the Council of Europe and party to the European Convention on Human Rights (ECHR)
Burma (Union of Myanmar)	No specific FoI legislation	N/A	N/A	The 1974 Constitution has no defined rights of access to official information.
Burundi (Republic of Burundi)	No specific FoI legislation	N/A	N/A	The 2005 revision of the Constitution omits any specific rights of access to information.
Cambodia (Kingdom of Cambodia)	No specific FoI legislation	N/A	N/A	The Constitution (1993) has no mention of rights to access to information.
Cameroon (Republic of Cameroon)	No specific FoI legislation	N/A	N/A	
Canada	Access to Information Act (Supported by the Privacy Act 1983) In addition, the ten provinces and 3 territories of Canada have separate FoI legislation (see Comments column for details).	Enacted	1983	In Canada the legislation differentiates between access to general records and records that contain personal information relating to the person making the request. Whereas the Privacy Act offers rights to access to personal information held about the person making the request, the Access to Information Act does not offer the right of access to personal information held about others. In practice,

Country	Legislation	Status	Date Passed	Comments
				this restricts the access to general information of a nonpersonal nature.
				The Access to Information Act is regulated at a national level by the Information Commissioner of Canada (Commissaire à l'information du Canada).
				Web: infocom.gc.ca
				Mail: The Information Commissioner of Canada Place de Ville, Tower B 112 Kent Street, 7th Floor Ottawa, Ontario K1A 1H3
				Email: general@infocom.gc.ca
				The following province and territory FoI laws are also in place:
				Nova Scotia
				Freedom of Information and Protection of Privacy Act (1977)—amended 1993
				Nova Scotia Freedom of Information and Protection of Privacy Review Office
				Web: foipop.ns.ca// legislation.html
				Mail: Box 181 Halifax, NS B3J 2M4
				New Brunswick
				Right to Information Act 1978
				The Office of the Ombudsman

Country	Legislation	Status	Date Passed	Comments
				Web: gnb.ca/0073/Index-e.asp
				Mail: P. O. Box 6000 Fredericton, NB E3B 5H1
				Email: nbombud@gnb.ca
				Newfoundland & Labrador
				Freedom of Information and Protection of Privacy Act (1981) & Access to Information and Protection of Privacy Act 2002
				The Office of the Information and Privacy Commissioner for Newfoundland and Labrador
				Web: oipc.gov.nl.ca/legislation.htm
				Mail: 2nd Floor, 34 Pippy Place P.O. Box 13004, Station A St. John's, NL A1B 3V8
				Email: commissioner@oipc.nl.ca
				Quebec
				An Act Respecting Access to Documents Held by Public Bodies and the Protection of Personal Information (1982)
				Commission on Access to Information For Quebec (Commission d'accès à l'information du Québec)
				Web: cai.gouv.qc.ca
				Mail: QUÉBEC CITY (Head Office) Bureau 1.10 575, rue Saint-Amable Québec (Québec) G1R 2G4

Country	Legislation	Status	Date Passed	Comments
				MONTREAL Bureau 18.200 500, boul. René-Lévesque Ouest Montréal (Québec) H2Z 1W7
				Email: cai.communications@cai.gouv.qc.ca
				Yukon
				Access to Information and Protection of Privacy Act (1984)
				The Access to Information & Protection of Privacy Act (ATIPP) Office
				Web: atipp.gov.yk.ca
				Mail: Government of Yukon Department of Highways and Public Works Information & Communications Technology Box 2703 Whitehorse, Yukon Y1A 2C6
				Email: atipp@gov.yk.ca
				Manitoba
				Freedom of Information and Protection of Privacy Act (1985)
				The Ombudsman
				Web: ombudsman.mb.ca
				Mail: 750–500 Portage Avenue Winnipeg, MB R3C 3X1
				202 Scotia Towers 1011 Rosser Avenue Brandon, MB R7A OL5

Country	Legislation	Status	Date Passed	Comments
				Ontario *Freedom of Information and Protection of Privacy Act (1988)* Ontario also has a separate municipal FoI Act: *Municipal Freedom of Information and Protection of Privacy Act (1991)* Information and Privacy Commissioner for Ontario. Web: ipc.on.ca Mail: 2 Bloor Street East Suite 1400 Toronto, Ontario M4W 1A8 Email: info@ipc.on.ca Saskatchewan *Freedom of Information and Protection of Privacy Act (1991)* Saskatchewan also has a separate municipal FoI Act: *Local Authority Freedom of Information and Protection of Privacy Act (1991)* Information and Privacy Commissioner of Saskatchewan Web: oipc.sk.ca/ Mail: Saskatchewan Information and Privacy Commissioner 503–1801 Hamilton Street Regina, Saskatchewan S4P 4B4 British Columbia *Freedom of Information and Protection of Privacy Act (1993)*

Country	Legislation	Status	Date Passed	Comments
				Office of the Information and Privacy Commissioner for British Columbia
				Web: oipc.bc.ca
				Mail: PO Box 9038, Stn. Prov. Govt. Victoria, BC V8W 9A4
				Email: info@oipc.bc.ca
				Alberta
				Freedom of Information and Protection of Privacy Act
				Office of the Information and Privacy Commissioner of Alberta
				Web: oipc.ab.ca
				Mail: # 410, 9925–109 Street Edmonton, Alberta T5K 2J8
				Email: generalinfo@oipc.ab.ca
				Northwest Territories
				Access to Information and Protection of Privacy Act (1994) Amended.
				Office of the Information and Privacy Commissioner of the Northwest Territories
				Mail: 5018, 47th Street, Yellowknife, Northwest Territories X1A 2N2
				Email: atippcomm@theedge.ca
				Prince Edward Island
				Freedom of Information and Protection of Privacy Act (2001)

Country	Legislation	Status	Date Passed	Comments
				Information and Privacy Commissioner
				Web: assembly.pe.ca
				Mail: J. Angus MacLean Building 180 Richmond Street P.O. Box 2000 Charlottetown, PE C1A 7K7
				Nunavut
				Access to Information and Protection of Privacy Act (Nunavut) (2000)
				The Information and Privacy Commissioner
				Web: info-privacy.nu.c
				Mail: 5018–47th Street P.O. Box 262 Yellowknife, NT X1A 2N2
				Email: AtippComm@theedge.ca
Cape Verde (Republic of Cape Verde)	No specific FoI legislation	N/A	N/A	Article 42(3) of the Constitution guarantees constitutional protection to access to information.
Cayman Islands (British Overseas Territory of the Cayman Islands)	Freedom of Information Law.	Enacted	2007	The Freedom of Information Unit is responsible for overseeing the implementation of the Freedom of Information Law, 2007.
	Freedom of Information (Information Commissioner) Regulations, 2008	Enacted	2008	
				Web: foi.gov.ky
				Mail: Government Administration Building, Grand Cayman, KY1-9000 Cayman Islands.
				Email: foi@gov.ky
				Information Commissioner
				Web: infocomm.ky

Country	Legislation	Status	Date Passed	Comments
				Mail: PO Box 10727 Grand Cayman KY1-1007

Email: info@infocomm.ky |
| Central African Republic | No specific FoI legislation | N/A | N/A | The Constitution was revised in 2005. However, we have been unable to trace a copy to determine if it contains any basic rights of access to official information. |
| Chad (Republic of Chad) | No specific FoI legislation | N/A | N/A | |
| Chile (Republic of Chile) | Law on Transparency of Public Functions and Access to Information of the Agencies of State

(Ley sobre Transparencia de la Función Pública y Acceso a la Información de los Órganos de la Administración del Estado) | Enacted | 2008 | Article 19, No 12 of the Constitution guarantees the right to freedom of expressions, including the "right to seek and impart" information. However, this does not necessarily confer a "right to receive" information. |
| China (People's Republic of China) | People's Republic of China Ordinance on Openness of Government Information (OGI Regulations)

The following municipality-related FoI regulations are also in place:

Guangzhou municipality

Guangzhou Municipal Provisions on Open Government | Enacted

Effective

Enacted | 2007

2008

2002 | The 1982 Constitution has no specific right of access to information. |

Country	Legislation	Status	Date Passed	Comments
	Information (Decree No. 8 of the Guangzhou Municipal People's Government, dated November 6, 2002) Shanghai municipality Shanghai Municipal Provisions on Open Government Information (Shanghai Municipal People's Government Decree No. 19, January 20, 2004)	Enacted	2004	
Colombia (Republic of Colombia)	The Law of Ordering the Publicity of Official Acts and Documents (Law 5 of 1985) (La Ley de Ordenación de la publicidad de los actos y documentos oficiales)	Enacted	1985	Articles 74, 20 and 23 of the Constitution establish rights to access public documents, impart and receive impartial and accurate information and to obtain a prompt response to requests for information.
Comoros (Union of the Comoros)	No specific FoI legislation	N/A	N/A	
Congo (Democratic Republic of the Congo—Congo-Kinshasa)	No specific FoI legislation	N/A	N/A	The revised 2006 Constitution states, under Article 24 that: *"Everyone has the right to information."*
Congo (Republic of the Congo—Congo-Brazzaville)	No specific FoI legislation	N/A	N/A	Article 27(4) of the Constitution provides access to information.
Cook Islands	Official Information Act 2008	Enacted Effective	2008 2009	The Act is based upon the equivalent New Zealand legislation. There is no right of access contained within the 1981 Constitution.

Country	Legislation	Status	Date Passed	Comments
Costa Rica (Republic of Costa Rica)	No specific FoI legislation but there is a right of access to information contained in the Constitution (please refer to the Comments column).	N/A	N/A	Article 30 of Part I of the Constitution of Costa Rico states: "Free access to administrative departments for purposes of information on matters of public interest is guaranteed. State secrets are excluded from this provision."
Croatia (Republic of Croatia)	Act on the Right of Access to Information (Zakon O Pravu Na Pristup Informacijama)	Enacted	2003	The 2001 Constitution has no right of access to information. Member of the Council of Europe and party to the European Convention on Human Rights (ECHR)
Cuba (Republic of Cuba)	No specific FoI legislation	N/A	N/A	The 1992 (last amended 2002) Cuban Constitution omits a specific right of access to information.
Cyprus (Republic of Cyprus)	No specific FoI legislation	N/A	N/A	The 1960 Constitution (restored in 1980) defines, under Article 19, that: "2. This right includes freedom to hold opinions and *receive and impart information* and ideas without interference by any public authority and regardless of frontiers. 3. The exercise of the rights provided in paragraphs 1 and 2 of this Article may be subject to such formalities, conditions, restrictions or penalties as are prescribed by law and are necessary only in the interests of the security of the Republic or the constitutional order or the public safety or the public order or the public health or the public morals or for the protection of the

Country	Legislation	Status	Date Passed	Comments
				reputation or rights of others or for preventing the disclosure of information received in confidence or for maintaining the authority and impartiality of the judiciary." Member of the Council of Europe and party to the European Convention on Human Rights (ECHR)
Czech Republic	Law on Free Access to Information (Zákon č. 106/1999 Sb., o svobodném přístupu k informacím)	Enacted Effective	1999 2000	Article 17 of the 1993 Charter of Fundamental Rights and Freedoms states: "Freedom of expression and the right to information are guaranteed." Member of the Council of Europe and party to the European Convention on Human Rights (ECHR)
Denmark (Kingdom of Denmark)	Access to Public Administration Files Act	Enacted	1985	There is no right of access to information contained within the 1953 Danish Constitution. Member of the Council of Europe and party to the European Convention on Human Rights (ECHR)
Djibouti (Republic of Djibouti)	No specific FoI legislation	N/A	N/A	The 1992 Constitution omits any specific right to access information.
Dominican Republic	Law number 200-04 Law on Free Access to Information (Ley No.200-04 - Ley General de Libre Acceso a la Información Pública)	Enacted	2004	The 2002 Constitution omits any specific right to access information. It is understood (as at 2009) that the government is considering a major revision of the Constitution.

Country	Legislation	Status	Date Passed	Comments
Ecuador (Republic of Ecuador)	Organic Law on Transparency and Access to Public Information (LOTAIP) (La Ley Orgánica de Transparencia y Acceso a la Información Pública (LOTAIP))	Enacted	2004	Article 81 of the Constitution grants a right to access information and establishes that information from public archives should not be reserved, except when national security or other laws provide the basis for exclusion.
Egypt (Arab Republic of Egypt)	No specific FoI legislation	N/A	N/A	The Constitution, last amended in 2007, has no defined right of access to official information. Some of the freedoms contained within the Constitution have, in practice, been restricted by the imposition of Emergency Powers.
El Salvador (Republic of El Salvador)	No specific FoI legislation	N/A	N/A	The 1983 Constitution (revised 2003) has no defined right of access to information.
Equatorial Guinea (Republic of Equatorial Guinea)	No specific FoI legislation	N/A	N/A	There is no right of access to information contained within the 1996 Constitution.
Eritrea (State of Eritrea)	No specific FoI legislation	N/A	N/A	Article 19(3) of the Constitution provides for freedom of access to information.
Estonia (Republic of Estonia)	Public Information Act (Avaliku teabe seadus)	Enacted Effective	2000 2001	The Estonian Data Protection Inspectorate (Andmekaitse Inspektsioon) is a national supervision agency for public information—complying with requests for information and publication of information on the Internet and elsewhere. Web: aki.ee Mail: Andmekaitse Inspektsioon; Väike-Ameerika 19, Tallinn 10129

Country	Legislation	Status	Date Passed	Comments
				Email: info@aki.ee

The right of access to information is defined in Article 44 of the Constitution.

Member of the Council of Europe and party to the European Convention on Human Rights (ECHR) |
| Ethiopia (Federal Democratic Republic of Ethiopia) | No specific FoI legislation but there is a right of access to information contained in the Constitution (refer to the comments column). | N/A | N/A | Article 29 of the Constitution (1994) states:

"2. Everyone has the right to freedom of expression without any interference. This right shall include freedom to seek, receive and impart information and ideas of all kinds, regardless of frontiers, either orally, in writing or in print, in the form of art, or through any media of his choice.

3. Freedom of the press and other mass media and freedom of artistic creativity is guaranteed. Freedom of the press shall specifically include the following elements:

(a) Prohibition of any form of censorship.
(b) Access to information of public interest."

Web: ethiopar.net |
| Fiji (Republic of the Fiji Islands) | No FoI legislation currently in place, although a draft Freedom of Information Bill was circulated in 2000 but was abandoned. Despite there being | N/A | N/A | Article 174 of the Constitution (1997) states "As soon as practicable after the commencement of this Constitution, the Parliament should enact a law to members of the public rights of access to official documents of the |

Country	Legislation	Status	Date Passed	Comments
	plans to develop a new Bill in 2004, there has been no further progress.			Government and its agencies." This Article is not contained in the Bill of Rights section of the Constitution, but under the heading of "Accountability"—accordingly there is some doubt that the present Constitution actually guarantees a right to information. In addition, Article 30(1) guarantees everyone a general right to "seek, receive and impart information and ideas".
Finland (Republic of Finland)	Act on the Openness of Public Documents (laki yleisten asiakirjain julkisuudeesta 9.3.1951/83) Act on the Openness of Government Activities (Laki viranomaisten toiminnan julkisuudesta 21.5.1999/621)	Enacted Enacted	1951 1999	Finland has a long established tradition of open access. During the time as a Swedish-governed territory, Finland had in place the Access to Public Records Act (1766). In addition, Section 12 of the Constitution (2000) declares that everyone has the right of access to public documents and recordings. Member of the Council of Europe and party to the European Convention on Human Rights (ECHR)
France (French Republic)	Law on Access to Administrative Documents. (Loi n°78-753 du 17 juillet 1978 portant diverses mesures d'amélioration des relations entre l'administration et le public et diverses dispositions d'ordre administratif, social et fiscal)	Enacted	1978	The 1958 Constitution (subsequently amended) has no right of access to information. Member of the Council of Europe and party to the European Convention on Human Rights (ECHR).

Country	Legislation	Status	Date Passed	Comments
Gabon (Gabonese Republic)	No specific FoI legislation	N/A	N/A	The 1991 Constitution (as subsequently amended in 1997 and 2003) has no right of access to information.
Gambia (Republic of The Gambia)	No specific FoI legislation	N/A	N/A	There is no right of access to information under the 1996 Constitution (as amended in 1997 and 2001).
Georgia (Democratic Republic of Georgia)	The General Administrative Code of Georgia—Chapter 3 of the Code is entitled "Freedom of Information"	Enacted Effective	1999 2000	The Constitution incorporates (Article 24(1)) the right to freely receive and impart information and (Article 41) the citizen's right to privacy of personal information and the right to become acquainted with information about themselves that is stored in state institutions as well as official documents. Member of the Council of Europe and party to the European Convention on Human Rights (ECHR)
Germany (Federal Republic of Germany)	Federal Freedom of Information Act (das Bundes Informationsfreiheitsgesetz)	Enacted	2005	The Virtual Privacy Office (Datenschutzbüro) website (datenschutz.de/privo) contains information on federal and state FoI legislation. The following links relate to sources of information regarding FoI legislation (Gesetze über Informationsfreiheit) in the constituent States. The Federal state of Berlin Berlin Commissioner for Data Protection and Freedom of Information (Berliner Beauftragter für Datenschutz und Informationsfreiheit)

Country	Legislation	Status	Date Passed	Comments
				Web: datenschutz-berlin.de
				The Federal state of Brandenburg Brandenburg State Commissioner for Data Protection and Access to Information
				(Die Landesbeauftragte für den Datenschutz und für das Recht auf Akteneinsicht Brandenburg)
				Web: lda.brandenburg.de
				The Federal state of Bremen The State Commissioner for Data Protection and Freedom of Information of the Free Hanseatic City of Bremen.
				(Der Landesbeauftragten für Datenschutz und Informationsfreiheit der Freien Hansestadt Bremen)
				Web: informationsfreiheit-bremen.de
				The Federal state of Hamburg The Hamburg officer for Data Protection and freedom of information
				(Der Hamburgische Beauftragte für Datenschutz und Informationsfreiheit).
				Web: hamburg.de/datenschut
				The Federal state of Mecklenburg-Vorpommern

Country	Legislation	Status	Date Passed	Comments
				Web: informationsfreiheit-mv.de The Federal state of <u>Nordrhein-Westfalen</u> State Commissioner for Data Protection and Freedom of Information North Rhine-Westphalia (Landesbeauftragte für Datenschutz und Informationsfreiheit Nordrhein-Westfalen) Web: ldi.nrw.de The Federal state of <u>Rheinland-Pfalz</u> Web: ism.rlp.de The Federal state of <u>Saarland</u> State Commissioner for Data Protection and Freedom of Information Saarland (Landesbeauftragter für Datenschutz und Informationsfreiheit Saarland) Web: lfdi.saarland.de The Federal state of <u>Saxony-Anhalt</u> State Commissioner for Data Protection and Freedom of Information Saxony-Anhalt (Landesbeauftragter für Datenschutz und Informationsfreiheit Sachsen-Anhalt)

Country	Legislation	Status	Date Passed	Comments
				Web: sachsen-anhalt.de/LPSA
				The Federal state of Schleswig-Holstein Web: datenschutzzentrum.de/material/recht/ifg.htm
				The Federal state of Thuringia Thuringian State Commissioner for Data Protection (TLfD)
				(Thüringer Landesbeauftragter für den Datenschutz (TLfD)
				Web: thueringen.de/datenschutz/tlfd/
				Germany is a member of the Council of Europe and party to the European Convention on Human Rights (ECHR)
Ghana (Republic of Ghana)	Right to Information Act	Enacted	2005	There is no specific single regulatory authority for the FoI legislation. Disputes about access requests are initially reviewed by the Minister responsible for the relevant service but can then be referred to the Courts for resolution.
				Web: ghana.gov.gh/right_to_information_act_2005
				The right to access information is contained within Article 21 of the Constitution.
Gibraltar (British Overseas Territory of Gibraltar)	No specific FoI legislation	N/A	N/A	The 2006 Constitution, under Protection of freedom of expression, Article 10(1) states:

Country	Legislation	Status	Date Passed	Comments
				"Except with his own consent, no person shall be hindered in the enjoyment of his freedom of expression, that is to say, freedom to hold opinions and *to receive and impart ideas and information without interference*, and freedom from interference with his correspondence."
Greece (Hellenic Republic)	Code of Administrative Procedure—Article 5	Enacted	1999	Hellenic Data Protection Authority (HDPA) (Αρχής Προστασίας Δεδομένων Προσωπικού Χαρακτήρα) Web: dpa.gr Mail: Data Protection Authority Offices: Kifissias 1-3, PC 115 23 Ampelokipi Athens, Greece Email: contact@dpa.gr Law No 2690— Ratification of the Administrative Procedure Code and other provisions defines the contents of Article 5 as: "Access to documents 1. Any interested party is entitled, by written application, to be informed of administrative documents. Administrative documents are documents drawn up by public services, such as reports, studies, minutes, statistical data, circulars, replies of the Administration, opinions and resolutions.

Country	Legislation	Status	Date Passed	Comments
				2. Any person having special legal interest is entitled, by written application, to be informed of private documents kept in public services that are related to his/her case pending before them or handled by them. 3. The right under the previous paragraph is not applicable in cases when the document concerns the private or family life of a third party or if there is violation of confidentiality stipulated by special provisions. The competent administrative authority may refuse to satisfy this right if the document refers to the discussions of the Cabinet of Ministers or if the satisfaction of this right may substantially obstruct the investigation of judicial, police or military authorities concerning the commission of a crime or an administrative violation." Member of the Council of Europe and party to the European Convention on Human Rights (ECHR)
Guatemala (Republic of Guatemala)	Law for Free Access to Public Information, 2008 (Ley de Acceso a la Informacion publica)	Enacted	2008	Article 31 of the Constitution (1985 amended 1993) states: "Access to files and state records. Everyone has the right to know what it recorded in files, files or any other form of state records, and the purpose for which this information is engaged and to

Country	Legislation	Status	Date Passed	Comments
				correction, modification and update. Are prohibited records and archives of political affiliation, except those pertaining to the electoral authorities and political parties."
Guernsey States of Guernsey (Including the islands of: Alderney, Sark Herm, Jethou, Brecqhou and Lihou).	No specific FoI legislation	N/A	N/A	
Guinea (Republic of Guinea)	No specific FoI legislation	N/A	N/A	
Guinea-Bissau (Republic of Guinea-Bissau)	No specific FoI legislation	N/A	N/A	Article 34 of the Constitution grants right of access to information.
Guyana (Co-operative Republic of Guyana)	No specific FoI legislation at present. However, a draft FoI Bill was prepared in 2005, which is still pending ratification and adoption.	N/A	N/A	There is no right of access to information guaranteed by the Constitution.
Honduras (Republic of Honduras)	Law of Transparency and Access to Public Information (Ley de Transparencia y Acceso a la Información Pública)	Enacted	2006	The Institute for Access to Public Information (IAIP) (El Instituto de Acceso a la Información Pública (IAIP)) Web: iaip.gob.hn
Hong Kong (Hong Kong Special Administrative Region)	No FoI legislation currently in place, but the Government of Hong Kong has introduced a "Code on Access to Information". However, the Code has only minimal legal status.			The Code can be accessed on the web via: access.gov.hk/en/code.htm. Section 1.8 of the Code requires that: "Each department will designate an Access to Information Officer who will be responsible for

Country	Legislation	Status	Date Passed	Comments
				promoting and overseeing the application of the Code."
				Annex A to the Code contains a list if all the departments to which the Code relates. The web-based version of this annex has hyperlinks to the contact details for each entry.
				Any person who believes that a department has failed to properly apply any provision of the Code may also complain to The Ombudsman. The Ombudsman's address is – 30/F, China Merchants Tower Shun Tak Centre 168–200 Connaught Road Central Hong Kong.
Hungary (Republic of Hungary)	Act on the Protection of Personal Data and Public Access to Data of Public Interest (Évi LXIII szóló 1992 a személyes adatok védelméröl és a nyilvánosság hozzáférése a közérdekű adatok nyilvánosságáról)	Enacted Effective	1992 1993	The Hungarian Parliamentary Commissioner For Data Protection and Freedom of Information. Web: abiweb.obh.hu/dpc/ Mail: H-1051 Budapest, Nádor u. 22., Hungary Email: adatved@obh.hu
	Act on the Freedom of Information by Electronic Means (Act XC of 2005). (Évi XC 2005 szabadságról szóló információk elektronikus úton)	Enacted	2005	The relevant citizen's rights to access information of public interest are contained within the Constitution of 1949. Member of the Council of Europe and party to the European Convention on Human Rights (ECHR)

Country	Legislation	Status	Date Passed	Comments
Iceland (Republic of Iceland)	Information Act No, 50.1996 (Upplysingalög)	Enacted Amended	1996 2003	Chapter V of the Information Act, under the following Articles specifies that an Information Committee will be established to review appeals against refusals to permit access to information. "Article 14 Right of appeal. Appeals against refusals by government authorities to grant access to materials under this Act may be referred to the Information Committee, which shall deliver rulings on disputes. The same shall apply to refusals by government authorities to furnish photocopies of documents or copies of other materials. The committee shall function independently and its rulings under this Act may not be referred to other government authorities. Article 15 The prime minister shall appoint three persons to the Information Committee for terms of four years, and an equal number of substitutes. Two of the committee members and their substitutes shall meet the requirements set for working as District Court judges. One of them shall be the chairman of the committee and the other the vice-chairman. Members of the committee may not be permanent employees of the Icelandic government ministries.

Country	Legislation	Status	Date Passed	Comments
				The committee may call in experts for advice and assistance if it considers this necessary."
Member of the Council of Europe and party to the European Convention on Human Rights (ECHR)
India (Republic of India)	Right to Information Act (RTI Act)	Introduced Effective	2000 2005	The Indian Constitution has no explicit right of access to information, although in cases brought before the Supreme Court since 1975 the Court has established that the citizen's right to know arises from the rights of freedom of speech and expression and of life contained with Articles 19(1) and 21(50) respectively. The National Right to Information legislation is augmented by local State arrangements, the details of which can be obtained from the State websites listed below. The Central Information Commission (CIC) deals with complaints relating to access to information. Web: cic.gov.in Mail: CIC, Club Building, Old JNU Campus, New Delhi – 110 067 The Department of Personnel and Training, Ministry of Personnel, Public Grievances and Pensions oversees the Right to Information Act and associated rights.

Country	Legislation	Status	Date Passed	Comments
				The following web portal provides national level information and hyper links to the various state government websites, some of which are specific to local Right to Information arrangements.
				Web: righttoinformation.gov.in/
				Email: rti@nic.in
				At a State level, the following local Right to Information (RTI) and State Information Commissioner (SIC) websites are in place:
				Andaman & Nicobar Islands
				Web (RTI): and.nic.in/Citizen%20Services/rti/rti1.htm
				Andhra Pradesh
				Web (RTI): aponline.gov.in/apportal/HomePageLinks/RTIA/RTIA-TreeMenu.htm
				Web (SIC): apic.gov.in
				Arunachal Pradesh
				Web (SIC): arunachalpradesh.gov.in/rti/directory_apsic.pdf
				Assam
				Web (SIC): sicassam.in
				Bihar
				Web (RTI): gov.bih.nic.in/Governance/DeptRTI.htm

Country	Legislation	Status	Date Passed	Comments
				Web (SIC): bsic.co.in
				Chandigarh
				Web (RTI): chandigarh.nic.in/citizen_right.htm
				Chhattisgarh
				Web (General): cicharyana.gov.in
				Web (RTI): cg.nic.in/rti
				Web (SIC): siccg.gov.in
				Delhi
				Web (RTI): delhigovt.nic.in/rti/
				Goa
				Web (RTI): egov.goa.nic.in/rtipublic
				Web (SIC): egov.goa.nic.in/rtipublic/sic.aspx
				Gujarat
				Web (SIC): gic.guj.nic.in
				Haryana
				Web (SIC): cicharyana.gov.in
				Himachal Pradesh
				Web (RTI and SIC): admis.hp.nic.in/sic/
				Jammu And Kashmir
				Web (general): jammukashmir.nic.in

Country	Legislation	Status	Date Passed	Comments
				Jharkhand
				Web (RTI): jharkhand.nic.in/right_to_info.htm
				Karnataka
				Web (RTI): dpar-rti.kar.nic.in
				Web (SIC): kic.cgg.gov.in
				Kerala
				Web (RTI): rti.kerala.gov.in
				Web (SIC): keralasic.gov.in
				Lakshadweep
				Web (RTI): lakshadweep.nic.in/rti.htm
				Madhya Pradesh
				Web (RTI): mp.gov.in/services/right2info.asp
				Web (SIC—Local language only): mp.gov.in/services/right2info.asp
				Maharashtra
				Web (RTI): maharashtra.gov.in/RightToInformation/indexEng.html
				Web (SIC—local language only): sic.maharashtra.gov.in
				Manipur
				Web (General): manipur.nic.in
				Meghalaya
				Web (RTI): megrti.gov.in

Country	Legislation	Status	Date Passed	Comments
				Mizoram
				Web (General): mizoram.nic.in
				Nagaland
				Web (RTI): nagaland.nic.in/rti-nag/main.htm
				Web (SIC): nlsic.gov.in
				Orissa
				Web (RTI): orissa.gov.in/rti
				Web (SIC): orissasoochanacommission.nic.in
				Puducherry
				Web (RTI): pon.nic.in/rti/
				Punjab
				Web (RTI): punjabgovt.gov.in/Punjabrti
				Web (SIC): infocommpunjab.com
				Rajasthan
				Web (RTI): rajasthan.gov.in/rajgovt/misc/righttoinformation.html
				Web (SIC): ric.rajasthan.gov.in
				Sikkim
				Web (RTI and SIC): cicsikkim.gov.in
				Tamil Nadu
				Web (RTI): tn.gov.in/rti
				Web (SIC): tnsic.gov.in

Country	Legislation	Status	Date Passed	Comments
				Tripura
				Web (RTI): rtitripura.nic.in
				Uttar Pradesh
				Web (RTI): upcmo.up.nic.in/rti_eng.htm
				Web (SIC—Local language only): upsic.up.nic.in
				Uttarakhand
				Web (SIC): uic.gov.in
				West Bengal
				Web (RTI): rtiwb.gov.in
				Web (SIC): wbic.gov.in
				The Right to Information Community Portal of India is a non-governmental organisation that provides further guidance on the Right to Information legislation and related issues within India:
				Right to Information Community Portal of India.
				Web: rtiindia.org
Indonesia (Republic of Indonesia)	Act No. 14/2008 Public Information Disclosure Act	Adopted	2008	The Act allows for the establishment of an Information Committee to deal with disputes over the refusal to provide requested information.
Iran (Islamic Republic of Iran)	Freedom of Information Law	Passed	2008	The amended Constitution (1989) has no specific right of access to government or official information
Iraq (Republic of Iraq).	No specific FoI legislation	N/A	N/A	The 2005 Constitution has no right of access to information.

Country	Legislation	Status	Date Passed	Comments
Ireland (Eire) (Republic of Ireland—Eire)	Freedom of Information Act 1997 Freedom of Information (Amendment) Act 2003	Enacted Amended	1998 2003	Data Protection Commissioner (An Coimisinéir Cosanta Sonraí). Web: //www. e/cln_118/EN/Home/ioner. dataprotection.ie Mail: Office of the Data Protection Commissioner. Canal House, Station Road, Portarlington, Co. Laois, Ireland. Email: info@dataprotection.ie Member of the Council of Europe and party to the European Convention on Human Rights (ECHR)
Isle of Man (Self-governing Crown Dependency)	No specific FoI legislation currently in place. However, in 2008 there were indications that an Access to Information Bill was being considered.	N/A	N/A	In 1996 the Isle of Man government published the *Code of Practice on Access to Government Information*. (available at gov.im/lib/docs/cso/codeofpractice.pdf)
Israel (State of Israel)	Freedom of Information Law (5758—1998) (Supported by the Freedom of Information Regulations, 5759-1999)	Enacted Effective Amended Amended Amended	1998 1999 2002 2005 2007	There is no oversight authority for dealing with access refusals or disputes; these are handled through the Magistrate Courts.
Italy (Italian Republic)	Law 241 of 7th August 1990 (Chapter V) provides for access to administrative documents.	Enacted	1990	Law 241 requires that those requesting information must have a legal interest. The Commission of Access to Administrative Documents was

Country	Legislation	Status	Date Passed	Comments
				established in 1991 following the entry into force of the Law 241/1990 and is the body responsible for overseeing the implementation of the Law.
				The Law 15/2005 amending and supplementing the law generally, has given the Commission's increased and new powers.
				Web: governo.it/Presidenza/ACCESSO/index.html
				Mail: Commissione per l'accesso ai documenti amministrativi
				c/o Presidenza del Consiglio dei Ministri, Dipartimento per il Coordinamento Amministrativo
				Via della Mercede, 9 00187 Roma
				Email: commissione.accesso@governo.it
				Italy is a member of the Council of Europe and party to the European Convention on Human Rights (ECHR)
Ivory Coast (Republic of Cote d'Ivoire)	No specific FoI legislation	N/A	N/A	The 2000 Constitution has no right of access to information.
Jamaica (Island Nation of Jamaica)	Access to Information Act No 21	Enacted	2002	The Access to Information Unit (A. T. I. U.) has been established to spearhead and guide the implementation and administration of the Access to Information Act by the following:

Country	Legislation	Status	Date Passed	Comments
				Providing guidance and training for government bodies on how to interpret and administer the Act;
				Identifying and addressing difficult or problematic issues arising from implementation of the Act;
				Monitoring compliance with the Act;
				Educating and guiding the public in respect of their rights and obligations under the Act.
				Web: ati.gov.jm
				Mail: Access To Information Unit, Unit 5–9 South Odeon Avenue, Half-Way Tree, Kingston 10, Jamaica W.I.
				Email: ati@cwjamaica.com
Japan	Law Concerning Access to Information Held by Administrative Organs.	Enacted Effective	1999 2001	Article 18 of the Law states: "1. The person who has an objection to a disclosure decision, etc. or to an inaction regarding a disclosure request shall make a motion for objection to the incorporated administrative agency, etc. in accordance with the Administrative Complaint Investigation Law (Law No. 160 of 1962)."

Country	Legislation	Status	Date Passed	Comments
Jersey (Bailiwick of Jersey)	Guarantee of Access to Information	Enacted	2005	
	A Draft Freedom of Information (Jersey) Law was presented to the States in 2007 for consultation, but has yet to be enacted.	Pending	N/A	Part 5 of the 2007 Draft law proposes making the present Data Protection Commissioner and the Data Protection Tribunal into the Information Commissioner and the Information Tribunal for both the Data Protection Law and the Freedom on Information Law. This extension of responsibilities is pending the ratification of the draft legislation.
Jordan (Hashemite Kingdom of Jordan)	Access to Information Law	Enacted	2007	
Kazakhstan (Republic of Kazakhstan)	No specific FoI legislation	N/A	N/A	The 1995 Constitution as amended by Law 284 (1998) did not originally recognise a general right to government-held information but permits access to specified categories of information as defined in Articles 18(3), 20(2) and 31(2). The Constitution was amended by: Law No. 284 in 1998, including the inclusion of Article 20(2), as follows: "Everyone shall have the right to freely receive and disseminate information by any means not prohibited by law. The list of items constituting state secrets of the Republic of Kazakhstan shall be determined by law."

Country	Legislation	Status	Date Passed	Comments
Kenya (Republic of Kenya)	No specific FoI legislation at present. However a Draft Freedom of Information Act was produced in 2007, although no legislation has yet been enacted.	Pending	N/A	The Draft FoI Act suggested the set up of the Information Commission of Kenya (ICK), but this action is pending awaiting the ratification of the proposed legislation. Article 79(1) of the 1992 Constitution (amended in 1998) states: "Except with his own consent, no person shall be hindered in the enjoyment of his freedom of expression, that is to say, freedom to hold opinions without interference, freedom to receive ideas and information without interference, freedom to communicate ideas and information' without interference"
Kosovo (Republic of Kosovo)	Law No. 2003 / 12—Law on Access to Official Documents.	Enacted	2003	The 2003 Law makes no provision for an oversight authority to deal with disputes and refusals to release information.
Kuwait (State of Kuwait)	No specific FoI legislation	N/A	N/A	The 1962 Constitution contain no specific right of access to information.
Kyrgyzstan (Kyrgyz Republic)	Law of the Kyrgyz Republic on Access to information Held by State Bodies and Local Self-Government Bodies of the Kyrgyz Republic	Enacted	2007	Appeals and disputes can be handled by either the National Ombudsman or through the courts.

Country	Legislation	Status	Date Passed	Comments
Latvia (Republic of Latvia)	Law on Freedom of Information	Enacted Amended	1998 2006	There appears to be no specific oversight authority in place, although The Data State Inspectorate (Data Valsts Inspekcija) does have responsibility for data protection. Web: .dvi.gov.lv Mail: Riga, Blaumana 11/13–15, LV-1011, Latvia Email: info@dvi.gov.lv Member of the Council of Europe and party to the European Convention on Human Rights (ECHR)
Lebanon (Republic of Lebanon)	No specific FoI legislation	N/A	N/A	The 1926 Constitution (last amended in 1990) omits any specific right of access to information. The Administrative Development Ministry created a Citizen's Charter in 2001 that grants a right to access public information. on the following basis: "Citizens are entitled to: 27. Access, at the site of the concerned administration, information of a public nature related to the work of the administration under the existing laws and regulations, providing that such information is not subject legally to the principle of confidentiality.

Country	Legislation	Status	Date Passed	Comments
				28. Access information and data on information networks, comment on it and discuss it. Citizens are also eligible to object to, correct or refuse the publication of any information related to themselves on networks provided they exhibit valid justification.''
Lesotho (Kingdom of Lesotho)	No specific FoI legislation at present. An Access and Receipt of Information Bill was placed before parliament in 2004, but the current status of the proposed legislation is unclear.	N/A	N/A	The 1998 amended Constitution provides, under Article 14 (Freedom of expression) that: ''(1) Every person shall be entitled to, and (except with his own consent) shall not be hindered in his enjoyment of, freedom of expression, including freedom to hold opinions without interference, *freedom to receive ideas and information without interference, freedom to communicate ideas and information without interference* (whether the communication be to the public generally or to any person or class of persons) and freedom from interference with his correspondence.''
Liberia (Republic of Liberia)	No specific FoI legislation	N/A	N/A	Article 15 of the 1983 Constitution relating to freedom of expression states: ''b) The right encompasses the right to hold opinions

Country	Legislation	Status	Date Passed	Comments
				without interference and the right to knowledge. It includes freedom of speech and of the press, *academic freedom to receive and impart knowledge and information and the right of libraries to make such knowledge available.* It includes non-interference with the use of the mail, telephone and telegraph. It likewise includes the right to remain silent. c) *In pursuance of this right, there shall be no limitation on the public right to be informed about the government and its functionaries.* e) This freedom may be limited only by judicial action in proceedings grounded in defamation or invasion of the rights of privacy and publicity or in the commercial aspect of expression in deception, false advertising and copyright infringement."
Libya (Socialist People's Libyan Arab Great Jamahiriya)	No specific FoI legislation	N/A	N/A	The original Constitution, which prevailed between 1951 and 1969, was abandoned following the coup in 1969 led by Colonel Gaddafi; and currently there is no formal documented Constitution in place.

Country	Legislation	Status	Date Passed	Comments
				A Constitutional Proclamation was in 1969 and amended in 1992) and declares that it "is made to provide a basis for the organization of the state during the phase of completion of the national and democratic revolution, until a permanent constitution is prepared, defining the objectives of the Revolution and outlining the future course". This Constitutional Proclamation makes no reference to rights over access to official information.
Liechtenstein (Principality of Liechtenstein)	The Information Act (Informationsgesetz)	Enacted Effective	1999 2000	Member of the Council of Europe and party to the European Convention on Human Rights (ECHR)
Lithuania (Republic of Lithuania)	Law on the Provision of Information to the Public (1999)	Enacted Amended	2000 2005	The citizen's right to information is included in Article 25 of the Constitution. Member of the Council of Europe and party to the European Convention on Human Rights (ECHR)
Luxembourg (Grand Duchy of Luxembourg)	No specific FoI legislation	N/A	N/A	The current Constitution includes a provision that "Everyone has the right to freedom of expression. This right includes *freedom to hold opinions and freedom to receive and impart information* and ideas without interference by having authorities and regardless of frontiers."

Country	Legislation	Status	Date Passed	Comments
				Member of the Council of Europe and party to the European Convention on Human Rights (ECHR)
Macedonia (Republic of Macedonia)	Law on Free Access to Information of Public Character	Enacted Effective	2006 2008	Free access to information and the freedom of reception and transmission of information are guaranteed in Article 16(2) of the Constitution. Commission for the Protection of the Right to Free Access to Information of Public Character (Комисијата за заштита на правото за слободен пристап до информации од јавен карактер) Web: sinf.gov.mk Mail: str. Goce Delcev, bb (building of the MRTV—14th floor) 1000, Skopje, Republic of Macedonia Email: sinf@sinf.gov.mk Member of the Council of Europe and party to the European Convention on Human Rights (ECHR)
Madagascar (Republic of Madagascar)	No specific FoI legislation	N/A	N/A	Article 11 of the Constitution states "(1) Information in all forms shall be subject to no prior restraint. (2) Conditions of freedom of information and its responsibility shall be determined by law and by codes of professional ethics."

Country	Legislation	Status	Date Passed	Comments
Malawi (Republic of Malawi)	No specific FoI legislation is currently enacted. A draft Access to Information Bill has been produced but has yet to be ratified	Pending	N/A	The right of access to all information held by the State of any of its organs at any level of Government in so far as such information is required for the exercise of a citizen's rights in stated in Article 37 of the Constitution.
Malaysia	No specific FoI legislation is currently enacted. There were attempts to table a private member's Bill on freedom of information in May 2008, but it was not considered then or since.	N/A	N/A	There is no Constitutional right to access official information.
Mali (Republic of Mali)	No specific FoI legislation	N/A	N/A	The 1992 Constitution has no specific right of access to information.
Malta (Republic of Malta)	Freedom of Information Act. The Act was passed by parliament in 2008 and is expected to be in force during 2010.	Passed Pending	2008	Article 41 (1) of the 1964 Constitution (amended up to 1994) provides a general right "To receive ideas and information without interference". Member of the Council of Europe and party to the European Convention on Human Rights (ECHR)
Mauritius (Republic of Mauritius)	No specific FoI legislation	N/A	N/A	The 1968 Constitution (amended 1991) contains, under protection of freedom of expression, the right of "freedom to hold opinions and to *receive and impart ideas and information* without interference."

Country	Legislation	Status	Date Passed	Comments
Mexico (United Mexican States)	Federal Law of Transparency and Access to Public Government Information (La Ley Federal de Transparencia y Acceso a la Información Pública Gubernamental)	Enacted Effective	2002 2005	In addition to the Federal Law, the majority of the constituent states and districts have adopted FoI laws. Federal Institute of Access to Public Information (IFIA) (Instituto Federal de Acceso a la información pública) Web: .ifai.org.mx Mail: Av. México # 151, Col. El Carmen, Coyoacán, C.P. 04100, Delegación Coyoacán, México D.F. Email: atencion@ifai.org.mx Article 6 of the revised 2007 Constitution states: "1) All information in possession of state institutions is public and only in exceptional cases may information be temporarily reserved, in the public interest and as defined by law. 3) All persons will have free access to public information without the need of justification or proving interest. All persons will have free access to their personal information and will be able to correct misinformation. 4) Procedures for accessing and revising information must be established."

Country	Legislation	Status	Date Passed	Comments
Micronesia (Federated States of Micronesia)	No specific FoI legislation	N/A	N/A	There is no specific right to access official information contained in the prevailing Constitution.
Moldova (Republic of Moldova)	Law of the Republic of Moldova on Access to Information	Enacted	2000	Rights to access information are declared in Article 34 of the republic's Constitution. Member of the Council of Europe and party to the European Convention on Human Rights (ECHR)
Monaco (Principality of Monaco)	No specific FoI legislation	N/A	N/A	There is no specific mention of a right to access information contained in the 1962 Constitution. Member of the Council of Europe and party to the European Convention on Human Rights (ECHR)
Mongolia	A Draft Law of Mongolia on Freedom of Information was produced in 2006, but has yet to be enacted. The timescale for the introduction of FoI legislation is unclear.	Not known	N/A	The draft Law provides for disputes arising out of requests for information to be considered by the National Human Right Commission.
Montenegro	Freedom of Information Law	Enacted	2005	The following articles of the 2007 Constitution contain the rights relating to accessing information: Article 51—relates to a right of access to information held by state authorities; Article 23—incorporates rights of access to information about the environment; and

Country	Legislation	Status	Date Passed	Comments
				Article 49—guarantees freedom of public information.

Member of the Council of Europe and party to the European Convention on Human Rights (ECHR) |
| Morocco (Kingdom of Morocco) | No specific FoI legislation | N/A | N/A | There is no provision in the 1996 Constitution of a right to access official information. |
| Mozambique (Republic of Mozambique) | No specific FoI legislation at present.

A draft Freedom of Information Bill was produced in 2006, but has yet to be enacted. The timescale for the introduction of FoI legislation is unknown. | N/A | N/A | Article 74 of the Constitution states:

"All citizens have the right to freedom of expression and to freedom of the press as well as the right to information." |
| Namibia (Republic of Namibia) | No specific FoI legislation in place at present.

There have been a number of attempts to bring into force legislation addressing freedom of and access to information, the last being in 2008. However, enactment of such laws is still awaited. | N/A | N/A | The Constitution (as amended in 1998) has no specific right of access to information. |
| Nauru | A draft Freedom of Information Act was promoted in 2004 but not passed in parliament. | N/A | N/A | The current Constitution, which is understood to be under review, has no specfic right of access to information. |
| Nepal (Federal Democratic Republic of Nepal) | Right to Information Act | Enacted | 2007 | Under the Act a National Information Commission was established. |

818　THE OPERATIONAL AUDITING HANDBOOK

Country	Legislation	Status	Date Passed	Comments
				Web: nic.gov.np
				Email: info@nic.gov.np
				An Interim Constitution came to effect from January 15, 2007 that replaced the previous Constitution of the Kingdom of Nepal, 2047 (1990). Article 27 of the Interim Constitution states:
				"(1) Every citizen shall have the right to demand or obtain information on any matters of his/her own or of public importance.
				Provided that nothing shall compel any person to provide information on any matter about which secrecy is to be maintained by law."
				However, Nepal currently has no permanent constitution.
Netherlands (Kingdom of the Netherlands)	Government Information (Public Access) (Act Wet openbaarheid van bestuur) (WOB).	Enacted (replaced 1978 Law) Amended	1991 2005	Article 110 of the current Constitution, which relates to the right of public access to information, is positioned in a section of the document entitled "Legislation and Administration" rather than the more usual Bill of Rights section. The prevailing opinion is that this does not guarantee a right to information as it is couched in terms of being consistent with statutes rather an a fundamental right. Member of the Council of Europe and party to the European Convention on Human Rights (ECHR)

Country	Legislation	Status	Date Passed	Comments
New Zealand	Official Information Act	Enacted	1982	The Office of the Ombudman (Te Tari-o-Nga Kaitiaki Mana Tangata) is an independent investigator who investigates complaints about the administrative acts and decisions of central and local government agencies; investigates complaints about the decisions of Ministers of the Crown and central and local government agencies on requests for official information. Web: ombudsmen.parliament.nz Mail: Auckland Level 10 55–65 Shortland Street PO Box 1960 Wellington 14th Floor 70 The Terrace PO Box 10 152 Christchurch 6th Floor 764 Colombo Street PO Box 13 482 Email: office@ombudsmen.parliament.nz The New Zealand Bill of Rights as amended by the associated Act of 1990 includes "Everyone has the right to freedom of expression, including the freedom to seek, receive and impart information and opinions of any kind in any form."
		Effective	1983	
		Amended	1993	

Country	Legislation	Status	Date Passed	Comments
Nicaragua (Republic of Nicaragua)	Law on Access to Public Information (Law No.621 of 2007) (Ley de Acceso a la Información Pública)	Enacted	2007	Article 66 of the Nicaraguan Constitution provides citizens with a right to truthful information and Article 26 includes a right of knowledge of all information held on them registered by state authorities, as well as to know why and for what purpose the information is held.
Niger (Republic of Niger)	No specific FoI legislation	N/A	N/A	The 1999 Constitution has no specific right of access to official information.
Nigeria (Federal Republic of Nigeria)	Freedom of Information Bill	Approved by Senate Awaiting signature	2006	Section 39(1) of the 1999 Constitution states that: "Every person shall be entitled to freedom of expression, including freedom to hold opinions and to receive and impart ideas and information without interference."
Norway (Kingdom of Norway)	Freedom of Information Act	Enacted Amended	1970 2006	The Parliamentary Ombudsman for Public Administration (Sivilombudsmannen) deals with complaints or disputes including those related to freedom of information request. Web: sivilombudsmannen.no Mail: P.O. Box 3 Sentrum, N-0101 Oslo Email: post@sivilombudsmannen.no A general right of access to information, limited by the normal privacy and other caveats, is contained in the 2004 Constitution (Article 100).

Country	Legislation	Status	Date Passed	Comments
				Member of the Council of Europe and party to the European Convention on Human Rights (ECHR)
Oman (Sultanate of Oman)	No specific FoI legislation	N/A	N/A	The 1996 Constitution has no specific right of access to official information.
Pakistan (Islamic Republic of Pakistan)	Freedom of Information Ordinance 2002	Enacted	2002	
Panama	Law on Transparency in Public Administration	Enacted	2002	The amended Constitution of 2004 provides a right to access information held by the state or by private companies involved in work of a public nature, limited where necessary by prevailing law (Article 43)
Papua New Guinea	A draft Freedom of Information Bill has been under consideration but has not yet been acted upon.	N/A	N/A	The citizen's rights to "access official documents, subject to the need for such secrecy as is reasonably justifiable in a democratic society" are contained in Article 51 of the Constitution. This Article also prescribes ten permissible exceptions to the right.
Paraguay (Republic of Paraguay)	No specific FoI legislation at present. A Draft Paraguayan Free Access to Public Information Law was considered in 2004, but its current status is unclear.	N/A	N/A	The citizen's rights to obtain information are enshrined in Article 29 of the Constitution (1992)
Peru (Republic of Peru)	Law of Transparency and Access to Public Information. (Ley de Transparencia y Acceso a la Información Publica)	Enacted Effective	2002 2003	Section 5 of Article 2 of the Constitution (1993) provides a right to request and access public information, except where prohibited by law.

Country	Legislation	Status	Date Passed	Comments
Philippines (Republic of the Philippines)	No specific FoI legislation at present. The Freedom of Information Act 2008 is, at the time of writing, still being considered by parliament.	Pending	N/A	The right of the people to information on matters of public concern is contained within Article III (Bill of Rights) of the Constitution dated 1987. In addition, the Constitution contains a provision (under Section 28) stating "Subject to reasonable conditions prescribed by law, the State adopts and implements a policy of full public disclosure of all its transactions involving public interest."
Poland (Republic of Poland)	Law on Access to Public Information	Enacted Effective	2001 2002	Section 61 of the Constitution grants rights of access to information. Member of the Council of Europe and party to the European Convention on Human Rights (ECHR)
Portugal (Portuguese Republic)	Law of Access to Administrative Documents (LADA). (Lei do Acesso aos Documentos Administrativos (LADA))	Enacted Amended	1993 1999	Committee of Access to Administrative Documents (Comissão de Acesso aos Documentos Administrativo (CADA)). Web: cada.pt Mail: Rua de São Bento, 148–2º 1200-821 Lisboa Email: geral@cada.pt The 1989 Constitution includes a right of access to information under Article 268. Member of the Council of Europe and party to the European Convention on Human Rights (ECHR)

Country	Legislation	Status	Date Passed	Comments
Puerto Rico (The Commonwealth of Puerto Rico)	No specific FoI legislation	N/A	N/A	
Qatar (State of Qatar)	No specific FoI legislation	N/A	N/A	
Romania	Law Regarding Free Access to Information of Public Interest (Legea numarul 544 din 12 octombrie 2001 privind liberul acces la informatiile de interes public)	Enacted	2001	The right of access to information is contained within Article 31 of the Constitution. Member of the Council of Europe and party to the European Convention on Human Rights (ECHR)
Russian Federation	Federal law on Providing Access to the Activities of Government Bodies and Bodies of Local Self-Government 2009	Enacted	2009	Articles 29(4) and 24(2) of the Constitution relate to the right of access to information and the right to review personal information respectively. The Institute for Information Freedom Development (IIFD) is a not for profit, nongovernmental organisation established in 2004 dedicated to investigating, identifying and solving problems of access to socially significant information in Russia. Web: svobodainfo.ru Mail: 196105, Saint-Petersburg, c/b 354 Email: institute@svobodainfo.ru Member of the Council of Europe and party to the European Convention on Human Rights (ECHR)

Country	Legislation	Status	Date Passed	Comments
Rwanda (Republic of Rwanda)	No specific FoI legislation at present. It is understood that the Media High Council is drafting a new bill that will oblige public officials to release information to journalists. The Access to Information Bill which will also give a time limit, within which officials should release information, is expected to be presented to parliament before the end of 2009	Pending	N/A	Article 34 of the Constitution states: "Freedom of the press and freedom of information are recognized and guaranteed by the State. Freedom of speech and freedom of information shall not prejudice public order and good morals, the right of every citizen to honour, good reputation and the privacy of personal and family life. It is also guaranteed so long as it does not prejudice the protection of the youth and minors."
San Marino (Republic of San Marino)	No specific FoI legislation	N/A	N/A	Member of the Council of Europe and party to the European Convention on Human Rights (ECHR)
Saudi Arabia (Kingdom of Saudi Arabia)	No specific FoI legislation	N/A	N/A	
Senegal (Republic of Senegal)	No specific FoI legislation	N/A	N/A	Article 8 of the Constitution includes "the right to a variety of information".
Serbia (The Republic of Serbia)	Law on Free Access to Information of Public Importance	Enacted Amended	2004 2007	Constitution Article 51 relates to the right to be informed and the right to access information maintained by state bodies as limited by other laws. Member of the Council of Europe and party to the European Convention on Human Rights (ECHR)

Country	Legislation	Status	Date Passed	Comments
Seychelles (Republic of Seychelles)	No specific FoI legislation	N/A	N/A	Section 28 of the Constitution confers rights of access to information subject to specified exceptions.
Sierra Leone (Republic of Sierra Leone)	A draft Access to Information Bill is being progressed but has yet to be enacted.	Pending	N/A	The Constitution of 1991, under article 25(1), states: "the freedom to hold opinions and to receive and impart ideas and information without interference".
Singapore (Republic of Singapore)	No specific FoI legislation	N/A	N/A	The revised (1999) Constitution has no specific rights of access to official information.
Slovakia (Slovak Republic)	Act on Free Access to Information (Law 211/2000)	Enacted Amended	2000 2008	Rights of access to information are defined in Article 26 of the Constitution (1992). Member of the Council of Europe and party to the European Convention on Human Rights (ECHR)
Slovenia (Republic of Slovenia)	Access to Public Information Act (Zakon o dostopu do informacij javnega značaja (ZDIJZ))	Enacted Amended	2003 2005	The Information Commissioner (Informacijske Pooblaščenke). Web: ip-rs.si Article 39 of the Constitution relates to freedom of expression and incorporates a right to obtain information of a public nature in which the citizen has a well founded legal interest under law. The legal interest is no longer defensible as the separate explicit access to information legislation overrides the necessity to prove a legal interest. Member of the Council of Europe and party to the European Convention on Human Rights (ECHR)

Country	Legislation	Status	Date Passed	Comments
Somalia (Federal Republic of Somalia)	No specific FoI legislation	N/A	N/A	There is no right to access information under the prevailing Constitution
South Africa (Republic of South Africa)	The Promotion of Access to Information Act 2000 (PAIA)	Enacted Effective	2000 2001	The Access to Information Commissioner (within the South Africa Human Rights Commission (SAHRC)) Web: sahrc.org.za The republic's current Constitution (1996) contains rights to access information not only held by the State but by "another person". This provision is unusual in the international FoI arena as it grants a right of access to privately-held information.
South Korea (Republic of South Korea)	Act of the Disclosure of Information by Public Agencies	Enacted Effective	1996 1998	There is no explicit right of access to information in the prevailing Constitution. However, the Constitutional Court has noted that in order to fulfil the freedom of speech and the press enshrined in Article 21 of the Constitution, it is necessary to access, collect and process appropriate information. This stance also supports the concept of the right to know. The subsequent passing of the Act of the Disclosure of Information by Public Agencies in 1996 provided the required legal framework of information access. Appeals against a refusal to provide information are handled under the Administrative Appeals Act involving the Administrative Appeals Commission.

Country	Legislation	Status	Date Passed	Comments
Spain (Kingdom of Spain)	Law on Rules for Public Administration	Enacted Amended	1992 1999	Article 105 of the 1978 Constitution states: "The law shall regulate ... b) *access by the citizens to the administrative archives and registers* except where it affects the security and defense of the State, the investigation of crimes, and the privacy of persons." The courts are initially used to deal with disputes or refusals to permit access to information, however, the Ombudsman (El Defensor del Pueblo) can also review cases of failure to follow the law. Web: defensordelpueblo.es Mail: Calle Zurbano, 42 28010 Madrid Email: registro@ defensordelpueblo.es Member of the Council of Europe and party to the European Convention on Human Rights (ECHR)
Sri Lanka (Democratic Socialist Republic of Sri Lanka)	In 2004 a draft Freedom of Information Act was discussed but has, as yet, not been enacted.	N/A	N/A	There is no general right of access to information contained in the Constitution.
Sudan (Republic of Sudan)	Right to Information Bill	Passed Pending	2009	
Swaziland (Kingdom of Swaziland)	No specific FoI legislation	N/A	N/A	Article 24 of the 2005 Constitution provides freedoms to receive and communicate ideas and information without interference.

Country	Legislation	Status	Date Passed	Comments
Sweden (Kingdom of Sweden)	The Principle of Public Access (Offentlighet-sprincipen) Freedom of the Press Act	Enacted Amended	1949 1976	The declaration that "all government documents are public in the absence of a statute that expressly regulates otherwise" was contained in the Constitution dated 1766. The current rights of access to information are contained in Article 1 of Chapter 2 of the 1949 Constitution. Member of the Council of Europe and party to the European Convention on Human Rights (ECHR)
Switzerland (Swiss Confederation)	Federal Law on the Principle of Administrative Transparency (Loi fédérale sur le principe de la transparence dans l'administration)	Enacted Effective	2004 2006	The Federal Data Protection and Information Commissioner (FDPIC) is responsible for overseeing Data Protection and verifying the implementation, effectiveness and cost of the Federal Law on the Principle of Administrative Transparency Web: edoeb.admin.ch Mail: Office of the Federal Data Protection and Information Commissioner FDPIC Feldeggweg 1 CH - 3003 Berne The 2002 Federal Constitution contains, in Article 16, some rather clipped definitions of rights to access information which exclude any specific right to access government held information. Member of the Council of Europe and party to the European Convention on Human Rights (ECHR)

Country	Legislation	Status	Date Passed	Comments
Syria (Syrian Arab Republic)	No specific FoI legislation	N/A	N/A	The 1973 Constitution omits any specific right to access information.
Taiwan	The Freedom of Government Information Law	Enacted	2005	
Tajikistan (Republic of Tajikistan)	Law of the Republic of Tajikistan on Information	Enacted	2002	
Tanzania (United Republic of Tanzania)	The 2006 Draft Freedom of Information Bill has not been enacted.	N/A	N/A	The right to seek, receive and impart information is incorporated within Article 18(1) of the Constitution.
Thailand (Kingdom of Thailand)	Official Information Act	Enacted	1997	The Office of the Information Commissioner (OIC). Web: oic.thaigov.go.th The following sections of the Constitution enacted by the King in 2007 following a coup in 2006, relate to the rights of access to information: Section 56—provides a right of access to data or information in the possession of a Government agency, a State agency, a State enterprise or a local government organisation. This right is tempered by the usual exceptions relating to matters of state security, public safety, etc., or those prescribed by other legislation.

Country	Legislation	Status	Date Passed	Comments
				Section 57—Relates to a right to receive data in respect of any project or activity which may affect the quality of the environment, health and sanitary conditions, the quality of life or any other material interest concerning a person or local community. Section 61—refers to the right to information in respect of a consumer complaint. Section 62—confers a right to monitor and make request for an examination of the performance of duties of persons holding political positions, State agencies and State officials.
Togo (Togolese Republic)	No specific FoI legislation	N/A	N/A	
Tonga (Kingdom of Tonga)	No specific FoI legislation	N/A	N/A	
Trinidad and Tobago (Republic of Trinidad and Tobago)	Freedom of Information Act	Enacted Effective	1999 2001	Web: foia.gov.tt The Office of the Ombudsman handles disputes relating to refusals to grant access to information. Web: ombudsman.gov.tt Trinidad Office Mail: 132, Henry Street, Port of Spain, Trinidad Email: feedback@ombudsman.gov.tt Tobago Office

Country	Legislation	Status	Date Passed	Comments
				Mail: Caribana Building, Bacolet Street, Scarborough, Tobago
				Email: tgoregion@ ombudsman.gov.tt
				San Fernando Office
				Mail: 1st Floor, FinGroup Place Cor. Hobson & Kelshall St. San Fernando
				Email: sandoregion@ ombudsman.gov.tt
Tunisia (Republic of Tunisia)	No specific FoI legislation	N/A	N/A	
Turkey (Republic of Turkey)	Turkish Law on the Right to Information (Bilgi Edinme Hakki Kanunu)	Enacted	2003	General information Web: bilgiedinmehakki.org Member of the Council of Europe and party to the European Convention on Human Rights (ECHR)
Uganda (Republic of Uganda)	Access to Information Act	Enacted Effective	2005 2006	Appeals against refusal to provide information are handled in the courts. The citizen's right of access to information held by the State is defined in Article 41(1) of the Constitution.
Ukraine (Ukrainian People's Republic)	Law on Information	Enacted Amended	1992 2002	Disputes are handled by the Ukrainian Parliament Commissioner for Human Rights. Web: ombudsman.kiev.ua Mail: 21/8, Instytutska Str., Kyiv, 01008 Email: omb@ombudsman.kiev.ua

Country	Legislation	Status	Date Passed	Comments
				Article 34 of the Constitution (1996) confers a right to access information limited, as is normal, by any restrictions defined in other legislation or for matters of national or social concern (such as security or crimes).
				Member of the Council of Europe and party to the European Convention on Human Rights (ECHR)
United Arab Emirates (UAE)	No specific FoI legislation	N/A	N/A	
United Kingdom (United Kingdom of Great Britain and Northern Ireland)	Freedom of Information Act 2000 Freedom of Information (Scotland) Act 2002	Enacted Enacted	2000 2002	Information Commissioners Office Web: ico.gov.uk Mail: Information Commissioner's Office , Wycliffe House, Water Lane, Wilmslow, Cheshire SK9 5AF Tel: +44 (0)8456 30 60 60 or +44 (0)1625 54 57 45 Regional Offices: Information Commissioner's Office—Scotland 93–95 Hanover Street Edinburgh EH2 1DJ Tel: 0131 301 5071 Email: scotland@ico.gsi.gov.uk Information Commissioner's Office—Wales Cambrian Buildings

Country	Legislation	Status	Date Passed	Comments
				Mount Stuart Square Cardiff CF10 5FL
				Tel: 029 2044 8044
				Email: wales@ico.gsi.gov.uk
				Information Commissioner's Office—Northern Ireland
				51 Adelaide Street Belfast, BT2 8FE
				Tel: 028 9026 9380
				Email: ni@ico.gsi.gov.uk
				Member of the Council of Europe and party to the European Convention on Human Rights (ECHR)
United States of America	Freedom of Information Act	Enacted	1966	The initial Freedom of Information Act (1966) has been amended several times, the last occasion being in 2008.
		Effective	1967	
	Electronic Freedom of Information Act Amendments	Enacted	1996	
				The Office of Information Policy (OIP) is responsible for encouraging agency compliance with the Freedom of Information Act (FOIA).
				Web: usdoj.gov/oip
				Mail: Office of Information Policy (OIP) Suite 11050 1425 New York Avenue, N.W. Washington, D.C. 20530
Uruguay (Eastern Republic of Uruguay)	Law on the Right of Access to Public Information	Enacted	2008	

Country	Legislation	Status	Date Passed	Comments
	(La Ley sobre el Derecho de Acceso a la Información Pública)			
Uzbekistan	Law on the Principles and Guarantees of Freedom of Information (The above law replaced the 1997 law of the same name)	Enacted Effective	2002 2003	
Venezuela (Bolivarian Republic of Venezuela)	No specific FoI legislation	N/A	N/A	A right of access to information and data held by government and private about citizens or their property is contained within Article 28 of the 1999 amended Constitution. The exception would be where other law specifies prohibiting the release of information.
Vietnam (Socialist Republic of Vietnam)	No specific FoI legislation is in place at present. However, it is understood that work has started in 2009 on drafting a right to information.	N/A	N/A	
Yemen (Republic of Yemen)	No specific FoI legislation at present, although it is understood that a draft law was being worked on in the last quarter of 2009.	N/A	N/A	
Zambia (Republic of Zambia)	No specific FoI legislation	N/A	N/A	
Zimbabwe (Republic of Zimbabwe)	Access to Information and Privacy Act (AIPPA)	Enacted	2002	

Appendix 5
Information Management Definitions

Term or Expression	Definition
Active (or current) Records	Records that are required frequently and that need to be accessible by staff on an ongoing basis. (An active record can be subsequently closed in accordance with the Retention and Disposal Policy and either stored or disposed of as required.)
Archival Records	These are records designated as having a long-term regulatory, historical, cultural or educational significance and requiring appropriate archiving (either within the organisation or with a recognised local or national body).
Compliance	In the context of Information Management, compliance relates to an organisation's need to operate in accordance with the existing legislation, regulations, standards and best practice.
Data	Data can be thought of as the smallest component of information but which, in itself, does not necessarily have meaning, such as individual letters and digits held in a random way. For example, 0850361974 is a string of numbers. On their own, and out of context, it can be almost impossible to tell what the numbers refer to, but they are data (in this case, perhaps, an ISBN number which identifies a book, a telephone number or a customer account number).
Data Controller	A Data Controller is the person or organisation controlling the contents and use of the data.
Data Quality	Data quality relates to the accuracy, integrity, completeness and reliability of data and information.
Data Subjects	Data Subject relates to the individual who is the subject of the personal data. In practice, we are all Data Subjects. The UK Data Protection Act (DPA) grants rights to Data Subjects to see the data stored about them and requires that any errors in the data be corrected. In some circumstances the Data Subject may have a right to compensation for damage or distress caused.

Term or Expression	Definition
Disposal	This is the final stage in the record lifecycle and can either relate to destruction or transfer of a record to a recognised archive for preservation.

A Retention and Disposal Policy will define any statutory or regulatory requirements for the internal retention of records for a noted minimum period (for example for taxation and accounting purposes). |
| Explicit Knowledge | Explicit Knowledge is the knowledge that has been captured somewhere, for example in documents or a database. It is knowledge that has, through some process, been laid down, and put into a re-usable format, so that other people or systems can work with it. |
| Information | Information is something which tells us something and can also be communicated to someone else in a meaningful way.

Information is data that is put into context, can be comprehended, understood and shared with other people and/or machines. |
| Information Asset | An Information Asset is a definable piece of information, stored in any manner, which is recognised as having value to the organisation.

In addition, information assets are not easily replaceable without cost, skill, time and resources and they are part of the organisation's corporate identity, without which, the organisation may be threatened. |
| Information Governance | Information Governance is an encompassing term that relates to all laws, regulations, policies, procedures and protocols for the creation, use, amendment, storage, release, sharing, reuse, disposal and destruction of all information held by an organisation. |
| Information Management | A management framework for the acquisition, organisation, storage, security, retrieval, use, sharing, dissemination and disposal of information. |
| Information Resources | Information resources are the physical objects and digital code and files that store information. For example:

– A book is a paper information resource
– A PDF format file is a digital information resource.

The term "information resource" is used as a generic term. It can mean a record within a database, or the whole of the database. An information resource can also be an html page, or the whole of an Internet or Intranet site. |
Information Security	The policies, procedures and practices required to maintain and provide assurance of the confidentiality, integrity and availability of information.
Information Steward (or Champion)	The officer responsible for the accuracy, integrity and quality of data within their domain. Information Stewards are trustees of information rather than the owners of the information and the related systems.
Knowledge	Knowledge implies understanding. Knowledge could be defined as information plus experience and opinion.
Knowledge Assets	Knowledge Assets are instances of knowledge related to the operations of an organisation, its customers, services and the regulatory framework that enable it to operate effectively and efficiently.

Term or Expression	Definition
Knowledge Management	This is the overall process responsible for gathering, analysing, storing and sharing knowledge within an organisation.
Logical Security	Logical security is a subset of computer security that consists of software safeguards for the organisation's systems which include the use of user ID and password access controls, forms of electronic or biometric authentication and the allocation and management of related access rights and authority levels. Logical security measures work in association with Physical Security measures to protect systems and data from unauthorised access, unlawful disclosure, loss, corruption or disruption.
Metadata	Metadata is data about data, giving details about the context, content and structure of the record. Metadata supports retrieval, establishes provenance, demonstrates linkages between documents and relationships between records, aids the integrity of records and the ongoing use of the record as technological platforms evolve over time. Metadata is also used in the classification of records as a means to identify the related security requirements.
Nonactive (or noncurrent) Records	These are records that are no longer referred to in the course of the organisation's operations, but that must be retained in accordance with the relevant Retention and Disposal Guidelines.
Personal Data	Personal Data is information that relates to a living individual who can be identified from that information (or from that and other information in the possession of the Data Controller), including any expression of opinion about the individual and, with very few exceptions, any indication of the intentions of the Data Controller in respect of the individual. **NB: This is the definition as applies to the UK Data Protection Act and related definitions in other national or state legislation may differ.**
Physical Security	In general terms and in relation to the context of information security, usage of the term "physical security" relates to the implementation of physical, logical and procedural obstacles in order to prevent unauthorised access to buildings, facilities or information with the intent to: • damage, destroy, disable, compromise or remove the fabric of the structure or its contents • injure or otherwise harm any persons located within or near the structure or • compromise, destroy, misuse or remove the organisation's information assets.
Processing	Any activity/operation performed on data, whether held electronically or manually, such as obtaining, recording, holding, disseminating or making available the data or carrying out any operation on the data. This includes organising, adapting, amending and processing the data, retrieval, consultation, disclosure, erasure or destruction of the data.

Term or Expression	Definition
Records	Information created, received and maintained as evidence and information by an organisation, in pursuance of legal obligations or in the transaction of business.
Records Management	The discipline and professional function of managing records in order to meet organisational needs, business efficiency and legal and financial accountability.
Semi-Active (or Semi-Current) Records	These are records that are required to support the organisation's operations but which are only accessed on an infrequent basis.
Sensitive Data	In terms of the UK Data Protection Act, Sensitive Data is any information about a living individual relating to his or her: • racial or ethnic origins • religious beliefs or other beliefs of a similar nature • political opinion • membership of trade unions • physical or mental health or condition • sexual life • the commission or alleged commission by them of an offence • proceedings for any offence committed or alleged to be committed by them, the disposal of such proceedings or the sentence of any Court in such proceedings. **NB: This precise definition may vary across national legal environments. In general terms, sensitive data can also mean any information which is commercially sensitive or could cause harm or disadvantage if disclosed.**
System Administrator	A system administrator (sometimes abbreviated as sysadmin) is a person who is responsible for managing a multi-user computing environment. Their responsibilities typically include installing and configuring system hardware and software, establishing and managing user accounts, upgrading software and backup and recovery tasks.
System Owner	Normally senior managers who have overall operational responsibility for the operation and security of the systems and information used within their service or functional areas.
Tacit Knowledge	Tacit Knowledge is personal knowledge that includes skills, insight and judgement. It is rooted in experience, ideals and values, and is difficult to capture in explicit form. For individuals, tacit knowledge is evidenced through the know-how they demonstrate.

Appendix 6
IT and Information Management Policies

Policy or Documentation	Purpose
Information Management Policy*	This overarching Policy defines the environment necessary to ensure that the organisation's information assets are appropriately managed during their usual lifecycle. Greater detail of the elements of the overall processes are defined within the supporting policies and procedures, which may include, for example: • Accessibility • Accuracy • Legal compliance • Information sharing • Records Management • Roles and responsibilities • Security and safety implications • Standards • Knowledge Management The IM Policy defines the basis upon which information is gathered, used, stored, shared, protected, disclosed and eventually disposed of. The Policy should also incorporate controls to ensure that any legislative or regulatory implications impinging on the use of information are appropriately addressed. In addition, processes applied to the management of information assets should, whenever possible, comply with recognised standards and best practice. The other key policy in relation to this one is the IT Security Policy which defines the control measures to support the provision of accurate, up-to-date, reliable and adequate information in order to support the organisation's operational and administrative requirements.

Policy or Documentation	Purpose
IT Security Policy*	Defines the corporate and cultural approach to matters of IT security, with the objective of ensuring the confidentiality, integrity and availability of information across the organisation. In addressing these requirements the Policy should provide a top-level overview of the measures that will be applied in all the key aspects of IT security (for example, Access Control, Physical Security and Network Management). Where relevant, these subcomponents of IT Security can be the subject of their own, more detailed, policy or ratified guidance material. A survey of UK companies published in 2008[1] noted that 55 % of the companies surveyed have a documented security policy in place, as compared to 27 % as at 2002.
Communications and Operation Management	This is a top-level Policy relating to maintaining management control over such issues as: • Change Management • Management of test systems • Capacity planning • Protection against threats • System patching • Back-up • Management of media • System documentation • Monitoring and logging • Network controls • IT health checks *Each or any of the noted topics can be the subject of further supporting documentation and guidance, as is the case illustrated in this table.*
Computer, telephone and desk use	This document outlines the basis for appropriate staff use of the provided facilities including computer and information resources, communication facilities and storage. The intention should be to prevent any misuse of such resources and to encourage good practice, for example in relation to: • Preventing fraud, theft or dishonesty • Storing, loading or executing software for non work-related purposes or where the organisation does not have a suitable licence in place • Storing, processing and printing of data for non work-related purposes • Code of practice for acceptable use of telephone facilities for private purposes • The application of a clear desk policy designed to protect information and records from loss, theft or authorised disclosure • The prevention of unauthorised disclosure of information due to unattended PC screens.

Policy or Documentation	Purpose
	• Basic conditions for storing and disposing of information in order to protect confidentiality etc. • Ensuring that the use, storage and protection of data is lawful.
Email*	This document should specify the do's and don'ts relating to the use of email facilities, including: • Recognising the associated risks and potential implications for the organisation and implicated staff members • Preventing the use of non work email addresses • Emails are to be considered as part of the organisation's official records and have the same legal status as any form of written communication • Defining the scope and limitations for private use of corporate email facilities • Care over the inclusion or attachment of personal, confidential or sensitive information • Not to include content that is, profane, defamatory, obscene or in any other way offensive or unlawful • Taking appropriate precautions when receiving unexpected or suspect emails • Alerting users to the possible virus infection of emails and their attachments • Advising of the monitoring of email usage
Human Resources Information Security Standards*	This document specifies the steps to be taken prior to granting new users access to IT facilities and resources, as a means of preventing inappropriate access that could jeopardise the integrity of the organisation's information. The required actions include: • Adherence to the procedural requirements for recruitment (i.e. obtaining satisfactory references, criminal record checks or bonding cover prior to joining the organisation). • Confirming the identity of the employee, their right to work and their claimed qualifications • Ensuring that the appropriate terms and conditions of employment are incorporated into the employment contracts and that the employee officially acknowledges their responsibilities and obligations for and to IT security etc. • Ensuring that the level of access is appropriate and proportional to the employee's duties and responsibilities • Only setting up valid and authorised IT users • Provision of appropriate and relevant information security awareness, education and training Ensuring that when the employee leaves the organisation, access to IT facilities and information resources is promptly terminated and access rights disabled (this is especially important in cases of disciplinary offences or dismissal)

Policy or Documentation	Purpose
	• Leavers should return all the organisation's assets provided to support their duties (i.e. laptops, PDAs, mobile phones, etc).
Information Protection	This document outlines the scope of affected information sources irrespective of their form (i.e. physical or electronic).
	The following key aspects are included:
	• Identifying and recording all the key information assets in use within the organisation • Establishing an 'owner' for each major information asset and it's characteristics such as format, location, acceptable uses and back-up regime • Details of the storage arrangements, access permissions and authorised disclosure arrangements • Classifying each information asset, taking into account it's relative sensitivity, level of protective marking and significance to the organisation • Specific identification of personal data (as defined by the prevailing Data Protection legislation) • Any restrictions on the access to information assets in relation to their categorisation.
Incident Management*	This document outlines how the organisation will identify any actual or suspected information or IT security incidents, taking into account the following aspects:

	• Clearly identifying the scope and range of potential incidents, that could include, for example:
	  • Breach of policy
	  • Compromise of control
	  • Virus infection
	  • Illegal or inappropriate action
	  • Use of IT resources for personal gain
	  • Loss or theft of data
	  • Unauthorised disclosure of information

	• Prompt identification, reporting, investigation and recording of incidents • Prompt action to remedy the situation and isolate the effects • Prompt escalation of major incidents • Systematic approach to investigating and resolving incidents • Learning lessons from incidents to inform the process of improving security
Internet Acceptable Usage*	Provides clarity on the appropriate and acceptable use of the Internet by staff during working hours.
	Clearly defining how the Internet should be used for work purposes. Defining the unacceptable uses of the Internet, such as:
	• Personal use only permissible in the employee's own time

Policy or Documentation	Purpose
	• Accessing chat rooms or social networking sites • Accessing or attempting to access unsuitable, pornographic, offensive or unlawful material • The downloading of software and files (that could harm the organisation's systems and records)
IT Access*	This document should state the basis upon which access to the organisation's systems and data is granted. Normally, such access is on a 'need to know' basis related to the user's operational duties and responsibilities. The policy or guidance should provide an overview of the main access controls applied (for example separate network and application access user IDs and associated passwords). In addition, it should define how such controls can be further strengthened by, for example, robust password standards, enforced periodic password changes and the requirement of employees never to share their passwords or attempt to access information to which they are not entitled.
IT Infrastructure Security*	This document augments the IT Security Policy and is often more directly related to the actions taken by IT Staff as opposed to general employees. These may include specialist roles such as Network Administrator. The contents relates to the establishment and application of appropriate standards for the physical and environmental security of the following key areas: • The protection of secure areas housing centralised IT equipment, the physical network infrastructure and centralised records. • Physical and other security measures will need to be identified and risk assessed as to their suitability and effectiveness. • Unauthorised access must be prevented so as to protect equipment, assets and information. • Deliveries of IT equipment should be checked for integrity and suitably protected. • The security measures should take account of the relative value, sensitivity and confidentiality of information and systems; and be proportionate. • Protection of cabling. • Ensuring that equipment is subject to regular and appropriate maintenance. • Controls should also be in place for the protection of IT hardware taken off the premises. • Processes should be in place for the secure disposal or re-use of equipment that completely remove all trace of any prior information.

Policy or Documentation	Purpose
Legal Responsibilities*	The range of relevant legal and regulatory obligations affecting an organisation will obviously depend on its country of operation and the sector in which it operates. There is likely to be a combination of mandatory elements and associated good practices, as defined, for example in either national, international or sector-specific standards. However, all such obligations and compliance requirements should be identified. In addition, the specific requirements, compliance issues and obligations will need to be clearly communicated to employees so that they can function accordingly and lawfully. Where appropriate, separate detailed procedures and guidance should be made available and maintained up-to-date. Ignorance of the law is no defence and with regard to specific legislation, such as that relating to Data Protection and Freedom of Information, the organisation and, in some instances, the implicated employees can be held liable. This top-level document should also aim to briefly describe how the organisation will ensure compliance with the necessary laws, regulations and standards.
Remote Working*	The organisation as a whole should have a Human Resources Policy which defines the circumstances where an employee could or would be allowed to work at home or off site but still able to access the organisation's IT facilities. The relevant HR Policy will also need to be backed up with an IT-related Remote Working document which addresses the technical and security issues surrounding remote access facilities. The key points for this document include: • Restricting remote access to authorised staff and clearly defining the conditions of use. • Only using approved and technically suitable and secure devices and software to gain access. • Ensuring that all corporate IT equipment and property is fully accounted for and returned when the employee leaves or changes role. • Ensuring the protection of the central facilities through the use of effective firewalls and other logical barriers to unauthorised access. • Stating the employee's physical security obligations.
Removable Media*	A combination of the increasing storage capacity of removable media devices and their ease of use does leave organisations vulnerable to the loss, misplacement or theft of such devices. Such

Policy or Documentation	Purpose
	devices can be simply connected to most computers and the data they contain, which may be personal or confidential in nature, becomes potentially accessible to anyone, whether or not they are unauthorised to view it. This document outlines the processes deployed for the protection of such media against loss, theft, unauthorised access or damage. The following key areas should be addressed: • Limit the use of removable media devices and control the issue of them to authorised personnel. • Only acquire and use reliable and technically suitable devices. • Apply encryption to the files contained on the devices. • Define the physical security measures to be applied. • Promptly identify, report and deal with actual or suspected breaches of information security involving removable and portable devices. • Define how the devices will be disposed at the end of their useful life and what specific measures will be taken to make them irreversibly unusable and unreadable.
Software*	This document should define the way in which the organisation acquires, registers, licenses, installs, develops and maintains software. The scope of the document will need to be related to the actual pattern of software usage apparent in the organisation, but the following examples of issues to address are provided as a guide: • Rigorous assessment, justification and authorisation of software acquisitions. • Adequacy of software testing. • Accurate records of software licenses and the ability to confirm ongoing compliance with the relevant terms and conditions. • Robust development standards and methods. • Effective project management. • Adequacy of system documentation. • Protection against malicious code. • Restricting the ability to load or upgrade software to qualified or experienced IT staff.
Change Management Policy (including Patch Management)*	Describes the processes required to control changes to systems and software including: • Documenting the reasons for change. • Assessment of all the implications, including costs and operational impacts. • Formal justification and approval process. • Controlled and universal application of patches and bug fixes.

Policy or Documentation	Purpose
	• Monitoring of the status of software versions deployed across the organisation. • Communication with all affected parties. • Prior comprehensive testing. • Arrangements for rolling back or aborting in the event of problems. • Controlled application to the live or production environment. • Subsequent monitoring and post implementation review.
Anti-Virus Update Policy*	Defines the processes to be applied to the periodic and consistent deployment and update of anti-virus precautions in order to prevent the introduction of malicious code into any aspect of the organisation's IT environment.
Capacity Management Policy*	Capacity management is inextricably linked to higher-level operational planning and IT strategic planning, based upon a clear vision of the corporate objectives and the linked requirements. This document should spell out how the organisation systematically goes about assessing the current and future IT requirements in order to keep in step with the broader operational and administrative objectives. This is not as easy as it sounds, partly because of the developments in the IT sector being relatively rapid and the associated difficulty of ensuring that the organisation doesn't become linked to a decaying or short-lived technical solution. It isn't an option to do nothing in this respect and any organisation will need a clear and consistent vision that spans operational, functional and technical aspects. If the underlying business plan changes, for example due to unforeseen market forces, then the IT Strategy and Capacity Plans will need to be actively reassessed, valued and justified.
Back-up Procedures*	Provides the basis for ensuring that all systems and data are adequately backed up at an appropriate frequency. Also incorporates the physical and logical security measures and environmental controls designed to protect key back-up media from loss, theft, corruption or damage. May also incorporate guidance on the appropriate handling, storage and management of media. Some degree of testing of the robustness and accessibility of back-up data and code should be considered so as to provide some assurance that the mechanisms of recovery would actually work in the event of a incident occurring.
Business Continuity Plan*	The Business Continuity Plan (BCP) is not solely about IT, although such technology is likely to play a large part in the efficient recovery of operations and services.

Policy or Documentation	Purpose
	The BCP should primarily identify all the components and facilities that would be required to support the critical operations and services. This will include premises, staff resources, communications, consumables, utility services as well as computing facilities and access to key application systems and data.
	Throughout the BCP there is a consistent thread of identifying the base operation(s), the related resource requirements and the means to deliver them within a critical timescale.
Disaster Recovery Plan*	The Disaster Recovery Plan (DRP) should define the mechanisms and arrangements in place to support the recovery of IT operations is association with the Business Continuity Planning process.
	The DRP will define the available options and how these will relate to the underlying nature and extent of any crisis or emergency situation. These options will depend on the nature of the organisation and its operations and the relative levels of significance of the required IT resources.
	The solutions will vary and be constrained by their associated costs and practicality. For example, one option may be to decamp the IT operations to either a warm or hot site provided by an external specialist contractor in return for a monthly service fee.
	Once again, doing nothing and to trust to luck that the organisation will never be affected by a disruptive or catastrophic incident is not an option.
Information Asset Register*	This guidance or procedural document should spell out the process to be applied to identify, record and categorise all the organisation's information assets.
	Ideally the Register or Inventory should be a consolidated central record across the entire organisation and contain all the key sets of records and files (in all forms).
	In one sense the onerous task of producing such a catalogue can be an epiphany as it often reveals unknown or long-forgotten information sources that may acquire a renewed significance. Alternatively, the process may reveal redundant, inaccurate or unreliable assets that need to be updated or abandoned.
	Creating the Information Asset Register or Inventory is just the beginning of the process of categorising and prioritising the entries as the basis for ensuring that proportional levels of protection and security are applied. This is a vital stage in the development of an Information Management Environment, which we explore in chapter 28.

Policy or Documentation	Purpose
Data Protection Policy*	• Maintaining an up-to-date registration or notification of the organisation's use of personal data. • Ensuring adherence to the Data Protection principles, in that: personal information is fairly and lawfully obtained; only used for specified and lawful purposes; is adequate, relevant and not excessive for the purpose for which it is processed; be accurate and kept up to date; not kept for longer than is necessary; is processed in accordance with the defined rights of Data Subjects; is kept secure; and not transferred to a country or territory outside the EU unless that country or territory has an adequate level of Data Protection. • Ensuring that requests from Data Subjects to access their personal information held by the organisation are dealt with promptly and lawfully. • Describing how proven errors in personal data are to be promptly corrected. Data Protection is addressed in Chapter 44. In addition Appendix 3 provides details, by country or state, of the current international Data Protection legislation and its status. Contact points are also provided so that further information can be sought.
Freedom of Information Policy*	The spread and creation of international Freedom of Information (FoI) legislation is moving ahead. Such legislation is also referred to as Access to Information or the Right to Information. Chapter 45 provides a discussion of the issues related to FoI and Appendix 4 provides details, by country, of the current situation with FoI legislation. The FoI Policy document should document how the organisation will comply with the specific requirements of the local law. This is likely to include the following key constituents: • Identifying what information can be released and that which must be restricted for matters of confidentiality. • Ensuring that all staff are aware of their FoI responsibilities and how to deal effectively, efficiently and lawfully with FoI requests.
Publication Scheme	A documented Publication Scheme is an established feature of local government authorities in the UK, although it could also be adapted for use in the private sector. Such UK local authorities and public bodies are obliged to document and make public details of the information they can provide to anyone upon request (for example to representatives of the press and media, researchers and members of the public). The Publication Scheme should also define the format(s) in which the information can be provided and any fees that may be due for the service (although many authorities waive the charging of a fee).

Policy or Documentation	Purpose
	The items contained within the Publication Scheme can obviously be released, without question, under the terms of the Freedom of Information Act and there should be administrative linkage with the mechanisms for dealing with FoI requests.
Physical Security Policy*	A Physical Security Policy should ideally contain an overview of the measures and controls that an organisation will have in place to adequately address any attempts to gain authorised access to its premises and to protect: • Staff, customer and visitors from harm or injury. • Premises from damage, vandalism, disruption or destruction. • Property and assets from loss, theft, damage or destruction. • Information assets and records from loss, theft, disruption, unauthorised disclosure or destruction. As can be seen from the above list of aspects to protect, the Physical Security Policy has operational implications that are wider than purely IT aspects.
Records Management Policy*	This Policy should outline the organisation's approach to the effective management of all of its records and the compliance with any relevant legislations, regulations and applicable standards. The document should specify what will be done in respect of the following: • The capture of accurate, complete, authentic and reliable records. • The maintenance of records to meet the organisation's operational and administrative requirements. • The secure disposal of unwanted records. • The retention of records for periods prescribed by laws and regulations and the prevention of premature disposal. • The application of security measures to protect records from unauthorised access, loss, alteration, destruction or leakage. • The ongoing accessibility of records to those authorised to use them. • Adherence to the requirements of Data Protection and Freedom of Information (or equivalent) legislation or regulations. • Establishing arrangements for the recovery of records in event of an unplanned event occurring. • Complying with prevailing legislation, regulation and government directives. • Appropriately preserving records of permanent interest. • Ensuring that all employees are aware of their responsibilities and of the importance of records and information management.
Knowledge Management Policy*	Knowledge Management is concerned with the establishment of an environment that encourages and supports the identification, creation, communication and exploitation of knowledge that is derived from a combination of information, intuition and insight.

Policy or Documentation	Purpose
	The KM Policy should set the cultural tone for such an environment so that potentially valuable knowledge, experience and skills are recognised, recorded, effectively harnessed and not lost to the organisation.
Data Quality Policy	The Data Quality Policy may operate at either an organisation-wide level or in a specific area where the quality, accuracy and integrity of data is critical, for example in relation to the calculation of key performance indicators (KPIs) or mandatory sector statistics.
	The Policy should define the steps to be taken to maintain the accuracy and related quality of data so that it can be relied upon for both internal and external purposes.
Data Transfer and Sharing Standards and Protocol Guidelines*	Data can be shared either internally within an organisation or externally with partners or stakeholders.
	Employees should be given clear guidance on how they should deal with all requests for information and the issues to consider. (For example, whether a work colleague is actually entitled and authorised to access such data or to confirm the validity and legality of an external request for information).
	It is preferable that such external arrangements are formalised and subject to a documented agreement that incorporates mechanisms capable of providing assurances over, *inter alia,* the defined use, movement, protection, logical security measures, disclosure and disposal of the data in question.
	This document should define the administrative requirements and this should be proportionate and relevant to the categorisation of the affected data recorded within the Information Asset Register/Inventory.
Protective Marking Scheme Guidance	In the UK, the Government has a detailed Protective Marking Scheme (PMS) in place that it is encouraging other public bodies to adopt. The PMS has a number of defined categories (e.g. Protected, Restricted, Secret and so on) and defines the security measures that should be applied to each category of information in relation to access, disclosure security etc.
	Conceptually the PMS level could be recorded for each set of data or records within the Information Asset Register as a means of ensuring that proportionate and appropriate security measures are applied. However, the PMS is bureaucratic and not necessarily ideally suited to all organisations as it could represent an unnecessary, costly and additional burden.

Policy or Documentation	Purpose
Roles and Responsibilities Guidance	Roles and Responsibilities in relation to IT, Information Management and related processes (as reflected in the documents contained within this table) can be specific to a given position or officer in relation to their duties (e.g. the IT Security Manager).
	Alternatively, responsibilities can be general and apply to the majority of staff who utilise IT facilities and resources (e.g. the need to adequately protect their access passwords from loss or misuse).
	The availability of a documented outline of both these categories of responsibility can provide a useful reference point and the basis for assessing levels of control assurance.
Record Retention and Disposal Guidelines*	This document should specify all the required retention periods for documents as specified by laws or regulations (for example retaining invoices or other financial records for taxation purposes).
	In addition it should outline the processes for the secure and irreversible disposure of unwanted records and electronic media.

NOTE

1. *2008 Information Security Breaches Survey*, Department for Business, Enterprise and Regulatory Reform (2008), www.berr.gov.uk.

Bibliography

American Institute of Certified Public Accountants (AICPA) (1948, published in 1949) *Internal Control—Elements of a Co-ordinated System and its Importance to Management and the Independent Public Accountant*. AICPA, New York.

Ashworth, J. H. and Adams Cleveland, B. (2007) *Freedom of Information ACT Guide, March 2007*. Office of Information and Privacy, Washington USA.

BS31100 (22 October 2008) *Code of Practice for Risk Management*, British Standards Institute Bali, R. K., Wickramasinghe, N. and Lehany, B. (2009) *Knowledge Management Primer*. (Routledge Series in Information Systems). Routledge, Florida USA.

Beasley, K. (1994) *Self Assessment—A Tool for Integrated Management*. Stanley Thornes, Cheltenham.

Best, D. (2002) *Effective Records Management: A management guide to the value of BS ISO 15489-1 Pt1*. British Standards Institution, London.

Birkinshaw, P. (2001) *Freedom of Information: The Law, the Practice and the Ideal (Law in Context)*. Cambridge University Press, Cambridge.

Brotby, K. (2009) *Information Security Governance*. (Wiley Series in Systems Engineering and Management). Wiley Blackwell, Hoboken NJ USA.

Bygrave, L. A (2002) *Data Protection Law, Approaching its Rationale, Logic and Limits*. Kluwer Law International, Netherlands.

Calder, A. and Watkins, S. (2008) *IT Governance: A Manager's Guide to Data Security and ISO 27001 / ISO 27002*. 4th edition. Kogan Page, London.

Canadian Institute of Chartered Accountants (November 2005) *Guidance on Control*, The Criteria of Control Board ("CoCo") of CICA, ISBN 0-88800-436-1, still in print. See also CoCo's *Preface to Guidance issued by the Criteria of Control Board* (November 1995) and *Guidance for Directors—Governance Processes for Control* (December 1995).

Carey, P. (2004) *Data Protection: A Practical Guide to UK and EU Law*. Oxford University Press, Oxford.

Carey, P. (2008) *Data Protection Handbook*. The Law Society, London.

Carey, P. and Turle, M. (2008) *Freedom of Information Handbook*. 2nd edition. The Law Society, London.

Cascarino, R. E. (2007) *Auditor's Guide to Information Systems Auditing*. John Wiley & Sons Ltd, Chichester UK.

Casler, D. J. and Crockett, J. R. (1982) *Operational Auditing: An Introduction*. IIA, Altmonte Springs, Florida.

Chambers, A. D. (1997) *Effective Internal Audits—How to Plan and Implement*. Management Audit, HB, www.management-audit.com.

Chambers, A. D. (2008) "The board's black hole—filling their assurance vacuum: can internal audit rise to the challenge", *Measuring Business Excellence*, Vol. 12, No. 1.

Chambers, A.D. (2009) *Tolley's Internal Auditor's Handbook*. LexisNexis, pp. 484–491.

Chambers, A. D. (2009) "The black hole of assurance", *Internal Auditor*, Vol. 66, No. 2.

Chambers, A. D. and Court, J. M. (1991) *Computer Auditing*. 3rd edition. Pitman, London.

Chambers, A. D. and Rand, G. (1997) *Auditing the IT Environment—Assessing and Measuring Risk and Control*. Management Audit, HB, www.management-audit.com.

Chambers, A. D. and Rand, G. (1997) *Auditing Contracts*. Management Audit, HB, www.management-audit.com.

Chambers, A. D., Selim. G. M. and Vinten, G. (1987, 1988 and 1990) *Internal Auditing*. Pitman Publishing, London.

Chapman, R. J. (2006) *Simple Tools and Techniques for Enterprise Risk Management*. John Wiley & Sons Ltd, Chichester UK.

Collins, A. (1904) *The Municipal Internal Audit*. Gee & Co., London.

Committee of Sponsoring Organizations of the Treadway Commisssion ("COSO") (1987) *Report of the National Commission on Fraudulent Financial Reporting,* "The Treadway Commission Report'' (National Commission on Fraudulent Financial Reporting, New York), available on COSO's website: www.coso.org.

Committee of Sponsoring Organizations (COSO) (1992) *Internal Control—Integrated Framework*, www.coso.org.

Committee of Sponsoring Organizations (COSO), (2004) *Enterprise Risk Management—Integrated Framework*, www.coso.org.

Crohy, M., Galai, D. and Mark, R. (2006) *The Essentials of Risk Management: The Definitive Guide for the Non-risk Professional*. McGraw-Hill Professional, New York.

Darch, C. and Underwood, P.G. (2009) *Freedom of Information in the Developing World: Demand, Compliance and Democratic Behaviours*. Chandos Publishing Ltd, Oxford.

Davenport, T. H. and Prusak, L. (2000) *Working Knowledge: How Organizations Manage What They Know*. 2nd revised edition. Harvard Business School Press, Boston.

Davis, C., Schiller, M. and Wheeler, K. (2007) *IT Auditing: Using Controls to Protect Information Assets*. McGraw-Hill Osborne, New York.

Davis, J. R., Alderman, C. W. and Robinson, L. A. (1990), *Accounting Information Systems—A Cycle Approach*. 3rd edition. John Wiley & Sons Inc., New York.

Drucker, P. F. (1977) *Management: Tasks, Responsibilities, Practices*. Pan UK edition.

Fayol, H. (1916) *Administration Industrielle et Générale* (General and Industrial Management). H. Dunod et E. Pinat, Paris. Trans. by Constance Storres (1949) Pitman, London.

Financial Reporting Council (1999 and 2005 (revised)) *Internal Control—Guidance for Directors on the Combined Code*, ("The Turnbull Report"), www.frc.org.uk.

Financial Reporting Council, (2008, 2010) *Combined Code on Corporate Governance*, http://www.frc.org.uk/.

Flinn, A. and Jones, H. (2009) *Freedom of Information: Open Access or Empty Archives?* Routledge, Kentucky USA.

Frappaolo, C. (2006) *Knowledge Management*. 2nd edition. Capstone Publishing, Oxford.

Gallegos, F. and Senft, S. (2008) *Information Technology Control and Audit*. Auerbach Publications, Abingdon UK.

Gleim, I. (2001) *CIA Review Book Part III* (Management Control and Information Technology). 10th edition. Gleim Publications.

HM Treasury (October 2004) *The Orange Book—Management of Risk, Principles and Concepts*, http://www.hm-treasury.gov.uk/d/orange_book.pdf.

HM Treasury (December 2006) *Internal Audit Quality Assessment Framework—A Tool for Departments*, http://www.hm-treasury.gov.uk/psr_governance_risk_iaqaf.htm.

Hayes, J. (2006) *The Theory and Practice of Change Management*. 2nd revised edition. Palgrave Macmillan, Basingstoke UK.

Henry, C. L. (2003) *Freedom of Information Act*. Nova Biomedical, Hauppauge USA.

Hertzberg, F. *et al.* (1959) *The Motivation to Work*. 2nd edition. Harper & Row, London.

Hibbert, G. and Graham M. (1979) "The boundaries of internal auditing", *Accountancy*, September.

Hill, D. G. (2009) *Data Protection*. CRC Press, Florida USA.

Hinton, M. (2005) *Introducing Information Management: the business approach*. Butterworth-Heinemann, Oxford.

Hislop, D. (2009) *Knowledge Management in Organizations: A Critical Introduction*. 2nd edition. Oxford University Press, Oxford.

Hopton, D. (2009) *Money Laundering*. 2nd edition. Gower, Farnham UK.

Hubbard, L. (2000) *Control Self-Assessment: A Practical Guide*. The Institute of Internal Auditors, www.theiia.org.

Hull, J. C. (2009) *Risk Management and Financial Institutions*. Pearson Education.

ISO 31000:2009: Risk management—Principles and Guidelines, in draft at September 2009, http://www.iso.org/iso/home.htm.

Institute of Internal Auditors Inc. (2005) *Sarbanes-Oxley Section 404 Work: Looking at the Benefits* (The IIA's Research Foundation), www.theiia.org.

Institute of Internal Auditors Inc. (January 2008) *Sarbanes-Oxley Section 404: A Guide for Management by Internal Controls Practitioners*. 2nd edition, www.theiia.org.

Institute of Internal Auditors Inc. (2009, and annual updates) *International Professional Practices Framework (IPPF)*, www.theiia.org.

Institute of Internal Auditors Inc. (2009) *Position Statement: The Role of Internal Audit in Enterprise-wide Risk Management*, www.iia.org.uk or www.theiia.org.

Institute of Internal Auditors Inc. (expected 2010) *Internal Audit Capability Maturity Model (IA-CMM)*, authored by Elizabeth MacRae (The Institute of Internal Auditors Research Foundation).

Johnson, K. P. and Jaenicke, H. R. (1980) *Evaluating Internal Control—Concepts, Guidelines, Procedures, Documentation*. John Wiley & Sons Inc., New York.

Jorion, P. (2009) *Financial Risk Manager Handbook*. 5th edition. John Wiley & Sons Ltd, Chichester UK.

Kelleher, D. (2006) *Privacy and Data Protection Law in Ireland*. Tottel Publishing Ltd, Dublin.

Keyser, T. and Dainty, C. (2004) *The Information Governance Toolkit: Data Protection, Caldicott, Confidentiality*. Radcliffe Publishing Ltd, Oxford.

Koontz, H. and O'Donnell, C. (1976) *Management—A Systems and Contingency Analysis of Managerial Functions*. 6th edition (International student edition). McGraw-Hill, Tokyo.

Koontz, H., O'Donnell, C. and Weinrich, H. (1976) Management. 8th edition. McGraw-Hill, Singapore.

Kuner, C. (2007) *European Data Protection Law: Corporate Compliance and Regulation*. 2nd edition. Oxford University Press, Oxford.

Lam, J. (2003) *Enterprise Risk Management: From Incentives to Controls*. John Wiley & Sons Ltd, Chichester UK.

Lawrence, P. and Lorsch, J. (1957) *Organization and its Environment*. Harvard University Press, Cambridge MA.

Lea Ginn, M. (2006) *Records Management*. 8th revised edition. South-Western, Div of Thomson Learning, Florence KY, USA.

Ledgerwood, G. Street, E. and Therivel, R. (1992) *The Environmental Audit and Business Strategy*. Pitman/Financial Times, London.

Leitch, M. (2008) *Intelligent Internal Control and Risk Management: Designing High-performance Risk Control Systems*. Gower Publishing Ltd, Farnham UK.

Likert, Rensis (1956) *New Patterns of Management*. McGraw-Hill, New York.

MacDonald, J., Crail, R. and Jones, C. (2009) *The Law of Freedom of Information*. 2nd edition. Oxford University Press, Oxford.

Macdonald, L. A. C. (2008) *Data Protection: Legal Compliance and Good Practice for Employers*. 2nd revised edition. Tottel Publishing, Haywards Heath UK.

MacRae, E. (expected 2010) *Internal Audit Capability Maturity Model (IA-CMM)*. The Institute of Internal Auditors Research Foundation.

McKilligan, N. and Powell, N. (2009). *Data Protection Pocket Guide—Essential Facts at Your Fingertips*. 2nd edition. BSI British Standards Institution, London.

Maslow, A. (1954) *Motivation and Personality*. Harper & Row, London.

Merna, T. and AlThani, F. F. (2008) *Corporate Risk Management*. 2nd edition. John Wiley & Sons Ltd, Chichester UK.

Min, Young-Woon (2009) *Understanding and Auditing IT Systems, Volumes 1 and 2*. Lulu.com, USA.

Mitnick, K. and Allsopp, W. (2009) *Unauthorised Access: Physical Penetration Testing for IT Security Teams*. John Wiley & Sons Ltd, Chichester UK.

Moeller, R. (2004) *Sarbanes-Oxley and the New Internal Auditing Rules*. John Wiley & Sons Ltd, Chichester UK.

Moeller, R. (2007) *COSO Enterprise Risk Management: Understanding the New Integrated ERM Framework*. John Wiley & Sons Ltd, Chichester UK.

Petrocelli, T. (2005) *Data Protection and Information Lifecycle Management*. Prentice Hall, New Jersey USA.

Pickett, S. (2001) *Internal Control: A Manager's Journey*. John Wiley & Sons Inc., USA [translated into other languages].

Pickett, S. (2002) *Financial Crime; Investigation and Control*. John Wiley & Sons Inc., USA [translated into other languages].

Pickett, S. (2003) *The Internal Auditor at Work: A Practical Guide to Everyday Challenges*. John Wiley & Sons Inc., USA.

Pickett, S. (2003) *Internal Auditing Handbook*. 2nd edition. John Wiley & Sons Ltd, Chichester UK.

Pickett, S. (2005) *Auditing the Risk Management Process*. John Wiley & Sons Inc., USA.

Pickett, S. (2005) *Auditing for Managers: The Ultimate Risk Management Tool*. John Wiley & Sons Ltd, Chichester UK.

Pickett, S. (2005) *The Essential Handbook of Internal Auditing*. John Wiley & Sons Ltd, Chichester UK [translated into other languages].

Pickett, S. (2006) *Enterprise Risk Management: A Manager's Journey*. John Wiley & Sons Inc., USA.

Pickett, S. (2006) *Audit Planning: A Risk Based Approach*. John Wiley & Sons Inc., USA.

Pickett, S. (2007) *Corporate Fraud: A Manager's Journey*. John Wiley & Sons Inc., USA.

Pickett, S. (2009) *Internal Investigations: A Basic Guide Anyone Can Use*. John Wiley & Sons Ltd, Chichester UK.

Protiviti (2009) *2009 Internal Audit Capability and Needs Survey,* (www.protiviti.com), *and Capability Maturity Model Based on the IIA Standards*.

Sadgrove, K. (2005) *Complete Guide to Business Risk Management*. 2nd revised edition. Gower Publishing Ltd, Farnham UK.

Schonberger, R. J. (1982) *Japanese Manufacturing Techniques—Nine Hidden Lessons in Simplicity*. Free Press, New York.

Shepherd, E. and Yeo, G. (2003) *Managing Records: A Handbook of Principles and Practice*. Facet Publishing, London.

Singleton, S. (2003) *Data Protection Law for Employers (Thorogood Professional Insights)*. Thorogood, Abingdon UK.

Smith, K. (2004) *Freedom of Information: A Practical Guide to Implementing the Act*. Facet Publishing, London.

Smith, K. (2007) *Public Sector Records Management: A Practical Guide*. Ashgate, Farnham UK.

Taleb, N. N. (2008) *The Black Swan: The Impact of the Highly Improbable*. Penguin, London.

Taylor, F. (1903) *Shop Management*. New York.

Taylor, F. (1911) *Scientific Management*. Harper & Brothers, New York, London.

Towers, S. (1994) *Business Process Re-Engineering—A Practical Handbook for Executives*. Stanley Thornes, Cheltenham UK.

Wade, K. and Wynne, A. (1999) *Control Self Assessment—for Risk Management and Other Practical Applications*. John Wiley & Sons Inc., New York.

Wadham, J., Griffiths, J. and Harris, K. (2007) *Blackstone's Guide to the Freedom of Information Act 2000*. 3rd edition. Oxford University Press, Oxford.

Webster, M. (2003) *Data Protection for the HR Manager*. Gower Publishing Ltd, Farnham UK.

Webster, M. (2006) *Data Protection in the Financial Services Industry*. Gower Publishing Ltd, Farnham UK.

Webster, M. (2006) *The ICSA Data Protection Troubleshooter*. ICSA Publishing Ltd, London.

Wiseman, L. and Gordon, J. (2009) *Data Protection: Guidelines for the use of personal data in system testing*. BSI British Standards Institution, London.

Index

absenteeism rates 325–7, 401–4, 425–7
access controls 43–4, 57–74, 136–7, 242–3, 273–4, 282–3, 372–5, 380–2, 392–5, 401–7, 453–62, 481–8, 489–92, 497–501, 504–10, 514–23, 527–41, 542–53, 555–69, 573–9, 585–9, 613–15, 620–6, 636–44, 661–6, 667–70, 680–7, 704–6, 763–834, 842–3
   see also data protection...; security
   data protection 620–6, 631–2, 639–44, 848
   data transfers and sharing 515–23, 542–53, 636–44, 704–6, 850
   freedom of information 479–88, 497–501, 503–10, 516–23, 525–41, 581–4, 590–1, 627–35, 646–7, 763–834, 848–9
   hacking 646, 671–9
   human resource information security 661–6, 667–70, 841–2
   information security incidents 487, 520–3, 671–9, 841–2
   Internet 599–604, 842–3
   life-cycle issues 661–6
   logging systems 487, 576–9, 588–9, 667–70
   physical security 555–8, 638–44, 661–6, 667–70, 849
   records management 527–41, 680–7, 849
   remote working 585–9, 844
   rights and responsibilities 661–6
   spreadsheets 704–6
   system access controls 8, 487, 576–9, 661–6, 707–9
   updated access rights 662–6
   user-screening processes 662–6, 667–70, 694–5
   verification tasks 662–6
access key devices 555–8
accessibility aspects of information management 515–23
accountabilities 33–4, 78, 84, 85–94, 100–15, 282–3, 448–50, 464–75, 493–5, 535–41, 559–61
accountancy profession 17
accounting controls *see* finance and accounting
accounts payable
   see also creditors; purchasing
   concepts 7, 11, 28–9, 33, 42, 45, 51, 240, 246–8, 436, 713
   control objectives 246

   risk/control questions 246–8
accounts receivable
   see also debtors; order processing
   concepts 7, 33, 42, 240, 248–51, 362, 372–5, 380–2, 713
   control objectives 248
   risk/control questions 249–51, 362
accruals 158–60
accurate information 57–74, 124–7, 242–51, 272–4, 283–9, 291–316, 493–5, 507–10, 514–23, 535–41, 559–61, 587–9, 600–4, 618–26, 705–6, 710–11, 835
action plans 71–4, 206, 212, 489–92
activators, systems concepts 131–5
activities
   categories of organisational activities 6–12
   control activities 117–46, 147–50, 157–8, 164–77
actuals
   sales performance and monitoring 359–62
   three Es (effectiveness, efficiency, and economy) 15–16, 19–23, 219–35
ad hoc internal requests, data transfer types 636, 638–9
adaptive control systems 133–5
added value 21–3, 76, 211–12, 219–35, 364–6, 370–1, 391–2
   see also value...
added value *(cont.)*
   CSAs 211–12
   definitions 22
   operational auditing 21–3, 76, 211–12, 219–35, 364–6, 370–1, 391–2
additional voluntary contributions (AVCs) 419
administrative controls, concepts 3, 6–7, 117
advertising *see* promotion and advertising
affiliates 158, 177
Afghanistan 729, 764
after sales support 5–6, 8, 43, 126–7, 343–4, 348, 350, 366, 375–82, 389–92, 714–15, 724
   see also maintenance and servicing; marketing and sales; spare parts...; warranty arrangements
   concepts 8, 343–4, 375–82, 389–92, 714–15, 724
   control objectives 375–6, 377–8, 380–1, 389
   risk/control questions 376–7, 378–80, 381–2, 389–92

860 INDEX

after sales support (*cont.*)
   SAPG   714–15, 724
agents   8, 343, 350, 351–3, 362, 368–71, 404–7, 714
   concepts   350, 351–3, 362, 368–71
   conflicts of interest   369–71
   control objectives   368–9
   remuneration   368–71
   responsibilities   369–71
   risk/control questions   369–71
AGMs   93
AICPA   116–18
air conditioning systems, systems concepts   130–5
Albania   729, 764
allowances, taxation   264–6
annual reports   92–4, 117, 151–77, 251–3, 710–11
   see also Sarbanes-Oxley Act 2002
anonymous voting systems   205, 207–8
anti-discrimination laws   406–7, 594–5
appendices   616, 712–851
Apple Corporation   570–1
appointments, auditors   17, 176
approval issues
   boards of directors   17, 73–4, 164, 166, 211
   lists of contractors   9, 290, 297–9, 316
archives   514–23, 538–41, 680–7, 835
Argentina   730, 765
Armenia   730, 765
ARPANET   598
Ashby's cybernetics law of requisite variety   131–5
asset management   481–8, 710–11
asset registers   497, 502–10, 515–23, 527–41, 556–8, 681–7, 700–1, 710–11, 847, 850
assets
   see also hardware...; information...; software...
   fixed assets (and capital charges)   7, 240, 253–6, 432–6, 447, 502, 710–11
   risk management   3, 5–6, 10, 17, 22, 25, 29–30, 36–7, 40, 41–74, 76–94, 95–115, 143–5
assurance issues   8, 17–19, 22, 76, 82–4, 100, 115, 117–46, 171–3, 182–7, 212, 214–35, 240–75, 286–9, 306–10, 314–16, 318, 319–42, 345–81, 468–75, 714, 721
   see also quality assurance...
   boards of directors   82–4
   resourcing decisions   17–19, 232–5
ATMs   10
attachments, emails   593–7, 691–3
audit approaches to operational auditing   12–16
audit committees   32–3, 82–4, 86–7, 88–90, 114, 127–8, 143–5, 153–77, 211–12, 214–35
   see also boards of directors
   chief audit executives   82–4, 143–5, 232–3
   complaints   160
   CSAs   211–12
   financial experts   158–62, 172–3
   monitoring functions   127–8, 143–5, 158–77
   responsibilities   158–73, 176–7, 211, 214–35
   Sarbanes-Oxley Act 2002   153–77
   statutory requirements   158–60

audit findings   13–14
audit logs *see* logging systems
audit reports   13–14, 200–1, 218, 226–35
audit review programmes, joint ventures   283
audit trails, concepts   35, 36, 168–70, 247–8
audit universes
   business processes   27–39, 41, 240
   concepts   6, 9, 11, 27–39, 41, 290
   contracting   9, 290
   hybrid audit universe   30
audit visits   45, 277–84
auditors
   appointments   17, 176
   credibility issues   11–12, 16–18
   knowledge/skills/competencies requirements   16–18, 86–7, 158–60, 218, 233–4
   recruitment issues   17, 176
   remuneration   176, 233
   technical activities   16–19
Australia   534, 581, 685, 730, 765–6
Austria   731, 767
authority to make organisational commitments   136–7, 147–50, 183–5, 203–4, 208–13, 550–3, 554–8
automated controls   130–5, 195–8

back-up and media management   8, 43–4, 67–74, 486, 497–501, 505–10, 521–3, 537–41, 558, 562–5, 584, 658–60, 846
   concepts   562–5, 584, 588–9, 846
   control objectives   563
   procedures   563–5, 846
   risk/control questions   563–5
BACS   245, 261, 487, 696–8
bad debts   33, 249–51
BAE   97–8
balance sheets   54, 67–74
bank account reconciliations   258–61
bank accounts and banking arrangements
   concepts   7, 240, 258–61, 283, 713
   control objectives   258–9
   risk/control questions   259–61
banks   29, 42, 51, 97–8, 283
Barbados   731, 768–9
batch processing   559–61
Belarus   731, 769
Belgium   732, 770
benchmarking, concepts   16, 23–4, 92, 172–3, 349–50, 354
Bermuda   732–3, 770–1
BERR   481, 585, 590–1, 599, 658, 671–2, 691, 851
'best' row in control matrices   58–74
bibliography   852–7
Blair, Tony   151
boards of directors   4–5, 9–10, 12–14, 17, 32, 44, 73–4, 75–94, 102–8, 112–15, 117–46, 147–50, 153–77, 211–12, 215–35, 470, 524–41, 552–3
   see also audit committees
   approval requirements   17, 73–4, 164, 166, 211
   assurance vacuums   82–4

committees 32–3, 82–4, 86–7, 88–90, 93, 114
corporate governance 81–94, 176–7, 470
CSAs 211–12
direction-setting objectives 81–2, 87–8, 147–50
internal controls 117–46, 151–77, 470
objectives 81–4, 87–90, 112–15, 117–46, 147–50, 176–7, 470, 552–3
organisational objectives 81–2, 87–90, 112–15
risk management 102–8, 112–15, 470
risk registers 107–8, 115
bomb threats 556–8
Bosnia and Herzegovina 733, 771–2
'both' row in control matrices 58–74
Botswana 733, 772–3
bottom-round management, concepts 196–8
bought-in expertise, technical activities 17–18
boundaries, systems concepts 131–5
BPR *see* business process re-engineering
brainstorming sessions 57, 106–7, 183, 207–8
Brazil 733, 774
break-even points 269–70
breakdown services, company vehicles 435–6
bribery 84–5
British Petroleum (BP) 17–18, 199
British Security Industry Association (BSIA) 684
British Standards Institute (BSI) 182, 183–4, 466–7, 480–8, 526
 see also ISO...
 background information 182, 183–4, 466–7, 480, 526
 BS 4783 526
 BS 5454 526
 BS 7499 555
 BS 7750 467
 BS 7799 480–1, 526
 BS 8555 466–7, 475
 BS 15000 483
 BS EN 15713 684
 DISC PD0010 526
 DISC PD0012 526
'budget/actual comparisons', operational auditing evaluations 223–33
budgeting and monitoring 7, 51, 71–4, 223–35, 240, 256–8, 268–70, 276–84, 287–9, 293–316, 351–3, 388–92, 406–7, 413–15, 442–5, 490–2, 652–4, 710–11, 713
 control objectives 256, 443–5
 IT accounting 710–11
 risk/control questions 257–8, 443–5
buildings
 IT sites and infrastructure 555–8, 658–60, 681–7, 843
 portable buildings 111
builds of software, concepts 571–5
Bulgaria 734, 774–5
business continuity plans (BCPs) 497–501, 521–3, 846–7
 see also contingency plans
business cycles, concepts 32–5, 240
business management techniques

see also delayering...; empowerment...; outsourcing...; quality assurance... concepts 178–98
JIT 178, 195–8
business plans 282–3
business process re-engineering (BPR), concepts 178–81, 188–90, 199
business processes
 concepts 3–4, 27–39, 41, 116–46, 167–73, 178–81, 199–213, 240, 712–28, 837
 contracting 32
 CSAs 30, 199–213
 definitions 32–5, 837
 hallmarks of robust business processes 36, 141–2, 507–10, 521–3, 587–9
 identification approaches 32–5
 lists 32–5
 SAPGs 35–6, 712–28
 Sarbanes-Oxley Act 2002 167–73
 university case study 37–9
 weaknesses 30–2

Cadbury, Sir Adrian 116
CAE 13, 18
'calculated risk score' row in control matrices 58–74
campus area networks (CANs) 609
Canada 117, 129–30, 154, 199, 685, 734–7, 775–81
 see also CoCo
capacity management 486, 497, 511–13, 520–3, 715, 725, 846
 control objectives 512
 definition 511–12
 risk/control questions 512–13
Cape Verde 737–8, 781
capital expenditure, hardware assets 502, 713, 721
carbon trading 464–5
cash 7, 11, 32–6, 42, 54, 135–6, 240, 245–6, 258–61, 270–2, 274–5, 720–8
 see also petty cash...
cash flow management 33–4
Cayman Islands 738, 781–2
CCTV 554–5, 673
CDs 497, 533, 566–7, 637, 672
CEOs 97–8, 117, 128–9, 163–77, 229, 232–3
CERN 598
certification requirements
 CSAs 200
 Sarbanes-Oxley Act 2002 151–77
Certified Internal Auditors (CIAs) 204
CFOs 117, 128–9, 163–77
change management 497–501, 506–7, 520–3, 547–53, 605–8, 845–6
CHAPS 261
Chartered Institute of Public Finance and Accountancy (CIPFA) 228–30
Charters, operational auditing 217–35
cheques 259–61
chief accountants 4, 58, 69, 164–77

chief audit executives 18–19, 82–4, 143–5, 171, 216–35, 470
  audit committees 82–4, 143–5, 232–3
  'for pay and rations' reports 83–4
  resourcing considerations 18–19, 232–3
Chile 738, 782
China 581, 739, 782–3
CIAs *see* Certified Internal Auditors
CIPFA *see* Chartered Institute of Public Finance and Accountancy
classifications of organisational activities, concepts 6–12
cleaning firms, outsourcing considerations 192, 193
'clear desk' policies 539–40, 840–1
clearing banks 29
clients 13–14, 222–35
  see also customer...
closed systems, concepts 131–5
CoCo internal control framework 117–18, 129–30, 141–3, 144, 157–8, 208–10
  see also Canada
Codes of Conduct, ethics 148–9, 161–3, 172, 215–35
collection aspects
  data protection 618–26
  information asset registers 505–6, 847
  information management 515–23, 542–53, 618–26
collusion, fraud 149–50
colour codes and numeric scores, risk matrices 104–6
comfort letters 164
commitment factors 136–7, 147–50, 183–5, 203–4, 208–13, 550–3, 554–8
Committee of Sponsoring Organizations (COSO) 4–5, 15, 75–81, 96–9, 103, 111, 115, 117–28, 140, 142, 144, 147–50, 157–77
Common Law Duty of Confidence 640
communications 17–18, 20, 28–9, 78, 81–4, 85–7, 89–94, 99–115, 120–1, 124–7, 196–8, 208–13, 234, 277–84, 366–8, 430–2, 487, 489–92, 497, 515–23, 542–53, 554–8, 581–4, 590–7, 840
  emails 487, 497, 520–3, 581–4, 590–7, 691–3, 841
  JIT coordination 196–8
  knowledge management 542–53
  labour relations 430–2
  sharing aspects of information management 515–23, 542–53, 636–44
  subsidiaries/joint ventures 277–84, 366–8
Communities of Practice (CoPs) 547
Companies Act 2006 464, 473–5
company vehicles 7, 399, 432–6, 556–8, 714
  control objectives 433
  risk/control questions 433–6
comparators, systems concepts 130–5
competencies 9, 16–18, 84–5, 122, 129–30, 147–50, 158–77, 208–13, 290, 295–7
competitive advantages 71–4, 279–80, 344–55, 362–6, 368–9, 388–92, 411–13, 468–75, 489–92
competitive disadvantages 57–74
complaints 126–7, 160, 350, 356–7, 362, 406–7

completeness of information flows 14, 124–7, 168–73, 272–4, 283–9, 291–316, 507–10, 515–23, 535–41, 559–61, 587–9, 705–6, 710–11, 835
compliance issues 4–5, 46–50, 55, 60–74, 77–94, 96–115, 117–46, 151–77, 202, 226–35, 242–75, 291–316, 319–42, 400–36, 439–52, 463–75, 479–88, 496–501, 514–41, 616–35, 640–4, 665–6, 707–11, 713–14, 721, 835
  see also legislation; regulations
'compliance testing' column of SAPG risk/control section 48–50
Computer Misuse Act 1990 581, 646
concealed risks 107–10
confidentiality 57–74, 124–7, 220–1, 242–3, 272–4, 299–302, 345–8, 351–5, 401–7, 438–42, 453–62, 503–10, 515–23, 533–41, 560–1, 566–9, 586–9, 592–7, 637–44, 663–6, 671–9, 680–7, 688–90, 700–6, 729–62
configuration management database (CMDB) 572
conflicts of interest
  agents 369–71
  distributors 362–6, 389–92
  ethics 162–4
consistency of information flows 14, 124–7, 272–4, 705–6
consulting roles 100, 115, 180–1, 212, 232, 542
contingency plans 43–4, 69–74, 91, 103, 368, 397–8, 453–62, 487, 497–501, 512–13, 528–41, 561, 658–60, 671–9, 689–90, 707–9, 846–7
  see also business continuity plans
  concepts 658–60, 689–90
  control objectives 658–9
  risk/control questions 659–60
  security 453–62, 528–41, 658–60
  subsidiaries 368
  tests 658–60, 689–90
continuous improvements 16, 77–80, 91–4, 140–1, 179–81, 182–7, 210–13, 315–16, 466–7
  see also total quality management
contract management environment
  concepts 9, 290–5
  control objectives 291–2
  risk/control questions 292–5
contracting 6, 7, 9, 22–3, 32, 44, 143–5, 191–5, 220–1, 234, 285, 289–316, 385–92, 648–50, 655–7, 683–7, 716–17, 727–8
  see also outsourcing...; procurement; tendering
  approved lists of contractors 9, 290, 297–9, 316
  audit universes 9, 290
  business processes 32
  concepts 285, 385–92, 648–50, 655–7, 683–7, 716–17, 727–8
  control objectives 291–316, 388–9, 655
  costs and benefits analysis 291–316, 648–50, 655–7
  definition 289–90
  disposal of records 683–7
  documentation 300–1, 302–10, 314–16
  final accounts 9, 290, 310–13
  insurance cover 296, 389–92

interim payments 9, 44, 290, 308–13
overview of audit universes 9, 290
performance/productivity measurement systems 9, 290, 306–8, 313–16, 385–92
reviews of project outturn/performance 313–16
risk/control questions 292–316, 649–50, 656–7
SAPG 716–17, 727–8
selection and letting issues 9, 290, 304–6
viability/competence assessments of contractors 9, 290, 295–7
contracts of employment 405–7, 441–2
control activities
  concepts 117–46, 147–50, 157–8, 164–77, 207–13, 281–4, 707–9
  dimensions 123–4
  joint ventures 281–4
'control activities' component, COSO internal control framework 120–1, 123–4, 142, 144, 147–50, 157–8, 164–77
'control environment' component, COSO internal control framework 120–2, 147–50, 157–77
control environments 120–2, 147–50, 152–77, 453–5, 712–13, 721
control matrices
  see also inherent risk
  concepts 40, 53–4, 56–74
  examples 56–74
  MISs 56–74
  planning 64, 71–4
control registers, Sarbanes-Oxley Act 2002 168–70, 173
control self assessments (CSAs)
  see also standard audit programme guides
  action plans 206, 212
  anonymous voting systems 205, 207–8
  audit committees 211–12
  business processes 30, 199–213
  CoCo internal control framework 208–10
  concepts 18–19, 30, 41, 102–3, 128, 199–213, 718
  control objectives 210–12
  costs and benefits analysis 202–4, 205–6, 211–12
  critique 205–6
  definition 18–19, 41, 199–200
  hybrid approaches 206–7
  IIA CCSA programme 204, 210
  management commitment needs 202–3
  negative perspectives 202–3
  origins 199
  questions 208–12
  readings 210
  reassurance aspects 206
  responsibilities 200–2
  suitable focus areas 200–1
  top-down commitment 203–4
  training 204–5, 212
  Word tables 206
  workshop/survey approaches 200–1, 204–12
control systems, concepts 130–5

control-effectiveness measurements 54–6, 57–74, 78, 84, 85, 127–8, 141–3, 151–77, 209–13, 219–35
control-risk self assessments *see* control self assessments
controls, concepts 116–46
conversion business process, concepts 720–8
Coopers & Lybrand 118
coordinated sections within businesses 3–26, 27–39, 78–94, 116, 118–20, 196–8, 200–1, 218
Copyright Designs and Patents Act 1988 581, 646
core/non-core activities, outsourcing considerations 193–4, 195
corporate framework business process, concepts 34–5, 720–8
corporate governance 3, 5–6, 9–10, 17, 22, 25–6, 29–30, 34, 44, 75–94, 176–7, 205, 232–5, 470–5, 509–10, 718, 836
  best practices 93, 228–30
  boards of directors 81–94, 176–7, 470
  communications 78, 81–4, 85–7, 89–94
  concepts 75–94, 176–7, 205, 470–5, 509–10, 718, 836
  external governance processes 75, 81–4, 90–4, 116
  internal controls 76–94
  internal governance processes 78, 81–2, 84–7
  international conflicts of standards 176–7
  objectives 77–94
  risk management 76–94, 110
  SAPG 718
  stakeholders 75–82, 90–4
corporate memory, concepts 545–53
corporate social responsibilities 16, 21, 91–4, 463–75
corrective category of control 139, 168–70
corrective control systems 135
corrupted data 57–74
COSO *see* Committee of Sponsoring Organizations
costing methods 268–70, 321, 345–8, 354–5, 438–42, 445–50, 710–11, 720–8
costs and benefits analyses 151, 154–5, 171–2, 183–5, 188–9, 192–4, 197–8, 202–4, 205–6, 211–12, 219–35, 286–9, 291–316, 327–30, 349–50, 360–2, 411–13, 442–5, 460–2, 466–75, 507–10, 648–50, 651–7
  see also budget...
CRB *see* Criminal Records Bureau
credibility issues, auditors 11–12, 16–18
credit cards 272
credit notes 249–51
credit-granting business process 32–3, 136, 138, 194, 249–51, 371–5
  see also order processing
creditors 33–4, 91–4, 242–3, 246–8
  see also accounts payable
creditworthiness appraisals 249–51
Criminal Justice and Public Order Act 1994 617
Criminal Records Bureau (CRB) 663, 665–6, 841–2
criminal sanctions
  data protection 617–18, 625–6
  Sarbanes-Oxley Act 2002 152–4, 164–77

crisis response plans 91, 494–5, 497–501, 536–41, 556–8, 658–60, 671–9, 707–9, 842, 847
Croatia 740, 784
CSAs *see* control self assessments
cultural issues 29–30, 34, 57–8, 85–6, 110, 115, 121–2, 183–7, 220–1, 277–84, 496–501, 532–41, 547–53, 598, 678–9, 840
   JIT 196
   joint ventures 280–1
   knowledge management 547–53, 849–50
   outsourcing considerations 192, 193, 220–1
   quality assurance systems 183–7
   subsidiaries 277–84, 366–8
'current control/measure' column of SAPG risk/control section 48–50
customer-focused marketing 344, 348–50, 356–9, 369
customers 91–4, 126–7, 180–1, 222–5, 344–82
   after sales support 5–6, 8, 43, 126–7, 343–4, 348, 350, 366, 375–82
   complaints 126–7, 350, 356–7, 362
   credit-granting business process 32–3, 136, 138, 194, 249–51, 371–5
   requirements 344–50, 388–92
Customs and Excise (C&E) 262–3, 622
cybernetics 130–5
cycles
   concepts 27–39, 372–5, 468–75, 544–5, 547–9, 661–6, 680–7
   definition 32
   university case study 37–9
Cyprus 740, 784–5
Czech Republic 740, 785

damage or distress to data subjects situations, data protection 617, 620, 625, 835
data controllers, data protection 617–26, 729–62, 835
data definitions 542–5, 835–6
   see also knowledge...
data protection 9, 43–4, 404–7, 479–88, 496–501, 503–10, 514–23, 525–41, 562–5, 581–4, 590–7, 616–26, 631–2, 639–44, 646–7, 700–6, 729–62, 835, 842, 848
   see also access...; sensitive...
   access requests 619–26
   concepts 479–88, 514–23, 525–41, 581–4, 590–1, 616–26, 631–2, 639–44, 646–7, 700–6, 729–62, 835, 842, 848
   control objectives 625
   criminal sanctions 617–18, 625–6
   damage or distress to data subjects situations 617, 620, 625, 835
   errors 617, 620, 625, 626, 848
   exemptions 621, 624
   international legislation 616, 729–62, 848
   objectives 617
   principles 618–26, 631–2, 639–41, 848
   processes 619–26
   risk/control questions 625–6
   time limits 620, 625

Data Protection Act 1998 616–26, 639–44, 646, 759–60, 835, 838, 842, 848
data retention and disposal 487, 497, 524–41, 562–5, 620–6, 638–44, 680–7, 836, 851
   see also disposal...; retention...
   concepts 680–7, 836, 851
   control objectives 685
   life-cycle issues 680–7
   risk/control questions 685–7
   standards 684–5
data subjects, data protection 617–26, 642, 729–62, 835
data transfers and sharing 487, 497, 515–23, 542–53, 636–44, 688–90, 704–6, 850
   ad hoc internal requests 636, 638–9
   concepts 636–44, 688–90, 704–6, 850
   control objectives 642, 688–9
   exemptions/exceptions 637–8
   ISAs 639–44
   regular transfers with external parties 636–7, 639–44
   risk/control questions 643–4, 689–90
   types 636–8
databases 9, 43, 57–74, 136–7, 487, 502–10, 544–53, 613–15
   see also information asset registers
   concepts 613–15
   control objectives 613–15
   risk/control questions 614–15
debt collectors 194
debtors 33, 194, 248–51, 371–5, 378–82
   see also accounts receivable; order processing
delayering considerations, concepts 178, 187–9
Denmark 740, 785
depreciation 253–6, 434–6
detailed issues, SAPG questions 46–50
detective category of control 138–9, 144, 168–70
detectors, systems concepts 130–5
developing world, environmental issues 465–6
development project management 8, 437, 447–50, 715
   control objectives 447–8
   definition 447
   risk/control questions 448–50
digital cameras 567
digital preservation
   concepts 531, 532–41, 681–7
   definition 532
direct marketing, data protection 620
directive category of control 138
directors 4–5, 9–14, 17, 32, 44, 73–4, 75–94, 102–3, 107–8, 112–15, 117–46, 147–50, 153–77, 211–12, 215–35, 464, 470, 524–41
   see also boards...
disaster recovery plans (DRPs) 91, 494–5, 497–501, 536–41, 556–8, 563–5, 574–5, 658–60, 671–9, 707–9, 842, 847
disciplinary/grievance procedures 7, 85, 149, 399, 400–4, 424–7, 594–7, 604, 641–4
   concepts 424–7, 594–7, 604
   control objectives 425
   risk/control questions 425–7, 597, 604

disclosures
　information management　515–23
　Sarbanes-Oxley Act 2002　151–77
discount policies *see* pricing and discount policies
discussion boards　600–4
disposals　433–6, 447, 487, 497, 505–6, 514–23,
　　524–41, 562–5, 620–6, 638–44, 680–7,
　　836, 851
　company vehicles　433–6
　control objectives　685
　information asset registers　505–6, 515–23, 681–7
　R&D equipment　447
　records management　527–41, 680–7, 849, 851
　removable media　567–9
　resurrected deleted files　562, 567, 682–7, 851
　risk/control questions　685–7
　standards　684–5
dissemination *see* sharing…
distribution
　see also logistics; stock…; transport; warehousing…
　concepts　7–8, 383–98, 714
　control objectives　384–98
　insurance cover　385–98
　operational auditing　7–8, 383–98
　overview　383–4
　risk/control questions　384–98
distributors　3, 8, 33, 35, 42–3, 343, 362–6, 382, 383,
　　388–92, 714
　concepts　362–6, 382, 383, 388–92
　conflicts of interest　362–6, 389–92
　control objectives　362–3, 388–9
　definition　362, 388
　performance/productivity measurement systems
　　362–6, 388–92
　risk/control questions　363–6, 389–92
diversity issues　16, 21, 84–5, 93, 406–7, 594–7
　see also anti-discrimination…; equal opportunity…;
　　equity… boards of directors　93
　three Es of equity, environment, and ethics, concepts
　　16, 21, 84–5, 93
division-with-supervision opportunities, internal controls
　　135–7, 142–3, 150
documentation　36–7, 40–74, 167–73, 182–7, 197–8,
　　218, 241–3, 262–3, 272–5, 286–9, 291–316,
　　335–42, 375–82, 411–13, 443–5, 494–5, 535–41,
　　544–53, 606–8, 652–4, 681–7, 695, 701–6,
　　712–28, 839–51
　see also standard audit programme guides
drivers, definition　571
Drucker, P.F.　111
due diligence　87–8
DVDs　497, 566–7, 637

Eastern Europe　280–1
economy issues
　concepts　4, 15–16, 19–23, 29–30, 77–9, 219–35,
　　319–42
　performance/productivity measurement systems
　　19–23, 219–35, 319–42

three Es (effectiveness, efficiency, and economy)
　15–16, 19–23, 29–30, 219–35
EDI *see* electronic data interchange
EDMS *see* electronic document management systems
'effective yes/no' column of SAPG risk/control section
　48–50
effectiveness issues
　concepts　4–5, 15–16, 19–23, 29–30, 54–6, 76, 78,
　　84, 85, 88–9, 95–115, 117–46, 209–13, 219–35,
　　313–16, 319–42, 352–3, 557–8, 612
　control-effectiveness measurements　54–6, 78, 84, 85,
　　127–8, 141–3, 151–77, 209–13, 219–35
　corporate governance　78, 84, 85, 88–9
　performance/productivity measurement systems
　　19–23, 78, 84, 85, 219–35, 313–16, 319–42
　three Es (effectiveness, efficiency, and economy)
　　15–16, 19–23, 29–30, 117–46, 215–35
efficiency issues
　concepts　4–5, 15–16, 19–23, 29–30, 77–9, 95–115,
　　117–46, 215–35, 319–42, 595–7
　performance/productivity measurement systems
　　19–23, 219–35, 319–42
　personnel　15–16
　three Es (effectiveness, efficiency, and economy)
　　15–16, 19–23, 29–30, 117–46, 215–35
Electronic Communications Act 2000　581, 646
electronic data interchange (EDI)　43–4, 198, 248–50,
　　487, 688–90
　control objectives　688–9
　risk/control questions　689–90
electronic document management systems (EDMS)　531
electronic funds transfers　242–5, 259–61, 487, 696–8
electronic records, types of records　496–7, 502–3,
　　524–41, 545–53, 566–9, 622–6, 631–2, 681–2,
　　712–28
emails　487, 497, 520–3, 581–4, 590–7, 646, 691–3,
　　841
　see also information technology
　attachments　593–7, 691–3
　concepts　590–7, 691–3, 841
　control objectives　595–6
　policies　591–7, 841
　Regulation of Investigatory Powers Act 2000　581,
　　592, 646
　risk/control questions　596–7
　spam　590–7, 602, 707–9
　standard formats　593–7
　statistics　590–1
　viruses　691–3, 841
embedded microchips　567
emergency/evacuation drills　428–30, 455–62, 556–8
　see also disaster…
empowerment considerations, concepts　178, 188,
　　189–91, 195–6, 211–12
encrypted data　566–9, 610–12, 638–44, 646, 673, 845
energy *see* materials and energy
Enterprise Risk Management framework (COSO)　75–6,
　　96–115, 119, 120–1, 140, 157–8
environmental auditing, concepts　465–75

Environmental Information Regulations 2004 526, 646
environmental issues 8, 16, 41, 42–3, 219–35, 318,
    335–8, 463–75, 713–14, 721
  assessments 468–9
  control objectives 335–6, 465, 471
  developing world 465–6
  EMAS 464, 466–70, 475
  emergence of concerns 465–6
  example programmes 470–5
  experts 469–70
  hazardous materials 332–8, 395–8, 428–30, 457–60,
      463–75, 554–8
  legislation 463–75
  physical security 332–5, 428–30, 454–62, 495,
      496–501, 520–3, 554–8, 588–9, 638–44, 849
  production/manufacturing 8, 318, 335–8
  responsibilities 463–75
  risk/control questions 336–8, 465, 471–5
  strategic objectives 467–8
  supply chains 468–75
  sustainability reports 470–5
  systems concepts 131–5
  three Es of equity, environment, and ethics 16, 21,
      84–5, 463–75
  waste management 335–8
equal opportunity laws 406–7
equity issues
  see also diversity...
  three Es of equity, environment, and ethics 16, 21,
      84–5
errors
  data protection 617, 620, 625, 626
  keying errors 57–74, 699–700
  spreadsheets 699–700, 702
estates management 430, 712–13
estimates 158–60
Estonia 741, 786–7
ethics 16, 34, 78, 84–5, 121–2, 147–50, 161–3, 172–3,
    209–13, 215–35, 288–9, 415–22, 437, 464–75,
    594–7
  Codes of Conduct 148–9, 161–3, 172, 215–35
  conflicts of interest 162–4
  environmental issues 464–75
  management 147–50, 161–3, 172–3, 209–13
  pension schemes 415–22
  questions 147–50, 172
  research and development 437
  Sarbanes-Oxley Act 2002 161–3, 172
Ethiopia 742, 787
Europe
  see also individual countries
  contracts 300
  data protection legislation 729, 742
  digital preservation 535
  freedom of information 627–8, 763
European Commission's Eco-Management and Audit
    Scheme (EMAS) 464, 466–70, 475
European Convention on Human Rights (ECHR) 628,
    763

European Economic Area 621–6
European Union Directive on Data Protection (95/46/EU)
    742
Excel 702–4
  see also spreadsheets
exemptions from VAT 263
expenditure business process, concepts 33–4, 36, 720–8
expenses 7, 11, 240, 270–2, 356–9, 433–6
  control objectives 271, 356–9
  petty cash and expenses 7, 240, 270–2
  risk/control questions 271–2, 356–9
expert systems 9, 44
experts
  environmental issues 469–70
  research and development 437–52
external auditors 151–77
external governance processes, concepts 75, 81–4,
    90–4, 116
external hard drives 566–7
external reviews, operational auditing 214, 216–17
extranets 610

facilitation roles, operational auditing 201–6, 212
facilities management (FM) 9, 43–4, 192, 487, 648–50,
    655–7
  see also information technology; outsourcing...
  concepts 192, 648–50
  control objectives 648–9
  definition 192, 648
  risk/control questions 649–50
facilities, plant and equipment
  see also maintenance
  concepts 8, 318, 319–24, 339–42, 427–30, 445–7,
      457–60, 486, 554–8, 714
  R&D equipment 8, 437, 445–7
fact-finding programmes 45, 277–8
failures 91, 141–3, 151–77, 315–16, 317–42, 375–82,
    494–5, 497–501, 512–13, 523, 536–41, 556–8,
    563–5, 574–5, 658–60, 671–9, 699–700, 707–9
Fayol, Henri 116, 118, 187–8, 198
feed system direct interfaces 57–74
feedback systems 130–5, 234, 350, 356–7, 362, 545–53
feedforward, systems concepts 132–5
fees 158–60, 164–77
FEI surveys 155
Fiji 742, 787–8
file headers 68–74
final accounts for contractors 9, 290, 310–13
finance and accounting
  accounting policies 710–11
  concepts 3, 6, 7, 27, 32–5, 42, 117, 143–5, 192,
      197–8, 239–75, 710–11, 713, 722
  control objectives 240–75
  cyclical definition 240
  definition 117, 239–40
  functional definition 240
  IT accounting 710–11
  JIT 197–8
  management 239–75

overview of functions 7, 240
risk/control questions 240–75
SAPG 713, 722
system/function components 239–40
finance directors 4
financial controls 3, 143–5
financial experts, audit committees 158–62, 172–3
financial information and reporting
 concepts 7, 240, 272–4, 710–11, 713
 control objectives 272–3
 risk/control questions 273–4
 standards 272–4, 710–11
financial institutions 10–11, 717
financial reporting, concepts 7, 34–5, 51, 117–46, 151–77, 240, 710–11, 720–8
Financial Services Authority (FSA) 672–3
financial statements 151–77, 251–3
Finland 742, 788
fire hazards 332–5, 428–30, 454–62, 554–8, 660
firewalls 707–9
fixed assets (and capital charges)
 concepts 7, 240, 253–6, 432–6, 447, 462, 502–3, 710–11, 713
 control objectives 253–4
 risk/control questions 254–6
fixed standard types of data transfers 636–44
floats, petty cash and expenses 271–2
flood risks 557
floppy disk drives 497, 575
flowcharts 48–50, 167–70
FoI *see* freedom of information
'for pay and rations' reports, chief audit executives 83–4
forecasts 15–16, 19–23, 219–35, 359–62
formal procedures, informal coalitions 31–2
France 154, 743, 788
fraud 47, 53–4, 57–8, 84–5, 142–4, 149–50, 153–77, 242–8, 259–61, 271–2, 291, 294, 315–16, 327, 355–9, 375, 377, 392–5, 397–8, 415–24, 434–6, 446–7, 453–62, 494–501, 523, 537–41, 554–8, 566–9, 580–4, 588–604, 661–79, 683–7, 696–700, 710–11, 840–51
 categories 150
 collusion 149–50
 concepts 149–50, 153–77, 259–61
 definition 149
'free-standing' context, SAPG uses 45
Freedom of Information Act 2000, UK 627–35, 640–1, 646, 832–3, 848–9
Freedom of Information Acts, US 833
freedom of information (FoI) 479–88, 497–501, 503–10, 516–23, 525–41, 581–4, 590–1, 627–35, 640–1, 646, 763–834, 848–9
 concepts 627–35, 640–1, 763, 848–9
 control objectives 632–3
 definition 627, 763
 exemptions 628, 630, 631–3
 international legislation 627–8, 763–834, 848
 objectives 628–9, 763

publication schemes 536–41, 628–35, 848–9
risk/control questions 633–5
terminology 631–2
time limits 630, 634
frequency issues, internal controls 169–70
Friedman, Milton 464
fuel cards, petty cash and expenses 272
functional approaches to defining the audit universe 3–26, 27, 30, 41–5, 240–75, 712–28

gateway PCs 611–12, 707–9
gathering *see* collection...
GEC 97
general ledger/management accounts
 concepts 7, 28, 33–4, 42, 51, 240, 251–3, 462, 713
 control objectives 251
 risk/control questions 252–3, 462
generally accepted accounting principles 158–60
Georgia 743, 789
Germany 170, 581, 744, 789–92
Ghana 744, 792
Gibraltar 744, 792–3
global area networks (GANs) 609–12
global financial crisis from 2007 82–3, 219–20
globalisation 344
good management practices
 operational auditing 228–30, 251–75, 699–706
 spreadsheets 699–706
grant funding schemes, research and development 450–2
Greece 744, 793–4
grievance procedures *see* disciplinary/grievance procedures
gross risk
 see also inherent...
 concepts 101–15, 208–13
group loyalties/rivalries, process weaknesses 30–1
Guatemala 745, 794–5
Guernsey 745, 795

hacking 646, 671–9
hardware assets 502–10, 511–13, 554–8, 566–9, 580–9, 610–12, 648–50, 694–5, 710–11
 see also removable media
hazardous materials 332–8, 395–8, 428–30, 457–60, 463–75, 554–8
health checks, IT 487, 707–9
health insurance 7, 42, 399, 422–4, 713
 see also pension schemes and other benefits
 concepts 422–4
 control objectives 423
 definition 422
 risk/control questions 423–4
health and safety at work 7, 8, 42, 318, 319, 322–4, 332–5, 339, 399, 413–15, 427–30, 454, 457–60, 554–8, 682, 713
 see also security; welfare...
 concepts 413–15, 427–30, 454, 457–60, 554–8

health and safety at work (*cont.*)
    control objectives 427–8, 457–8
    risk/control questions 428–30, 458–60
health sector 10–11, 47, 717–18
hedging 243
Helpdesks 587, 594, 674–5,
    694–5
Herzberg's bipolar analysis of job satisfaction 190
high level review programmes, concepts 41, 45,
    147–50, 278–9, 470–5
HMRC 622, 672–3
holiday/sickness payments 245
home loans 110, 194
Hong Kong 155, 745, 795–6
HR *see* human resource...
Hubbard, Larry 207–10
human resource management 3, 5, 6, 7, 27–8, 103, 113,
    121–2, 399–436, 661–6, 713–14
    see also personnel
    concepts 7, 399–436, 661–6
    control objectives 399–436, 664
    definition 399
    information security 661–6, 841–2
    operational auditing 399–436
    overview 399
    risk/control questions 399–436, 665–6
human resources department 7, 399, 400–4, 661–6,
    713–14
    concepts 400–4, 661–6
    control objectives 400–1, 664
    definition 400
    risk/control questions 401–4, 665–6
Human Rights Act 1998 525, 581, 592, 640–1, 646
Hungary 746, 796
hybrid audit universe 30
hygiene factors of job satisfaction 190

IBM 199
ICAEW
    PCAOB 157, 174–6
    spreadsheet best practices 70
Iceland 746, 797–8
ICQs *see* internal control questionnaires
ICRP, British Petroleum 199
identity theft 672–9
IEC *see* International Electrotechnical Commission
IM *see* information management
impact assessments, concepts 52–6, 101–15, 122–3,
    207–8, 460–2, 471–5
improvement programmes, operational auditing 214–35
inaccurate information 57–74, 124–7, 242–51, 272–4,
    283–9, 291–316, 493–5, 507–10, 514–23, 705–6,
    710–11
incident management 487, 520–3, 646, 671–9, 681–2,
    707–9, 842
    see also disaster...; information security...
independence issues 25, 94, 151–77, 205–6, 215–35,
    241–2
    see also objectivity...

India 581, 746, 798–803
induction processes, personnel 661–2
induction training 411–13
informal coalitions, formal procedures 31–2
informal organisations, concepts 189
information asset registers
    collection methods 505–6
    concepts 497, 502–10, 515–23, 527–41, 681–7,
        700–1, 715, 725, 847, 850
    control objectives 505–6, 507–8
    costs and benefits analysis 507–10
    data fields 504–6, 700
    definition 502–7
    ownership issues 504–5, 507–10, 701–2, 847
    responsibilities 503, 507–10, 847, 851
    risk/control questions 509–10
    security issues 504–10, 847
information business process, concepts 34
Information Commissioner 617–26, 628–35, 759–60
    see also data protection; freedom of information
'information and communication' component, COSO
    internal control framework 120–1, 124–7, 157–8,
    170–7
information definitions 543–5, 836
information management (IM) 479–88, 496–501,
    506–10, 514–23, 524–5, 587–9, 613–15, 645–7,
    715, 725, 836, 839
    see also knowledge...; records...
    control objectives 521–2
    definition 514–16, 836
    risk/control questions 521–3
information requirements 12–14, 47–50, 82–4, 120–1,
    124–7, 151–77, 188–9, 208–13, 242–3, 272–4,
    286–9, 401–36, 448–52, 502–10, 514–23, 613–15,
    710–11
    see also financial information...
    material information 151–77
    subsidiaries 277–84, 366–8
information security incidents 487, 520–3, 646, 671–9,
    681–3, 707–9, 841–2
    concepts 520–3, 671–9, 681–3, 841–2
    control objectives 676–7
    examples 671–3, 674–5, 681–3
    management 487, 520–3, 673–9, 681–2
    risk/control questions 677–9
    statistics 671–2
    UK examples 672–3
    US examples 673, 682–3
information sharing agreements (ISAs) 639–44
information technology (IT) 6, 8–9, 43–4, 56–74, 103,
    113, 121–4, 136–7, 179–81, 188–9, 192, 195,
    233–4, 479–711, 712–28
    see also facilities management; hardware...;
        software...
    accounting 710–11
    back-up systems 8, 43–4, 67–74, 486, 497–501,
        505–10, 521–3, 537–41, 558, 562–5, 584,
        588–9, 846
    BACS 245, 261, 487, 696–8

best practices 480–8, 521–3
capacity management 486, 497, 511–13, 520–3, 715, 725, 846
concepts 479–88, 712–28
contingency plans 497–501, 512–13, 528–41, 561, 658–60, 671–9, 689–90, 707–9
data retention and disposal 487, 497, 524–41, 562–5, 620–6, 638–44, 680–7, 851
databases 9, 43, 57–74, 136–7, 502–10, 544–53, 613–15
EDI 43–4, 198, 248–50, 487, 688–90
emails 487, 497, 520–3, 581–4, 590–7, 691–3, 841
health checks 487, 707–9
Helpdesks 587, 594, 674–5, 694–5
human resource information security 661–6, 667–70, 841–2
information security incidents 487, 520–3, 646, 671–9, 681–3, 707–9, 841–2
Internet 10, 35–6, 40, 44, 92–3, 121–2, 479, 487, 497, 581, 593–4, 598–604, 609–10, 646, 667–70, 842–3
legislation 9, 43–4, 404–7, 479–88, 496–501, 514–23, 525–41, 581–4, 645–7, 707–9, 729–834
logging systems 487, 576–9, 588–9, 667–70, 694–5
organisational structures 8, 486, 493–5, 524–41, 715, 725
overview 486–8
ownership issues 504–5, 507–10, 524–41, 578–9, 701–2, 838
personal computers 8–9, 43–4, 486–8, 562–5, 570–5, 580–9
policies 479–88, 489–501, 506–10, 511–13, 514–41, 554–8, 566–9, 576–9, 580–4, 585–9, 591–7, 599–604, 715, 725, 839–51
processing operations 559–61
remote working 487, 497–501, 520–3, 585–9, 844
removable media 487, 497–501, 520–3, 533, 566–9, 844–5
responsibilities 493–5, 497–501, 503, 518–23, 524–41, 556–8, 563–5, 585–9, 601–4, 616–26, 627–44, 645–7, 661–6, 691–3, 851
SAPG 715–16, 725–7
service management 483–4
sites and infrastructure 486, 554–8, 715, 725, 843
spreadsheets 40, 53–4, 56–74, 487, 699–706
standards 480–8, 493–5, 515–41, 581–4, 645–7, 652–4, 701–6
strategic planning 8, 486, 489–92, 511–13, 582–4, 715, 725
system development 487, 651–7, 699–706
systems and operating software 9, 43–4, 64, 71–4, 487, 559–61, 570–5, 667–70
terms of reference 493–5
user support services 487, 694–5
inherent risk
see also control matrices; gross...; risk
concepts 52–4, 55–6, 57–74, 101–15, 122–3, 208–13, 275
definition 52–3, 101

inputs
operational auditing evaluations 219–35
systems concepts 131–5
three Es (effectiveness, efficiency, and economy) 15–16, 19–23, 29–30, 219–35
VAT 261–3
Institute of Internal Auditors (IIA) 3–5, 11–12, 16–19, 21–6, 76–82, 93, 95–8, 115, 121–2, 139–41, 157, 171, 176–7, 204, 210, 212, 214–19, 225, 229, 232–5, 570
1000 (Purpose, Authority, and Responsibility) 217
1010 (Recognition of the Definition of Internal Auditing...) 217
1100 (Independence and Objectivity) 25, 94, 176, 215
1130 17, 171
1210 16
2010 176, 212, 234
2020 17
2100 (Nature of Work) 76–7, 93
2110 (Governance) 16, 25–6, 77–82
2120 (Risk Management) 77–9, 95–9, 176
2130 (Control) 77–9
2210 176
2600 25
CCSA programme 204, 210
internal control framework 139–41, 157, 176
Quality Assurance and Improvement Program 214–17
standards 3, 11–12, 16–19, 21–6, 76–80, 95–8, 115, 121–2, 139–41, 171, 176, 214–17, 225, 229, 232–5
insurance cover 296, 385–98, 413–15, 430, 434–6, 457, 458–62, 555–8, 671–9, 713, 721
see also security
claims 460–2
concepts 296, 389–92, 454, 460–2, 555–8
contracting 296, 389–92
control objectives 460–1
costs and benefits analysis 460–2
distribution 385–98
risk/control questions 461–2
types 460–2
integrity business process, concepts 34, 96–115, 121–4, 147–50, 248, 493–5, 610–12
intellectual property 345–8, 366, 439–42, 450–2, 453–62, 533, 594–7, 646, 672–9
see also patents
inter-group rivalries, intra-group loyalties 30–2
interim payments for contracts, concepts 9, 44, 290, 308–13
internal auditors, CIA designation 204
internal audits *see* operational auditing
internal checks, concepts 116–17
internal control questionnaires (ICQs) 40–74
internal controls
see also Sarbanes-Oxley Act 2002
BPR 181

internal controls *(cont.)*
  business processes 34–9, 116–46
  categories of control 137–9, 144, 168–70
  CoCo framework 117–18, 129–30, 141–3, 144, 157–8, 208–9
  concepts 3–26, 29–30, 34–9, 40–74, 75–94, 96–8, 116–46, 147–50, 151–77, 201–13, 226–35, 281–4, 470–5, 718
  contemporary understanding 116, 117–18
  control-effectiveness measurements 127–8, 141–3, 151–77, 209–13
  corporate governance 76–94
  COSO framework 117–28, 140, 142, 144, 157–77
  definitions 5–6, 15, 77–9, 116–20, 128–30, 140–1
  division-with-supervision opportunities 135–7, 142–3, 150
  failures 141–3, 151–77
  frequency issues 169–70
  IIA framework 139–41, 157, 176
  joint ventures 281–4
  objectives 77–81, 96–9, 116–20, 123–30, 139–41, 151–77
  process issues 143–4
  risk management 75–94, 96–8, 112–15, 122–3, 137–42, 147–50, 151–77, 232–5
  'Rubik cube' 120–1
  SAPG 718
  ship analogy 119–20
  systems/cybernetics model 130–5
  Turnbull framework 117–18, 120, 128–9, 140–2, 144, 157–8, 170–1
internal environment 98–115
internal governance processes, concepts 75, 78, 81–2, 84–7
internal telephone directories 28
International Electrotechnical Commission (IEC)
  see also ISO...
  background information 480–8
international legislation 616, 627–8, 729–834, 848
  data protection 616, 729–62, 848
  freedom of information (FoI) 627–8, 763–834, 848
International Professional Practices Framework (IPPF) 76, 215, 225
Internet 10, 35–6, 40, 44, 92–3, 121–2, 479, 487, 497, 581, 593–4, 598–604, 609–10, 646, 667–70, 842–3
  see also information technology
  access controls 599–604, 667–70, 842–3
  concepts 598–604, 609–10, 646, 667, 842–3
  control objectives 602
  historical background 598–9
  policies 599–604, 842–3
  risk/control questions 603–4
  statistics 598–9
  websites 10, 35–6, 40, 44, 92–3, 218, 712, 729–834
interviews 57–8
intra-group loyalties, inter-group rivalries 30–2
intranets 546–8
inventories 7–8, 33–4, 42, 51, 195–8, 240, 266–8, 321, 327, 362–6, 380–2, 383–98, 681, 713

  see also stock...
  concepts 7–8, 195–8, 266–8, 383–98
  control objectives 266
  key spreadsheets 700–1
  risk/control questions 266–8
  valuations 266–8
investigative category of control 139, 144
investments
  concepts 7, 240, 274–5, 713
  control objectives 274
  risk/control questions 274–5
investors 33–4, 42, 93
invoices 246–51, 268, 354–5, 372–5, 389–92, 446–7, 688–90
  see also accounts payable; accounts receivable
inward focus of benchmarking 24
IP addressable devices 707
Iran 747, 803
Iraq 747, 803
Ireland (Eire) 747, 804
irregular tests of information flows, operational auditing definition 14
ISAs *see* information sharing agreements
Isle of Man 747, 804
ISO 182, 183–4, 466–7, 480–8, 496, 526, 640, 707
  see also British Standards Institute
  14000 series 466–7, 475
  15489 (Information and Documentation–Records Management) 484–6, 526
  background information 182, 183–4, 466–7, 480–8
ISO/IEC 17799 481, 526, 640
ISO/IEC 20000–1 484
ISO/IEC 27000 series 480–4, 526, 640, 707
ISO/IEC, background 480–8, 496
Israel 747–8, 804
IT *see* information technology
Italy 748, 804–5

Jaenicke, H.R. 34
Jamaica 748, 805–6
Japan 154, 195, 466, 581, 748, 806
JCL 560–1, 575
Jersey 748, 807
Jikoda ('stop everything...') 195–6
JIT... *see* just-in-time...
job descriptions/specifications 144, 149, 401–4, 405–7, 493–5
job satisfaction 190–1
Johnson, K.P. 34
Joint Information Systems Committee (JISC) 534
joint ventures
  concepts 279–84
  cultural issues 280–1
  definition 279–80
just-in-time management (JIT)
  concepts 178, 195–8, 285, 317, 383
  costs and benefits analysis 197–8
  cultural issues 196
  definition 195

operational auditing   196–8, 285
just-in-time purchasing (JITP), concepts   196–8, 285

Kanban cards   196–8
Kazakhstan   807
Kenya   749, 808
key issues, SAPG questions   46–50
keying errors   57–74, 699–700
King Report on Corporate Governance, South Africa   140, 141
KM *see* knowledge management
know-how   543–53, 838
knowledge management (KM)
   see also data...; information...
   benefits   542–5
   best practices   485–8
   BSI guidance publications   486
   concepts   479–88, 497–501, 519–23, 542–53, 715, 725, 836–8, 849–50
   control objectives   550–1
   definitions   485–6, 542–5, 836–8, 849
   information sources   542–6
   lessons learned   549–53
   life-cycle issues   544–5, 547–9
   policies   549–53, 849–50
   responsibilities   550–3, 849–50, 851
   risk/control questions   551–3
   tacit/explicit knowledge   544–53, 836, 838
   why-what-who-how questions   549–50
knowledge/skills/competencies requirements of auditors   16–18, 86–7, 158–60, 218, 233–4

labour relations   7, 399, 400–4, 430–2, 714
   concepts   430–2
   control objectives   431
   risk/control questions   431–2
LANs *see* local area networks
laptop computers   580–9, 672–3
Latvia   749, 809
law and regulatory compliance
   see also compliance...; legislation; regulations
   concepts   4–5, 8, 318, 338–9, 665–6, 714
   control objectives   338
   risk/control questions   338–9
law of requisite variety   131–5
leadership qualities   118–20
learning   129–30, 144, 208–13, 542–53
least cost basis   22–3
Lebanon   749, 809–10
legal departments   6, 27, 41, 43, 368, 450–2, 645–7, 712–15, 721
legislation   46, 77–9, 96–115, 117–46, 242–3, 261–6, 272–5, 287–9, 291–316, 319–42, 363–82, 385–98, 400–36, 439–52, 463–75, 479–88, 496–501, 514–23, 524–41, 602–4, 616–35, 640–4, 645–7, 674–9, 680–7, 707–11, 712–15, 721, 729–834
   see also individual Acts
   data protection   9, 43–4, 404–7, 479–88, 496–501, 514–23, 524–41, 581–4, 590–7, 616–26, 631–2, 639–44, 646, 729–62, 835, 838, 842, 848

   freedom of information   627–8, 763–834, 848
   international legislation   616, 627–8, 729–834, 848
   IT   9, 43–4, 404–7, 479–88, 496–501, 514–23, 525–41, 581–4, 645–7, 707–9, 729–834
   list of IT legislation   525–6, 581, 645–7, 729–834
   records management   524–41, 646–7, 680–7, 849
Lesotho   749, 810
lessons learned   549–53
Liberia   749, 810–11
Libya   749, 811–12
Liechtenstein   749, 812
life-cycle issues   372–5, 468–75, 544–5, 547–9, 661–6, 680–7
Likert's linking pins, concepts   31–2
Limitation Act 1980   646
line marketing, definition   344
linking pins, concepts   31–2
listed companies   151–77
Listing Rules   176
Lithuania   749, 812
loans   10–11, 110, 194, 259–61
local area networks (LANs)   9, 43–4, 489, 584, 609–12, 673, 693
Local Government Acts   646
logging systems   487, 576–9, 588–9, 667–70, 694–5
logical security *see* system access controls
logistics   8, 42, 383, 384–8, 714
   see also distribution
London listings   155
Luxembourg   749, 812–13

Macedonia   750, 813
McRae, Elizabeth   218
maintenance   8, 9, 44, 318, 339–42, 377–80, 435–6, 487, 504–10, 528–41, 570–5, 605–8, 651–7, 699–706, 714
   see also facilities, plant and equipment; software...
   contracting obligations   9, 44
   control objectives   340, 377–8
   MISs   57–74
   production/manufacturing   8, 318, 339–42
   records management   528–41, 849
   risk/control questions   340–2, 378–80
maintenance and servicing   8, 343, 377–80, 715
   see also after sales support
   concepts   377–80
   control objectives   377–8
   risk/control questions   378–80
Malaysia   750, 814
malicious software   9, 43, 497–501, 520–3, 563–9, 570–5, 583–4, 590–7, 601–4, 671–9, 691–3, 707–9, 841, 846
   see also malware; spyware; viruses
malpractice   57–74, 84–5, 142–4, 149–50, 151–77, 242–8, 259–61, 271–2, 288–9, 291, 294, 298–9, 315–16, 327, 352–9, 363–6, 375, 377, 389–95, 397–8, 415–24, 434–6, 446–7, 453–62, 494–501, 523, 537–41, 554–8, 566–9, 580–4, 588–604, 661–79, 683–7, 696–700, 710–11, 840–51

Malta 750, 814
malware 9, 43, 497–501, 520–3, 563–9, 570–5, 596–7, 601–4, 671–9, 691–3, 707–9
management
 see also Sarbanes-Oxley Act 2002
 back-up and media management 8, 43–4, 67–74, 486, 497–501, 505–10, 521–3, 537–41, 558, 562–5, 584, 588–9, 846
 business management techniques 178–98
 capacity management 486, 497, 511–13, 520–3, 846
 concealed risks 107–10
 CSAs 199–213
 data protection 9, 43–4, 404–7, 479–88, 496–501, 503–10, 514–23, 525–41, 562–5, 581–4, 590–7, 616–26, 631–2, 639–44, 848
 delayering considerations 178, 187–9
 EDI 43–4, 198, 248–50, 487, 688–90
 emails 487, 497, 520–3, 581–4, 590–7, 691–3
 environmental issues 463–75
 ethics/competencies 147–50, 158–77, 209–13, 215–35
 facilities management 9, 43–4, 192, 648–50
 fraud 149–50, 153–77
 freedom of information 479–88, 497–501, 503–10, 516–23, 525–41, 581–4, 590–1, 627–35, 640–1, 646–7, 763–834, 848
 human resource information security 661–6, 667–70, 841–2
 human resource management 3, 5, 6, 7, 27–8, 103, 113, 121–2, 399–436
 information asset registers 502–10, 515–23, 527–41, 681–7, 700–1, 847, 850
 information management 479–88, 496–501, 506–10, 514–23
 information security incidents 487, 520–3, 671–9, 681–2, 707–9, 841–2
 internal controls 3–26, 29–30, 34–9, 40–74, 75–94, 96–8, 116–46, 147–50, 151–77, 201–13
 Internet 10, 35–6, 40, 44, 92–3, 121–2, 479, 487, 581, 593–4, 598–604, 842–3
 IT overview 479–88
 joint ventures 279–84
 knowledge management 479–88, 497–501, 519–23, 542–53, 849–50
 legal responsibilities 645–7, 844
 objectives 12–14, 16–17, 29–30, 47, 118, 147–50, 201–13, 214–35
 records management 479–88, 496–501, 502–10, 511–13, 515, 517–23, 524–41, 680–7, 849
 software maintenance/development controls 9, 43–4, 64, 67–74, 487, 605–8, 651–7, 699–706
 software selection 655–7, 845
 span of control 118–20, 187–8
 spreadsheets 40, 53–4, 56–74, 487, 699–706
 subsidiaries 3, 265, 276–84, 366–8
 system access controls 8, 487, 576–9, 661–6, 707–9
 system development 487, 651–7, 699–706
 systems and operating software 570–5, 667–70
 user support services 487, 694–5
management and administration 6–7, 41, 51, 712–13, 721
management controls *see* internal controls
management information systems (MISs)
 concepts 41–4, 51, 56–74, 125–7, 362, 367, 368, 548–9, 710–11, 721
 control matrices 56–74
 risk exposures 56–74
managing customers as strategic assets (MCSA) 344
mandatory/regulatory/statutory data transfers 636–44
manpower and succession planning
 concepts 7, 399, 407, 408–10, 713
 control objectives 408
 risk/control questions 408–10
manual logs, concepts 667–70
manufacturing *see* production...
Marconi 97–8
market research
 concepts 8, 43, 346–7, 348–50, 442, 714
 control objectives 348–9
 costs and benefits analysis 349–50
 definition 348
 risk/control questions 349–50
market shares 268–70, 279, 363–4, 389–92
marketing and sales 3, 5–6, 8, 27–8, 32–5, 43, 51, 113, 136, 194, 343–82, 438–42, 620, 714, 724
 see also after sales...; agents; distributors; order processing; pricing...; product...; promotion...; sales...
 concepts 8, 343–82, 620, 714, 724
 control objectives 344–81
 data protection 620–6
 definition 343–4
 overview 343–4
 parent company relationships 366–8
 risk/control questions 344–81
 SAPG 714, 724
Maslow's hierarchy of needs 190–1
material information 151–77
'material weaknesses', definitions 153, 156–7, 172
materials and energy
 concepts 8, 318, 327–30, 392–5, 463–75, 714
 hazardous materials 332–8, 395–8, 428–30, 457–60, 463–75, 554–8
maturity models, operational auditing 218–19
Maxwell, Robert 415
media 8, 43–4, 67–74, 91, 486, 496–501, 505–10, 520–3, 537–41, 558, 562–5, 713, 721
metadata 497, 502–10, 515–23, 527–41, 837
 see also information asset registers
metropolitan area networks (MANs) 609–12
Mexico 751, 815
milestones 294–5, 306–16, 510
minutes of meetings 128
mission 71–4, 95–8, 112–15, 209–13
misstatements 109, 151–77, 259–61, 271–2, 315–16
mobile phones 585–9
Mongolia 751, 816

monitoring 7, 8, 14, 51, 71–4, 99–115, 120–1, 127–30, 142, 144, 157–8, 170–7, 185–7, 208–13, 214–15, 223–35, 240, 256–8, 306–8, 343, 346, 359–62, 437, 442–5, 487, 517–23, 592–7, 652–4, 667–70, 694–5, 710–11
 emails 592–7
 information flows 14, 99–115, 120–1, 127–30, 170–1, 208–13, 272–4, 667–70
 information management 517–23, 667–70
 logging systems 487, 576–9, 588–9, 667–70, 694–5
 ongoing monitoring 214–35
 project appraisal and monitoring 8, 437, 442–5, 651–4
 risk matrices 102–6
 sales performance and monitoring 8, 343, 346, 359–62
'monitoring' component, COSO internal control framework 120–1, 127–8, 142, 144, 157–8, 170–7
moral hazard 144
mortgages 10, 110
motivation levels 71–4, 120–2, 148–50, 181, 184–7, 190–1, 196–8, 203–4, 400–36, 547
Mozambique 752, 817
multinational enterprises 5–6, 12–14

NAID 684–5
Namibia 752, 817
National Environmental Policy Act 465–6
Nationwide Building Society 672
Nepal 752, 817–18
NESTOR 534
Netherlands 534, 752, 818–19
nett risk *see* residual risk
networks 9, 43–4, 487, 489, 511–13, 546–53, 554–8, 580–9, 609–12, 673, 693, 707–9
 concepts 609–12, 707–9
 control objectives 610–11
 MISs 68–74
 risk/control questions 611–12
 statistics 609–10
 types 609–10
new products 8, 34–5, 343, 345–8, 438–52, 473
 see also product development
New Zealand 752
news groups 600–4
Nicaragua 752, 820
Nigeria 752, 820
non-audit services 163–77
nonexecutive directors 87–90, 127–8
Norway 752, 820–1
Novell networks 68
nuclear industry 109
'number of auditors per 1000 staff', operational auditing evaluations 223–33

objectives
 mission 112–15
 perspectives 12–14, 16–17, 25, 64, 71–4
 'triple bottom line' objectives 464, 473

objectivity issues 14, 17, 25, 94, 176, 205–6, 215–35
 see also independence...
Obscene Publications Acts 646
obsolescence 380–2, 532–41, 681–7
omissions 57–74, 151–77
ongoing monitoring, operational auditing 214–35
Open Document Management API (ODMA) 531–2
open systems, concepts 131–5
operational auditing
 added value 21–3, 76, 211–12, 219–35, 364–6, 370–1, 391–2
 approaches 3–26
 assessments 214–35, 470
 audit approaches 12–16
 'budget/actual comparisons' 223–33
 business management techniques 178–98
 business processes 3–4, 27–39, 240, 712–28
 Charters 217–35
 concepts 3–26, 27–39, 76–94, 99–115, 170–3, 178–98, 201–13, 214–35, 470, 712–28
 corporate governance 3, 5–6, 9–10, 17, 22, 25–6, 29–30, 34, 44, 75–94, 176–7, 205, 232–5, 470–5, 509–10, 718
 costs and benefits analysis 219–35
 CSAs 18–19, 30, 41, 102–3, 128, 199–213, 718
 data protection 9, 43–4, 404–7, 479–88, 496–501, 503–10, 514–23, 525–41, 562–5, 581–4, 590–7, 616–26, 631–2, 639–44, 729–62, 848
 data retention and disposal 487, 497, 524–41, 562–5, 620–6, 638–44, 680–7, 851
 data transfers and sharing 515–23, 542–53, 636–44, 688–90, 704–6, 850
 databases 9, 43, 57–74, 136–7, 502–10, 544–53, 613–15
 definitions 3–5, 12–13, 14, 21–2, 76, 95, 835–8
 EDI 43–4, 198, 248–50, 487, 688–90
 emails 487, 497, 520–3, 581–4, 590–7, 691–3
 empowerment considerations 191
 environmental issues 463–75
 evaluations 214–35
 external reviews 214, 216–17
 facilitation roles 201–6, 212
 finance and accounting 3, 6, 7, 27, 32–5, 42, 117, 143–5, 192, 197–8, 239–75, 713, 722
 freedom of information 479–88, 497–501, 503–10, 516–23, 525–41, 581–4, 590–1, 627–35, 763–834, 848
 functional approaches 3–26, 27, 30, 41–5, 240–75, 712–28
 good management practices 228–30, 251–75, 699–706
 human resource information security 661–6, 667–70, 841–2
 improvement programmes 214–35
 information asset registers 497, 502–10, 700–1, 847, 850
 information management 479–88, 496–501, 506–10, 514–23

operational auditing *(cont.)*
  information requirements 12–14, 47–50, 82–4, 120–1, 124–7, 170–1, 272–4, 514–23, 710–11
  information security incidents 487, 520–3, 671–9, 707–9, 841–2
  input performance measures 221–35
  Internet 10, 35–6, 40, 44, 92–3, 121–2, 479, 487, 581, 593–4, 598–604, 842–3
  IT overview 479–88, 715–16
  IT strategic planning 489–92, 511–13, 582–4, 715, 725
  joint ventures 282–4
  knowledge management 479–88, 497–501, 519–23, 542–53, 849–50
  legal responsibilities 645–7, 844
  management and administration 6–7, 41, 51, 712–13, 721
  maturity models 218–19
  networks 487, 511–13, 546–53, 554–8, 580–9, 609–12, 707–9
  'number of auditors per 1000 staff' 223–8
  objectives 12–14, 16–17, 25, 230–5, 470
  ongoing monitoring 214–35
  output performance evaluations 219–35
  performance/productivity measurement systems 9, 19–23, 31, 78, 84, 85, 219–35, 290, 306–8, 313–16, 319–42, 359–66, 424–7
  periodic internal reviews 214–35
  profitability contributions 219–35
  quality assurance 182–7, 214–35, 330–2
  quantitative/quasi-quantitative/qualitative performance measures 221–8
  'ratio of payroll to other costs' 223–33
  'ratio of productive/unproductive audit time' 223–33
  recessions 82–3, 219–20
  recommendations 226–35
  records management 479–88, 496–501, 502–10, 511–13, 515, 517–23, 524–41, 680–7, 849
  responsibilities 29–30, 47, 87, 100, 112–15, 118–20, 125–30, 135–7, 144, 148–50, 170–3, 201–2, 493–5, 497–501, 503, 518–23, 661–6, 691–3, 851
  reviews 214–35
  SAPG 10, 35–6, 40–74, 240–1, 285, 318, 345, 384, 400, 438, 454, 470, 488, 712–28
  scope 3–12, 16–17, 27–39, 152, 164, 166–7, 170–3, 201–2, 218–35, 239–40, 469–75, 707–9
  software maintenance/development controls 9, 43–4, 64, 67–74, 487, 605–8, 651–7, 699–706
  software selection 655–7, 845
  spreadsheets 40, 53–4, 56–74, 487, 699–706
  subsidiaries 3, 265, 276–84, 366–8
  system access controls 8, 487, 576–9, 661–6, 707–9
  system development 487, 651–7, 699–706
  systems and operating software 570–5, 667–70
  value for money auditing 21–3, 230–3, 353
  weaknesses 217–18
operational level of risk, concepts 52

operational review programmes, development issues 40–74
operations logs for MISs 68–74
operations and resource management
  see also production/manufacturing
  concepts 317–42
opportunities, risk management 111, 113–15, 226–8
optical disks 566–7
order processing 8, 343, 362, 366, 371–5, 385–8, 398, 714
  see also accounts receivable; credit-granting...; debtors; marketing...
  concepts 362, 366, 371–5, 388
  control objectives 372
  definition 371–2
  life-cycle issues 372–5
  risk/control questions 373–5
organisational structures
  concepts 5–6, 8, 31–2, 47–50, 110, 118–22, 178–98, 486, 493–5, 524–41
  IT organisation 8, 486, 493–5, 524–41
organising 5–6, 116, 118–20
out-of-date information 57–74
out-of-stock situations 380–2, 392–5
outputs
  operational auditing evaluations 219–35
  systems concepts 131–5
  three Es (effectiveness, efficiency, and economy) 15–16, 19–23, 29–30, 219–35
  VAT 261–3
outsourcing considerations 18–19, 22–3, 116, 144, 178, 191–5, 220–1, 234, 648–50, 651–7, 683–7, 716–17, 726–8
  see also contracting...; facilities management
  cleaning firms 192, 193
  core/non-core activities 193–4, 195
  costs and benefits analysis 192–4, 220–1, 648–50, 655–7
  cultural issues 192, 193, 220–1
  definition 191–2
  disposal of records 683–7
  personnel impacts 192, 193–4
  public sector 192
  risk/control questions 192, 193, 194–5, 220–1, 649–50
outward focus of benchmarking 24
overdrafts 258–61
overhead costs 317–42
overseas operating units 3
ownership issues
  information asset registers 504–5, 507–10, 701–2, 847
  IT 504–5, 507–10, 524–41, 578–9, 701–2, 838
  policies 498–501, 578–9, 701–2

P11D returns 424
packaging, environmental issues 468–75
Pakistan 753, 821
paper records, retention issues 680–7

parameters to MISs 57–74
parent companies
   see also subsidiaries
   concepts 265, 276–84, 366–8, 714
passwords 58–74, 518–23, 527–41, 576–9, 585–9, 601–4, 623–6, 638–44, 707–9, 843
patch management 487, 520–3, 570–5, 707–9, 845–6
patents 345–8, 439–42, 450–2, 581, 594–5, 646
   see also intellectual property
payments business process, concepts 34–5
payroll
   see also remuneration
   concepts 7, 27–8, 33–4, 42, 53–4, 223–33, 240, 243–5, 362, 405–7, 415, 713
   control objectives 243–4
   risk/control questions 244–5, 362
PCAOB *see* Public Company Accounting Oversight Board
PCs *see* personal computers
PDAs 567, 580–9
peer groups, knowledge management 546–53
pension schemes and other benefits 7, 42, 399, 415–24
   see also health insurance
   concepts 415–22
   control objectives 416–17
   ethics 415–22
   risk/control questions 417–22
performance category of control 138
performance-related compensation schemes
   see also pension schemes...
   concepts 415–22, 713
performance/productivity measurement systems 9, 19–23, 31, 78, 84, 85, 219–35, 290, 306–8, 313–16, 319–42, 359–66, 424–7
   concepts 8, 9, 19–23, 31, 44, 74, 78, 84, 85, 209–13, 219–35, 270, 290, 306–8, 313–16, 319–42, 343, 346, 359–66, 424–7, 652–7
   contracting 9, 290, 306–8, 313–16, 385–92
   distributors 362–6, 388–92
   milestones 294–5, 306–16
   personnel 234, 314–16, 324–7
   policies 20–1, 85
   reviews of project outturn/performance 313–16
   sales performance and monitoring 8, 343, 346, 359–62
   staff appraisals 7, 234, 314–16, 324–7, 399, 400–4, 413, 424–7
   three Es of effectiveness, efficiency, and economy 19–23, 77–9, 84, 85, 117–46, 215–35
perimeters and external environs, IT sites and infrastructure 555–8, 843
periodic internal reviews, operational auditing 214–35
personal computers (PCs) 8–9, 43–4, 486–8, 562–5, 570–5, 580–9, 608, 623–6, 699–706, 840–1
   see also information technology
   concepts 580–4
   control objectives 582
   risk/control questions 582–4
   statistics 580–1

personal data, data protection 617–26, 636–44, 646, 729–62, 837, 848
personnel 3–8, 15–16, 20–1, 27–8, 33–4, 42, 53–4, 71–4, 84–5, 91–4, 112–15, 118–22, 125, 144, 147–50, 178, 188, 189–98, 241–5, 291, 294, 317–42, 343, 355–9, 399–436, 454–62, 489–501, 510, 516–41, 661–6, 713–14, 722–3
   see also health...; human resource...; manpower...; pension schemes...; recruitment...; training...
   absenteeism rates 325–7, 401–4, 425–7
   Codes of Conduct 148–9
   company vehicles 7, 399, 432–6, 556–8
   concepts 7, 399–436, 661–6, 713–14, 722–3
   contracts of employment 405–7, 441–2
   control objectives 325, 399–436, 664
   data protection 616–26, 631–2, 639–44
   definition 399–400
   disciplinary/grievance procedures 7, 85, 149, 399, 400–4, 424–7, 594–7, 604, 641–4
   efficiency issues 15–16, 20–1
   emails 487, 497, 520–3, 581–4, 590–7
   empowerment considerations 178, 188, 189–91, 195–6
   fraud 149–50, 242–5, 291, 294, 327, 355–9, 494–5, 588–97
   freedom of information 631–5, 848
   group loyalties/rivalries 30–1
   induction processes 661–2
   information security 487, 520–3, 646, 661–6, 667–70, 671–9, 841–2
   Internet 10, 35–6, 40, 44, 92–3, 121–2, 479, 487, 581, 593–4, 598–604, 842–3
   JIT 195–8
   job descriptions/specifications 144, 149, 401–4, 405–7, 493–5
   job satisfaction 190–1
   labour relations 7, 399, 400–4, 430–2
   legal responsibilities 645–7, 844
   maintenance 8, 9, 44, 318, 339–42
   motivation levels 71–4, 120–2, 148–50, 181, 184–7, 190–1, 196–8, 203–4, 400–36, 547
   outsourcing impacts 192, 193–4
   overview 399
   payroll 7, 27–8, 33–4, 42, 53–4, 223–33, 240, 243–5
   performance/productivity measurement systems 234, 314–16, 324–7
   production/manufacturing 317–42
   quality assurance systems 182–7
   remote working 487, 497–501, 520–3, 585–9, 844
   removable media 487, 497–501, 520–3, 533, 566–9, 672–3, 844–5
   remuneration 325–7, 355–62, 400–7, 415–22
   retention rates 149–50, 325–7, 401–4, 441
   risk/control questions 325–7, 399–436, 665–6
   sales management 8, 343, 355–9
   SAPG 713–14, 722–3
   security policies 495, 496–501, 520–3, 554–8, 661–6, 839–43, 849
   share schemes 415–22

personnel (cont.)
  spreadsheets 40, 53–4, 56–74, 487, 699–706
  staff appraisals 7, 234, 314–16, 324–7, 399, 400–4, 413, 424–7
  succession planning 7, 399, 407, 408–10
  system access controls 8, 487, 576–9, 661–6, 667–70, 707–9
  tacit knowledge 544–53
  termination of employment 400–4, 410, 425–7, 662–6, 841–2
  turnover rates 149–50, 325–7, 401–4
  user support services 487, 694–5
  welfare 7, 399, 400–4, 413–15
  whistleblowing policies 84–5, 121–2, 149
Peru 753, 821
petty cash and expenses, concepts 7, 240, 270–2, 713
Philippines 753, 822
physical security 332–5, 428–30, 454–62, 486, 495, 496–501, 520–3, 554–8, 588–9, 638–44, 658–66, 667–70, 681–7, 707–9, 837, 849
  see also security
  control objectives 556, 664
  fire hazards 332–5, 428–30, 454–62, 554–8, 660
  IT health checks 487, 707–9
  IT sites and infrastructure 486, 487, 520–3, 554–8, 658–60, 671–9, 681–7, 715, 725, 843
  risk/control questions 557–8, 665–6
  security policies 495, 496–501, 520–3, 554–8, 661–6, 839–43, 849
pilot exercises 71–4
PLANETS Project 535
planning 5–6, 8, 11–16, 19–21, 34–5, 41–5, 110, 116, 118–20, 207, 219–35, 318–21, 350, 359–61, 442, 712–14, 721
  control matrices 64, 71–4
  control process concepts 8, 34–5, 219–35, 318–21, 350
  production control concepts 8, 318–21, 714
  three Es (effectiveness, efficiency, and economy) 15–16, 19–23, 219–35
plant and equipment
  see also facilities, plant and equipment
  concepts 8, 318, 319–24, 339–42, 427–30, 445–7, 457–60, 714, 715
  R&D equipment 8, 437, 445–7
Poland 753, 822
policies 20–1, 81–4, 85, 87–90, 211, 241–2, 332–5, 428–30, 457–60, 479–88, 489–501, 506–10, 511–13, 514–41, 549–58, 566–9, 839–51
  see also procedures
  boards of directors 81–4, 87–90, 211
  Data Protection Act 1998 616–26, 639–44, 646, 759–60, 835, 838, 842, 848
  emails 591–7, 841
  freedom of information 628–35, 763–834, 848
  information management 479–88, 496–501, 506–10, 514–23
  Internet 599–604, 842–3
  IT 479–88, 489–501, 506–10, 511–13, 514–41, 554–8, 566–9, 576–9, 580–4, 585–9, 591–7, 599–604, 839–51
  knowledge management 549–53, 849–50
  ownership issues 498–501, 578–9, 701–2
  performance/productivity measurement systems 20–1, 85
  personal computers 580–4
  remote working 585–9, 844
  removable media 566–9, 672–3, 844–5
  safety policies 332–5, 428–30, 457–60, 554–8
  security policies 495, 496–501, 520–3, 554–8, 661–6, 839–43, 849
  system access controls 576–9, 661–6
political/country risks 368
'polluter pays' principle 464–5
pollution 332–8, 463–75
portable buildings 111
Portugal 753–4, 822
post-implementation reviews 549–53
pre-approval requirements, non-audit services 164, 166
pre-emptive category of control, concepts 138
premises, security 272–4, 332–5, 428–30, 453–62
preventive category of control 137–8, 144, 168–70
PRF see profit-related pay schemes
pricing and discount policies 8, 286–9, 304–6, 308–13, 343, 345–81, 389–92, 438–42, 714
  see also product/project accounting
  concepts 353–5, 356–9
  control objectives 354
  definition 353
  risk/control questions 354–5, 357
prior research 11–12
Privacy Rights Clearinghouse 673, 679, 682–3
privatised industries 109
probabilities, risk 52–3, 54–6, 101–15, 122–3
problem identification/solving techniques, quality assurance systems 183–4
procedures 9, 31–2, 49, 123–4, 290, 299–302, 489–501
  see also policies
  back-up and media management 563–5, 846
  tendering 9, 290, 299–302
processes 131–5, 224–35, 559–61, 621–6, 837
  see also business...; efficiency...
  data protection 621–6
  definition 837
  operational auditing evaluations 224–35
  systems concepts 131–5
processing IT operations
  concepts 559–61
  control objectives 559
  risk/control questions 560–1
procurement 6, 7–8, 11, 22–3, 42, 285–316, 714, 723
  see also contracting; purchasing
product designs, concepts 345–8, 438–42, 473
product development
  see also marketing...; research and development
  concepts 8, 343, 345–8, 366, 438–42, 473, 714, 715
  control objectives 345–6, 438–9

definition 345, 438
risk/control questions 346–8, 440–2
product life business process, concepts 35
product/project accounting
see also pricing and discount policies
concepts 7, 240, 268–70, 353, 447–50, 713
control objectives 268
risk/control questions 269–70
production/conversion business process, concepts 33–4
production/manufacturing 3, 5–6, 8, 12–14, 27–8, 32, 33–4, 42–3, 195–8, 317–42, 385–8, 393–5, 398, 442, 463–75, 714, 723–4
see also facilities...; maintenance; materials...; personnel; planning...; safe...
concepts 8, 317–42, 442, 714, 723–4
control objectives 318–42
definition 317–18
environmental issues 8, 318, 335–8
law and regulatory compliance 8, 318, 338–9
overview of functions 8, 318
risk/control questions 319–42
SAPG 714, 723–4
proficiency requirements on auditors 16–18
profit and loss accounts 54, 67–74
profit-related pay schemes (PRP) 415–22
profitability contributions of operational auditing 219–35
profits warnings 91–4
project appraisal and monitoring 8, 437, 442–5, 447, 651–4, 715
concepts 442–5
control objectives 442–3
definition 442
risk/control questions 443–5
promotion and advertising
see also marketing...
concepts 8, 343, 347, 349, 350–3, 369–71, 391–2, 714
control objectives 350–1
definition 350
risk/control questions 352–3, 391–2
protective marking schemes (PMS) 497, 503, 506–7, 516–23, 556–8, 640, 850
Protiviti's website 218
Public Company Accounting Oversight Board (PCAOB) 120–2, 155–77
see also Sarbanes-Oxley Act 2002
Public Records Acts 526, 533
public sector 192, 542, 610–12, 627–35, 681, 763–834, 848–9, 850
publication schemes 536–41, 628–35, 848–9
pull/push production activities 195–8
purchasing 7, 11, 42, 45, 196–8, 246–8, 253–6, 285–316, 433–6
see also accounts payable; creditors; procurement; suppliers
concepts 196–8, 285–316
control objectives 285–6
costs and benefits analysis 286–9

JITP 196–8, 285
price considerations 286–9, 304–6, 308–13
risk/control questions 285, 286–9

qualifications, recruitment issues 404–7, 663–6, 841–2
quality assurance systems
see also total quality management
concepts 8, 182–7, 214–35, 286–9, 306–10, 314–16, 318, 319–42, 345–81, 469–70, 714, 721
control objectives 184–7, 330
costs and benefits analysis 183–5, 330–2
operational auditing 182–7, 214–35, 330–2
production/manufacturing 8, 318, 330–2
risk/control questions 185–7, 331–2
testing and inspection methods 330–2
'quality at source' approaches 195–6
quality audits, concepts 183–7
quality circles 195
quality of information, concepts 14, 57–74, 109, 124–7, 151–77, 850
quality of products/services 14–24
quantitative/quasi-quantitative/qualitative performance measures, operational auditing 221–8
query languages/software 69–74, 613–15
questions 10, 35–6, 40–74, 148–50, 169–73, 185–7, 208–12, 229–35, 240–75, 285, 286–9, 292–316, 318, 344–81, 384–98, 400, 438, 454, 470, 488, 712–28
CSAs 208–12
ethics/competencies 148–50
finance and accounting 241–75
operational auditing evaluations 229–35
purchasing 286–9
SAPGs 10, 35–6, 40–74, 240–1, 285, 318, 345, 384, 400, 438, 454, 470, 488, 712–28

R&D *see* research and development
radical changes 122–3, 178–81
'ratio of payroll to other costs', operational auditing evaluations 223–33
'ratio of productive/unproductive audit time', operational auditing evaluations 223–33
re-order levels 380–2, 393–5
Re-use of Public Sector Information Regulations 2005 526, 646
recessions 82–3, 219–20
reconciled input data 67–74, 125–7
record creation, records management 524–41, 849
record keeping, records management 524–41, 680–7, 849
record maintenance, records management 528–41, 849
record retention, records management 497, 524–41, 562–5, 620–6, 680–7, 849, 851
recording *see* storage...
records management (RM)
see also information asset registers; information management
best practices 485, 524–41

records management (RM) (*cont.*)
   concepts   479–88, 496–501, 502–10, 511–13, 515, 517–23, 524–41, 544–5, 646–7, 680–7, 715, 725, 838, 849, 851
   control objectives   535–6
   definition   484–5, 524–5, 838
   digital preservation   531, 532–41, 681–7
   ISO   15489 484–6, 526
   legislation   524–41, 646–7, 680–7, 849
   risk/control questions   536–41
   types of records   496–7, 502–3, 524–41, 566–9, 622–6, 631–2, 681–2
recruitment issues   7, 17, 33, 42, 149, 176, 399, 400–10, 439–42, 661–6, 713, 841–2
   auditors   17, 176
   complaints   406–7
   concepts   404–10, 439–42, 661–6
   control objectives   404–5, 664
   definition   404
   personnel   33, 42, 149, 400–7, 661–6, 841–2
   qualifications   404–7, 663–6, 841–2
   references   404–7, 663–6, 841–2
   risk/control questions   405–7
   tests   407
recycle/reuse/reduce environmental paradigm   463–75
redundancies   410, 662–6
reference points, systems concepts   132–5
references, recruitment issues   404–7, 663–6, 841–2
registration numbers, VAT   262–3
registration procedures, quality assurance systems   182–7
regular transfers with external parties, data transfer types   636–7, 639–44
Regulation of Investigatory Powers Act 2000   581, 592, 646
regulations   4–5, 8, 43, 46, 77–9, 96–115, 117–46, 151–77, 202, 242–75, 287–9, 291–316, 319–42, 363–82, 385–98, 400–36, 439–52, 463–75, 479–88, 496–501, 514–41, 602–4, 616–35, 640–7, 674–9, 707–11, 713–15, 721
   see also legislation; Sarbanes-Oxley Act 2002
   freedom of information   479–88, 497–501, 503–10, 516–23, 525–41, 581–4, 590–1, 627–35, 640–1, 646–7, 763–834, 848
   list of IT regulations   525–6, 645–7, 729–834
   records management   524–41, 680–7, 849
reliability issues   4–5, 88–9, 96–115, 117–46, 170–3, 232, 251–3, 314–16, 493–5, 507–10, 535–41, 556–8, 559–61, 587–9, 595–7, 600–4, 610–26, 651–7, 705–6, 711, 835
remote operating units
   see also subsidiaries
   concepts   276–84, 366–8
remote working   487, 497–501, 520–3, 585–9, 844
   concepts   585–9, 844
   control objectives   587–8
   definition   585–7
   policies   585–9, 844
   risk/control questions   588–9

statistics   585
removable media   487, 497–501, 520–3, 533, 566–9, 637–44, 672–3, 844–5
   concepts   566–9, 844–5
   control objectives   567–8
   disposals   567–9
   policies   566–9, 672–3, 844–5
   risk/control questions   568–9
   types   497, 566–7, 672–3
remuneration
   see also payroll; pension schemes...
   agents   368–71
   auditors   176, 233
   personnel   325–7, 355–62, 400–7, 415–22, 425–7
renewable energy   464–75
reporting facilities   67–74, 77–94, 96–115, 117, 124–7, 151–77, 206–7, 226–35, 272–4, 470–5, 673–9, 710–11
   see also financial information...
reputations   52–4, 67–74, 91–4, 113, 171–2, 222–35, 296, 330–2, 336–8, 389–92, 468–75, 529–41, 656–60, 676–9
research and development (R&D)   6, 8, 27, 34, 43, 268, 345, 437–52, 715, 724–5
   see also product development; project appraisal...
   concepts   437–52, 715, 724–5
   control objectives   437–52
   definition   437
   development project management   8, 437, 447–50
   ethics   437
   grant funding schemes   450–2
   legal and regulatory issues   8, 437, 450–2
   overview   437
   plant and equipment   8, 437, 445–7
   risk/control questions   437–52
   SAPG   715, 724–5
   specialist staff   437–52
   tests   448–52
reserves   158–60
residual risk
   see also risk...
   concepts   101–15, 142–3, 208–13
resourcing considerations, operational auditing   16–19, 30, 170–2, 220–1, 232–5, 289–316, 444–5
responsibilities   29–30, 47, 87, 100, 112–15, 118–20, 125–30, 135–7, 144, 148–50, 151–77, 195–8, 200–3, 214–35, 265, 369–71, 493–5, 497–501, 518–23, 524–41, 556–8, 563–5, 661–6, 691–3, 851
   agents   369–71
   audit committees   158–73, 176–7, 211, 214–35
   business processes   29–30, 118–20, 200–3
   contracting   291–316, 648–50
   corporate social responsibilities   16, 21, 91–4, 463–75
   CSAs   200–2
   data protection   9, 43–4, 404–7, 479–88, 496–501, 503–10, 514–23, 525–41, 562–5, 581–4, 590–7, 616–26, 631–2, 639–44, 646, 848
   environmental issues   463–75

freedom of information   479–88, 497–501, 503–10, 516–23, 525–41, 581–4, 590–1, 627–35, 640–1, 646–7, 763–834, 848
information asset registers   503, 507–10, 847, 851
IT   493–5, 497–501, 503, 518–23, 524–41, 556–8, 563–5, 585–9, 601–4, 616–26, 627–44, 645–7, 661–6, 691–3, 851
JIT   195–8
joint ventures   280–1
knowledge management   550–3, 849–50, 851
list of IT legislation   525, 581, 645–7, 729–834
Sarbanes-Oxley Act 2002   151–77, 202
security issues   454–62, 554–8, 661–6, 851
subsidiaries   276–7
taxation returns   265
viruses   691–3, 841, 846
restatements of prior year results   173
resurrected deleted files   562, 567, 682–7, 851
retention
  control objectives   685
  data retention and disposal   487, 497, 524–41, 562–5, 620–6, 638–44, 680–7, 849, 851
  personnel   149–50, 325–7, 401–4, 441
  risk/control questions   685–7
return on capital employed (ROCE)   194
returned goods   289, 361–2
returns   262–3, 264–6, 273–5, 424
revenue business process, concepts   32–6, 720–8
revenue expenditure, software assets   502–3
reviews
  operational auditing   214–35
  project outturn/performance   313–16
risk   3–6, 10, 17, 22, 25, 29–30, 36–7, 40, 41–74, 76–94, 95–115, 120–3, 137–9, 148–50, 168–70, 201–13, 453–62, 658–60, 667–70, 671–9
  appetites   95–115, 208–13
  aversion   111
  categories   102–6, 113–15, 122–3, 137–9, 168–70, 208–13
  concepts   40, 45–6, 50–74, 95–115, 120–3, 137–9, 148–50, 168–70
  control matrices   40, 53–4, 56–74
  definition   52, 101
  exposures   52–3, 55–74, 99–115, 453–62
  levels   51–2, 102–4, 113–15, 143–5
  matrices   101–6
  mitigation   101–15, 207–8, 211–12, 453–62, 658–60, 667–70, 671–9
  owners   107
  registers   101, 106–8, 115, 168–70
  responses   95–115, 122–3
  sponsors   107
'risk assessment' component, COSO internal control framework   120–1, 122–3, 142, 144, 147–50, 157–8, 163–77
risk assessments, concepts   51–74, 85–6, 95–115, 120–1, 122–3, 137–9, 148–50, 168–70, 201–13, 215–35, 277–84, 368, 427–30, 453–62, 481–8, 566–9, 658–60, 699–706, 707–9

risk management   3–6, 10, 17, 22, 25, 29–30, 36–7, 40, 41–74, 75–94, 95–115, 122–3, 137–9, 152–77, 202, 205, 207–8, 232–5, 453–62, 470–5, 481–8, 674–9, 712–13, 718, 721
  see also Sarbanes-Oxley Act 2002
  activities fan   99–100
  concealed risks   107–10
  concepts   75–94, 95–115, 122–3, 137–9, 152–77, 202, 205, 207–8, 453–62, 470–5, 481–8, 674–9, 718, 721
  control issues   75–94, 96–8, 112–15, 122–3, 232–5
  corporate governance   76–94, 110
  definition   95–8
  essential effective components   98–9, 120–3, 124–8, 142, 144, 147–50
  internal controls   75–94, 96–8, 112–15, 122–3, 137–42, 147–50, 151–77, 232–5
  limitations   107–15
  objectives   77–81, 85–6, 95–8, 112–15, 122–3
  opportunities   111, 113–15, 226–8
  organisational cultures   110, 115, 678–9
  processes   95–115
  'Rubik cube'   98–9, 120–1
  SAPG   712, 718
  scope of internal audit's role   99, 201–2
  simultaneous risks   110–11
  strategic objectives   96–8, 112–15
  subjective judgements   104
  tools   101–7
risk/control section of SAPGs, concepts   45–6, 47–50
robust systems   36, 141–2, 507–10, 521–3, 587–9
Romania   754, 823
Royal Dutch Shell   485–6
'Rubik cube', risk management   98–9, 120–1
Russian Federation   280–1, 754, 823
Rwanda   754, 824

safe production/manufacturing environment   8, 318, 319, 322–4, 332–5, 339, 413–15, 427–30, 457–60
safety policies   332–5, 428–30, 457–60, 554–8
sales   3, 5–6, 8, 27–8, 32–5, 43, 51, 113, 136, 194, 343–82, 385–8, 393–5
  see also marketing...; order processing
  quotas   356–9
sales management   8, 343, 355–62, 442, 714
  concepts   355–62, 442
  control objectives   356
  costs and benefits analysis   360–2
  definition   355–6
  remuneration   355–62
  risk/control questions   357–9
sales performance and monitoring   8, 343, 346, 359–62, 714
  concepts   359–62
  control objectives   360
  definition   359
sales tax see VAT
samples   168–70
SAP, IBM   199

SAPGs *see* standard audit programme guides
Sarbanes-Oxley Act 2002
  see also internal controls; Public Company Accounting
    Oversight Board
  breaches 152–4
  complacency dangers 167–8
  concepts 151–77, 202
  control registers 168–70, 173
  COSO internal control framework 157–77
  costs and benefits analysis 151, 154–5, 171–2
  criminal sanctions 152–4, 164–77
  documentation requirements 167–70
  overview of sections 151–4
  recognised suitable control frameworks 157–8
  s.101 166
  s.201 (Services Outside the Scope of Practice of
    Auditors) 152, 164, 166–7
  s.206 (Conflicts of Interest) 152, 163–4
  s.301 (Public Company Audit Committees) 152,
    158–60, 176
  s.302 (Corporate Responsibility for Financial
    Statements) 151, 153, 156–77, 202
  s.303 (Improper Influence on Conduct of Audits)
    152, 164–5
  s.404 (Management Assessment of Internal Controls)
    117, 141–2, 151–77, 202
  s.406 (Code of Ethics for Senior Financial Officers)
    152, 161–3
  s.407 (Disclosure of Audit Committee Financial
    Expert) 152, 158, 161
  s.906 (Corporate Responsibility for Financial
    Statements) 152–4
  SOX-Lite 155–6
  standardisation incentives 170
Saudi Arabia 755, 824
scientific management 198
SCL 560–1, 575
scope of operational auditing 3–12, 16–17, 27–39, 152,
  164, 166–7, 170–3, 201–2, 218–35, 239–40,
  469–75, 707–9
screensavers 623
SD memory cards 566–7
Securities & Exchange Commission (SEC) 117, 120,
  141–2, 151, 154–77
Securities Exchange Act 1934 152–4, 157–77
security 272–4, 332–5, 428–30, 453–62, 463–75,
  481–8, 489–95, 504–10, 514–23, 527–41, 554–8,
  576–9, 613–15, 636–44, 651–7, 671–9, 713, 721,
  836, 839–51
  see also access...; health and safety; insurance...
  contingency plans 43–4, 69–74, 91, 103, 368,
    397–8, 453–62, 497–501, 512–13, 528–41, 561,
    658–60, 671–9, 707–9
  control objectives 454–62, 664
  data protection 9, 43–4, 404–7, 479–88, 496–501,
    503–10, 514–23, 525–41, 562–5, 581–4, 590–7,
    616–26, 631–2, 639–44, 646, 729–62, 848
  data retention and disposal 487, 497, 524–41, 562–5,
    620–6, 638–44, 680–7, 851
  definition 453–4
  fire hazards 332–5, 428–30, 454–62, 554–8, 660
  information asset registers 504–10, 847
  information security incidents 487, 520–3, 671–9,
    681–3, 707–9, 841–2
  IT health checks 487, 707–9
  IT sites and infrastructure 486, 487, 520–3, 554–8,
    658–60, 671–9, 681–7, 843
  logging systems 487, 576–9, 588–9, 667–70
  overview 454
  passwords 58–74, 518–23, 527–41, 576–9, 585–9,
    601–4, 623–6, 638–44, 707–9, 843
  policies 495, 496–501, 520–3, 554–8, 661–6,
    839–43, 849
  records management 527–41, 849
  removable media 487, 497–501, 520–3, 533, 566–9,
    672–3, 844–5
  responsibilities 454–62, 554–8, 661–6, 851
  risk/control questions 454–62, 665–6
  spreadsheets 699–706
  system access controls 8, 487, 576–9, 661–6,
    667–70, 707–9
Security Industry Authority (SIA) 555
security services 555–8
selection and letting of contracts, concepts 9, 290,
  304–6
self-actualisation concepts 190–1
sensitive company data 57–74, 124–7, 220–1, 242,
  272–4, 299–302, 345–8, 351–5, 401–7, 438–42,
  453–62, 503–10, 515–23, 533–41, 560–1, 566–9,
  586–9, 592–7, 616–26, 636–44, 663–6, 671–9,
  680–7, 688–90, 700–6, 729–62, 838
  see also data protection
sensitive data, data protection 617–26, 636–44, 646,
  729–62, 848
'seq' column of SAPG risk/control section 48–50
Serbia 755, 824
servers 487, 548, 554–8
service level agreements, IT 493–5
service packs/releases 571–5
service provisions 5–6
share option schemes, personnel 415–22
share prices 93
share schemes, personnel 415–22
shareholders 81–2, 90–4, 97–8, 128–9, 464, 473–5
  see also corporate governance; stakeholders
sharing aspects of information management 515–23,
  542–53, 636–44
ship analogy, internal controls 119–20
shredders 683–4
'significant deficiencies', definitions 153, 156–7, 172
'significant misstatement', definitions 153, 156–7
signing-off procedures 49
simultaneous risks, risk management 110–11
Singapore 755, 825
sites and infrastructure for IT
  see also physical security
  concepts 486, 554–8, 715, 725, 843
'size' row in control matrices 58–74

skills 16–18, 84–90, 122, 148–50, 158–60, 204–5, 218, 233–4, 241–2, 294–5, 318–27, 337–42, 351–66, 385–8, 396–8, 400–4, 408–13, 439–42, 489–95, 559–75, 651–4, 684
Skills for Security 684
Slovakia 756, 825
Slovenia 756, 825
software 9, 43–4, 64, 67–74, 487, 489–92, 511–13, 520–3, 531–41, 559–61, 570–5, 585–9, 605–8, 648–50, 651–7, 691–3, 699–706, 845
  concepts 502–10, 554–8, 655–7, 691–3, 845
  malicious software 9, 43, 497–501, 520–3, 563–9, 570–5, 583–4, 590–7, 601–4, 671–9, 691–3, 707–9, 841, 846
  processing IT operations 559–61
  selection considerations 655–7, 845
  systems and operating software 9, 43–4, 64, 71–4, 487, 559–61, 570–5, 667–70
software maintenance/development controls 9, 43–4, 64, 67–74, 487, 605–8, 651–7, 699–706, 845
  concepts 605–8, 651–7, 845
  control objectives 606–7
  risk/control questions 607–8
South Africa 140, 141, 756, 826
South Korea 757, 826
SOX *see* Sarbanes-Oxley Act 2002
SOX-Lite, concepts 155–6
Spain 757, 827
spam 590–7, 602, 707–9
span of control, concepts 118–20, 187–8
spare parts and supply 8, 343, 380–2, 715
  concepts 8, 343, 380–2
  control objectives 380–1
  risk/control questions 381–2
specialisation 135–7, 142–3
specialist staff, research and development 437–52
specifications, system development 651–7, 706
sponsors 4–5, 15, 75–81, 96–9, 103, 107, 111, 115, 117–28, 140, 142, 144, 147–50, 157–77, 351–3
spreadsheets 40, 53–4, 56–74, 487, 699–706
  access controls 704–6
  concepts 70, 699–706
  control matrices 40, 53–4, 56–74
  control objectives 705
  documentation needs 701–6
  error types 699–700, 702
  good practice 70, 699–706
  ICAEW best practices 70
  inventories 700–1
  risk assessments 699–706
  risk/control questions 706
  tests 705–6
spyware 570–5, 596–7, 601–4, 672–9
staff appraisals 7, 234, 314–16, 324–7, 399, 400–4, 413, 424–7, 713
  concepts 424–7
  control objectives 425
  risk/control questions 425–7
stakeholders 22, 75–82, 90–4, 112–15, 464–75

added value definition 22
corporate governance 75–82, 90–4
environmental issues 464–75
types 91
standard audit programme guides (SAPGs)
see also control self assessments
  concepts 10, 35–6, 40–74, 240–1, 285, 318, 345, 384, 400, 438, 454, 470, 488, 712–28
  examples 41–5
  format proposals 45–51
  index 712–28
  objectives section 46–7
  practical uses 41–5, 240–1
  purposes 46, 240–1, 719–21
  questions 10, 35–6, 40–74, 240–1, 285, 318, 345, 384, 400, 438, 454, 470, 488, 712–28
  risk/control section 45–6, 47–50
  system interface section 46, 50
  title page section 46–7
standard cost variances 268–70, 711
standards 3, 11–12, 16–19, 21–6, 76–80, 95–8, 115, 121–2, 130–5, 139–41, 171, 176, 182, 183–4, 214–17, 225, 229, 232–5, 272–5, 276–84, 287–9, 295–7, 319–42, 400–36, 465–75, 480–8, 515–41, 554–8, 652–4, 707–9
see also British Standards...; ISO...
  data retention and disposal 684–5
  data transfers and sharing 515–23, 542–53, 636–44
  emails 593–7
  environmental auditing 465–75
  financial information and reporting 272–4, 710–11
  IIA 3, 11–12, 16–19, 21–6, 76–80, 95–8, 115, 121–2, 139–41, 171, 176, 214–17, 225, 229, 232–5, 570
  IT 480–8, 493–5, 515–41, 581–4, 645–7, 652–4, 701–6
  systems concepts 130–5
stock control
  concepts 7–8, 380–2, 392–5, 398, 714
  control objectives 392–3
  risk/control questions 393–5
stock and materials handling 6, 7–8, 11, 33–4, 42, 45, 51, 195–8, 240, 266–8, 321, 327, 362–6, 380–2, 383–98, 714, 723
see also inventories; spare parts...
  concepts 7–8, 383–98, 714, 723
  out-of-stock situations 380–2, 392–5
  overview 383–4
  re-order levels 380–2, 393–5
  SAPG 714, 723
storage aspects of information management 515–23, 544–53, 563–5, 586–9, 844–5
see also removable media
strategic objectives 96–8, 112–15, 178–81, 281–4, 291–316, 345–81, 388–92, 402–36, 438–52
  environmental issues 467–8

strategic objectives (cont.)
  risk management 96–8, 112–15
strategic planning
  concepts 8, 71–4, 281–4, 291–316, 345–81, 438–42, 486, 489–92, 511–13, 582–4, 715, 725
  IT 8, 486, 489–92, 511–13, 582–4, 715, 725
strengths and weaknesses analysis 71–4
subjective judgements, risk management 104
subsidiaries 3, 265, 276–84, 366–8
  see also parent companies; remote operating units
  concepts 276–84, 366–8
  cultural issues 277–84, 366–8
  fact-finding programmes 277–8
  marketing and sales 366–8
  responsibilities 276–7
  taxation 265, 366–8
'substantive testing' column of SAPG risk/control section 48–50, 56
succession planning, concepts 7, 399, 407, 408–10
Sudan 757, 827
suppliers 33–4, 91–4, 194–8, 286–316, 655–7
  see also purchasing
supply chains, environmental issues 468–75
sustainability reports 470–5
Sweden 627, 757–8, 828
Switzerland 758, 828
synergy 344, 469–75
system access controls
  see also access controls
  concepts 8, 487, 576–9, 642, 661–6, 667–70, 707–9, 837
  control objectives 577
  definition 576, 837
  risk/control questions 578–9
system administrators 576–9, 838
system development 487, 651–7, 699–706, 845
  concepts 651–7, 699–706, 845
  control objectives 651–2, 655, 705
  costs and benefits analysis 651–4
  risk/control questions 652–4, 656–7, 706
  sourcing considerations 651, 655–7
  spreadsheets 699–706
  tests 652–7
system interface section of SAPGs 46, 50–1
system risk
  see also risk
  definition 52–3
systems concepts 130–5, 719–20
systems and operating software 8, 43–4, 64, 71–4, 487, 559–61, 570–5, 667–70
  concepts 570–5, 667–70
  control objectives 573–4
  definition 570–1
  risk/control questions 574–5
  updates 570–5, 584

table PCs 585
tacit knowledge
  see also knowledge...

  concepts 544–53, 838
tactical level of risk, concepts 51–2
Taiwan 758, 829
taxation 7, 33, 42, 51, 53–4, 91, 164, 166, 240, 244–5, 246–51, 261–6, 269, 311, 312, 354–5, 366–8, 416–24, 434–6, 442, 517–23, 713, 722
  allowances 264–6
  concepts 261–6, 311–12
  control objectives 262, 264, 311–12
  parent companies 366–8
  returns 262–3, 264–6
  risk/control questions 262–3, 264–6, 311–12
  VAT 7, 51, 240, 246–51, 255–6, 261–3, 271–2, 312, 355, 713, 722
Taylor, Frederick 195, 198
TCP/IP 598, 707
teams 183–7, 200–1, 204–12
  see also personnel
technical activities, resourcing considerations 16–19
Telecommunications Regulations 2000 526, 646
telephones 28, 609, 840–1
temporary/short-term staff 403, 409, 576–9
tendering 7, 9, 22–3, 44, 191–5, 220–1, 290–316, 651–4, 716–17, 726–8
  see also contracting
  concepts 9, 290, 299–304
  control objectives 299–300, 302–3
  definition 299
  documentation 300–1, 302–5
  procedures 9, 290, 299–302
  risk/control questions 300–2, 303–4
termination of employment 400–4, 410, 425–7, 662–6, 841–2
termination/contingency plan options, risk matrices 102–6
terms of reference, IT function 493–5
'test' row in control matrices 58–74
test scripts, concepts 169–70
tests 14, 48–74, 125–7, 167, 168–73, 194–5, 330–2, 347–8, 442, 448–52, 652–60, 689–90, 705–6, 707–9
  concepts 168–73, 330–2, 347–8, 652–60, 689–90, 705–6, 707–9
  contingency plans 658–60, 689–90
  EDI 689–90
  information flows 14, 125–7, 167, 168–73, 689–90
  IT health checks 707–9
  production/manufacturing quality controls 330–2
  R&D 448–52
  recruitment issues 407
  spreadsheets 705–6
  system development 652–7
Thailand 758, 829–30
three Es of effectiveness, efficiency, and economy, concepts 15–16, 19–21, 29–30, 77–9, 84, 85, 117–46, 215–35
three Es of equity, environment, and ethics, concepts 16, 21, 84–5, 463–75
time business process, concepts 35

time divisions, internal controls 137, 227–8
timeliness of reports 272–4, 283, 289, 291–316,
   448–50, 514–23, 559–61, 710–11
timings, development project management 447–50
title page section of SAPGs 46–7
TJX Companies Inc. 672–3
Tokyo Stock Exchange 106
total quality management (TQM)
   see also continuous improvements; quality...
   concepts 178, 181–7, 330, 469–70
   costs and benefits analysis 183–5
   definition 181
   risk/control questions 185–7
Towers, Stephen 180–1
Toyota 195
TQM *see* total quality management
trade marks, distributors 366, 392
trades unions 91, 427, 431–2
training and development 7, 15–17, 64, 71–4, 90, 138,
   144, 149, 204–5, 212, 218, 234, 241–2, 294–5,
   314–16, 319–22, 324–7, 337, 339–42, 351–66,
   370, 396–8, 400–4, 408–13, 439–42, 448–50,
   489–501, 518–23, 536–53, 572–5, 614–15, 657,
   661–6, 699–706, 713
   concepts 410–13, 439–42, 448–50, 699–706
   control objectives 410–11
   costs and benefits analysis 411–13
   definition 410
   IT 489–92, 518–23, 536–53, 572–5, 583–4, 657,
      661–6, 699–706
   knowledge management 542–53
   risk/control questions 411–13
transparency issues 85–6, 91–4, 516–23, 628–35
transport 8, 383, 384–8, 714
   see also distribution
Treadway Report 118, 157
   see also Committee of Sponsoring Organizations
treasury
   concepts 7, 33–4, 36, 51, 240–3, 713, 720–8
   control objectives 241
   risk/control questions 241–3
trends 16
Trinidad and Tobago 758, 830–1
'triple bottom line' objectives 464, 473
Trojans 672, 691–3
trust levels, CSAs 209–13
Turkey 759, 831
Turnbull internal control framework 117–18, 120,
   128–9, 140–2, 144, 157–8, 170–1
   see also UK, Combined Code on Corporate
      Governance
turnover rates, personnel 149–50, 325–7, 401–4
'type' row in control matrices 58–74

Uganda 759, 831
UK 22–3, 109, 117–18, 120, 128–9, 140, 144, 157–8,
   170–1, 176–7, 218–19, 245, 464, 466, 526, 533–5,
   555, 581, 585–9, 590–2, 599, 609–10, 616–35,
   658, 671–9, 681, 684–5, 759–60, 832–3

Combined Code on Corporate Governance 128–9,
   140, 144, 157–8, 170–1, 176–7
Companies Act 2006 464, 473–5
Department of Trade and Industry 480
HM Treasury 218–19
Ukraine 759, 831–2
United States Code (USC) 154
university case study, cycles 37–9
untrue statements 151–77
up-to-date information
   data protection 619–26, 848
   information management 514–23, 619–26
updates
   access rights 662–6
   systems and operating software 570–5, 584
Uruguay 761, 833–4
US 117–28, 151–77, 465–6, 534–5, 581, 627, 671–3,
   682–3, 684–5, 760–1, 833
   see also Committee of Sponsoring Organizations;
      Sarbanes-Oxley Act 2002
   Environmental Protection Agency 465–6
USB memory sticks 566–7, 637
users
   screening processes 662–6, 667–70, 694–5
   support services 487, 694–5
utilisation aspects of information management 515–23,
   544–53
Uzbekistan 834

validation tasks 13–14, 241–75, 291–316, 405–7, 698,
   702–6, 710–11
valuations
   interim payments 9, 44, 290, 308–10
   inventories 266–8
value for money auditing (VFM), concepts 21–3,
   230–3, 353
values 16, 34, 78, 84–5, 121–2
variables, systems concepts 131–5
variances 268–70, 278, 382, 395, 711
VAT 7, 51, 240, 246–51, 255–6, 261–3, 271–2, 312,
   355, 713, 722
   control objectives 262
   registration numbers 262–3
   returns 262–3
   risk/control questions 262–3, 312
VBA 703
Venezuela 761, 834
verification tasks 13–14, 241–75, 291–316, 405–7,
   468–75, 576–9, 662–6, 698, 702–6
versions of software 571–5
vertical integration 194
VFM *see* value for money auditing
viability/competence assessments of contractors, concepts
   9, 290, 295–7
Vietnam 762, 834
virtual private networks (VPNs) 585–9, 609–12
viruses 9, 43, 487, 497–501, 520–3, 563–9, 570–5,
   583–4, 590–7, 601–4, 671–9, 691–3, 707–9, 841,
   846

viruses (*cont.*)
    concepts   691–3, 846
    control objectives   691–2
    emails   691–3, 841
    risk/control questions   692–3
vision   209–13
Voice over IP telephony (VoIP)   609

walkthrough tests   168–70
WANs *see* wide area networks
warehousing and storage   7–8, 42, 51, 327, 383–4, 395–8, 714
    see also distribution; stock...
    concepts   395–8
    control objectives   396
    definition   395
    risk/control questions   396–8
warranty arrangements   8, 43, 51, 343, 375–7, 381–2, 714
    see also after sales support
    concepts   8, 43, 51, 343, 375–7, 381–2
    control objectives   375–6
    risk/control questions   376–7
waste management   335–8, 463–75
'weakness to report' column of SAPG risk/control section   48–50
websites   10, 35–6, 40, 44, 92–3, 218, 712, 729–834

Weinstock, Lord   97–8
welfare of personnel   7, 399, 400–4, 413–15, 457–60, 555–8, 713
    see also health and safety at work; security
    concepts   413–15, 457–60, 555–8
    control objectives   413
whistleblowing policies   84–5, 121–2, 149
why-what-who-how questions, knowledge management   549–50
wide area networks (WANs)   489, 609–12, 693
Wiley website   10, 35–6, 40, 44, 712
Windows   570–1
Word tables   206
working capital   242–3
workshop/survey approaches to CSA   200–1, 204–12
worms   672
'WP' (working paper) column of SAPG risk/control section   48–50

Yemen   762, 834

Zimbabwe   762, 834

Indexed by Terry Halliday